FLAYING
in the Pre-Modern World

Practice and Representation

FLAYING

in the Pre-Modern World

Practice and Representation

Edited by
Larissa Tracy

D. S. BREWER

First published 2017
D. S. Brewer, Cambridge

ISBN 978 1 84384 452 5

D. S. Brewer is an imprint of Boydell & Brewer Ltd
PO Box 9, Woodbridge, Suffolk IP12 3DF, UK
and of Boydell & Brewer Inc.
668 Mt Hope Avenue, Rochester, NY 14620–2731, USA
website: www.boydellandbrewer.com

A catalogue record for this book is available from the British Library

The publisher has no responsibility for the continued existence
or accuracy of URLs for external or third-party internet websites
referred to in this book, and does not guarantee that any content
on such websites is, or will remain, accurate or appropriate

This publication is printed on acid-free paper

Designed and typeset in Adobe Arno Pro and Charlemagne by
David Roberts, Pershore, Worcestershire

Printed and bound in Great Britain by
TJ International Ltd, Padstow, Cornwall

Contents

Illustrations

The editor, contributors and publishers are grateful to all the institutions
and persons listed for permission to reproduce the materials in which they
hold copyright. Every effort has been made to trace the copyright holders;
apologies are offered for any omission, and the publishers will be pleased to
add any necessary acknowledgement in subsequent editions.

Acknowledgments

T HIS project was first inspired by a conversation with Asa Simon Mittman, who suggested the possibility of a volume on flaying in the Middle Ages – specifically, human flaying – as there was an interesting image of St Bartholomew that he wanted to write on. So, we put our heads together and proposed a session for the annual International Medieval Congress at Kalamazoo in May 2013. This volume developed from that session: 'MONSTERS II: Down to the Skin: Images of Flaying in the Middle Ages', sponsored by MEARCSTAPA (Monsters: The Experimental Association for the Research of Cryptozoology through Scholarly Theory and Practical Application). I owe a considerable debt to Professor Mittman for his editorial guidance and support during the course of this project. I would also like to thank Thomas D. Hill and Paul R. Hyams for sending me research materials on aspects of medieval violence over the years. A great deal of work goes into assembling a volume like this, and so my gratitude goes out to Tina Boyer, Kelly DeVries, Martin Foys, Jay Paul Gates, David F. Johnson, Jeff Massey, and the MEARCSTAPA executive board (Boyer, Massey, Mittman, Stefanie Goyette, Ana Grinberg, Mary Kate Hurley, Mary Leech, Derek Newman-Stille, Melissa Ridley-Elmes, Thea Tomaini and Renée Ward) for their editorial input over the course of this project. I am grateful to Mary Rambaran-Olm for her help in compiling the initial bibliography and to Shannon Ambrose, without whose editorial and proofreading eye this volume would not have been possible. My parents, Nina Zerkich and Robert Tracy, are an unwavering source of support in all my endeavours, and the denizens at the Patrick Henry Tavern in Richmond, Virginia, have provided endless inspiration. I would also like to thank Caroline Palmer for her constant encouragement and the anonymous readers of this volume in its various stages for their pertinent suggestions and constructive comments.

The research for Peter Dent's article was supported by a Leverhulme Trust Research Fellowship. This volume was made possible by a funding grant from Longwood University's Cook-Cole College of Arts and Sciences and support from the School of Arts & Humanities at Methodist University.

Because this volume would be almost impossible were it not for her substantial body of work on early medieval legal traditions, and because she was such an inspirational and energetic force who had a profound impact on modern understandings of the Middle Ages, I would like to dedicate this volume to the memory of Lisi Oliver (1951–2015). A bright light has gone out.

Contributors

Frederika Bain (PhD, English, University of Hawai'i at Mānoa) wrote her dissertation on dismemberment and identity-formation in medieval and early modern England. She has published an edition of four early modern fairy spells and a chapter in *The Renaissance of Emotion* (ed. Richard Meek and Erin Sullivan [Manchester University Press, 2015]) on affective scripts in accounts of execution and murder. Her chapter on the iconography of the medieval fairy-woman Melusine is forthcoming from Brill. She works for the University of Hawai'i's College of Tropical Agriculture, writing on far different topics.

Peter Dent (PhD, Art History, The Courtauld Institute of Art) is a lecturer in Art History in the Department of History of Art, University of Bristol. He wrote his doctoral thesis (also at the Courtauld) on representations of the body of Christ in fourteenth-century Tuscan sculpture (2005). He has since held research fellowships from the British Academy, the Henry Moore Foundation and the Leverhulme Trust. He edited the collection *Sculpture and Touch* (Ashgate, 2014) and is currently one of the editors of *The Sculpture Journal.*

Kelly DeVries (PhD, Medieval Studies, University of Toronto) is Professor of History at Loyola University, Maryland, and Honorary Historical Consultant for the Royal Armouries, UK. He has published and edited numerous books, articles and bibliographies on military history, medieval history and the history of technology, for academic and popular historical audiences; these include *Wounds and Wound Repair in Medieval Culture*, with Larissa Tracy (Brill, 2015); *The Battle of Crécy: A Casebook*, with Michael Livingston (Liverpool University Press, 2015); *Medieval Military Technology*, 2nd edn (University of Toronto Press); *Rhodes Besieged* (History Press, 2011); *Medieval Weapons* (ABC-CLIO, 2007); *The Artillery of the Dukes of Burgundy, 1363–1477* (Boydell, 2005); and *Joan of Arc: A Military Leader* (Sutton, 1999). He has appeared on more than thirty television shows for PBS, History, History International, Military History and National Geographic Channels. He travels and lectures throughout the world.

Valerie Gramling (PhD, English, University of Massachusetts) is currently a lecturer in the Department of English at the University of Miami. Her research interests include performance studies, theatre and performance history, and contemporary adaptations of medieval literature and drama. She has directed productions of *Everyman* and the Chester *Noah* and *Harrowing of Hell* plays, and her adaptation of the Chester *Noah*, with added dialogue from George Gordon Byron's *Heaven and Earth*, was published in the *Massachusetts Center for Interdisciplinary Renaissance Studies Newsletter* (Spring 2011).

Perry Neil Harrison (Doctoral Fellow, English, Baylor University) is a specialist in Medieval Studies and Anglo-Saxon language and culture. He received his MA in Literature from Abilene Christian University in 2010 and trained in Folklore Studies at the University of Louisiana at Lafayette. His specific research interests include representations of the body and identity in medieval culture, Germanic linguistics and philology, and medieval outlaw ballads. He is also the author of the article 'Seascape and the Anglo-Saxon Body Frame', in *Medieval Perspectives* 28 (2013), and a chapter in the forthcoming collection *Robin Hood and the Outlaw/ed Literary Canon.*

Jack Hartnell (PhD, Art History, The Courtauld Institute of Art) is Lecturer and Mellon Postdoctoral Fellow at Columbia University, New York, where his teaching and research focuses on the visual culture of late medieval and early Renaissance medicine. In 2015 he was Andrew W. Mellon Postdoctoral Fellow at The Courtauld Institute of Art, and has also held fellowships at the Victoria and Albert Museum and the Max-Planck-Institut für Wissenschaftsgeschichte in Berlin. He is currently completing a monograph exploring the relationship between art and early anatomical practice in Western Europe, as well as another on the cryptic medieval image of the Wound Man.

Emily Lavin Leverett (PhD, Medieval Literature, The Ohio State University) is Associate Professor of English at Methodist University. Her scholarship has focused on romances in the London Thornton Manuscript, including *The Siege of Jerusalem.* She is currently working on medievalism in modern fantasy culture.

Sherry C. M. Lindquist (PhD, Art History, Northwestern University) is Associate Professor of Art History at Western Illinois University. She has published *Agency, Visuality and Society at the Chartreuse de Champmol* (Ashgate, 2008), and *Meanings of Nudity in Medieval Art* (Ashgate, 2012), and has articles in *Gesta, Studies in Iconography, Winterthur Portfolio, Different Visions* and numerous anthologies. She is co-curator, with Asa Mittman, of the exhibit *Medieval Monsters: Terrors, Aliens and Wonders* at the Morgan Library and Museum, New York (2018).

Michael Livingston (PhD, English, University of Rochester) holds degrees in History, Medieval Studies and English. He currently serves as Associate Professor of English at The Citadel, is Associate Editor of the Secular Commentary Series of the Consortium for the Teaching of the Middle Ages (TEAMS), and sits on the Advisory Board of the TEAMS Middle English Texts Series. His most recent books are *Owain Glyndŵr: A Casebook* (Liverpool University Press, 2013), *The Battle of Brunanburh: A Casebook* (University of Exeter Press, 2011), an edition of *The Middle English*

Metrical Paraphrase of the Old Testament (Medieval Institute Publications, 2011), and, with Kelly DeVries, *The Battle of Crécy: A Casebook* (Liverpool University Press, 2015).

Asa Simon Mittman (PhD, Art History, Stanford University) is Professor and Chair of Art History at California State University, Chico. He is author of *Maps and Monsters in Medieval England* (Ashgate, 2006), co-author with Susan Kim of *Inconceivable Beasts: The Wonders of the East in the Beowulf Manuscript* (Arizona Center for Medieval and Renaissance Studies, 2013), and author and co-author of a number of articles on monstrosity and marginality in the Middle Ages, including pieces on Satan in the Junius 11 manuscript (*Gesta*, with Kim) and 'race' in the Middle Ages (*postmedieval*). He coedited the *Research Companion to Monsters and the Monstrous* (Ashgate, 2012), and is the founding president of MEARCSTAPA and a founding member of the Material Collective. Mittman is co-director of *Virtual Mappa*. He edits book series for Boydell and Brill. His current research includes the Franks Casket and images of Jews on medieval maps.

Mary Rambaran-Olm (PhD, Old English Language and Literature, University of Glasgow) continues research on the Exeter Book at the University of Glasgow after assisting on the AHRC funded 'Cullen Project'. Recent publications include *'John the Baptist's Prayer'* [*'Descent into Hell'*] *from the Exeter Book* (D. S. Brewer, 2014), as well as the articles 'The Advantages and Disadvantages of Digital Work in Anglo-Saxon Studies', *Digital Medievalist* 9.3 (2013); and 'Trial by History's Jury: Examining Æthelred II's Legislative Legacy from AD 993–1006', *English Studies* 95.7 (2014). Her research interests include: the Exeter Book, digital humanities, textual criticism, manuscript studies, Æthelred II and medievalism.

William Sayers (PhD, Romance Languages & Literatures, University of California, Berkeley) writes primarily on Old Norse, Old Irish, French, Norman and Anglo-French languages and literatures, and works in English etymology as a sideline. Recent studies of relevance to the present contribution are 'Extraordinary Weapons, Heroic Ethics, and Royal Justice in Early Irish Literature', *Preternature* 2.1 (2013): 1–18; 'Fantastic Technology in Early Irish Literature', *Études Celtiques* 40 (2014): 85–98; and 'Qualitative and Quantitative Criteria for Prosperous Royal Rule: Notes on *Audacht Morainn* and a Vedic Indian Analogue', *Studia Celtica* 48 (2014): 93–106.

Christine Sciacca (PhD, Art History, Columbia University) is Assistant Curator in the Manuscripts Department at the J. Paul Getty Museum. Her research concentrates on Italian, German and Ethiopian manuscript illumination, with a focus on liturgy, devotional practice and patronage. She has published articles on the role of textile curtains in illuminated manuscripts and on embroidered repairs in manuscripts, and is the author of *Building the Medieval World* (J. Paul Getty Museum / British Library), on images of architecture in illuminated manuscripts. Her international loan exhibition and accompanying catalogue, *Florence at the Dawn of the Renaissance: Painting and Illumination, 1300–1350,* appeared at the Getty Museum and the Art Gallery of Ontario in Toronto. Her most recent exhibitions have focused on gift-giving in the Middle Ages, and the role of food in medieval and Renaissance society as depicted in manuscript illumination.

Susan Small (PhD, Medieval French Literature, University of Western Ontario) is Associate Professor of French at King's University College at Western University, Canada. Her recent publications include 'The Medieval Werewolf Model of Reading Skin', in *Reading Skin in Medieval Literature and Culture,* ed. Katie L. Walter (Palgrave, 2013); and 'Frontier Girl Goes Feral in Eighteenth-Century France: The Curious Case of Marie-Angélique Memmie Le Blanc, the Wild Girl of Champagne', in *Making Monstrosity: Exploring the Cultural History of Continental European Freak Shows,* ed. Anna Kérchy and Andrea Zittlau (Cambridge Scholars, 2012).

Larissa Tracy (PhD, Medieval Literature, Trinity College, Dublin) is Associate Professor of Medieval Literature at Longwood University, Farmville, VA. She is the author of *Torture and Brutality in Medieval Literature* (D. S. Brewer, 2012) and *Women of the Gilte Legende* (D. S. Brewer, 2003). She co-edited, with Jeff Massey, *Heads Will Roll: Decapitation in the Medieval and Early Modern Imagination* (Brill, 2012), edited *Castration and Culture in the Middle Ages* (D. S. Brewer, 2013), and co-edited, with Kelly DeVries, *Wounds and Wound Repair in Medieval Culture* (Brill, 2015). She has published articles on violence, fabliaux, romance, gender and hagiography, and teaches a variety of courses (including studies abroad) on various aspects of medieval literature. She is the series editor for Explorations in Medieval Culture (Brill), and edits *Eolas: The Journal for the American Society of Irish Medieval Studies.*

Renée Ward (PhD, English Literature, University of Alberta) is a Senior Lecturer in Medieval Literature at the University of Lincoln. Her primary areas of research are in medieval literature, monster studies and medievalism, especially in the romance and young-adult fantasy genres. She has published articles on Middle English romances such as *Lybeaus Desconus, Octavian* and *William of Palerne,* and is currently preparing a monograph on werewolves in medieval romance. She has also published widely on the medievalism of J. K. Rowling's *Harry Potter* series.

Abbreviations

DIL   *Dictionary of the Irish Language*, ed. E. G. Quin *et al.* (Dublin: Royal Irish Academy, 1913–76)

EA   *Egils saga einhenda og Asmundar saga berserkjabana*, in *Fornaldarsögur Norðurlanda*, ed. Guðni Jónsson and Bjarni Vilhjálmsson, vol. 3 (Reykjavík: Bókútgáfan forni, 1943), pp. 153–89

EETS e.s.   Early English Text Society, Extra Series

EETS o.s.   Early English Text Society, Original Series

EETS s.s.   Early English Text Society, Supplementary Series

MED   *Middle English Dictionary*, The Regents of the University of Michigan (18 Dec. 2001). http://quod.lib.umich.edu/m/med/

OED   *Oxford English Dictionary* (Oxford: Oxford University Press, 2015). http://www.oed.com/

ÖO   *Örvar-Odds saga*, in *Fornaldarsögur Norðurlanda*, ed. Guðni Jónsson and Bjarni Vilhjálmsson, vol. 1 (Reykjavík: Bókútgáfan forni, 1943), pp. 283–399. http://www.snerpa.is/net/forn/orvar.htm

RCL   *Richard Coer de Lyon*, ed. Karl Brunner, in *Der Mittelenglische Versroman über Richard Löwenherz*, Wiener Beiträge zur Englischen Philologie 42 (Vienna and Leipzig, 1913)

SD   Stage direction

INTRODUCTION

Rending and Reading the Flesh

Larissa Tracy

S KIN is the parchment upon which identity is written. Class, race, ethnicity and gender are read upon the human surface. Removing skin tears away identity and leaves a blank slate upon which law, punishment, sanctity or monstrosity can be inscribed. Flaying strips away the means by which people see themselves or are viewed by others. Modern popular culture is fascinated with flaying – it often appears as a motif in horror films or serial crime dramas because, as Judith Halberstam writes, '[s]kin is at once the most fragile of boundaries and the most stable of signifiers; it is the site of entry for the vampire, the signifier of race for the nineteenth-century monster'.[1] In the 1991 film *Silence of the Lambs*, the serial killer branded 'Buffalo Bill' by the sensational media dresses up in a patchwork of skin sewn together to make a 'woman suit'; prancing in front of a mirror, he becomes 'a layered body, a body of many surfaces laid upon one another'.[2] For 'Bill' flaying is part of the transformative act through which he can emerge from a chrysalis of conflicting identities into a fully formed entity. The voyeuristic act of watching 'Bill' watching himself 'transformed' horrifies and, at the same time, captivates. In this sense, skin becomes 'a metaphor for surface, for the external; it is the place of pleasure and the site of pain; it is the thin sheet that masks bloody horror'.[3] This metaphor of skin as a surface for touch, pain, pleasure, torment and suffering is not exclusively a modern phenomenon.

Frequently when flaying is employed in modern popular culture (though not in *Silence of the Lambs*) it evokes a sense of the medieval – or what is assumed to be medieval. Like torture, flaying is one of those acts that modern audiences generally prefer to locate in a distant past, the product of a less enlightened age. Thus, it is often – erroneously – enumerated as one of many 'medieval' horrors, and it is used in fantasy and popular culture to evoke a particularly 'medieval' kind of atrocity. In George R. R. Martin's wildly popular modern fantasy series *Song of Ice and Fire*, a flayed man acts as a sigil for one of the more brutal houses. The HBO film adaptation, *Game of Thrones*, treats modern viewers to the display of banners adorned with a stylistic image of a skinless corpse. One of the more sadistic members of the House of Bolton, the illegitimate Ramsay

---

[1] Judith Halberstam, *Skin Shows: Gothic Horror and the Technology of Monsters* (Durham, NC: Duke University Press, 1996, repr. 2006), p. 163.

[2] Ibid., p. 1.

[3] Ibid., p. 165.

Snow, delights in honing his family reputation by systematically flaying the traitorous Theon Greyjoy, piece by piece, until Theon has lost any sense of himself. Repeatedly in later seasons, viewers are witness to other bloody, skinless trophies of Ramsay's sadism. In *Song of Ice and Fire* and its television adaptation, flaying is a medievalism that perpetuates a fantasy of medieval brutality and cruelty.

Barbara Tuchman imprinted the modern imagination with images of a bloody Middle Ages in which the 'tortures and punishments of civil justice customarily cut off hands and ears, racked, burned, flayed, and pulled apart people's bodies'.[4] Flaying is among the litany of tortures Tuchman ascribes to Bernabó Visconti, who ruled jointly with his brother Galeazzo in Lombardy and established a regime in which murder, cruelty, avarice and savage despotism alternated with effective government, respect for learning and encouragement of the arts.[5] She provides a lurid description of the *Quaresima*, 'a forty-day program of torture attributed to Bernabó and his brother, supposedly issued as an edict on their accession', which she hopes was intended to frighten, 'rather than for actual use': 'With the *strappado*, the wheel, the rack, flaying, gouging of eyes, cutting off of facial features and limbs one by one, and a day of torture alternating with a day of rest, it was supposed to terminate in death for "traitors" and convicted enemies'.[6] Thanks in part to studies like Tuchman's, flaying is often associated with spectacular displays of medieval cruelty. But it was actually a fairly rare punitive practice and not all aspects of flaying are simply barbaric, or even damaging. There are profound cultural, aesthetic, medical and ideological ramifications of skin removal.

In the Middle Ages the body was '*the* preeminent symbol of community'.[7] Suzanne Conklin Akbari and Jill Ross write: 'Body was not only that which was most intimately personal and most proper to the individual, but also that which was most public and representative of the interlocked nature of the group'.[8] Abruptions and disruptions of the body begin with the skin – the locus for touch, for beauty and for reverence. Its removal or restoration, by any means, has inspired countless artists and poets to render it on canvas – as canvas – or in literature as a site for divine sacrifice or penal justice. Skin is imbued with power; its removal and reuse acts as a means of transferring power in certain shamanistic rituals,

---

[4] Barbara W. Tuchman, *A Distant Mirror: The Calamitous Fourteenth Century* (New York: Ballantine Books, 1978), p. 135.

[5] Ibid., p. 240.

[6] Ibid., p. 241.

[7] Suzanne Conklin Akbari and Jill Ross, 'Limits and Teleology: The Many Ends of the Body', in *The Ends of the Body: Identity and Community in Medieval Culture*, ed. Akbari and Ross (Toronto: University of Toronto Press, 2013), pp. 3–21 at p. 3.

[8] Ibid., p. 3.

as transformative and purifying, while removing human skin in an act of judicial brutality, as a comic device or as a sign of spiritual sacrifice, leaves lasting impressions about the qualities and nature of humanity. Human excoriation often functioned as an *imaginative* resource for medieval and early modern artists and writers, even though it seems to have been a rare occurrence in practice. Skin makes identity; its removal erases and strips away that identity, or remakes it into something new. As Steven Connor writes, skin provides 'a model of the self preserved against change, and also reborn through change', because flaying is always accompanied or followed by the 'possibility of re-assumption: either the assumption of another skin, or the resumption of one's own skin (through healing)'.[9] Yet the skin can be changed, marked for or with new meanings, especially in the case of judicial mutilation and ordeal. Monstrosity that is embedded in the skin can be removed with the skin as surely as monstrous identity can be inscribed by removing the skin, rendering the beautiful into something horrific. When beautiful skin is removed, the product is monstrous; when monstrous skin is removed, it yields the potential for beauty. It is this contradiction that informs medieval artistic and literary depictions of flaying.

In his influential analysis of torture and pain in medieval art, Robert Mills explains medieval notions of skin as memory. He writes that 'to flay someone alive would be to tear away the bodily surface onto which transitory memories and identities could be inscribed – only to fashion an etched parchment in its place (the dead skin), from which "timeless" moral lessons could be read'.[10] Other recent studies, like that edited by Katie Walter, read skin as a legible text upon which various identities and anxieties are inscribed.[11] Walter's volume explores the 'dense tissue of associations of skin in medieval culture'[12] through essays on the monstrous touch of the Blemmye, touch in religious literature and art, the transformative properties of werewolves, reading the skin during confession and disfiguring diseases of the skin. But only Mills' essay deals with the concrete act of flaying a living person, in his analysis of

---

[9] Steven Connor, *The Book of Skin* (Ithaca, NY: Cornell University Press, 2004), pp. 31, 32.

[10] Robert Mills, *Suspended Animation: Pain, Pleasure and Punishment in Medieval Culture* (London: Reaktion, 2005), p. 68.

[11] Katie L. Walter, ed., *Reading Skin in Medieval Literature and Culture* (New York: Palgrave, 2013). Also see: Sarah Kay, 'Flayed Skin as *objet a*: Representation and Materiality in Guillaume de Deguileville's *Pèlerinage de vie humaine*', in *Medieval Fabrications: Dress, Textiles, Clothwork, and other Cultural Imaginings*, ed. E. Jane Burns (New York: Palgrave, 2004), pp. 193–205; Sarah Kay, 'Original Skin: Flaying, Reading, and Thinking in the Legend of Saint Bartholomew and other Works', *Journal of Medieval and Early Modern Studies* 36.1 (2006): 35–73.

[12] Katie L. Walter, Introduction to *Reading Skin*, ed. Walter, p. 1.

the thirteenth-century Middle English *Havelok the Dane*.[13] In addition to Walter's compelling collection, there have been several important studies on skin and on touch, like Connor's *Book of Skin* and Constance Classen's *The Deepest Sense*.[14] But within those texts discussions of flaying are limited and often repeat the same sources, the same mythologies, and analyse the same iconography and texts. To date, no study has looked comprehensively at the actual practice of excoriation in relation to the artistic and literary representations, nor has any study approached this question through a multidisciplinary lens. In Karmen MacKendrick's words, it is possible to 'thematize that which is both fragmentation and joining, schism and suture', and to do so 'in a philosophy of touches and folds and scars, surfaces marked without depths revealed'.[15] But while there are many modern theoretical paradigms through which flaying can be discussed, this collection focuses more on literal flaying, both human and animal – the act, the laws, the instruments, the implications, the representations, the reality – within the context of the Middle Ages. In some instances, we will deal with the same sources and mythologies as previous studies, but we hope to offer a more textured understanding of flaying and its functions in medieval literature and culture by presenting them in tandem with more unusual or unique episodes and by analysing practice and representation together.

Framed in the discourse of modern misconceptions and medievalisms, this volume explores literal skin removal from the eleventh century to the early seventeenth century, across a variety of cultures (Ireland, England, France, Italy and Scandinavia), interrogating the connection between practice and imagination in depictions of literal skin removal (rather than figurative or theoretical interpretations of flaying), and offering a multilayered view of medieval and early modern perceptions of flaying and its representations in European culture.

Forms of Flaying and the Mythology of Excoriation

Flaying refers to any act of skin removal, for any purpose, whether in its entirety or in strips during the process of flogging, scourging or (in rare instances) scalping. The term 'flaying' generally applies to the removal of human integument; animals were usually 'skinned', though at times the linguistic division between human and animal was as porous as their hides, and in their removal those boundaries collapsed. In Latin, *pellis* refers

---

[13] Robert Mills, 'Havelok's Bare Life and the Significance of Skin', in *Reading Skin*, ed. Walter, pp. 57–80.

[14] Connor, *Book of Skin*, pp. 10, 31, 67, 284 n. 44; Constance Classen, *The Deepest Sense: A Cultural History of Touch* (Chicago: University of Illinois Press, 2012).

[15] Karmen MacKendrick, *Word Made Skin: Figuring Language at the Surface of Flesh* (New York: Fordham University Press, 2004), p. 7.

specifically to dead, flayed skin – this word was used for animal skins and 'evokes disgust, disgrace and horror'; in contrast is *cutis*, living skin that 'protects, that expresses and arouses and that is the subject of care and beautiful attention'.[16] The act of cutting away the skin has an independent life in romance languages: Old French *escorcier*, 'to skin (an animal), to flay (a person)', has its root in the Latin *excorticare*, 'to strip of bark or skin'.[17] The term appears in Old English as *flēan, flōg, be-flagen*, and in Old Norse/Icelandic as *flā, flō, flōgum, fleginn*. According to the *Middle English Dictionary, flen*, or *flowen*, means:

1 (a) To strip the skin from (a person, a part of someone's body); also, to tear the skin to shreds (by blows, scourging, etc.); to strip (the skin from the flesh); ~ **of**, to flay off (the skin); ~ **out of skin**, to flay (someone) completely; also *fig.*; (b) ~ **quik**, to skin (someone) alive, to strip off (the skin) while the victim lives; (c) ~ **of berd**, to remove (someone's) beard with the skin.

2 (a) *Surg.* To remove or peel back the skin from (part of the body); also, to expose (something) by cutting and drawing back the flesh; (b) to circumcise.

3 To break the skin or the mucous membrane of (a part of the body); abrade, bruise, excoriate; to tear or corrode (the skin).

4 (a) To remove the hide from (an animal, part of an animal), to skin; to peel back (an animal's skin); (b) **fleing knif**, a skinning knife.[18]

From images of St Bartholomew holding his skin in his arms (or wearing it like a cloak), to the scourging of Christ and Christian saints, to scenes of execution in *Havelok the Dane* and skins worn to channel divine power, to laws that prescribed it as a rare punishment for treason, flaying takes a variety of forms in medieval and early modern culture. The primary concern here is the physicality of flaying – the instruments used to achieve it, the uses to which the flayed skin was put, the textual implications of inflicting it as well as its existence as an aspect of literature and art.

To remove the flesh rendered criminals unrecognizable – or clarified that damning label; it neutralized the threat of a 'barbarian Other'. As such, several myths regarding the frequency of medieval flaying emerge in later centuries, creating an impression of cruelty and barbarism in a darker, less civilized age. Marsyas, the satyr flayed (justly, many argue) for his presumption in challenging Apollo to a musical duel, is a touchstone for

---

[16] Connor, *Book of Skin*, p. 11.

[17] *Dictionnaire de l'ancien français, le Moyen Âge*, ed. A. J. Greimas (Paris: Larousse, 1995), p. 231. I am grateful to Daniel O'Sullivan and Jeff Massey for their input on this matter.

[18] *The Middle English Dictionary*, online at http://quod.lib.umich.edu/m/med (accessed 2 May 2014).

many medieval discussions of this judicial punishment. Ovid only briefly tells his tale in the *Metamorphoses* (vi.383–400), but Marsyas' suffering informs medieval penal imagery, 'the network of visual and textual significations that transform the violated bodies of executed criminals into discourse and fantasy'.[19] As a punishment, flaying is an arresting motif in medieval iconography, particularly in visual renderings of St Bartholomew's martyrdom – the only prominent saint condemned to be entirely flayed alive. Gerard David's triptych *The Judgement of Cambyses* (1498), installed in the Judgement Chamber of the Bruges Town Hall, adroitly analysed by Mills, captivates its audience with its grisly public flaying of the corrupt judge Sisamnes. His criminal-skin 'communicates the horror of death in the minds of the viewers' and, equally, 'mediates something immaterial and abstract: the intangible "truth" of just judgment'.[20] In mythologies of medieval flaying, justice is often the aim – even if it is not the product.

As Akbari and Ross suggest, the dynamic aspect of embodiment is often expressed in medieval sources through engagement with the processes of the body; at other times, it is expressed 'through performance, whether literally acted out within the text or used as a metaphorical system that employs the body as a flexible symbol to denote religious, civic, national, or ethnic communities'.[21] The body as a whole is often the site for these discourses, but sometimes the focal point is only skin-deep. This volume probes beneath the surface aspects of embodiment and considers both the practice and the representation of flaying in two parts. Within each section, the chapters are arranged thematically to capture the transformation of flaying as both an idea and a practice in the premodern world, crossing the gap between practice and cultural representations in art and literature. The articles in the first part have counterparts in the second, where practice is envisioned in fantasy and representation. Thus, the chapters function as interlocking parts that build upon one another and speak to each other. The first section deals with the instruments used to remove skin, the specific processes involved, and the medical effects on the flayed body, as well as early modern accounts of human skin as a material object worn as clothing for divination. Other pieces in this section investigate the reality of flaying in historical and legal practice, often revealing an absence rather than a presence. Representations of flaying in religious and secular contexts, including art, literature and performance, follow in the second section, with particular attention to depictions of St Bartholomew. The discourse is wrapped up in the Epilogue, on book-binding with human skin, tying

---

[19] Mills, *Suspended Animation*, p. 65. Mills lays a great deal of the groundwork for subsequent discussions of flaying in medieval representation and practice.

[20] Ibid., p. 70.

[21] Akbari and Ross, 'Limits and Teleology', p. 4.

together threads of discussion throughout and bringing the issue of flaying into a modern context.

Flaying in Practice

While flaying is a feature of modern folklore about pre-modern judicial or medical procedure, chronicles and legal texts make scant reference to it as an *actual* practice. Medically speaking, the skin was the organ penetrated in wounding and through which surgeons and physicians probed in order to heal. Skin is debrided to remove dead or infected tissue and to promote healing. The skin must also be cut in order to access the inner depths of the body for care and for cure, as Jack Hartnell explains in the first chapter of this volume. In the 'flayed figure' woodcut in Juan de Hamusco's *Historia de la composicion del cuerpo humano* (1556), the subject holds both his skin – like a discarded garment complete with eye holes – and the knife with which it was removed, striking a pose so that the musculature underneath is visible and accessible to the medical student.[22] Henri de Mondeville (*c.* 1260–1320), in his unfinished *Cyrurgia* (started in 1306), dealt thoroughly with wound treatment[23] and opposed the Hippocratic view that advocated suppuration – pus formation – preferring dry healing instead; that is, the simple bathing of wounds, immediate closure by suture, and dry dressings with minimal loss of flesh or skin.[24] Hartnell points out that the skin was simply a casing for the body that must be healed, and knives were simply the tools used to access it, though some surgeons had specialist instruments commissioned as a mark of their status. Of course, anxieties about the integrity of the soul developed with the rise of surgery as a discipline. Any breaking of the skin through blunt or sharp-force trauma, any puncture or slash, laceration or abrasion, threatens the interior systems of the body and so the removal of that skin destabilizes the symbiotic relationship between skin and soul.[25]

According to Sarah Kay and Miri Rubin, the 'body/soul opposition was deployed regularly in medieval rhetoric to denote a troubling proximity of incommensurable, yet coexisting entities'.[26] Caroline Walker Bynum highlights this relationship, writing that the 'experiences of souls were

---

[22] See: Mills, *Suspended Animation*, p. 75 fig. 36.

[23] Roy Porter, *The Greatest Benefit to Mankind* (New York: W. W. Norton, 1999), pp. 116–17.

[24] Pierre Huard and Mirko Drazen Grmek, *Mille ans de chirurgie en occident: Vᵉ–XVᵉ siècles* (Paris: R. Dacosta, 1966), p. 40.

[25] Larissa Tracy and Kelly DeVries, Introduction to *Wounds and Wound Repair in Medieval Culture*, ed. Tracy and DeVries (Leiden: Brill, 2015).

[26] Sarah Kay and Miri Rubin, Introduction to *Framing Medieval Bodies*, ed. Kay and Rubin (Manchester: Manchester University Press, 1994), pp. 1–9 at p. 5.

imaged as bodily events', pointing to the use of bodily metaphors for spiritual states in many societies.[27] In this context, flaying peels away the body from its frame – pulling away from the soul. Even after the separation of 'the inside and the outside of the body, the role of the skin is to maintain the integrity of the soul – to be, as it were, the soul's body'.[28] As MacKendrick explains in terms of the Gospel of John, flesh 'is not simply that which blocks the light but that which makes possible the very fact of illumination as both medium and object of luminosity'.[29] Flaying also reveals the humanity underneath, the flesh and blood that signified mankind's divine origins and separation. As early as 1109, Guibert of Nogent weighed in on debates about the physical manifestation of Christ, specifically the efficacy and legitimacy of his relics.[30] The skin that is flayed remains intact as an object of devotion. Martyrs were willing to sacrifice their bodies 'because they know every particle will return in the end'; they participate in a 'vision of last things in which not just wholeness but reassemblage is the ultimate promise'.[31] To medieval minds, the basic idea of flesh and flaying often evoked the sacred flesh of Christ. After the Fourth Lateran Council, in 1215, the Eucharist and the doctrine of transubstantiation are directly tied to the *idea* of Christ's flesh – removed, combined, reconstituted, consumed and, yet, whole and intact. Flesh, and flesh made Word, were centralizing features of medieval Christian devotion; flesh that was both 'Light and Word, is also the medium of *touch*, which enfolds and cuts across a nearly bewildering array of meanings'.[32] To touch the flesh was to touch the divine; to witness sacrifices of the flesh was often perceived as a means of participating in divine sacrifice.

Part of reconciling these disparate, conflicting entities – flesh and divinity – involved subordinating the body to the soul, and moderation of the body could help achieve greater control over the soul.[33] Prayer manuals, devotional works and the rules of religious Orders, like the Dominican treatise *The Nine Ways of Prayer of St Dominic* (1260–88),

---

[27] Caroline Walker Bynum, *Fragmentation and Redemption: Essays on Gender and the Human Body in Medieval Religion* (New York: Zone, 1992), p. 234.

[28] Connor, *Book of Skin*, p. 10.

[29] MacKendrick, *Word Made Skin*, p. 27.

[30] Steven F. Kruger, 'Becoming Christian, Becoming Male', in *Becoming Male in the Middle Ages*, ed. Jeffrey Jerome Cohen and Bonnie Wheeler (New York: Garland, 2000), pp. 21–41 at p. 22. See also: Guibert of Nogent, *The Deeds of God through the Franks*, trans. Robert Levine (Woodbridge: Boydell Press, 1997), p. 38.

[31] Bynum, *Fragmentation and Redemption*, pp. 12, 13.

[32] MacKendrick, *Word Made Skin*, p. 27.

[33] Walter Simons, 'Reading a Saint's Body: Rapture and Bodily Movement in the *Vitae* of Thirteenth-Century Beguines', in *Framing Medieval Bodies*, ed. Kay and Rubin, pp. 10–23 at p. 14.

included flagellation, though its use was contested throughout the Middle Ages and is more correctly thought of as penance rather than prayer.[34] An anchoress was permitted to beat herself with scourges weighted with lead, with holly, or with thorns, but only with her confessor's permission; however, she 'should not sting herself anywhere with nettles, or scourge the front of her body, or mutilate herself with cuts, or take excessively severe disciplines at any one time, in order to subdue temptations'.[35] Thus, the anchoress could share the suffering of Christ, and it could be 'internalised as a punitively penitential inscription on the body'.[36] But that was as far as she could go in her mimetic devotions. As far as surviving sources indicate, actual martyrdom by flaying was solely a facet of religious literature and iconography.

Though it is often described as such, flaying was not a form of torture; its use was strictly punitive rather than interrogative, and then it was generally reserved (in limited cases) as a punishment for treason or other heinous crimes.[37] In each of these instances, flaying is part of the process of punishment, a final outcome after sentence is passed or the victim condemned – guilty or innocent. Emanuel J. Mickel writes, 'that the popular imagination condemned treason in the strongest terms can be seen in the literature of the period where [...] flaying was also thought to be a traditional way of punishing traitors'.[38] Punishments for treason publicly inscribed the crime against the body politic – or the body of the king – upon the body of the traitor. This revealed, above all else, 'the constant interplay of the somatic and the conceptual that served to explain

---

[34] Ibid., pp. 14–15.

[35] Part 8 of the outer rule of *Ancrene Wisse*, in *Medieval English Prose for Women: 'Ancrene Wisse' and the Katherine Group*, ed. and trans. Bella Millett and Jocelyn Wogan-Browne (Oxford: Oxford University Press, 1990), p. 136, ll. 13–19.

[36] Jocelyn Wogan-Browne, 'Chaste Bodies: Frames and Experiences', in *Framing Medieval Bodies*, ed. Kay and Rubin, pp. 24–42 at p. 33.

[37] In *Torture* (Philadelphia: University of Pennsylvania Press, 1985), Edward Peters points out that to the medieval mind *torture* meant something very specific – judicial torture was the *only* kind of torture, however it was administered, and any other form of punishment not designed to elicit a confession should not be called torture (p. 7). Canon law required at least two 'half-proofs' before the accused could be subjected to torture to obtain the 'Queen of Proofs' – the confession. Between 1150 and 1250 jurists raised confession of the accused up as the most valuable proof, with other proofs arranged in a hierarchy below it – a hierarchy that provided the essential background for the use of torture, especially in capital crimes (p. 46). We employ Peters' definition of *torture* as distinct from *punishment*, throughout this volume.

[38] Emanuel J. Mickel, *Ganelon, Treason, and the 'Chanson de Roland'* (University Park: Pennsylvania State University Press, 1989), p. 147.

everyday social interaction'.[39] Flaying was supposedly the punishment meted out to Bertram de Gurdun, the man whose quarrel found its mark in the body of Richard I. According to Roger de Hoveden, Bertram was flayed alive, despite the pardon of the dying king.[40] While Roger's account conflicts with others regarding Richard's death, the story became very popular in later centuries. As Emily Leverett points out in this volume, Richard develops an equally legendary association with flaying, which may have developed from this 'historical' event, but which belongs securely in the realm of literary fantasy. Acts of treason often merited the worst punishments, even if they were only threatened rather than actually carried out. In 1176, Henry, the 'Young King', condemned his vice-chancellor Adam to be hung up and flayed alive for reporting the young king's activities to his father, Henry II.[41] Adam escaped this punishment, claiming benefit of the clergy.[42] Violating the king's body, or those of his royal daughters, was also considered an act of treason, for which flaying may have figured as a punishment in select cases. In 1314, Philip and Walter de Launoy were supposedly condemned to be flayed by degrees after being convicted of adultery with the two daughters-in-law of King Philip IV of France.[43]

The presence of flaying in legal discourse is more problematic. Anthony Musson points out that 'ideologies of law' are multidimensional, operating on several different levels.[44] Nor were all laws confined to identifiable legal texts. Musson writes that institutions 'forming the royal judicial and administrative machine and other bodies, such as parliament, the county, urban and manorial courts, the Church, and the universities, could also create and disseminate ideology by providing an interface for the communication and exchange of ideas, beliefs and opinions'.[45] As such, medieval law was not a uniform entity; not every society shared the same views on punishment or the integrity of the body, and if they did, not every community wrote them down. Thus, legal references to any form of

---

[39] Danielle M. Westerhof, 'Amputating the Traitor: Healing the Social Body in Public Executions for Treason in Late Medieval England', in *The Ends of the Body*, ed. Akbari and Ross, pp. 177–92 at p. 178.

[40] M. J. Swanton, '"Dane-Skins": Excoriation in Early England', *Folklore* 87.1 (1976): 21–8 at p. 22.

[41] Ibid. The actual account appears in *Placita Anglo-Normannica: Law Cases from William I to Richard I Preserved in Historical Records*, ed. Melville Madison Bigelow (London: George Olms, 1879), pp. 314–15.

[42] Swanton, '"Dane-Skins"', p. 22.

[43] Ibid.

[44] Anthony Musson, *Medieval Law in Context: The Growth of Legal Consciousness from Magna Carta to the Peasants' Revolt* (Manchester: Manchester University Press, 2001), p. 7.

[45] Ibid.

flaying – flogging, flagellation, complete excoriation (pre- or post mortem) or scalping – are scattered and varied.

According to Peter Baker, the Latin *Life of St Swithun* refers to a law from a lost law code of Edgar *reported* to have dictated that thieves and robbers should be tortured, then the skin and hair of their heads flayed off.[46] Baker cautions, however, that while the spirit, if not the letter of this law, seems to have been confirmed by later laws that included similar penalties for theft, 'one may doubt how often the state was able both to apprehend and punish such criminals', potentially leading to a certain amount of localized vigilante justice.[47] In her studies of early English and Continental law, Lisi Oliver discusses scalping as a punishment, but also the amount of restitution that could be claimed for *wælt wund*, potentially 'a wound that detaches a strip of skin'.[48] Cnut's code, drafted by Archbishop Wulfstan, includes removal of the scalp among a catalogue of possible corporeal punishments where survival of these mutilations might be uncertain (or undesired), but there was a chance that the victim would live to repent.[49] Scalping as punishment was meant to leave a permanent scar rather than kill. Oliver writes that because hair cannot grow back on the scalped portion of the head, 'not only is the transgressor publicly humiliated and physically tortured, but he is branded for life'.[50] Michael Swanton points out that after the Conquest scalping appears in the English customary law collection *Leges Henrici Primi* (*Laws of Henry I*) as a punishment for the crime of *lèse-majesty* where a man is found guilty of slaying his lord.[51] Swanton suggests that 'enthusiastic executioners' might have overstepped their mark and resorted to flaying the whole body, contending that 'it is but

---

[46] Peter S. Baker, *Honour, Exchange and Violence in 'Beowulf'* (Cambridge: D. S. Brewer, 2013), pp. 5–6.

[47] Ibid., p. 6.

[48] Lisi Oliver, *The Beginnings of English Law* (Toronto: University of Toronto Press, 2002), p. 103. See also: Lisi Oliver, *The Body Legal in Barbarian Law* (Toronto: University of Toronto Press, 2011), p. 84, which deals specifically with injuries to the scalp. On scalping and scourging as punishment, see: *The Body Legal*, pp. 175–6. Visigothic law adds scalping to the humiliation of public beating (p. 176).

[49] Patrick Wormald, *The Making of English Law: King Alfred to the Twelfth Century*, vol. 1: *Legislation and its Limits* (Oxford: Blackwell, 2001), p. 126.

[50] Oliver, *The Body Legal*, p. 176. Swanton claims that 'judicial excoriation seems to have been known since earliest times on the Continent of Europe – where it may be related to the much-debated Merovingian practice of scalping', but says that the practice makes 'only a relatively belated appearance in England' ('"Dane-Skins"', p. 21). However, he further explains that 'excoriation' means superficial lacerations on the skin rather than flaying.

[51] Swanton, '"Dane-Skins"', p. 21.

a small step from flaying the head to flaying the entire body'.[52] However, it is a great leap from scalping to flaying. W. R. J. Barron 'concedes that the punishment was not common in reality, for it is not found in chronicles or the law'.[53] It was always an *exceptional* penalty, one that does not seem to have been performed regularly, if at all, despite Barron's contention that it was an ancient practice.[54] Mickel rejects the idea that flaying was born of 'ancient usage' and quite correctly points out that such 'an assumption comes from our natural inclination to ascribe harsher penalties to an earlier, less enlightened age'.[55]

Flaying was rarely used as a method of capital punishment in the medieval period; when it was – either legitimately or illegitimately – the flayed body was an eloquent canvas upon which the punitive excesses of the secular authority may be written. As Mitchell Merback writes, 'the maimed body of the condemned spoke an arresting language of pain that spectators understood not as an unfortunate by-product of the performance of justice, but as a portentous source of information'.[56] Here, Susan Small analyses the graphic execution of Peter Stubbe, who was condemned as a sorcerer, sexual predator, serial killer and werewolf, to be beaten on a wheel, flayed, dismembered, decapitated and burned at the stake. Stubbe was accused of effecting his transformation into a werewolf by wearing a magic girdle secured through a deal with the devil. Skin – the loss of the human and appropriation of the wolf – is intimately connected to the narrative of Stubbe's crimes and punishment. There were also extraordinary circumstances where the 'wolf' was not the one who was flayed, but the one who did the flaying. In this collection Kelly DeVries provides a concise case study of the Venetian Marcantonio Bragadin, who was flayed by Turkish invaders of Crete and had his skin stuffed with straw, simply for being an able general who refused to surrender. This account provides one of the few surviving narratives of *actual* punitive flaying.

One of the most infamous myths regarding medieval flaying, one which persisted well into the modern era, was enshrined by Samuel Pepys on 10 April 1661. Visiting Rochester Cathedral, Pepys observed the great doors of the cathedral that were said to have been covered with the skins of Danes, flayed by the Anglo-Saxons as a punishment for sacrilege.[57]

---

[52] Ibid.

[53] W. R. J. Barron, 'The Penalties for Treason in Medieval Life and Literature', *Journal of Medieval History* 7 (1981): 187–202 at p. 197.

[54] Ibid.

[55] Mickel, *Ganelon, Treason*, p. 147 n. 303.

[56] Mitchell B. Merback, *The Thief, the Cross and the Wheel: Pain and the Spectacle of Punishment in Medieval and Renaissance Europe* (London: Reaktion, 1999), p. 19.

[57] Lawrence S. Thompson, *Bibliologia comica; or, Humorous Aspects of the Caparisoning and Conservation of Books* (Hamden, CT: Archon, 1968).

Lawrence S. Thompson gives credence to this report, claiming that Pepys was 'not merely propagating idle rumor' and citing the nineteenth- and early twentieth-century debates in the pages of *Notes & Queries* as evidence that '[o]ur Anglo-Saxon forebears' were no less savage than the Romans in 'their treatment of marauding Danes who violated their places of worship'.[58] Allegedly, church doors in Hadstock, Copford, Worcester and Southwark, in addition to Rochester, were decorated with the skins of Danes.[59] In her contribution to this volume, Mary Rambaran-Olm tackles the persistence of this myth as part of a nationalizing medievalism in the seventeenth and eighteenth centuries that continued well into the twentieth century. These myths, coupled with a profound sense of alienation from the past, have created the image of the medieval world perpetuated in modern popular culture, as in *Game of Thrones*. But the reality of flaying in the medieval period was quite different.

Medieval representations and interpretations of the body and human identity were complex. Anxieties about community, inclusion and exclusion were often embodied in the skin. As such, the occurrence of flaying is not restricted to accounts of punishment or brutality, or even human practice. As Connor writes, 'nothing is deader than a skin, peeled, shucked or sloughed. And yet skins are often imagined as containing or preserving life and therefore having the power to restore it'.[60] Thompson enumerates 'folk beliefs which may have their roots in times we do not care to recall in all their details', beliefs that are supposedly full of 'human skin legends'.[61] Here, Frederika Bain re-examines this folkloric evidence and offers a far more current and nuanced analysis of traditions that involved wearing human skin, including narratives where skin is presented as having both curative and transformative properties. Bain's chapter emphasizes the transgressive potential of wearing skin – animal or human – crossing the boundary between literal and literary. Bridging the gap between practice and representation, Bain investigates accounts of wearing animal skin to absorb the essence and traits of the animal, juxtaposing them with similar accounts where a human skin was worn to absorb its power. References to flaying in medieval tradition imply both a fascination with and revulsion from such excessive brutality among medieval populations. Some scant physical as well as textual evidence does survive that suggests that flaying was carried out for a variety of legitimate and illegitimate reasons during the Middle Ages, though most of the recorded episodes covered here occur in the sixteenth century and the myths of flayed skins largely emerge in the seventeenth century. Medieval Europe seems to have had a distaste for it, except in apocryphal accounts and spurious reports. This scarcity in reality

---

[58] Ibid., p. 120.

[59] Ibid. See also: Swanton, '"Dane-Skins"'.

[60] Connor, *Book of Skin*, p. 31.

[61] Thompson, *Bibliologia comica*, p. 120.

raises complicated questions about its prevalence as an artistic and literary motif – in many instances, flaying seems only to exist in the pre- or early modern imagination.

Representations of Flaying

While flaying was limited in practice, it widely featured in representations of pain, suffering and sanctity throughout the Middle Ages. Flayed bodies were displayed on canvas, parchment, in churches, described in romances as criticism of illegitimate power, or used as aspects of Otherworldly monstrosity. Flaying is a popular literary motif that occasionally reflects or distorts actual practice. Representations of flaying intersect with medieval notions of the body as an intact or inviolate vessel for the soul. The hagiographical experience of flaying – particularly that associated with St Bartholomew, who was said to have been flayed by a non-Christian tyrant during his missionary endeavours in India – its participation in the spectacle of pain associated with the sacrifice of martyrdom,[62] featured abruptions of the skin, penetrating wounds, and occasionally skin removal. The twelfth and thirteenth centuries saw a renewed debate over theological matters 'in which the relationship of the part to the whole was crucial, and [there was] a new emphasis on miracles [...] in which bodies are the mediators between earth and heaven'.[63] As a consequence, religious iconography and texts were filled with torture imagery and narratives about rending the body and the flesh – tearing away layers of both meaning and being with the hope, the assumption, that upon salvation all would be whole again. Flesh rendered would be flesh restored. For many medieval people, witnessing this spectacle in artistic depictions, 'the experience of *seeing and imagining* a body that was ravaged and bleeding from tortures inflicted upon it lay at the centre of a constellation of religious doctrines, beliefs and devotional practices'.[64] A body of medieval hagiography, the most popular collection of which was Jacobus de Voragine's *Legenda aurea* (1255–66) [*LgA*],[65] circulated throughout medieval Europe and codified

---

[62] Mills highlights the medieval cultural associations surrounding the removal of skin, specifically the place of flaying within medieval penal imagery – 'the network of visual and textual significations that transform the violated bodies of executed criminals into discourse and fantasy' (*Suspended Animation*, p. 65).

[63] Bynum, *Fragmentation and Redemption*, p. 13.

[64] Merback, *The Thief, the Cross, and the Wheel*, p. 19.

[65] The *Legenda aurea* has been translated and edited by both William Granger Ryan and Christopher Stace. See: Jacobus de Voragine, *The Golden Legend: Readings on the Saints*, ed. and trans. William Granger Ryan, 2 vols. (Princeton: Princeton University Press, 1993); *The Golden Legend*, ed. Christopher Stace with an introduction by Richard Hamer (Middlesex: Penguin, 1998).

the sufferings of countless martyrs to the Christian faith, many of whom simply existed as stock, formulaic characters, reinforcing the polemic of holy sacrifice.

More than 1,000 manuscripts of the *LgA* survive. It was translated into French (*Legende doreé*, 1380–1480)[66] and Middle English (the *Gilte Legende*, c. 1438)[67] and later printed by William Caxton as *The Golden Legend* (1483). The Middle English *South English Legendary* (1270–80) evolved independently of the *LgA*; it was assembled in the southwest Midlands during the second half of the thirteenth century and was revised and supplemented around 1380–90. There are more than sixty extant manuscripts, making it one of the best-represented works in Middle English, next to *Prick of Conscience*, the *Canterbury Tales* and *Piers Plowman*. Its adaptation of Latin material is marked by a specific attention to native English saints' lives.[68] These collections circulated widely and popularized legends devoted to the tribulations of saints, providing a scintillating spectacle of violence and torture, including flogging and flaying. The martyrdom of these saints was specifically and deliberately inscribed on their skins – or inscribed in the inefficacy of torments that failed to mark the beautiful skin of a martyr who had to be dispatched by more conventional means, like beheading.[69] Sinners are often afflicted with skin

---

[66] See: Genevieve Hasenohr, 'Religious Reading amongst the Laity in France in the Fifteenth Century', in *Heresy and Literacy, 1000–1530*, ed. Peter Biller and Anne Hudson (Cambridge: Cambridge University Press, 1994), pp. 205–21.

[67] See: *Three Lives from the Gilte Legende, Edited from MS BL Egerton 876*, ed. Richard Hamer (Heidelberg: Universitätsverlag Carl Winter, 1978); *Gilte Legende*, ed. Richard Hamer with the assistance of Vida Russell, 3 vols., EETS o.s. 327, 328 and 339 (Oxford: Oxford University Press, 2006, 2007 and 2012); and *Supplementary Lives in some Manuscripts of the Gilte Legende*, ed. Richard Hamer and Vida Russell, EETS o.s. 315 (Oxford: Oxford University Press, 2000).

[68] Karen Winstead, *Virgin Martyrs: Legends of Sainthood in Late Medieval England* (Ithaca, NY: Cornell University Press, 1997), pp. 71–2. See also: Manfred Görlach, *The South English Legendary, Gilte Legende and Golden Legend* (Braunschweig: Institut für Anglistik und Amerikanistik, 1972), reiterated in *Studies in Middle English Saints' Legends* (Heidelberg: Universitätsverlag Carl Winter, 1998); and Oliver Pickering, 'The Temporale Narratives of the *South English Legendary*', *Anglia* 91 (1973): 425–55; *The South English Ministry and Passion: Ed. from St John's College, Cambridge, MS B.6*, ed. Oliver Pickering, Middle English Texts (Heidelberg: Universitätsverlag Carl Winter, 1984); and Oliver Pickering, 'The Outspoken *South English Legendary* Poet', in *Late Medieval Religious Texts and their Transmission: Essays in Honor of A. I. Doyle*, ed. A. J. Minnis (Cambridge: D. S. Brewer, 1994), pp. 21–37.

[69] See: Larissa Tracy, *Torture and Brutality in Medieval Literature: Negotiations of National Identity* (Cambridge: D. S. Brewer, 2012).

diseases, flaying off their skin with their own fingernails, like Sir William Tracy, one of the murderers of Thomas á Becket, who could not be cured until he repented his crime against the saint and sought forgiveness (just before death).[70] Flaying functions as an important and popular motif of sanctity and hagiography. Whenever it is employed, flaying is a stunning visualization of the contradictions of fragility and durability of the flesh. In Chapter 6, Asa Simon Mittman and Christine Sciacca explore the visual aspects of the flayed Bartholomew in the Laudario of Sant'Agnese, in which the saint is depicted wearing his own skin as a garment, and analyse the visual implications of this scene. In the following essay, Sherry Lindquist similarly investigates images of St Bartholomew in the *Belles Heures* of the Duc de Berry and considers the representations of flaying and flagellation in terms of masculinist devotion. Next, Peter Dent looks through 'a window of pain' at questions of surface, interiority and Christ's flagellated skin in late medieval sculpture. Artistic representations of flaying as the locus for devotional practice are mirrored in performance, as Valerie Gramling then explains in regard to the English Passion Plays in Chapter 9. These pieces are all connected by the emphasis on flagellation as a means of wounding the body – of saint, saviour or sinner – and reflect back on the practices examined by Small.

In Chapter 10, William Sayers juxtaposes Irish literary and hagiographical accounts of flaying, including that of Bartholomew and *Togail Bruidne Da Derga* (*The Destruction of Da Derga's Hostel*), with the absence of flaying in Irish legal texts. While representations of flaying are important modes of religious devotion, flaying appears most frequently as a literary motif in medieval romance. The chivalric world is visible to medieval and modern audiences through a thin film of associations and realities. Knights fulfil their quests in a world that bears a hazy resemblance to that in which people actually lived and operated. Medieval romance is populated by the fantastic (both creatures and feats), and often critiques the savage deeds of its actors. In romance, knights and kings, and even Vikings, exact justice in the pursuit of chivalry, but occasionally they go too far and perpetuate needless brutality in the name of law. Kings who resort to torture or excessive judicial brutality – specifically flaying – are potentially tarnished by their cruelty and inhuman justice. In her essay, Leverett considers the intersections of flaying, religious and national identity in *The Siege of Jerusalem* and *Richard Coer de Lyon*, where

---

[70] Sir William's tale is told as the last miracle story of St Thomas' *vita* in the *South English Legendary*. William tries to find repentance in England, but his skin breaks out in foul, stinking boils that fester and he pulls off the skin from his hands and arms until there is nothing but sinew and bare bone. Yet he cannot not die, so he calls on Thomas' mercy and dies, possibly forgiven. *The Life of St Thomas of Canterbury*, in *The South English Legendary, or Lives of Saints*, ed. Carl Horstmann, EETS o.s. 87 (London: Trübner, 1887), pp. 106–77 at p. 175 (ll. 2382–416).

Christians flay Muslims and dine on their flesh, an inversion of the historical episode of Bragadin examined by DeVries: 'The flayed, skinless bodies are consumed, either literally or metaphorically, like parchment manuscripts meant to be read, digested, and, in some cases, burned'.[71] Next, Michael Livingston returns to the *Siege of Jerusalem*, but with particular regard to beard-flaying in this text and the wider Arthurian tradition. Flaying off the beards of defeated enemies has profound implications for masculinity and appears as a facet of shaming. As such, the loss of face – literally, when the skin of the face is torn, ripped or burned off – also results in a loss of identity. But in Norse romances, as Larissa Tracy explains in Chapter 13, the loss of a monstrous identity through flaying as part of a combat or quest provides a fresh tableau for the inscription of a different identity, that of ally instead of enemy. Tracy's analysis of flaying in Norse texts as an aspect of magical transformation contradicts the perception of Viking cruelty that the seventeenth- and eighteenth-century antiquarians breathed into life with their tales of 'Dane-skins' flayed off savage, sacrilegious Vikings by just and righteous English Christians.

In a reflection of Bain's piece concerning the practice of wearing flayed remains and the literary use of horsehide, Renée Ward's essay investigates the intersection of animal and human skin in *Robin Hood and Guy of Gisborne*, especially where animal skin masks human identity, or human identity is further effaced through facial flaying. Animal skin was a staple of medieval life, particularly in the production of manuscripts and clothes.[72] In her work on reading texts written on animal skins, Sarah Kay maintains that, 'wounds in [a manuscript's] parchment may have been seen as a graphic realization of the text's content, an uncanny precipitate of its ideas in concrete form'.[73] Most human clothing was made from animal skin or hair, so wearing clothing involved a close physical contact with animals, as did many other aspects of medieval life. In the Old Norse/Icelandic *Völsunga saga* (*Saga of the Volsungs*), Sigmund and Sinfjötli train for vengeance by donning wolf skins they take from men they find sleeping in a

---

[71] Emily Leverett, 'Reading the Consumed: Flayed and Cannibalized Bodies in *The Siege of Jerusalem* and *Richard Coer de Lyon*', p. 287.

[72] See: Sarah Kay, 'Legible Skins: Animals and the Ethics of Medieval Reading', *postmedieval: a journal of medieval cultural studies* 2.1 (2011): 13–32, and several works by Bruce Holsinger, including: *Music, Body and Desire in Medieval Culture: Hildegard of Bingen to Chaucer* (Stanford, CA: Stanford University Press, 2001); 'Parchment Ethics: A Statement of More than Modest Concern', *New Medieval Literatures* 12 (2010): 131–6; and 'Of Pigs and Parchment: Medieval Studies and the Coming of the Animal', *PMLA* 124.2 (2009): 616–23.

[73] Kay, 'Original Skin', p. 36.

hut in the forest – after they kill the previous owners.[74] In *Hrólfs saga kraka* (*Saga of King Hrolf Kraki*) (*c.* 1400) the evil queen transforms her stepson by striking him with wolfskin gloves and uttering a curse that will lead to his death (in bear form) by hounds, after which he is flayed and fed to his wife.[75] Here, Hartnell, Bain and Ward all consider the symbiosis between animal and human flesh, both in how it is taken and how it is worn.

Skin as a boundary is crossed, erased and effaced in the act of flaying. Skinning an animal or a human removes the essential identity that separates one species from another. Consider the difficulty – before the era of genetic testing – of identifying the flayed remnants on English church doors as either definitively human or definitively cow. Another persistent myth that bleeds into practice is the 'tradition' of anthropodermic book binding, from supposed examples from the medieval period through World War II. In the Epilogue, Perry Neil Harrison challenges many of the older assumptions about the prevalence of this practice and offers new insights into the mythology of binding books in human skin, while gathering together the threads of inquiry from the other chapters.

T HIS collection includes a selection of widely diverse examples of flaying, probing the layered responses to skin-removal in art, history, literature, manuscript studies and law. The sources cover a broad geographical and linguistic range: French (Lindquist, Tracy), Irish (Sayers), Italian (Bain, DeVries, Dent, Mittman and Sciacca), Middle High German (Bain, Small), Old Norse (Bain, Tracy), Welsh (Livingston), Old English (Rambaran-Olm) and Middle English (Gramling, Leverett, Livingston, Tracy, Ward). They deal with issues of race and religious identity (DeVries, Leverett), misogyny (Bain) and mysticism (Gramling). Some follow the fascination with skin into the modern era (Bain, Rambaran-Olm, Harrison). But overall, the individual articles re-evaluate the commonality of flaying, how art reflects spiritual responses to skin removal and how flaying, in any form, was used to further political or religious goals. They often share sources, or refer to the same events, and aim to communicate with each other as much as possible – highlighting the intersections within their own scholarship and the material at hand. We have, therefore, gathered all the sources together in a select bibliography of primary sources and shared secondary texts with a particular emphasis on the various aspects of flaying. As a whole, this collection literally gets beneath the skin of medieval sensibilities regarding punishment and sacrifice in a nuanced discussion of medieval flaying.

---

[74] See: *Saga of the Volsungs: The Norse Epic of Sigurd the Dragon Slayer*, trans. Jesse Byock (Berkeley: University of California Press, 1990).

[75] *The Saga of King Hrolf-Kraki*, trans. Jesse Byock (London: Penguin, 1998), pp. 37–9.

I
FLAYING IN PRACTICE

1

Tools of the Puncture: Skin, Knife, Bone, Hand

Jack Hartnell

[…] a descrete leche schal openly knowen
þe tortuouse depnesse of his enserchinge.[1]

A HAIRLESS figure stands at the centre of a manuscript illumination,
his curved body delicately tinted pink and apparently naked (Fig. 1.1).
He seems to be looking vacantly outwards, staring into the empty space
immediately to his left. Yet, on closer inspection, this cannot be; he has no
eyes or eyelids, only empty sockets. In fact, his body sports no outer layer
at all: His skin is folded in two like a piece of stiff fabric, slung over a long
stick he carries at his shoulder. Amongst the flaps and folds, his arms and
legs are still distinguishable by their intact hands and feet, as is the body's
once-full head of hair which spirals out in strange black weaves from a
central corona-like scalp.

Despite the singular and static depiction in front of a traditional
checker-work background, this is not a devotional image from a religious
text. It certainly resembles depictions of St Bartholomew, rendered
unflinching despite his absent skin through a sense of anaesthetizing
spirituality, but this is not the saint inventively presenting his pelt on a
pole.[2] Neither is this a figure from more mythic or historical sources: the
corrupt Persian judge Sisamnes, for example, whom Gerard David depicts
so vividly in a 1498 diptych, flayed alive with his skin draped across his
chair of judgement.[3] Nor is this figure intended as a more playful marginal

---

[1] From an anonymous Middle English surgical manual, *c.* 1392, London,
Wellcome Library, MS 564. An edited version of the text appears in Richard
Grothé, 'Le MS. Wellcome 564: deux traites de chirurgie en Moyen-Anglais',
PhD dissertation (University of Montreal, 1982). The phrase is further
discussed in Virginia Langum, 'Discerning Skin: Complexion, Surgery, and
Language in Medieval Confession', in *Reading Skin in Medieval Literature
and Culture*, ed. Katie L. Walter (Basingstoke: Palgrave, 2013), pp. 141–60.

[2] On Bartholomew in this volume, see: Asa Simon Mittman and Christine
Sciacca, 'Robed in Martyrdom: The Flaying of St Bartholomew in the
Laudario of Sant'Agnese', pp. 140–72; and Sherry C. M. Lindquist,
'Masculinist Devotion: Flaying and Flagellation in the *Belles Heures*',
pp. 173–207. On the 'anaesthesia' of saintly glory, see: Caroline Walker
Bynum, *The Resurrection of the Body in Western Christianity* (New York:
Columbia University Press, 1995), p. 252.

[3] On the Sisamnes myth, especially David's diptych, see: Robert Mills,
Suspended Animation: Pain, Pleasure, and Punishment in Medieval Culture
(London: Reaktion, 2005), p. 59.

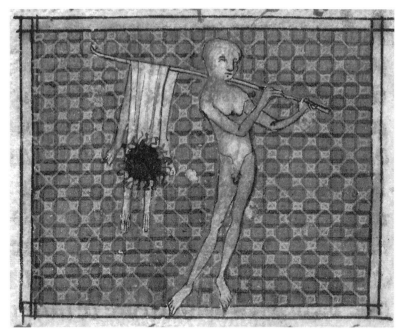

Fig. 1.1 Anatomical figure of a flayed man holding his skin on a stick over his shoulder, from a copy of Henri de Mondeville's *Cyrurgie*, 1314, France (Paris, Bibliothèque nationale de France, MS Fr. 2030 (formerly Colbert 4478), fol. 10v)

image, parodying or punning on the grotesque. Unlike the two miniature wide-eyed rabbits who flay a bound man in the *bas-de-page* of the Metz Pontifical, this skinned man is central to his manuscript context, spanning with bold prominence an entire column of text.[4] Instead, this image stems from a sphere of visual culture that provides an important counterpoint to the punitive and saintly narratives of skin removal: the emergent medieval discipline of surgery. Rather than exclusively embodying flaying's violent aspects – an idea that chapters later in this collection will go on to explore – this skinless man was used instead for instruction in healing. This is a flayed figure of repair, rather than removal.

The flayed man is fourth in a series of small diagrams from a 1314 copy of the French master surgeon Henri de Mondeville's *Chirurgia magna*. An accompanying caption illuminates something of its function:

le 4 figure. un home escorchie portant son cuir sus ses espaulles o un baston et la pert le cuir du chief eschevele, le cuir des mains, et des pies et la char lacerueuse et glandeuse qui est par le cors et la blance qui est es mamelles et es emuptoires, et par la fixeure du ventre apert la gresse le sain loint.

[4] The Metz Pontifical, 1302–16, Cambridge, Fitzwilliam MS 298, fol. 74r.

[The fourth figure, a flayed man carrying his skin over his shoulders on a stick; and the skin of his head with hair, the skin of his hands, and his feet; and the lacerated flesh that is on the body, and the white which is the breasts and the emunctories, and by the opening of the venter is the fat and the lard.][5]

Exposing the whitish hue of the subcutaneous fat [*la gresse*] that lies under the body's outer layers, the depiction of the flayed figure outside his skin [*le cuir*] is deliberately revelatory, displaying the subtle gradations of colour and texture found in the body beneath. The thirteen illustrations that feature in the *Chirurgia* are perhaps related to several larger sketches of individual internal organs, now lost, used by Henri in his lectures at the University of Montpellier in 1304.[6] Like these larger sheets, the smaller 1314 manuscript also functioned didactically, allowing practitioners or students consulting the learned surgeon's texts to acquaint themselves with the body's internal workings through evocative visualization, as well as to find their way to relevant sections of the surgical material.

Whilst restrictions on anatomizing bodies in later medieval France mean it is unlikely that Henri himself would have so deliberately flayed a human figure, surgical discussions of skin frequently surface in the medical literature of the period.[7] Considered to have a twofold face, skin consisted of two separate elements dubbed 'skin proper' and the 'pannicule', outer and inner layers that doubly protected the body's internal workings.[8] Medically, skin was many things: to quote Henri, it was 'nervosum, forte,

---

[5] Paris, Bibliothèque nationale de France, MS Fr. 2030, folio 9v. A similar series of surgical figures appear as uncoloured line drawings in Cambridge, Trinity College, MS O.2.44. My translation.

[6] Loren C. MacKinney, 'The Beginnings of Western Scientific Anatomy: New Evidence and a Revision in Interpretation of Mondeville's Role', *Medical History* 62.3 (1962): 233–9. On medical illustrations like these more broadly, see: Loren C. MacKinney, *Medical Illustrations in Medieval Manuscripts* (London: Wellcome Library, 1965); Rudolph Herrlinger, *A History of Medical Illustration* (London: Pitman, 1970); Peter Murray Jones, *Medieval Medicine in Illuminated Manuscripts*, rev. edn (London: British Library, 1998); Hilde-Marie Gross, 'Illustrationen in medizinischen Sammelhandschriften', in *Ein teutsch puech machen: Untersuchungen zur landessprachlichen Vermittlung medizinischen Wissens*, ed. Gundolf Keil (Wiesbaden: Reichert, 1993), pp. 172–348.

[7] On restrictions and allowances for human dissection in the period, see: Katharine Park, *The Secrets of Women: Gender, Generation, and the Origins of Human Dissection* (New York: Zone, 2006); and Elizabeth A. R. Brown, 'Death and the Human Body in the Later Middle Ages: The Legislation of Boniface VIII on the Division of the Corpse', *Viator* 12 (1981): 221–70.

[8] For more on skin's taxonomies see: Katie L. Walter, 'The Form of the Formless: Medieval Taxonomies of Skin, Flesh and the Human,' in *Reading Skin*, ed. Walter, pp. 119–39.

tenax, mediocre in duritie et mollitie, flexibile, multum sensibile, tenue temperatum in complexione, totum corpus in parte exteriori circumdans' [nervous, tough, resistant, medium-hard, flexible, very sensitive, thin and temperate in complexion; it covers the entire surface of the body].[9] And as well as various physical characteristics, skin imparted itself to a whole host of wider meanings and interpretations in a varied medical discourse. It was a surface to be read for signs and symptoms in its colour, temperature and texture – an important interface for uncovering underlying causes lurking beneath. Like many diagnostic tools in medieval medicine, examination of the skin was as likely to highlight defects in the patient's moral or spiritual integrity as it was to expose more corporeal flaws in their diet or humoral balance.[10]

Skin removal featured in discussions of surgical technique too. Limb amputations (often unsuccessful) necessitated the stripping back of the skin to access and saw through bone; cauterizing or suturing the skin was common to stop bleeding or infection; incisions or counter-incisions into the skin could be made to enlarge entry wounds for removal of foreign bodies or relax separated body parts; skin could be etched away with corrosives; growths or ulcers were cut directly out of the skin; and the frequently prescribed practice of phlebotomy also called for the partial removal of the skin to let blood flow, an act sometimes referred to in the French literature as *flagellation*.[11] From the 1450s onwards, surgeons like the Brancas dynasty from Catania in Sicily contributed to a growing market in plastic surgery, especially rhinoplasty and other facial treatments to repair

---

[9] For the Latin, see: Julius Pagel, ed., *Die Chirurgie des Heinrich von Mondeville* (Berlin: Hirschwald, 1892), p. 22; for a French translation, Edouard Nicaise, ed., *Chirurgie de maître Henri de Mondeville* (Paris: Félix Alcan, 1893); for an English translation, Leonard D. Rosenman, ed., *The Surgery of Henri de Mondeville*, 2 vols. (Bloomington, IN: Xlibris, 2003).

[10] For an interesting discussion of the liminal position skin occupied in medieval medicine, see the many contributions to *La pelle umana / The Human Skin*, a special issue of the journal *Micrologus* 13 (2005); Luke Demaitre, 'Skin and the City: Cosmetic Medicine as Urban Concern', in *Between Text and Patient: The Medical Enterprise in Medieval and Early Modern Europe*, ed. Florence Eliza Glaze and Brian K. Nance (Florence: Sismel – Edizioni del Galluzzo, 2011), pp. 97–120. On skin and reading, see: the works of Sarah Kay, in particular 'Original Skin: Flaying, Reading, and Thinking in the Legend of Saint Bartholomew and other Works', *Journal of Medieval and Early Modern Studies* 36.1 (2006): 35–74.

[11] On the affective appearance of flagellation – beating or tearing the skin from the body – as a variation on flaying, particularly in terms of Christ's scourging, see in this volume: Peter Dent, 'A Window for the Pain: Surface, Interiority and Christ's Flagellated Skin in Late Medieval Sculpture', pp. 208–39; and Valerie Gramling, '"Flesche withowtyn hyde": The Removal and Transformation of Jesus' Skin in the English Cycle Passion Plays', pp. 240–60.

or replace scarred features and absent skin.[12] Animal skin similarly featured
in surgical treatments, not only as leather bags for administering drugs to
patients, or straps to bind the body and help in the healing of bones, but
also sometimes in more graphic treatments that strangely juxtaposed the
flayed skins of man and beast.[13] Henri de Mondeville sceptically cites a
cure for skin lesions that recommends the burial of the patient for three
days and nights, neck-deep inside the stripped skin of a horse [*equi statim
excoriata*] stuffed with hot manure, so that portions of their own skin
might in turn be 'flayed off' [*flagellis*] by the heat.[14] Although seemingly
unusual, Henri was not the first to acknowledge this treatment, nor the
last. His Italian predecessor Guglielmo da Saliceto states that wrapping
the patient in the skin of a recently flayed horse is particularly efficacious
for treating victims whose skin had been removed.[15] Early modern
medical treatises, too, prescribe immediately covering new mothers
after giving birth in the skin of a black sheep which has been flayed

[12] Jacques Joseph, *Nasenplastik und sonstige Gesichtsplastik* (Leipzig:
Kabitizsch, 1931). On the long history of aesthetic surgery, see: Sander L.
Gilman, *Making the Body Beautiful: A Cultural History of Aesthetic Surgery*
(Princeton: Princeton University Press, 2000). On its medieval history
in particular, see the chapter 'Surgery Between Alchemy and Cosmetics',
in Michael McVaugh, *The Rational Surgery of the Middle Ages* (Florence:
Sismel – Edizioni del Galluzzo, 2006), as well as Demaitre, 'Skin and
the City'. As a contemporary counterpoint to surgical beautification,
compare such restorative rhinoplasty with the deliberately punitive facial
interventions discussed in Patricia Skinner, 'The Gendered Nose and its
Lack: "Medieval" Nose-cutting and its Modern Manifestations', *Journal of
Women's History* 26.1 (2014): 45–67.

[13] On the medieval concept of skin as both bodily facet and raw material, see:
Isabel Davis, 'Cutaneous Time in the Late Medieval Literary Imagination',
in *Reading Skin*, ed. Walter, pp. 99–118; Renée Ward, '"Thou shalt have the
better cloathe": Reading Second Skins in *Robin Hood and Guy of Gisborne*',
pp. 349–65, in this volume.

[14] Pagel, *Chirurgie*, p. 394. Mondeville is himself not keen on this elaborate
treatment. It was also a prescribed treatment for shock among the medieval
Mongols. See: Timothy May, 'Spitting Blood: Medieval Mongol Medical
Practices', in *Wounds and Wound Repair in Medieval Culture*, ed. Larissa
Tracy and Kelly DeVries (Leiden: Brill, 2015), pp. 175–93.

[15] For the Latin, see: Christian Heimerl, ed., *The Middle English Version of
William of Saliceto's 'Anatomia'* (Heidelberg: Universitätsverlag, 2008); for
a French translation, Paul Pifteau, ed. and trans., *Chirurgie de Guillaume
de Salicet* (Toulouse: Saint-Cyperien, 1898); for an English translation,
Leonard D. Rosenman, ed., *The Surgery of William of Saliceto* (Bloomington,
IN: Xlibris, 2002). For more on William of Saliceto, see: Jole Agrimi and
Chiara Crisciani, 'The Science and Practice of Medicine in the Thirteenth
Century according to Guglielmo da Saliceto, Italian Surgeon', in *Practical
Medicine from Salerno to the Black Death*, ed. Luis García-Ballester *et al.*
(Cambridge: Cambridge University Press, 1994), pp. 60–88.

alive.[16] Mary Rambaran-Olm notes the prescription in the *Anglo-Saxon Leechbook* for using porpoise skin as a cure for lunacy.[17]

Clearly these forms of medical flaying, a means of providing relief to the diseased or cure to the battle-wounded, must at their simplest be considered quite distinct from the penal or more aggressively grotesque removal of skin known from contemporary flaying legends and saintly martyrdoms. The two clash fundamentally in their ideology. One is about the careful alleviation of pain and the other about pain's deliberate extension; one leaves behind a renewed and enlivened patient and the other a corpse (or soon-to-be corpse), ultimate in its despoiled nakedness. And yet, the similarities between Henri's flayed man with the iconography of the skinless St Bartholomew suggest that, in certain fundamentals, the two processes of removing skin are linked. Both practices court notions of fear, power and the stripped body. After all, whether carried out by surgeon or executioner, there remains in both a figure of control who removes skin from the body of another. At times there was even a blurring of these personages to match a blurring in practice: the surgeon of the fourteenth-century Pope John XXII, Jean d'Amand, was amongst several figures accused of poisoning the pontiff and was ordered to be flayed alive, the surgical flayer becoming the flayed.[18] But most telling in the correlations between these two practices are their very simplest components: their instruments, the tools of the puncture, rip and slash. Little has been said about these flaying accoutrements. Perhaps it is because, by thinking about the act of flaying as something that invites or even requires careful instrumentation, we are brought back to the uneasy conceptual conflation between a deliberately punitive, fantastical barbarism and a skilful, genuine craft. It is certainly possible that flaying's ability to inspire fear and discipline – features so prized in flaying's myth in late medieval society – might be mediated or nullified by any sense of it as an exquisite craft. Yet in considering penal flaying alongside surgery, it becomes clear

---

[16] This practice was sometimes known as 'binding the mother', and is mentioned in French midwife Louise Bourgeois' *Diverse Observations on Sterility, Miscarriages, Fertility, Childbirth, and Diseases of Women and Newborn Children (1626)*, notes and ed. Alison Klairmont Lingo, trans. and ed. Stephanie O'Hara, The Other Voice in Early Modern Europe 33 (Toronto: University of Toronto Press, 2013).

[17] Mary Rambaran-Olm, 'Medievalism and the "Flayed-Dane" Myth: English Perspectives between the Seventeenth and Nineteenth Centuries', in this volume, pp. 91–115.

[18] Edouard Nicaise, ed., *La Grande Chirurgie de Guy de Chauliac* (Paris: Félix Alcan, 1890), p. lxx. On the moral, legal and gendered implications of such bodily disfigurement as punitive measure, see: Patricia Skinner, 'Marking the Face, Curing the Soul? Reading the Disfigurement of Women in the Later Middle Ages', in *Medicine, Religion and Gender in Medieval Culture*, ed. Naoë Kukita Yoshikawa (Woodbridge: Boydell Press, 2015), pp. 181–202.

that the two fields erect and transgress many related intellectual, technical and personal boundaries. By setting into dialogue medical and punitive flaying, the mechanical and material intricacies involved in removing skin in the Middle Ages can be better understood. Just as no consideration of artistic practice is rounded or complete without some consideration of the materials and tools at its core and which shape its outcomes, so too a consideration of the practice of flaying is not complete without thinking more about the knives wielded when removing the skin.

Surgical instruments are exceptionally rare historical survivals, as are many tools from the medieval period.[19] Not only did their utilitarian function leave them open to damage and obsolescence during use, but also their often-unremarkable appearance has meant they are rarely preserved amongst the prized and precious collections of objects passed down from the Middle Ages. In archaeological settings, the deterioration of their largely iron or steel components mean it can be hard to discern the individual function of a tool, let alone whether or not it stems from the medical realm.[20] Historiography is a factor here, too. As the historian of surgery Ghislaine Lawrence has suggested, literature on the history of medicine has been 'inconsistent on the value of artefacts to the historical enterprise'.[21] Concerned primarily with bolstering existing chronologies and fitting newly discovered historical objects into the extant modern categories of surgical equipment, medical historians tend not to consider such artefacts inventively as 'the outcome of processes of invention or innovation, or as product or commodity'.[22] Despite the efforts of writers like John Kirkup or Marie-Véronique Clin, who for some time have been charting both the broader evolution and the micro-histories of surgical instruments with increasing accuracy, medical tools are usually made to toe the line, not forge a new path.[23] Thus, with limited support, either primary

[19] For a thorough bibliographic and conceptual introduction to medieval tools, see: Johan David, *L'Outil* (Turnhout: Brepols, 1997). For a broader anthropological background to tools, see the works of Tim Ingold, especially 'Tools, Minds and Machines: An Excursion in the Philosophy of Technology', *Techniques & Culture* 12 (1989): 151–76.

[20] See, for example, the state of preservation in examples of knives excavated in London, in J. Cowgill, M. de Neergaard and N. Griffiths, *Knives and Scabbards: Medieval Finds from Excavations in London* (London: HMSO / Museum of London, 1987).

[21] Ghislaine Lawrence, 'The Ambiguous Artifact: Surgical Instruments and the Surgical Past', in *Medical Theory, Surgical Practice: Studies in the History of Surgery*, ed. Christopher Lawrence (London: Routlege, 1992), p. 295.

[22] Ibid.

[23] John Kirkup, *The Evolution of Surgical Instruments: An Illustrated History from Ancient Times to the Twentieth Century* (Novato, CA: Norman, 2006); Marie-Véronique Clin, 'Surgical Instruments as Art Objects', in *Antique Tools and Instruments from the Nessi Collection* (Milan: 5 Continents, 2004),

or secondary, for fleshing out these fragmented discoveries of surgical practice, evidence must be drawn from a broad historical context.

Discussions of surgery in the late Middle Ages and the early Renaissance are largely absent from the rich university sources that have helped scholars expatiate the histories of more academic forms of science, religion or philosophy. At that moment in its re-emergence into the Western medical canon, surgery was considered a discipline quite separate from pharmaceutical or more theoretical medicine.[24] This is not to say that some surgical authors, acquainted with the potential prowess of physicianship and sometimes even trained as physicians themselves, did not take an intellectual approach to their work. Engaged in a long-standing process of differentiating the craft from barber-surgeons and other 'lowly' craftsmen, some practitioners – like Henri de Mondeville, his French successor Guy de Chauliac, or Italian surgeons like Roger Frugardi or Roger of Saliceto – did attempt to assert surgical practice as part of a more academic discipline. Drawing on historic textual sources, they wrote Latinate surgical treatises that sought to place them on a social and intellectual par with university professionals, their theoretically minded academic counterparts. At the same time, however, surgical authors were also consciously trying to differentiate themselves from these same academics, who rarely engaged in actual dissections of the body, if at all.[25] Emphasizing their manual practice of a craft-based surgery, they saw themselves as having a unique

pp. 103–14. For several atypical essays that work against the generalizing ethic of historical writing on instruments, see: R. G. W. Anderson, J. A. Bennett and W. F. Ryan, eds., *Making Instruments Count: Essays on Historical Scientific Instruments Presented to Gerard L'Estrange Turner* (Aldershot: Ashgate, 1993).

[24] Several thorough studies have been undertaken on medieval surgery: Michael McVaugh, 'Therapeutic Strategies: Surgery', in *Western Medical Thought from Antiquity to the Middle Ages*, ed. Mirko D. Grmek (Cambridge, MA: Harvard University Press, 1998), pp. 273–90; Pierre Huard and Mirko D. Grmek, *Mille ans de chirurgie en Occident: Ve–XVe siècles* (Paris: Dacosta, 1966); Michael McVaugh, 'Surgical Education in the Middle Ages', *Dynamis* 20 (2000): 283–304; Mario Tabanelli, *La chirurgia italiana nell'alto medioevo*, 2 vols. (Florence: Olschki, 1965); Helen E. Valls, 'Studies on Roger Frugardi's *Chirurgia*', PhD dissertation (University of Toronto, 1995). On English traditions, see: Faye Getz, *Medicine in the English Middle Ages* (Princeton: Princeton University Press, 1998); on Dutch traditions, see: Erwin Huizenga, 'Cutting and Writing: Medieval Dutch Surgeons and their Books', in *Manuscript Studies in the Low Countries*, ed. Anne Margreet *et al.* (Groningen: Egbert Forsten, 2008), pp. 81–102.

[25] On the position of surgeons, see various works by McVaugh and Cornelius O'Boyle, especially: McVaugh, *Rational Surgery*; O'Boyle, 'Surgical Texts and Social Contexts: Physicians and Surgeons in Paris, *c.* 1270 to 1430', in *Practical Medicine*, ed. García-Ballester *et. al.*, pp. 156–86. For the surgeon's place within the broader medical world of medieval Paris, see: Danielle

capacity for the physical treatment and manipulation of the body that was absent from intellectual medicine at the time, setting them apart from the entirely abstract and specifically textual discussions of medicine found in academic circles. Broadly speaking, the medieval surgeon's position was liminal, between barber-surgeon and physician, between pure craft and pure concept. Therefore surgical texts, whilst politically potent, were not necessarily the primary means of communicating practice amongst surgeons; the craft also dwelled in the less literate, more practical worlds of workshops, guilds and oral transmission.[26]

Such a textual scarcity means that direct sources for understanding surgery's instrumentation are uncommon. Even when such texts themselves are preserved, they tend to offer few specifics on surgery's tools. Take, for example, the descriptions by French medieval writers of objects used in skin removal. When Henri or Guy mention the knives used in surgical practice, they use ambiguous and often interchangeable terminology, sometimes citing a simple *couteau*, other times a *rasoir*, *phlebotome* or *faucille* depending on the context or detail.[27] By their time, these seemingly concrete terms had already been much transcribed and translated, and shifted further in later fifteenth- and sixteenth-century terminology.[28] Between 1350 and 1550 a surgical knife might appear as the Latin *novacula* or *cutellus*, the Arabic *mokhdea*, the French *bistouri*, the German *messer*, the English *launcet*, *flytme* or *catlin*, and a variety of other hybrid names like *sarmgatoria bicops*.[29] Whilst each term doubtless brought

---

Jacquart, *La Médecine médiévale dans le cadre parisien, XIVe–XVe siècle* (Paris: Fayard, 1998).

[26] On the epistemics of this kind of knowledge, see: Pamela H. Smith, Amy R. W. Meyers and Harold J. Cook, eds., *Ways of Making and Knowing: The Material Culture of Empirical Knowledge* (Ann Arbor: University of Michigan Press, 2014); and Pamela H. Smith, *The Body of the Artisan: Art and Experience in the Scientific Revolution* (Chicago: University of Chicago Press, 2004).

[27] 'Glossaire des Instruments', in Nicaise, *Henri de Mondeville*, p. 686; 'Des Instruments de Chirurgie', in ibid., p. 869. For the original Latin of Chauliac's *Chirurgia magna*, see: Guigonis de Caulhiacho, *Inventarium sive Chirurgia magna*, ed. Michael McVaugh, 2 vols. (Leiden: Brill, 1997); for a French translation, Nicaise, *Guy de Chauliac*; for an English translation, Leonard D. Rosenman, ed., *The Major Surgery of Guy de Chauliac* (Bloomington, IN: Xlibris, 2007).

[28] On vernacular translations of medical works, particularly in English, see: Linda Ehrsam Voigts, 'Multitudes of Middle English Medical Manuscripts, or the Englishing of Science and Medicine', in *Manuscript Sources of Medieval Medicine: A Book of Essays*, ed. Margaret T. Schleissner (New York: Taylor & Francis, 1995), pp. 183–95.

[29] For Old English and Middle English translations of this medical terminology, see: Marta Sylwanowicz, '"And this is a wonderful

with it certain nuances to practitioners at particular moments or in certain regions, these words were used generically in the highly diffuse atmosphere of medieval textual translation. Knowledge of knives came primarily from experience and personal choice.

Given this etymological ambiguity, imagery produced alongside such documentary evidence proves unusually fruitful in understanding tools. Illustrations were by no means the norm in surgical tracts, including diagrams of instrumentation, but some traditions can be traced. Cautery texts, for example, which directed the burning of the body to balance the humours, replicated images of both procedures and specialist equipment, as did illustrated copies of Frugardi's *Cirurgia*, depicting a relatively consistent surgical instrumentation.[30] Perhaps most visually prominent was an influential Arabic tract by the eleventh-century author al-Zahrāwī (known in the West as Albucasis), specifically the last volume of his thirty-part treatise *Kitāb al-Tasrīf li-man 'an at-ta'līf* (*The Method of Medicine*) addressing surgery.[31] Repeatedly transcribed and translated well beyond the Middle Ages, different manuscript copies of this work preserve around 200 depictions of surgical tools, often elongated and woven strip-like

instrument ...": Names of Surgical Instruments in Late Middle English Medical Texts', in *Foreign Influences on Medieval English*, ed. Jacek Fisiak and Magdalena Bator (Frankfurt: Peter Lang, 2011). For the German, see: Chiara Benati, '*Dat Boek der Wundenartzstedye*' *und der niederdeutsche chirurgische Fachwortschatz* (Göppingen: Kümmerle, 2012). On medical terminology, see: Michael McVaugh, 'Surface Meanings: The Identification of Apostemes in Medieval Surgery', in *Medical Latin from the Late Middle Ages to the Eighteenth Century*, ed. Wouter Bracke and Herwig Deumens (Brussels: Koninklijke Academie, 2000), pp. 13–29.

[30] On depictions of Cautery, see: Peter Murray Jones, 'Image, Word, and Medicine in the Middle Ages', in *Visualizing Medieval Medicine and Natural History, 1200–1550*, ed. Jean A. Givens, Karen M. Reeds and Alan Touwaide (Aldershot: Ashgate, 2006), pp. 1–25; Antonio Fornaciari and Valentina Giuffra, 'Surgery in the Early Middle Ages: Evidence of Cauterisation from Pisa', *Surgery* 151 (2012): 351–2. For illustrations of surgical tools outside of Albucasis, see, for example, a twelfth-century edition of Constantine the African's *Chirurgia* (Book IX of the *Pantegni, Practica*) now in Monte Cassino (MS 200). On Frugardi and instruments, see: Valls, 'Studies on Roger Frugardi'. On older histories of surgical instruments, see: Lawrence J. Bliquez, *The Tools of Asclepius: Surgical Instruments in Greek and Roman Times* (Leiden: Brill, 2014).

[31] For more on Al-Zahrāwī see: M. S. Spink and Geoffrey Lewis, eds., *Albucasis on Surgery and Instruments: A Definitive Edition of the Arabic Text* (London: Wellcome Institute of the History of Medicine, 1973). On the text's circulation, see: Monica H. Green, 'Moving from Philology to Social History: The Circulation and Uses of Albucasis's Latin *Surgery* in the Middle Ages', in *Between Text and Patient*, ed. Glaze and Nance, pp. 331–72.

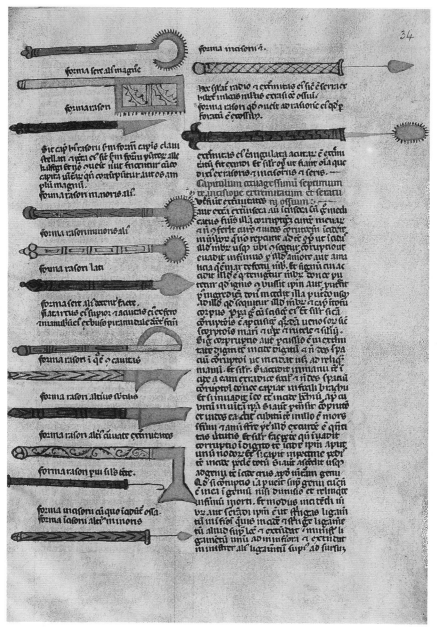

Fig. 1.2 Surgical instruments interspersed with the text of a Latin copy of al-Zahrāwī's treatise on surgery from *Kitāb al-Tasrīf li-man ʾan at-taʾlīf* (*The Method of Medicine*), late fourteenth century, Italy (London, British Library, Add. MS 36617, fol. 34r)

Fig. 1.3 A pair of scissors and a knife interspersed with the text of a small surgical manual in Flemish, based on the *Cyrurgie* of Jan Yperman, last quarter of the fifteenth century, Flanders (Leiden, Universiteitsbibliotheek, MS BPL 3094, fols. 97v–98r)

between passages of text (Fig. 1.2). These illustrated tools are far from direct likenesses intended to convey precise shapes and dimensions to the reader; whether in original manuscripts, Latin translations, or even later printed editions, al-Zahrāwī's instruments appear for the most part impossibly thin, or with toothed blades of exaggerated size or a strange feather-like softness.[32] Sometimes mistakenly taken at face value, these are, in fact, schematic depictions, indicatory images that relied on further knowledge for detailed identification or use. Several surgical manuals of the later Middle Ages continued in this abstract style; fourteenth- and fifteenth-century instrumental images were most often found woven between lines of text.[33] That such images are not concerned with a modern sense of precise accuracy does not mean they are useless in understanding the tools they depict. Take, for example, an illustration of a knife and pair of scissors from around 1300, presented alongside a surgical text based on the work of the Flemmish surgeon Jan Yperman (Fig. 1.3). Here, both the material

[32] On the influence of Albucasis' instruments on later printed texts, see: Martha Driver, 'The Illustrated Instrument: Early Surgical Manuals', *American Book Collector* 6 (1985): 3–9.

[33] See, for example, the manuscripts from various centuries containing Chauliac's work in Bristol (City Reference Library MS 10), Montpellier (Bibliothèque interuniversitaire, Section Médecine, MS Fr. 184), and Paris (Bibliothèque nationale de France, MSS Lat. 17846 and Lat. 6910).

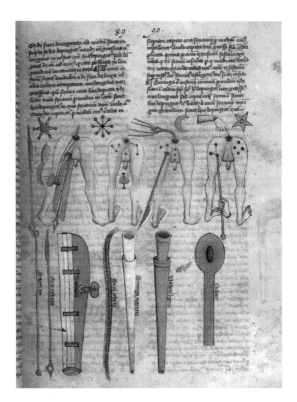

Fig. 1.4 The process of operating on an anal fistula, and the instruments involved, from a copy of John Arderne's *Practica*, *c.* 1420–30, England (London, British Library, Add. MS 29301, fol. 25r)

essence of the objects and their careful craft are preserved. The sharpened, biting nature of the scissors is represented in a typically exaggerated set of jagged teeth, a visual strategy often found in schematic images of serrated cutting instruments. Similarly, the ornate carving of the knife's handle, complete with an embossed maker's mark on the blade, affirms its status as a carefully crafted item.

Some notable exceptions to this generalizing aesthetic likewise suggest something more concrete in depictions of instruments, as well as their relationship to the flaying of skin. Key amongst these are the instrumental and surgical diagrams of the English surgeon John Arderne, created in the fourteenth century and diffused with precision across subsequent versions of his treatises.[34] Convincingly shown by Peter Murray Jones to stem from the surgeon's own depictive schema, Arderne's illustrations are ground-breaking in surgical terms and contain perhaps the first images of an actual surgical operation, especially his pioneering treatment of anal fistula (Fig. 1.4).[35] The operation is displayed in narrative sequence

[34] Peter Murray Jones, 'John of Arderne and the Mediterranean Tradition of Scholastic Surgery', in *Practical Medicine*, ed. García-Ballester *et al.*, pp. 298–321.

[35] Peter Murray Jones, '*Sicut hic depingitur ...*: John of Arderne and English Medical Illustration in the 14th and 15th Centuries', in *Die Kunst und das*

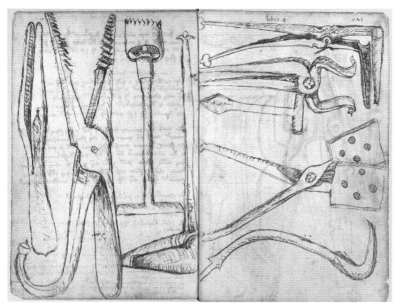

Fig. 1.5 The surgical instruments of Jean Gispaden, from his notebook containing excerpts from surgical textbooks, itineraries and case descriptions, second half of the fifteenth century, eastern France (perhaps Grenoble) (Paris, Bibliothèque nationale de France, MS Lat. 7138, fols. 199v–200r)

complete with the disembodied hand of the surgeon working his tools, a precisely rendered inventory of which is shown neatly labelled in isolation below, the knives and probes arranged in the order they are needed by the surgeon.[36] Similar specific evidence can also be found in a more personal fifteenth-century source, the handwritten notebook of a surgeon operating in Grenoble and named as Jean Gispaden. Comprised mostly of transcribed treatises by important early physicians, the final third of the manuscript contains detailed notes of Gispaden's own clinical work, including records of operations, journeys undertaken for practice and four pages with delicate line drawings of his own instruments (Fig. 1.5).[37] Taking care to make clear their comparative size, as well as the details of their

Studium der Nature vom 14. zum 16. Jahrhundert, ed. Wolfram Prinz and Andreas Beyer (Weinheim: VCH, 1987), pp. 103–26; and Peter Murray Jones, 'Staying with the Programme: Illustrated Manuscripts of John of Arderne, *c.* 1380–*c.* 1550', in *Decoration and Illustration in Medieval English Manuscripts*, ed. A. S. G. Edwards (London: British Library, 2002), pp. 204–27.

[36] A more elaborate page of illustrated instruments can also be found in a treatise of Arderne's writings: London, British Library, MS Sloane 6.

[37] Ernest Wickersheimer, *Maître Jean Gispaden, chirurgien annécien et grenoblois de la fin du XVe siécle* (Geneva: Imprimerie A. Kundig, 1926).

handles, hinges and decorated ends, these images are prominent and proud, intended to be as informative of Gispaden's practice as are the personal accounts of his treatment and travel. Increasingly accurate images of surgical instruments came into further prominence in the era of early print, intellectual descendants of the more veristic traditions in which Arderne and Gispaden were working. Depictions of so-called surgical *armamentaria* survive in the printed works of some early German battlefield surgeons, depicting groups of surgical instruments with enough interest in accuracy that it is possible to discern their specific functions.[38] The *armamentarium* found in the German surgeon Hieronymus Brunschwig's *Buch der Cirurgia* (1497) is the earliest known printed image of this type, a gathering of surgical instruments hanging about a folding wooden structure (Fig. 1.6).[39] Displayed in much the same visual style as printed inventories of church treasuries or *wunderkammer*, and doubtless with the same purpose of reification, it depicts some twenty or so different specialist tools including a folding knife, bow saw, scissors, syringe, probes and various implements for the extraction of arrows and bullets.[40]

All of these images suggest just how important a surgeon's instruments were to their owner. At their most basic Arderne, Gispaden and Brunschwig's visualizations function as inventories, emphasizing the sheer financial value of such tools. The more detailed depictions make clear that these objects were intricately crafted and must have been expensive, complete as they are with etched grips, animalistic foliate-ended handles and *cuir bouilli* cases, features that link the manual craft of surgery to the output of other comparable artisans, working not with muscle and skin but with metal and leather. The monetary value ascribed to such knives and tools is made even clearer by their presence in wills of medieval surgeons. Antony Copage, a practitioner from London, left 'all my enturmentes [instruments] of stele' to his servant George on the condition that 'he be of the same crafte', placing these objects on a par with his books of surgery, sold to the city's Company of Surgeons, and his most personal possessions:

---

[38] Kirkup, *Surgical Instruments*, p. 21.

[39] Brunschwig's image appears again in several later printed surgical treatises, for example Hans von Gersdorff's *Feldbuch der Wundarznei* (1517). On Brunschwig, see: Gustav Klein, *Das Buch der Cirurgia des Hieronymus Brunschwig* (Munich: Kuhn, 1911); Henry Sigerist, *Hieronymus Brunschwig and his Work: A Fifteenth-Century Surgeon* (New York: Abrahamson, 1946); and Pierre Bachoffner, 'Jérôme Brunschwig, chirurgien et apothicaire strasbourgeois, portraituré en 1512', *Revue d'histoire de la pharmacy* 81.298 (1993): 269–78.

[40] Note also the lack of labels or descriptors of the various instruments in this image, a move that perhaps brings the surgical knowledge on display in line with other shrouded and deliberately opaque markers of medieval knowledge, for example the alchemical.

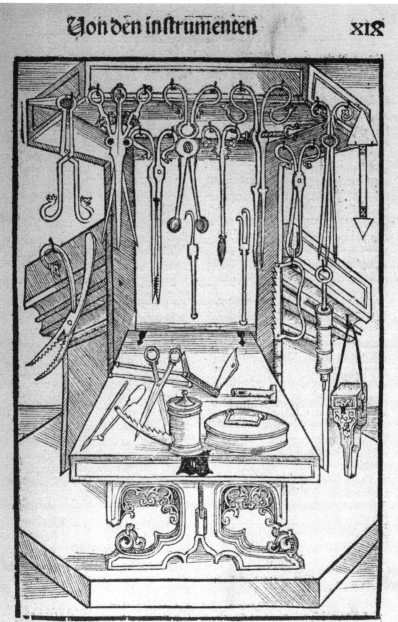

Fig. 1.6 Surgical armamentarium from Hieronymus Brunschwig's *Buch der Cirurgia* (Strassburg: Johann Grèuninger, 1497)

rings, gloves and finest clothes were all bequeathed to his wife.[41] Perhaps more importantly, by displaying the tools of their trade within their texts, medieval surgeons implied that their knives, saws and scissors possessed a more intricate, symbolic power. For the surgeons themselves, showing that they were in possession of such objects had a double edge, at once practical and epistemological. On the one hand, displaying an inventory indicated quite simply that they were in possession of the tools needed to perform a surgical operation, an aspect more important than it sounds. As late as 1554, the mere possession of carpentry equipment occasioned a woodworker named Galop to be called to St Bartholomew's Hospital in London to 'practyse surgery' on a patient whose limb needed amputating.[42] In this sense, the collective nature of the instruments' depiction is vital: a deliberate display of a full arsenal of tools suggested the extensive range of services a surgeon had to offer. As was the case with many contemporary guild-oriented crafts, to control access to instruments was, in a very real sense, to control practice; possession of tools conferred social standing and professional power.[43] On the other hand, this power or ownership was also closely intertwined with a sense of technical command, the display of instruments directly linked to the display of knowledge. To own such an instrument and to advertise this fact also made clear that a surgeon knew how to use it. Although necessarily sparse, drawn from different countries at wide-ranging moments across the period, the examples above suggest such values were widespread for the medieval surgeon. Knives embodied both action and expertise, as non-textual carriers of artisanal surgical intention poised to be dragged across the patient's skin.

Given this deep connection between surgeons and their tools, by the later Middle Ages a comparatively developed technical and conceptual language was in place that considered instruments as, quite literally, a part of the surgeon himself. Present as early as the Hippocratic collection of writings from the fourth century BCE, ancient and medieval authors alike often discussed probes, scissors and knives as direct extensions of their operator's hands.[44] Both Greek and Latin preserve an inextricable bond between body and action in the very terminology of surgery – *kheirourgos* or *chir-urgia*, combining 'hand' and 'work' – and although this wordplay might seem pedantic, the breaking down of such terms was of vital importance to medieval surgeons. Amongst Henri de Mondeville's

---

[41] Ida Darlington, ed., *London Consistory Court Wills, 1492–1547* (London: London Record Society, 1967), p. 108, online at http://british-history.ac.uk/ source.aspx?pubid=573 (accessed 9 Oct. 2014).

[42] R. T. Beck, *The Cutting Edge: Early History of the Surgeons of London* (London: Lund Humphries, 1974), p. 8.

[43] Lawrence, 'The Ambiguous Artifact', pp. 308–9.

[44] C. J. S. Thompson, *The History and Evolution of Surgical Instruments* (New York: Schuman's, 1942), p. 9.

five conditions of a good surgical practitioner, listed in his treatise on anatomy, the third concerns knowledge of the origins of the term 'anatomy' itself: 'anatomia dicitur ab ana. quod set rectum et tomes quod set division' [*anatomia* derives from 'ana' which means exact, and 'tomos' which means to cut into pieces].[45] Beginning with Old English texts, direct conflations had similarly been made between tools, instruments and the people who wielded them; the terms for surgeon and surgical object were often interchangeable with one another.[46] In Middle English texts too, the agency of the medical professional was caught up in common bodily terminology, the ring finger often dubbed the *leche finger*, or 'doctor finger'.[47] Later medieval surgeons took this sense of physicality one step further in their constant invocation of digits, hands and tools: Lanfranc of Milan writes of a surgeon's 'wel shaped' hands with 'long smale fyngres';[48] Jan Yperman of surgeons' firm fingers, 'vingheren ende lanc sterc van lichame, niet bevende' [fingers extending long from the body, not trembling];[49] and Henri even directly likens the iron joints and blades of the knife to a surgeon's fingernails and digits.[50] By the sixteenth century medical writers like Jacques Guillemeau voiced concern that surgical tools should not become too extensive lest they overtake the hands from which they themselves are formed.[51] In short, knives were considered tactile, almost fibrous, growths that acted as a surgeon's new fricative fingers.

With this utilitarian conflation in mind, images of surgical instruments not simply displayed but actually in use, records of them in action opening the body and flaying the skin as the surgeon's extended hands, are extremely valuable. The majority of such depictions are, again, difficult to interrogate because of their largely schematic rendering; the practice of phlebotomy, for example, was the most frequent reason for medieval physicians and surgeons to puncture the skin, but on the whole appears undetailed in its depiction of both patients and tools.[52] Just

---

[45] Mondeville himself did not know Greek, hence the slight inaccuracy in his listing of the word's components. Pagel, *Chirurgie*, p. 17.

[46] Sylwanowicz, 'Wonderful Instrument', p. 236.

[47] See, for example, its use in Heimerl, *The Middle English … Anatomia*, p. 90.

[48] Thompson, *History and Evolution*, p. 10.

[49] A. DeMets, *La Chirurgie de Maître Jehan Yperman (1260?–1310?)* (Paris, Editions Hippocrate, 1936), p. 43; for an Italian translation, Mario Tabanelli, *Jehan Yperman, padre della chirurgia fiamminga* (Florence: Olschki, 1969); for an English translation, Leonard D. Rosenman, ed., *The Surgery of Jehan Yperman* (Bloomington, IN: Xlibris, 2002).

[50] Marie-Christine Pouchelle, *Corps et chirurgie à l'apogée du Moyen Age* (Paris: Flammarion, 1983), p. 106.

[51] Kirkup, *Surgical Instruments*, p. 381.

[52] For a brief history of phlebotomy and examples of its tools, see: Daniela Krause, *Aderlass und Schröpfen. Instrumente aus der Sammlung des*

as the act of flaying was a rare event in the reality of medieval punitive life, so too the actual dissection of the human body was a comparatively uncommon undertaking. Despite the annualized regularity implied by university decrees and statutes, the availability of bodies and the relative unimportance of actual anatomy instruction to intellectual medicine suggests that academic dissection was practised relatively infrequently.[53] Similarly, the more frequent dissective practices of Italy and Northern France in non-university contexts – embalming, autopsy and *sectio in mortua* [caesarean section] – were largely private events, unavailable to the prying eyes of a general populace.[54] However, several images do exist portraying visually arresting, medicalized procedures of removing the skin. One is an earlier trope showing a single surgeon at work on a patient or cadaver in dissection. In the *Anathomia* of Guido da Vigevano, a section of his ten-part *Liber notabilium* written in 1345 for his patron, Philip VI of France,[55] Guido presents a series of images of anatomical dissection which he considered 'rather better than can be seen in the human body itself, because when we do an anatomy on a man, it is necessary to make haste because of the stench'.[56] Initial concern is for the surfaces of the body; an opening image shows the locations of internal organs and members etched in strips across the stomach of *homine vivo*, a living man. But as soon as the anatomical series begins in earnest, the figure of the doctor quickly appears as a dissective mediator. Making a series of deliberate incisions in the same man (now a corpse), a physician fully dressed in academic robes (perhaps intended to depict Guido himself) gives access to various 'venters' of the body as originally described by Galen.[57] In each case, the focus is on the skin being cut, first the opening of the abdomen – 'the belly is slit

---

Karl-Sudhoff-Instituts (Aachen: Shaker Verlag, 2004); Pedro Gil-Sotres, 'Derivation and Revulsion: The Theory and Practice of Medieval Bloodletting', in *Practical Medicine*, ed. García-Ballester *et al.*, pp. 110–56. See also: Mariacarla Gadebusch Bondio, ed., *Blood in History and Blood Histories* (Florence: Sismel, 2005).

[53] On dissection and the university, see: Andrea Carlino, *La fabbrica del corpo* (Milan: Einaudi, 1994); Roger French, *Dissection and Vivisection in the European Renaissance* (Aldershot: Ashgate, 1999); Cornelius O'Boyle, *The Art of Medicine: Medical Teaching at the University of Paris, 1250–1400* (Leiden: Brill, 1998); Jacquart, *Médecine médiévale*.

[54] For a unique and revealing inclusion of these dissective practices within the broader context of medieval anatomy, see: Park, *Secrets of Women*.

[55] Ernst Wickersheimer, *Anatomies de Mondino dei Luzzi et de Guido de Vigevano* (Paris: Droz, 1926).

[56] Translation taken from 'Academic Dissection as "Material Commentary" (2): Anatomical Illustration, b. The *Anatomy* of Guido Vigevano', in *Medieval Medicine: A Reader*, ed. Faith Wallis (Toronto: University of Toronto Press, 2010), pp. 238–47.

[57] 'Academic Dissection', in *Medieval Medicine*, ed. Wallis, p. 231.

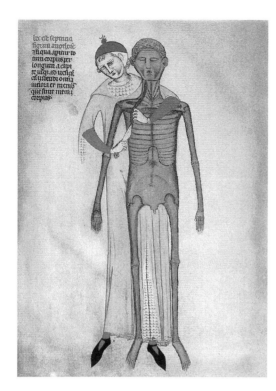

Fig. 1.7 Surgeon
dissecting a corpse
at the chest, from the
Anathomia of Guido da
Vigevano, 1345, Paris
(Chantilly, Musée Condé,
MS 334)

in order that all the members which are in the belly may be seen', reads
the accompanying text – and then the chest.[58] In one image, the surgeon
stands in a demonstrative position behind the cadaver, making an incision
from the chin down the side of the ribs (Fig. 1.7). His left hand extends
around the shoulder of the cadaver in an awkward embrace, gripping the
newly loosed flap of skin in preparation to peel it back across the body,
opening the rib cage and giving access to the lungs beneath. Knife and
hand are not only presented as working in tandem – one slicing, the other
pulling and flaying the skin – but are also rendered in such similar shape
and shade that the tool appears as an extended first finger of the surgeon,
echoing Henri de Mondeville's conflation of blades and fingernails.
Although conceptually evocative, the knives used in Guido's dissections
are not detailed enough to indicate his specific tools. While they are clearly
shown as different from one another in his different anatomical scenarios,
suggesting an effort to make at least some distinction between types of
tool, the treatment of the body and not surgical instrumentation is the
primary focus of such an image. This is borne out in other contemporary
depictions of the dissection scene, for example the well-known image of
academic dissection found in the *Fascicolo di medicina*, the second edition
of a printed medical book published in Venice in 1494 (or 1493, to use the

---

[58] Ibid., p. 243.

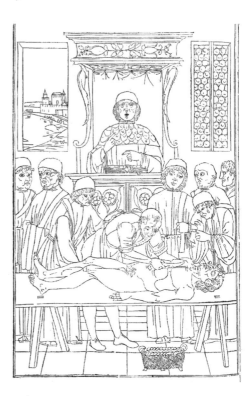

Fig. 1.8 Dissection scene
from a later edition of the
Fascicolo di medicina
(Venice: Gregorium de
Gregoriis Fratres, 1495)

local Venetian calendar) (Fig. 1.8). Detail is lavished on the structure of the anatomical action rather than the accoutrements of surgery.[59]

A lack of focus on instrumentation may not be the primary reason that such tools lack detail: in some urgent surgical occasions these objects might actually have been generic, quotidian knives with no specifically medical function, taken in emergency from contexts outside of medicine and used on the human body. Some evidence suggests that a surgeon might have used tableware, for example, at least *in extremis* in the absence of more specialized equipment.[60] Clearly, the more lavish examples of medieval cutlery, with their delicately rendered visual elements, would not fare well during the highly physical atmosphere of the operation; but

[59] The Latin original, the *Fasciculus medicinae*, was published three years earlier in 1491. See: Tiziana Pesenti, *Fasiculo de medicina in volgare: Venezia, Giovanni e Gregorio De Gregori, 1494*, especially vol. 2, *Il 'Fasciculus medicinae' ovvero, le metamorfosi del libro umanistico* (Treviso: Antilia, 2001).

[60] Kirkup, *Surgical Instruments*, p. 379. On medicine and dining, see: Joseph Zeigler, 'Medicine and the Body at the Table in Fourteenth-Century Italy: Book One of Philip Ferrara's *Liber de introductione loquendi*', in *Between Text and Patient*, ed. Glaze and Nance, pp. 121–36. On cutlery, see: Klaus Marquardt, *Europäisches Essbesteck aus acht Jahrhunderten* (Stuttgart: Arnoldsche, 1997); Bridget Ann Henisch, *Fast and Feast: Food in Medieval Society* (University Park: Pennsylvania State University Press, 1976).

Fig. 1.9 The knife-maker
Linhart Lebenbrüst,
from the *Hausbuch
der Mendelschen
Zwölfbrüderstiftung*,
1476, Nuremberg
(Nuremberg,
Stadtbibliothek,
MS Amb. 317.2°
(Mendel I), fol. 95v)

material lavishness clearly did not put surgeons off particular tools for their
highly manual tasks. Both Henri de Mondeville and Guy de Chauliac offer
a textual basis for this in their description of amputations, calling for knives
and cauteries not just of iron but also of gold: 'cum ferreo instrumento aut
aureo optime calefacto' [with a well-heated instrument of iron or gold].[61]
Solid gold, of course, could not have been sharpened enough to cut the
skin, but the phrase certainly intimates the use of fine, gilded instruments.
Whether destined for anatomy table or dinner table, it is increasingly
clear that such knives were crafted by the same specialist cutlers, as was
confirmed by finds at a medieval knife workshop uncovered in Paris in
2001.[62] Many medieval cities would have had access to such an established
workshop, or at least to an itinerant knife-maker, like the figure depicted
in the fifteenth-century *Hausbücher der Nürnberger Zwölfbrüderstiftungen*
(Fig. 1.9).[63] Surrounded by fighting daggers, flat serving knives and

---

[61] Pagel, *Chirurgie*, p. 389.

[62] M. Michel Fleury, 'Lecture, par M. Michel Fleury, d'une note de Mme
Catherine Brut sur des découvertes de céramiques et de restes de
coutellerie du XIVᵉ siècle faites 34, rue Greneta (2e arr.)', in *Commision du
Vieux Paris*, procès-verbal de la séance du Mardi, 9 Janvier 2001, pp. 14–21.

[63] On the *Handbücher*, see the online resource by Christine Sauer: http://
nuernberger-hausbuecher.de (accessed 8 Oct. 2014).

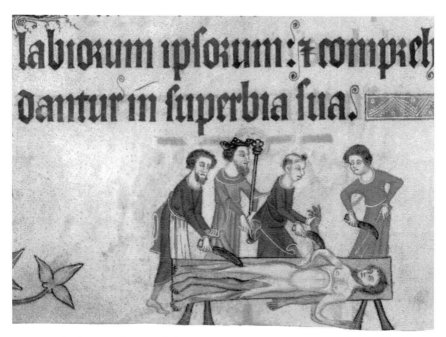

labiozum ipfozum: + compzeh
dantur in fuperbia fua.

Fig. 1.10 The flaying of St Bartholomew, from the Luttrell Psalter, *c.* 1325–40, England (London, British Library, Add. MS 42130, fol. 103v)

wooden-handled table cutlery, such images hint at the wealth of variation within a single cutler's craft. The examples in his display cabinet, complete with metal rear bolsters at the butt of their handles, are the same specific type wielded by the four surgical flayers of Sisamnes in Gerard David's 1498 diptych, mentioned above.

Indeed, non-medical images of flaying present several remarkable similarities to scenes of surgical dissection. Bartholomew and his mutilated peers are mostly shown on the makeshift wooden table of early anatomies, and scenes of both surgery and torture often display clear figures of power directing the action, reminiscent of the academic setting of the *Fasciculus medicinae*. The expressive depictions in hagiographic images provide only a certain type of imaginative evidence for flaying, but not necessarily its reality.[64] However, even so, an identical, commanding gesture links King Astyages ordering the flaying of Bartholomew in the margins of the Luttrell Psalter (Fig. 1.10) with the robed figure of Mondino in a printed edition of his *Anathomia* from 1493, proclaiming *ex cathedra* to the sector below

[64] On the caution with which hagiographic evidence should be considered, see: Candida Moss, *The Myth of Persecution* (New York: Harper Collins, 2013); Barbara H. Rosenwein, Thomas Head and Sharon Farmer, 'Monks and their Enemies: A Comparative Approach', *Speculum* 66.4 (1991): 764–96.

Fig. 1.11 Mondino da Luzzi
directing an anatomical
dissection, from a copy
of the *Anatomia Mondino*
(Melerstadt: 1493)

(Fig. 1.11).[65] Onlookers, too, are shown gathered at the scene of execution in the same way as crowds of scholarly observers gather around the dissection table (see Fig. 1.8). Whether it is meant to create and conserve knowledge or to mete out punishment, flaying is, above all, an act to be witnessed.

As is the case with surgical imagery, these non-medical flaying scenes are largely generic in their depiction of the instruments used to strip skin. Knives are simply rendered and lack individual detail. But as with surgical models, a schematic figuring should not necessarily preclude any potency in their presentation. Echoing the symbolic appearance of teeth on objects like Yperman's scissors, designed to preserve the essence of the instrument if not its direct form, the tools depicted in images of flaying also serve an emotive function. In the Luttrell Bartholomew scene, knives are objects of serious symbolic power. Not only are their blades extended and threatening – greatly exaggerated in size to almost the length of the flayers' forearms – but they are even highlighted with gold leaf to catch the eye in the light of the turning page, recalling Guy and Henri's 'golden instruments'.

---

[65] On gesture in medieval medicine, see: Cornelius O'Boyle, 'Gesturing in the Early Universities', *Dynamis* 20 (2000): 249–81.

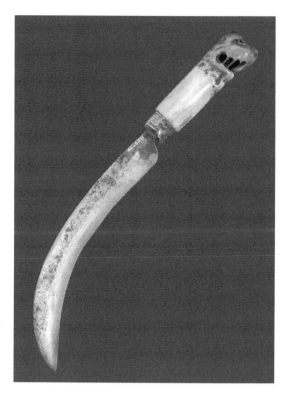

Fig. 1.12 Amputation
knife with bone
handle, late fifteenth
or sixteenth century
(London, Science
Museum (on long-term
loan to the Wellcome
Collection), museum
no.A648001)

Here knives are not a mere feature of the scene, but are rather a significant
function of the image itself: emphasizing the cutting context of the tableau,
they draw focus to the key index of the act of flaying.

One of the most intriguing examples that showcases both the highly
practical and highly conceptual avenues surgical instruments might open
up for the historian of flaying is a bone-handled knife from the collections
of the Science Museum in London, now on permanent display at the
Wellcome Collection (Fig. 1.12). Measuring 26 cm from blade-tip to handle,
it is neither the most decorated nor the plainest knife to survive from the
period, its principal figurative element being an animal-head grotesque at
the handle's end. Variously described as a wolf, bear or lion, the teeth of its
gaping mouth are abstractly tooled out, perhaps with a drill, its eyes, ears,
snout and fur all lightly incised into the uncoloured bone.

The slightly darkened, shiny patina of the handle makes clear this is a
well-used object, but its function as a medical accoutrement is not instantly
apparent. Its sculpted imagery suggests possible use in a hunting context,
but extant sets of such equipment are consistent in the types of knives and
saws they contain, and none has such a pronounced, curved blade.[66] It is, in

---

[66] See, for example, the hunting sets at the Victoria and Albert Museum,
London (museum no. M.627–1910), and the Metropolitan Museum of Art,
New York (accession no. 68.141.247a–g).

Fig. 1.13 Amputation saw (with detail below), metal frame and ivory handle, sixteenth century (London, Science Museum (Hamonic Collection, on long-term loan to the Wellcome Collection), museum no. A121435)

fact, this blade which provides the most convincing evidence for the knife's medical function, its downward 'falciform' or 'crooked' shape identifying it quite specifically for use in amputation, as described by writers from Henri de Mondeville to Ambroise Paré in the sixteenth century, allowing for a more accurate, circular incision to be made around the limb.[67] Certainly its decoration, which might at first appear inappropriate for an instrument of cure, does not exclude a medical context. On the contrary, animalistic grotesques feature on many surgical objects, for example the handles of tools in Brunschwig's *armamentarium* (see Fig. 1.6), or at the ends of a sixteenth-century bow saw, also in the Wellcome Collection, where the two catches of its removable blade have been fashioned as scaly, biting dragons (Fig. 1.13). Given problems of survival and sources, however, specifically

---

[67] Pagel, *Chirurgie*, p. 389. Precisely this sort of amputation knife is illustrated in later medical treatises, like Ambroise Paré's *Ouvres* of 1575. For scholarly work on Paré see: Évelyne Berriot-Salvadore and Paul Mironneau, eds., *Ambroise Paré (1510–1590): pratique et écriture de la science à la Renaissance. Actes du Colloque de Pau (6–7 mai 1999)* (Paris: Honoré Champion Éditeur, 2003).

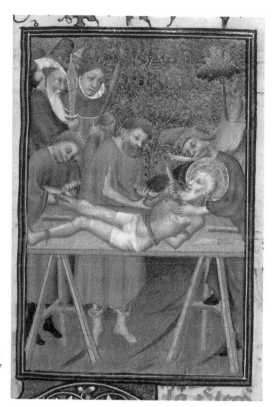

Fig. 1.14 The flaying of
St Bartholomew, from
the Breviary of John the
Fearless and Margaret of
Bavaria, 1410–19 (London,
British Library, MS Harley
2897, fol. 379r)

dating and locating an object like this curved knife with any degree of
accuracy is difficult. Guy de Chauliac mentions a curved *facuille* as early as
the fourteenth century, and the blade in the Wellcome Collection certainly
bears resemblance to the knives stripping the saintly skin of Bartholomew
in the French fifteenth-century Breviary of John the Fearless and Margaret
of Bavaria (Fig. 1.14).[68] Brunschwig also discusses a similar sickle-shaped
knife in his *Chirurgia* of 1497, and Paré adopted just such a *cutler falcato*
from the earlier *Chirurgie* of Pierre Franco in 1556. But for whom the knife
might have been made is impossible to know from the current evidence. It
could have been created in any one of the burgeoning medical centres in
Bologna, Paris, Montpellier, Leiden, Lerida, London – the list goes on.

Despite this lack of provenance, however, the extensive network of
underlying meanings and contexts emerging from the various sources for
medical instrumental knowledge suggests there is still much that can be
learned from such an object. Of particular interest is a specific moment
in the object's use: the grip and the action of the surgeon taking the
instrument in his hand. For in this specific knife, there is a fundamental
problem of design in the relationship between object and user, a tension

[68] London, British Library, MS Harley 2897.

between use, threat and function that was integral to how it might have worked.

The knife would have been used to cut through skin, the prime instrument in the act of surgical flaying. With only a little pressure on the keen, razor-sharp blade, the attendant surgeon would have been able to slice speedily through the epidermis of arm or leg before peeling it back and working further through flesh until the knife's metal hit the skeleton beneath. Thus, in material terms, metal bit through skin to meet bone. Such biting was at once literal and metaphorical. Medieval surgical treatises often designated the act of surgery itself as a 'biting' craft, and Henri de Mondeville returns repeatedly to the action of 'gnawing' in his texts, not just to describe corrosives on the skin or spreading diseases like cancers or herpes, but also to describe the surgical operation and its instrumentation as something that gnawed into the patient.[69] Yperman's toothy scissors (see Fig. 1.3) or the dragons of the Wellcome saw that take the blade's teeth as their own (see Fig. 1.13) all draw on this idea, as does the growling grotesque at the end of the Wellcome knife with its deliberately tooled teeth. Indeed, if used in the same fashion as the flayers of Bartholomew in the fourteenth-century Breviary (see Fig. 1.14), biting would play an even more dramatic role in the object. Not only does the tormentor positioned furthest to the right in this scene hold a knife in his own mouth (a pose also adopted by the flayers of Gerard David's Sisamnes), but with his other hand he is using the white handle of another knife to rip away the skin from the body. Were this second knife the Wellcome example, the mouth of the bone handle would be quite literally sinking its teeth into the saint's skin, flaying it from the body.

At the same time, the ornament and design of the Wellcome knife suggest a more complex interplay of tissues and intentions, one that complicates an initial sense of control in cure or punishment. Throughout its use in surgical amputation, the hand of the operator would have been gripped around the knife's handle. The bone end is only 10 cm long, so as the surgeon hit the tougher sections of muscle and tendon at the limb's core, his grip would have had to tighten, fingers wrapping increasingly hard around the teeth of the animalistic grotesque itself. Exerting a force of its own, the mouth of the handle would have bitten down into the surgeon's own fingers as he steadied the blade, completing a union of surgeon and knife. Such an overly complex or uncomfortable design was clearly no deterrent for surgeons, especially not in the extravagant cases of other extant surgical objects. Amputation saws that survive from the period are flourished with complex coiled frills sprouting from elephantine details, or beak-like lips shooting out at right angles from the steel framework (Fig. 1.15). These artistic elements are recorded as complicating amputation, snaring dangerously on inner tissues or catching unnecessarily on loose

---

[69] Pouchelle, 'Appendix: Metaphorical Tables', in *Corps et Chirurgie*.

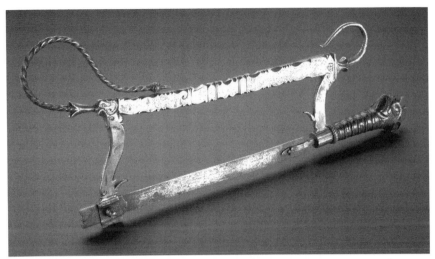

Fig. 1.15 Amputation saw, early sixteenth century (London, Science Museum [on long-term loan to the Wellcome Collection], museum no. A241432)

flaps of skin; yet their virtue was still extolled by some surgeons, and they were used well into the later Renaissance.[70] As discussed above, they were literally conflated with the surgeon's own hands, manipulable extensions practitioners were apparently reluctant to jettison. Thus, in the Wellcome knife, metal bites skin towards bone at the knife's tip, while bone in turn bit back into flesh at the handle, a circular, antagonistic back-and-forth of effort and material that bound together the bodies of doctor and patient, the whole action mediated by the knife.

This paired physicality is matched by the knife's material connections too. Bone did not feature in the medieval medical world only as material for knife handles but also as a cure for various ailments: as a blanching treatment for darkened teeth, as a remedy for haemorrhoids, as a lung preservative when mixed with poppy juice or coriander, or as a purgative if used with quince to cleanse the stomach. The raw medicinal power of ancient bone was also clearly prized; a small figure in a coffin labelled 'MUMIÉ' – an embalmed mummy – appears in Robinet Testard's late fifteenth-century illustration of a pharmacist's shelf, ready for grinding into various remedies.[71] In the Wellcome knife, therefore, bone might

---

[70] Kirkup, *Surgical Instruments*, p. 380.

[71] The image appears in a fifteenth-century French edition of Matthaeus Platearius' *Liber de simplici medicina dictus circa instans*. On this text, see: Paul Dorveaux, *Livre des simples médecines* (Paris: Société française d'histoire de la médecine, 1913). On *mumia*, see: Michael Camille, 'The Corpse in the Garden: *Mumia* in Medieval Herbal Illustrations', *Micrologus* 7 (1999): 296–318. The substance's proximate ability to indicate sites of healing is also preserved in a seventeenth-century London pharmacist's

be considered a rhetorical material that couples hand and instrument beyond the fused double-bite of their use. Scholarship has highlighted the relationship between skin and ivory or bone, drawing attention to various textual descriptions – as diverse as Petrarch, the Pygmalion myth and the Song of Solomon – in which the two organic materials are often likened to one another, conceptually aligned in theoretical, romantic and classicizing traditions.[72] Common to both are physical characteristics, like their white pallor or surface texture, as well as more inherent intellectual properties, for example, the indication of purity, chastity or a more sensual amorousness. Skin and decorative bone are conflated in much the same way as the surgeon and his instrument. The knife was not a foreign implement but one that almost melted into the palm.[73] Absorbing the surgeon's movement, his authority and his knowledge, it was a combinatory, material-based welding of forms, matched by the constant biting of the grotesque deep into the skin.

The merging of hand and handle is, thus, deliquescent, bordering on the liquid, a notion key to actions of both amputation and flaying. The practitioner is, of course, hardly the most fluid figure in the surgical scene: bleeding profusely, the soon-to-be amputee becomes liquid themself. His skin lacerated, the arm or leg in question would have begun to pour blood, draining the body from beneath its protective *pannicule* and merging with the blade. So vivid was this liquid phenomenon that it was a deep anxiety to attendant surgeons; both Henri de Mondeville and Guy de Chauliac offer guidance on how to stem blood flow, as well as the advice to remove non-essential persons from the room lest they should faint at the sight or encourage the patient to do so. Guy speaks in grave terms of the success rate of medieval amputations, fearing for both the health and sanity of his patients: 'car i'ay ouy dire, que pour le grand combat de la vertu animale et naturelle, quelques-vns ont encouru manie, et consequemment la mort' [for I have heard it said, that in the great fight of animal and natural virtue, some have become manic and subsequently died].[74] Just like the open, roaring mouth of the grotesque on the knife's handle, far from being

street sign featuring a unicorn complete with tusk wrought from narwhal horn (now Wellcome Collection, no. A631343).

[72] W. Monroe, 'A French Gothic Ivory of the Virgin and Child', *Museum Studies* 9 (1978): 6–29; Susan L. Smith, 'The Gothic Mirror and the Female Gaze', in *Saints, Sinners, and Sisters: Gender and Northern Art in Medieval and Early Modern Europe*, ed. Jane L. Carroll and Alison G. Stewart (Aldershot: Ashgate, 2003), pp. 73–93; Sarah M. Guérin, 'Meaningful Spectacles: Gothic Ivories Staging The Divine', *Art Bulletin* 95.1 (2013): 53–77.

[73] Brunschwig, in his *Cirurgia*, describes knives as 'kalte Waffen', humoristically cold weapons, heated by the hand of the surgeon (Klein, *Brunschwig*, p. xiii). Bone itself is a material particularly receptive to heat.

[74] Nicaise, *Guy de Chauliac*, p. 436.

blessed with saintly anaesthesia, the amputee – like the torture victim – would surely have been screaming.

Lending the instrument as a whole a sense of activity and agency, the animalistic bone handle gives the object not just an alert, biting vigour, but also a sense of doubled strength, and perhaps even brings animated hope to the entire surgical enterprise. Such a complex multifaceted meaning does not dwell in the Wellcome knife alone, but rather prompts us to think about all accoutrements used in multiple types of flaying. Might the wielder of a fourteenth-century knife handle depicting the Green Man, discovered in the ground in Scotland, also be slipping into nature when he cuts, matching the bone handle's foliage-covered features?[75] Maybe medieval and Renaissance users of popular cutlery, carved with ideal courtly ladies and suitors, were aware of the slippage of skin and implement, especially in the distinctly sensuous atmospheres of upper-class dining. Perhaps, too, the wielders of more torturous blades might have recognized the literal and conceptual slippage between themselves, their knives and their victims. Evidence from medieval knives holds the tantalizing suggestion that they might act as a sort of exquisite bridge between bodies, materials and their morphologies, their solid or liquid states of being. Crafting a clear bond between surgery and flaying, both medical and punitive moments are so avowedly actions of the knife that the object might even proudly stand as index for them. Guy de Chauliac repeatedly urges the surgeon to question 'when to use the knife', the phrase not necessarily meaning specifically when to cut, but rather when to engage in any form of operation, the tool standing for the act of surgery itself. So too, the flayed Bartholomew often stands not holding his flayed skin but simply the knife that flayed it, the device symbolic of his endured punishment and the whole flaying process.

Like surgery, flaying itself might be extended and refined through an understanding of its tools. Murderous and violent or medicalized and delicate, regardless of aggression or intention, there is an interplay of different materials and of different moments in the actions of both, the knife simultaneously inside and outside of the bodies of patient and doctor, victim and executioner. Whilst one removes skin to maintain life and the other does so in order that life may slowly and distressingly ebb away, medicine offers access to what removing skin meant in both contexts during the Middle Ages. Formulating a multifaceted relationship between the metal of the knife, the bone of its handle, the skin of the flayed and the hand of its wielder, it puts forward an incisive form of medieval thinking that could bite with as much physical and conceptual conviction as its piercing, instrumented blade.

[75] M. A. Hall, 'An Ivory Knife Handle from the High Street, Perth, Scotland: Consuming Ritual in a Medieval Burgh', *Medieval Archaeology* 45 (2001): 169–18.

2

A Tale of Venetian Skin:
The Flaying of Marcantonio Bragadin

Kelly DeVries

O N 24 November 1961, with very little fanfare and almost no audience – only far-removed descendants and a few scientists – a niche tomb in the Basilica di Santi Giovanni e Paolo was opened. It was not entirely known what would be found. For many years, locals suspected that there would be nothing, that the legends were false. The tomb, marked on its outside by an urn, a bust and an identifying inscription, was that of Marcantonio Bragadin, the heroic Venetian defender of Famagusta during the attack of the Ottoman Turks in 1570–1.

Inside the tomb was a leaden casket, too short to carry a body. But, then again, it was not a body that had been interred. When opened, several pieces of skin were revealed – the skin of one who had been flayed alive.[1] Beyond the presence of skin, however, accounts from 1961 report little else. For this, one must go to a description from the 1596 transmission of Bragadin's skin from the Venetian church where it first rested, San Gregorio, to the Basilica di Santi Giovanni e Paulo:

> Esa era piegata in ampiezza d'un foglio di carta, salda e palpabile come fosse un pannolino; vi si vedevano i peli del petto ancora attaccati, et alla mano destra, che era scorticata, la dita non compiute di scorticare con l'unghie che sembravano ancora vive.

> [[The skin] was folded to a size of a sheet of paper, solid and palpable as a napkin; they could see his chest hair still attached, and on the right hand, which was flayed, was a nail that still seemed alive].[2]

Between 1571 and 1596 the flayed skin had already travelled widely and, at a time when the Venetian governmental leadership was touting victory at Lepanto as a sign of future success, Bragadin's skin reminded the citizens of Venice of their defeat at Cyprus and what the past had already brought. Bragadin's skin was a testament to his people that flaying was one vicious,

---

[1] Cecilia Gibellini, *L'immagine di Lepanto: la celebrazione della vittoria nella letteratura e nell'arte veneziano* (Venice: Marsilio, 2008), p. 92; and John Julius Norwich, *The Middle Sea: A History of the Mediterranean* (London: Vintage Books, 2007), pp. 319–20.

[2] Giuseppe Tassini, *Curiosità veneziane, ovvero Origini delle denominazioni stradali di Venezia* (Venice: Grimaldo, 1872), pp. 358–9. Tassini has no reference other than 'una cronaca già dai Bragadin posseduta' [a chronicle previously held by Bragadin].

inhumane effect of fighting a vicious, inhumane enemy; the maintenance of this legendary artefact was a powerful reminder to Venetians of their constant foe, the Ottoman Turks. Unlike countless medieval narratives where flaying is threatened or supposedly sentenced as a punishment for grievous crimes, the story of Marcantonio Bragadin is one that can actually be verified in the survival of the skin itself. Therefore, it is a unique – and relatively unknown – case study for considering the context and circumstances of punitive flaying.

Flaying was not a frequent punishment, and was never previously recorded in the many violent encounters between Turks and Europeans from the early fourteenth century to 1571. Several medieval literary texts, like the Middle English *Sowdone of Babylone* and *The Siege of Jerusalem*, ascribe flaying to Muslim enemies as a means of Othering them, a form of anti-Muslim propaganda, but there is no evidence that they ever practised it other than in the Bragadin episode.[3] Nor, it seems, was it planned at the beginning of 5 August, the day Bragadin had arranged to 'conditionally surrender' Famagusta, with the promise from the Ottoman general, Lala Mustafa Pasha, that no executions would follow. That changed, however, when Mustafa, in the middle of the surrender ceremony, without any explained provocation, suddenly ordered the mutilation and flaying of Bragadin and the execution of all Venetians in the town. Indeed, one of the reasons so many eyewitness accounts remain is because many Ottoman soldiers were so surprised by the sudden change of events that they failed to follow their commander's order to kill those they were escorting to ships in the harbour. Unfortunately, as there are no remaining Turkish accounts of the flaying, it will never be known what changed Mustafa's mind so quickly. That part of the story will have to remain conjecture. However, the flaying of Bragadin was the result of more than a century of military dispute over Cyprus as much as it was a product of tensions on the day of surrender. The skin that survived into the twentieth century is a testament to the complexity of relationships in the medieval Mediterranean and to the profound symbolism of this spectacular punishment.

One Hundred Years of Escalating Tensions and Tenuous Treaties

Venice acquired Cyprus in 1473 when the last Lusignan king, James II, died and his widow, Queen Caterina Cornaro, a Venetian, inherited the island. Not interested in ruling, and much preferring to reside in the city of her birth, she essentially ceded Cyprus to Venice at that time, though it only

---

[3] In this volume, see: Emily Leverett, 'Reading the Consumed: Flayed and Cannibalized Bodies in *The Siege of Jerusalem* and *Richard Coer de Lyon*', pp. 285–307; Michael Livingston, 'Losing Face: Flayed Beards and Gendered Power in Arthurian Literature', pp. 308–21; and Larissa Tracy, 'Face Off: Flaying and Identity in Medieval Romance', pp. 322–48 at n. 35.

became official in 1489 at her titular abdication.[4] Cyprus was, thus, a late addition to Venice's Aegean Sea Empire, which also included Crete. Almost immediately Cyprus became one of the city-state's most prosperous economic centres, as trade flowed via the island from the Middle East and Asia to Venice and vice versa. Yet, at the same time, and maybe because of its increased prosperity, Cyprus became a key target of the Ottoman Empire, then in the midst of its conquest of the Eastern Mediterranean.

This conquest had begun at the turn of the fourteenth century and progressed steadily after that.[5] Within the initial decade the Ottomans had their first major military victory – when the Turkish dynast Ghazi Osman, from Asia Minor, used mainly familial forces to defeat a much larger Byzantine army at the Battle of Baphaeum in 1301 – and captured their first major city, Nicaea. Within their first century, the Ottomans had conquered all, or the majority, of the Byzantine Empire, Bulgaria, Macedonia, Greece, Montenegro, Bosnia and Serbia, and in two major battles (at Kosovo in 1389 and Nicopolis in 1396) Ottoman armies crushed Western opponents. At Kosovo they defeated a large Serbian army, killing the Serbian ruler, Prince Lazar; at Nicopolis they destroyed a crusading force drawn from England, Burgundy, France, Germany, Hungary, Wallachia, Transylvania and the Teutonic Knights. Defeats were few during these years, although the fifteenth century opened with one of the most significant ones, at Ankara in 1402, when Tamerlane (Timur 'the Lame') and his Mongols routed the Ottoman army in battle and captured their sultan, Bayezid I, who – after being paraded in a cage around the Timurid lands for more than a year – committed suicide.[6]

A succession crisis between Bayezid's sons, Suleyman and Musa, halted Ottoman expansion for several years, but Murad II, who ruled from 1421

---

[4] Kenneth Setton, *The Papacy and the Levant (1204–1571)*, vol. 2: *The Fifteenth Century* (Philadelphia: The American Philosophical Society, 1978), p. 258; Jean Richard, 'Chypre du protectorat à la domination vénetienne', in *Venezia e il Levante fino al secolo XV*, ed. Agostino Pertusi (Florence: Leo S. Olschki Editore, 1973), pp. 657–77; and Benjamin Arbel, 'A Fresh Look at the Venetian Protectorate of Cyprus (1474–89)', in *Caterina Cornaro: Last Queen of Cyprus and Daughter of Venice / Ultima regina di Cipro e figlia di Venezia*, ed. Candida Syndikus and Sabine Rogge (Münster: Waxmann Verlag, 2013), pp. 213–31.

[5] The best books covering the rise of the Ottomans are: Halil Inalcik, *The Ottoman Empire: The Classical Age, 1300–1600*, trans. Norman Itzkowitz and Colin Imber (New York: Praeger, 1973); and Colin Imber, *The Ottoman Empire, 1300–1650* (New York: Palgrave, 2002). But for a strictly military focus, see: Stephen Turnbull, *The Ottoman Empire, 1326–1699* (London: Osprey, 2003); and Mesut Uyar and Edward J. Erickson, *A Military History of the Ottomans from Osman to Atatürk* (Santa Barbara, CA: Praeger Security International, 2009), pp. 1–26.

[6] Justin Marozzi, *Tamerlane: Sword of Islam, Conqueror of the World* (London: Harper Perennial, 2004), pp. 318–46.

to 1451, began once again to campaign, primarily in the remains of the Byzantine Empire and south-eastern Europe. Smyrna fell in 1424, Salonika in 1430 and Albania in 1432, with a large Hungarian army defeated on the Upper Danube in 1428, forcing the Hungarians to retreat to fortifications protecting their borders. A period of Ottoman defeats followed: in 1441, Vladislav of Poland and Hungary raised the siege of Belgrade; the next year the Hungarian János Hunyadi defeated them, invading Transylvania; in 1443 the Albanians revolted and regained their independence; and in 1444 Hunyadi won the Battle of Mount Kunovica. However, Murad quickly bounced back, with victories against a Western European 'crusading' army at the Battle of Varna in 1444 and against Hunyadi at the Second Battle of Kosovo in 1448. With these victories, the Turks recovered control of the Balkans, except for Albania, an area they would hold securely for the next four centuries.[7]

On 3 February 1451, Murad died and the sultanship passed fairly smoothly to his son, Mehmed II. Mehmed's greatest achievement was the successful siege of Constantinople in 1453, therefore awarding him the title by which he would be known throughout history, 'the Conqueror'.[8] He did have other victories: Athens in 1456, Serbia in 1459, the Morea in 1460, Trebizond in 1461, Herzegovina in 1467, Kaffa in 1475 and Albania in 1478; but also some major defeats: at Belgrade in 1456, Jaysca in 1463, Savacz in 1475, Rhodes in 1480 and – although it was held for several weeks – Otranto in 1480–1.[9]

Surprisingly, during the first 180 years of Ottoman expansion, the islands of the Eastern Mediterranean were relatively safe. Some had been captured, but only those that did not necessitate a full-scale amphibious operation, leaving us to wonder if Turkish naval capabilities lagged significantly behind their military ones, either technologically (they lacked sufficient transport ships and galleys to deliver the number of men and siege machines it would take to conquer a fortified naval target), logistically (there were insufficient naval bases to restock the typically short-journeying galleys with food and water), or economically (the Ottomans did not want to spend the finances required to launch amphibious operations against naval targets perceived to be less valuable

---

[7] Turnbull, *The Ottoman Empire*, pp. 30–6; and Uyar and Erickson, *A Military History of the Ottomans*, pp. 28–30.

[8] The standard text for almost half a century had been Steven Runciman's *The Fall of Constantinople, 1453* (Cambridge: Cambridge University Press, 1965), but it has been very effectively replaced by Marios Philippides and Walter Hanak, *The Siege and Fall of Constantinople in 1453: Historiography, Topography, and Military Studies* (Burlington, VT: Ashgate, 2011).

[9] Turnbull, *The Ottoman Empire*, pp. 36–45. On the losses at Belgrade and Rhodes, see: Kelly DeVries, 'Conquering the Conqueror at Belgrade (1456) and Rhodes (1480): Irregular Soldiers for an Uncommon Defense', *A Guerra, Revista de História das Ideias* 30 (2009): 219–32.

than land targets).[10] That had clearly changed by 1480, when both Rhodes and Otranto were deemed valuable enough to be attacked by amphibious operation. Both were significant undertakings, requiring large numbers of military and naval personnel.

By 1480 Cyprus had never been attacked by the Ottomans. The Lusignan kings, who had held the island since 1192, were hardly ever threatened by outside forces, although they had paid the Egyptian Mamluks a tribute for some of the fifteenth century before the Venetians took control of the island. The Ottomans were clearly a threat, simply by their proximity and expansionist goals, but they had not acted.[11] Or, perhaps better put, the Ottomans had not acted *yet*. There was every anticipation they would do so soon – even though the failure to conquer Rhodes certainly demoralized the two Ottoman sultans who followed Mehmed's death in 1481, they could still have rationalized that the Catholic military order the Knights Hospitaller put on an extremely valiant defensive effort, turning back several assaults of the city's walls and fortresses before an exhausted and depleted Ottoman force retreated to Turkey.[12] Cyprus could not similarly be defended. Beyond the fact that there were two major cities – Nicosia and Famagusta – that would need defending, instead of just the one on Rhodes, the island was simply larger and could not be abandoned to the Turks, as the Hospitallers had done with the territory around the city of Rhodes. In addition, Cyprus was not defended by a military force fanatically willing to die for its religious beliefs, as were the Knights Hospitaller. No doubt Queen Caterina Cornaro pondered this (and not just her Venetian birth) before she passed effective control of the island to Venice in 1473.

By then, Venice knew exactly what to anticipate from the Ottomans. At the time they took over Cyprus, the Venetians were enmeshed in a war that had begun in 1463 and would not end until 1479. Although most of this war had been fought over the Venetian holdings on the Balkan Peninsula, the improving Ottoman navy was playing its role, too. It could even be said that the Ottomans were using this war against the greatest naval power in

---

[10] John H. Pryor, *Geography, Technology, and War: Studies in the Maritime History of the Mediterranean, 649–1571* (Cambridge: Cambridge University Press, 1988), p. 177; and Rhoads Murphey, *Ottoman Warfare, 1500–1700* (London: University College London Press, 1999), pp. 17–18, 22–3.

[11] This period is covered in volume 2 and the first half of volume 3 of George Hill, *A History of Cyprus*, 4 vols. (New York: Macmillan, 1948; repr. Cambridge: Cambridge University Press, 2010). On the relationship between Venice and the Mamluks, both before and after the acquisition of Cyprus, see: Deborah Howard, 'Venice and the Mamluks', in *Venice and the Islamic World, 828–1797*, ed. Stefano Carboni (New Haven: Yale University Press, 2007), pp. 72–89.

[12] Robert Douglas Smith and Kelly DeVries, *Rhodes Besieged: A New History* (Stroud: The History Press, 2011), pp. 42–63.

the Mediterranean as a 'proving ground' to test and improve their naval technology and logistics. Ultimately, their conquest of Negroponte, lost by Venice in 1470 (the republic's most costly loss), showed that the Ottoman navy was prepared for bigger amphibious operations in the future. The Venetians were certainly not wrong in thinking one of those would be directed at Cyprus.[13]

Venice lost the war of 1463–79 badly; they would also lose the next war they undertook against the Ottoman Turks, between 1499 and 1503. This second war was almost entirely fought on sea and showed that the Turks had completely changed their policies. Their navy was well funded and provided with the most sophisticated technology – ships and gunpowder weapons – and logistical support, probably better than any other navy in the Mediterranean. The initial engagement (1499) was the Battle of Zonchio, off the coast of Lepanto, where a very large Venetian fleet, estimated at eighty-eight galleys and other vessels, lost to an even larger Ottoman fleet estimated at more than 260 vessels. Many Venetian ships were sunk, including the first recorded sinking of a ship by naval gunfire. As a result of this defeat, Venice lost its port at Lepanto. A second naval battle was fought in 1500 off the coast of Coron, where the Venetian fleet was trying to prevent the capture of yet another port. Once again, the Venetians lost and the city fell. A third naval engagement was fought that same year off the coast of Modon, and with the same results; Venice lost yet another port. Venice quickly signed a treaty with Vladislaus II, King of Hungary (who promised troops), and Pope Alexander VI (who promised money), but their allies could not respond in time, and in 1501 Venice lost Durazzo in Albania, another port. Armistices with the Turks were attempted, but their ineffectiveness was such that, in 1503, Turkish cavalry carried out raids on Venetian territories in northern Italy from the Balkans. Finally, Venice buckled and signed a peace treaty with the Ottoman Turks.[14]

---

[13] On the Venetian-Ottoman war of 1463–79, see: Setton, *The Papacy and the Levant*, II.271–313; and Thomas F. Madden, *Venice: A New History* (New York: Viking, 2012), pp. 286–9. An interesting primary account of the naval war can be found in the history of Pietro Mocenigo, a Venetian galley commander. Coriolano Cippico, *The Deeds of Commander Pietro Mocenigo*, ed. Kiril Petkov (New York: Italica Press, 2014).

[14] There is a need for a good scholarly treatment of this war. For the moment, the best overview of the war, although discussing very little about the military campaigns, is Setton, *The Papacy and the Levant*, II.514–39, but see also: Daniel Goffman, *The Ottomans and Early Modern Europe* (Cambridge: Cambridge University Press, 2002), pp. 142–4. Zonchio is the most discussed battle: L. Fincati, 'La deplorabile battaglia navale del Zonchio (1499)', *Rivista marittima* 16 (1883): 187–201; Roger Crowley, 'Fireball at Zonchio', *Military History Quarterly* 24 (Sept. 2012): 36–43; and Kelly DeVries, 'The Effectiveness of Fifteenth-Century Shipboard Artillery', *The Mariner's Mirror* 84 (1998): 389–99.

Cyprus had been spared direct involvement in these wars as they were both fought in the north-eastern Mediterranean. Nevertheless, the island's indirect involvement had been extensive. Venice had used Cypriot ports frequently to house and restock their fleets, and had begun garrisoning all of the fortifications, reconstructing and repairing the walls around Nicosia and Famagusta. Perhaps more importantly, it was through Cyprus that Venice increased its trade with the Mamluks, whom the Ottomans considered one of their most feared enemies. The Venetians also continued paying the Cypriot tribute to the Mamluks, which reached 8,000 gold ducats *per annum* in the late fifteenth century.[15]

The Ottoman Turks noticed this activity; the treaty ending the 1499–1503 war was the first to imply a threat against Crete and Cyprus. This threat was pacified only when the Venetians agreed to make extraordinary concessions. First, the Venetians were to recognize the loss of lands captured during the war by the Ottomans. Second, the Venetians could continue trading with the Mamluks, but under the oversight of the Turks. Third, both the Turks and the Venetians would trade prisoners and slaves captured (which proved to be a problem for the Venetians as they had sold all those whom they had captured, thus delaying the signing of the treaty). Fourth, the Venetians would promise not to pirate Turkish ships, while ignoring the Ottoman piracy of non-Venetian Christian ships – even papal ones – and enslavement of non-Venetian Christians.[16] Fifth, the Venetians were prohibited from holding or capturing Ottoman slaves, including those that might already be rowing Venetian galleys (another common practice of Eastern Mediterranean states). Sixth, the Venetians were not to free any Christian captives they found on Ottoman vessels. Seventh, the Venetians were also to discourage anti-Ottoman activities by other European powers. Finally, the Venetians were to pay the Turks an annual tribute of 10,000 gold ducats.

And so it continued for most of the next seven decades. Venice only rarely resisted this treaty's requirements and the city signed new treaties that added even more provisions in 1513 and 1517. By doing so, though, Cyprus and Crete remained Venetian. This was, however, a very fragile peace; the Venetians constantly anticipated an invasion of either or both islands, evidenced in the 1507 provisions assigned to the Cypriots by the Venetian senate. Nicosia seems to have been in acceptable defensive shape, but Famagusta, with a much smaller population, was less so. The senate

---

[15] Arbel, 'A Fresh Look', pp. 214–15. Arbel's focus is on Cyprus during the First Venetian–Ottoman War, but his points are equally valid for the Second War as well.

[16] While this is difficult to understand from a modern perspective, the pirating of ships and taking of slaves was a thriving economic system, practised by governments and outlaws. See: Molly Greene, *Catholic Pirates and Greek Merchants: A Maritime History of the Early Modern Mediterranean* (Princeton: Princeton University Press, 2013).

demanded the Cypriots first improve the fortifications of the city. Then, to guarantee its garrison was fully manned, the old feudal obligations were to be enforced, with all Cypriot men serving as militia for four months a year. Those who refused to comply could lose their estates and goods. Huge tariffs were also imposed on all trade goods to increase funding. The Cypriots were not pleased, but they did comply.[17]

Trade with the Mamluks remained very prosperous, seeming to justify the concessions made by the Venetians to the Ottomans. However, in 1512, Sultan Bayezid II died and his son, Selim II, inherited his empire. As soon as he took over, Selim quickly changed the Ottoman expansionist direction towards the Middle East and Egypt. In 1513 he approached the Venetians, asking to use Cyprus as a base to launch his operations against the Mamluks. Bayezid had made a similar request in 1488, but the Venetians had refused, choosing to privilege their economic relationship with the Mamluks over their worry that the Turks might invade Cyprus.[18] They clearly felt the reverse in 1513 because they quickly agreed to the Ottoman demands. Within four years Selim had conquered Syria, Palestine, Egypt and the holy cities of Mecca and Medina.[19] With the latter came responsibilities to protect pilgrims on the *hajj*; it was a responsibility that the sultans would take very seriously. In renegotiating their treaty with Venice in 1517, attacks of pilgrimage vessels going to or from the holy cities were absolutely forbidden. The Venetians were also made to inform other European states that, should they attack pilgrimage ships, Venice would suffer.[20] The Venetians also agreed to continue paying the yearly tribute of 8,000 gold ducats, but only to the Ottoman Turks now.[21]

The delicate peace returned. And, once more, Venice returned to

---

[17] Kenneth Setton, *The Papacy and the Levant (1204–1571)*, vol. 3: *The Sixteenth Century to the Reign of Julius III* (Philadelphia: The American Philosophical Society, 1984), pp. 45–6.

[18] On the 1488 refusal, see: Caroline Finkel, *Osman's Dream: The History of the Ottoman Empire* (New York: Basic Books, 2005), p. 91; and on the 1513 compliance, see: Palmira Brummett, *Ottoman Seapower and Levantine Diplomacy in the Age of Discovery* (Albany: State University of New York Press, 1994), pp. 108–9.

[19] Andrew C. Hess, 'The Ottoman Conquest of Egypt (1517) and the Beginning of the Sixteenth-Century World War', *International Journal of Middle Eastern Studies* 4 (1973): 55–76.

[20] Niccolò Capponi, *Victory of the West: The Great Christian–Muslim Clash at the Battle of Lepanto* (New York: Da Capo Press, 2006), p. 121; Colin Imber, 'Ideals and Legitimation in Early Ottoman History', in *Süleyman the Magnificent and his Age: The Ottoman Empire in the Early Modern World*, ed. Metin Kunt and Christine Woodhead (London: Longman, 1995), p. 149; and S. Faroqhi, *Pilgrims and Sultans: The Hajj under the Ottomans, 1517–1683* (London: I. B. Tauris, 1994), pp. 7–10.

[21] Finkel, *Osman's Dream*, p. 113, and Setton, *The Papacy and the Levant*, III.184.

anticipating the imminent attack of Cyprus, which, of course, meant continuing to follow the provisions of the treaties they had with the Ottomans. When Suleyman the Magnificent came to throne in 1521 and turned his military might against Rhodes the following year, the Venetians refused to help. They would not even allow provisions or reinforcements to sail through or from Crete and Cyprus; indeed, the great military engineer Gabriel Tadini di Martinengo, whose presence had been requested by the Grand Master of the Hospitallers, Philippe de l'Isle Adam, had to sneak over to Rhodes when the Venetian officials denied his request to go there.[22] That same year, when the Hungarians, supported by the papacy, asked for financial aid to help them resist Suleyman's attacks, the Venetians also refused to reciprocate what had been given them by the Hungarians during the 1499–1503 war. The senate's official reason: were they to do so, Cyprus might be attacked.[23]

Of course, when the Ottomans were fighting elsewhere, as in Hungary and Austria or against the Safavid Persians, the Venetians were able to relax a little. However, in 1537 they let that relaxation lead them to do something that Suleyman did not like: the Venetians signed a treaty with Holy Roman Emperor Charles V and the result was a war that continued until 1540, which they again lost. The cost for that defeat was 300,000 ducats, as well as the 8,000 due annually for Cyprus, and the loss of two more Eastern Mediterranean ports.[24] Two years later the Venetians had paid that debt down to 75,000 ducats (plus the 8,000 owed that year), but Suleyman added 12,000 more ducats, claiming that two Ottoman galliots had been pirated by Venetians off the Barbary coast, leading to the death of twenty-nine Muslims. The Venetians agreed to pay that, too.[25]

Between then and the actual attack of Cyprus in 1570, the Venetian senate frequently issued warnings of impending invasion, due to news that the Ottomans were amassing a fleet, or other 'intelligence': such warnings came in 1551, 1558, 1561, 1564 (the Turks attacked Malta instead), 1566, 1567 (they attacked Chios) and 1568.[26] So sure were the Venetians that Cyprus was soon to be invaded that, in 1567, large amounts of money were sent to the island to update the fortifications at Nicosia and Famagusta and to

---

[22] This is reported by both the eyewitness chroniclers of the siege, Jean de Bourbon and Jacobus Fontanus, who marvel at the Venetians' 'heresy' in siding with the Ottomans rather than the Knights Hospitallers. See: Smith and DeVries, *Rhodes Besieged*, pp. 109–10. A proposal to aid the Hospitallers was brought before the Venetians, but it resoundingly was defeated. See: Setton, *The Papacy and the Levant*, III.207.

[23] Setton, *The Papacy and the Levant*, III.200.

[24] Ibid., pp. 433–49.

[25] Ibid., p. 465.

[26] Ibid., p. 536, and Kenneth Setton, *The Papacy and the Levant (1204–1571)*, vol. 4: *The Sixteenth Century from Julius III to Pius V* (Philadelphia: The American Philosophical Society, 1984), pp. 700, 766, 842, 880, 891, 919.

establish cannon foundries and gunpowder factories in those cities so that the Cypriots did not need to rely solely on what could be sent to them from Venice.[27]

The warnings finally proved prophetic on 27 June 1570, when an Ottoman fleet, said by eyewitnesses to number 350–400 ships and 60,000–100,000 men (probably exaggerating the numbers of both),[28] set sail for Cyprus from Turkey, arriving six days later. What had changed for the Turks to do what was unprecedented in Venetian–Ottoman relations – breaking the treaty of 1540, which was still in effect – is not known. Suleyman died in 1566 and there was a rumour that the new sultan, Selim II, whose drinking habits had already been established by the time he took the throne, especially loved Cypriot wines. Although dismissed, it is a story frequently repeated by historians.[29] More likely, the new sultan was looking for a quick victory to legitimize his rule in the eyes of the many Turks who did not feel he could fill his father's shoes. That Suleyman was known as 'the Magnificent' and Selim as 'the Sot' indicates that the judgement of those Turks was correct.

At the outset it looked as if Selim was going to have his easy victory. Nicosia fell after only a seven-week siege. Lala Mustafa Pasha led a marvellous attack of the walled city, but blame for its fall is accorded to the poor defensive generalship of Nicolò Dandolo by all three of the eyewitnesses who report the siege – Fabriano Falchetti, Giovanni Sozomeno and Angelo Calepio – rather than credit being given to Mustafa. Mustafa did lead fifteen assaults of the walls over forty-five days and attacked all the bastions, which, when not being assaulted, were heavily bombarded. But Nicosia's walls were strong and, with any kind of defence, should have held out longer. The garrison was massacred, the population enslaved and the city pillaged; barrels of unused gunpowder went into invaders' stores.[30] The Turkish army, having suffered few losses, moved to Famagusta. It was there that the easy victory became much more difficult. For, rather than facing an incapable leader, the Ottomans faced Marcantonio Bragadin.

---

[27] Setton, *The Papacy and the Levant*, IV.907.

[28] Ibid., p. 1000.

[29] For example, Madden, *Venice*, p. 328; Stephen Turnbull, *The Art of Renaissance Warfare: From the Fall of Constantinople to the Thirty Years War* (London: Greenhill Books, 2006), p. 131; and John Francis Guilmartin, Jr., *Gunpowder and Galleys: Changing Technology and Mediterranean Warfare at Sea in the Sixteenth Century*, 2nd edn (London: Conway Maritime Press, 2003), p. 249.

[30] The best comprehensive account of the attack and fall of Nicosia is Setton, *The Papacy and the Levant*, IV.974–1003. Capponi's *Victory of the West*, pp. 136–44, contains the best military history.

A Capable, Experienced Opponent

Bragadin was an old, experienced soldier, the kind rarely produced by Venice, which still relied largely on mercenaries to provide its warriors.[31] He had not initially sought military service, but he soured early on in his career as a lawyer, and in 1543 he joined the city's navy. Immediately an officer, due to his familial connections and wealth, his leadership skills were recognized and he quickly rose to the rank of *vicegovernatore di galera* (essentially, second in command of a galley). He would be at sea for most of the next seventeen years, where he undoubtedly came into frequent contact with the Ottoman Turks, although, at the time, the majority of these encounters would have been peaceful. In 1560, Bragadin returned to Venice, perhaps wishing to settle down and have a family with his wife, Elisabetta di Almorò Morosini, whom he married in 1556. He was named city magistrate. But, once again, inactivity seems to have driven him back to the navy, where, in 1566, he was named *governatore di galea* and placed in command of a galley. This was only a temporary position, however, as in three years, on 31 May 1569, he was elected *capitano del regno di Cipro* (Captain of the Kingdom of Cyprus) and went to Famagusta with 300 men and 6,000 ducats (1,000 to upgrade the garrison's accommodations and 5,000 to upgrade the walls).[32]

For two years Bragadin did what he could to prepare for the impending conquest. The walls of the cities were strengthened, supplies were stocked, cannons were cast, gunpowder made and the militia trained. What the Captain of Cyprus could not do, however, was increase the numbers of experienced soldiers he had at hand. A tally from the beginning of the siege showed only 2,200 in Famagusta. Relief and reinforcements would have to come from Venice. Until then, the defenders would hunker down behind the very powerful walls.

On 9 September 1570, Nicosia fell. By the next day Bragadin received news of this – and of the massacre of troops that followed – by letter from Mustafa Pasha, who recommended that the city surrender. Zaccaria Mudazzo, the commander of the third largest city, Kyrenia, received the same letter and did surrender, and the Venetian citizens were allowed to leave Cyprus unharmed, although Mudazzo, accused of treason, would spend the rest of his life in prison.[33] The letter to Bragadin was followed

---

[31] See: M. E. Mallett and J. R. Hale, *The Military Organization of a Renaissance State: Venice, c. 1400 to 1617* (Cambridge: Cambridge University Press, 1984).

[32] The *Dizionario biografico degli Italiani* biography of Marcantonio Bragadin was written by Angelo Ventura and published in volume 13 in 1971. It is available online through http://www.treccani.it/enciclopedia (accessed 13 Jun. 2015). On the moneys and men allocated by the Venetian Senate in 1569, see: Setton, *The Papacy and the Levant*, IV.941.

[33] Capponi, *Victory of the West*, p. 144, and Setton, *The Papacy and the Levant*, IV.1004.

up on the same day by the delivery of the head of Dandolo on a platter. Neither message affected Bragadin's determination to defend the city. He responded to Mustafa:

> Milord pasha of Caramania. I have seen your letter. I have also received the head of the lord lieutenant of the city of Nicosia, and I tell you herewith that even if you have so easily taken the city of Nicosia, with your own blood you will have to purchase this city, which with God's help will give you so much to do that you will always regret having encamped here. From Famagusta, 10 September.[34]

The Ottoman army arrived outside the walls of Famagusta on 16 and 17 September.

The Siege of Famagusta

Within the next few days the Turks began bombarding the city. They also began digging trenches and traverses to the large moat surrounding it. The city's guns kept up constant counter gunfire, certainly at a lesser rate than their opponents', but sufficient to slow the progress of the siege. This remained the situation for two and a half months. Then, on 26 January 1571, a small Venetian fleet of thirteen galleys and four transport ships successfully ran the Turkish blockade around the harbour: 1,700 men, 1,400 kegs of gunpowder, cannonballs, 800 kegs of wine and grain were off-loaded, to the absolute joy of the Famagustans. A second relief fleet brought 1,270 more men a short time later. Venice had heard of the city's plight, and all judged it necessary to send relief; this, Bragadin was told, was but the initial outpouring of support that would eventually force the Ottomans from the island, dispirited by the Venetian commitment to control of Cyprus.[35] But these were to be the last supply ships to reach besieged Famagusta. February's tally of 4,000 infantry, 800 militia, 3,000 townspeople and villagers, and 200 Albanian mercenaries, made by another eyewitness, Nestor Martinengo, was to be Famagusta's largest population until its fall.[36]

Mustafa was undoubtedly dispirited by these reinforcements, especially as the galleys in the first fleet constantly harassed his ships. Still, reinforcements and supplies arrived for him almost every day. Mustafa knew that Selim II would see to it that his expeditionary force in Cyprus

---

[34] This letter was copied by an eyewitness in Famagusta, Pietro Valderio. I am using the translation into English by Setton, *The Papacy and the Levant*, IV.996. Historians are fortunate in having five accounts of the siege from survivors.

[35] Ibid. pp. 1004–6.

[36] Ibid., p. 1027.

did not lack men, guns, powder, shot or food. The Turkish soldiers were also making more and more progress in approaching the walls. Mustafa had intensified his bombardment. Martinengo counted seventy-four large cannons firing constantly, while Alessandro Podacatero, another eyewitness, counted eighty.[37] In late April, Bragadin was forced to expel the 'useless mouths' from the city (mostly Greek peasants and the elderly). This was done at every lengthy siege and was generally a death sentence for those expelled; opposing troops would not allow them to pass, so that the plight of their suffering and slow starvation could be observed by those inside, reminders of what awaited them should the siege persist. However, Mustafa was confident enough not to worry about such matters; after all, the Turks would soon occupy Cyprus and he felt that kindness should be extended to the native inhabitants who would soon be Ottoman subjects. All were given food and guided by janissaries to nearby villages.[38]

On 25 May, Mustafa again offered peace terms but was refused. He knew that the garrison was running low on food, gunpowder and cannonballs, but he also knew that once his men reached the counterscarp of the moat, which would happen on 8 June, his casualty rates would increase as it would take him a long time to fill in the moat and begin assaulting the walls. These assaults began on 21 June. Weak spots in the walls were identified, and mines were dug under them, which were filled with gunpowder and set alight. Soldiers would then climb over the ruins and into the breaches attempting to enter the city. This first assault was unsuccessful – after several hours the Ottoman Turks were driven back to their camps – but seven more assaults would follow between then and 29 July.[39]

The besieged were now truly suffering. They had eaten everything in the city; the old, but not untrue, *topos* of having consumed all 'cats, dogs, horses, asses, mice and every other unclean animal' is repeated by every eyewitness – although it was apparent at the end of the siege that some of the wealthier citizens had been hoarding victuals.[40] Gunshot and powder were meted out in very small amounts. On 8 July, Martinengo noted that Famagusta received 5,000 cannonballs from the Turks that day, but was only able to respond with twenty of its own.[41] Large numbers of Ottomans continued to be killed daily; it is estimated that as many as 50,000 lost their lives by the end of the siege. But Ottoman soldiers could be replaced and Venetian defenders could not. The loss of any Venetian soldier was felt far more strongly than any number of the enemy that were killed. Everyone left in Famagusta was helping defend the town, including the women and children, but there were simply not enough of them to make up for the lost

---

[37] Ibid., pp. 1028–9.

[38] Ibid., p. 1028.

[39] Ibid., pp. 1028–36.

[40] Ibid., p. 1030. The quote here comes from Pietro Valderio.

[41] Ibid., pp. 1030–1.

soldiers. By 20 July, Angelo Gatto, one of the soldiers still alive, counted only 500 remaining of his fellow Italian soldiers; all of the mercenaries and militia had been killed. Only seven barrels of gunpowder remained, five for cannon and two for *haquebusses* (handheld guns).[42]

On 23 July, Mustafa again petitioned for peace. This time there was more discussion. Bragadin wished to hold out, although by this time he must have known it was futile. The Famagustans assented to his decision, although they preferred to seek peace terms.[43] However, after the Turks launched three more assaults against the now barely standing walls on 29 July, even Bragadin agreed to peace. On 2 August, negotiations began. Although he did not have to, as his troops were on the verge of entering the city, Mustafa agreed to a conditional surrender. The conditions of surrender were in fact quite merciful: all Italians would be allowed to leave the city on the ships in the harbour, taking whatever personal goods they could carry, and all Greeks could decide over the next three years to leave or stay under Ottoman governance. No one would be killed and the city would not be sacked.[44]

Treaty and Betrayal

Ostensibly, Mustafa agreed with all of these terms, even letting the Italians begin to leave before the official day of surrender on 5 August. Several writers who witnessed it said that Mustafa had begun the official ceremony in good spirit. After all, the siege was over, and he had been successful. Cyprus was now Ottoman and Mustafa was sure to gain wealth and titles when he presented the conquest to Selim II. But then something went terribly wrong. Judging from the eyewitness accounts, it cannot be determined exactly what was said or done to send Mustafa in an uncontrollable rage. Perhaps it was the pomp with which Bragadin and his lieutenants had come to the ceremony: he was wearing his finest clothes and insignia, with a parasol carried over his head as a symbol of his office – not, perhaps, the clothing or demeanour a defeated general should display. But the Ottoman delegation had placed colourfully decorated chairs next to a table covered with fine cloth for Bragadin and others to sit on, so Bragadin's ostentation should probably not have bothered them. It may also have been that Mustafa discovered the execution of several Ottoman prisoners captured by the besiegers; the Turkish general may have been upset by the perceived lie when Bragadin claimed these had either escaped or were taken away by ship – one of these was a friend of Mustafa's who had not been seen since capture. Another possibility is that Mustafa demanded a Venetian officer remain as hostage to see the surrender terms

[42] Ibid., p. 1032.

[43] Ibid., pp. 1032–4.

[44] Ibid., pp. 1036–8.

carried out, and that he became outraged when Bragadin argued that this had not been in the surrender agreement.[45]

Whatever caused it, the Lala Mustafa Pasha suddenly arose and clapped his hands, demanding that all those in the surrender delegation, Venetians and Greeks, be tied up, and everyone in the process of leaving be restrained. A second clap, following only seconds after the first, showed that his anger had increased: all Christian soldiers were now to be killed, as well as any Greeks who were in the company of Bragadin. It had all happened so quickly that no one on either side knew exactly what to do. Some Ottoman soldiers began killing those nearby them. Others did not, probably because they were so shocked by the change of events; both Valderio and Martinengo claim that this is why they were spared, while Podacatero said he paid his captors for his freedom.[46] The janissaries, who had been instructed to protect the city from looting, quickly heard about Mustafa's refusal to accept his own peace proposal and they turned aside, allowing the Turkish troops to flood into the city. It was completely looted and any citizens who resisted were killed.[47]

Bragadin had continued to sit at the table while this was going on, although he seems not to have been immediately restrained. He was shouting, cursing and praying. When two Ottoman soldiers approached him, he extended his neck for their swords. But they only cut off his ears, and perhaps his nose, at Mustafa's specific order. The Venetian captain was then dragged back into the city, bound and placed under guard.[48] He remained that way for twelve days. During that time the killing had stopped and the looting of the city had ended. Citizens of the town were clearing the rubble of the siege's destruction, yet so, too, were Ottoman soldiers. But Mustafa's anger towards his opposing general had not diminished. Some sources claim that during his imprisonment Bragadin was offered mercy if he would convert to Islam, but he refused.[49] His wounds went untreated and so infection set in.

---

[45] Ibid., pp. 1039–40, goes through all the accounts.

[46] Ibid., pp. 1040–1.

[47] Capponi, *Victory of the West*, pp. 233–4.

[48] Setton, *The Papacy and the Levant*, IV.1041–2; Capponi, *Victory of the West*, p. 234; and Madden, *Venice*, p. 331.

[49] Setton, *The Papacy and the Levant*, IV, does not record this event, but Capponi, *Victory of the West*, p. 234, and Madden, *Venice*, p. 331, claim that it did happen.

Making a Spectacular Example of Bragadin

Perhaps because it was known that the infection would soon take his life, Bragadin was suddenly brought into the open city on 17 August. Podacatero has him *como morto* 'like death' in his account.[50] Although infection would have been an extremely painful way to die, it was not the brutal spectacle that Mustafa had in store for the Venetian captain. First, Bragadin was made to carry a large, heavy sack of earth on his shoulders from one end of Famagusta to the other, while trumpets and other musical instruments blared and he was taunted and threatened at every step. Evidently, this was in response to Bragadin's claim that he would make Mustafa do the same. He was then taken to the harbour and hoisted up a mast for all to see, before being taken down and dragged to the pillory in the centre of the city.

There, Bragadin was stripped and hung upside down. Two Turks began to flay his skin with very sharp knives.[51] No doubt these were butchers travelling with the Ottoman army. As several contributions to this volume point out, flaying seems not to have been a frequent practice anywhere in the sixteenth century.[52] But every army had butchers, and they could probably have removed the hide of a man as easily as that of a cow, horse or sheep. Of course, the very best flayers seem to have been able to remove the skin without ripping it or killing the victim, even after the entire skin was removed. Bragadin's flayers were not that good; he died in the process. The flayers successfully stripped off the skin of his face and head, then his torso and arms, and had reached the navel when the defender of Famagusta is said to have cried out in Latin: 'Into Your hands, Lord, I commend my spirit.'[53] Even if he did not actually utter these words, there can be little doubt that this is what Bragadin was probably thinking as he breathed his last. Valderio, who claims to have witnessed this vicious death, includes his own summary: 'Truly he may be canonized and put among the saints, and certainly if the legends of the saints are true, as they are, this honoured and blessed martyr deserves to be preferred to any other.'[54]

---

[50] Setton, *The Papacy and the Levant*, IV.1042.

[51] Cf. Jack Hartnell's article in this volume on knives and surgical skin removal. 'Tools of the Puncture: Skin, Knife, Bone, Hand', pp. 20–50.

[52] Bragadin appears to be the first example of such an Ottoman punishment mentioned in the sources. William Sayers analyses the absence of flaying in Irish sources, while several contributors discuss its rarity in practice juxtaposed with its frequency in representation. Leverett and Livingston each consider flaying episodes associated with Saracens in *The Siege of Jerusalem*. See in this volume: Sayers, 'No Skin in the Game: Flaying and Early Irish Law and Epic', pp. 261–84; Leverett, 'Reading the Consumed', pp. 285–307; and Livingston, 'Losing Face', pp. 308–21.

[53] This according to Valderio, in Setton, *The Papacy and the Levant*, IV. 1041.

[54] Ibid., p. 1042.

But the flayers had not completed their work. They lowered Bragadin's dead body to the ground and finished skinning his corpse. The body was then quartered and a section borne with pomp and fanfare to each of the four defensive strongholds of the city. The dismembered, skinless segments were raised there as symbols that the fortifications could no longer be used to fight against Ottoman Turks. Bragadin's skin was stuffed with hay and sewn together like a scarecrow, similar to the account of the prophet Mani's punishment related in the *Shāhnāma* and depicted in a sixteenth-century Persian manuscript (see Fig. 6.6).[55] Mounted on an ox, this skin-effigy was led around Famagusta, cheered and taunted by all onlookers. Several days later, although it is not exactly known when, the skin was taken to Constantinople, where Lala Mustafa Pasha, the victorious, conquering Ottoman general, presented it to Sultan Selim II.[56]

News of the horrific death Bragadin had suffered quickly made its way to Venice, where he was acclaimed a hero and martyr. The city mourned loudly, tears were shed and masses said. Jeers of cowardice and accusations of treason assailed the doge, members of the senate and other Venetian officials. However, several of the city leaders were not in Venice to hear the complaints of the citizens at this time, but in the harbour of Messina on the city's galleys. There the Holy League, in which Venice played a major part, was gathering to campaign against the Turks. The huge fleet that eventually amassed would catch the Ottomans off the coast of Lepanto, where the Holy League would gain an impressive victory. To many that day and in the centuries that followed, this was apt revenge for the loss of Cyprus and the flaying of Marcantonio Bragadin.[57] Yet Cyprus was never regained.

[55] See in this volume: Asa Simon Mittman and Christine Sciacca, 'Robed in Martyrdom: The Flaying of St Bartholomew in the Laudario of Sant'Agnese', pp. 140–72 at pp. 157–8.

[56] Setton, *The Papacy and the Levant*, IV.1042.

[57] Capponi's *Victory of the West* is the best account of this battle. While it was undoubtedly impressive, I am reluctant to accord it the 'decisive battle' tag that so many others have, for example Victor Davis Hanson, *Carnage and Culture: Landmark Battles in the Rise of Western Power* (New York: Doubleday, 2001), pp. 233–78. Clearly forgetting the loss of Cyprus, Hanson uses Lepanto as evidence that the 'Western Way of Warfare' historically has defeated non-Western ways of war. But besides managing to retain Cyprus, the Ottomans were also able to replace their fleet in a year, and the Venetians returned to paying them tribute in two years; it is therefore difficult to see Lepanto as 'decisive'.

The Legacy of Bragadin's Skin

Sometime after these events in Cyprus, Titian painted *The Punishment of Marsyas*, in which two men with sharp knives cut the hide off of a satyr. The vicious brutality of Titian's sixteenth-century painting pulls the viewer into the canvas. Here the satyr Marsyas hangs upside down, dangling from a tree, hooves tied to separate branches. His hands and head look as if he is dead, but anyone who knows the story also knows that he is very much alive and he is suffering. The lower half of the satyr, legs and groin, remain covered with fur. But someone stands behind him, the hilt of a knife held in his hand. What he is cutting cannot be determined. In front of Marsyas, also wielding a knife, is the god Apollo, and what he is cutting can be seen – Marsyas' skin. His skin has already been removed from his navel to his armpits. Marsyas is being flayed.

Titian did not generally paint dark subjects. In fact, in most of his art he seems oblivious to the ruthless violence that was so prevalent in the sixteenth century. Titian's paintings are usually filled with brightness and colour. They are joyful, abounding in life, vitality and hope. His portraits – of Charles V, Federico II Gonzaga, Isabella d'Este, Pope Paul III, Philip II, to name only the most famous – are strong and majestic. Among Titian's most famous paintings are undoubtedly his nudes: a couple of Danaë and several of Venus, among many others. Evidenced in these paintings is Titian's love of skin. The Danaës and the Venuses are all voluptuous women, boldly showing almost every bit of their lovely skin: sometimes a slip of cloth is draped across the body; sometimes a hand is placed over the genitalia; and at other times, the subject is completely bare. Clearly skin was beautiful to Titian.[58]

Titian enjoyed painting stories of the ancient gods and myths – although he also did his fair share of religious art. But the story of the flaying of Marsyas was not as popular a myth as those of Diana, Venus, Lucretia or any of the others he painted. As Ovid tells it, Marsyas was a very egotistical satyr who believed that his musical abilities surpassed even those of the gods. In a display of exceedingly stupid hubris – although not entirely unprovoked – Marsyas challenges Apollo to a musical duel. He loses to the god and receives what seems to have been a previously undetermined punishment. Apollo flays him. The god then, with equal hubris it should be noted, displays Marsyas' hide for all to see, the most grotesque of trophies.[59]

Of course, few would say this punishment fit the crime, most likely Titian included. He does not depict anything to suggest Marsyas' hubris

---

[58] There are several excellent studies of Titian, beginning perhaps with Carlo Ridolfi's seventeenth-century biography, *The Life of Titian*, trans. Julia Conaway Bondanella and Peter E. Bondanella (State College: Pennsylvania State Press, 1996). These, however, are my own observations.

[59] Ovid, *Metamorphoses*, vi.383–400.

other than a flute hanging from the tree. As far as the viewer can determine, Apollo flays the satyr for the fun of it, because he can, for that is what the gods, cruel tyrants, could do to all those beneath them. *The Punishment of Marsyas* does not depict human brutality, but instead the brutality of gods.[60] Titian could have chosen to depict a human being flayed, rather than the satyr. As several essays here explain, St Bartholomew was a favourite subject for religious art.[61] Bartholomew's first-century flaying at the hands of the Armenians was so widely known and accepted that he had, rather ironically, become the patron saint of tanners. Had Titian painted him, the action would have been presented as holy, a welcome martyrdom for the saint who endures the process stoically. Instead, Titian depicts Marsyas, a character whom he knew never existed, flayed by a god whom he also knew never existed. His message to the observer is clear: no human would ever flay another human; the brutality is simply too inhumane. Except that a prominent Venetian, Marcantonio Bragadin, had just been publicly flayed. This punishment, ordered by the Ottoman general Lala Mustafa Pasha following the surrender of the city of Famagusta on the island of Cyprus, the defence of which Bragadin had overseen during an eleven-month siege, may well have inspired the dark violence of Titian's painting.[62] Regardless, the spectacle of Bragadin's skin was well attested by eyewitness accounts, and the relic had a lasting legacy in popular lore.

Titian died in 1576, so he would not have known that Bragadin's skin did not stay in Constantinople. In 1580, with Venice once again in a temporary

---

[60] Gerard David's *The Judgement of Cambyses* (1498) is one of the earliest surviving depictions of this motif – the corrupt Persian judge Sisamnes is executed (justly) by Cambyses in this horrible manner. Later painters certainly took up the theme of Marsyas' execution, notably Jusepe de Ribera's *Apollo Flaying Marsyas* (1637). See also: Mittman and Sciacca, 'Robed in Martyrdom', p. 152. For a detailed discussion on David's painting, see: Robert Mills, *Suspended Animation: Pain, Pleasure and Punishment in Medieval Culture* (London: Reaktion, 2005).

[61] For more on the Flaying of St Bartholomew in this collection see: Mittman and Sciacca, 'Robed in Martyrdom'; Sherry C. M. Lindquist, 'Masculinist Devotion: Flaying and Flagellation in the *Belles Heures*', pp. 173–207; and Sayers, 'No Skin in the Game', pp. 261–84.

[62] Some art historians disagree that it was Bragadin's flaying that inspired Titian's *Punishment of Marsyas*, although that view is gaining acceptance. See, for example: Mark Hudson, *Titian: His Last Days* (London: Bloomsbury, 2009), p. 263; and John T. Paoletti and Gary M. Radke, *Art in Renaissance Italy* (London: Laurence King, 2005), p. 485. Far more willing to link Titian's painting to Bragadin's flaying are historians of Venice: i.e. Garry Wills, *Venice: Lion City: The Religion of Empire* (New York: Simon and Schuster, 2001), pp. 69–71. My thanks to Ruth Rhynas Brown for introducing me to this painting and suggesting its connection with Bragadin's flaying.

peace with the Ottoman Turks, Girolamo Polidori, sometimes described as an adventurer, sometimes as a veteran of Famagusta, was visiting Constantinople and discovered that Bragadin's skin was still there, on display, it seems, in one of the city's arsenals. In what was clearly a daring and risky act, he stole it and returned with it to Venice.[63] Bragadin's skin was given to his sons, who initially put it into a pillar in the church of San Gregorio,[64] and then, in 1596, it was interred with other Venetian heroes in the Basilica di Santi Giovanni e Paolo.

Unfortunately, Polidori never wrote the story of his adventure in retrieving the flayed skin; in fact, not much is known about him, including whether he was a survivor of the conquest of Cyprus. Nor would this be the first time in history that a relic was lied about, especially if the family was interested in having their father (who definitely deserved it) buried with other Venetian military and political heroes. Sufficient doubt had arisen by the twentieth century for Bragadin's descendants to give permission for his tomb to be opened in 1961. Other than the various surviving accounts of his execution – none of which specify the reasons for such a brutal punishment, one that seems to have been out of character for the Turks – there is no further evidence of Bragadin's flaying. Except that the skin itself exists, unlike those in other myths that persist about the flaying in the Middle Ages.[65] Today, encased in a lead casket, Bragadin's flayed skin remains, a symbol of the evils and brutality of a war fought over an island in the Eastern Mediterranean for centuries between the Venetians and the Ottoman Turks.[66]

---

[63] The conventional story is that given in Tassini, *Curiosità veneziane*, p. 358.

[64] Presumably a niche tomb, though that cannot be determined by the sources.

[65] In this volume, see Mary Rambaran-Olm's discussion on the 'flayed-Dane' myth: 'Medievalism and the "Flayed-Dane" Myth: English Perspectives between the Seventeenth and Nineteenth Centuries', pp. 91–115; and Frederika Bain's discussion of flayed remains and folklore: 'Skin on Skin: Wearing Flayed Remains', pp. 116–37.

[66] Gibellini, *L'immagine di Lepanto*, p. 92, and Norwich, *The Middle Sea*, pp. 319–20.

3

Flesh and Death in Early Modern Bedburg

Susan Small

Is my body then / But penetrable flesh?[1]

And then no wolf at all lay in front of the hunter but the bloody trunk of a man, headless, footless, dying, dead.[2]

G ERMANY in the late sixteenth century was marked by a volatile conflict between witches and werewolves (who inflamed the popular imagination), and the authorities who sought to destroy them.[3] The Continental witch trials, with their reports of shape-shifting, sexual perversion and cannibalism, filled the pages of the popular press, and public executions were staged as both a sop to the public's bloodlust and a powerful deterrent. Read in terms of the sixteenth-century concept of *convenientia*, or resemblance by contiguity, the tools of the executioner – axes, hatchets, swords, hammers, tongs – used at each stage of the punishment invoke specific aspects of the crimes they punish, thereby mapping the misdeeds onto the body of the criminal.

Moreover, concurrent with the rise of witch hysteria in late-sixteenth-century Germany was the growth of the science of anatomy. The dissection tools of its most famous practitioner, Vesalius, bear a remarkable resemblance to the instruments used by the executioner (Fig. 3.1).[4] Indeed, anatomists and executioners shared a common purpose: to dismantle the

---

[1] George Chapman, *Bussy D'Ambois* (1607), V.iii.125–6. Qtd. in Maik Goth, 'Killing, Hewing, Stabbing, Dagger-Drawing, Fighting, Butchery: Skin Penetration in Renaissance Tragedy and its Bearing on Dramatic Theory', *Comparative Drama* 46.2 (Summer 2012): 139–62 at p. 19. Available online through http://muse.jhu.edu (subscription needed; accessed 13 Nov. 2014).

[2] Angela Carter, 'The Company of Wolves', in *The Bloody Chamber and other Stories* (New York: Penguin Books, 1993), available online at http://www.angelfire.com/falcon/rote/CARTER.html (accessed 13 Nov. 2014).

[3] For a detailed discussion on the significance of skin, both human and animal, in medieval werewolf narratives see: Susan Small, 'The Medieval Werewolf Model of Reading Skin', in *Reading Skin in Medieval Literature and Culture*, ed. Katie L. Walter (New York: Palgrave, 2013), pp. 81–97. In this volume, see: Frederika Bain, 'Skin on Skin: Wearing Flayed Remains', pp. 116–37.

[4] See Jack Hartnell's discussion in this volume of penetrating surgical tools used in skin removal and their medical and art-historical presence in the Middle Ages. Hartnell draws several comparisons between the tools of the surgeon and the executioner, including Vesalius. 'Tools of the Puncture: Skin, Knife, Bone, Hand', pp. 20–50.

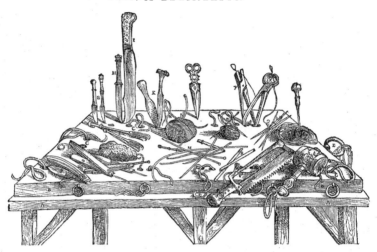

DE HVMANI CORPORIS FABRICA LIBER II.   237

DE INSTRVMENTIS, QVAE SECTIONI-
bus administrandis parari possunt.   *Caput VII.*

ANATOMICORVM INSTRVMEN-
TORVM DELINEATIO.

CHARACTERVM SEPTIMI CAPITIS FIGVRAE INDEX.

PRAESENTI figura mensæ cuidam incumbentem finximus asserem, quo in ut uorum sectionibus opportune utimur, dein huic asseri omnia propemodum accōmodauimus, qui- bus in dissectionum administrationibus, adeoq̃ tota Anatome quis posset uti. Quo autem singu la leuiori opera assequaris, huic etiam figuræ characteres, ac demum eorum indicem adhibere non grauatus sum. Indicetur itaq̃

A, A *Mensa, cui reliqua omnia modo seriatim indicanda supersternuntur.*

B, B *Asser uiuis sectionibus administrandis idoneus.*

C, C *Varia foramina, quibus laqueos pro animalis mole adhibemus, quū femora et brachia uincimus.*

D, D *Eiusmodi anuli, summis manibus pedibusq̃ ligandis adaptantur.*

E *Huic anulo maxilla superior, libera inferiori, catenula alligatur, ut caput immotum seruetur, ac interim neq̃ uox, neq̃ respiratio uinculorum occasione præpediantur.*

F, F *Diuersa nouacularum genera, quibus spongia accumbit.*

G *Cultelli ad earum speciem formati, quibus calami adaptantur.*

H *Vulgaris qui mensæ adhibetur culter.*   I. *Grandis ac ualidus culter.*

K *Cultri é buxo parati.*   L *Hamuli.*   M *Varij styli unā cum siphone.*

N, N *Obliquatæ acus cum filo crassiore, quibus literarum fasciculos colligamus.*

n *Minores acus, quas uulneribus suendis accommodamus.*

O *Serra*   P *Forficula.*   Q *Malleus ligneus.*

R *Arundines inflandis pulmonibus, & alijs quibusdam partibus idoneæ.*

S *Filum æneum, ossibus medendis aptum.*   T *Subula forandis ossibus parata.*

V *Varia subularum ferra.*   X *Forpex intorquendis filorum extremis comparatus.*

Y *Forpex, quo intorti, & ossa iam committentis fili reliquias præscindimus.*

                                                V 4   QVAN-

Fig. 3.1 A table with an array of anatomical instruments used for vivisection, photolithograph, 1940 (Bern: Dr A. Wander, 1940), after a woodcut, 1543 (Wellcome Library, museum no. 24377i)

human body, albeit for very different purposes. Early-modern anatomy's fascination with probing the inner workings of the body was countered by the public's fear of slipping into the morass of dark forces operating just beneath the skin of the world. One of the driving forces behind the witch-hunts was, in fact, the fear of metamorphosis or shape-shifting, which threatened the already uneasy balance between appearance and reality. It was a phenomenon that galvanized religious and secular authorities, electrifying a populace that was both terrified and transfixed by accounts of a devil that could cross the borders of the human body and turn ordinary men and women into ravening beasts.[5] This, then, was the uneasy episteme which permeated the sixteenth-century German psyche when, in 1589, in Bedburg, a small town near Cologne, authorities arrested a man suspected of turning into a werewolf and savagely abducting, raping and murdering more than sixteen men, women, and children over a twenty-five-year period.

Fuelled by the public's need for both reassurance and retribution, the trial, punishment and execution of Peter Stubbe[6] were designed to showcase the monster's degradation and ultimate annihilation. Stubbe was tied to the wheel, flayed,[7] and his limbs were broken; he was then decapitated and the body was burned at the stake. His daughter, Beell Stubbe, and his gossip,[8] Katherine Trompin, both convicted on charges of lewd and lascivious behaviour and accessory to murder, were burned alive beside his headless body. Stubbe's severed head was mounted on a stake above the likeness of a wolf 'to shewe vnto all men the shape wherein he executed those cruelties'.[9] Not specified in the charges laid against Stubbe,

---

[5] The emergence of witch-hunts and the superstitions surrounding them is well attested. See, for example: Alan Charles Kors and Edward Peters, eds., *Witchcraft in Europe, 400–1700: A Documentary History* (Philadelphia: University of Pennsylvania Press, 2001); Jeffrey Burton Russell, *Witchcraft in the Middle Ages* (Ithaca, NY: Cornell University Press, 1972); Bengt Ankarloo and Stuart Clark, eds., *Witchcraft and Magic in Europe: The Middle Ages* (Philadelphia: University of Pennsylvania Press, 2002); and Robin Briggs, *Witches and Neighbors: The Social and Cultural Context of European Witchcraft* (New York: Penguin, 1996), to name only a few.

[6] The name has various spellings, including: Peter, Peeter, Petter, or Petrus, Stub, Stubbe, Stube, Stumfius, Stump, Stumpf, Stumpff, Stumpp or Stupe. The most common English version, and the one that will be used in this chapter, is 'Peter Stubbe'.

[7] *OED*: '1. *trans.* To strip or pull off the skin or hide of; to skin'; and '2. To strip off or remove portions of the skin (or analogous membrane) from'. Flaying includes the preparatory act of 'skin penetration'. See: Goth, 'Killing, Hewing', p. 139 n. 1.

[8] *OED*: 'late old english godsibb, "godfather, godmother, baptismal sponsor", literally "a person related to one in God", from god "God" + sibb "a relative".'

[9] *A true discourse. Declaring the damnable life and death of one Stubbe Peeter, a most wicked sorcerer who in the likenes of a woolfe, committed many murders,*

but detailed in records of the trial, were the crimes of cannibalism, incest, rape and carnal copulation with the devil.

Stubbe's insatiable bloodlust, combined with his hunger for notoriety and a lifelong fascination with the dark arts, led him to strike a Faustian bargain in which he 'gaue both soule and body to the deuil for euer' (p. 3) in return for a magic girdle that would allow him to turn into a huge, ravening wolf and satisfy his monstrous appetites at will 'without dread or danger of life, and vnknowen to be the executor of any bloody enterprise' (p. 4). This girdle was the mechanism that supposedly transformed his murderous intent into action and wrapped his human form in an impenetrable overlay of teeth and fur that concealed his true identity. Indeed, 'so muche he had practised this wickednes, that yᵉ whole Prouince was feared by the cruelty of this bloody and deuouring Woolfe' (p. 6). He lured his own son into the woods, slew him and feasted upon his brains. When his lust outran even his wolfish form, 'as an insaciate and filthy beast' (p. 8) in human form he slept with his sister, his gossip, a succubus and numerous other women, even impregnating his own daughter. Stubbe's murderous rampages finally ended in 1589, when he was hunted down 'in his wooluishe likenes' (p. 15) and, in an attempt to escape, slipped off his girdle and metamorphosed in front of his captors, who, 'finding him to be the man indeede, and no delusion or phantasticall motion' (p. 16), immediately apprehended him.

The case was sensational and immediately hit the headlines. A seven-page pamphlet with the long but incendiary title, *Warhafftige und erschreckliche Beschreibung, von einem Zauberer (Stupe Peter genandt) der sich zu einem Wehrwolff hat können machen ...* (*The True and Terrifying Story of a Sorcerer (named Stupe Peter), who Could Turn Himself into a Werewolf ...*), was rushed into print in nearby Cologne.[10] In Antwerp a month later, the story took up two entire pages of an eight-page pamphlet, *Warachtighe ende verschrickelijcke beschrijvinge van vele toovenaers ende toovenerssen ...* (*The True and Shocking Story of Many Witches and*

continuing this diuelish practise 25. yeeres, killing and deuouring men, woomen, and children. Who for the same fact was taken and executed the 31. of October last past in the towne of Bedbur neer the cittie of Collin in Germany. Trulye translated out of the high Duch, according to the copie printed in Collin, brought ouer into England by George Bores ordinary poste, the xi. daye of this present moneth of Iune 1590. who did both see and heare the same (London: E. Venge, 1590), p. 19. Online text available at http://quod.lib.umich.edu/cgi/t/text/text-idx?c=eebo;idno=A13085.0001.001. Hereafter, page numbers will be given in parentheses.

[10] *Warhafftige und erschreckliche Beschreibung, von einem Zauberer (Stupe Peter genandt) der sich zu einem Wehrwolff hat können machen, welcher zu Bedbur (vier meilen von Cölln gelegen) ist gerichtet worden., den 31. October, dieses 1589. Jahrs, was böser Thaten er begangen hat ...* (Cologne: Nikolaus Schreiber, 1589).

Wizards ...).[11] On 11 June 1590, George Bores, an English witness to Stubbe's punishment and execution, brought over to London a nineteen-page document entitled *A true discourse. Declaring the damnable life and death of one Stubbe Peeter, a most wicked sorcerer ... Trulye translated out of the high Duch* [*sic*], *according to the copie printed in Collin*.[12] A summary of the case appeared in Martín Antonio Delrío's *Disquisitionum magicarum libri sex* in Mainz the same year,[13] and another in F. Claude Prieur's *Dialogue de la lycanthropie* in Louvain six years later.[14] Contemporary interest in the case lasted well into the seventeenth century both in continental Europe and in England; one version, in Richard Verstegan's *Restitution of Decayed Intelligence*, was published in London as late as 1628.[15] It is clear that this sustained attention was due, at least in part, to the fact that Stubbe was tried as a werewolf; Prieur's treatise deals specifically with lycanthropy, and Verstegan cites Stubbe as an example in his dictionary entry for the word 'werewolf'.

A true discourse ... Trulye translated out of the high Duch, according to the copie printed in Collin, published as a chapbook for Peter Venge in London in 1790, remains the most important English-language record of the Stubbe case.[16] Copies of the document, signed by George Bores and fellow witnesses Tyse Artyne, William Brewar and Adolf Staedt, '[w]ith divers others that have seen the same', are now housed in the British Library and the Lambeth Palace Library. Folded and fastened to the inside cover

[11] Jan van Ghelen, *Warachtighe ende verschrickelijcke beschrijvinge van vele toovenaers ende toovenerssen: een uniek Antwerps vlugschrift uit 1589 over Duitse heksenprocessen en weerwolf Stump*, ed. Dries Vanysacker (Wildert: Carbolineum, 2003), Seite 7 and 8.

[12] See n. 9.

[13] Martín Antonio Delrío, *Disquisitionum magicarum libri sex: quibus continetur accurata curiosarum artium, et vanarum superstitionum confutatio: utilis theologis, jurisconsultis, medicis, philologis*, repr. edn (Moguntiae: Petri Henningii, 1617), p. 190.

[14] Claude Prieur, *Dialogue de la lycanthropie ou Transformation d'hommes en loups vulgairement dits loups-garous, et si telle se peut faire ...* (Louvain: Iehan Maes and Philippe Zangre, 1596; repr. Paris: Hachette / Bibliothèque nationale, 1975).

[15] Richard Verstegan, *Restitution of decayed intelligence in antiquities, concerning the most noble and renowned English nation. By the study and travel of R. V.* (London: Samuel Mearne, John Martyn and Henry Herringman, 1628), pp. 236–7.

[16] The account will be variously referred to in this study as 'the London account', 'the London chapbook', 'the London document', the London pamphlet' or 'the English broadsheet'. A Danish translation of this account was published in Copenhagen the following year, under the title *En forskreckelig oc sand bescriffuelse om mange troldfolck som ere forbrends for deris misgierninger skyld fra det aar 1589* (Copenhagen: Flugschrift im Verlag Laurentz Benedicht, 1591).

of the chapbook is an unattributed woodcut consisting of two rows of four panels each, depicting Stubbe's crimes, capture, trial, punishment and execution.[17] The illustrated broadsheet, or *Bilderbogen*, is described by the historian Julius R. Ruff as 'a sequence of pictures printed from woodblocks illustrating an act of violence from its inception to its final consequences'.[18] The eight-panel British Library woodcut is a sequenced composite of three original panels (2, 3 and 4) and five (1, 5, 6, 7 and 8) which appear to have been copied from an earlier single-leaf woodcut entitled 'Of a Peasant Who Turned Himself into a Wolf near Cologne, and His Punishment, 1589', which was published on a broadsheet produced by Lucas Mayer in Nuremberg in 1589 (Fig. 3.2).[19] What seems to be a copy of the Mayer woodcut was published by Johann Negele under the same title in Augsburg the same year.[20]

Julius Ruff suggests that the luridness of the illustrations on broadsheets served to attract the illiterate and uneducated, feeding their hunger for sensationalism and spectacle. Stubbe's trial, punishment and execution

[17] The British Library woodcut, with accompanying captions, is reproduced in various sources, including Caroline Oates, 'Metamorphosis and Lycanthropy in Franche-Comté [*sic*] 1521–1643', in *Fragments for a History of the Human Body: Part I*, ed. Michael Feher, Ramona Naddaff and Nadia Tazi (New York: Zone, 1989), pp. 315–6 (fig. 3), 305–15, 313; and Susan Wiseman, *Writing Metamorphosis in the English Renaissance, 1550–1700*, (Cambridge: Cambridge University Press, 2014), p. 142, fig. 12.

[18] Julius R. Ruff, *Violence in Early Modern Europe, 1500–1800* (Cambridge: Cambridge University Press, 2001), p. 17.

[19] Walter L. Strauss, *The German Single-Leaf Woodcut, 1550–1600: A Pictorial Catalogue*, 3 vols. (New York: Abaris, 1975), 2:701, fig. 6. For a discussion of the terminology relating to early modern broadsheets and narrative strips, and the practice of cutting and pasting, see: David Kunzle, *The Early Comic Strip: Narrative Strips and Picture Stories in the European Broadsheet from c. 1450 to 1825* (Berkeley: University of California Press, 1973), pp. 4–5. For a discussion of the role of pamphlets, broadsheets and woodcuts in the popularization of criminal trials in Early Modern Germany, see: Kunzle, *The Early Comic Strip*, pp. 157–96; Ruff, *Violence*, pp. 17–18; and Strauss, *Single-Leaf Woodcut*, 1:2–5. For a lively journalistic take on the same subject, see: 'Social Media in the 16th Century: How Luther went Viral', *The Economist* (17 Dec. 2011), available to registered users through http://www.economist.com (accessed 4 Nov. 2014).

[20] Strauss, *Single-Leaf Woodcut*, 2:795, fig. 1. Strauss notes that, because of their popularity and profitability, '[b]roadsheets were being copied constantly' (p. 8). The Negele coloured woodcut is reproduced, with accompanying four-column, sixteen-line German text, in Wolfgang Harms and Cornelia Kemp, *Deutsche illustrierte Flugblätter*, Band IV (Tübingen: Max Niemeyer Verlag, 1987), 4:301, p. 413. For an excellent overview of Renaissance and early modern werewolf iconography, see: John Block Friedman, 'Werewolf Transformation in the Manuscript Era', *The Journal of the Early Book Society* 17 (2014): 36–93.

Fig. 3.2 Lukas Mayer, *Hinrichtung Peter Stump* (*The Execution of Peter Stubbe*), woodcut, 1589

certainly provided salacious fodder. Even in the midst of such a virulent campaign of persecution as the early modern European witch-hunts (Richard Verstegan notes, for example, that '[o]f such [werewolves], sundry haue bin taken and executed, in sundry partes of *Germanie*, and the *Netherlands*'),[21] accounts of Stubbe's life and death are marked by a tone of singular horror and hyperbole. The London version (1590) reads: '[O]f all other that ever lived, none was comparable unto this Hell hound'; Prieur (1596) says: [Stubbe] 'a esté executé d'une mort & supplice non vulgaire pour ses meschancetez excessives' [was executed by an uncommon method of punishment and death for his excessive misdeeds].[22] Later, and only somewhat more laconically, Verstegan writes that Stubbe was 'put unto a very terrible Death'.[23] The sixteen murders with which Stubbe was charged were compounded by the equally sensational charges of cannibalism, sorcery, incest, rape and sex with the devil. Murder and sorcery were capital crimes in sixteenth-century Germany, and, as historian Valérie Toureille observes, incest, rape and carnal copulation with the devil fell under the category of 'actes sexuels contre nature',[24] for which the death penalty

[21] Verstegan, *Restitution*, p. 237. Original spelling, punctuation and emphasis.

[22] Prieur, *Dialogue*, p. 37.

[23] Verstegan, *Restitution*, pp. 236–7.

[24] Valérie Toureille, *Crime et châtiment au Moyen Âge (V^e–XVe siècle)* (Paris: Seuil, 2013), p. 253. Stubbe's daughter Beell, with whom he had a child, and his gossip, Katherine Trompin, a relative with whom he had had a long sexual relationship, were arraigned on charges of 'accessory to divers

could also be invoked. Accessory crimes, moreover, entailed accessory punishments, which could be aggravated in accordance with the nature and gravity of the offence.[25]

Stubbe's sentence was handed down on 28 October 1589. In addition to capital punishment, it included three accessory punishments and one post-mortem directive [numbering added]:

> Stubbe Pee|ter as principall mallefactor, was iudged [1] first to haue his body laide on a wheele, [2] and with red hotte burning pincers in ten seue|ral places to haue the flesh puld off from the bones, [3] after that, his legges and Armes to be broken with a woodden Are [*sic*] or Hatchet, [4] afterward to haue his head strook from his body, [5] then to haue his carkasse burnde to Ashes.   (pp. 17–18)

Each step in this process is associated with an object (wheel, pincers, wooden axe or hatchet, sword, fire) that could be classified as a tool; what classifies it as a weapon in this context is, as Elaine Scarry puts it, 'not the object itself but the surface on which they [*sic*] fall'.[26] And the surface on which they fall here is Peter Stubbe's body: they pin down his torso, sear and slice through his skin, rupture his flesh, smash his sinews, tendons and bones, sever skin, cords and tissue, and obliterate the scraps that are left. And in so doing, they leave behind traces which bear a striking resemblance to the carnage left in the wake of Stubbe's own murderous rampage. The resemblance between the weapons themselves (wheel, pincers, axe, sword, fire) is not physical, but can be read in terms of the sixteenth-century concept of *convenientia*, which Michel Foucault describes as 'not an exterior relation between things, but the sign of a relationship'.[27] That is to say, the

---

> murders committed [...] as also for their lewd life otherwise committed [...] and were judged to be burned quick to ashes, the same time and day with the carcass of the aforesaid Stubbe Peeter'. Incest is also, with buggery and sodomy, listed in the *Trias judiciel du second Notaire de Jean Papon, conseiller du roy* as a capital crime of 'luxure abominable': 'La peine du feu est reseferuee seulement contre les bougres, sodomites, & convaincus d'inceste, selon ce que cy dessus est déclaré, & aussi en trois chapitres dudit recueil au tiltre de luxure abominable' [Death by fire is reserved only for homosexuals, sodomites, and those convicted of incest, according to that which is declared above, and also in three chapters of the said collection regarding abominable lust] (Lyons: Jean de Tournes, 1580), p. 459. Unless otherwise noted, all translations are mine.

[25] See: Toureille, *Crime et châtiment*, p. 253.

[26] '[A]n ax that cuts through the back of a wolf is a weapon', for example, 'and the ax that cuts through a tree is a tool'. Both quotes from Elaine Scarry, *The Body in Pain: The Making and Unmaking of the World* (Oxford: Oxford University Press, 1985), p. 173.

[27] Michel Foucault, *The Order of Things: An Archeology of the Human Sciences*, trans. Alan Sheridan (New York: Routledge, 2002), p. 20. *Convenientia* is, in other words, 'a resemblance connected with space in the form of a

way these weapons function within the punishment sequence lays out a pattern of adjacency, and this pattern operates according to the same paradigm as that which structured Stubbe's crimes. It is, then, possible to construct a similarity model between Stubbe's crimes and his punishments anchored by the categories of: 1) punishment weapon; 2) function; and 3) crime. It would play out as follows: 1) wheel: constraint: criminal confinement; 2.1) pincers: penetration: rape; and 2.2) pincers: flaying: cannibalism; 3) axe: disjunction: dismemberment; 4) sword: severance: throat-slitting; and 5) fire: smoke screen: sorcery. Of course, there are overlaps and also other possible configurations; flaying, for example, must be involved not only in cannibalism ('[he] most cruelly slewe him, which doon, he presently eat the brains out of his head' [p. 10]); and 'she the caitife had most raue|noullye [*sic*] deuoured, whose fleshe he estéemed both swéet and dainty in taste' [p. 12]), but also in disembowelling ('he had murdered [...] two goodly yong women bigge with Child, tearing the Children out of their wombes, in most bloody and sauedge sorte, and after eate their hartes panting hotte and rawe' [p. 7]), and dismemberment ('he would presentlye in|counter them, and neuer rest till he had pluckt out their throates and teare their ioyntes a sunder' [p. 5]). The paradigm, however, does not change.

This is not to suggest that there existed a sixteenth-century German penal typology into which the details of Stubbe's case could be slotted so as to determine his particular punishments. Indeed, as the historian Florike Egmond remarks, '[i]t would have been extremely helpful if early modern magistrates had ever explained why they regarded breaking on the wheel as a harsher punishment than, for instance, hanging, or why they saw drowning and burning as roughly equivalent to each other'.[28] Without

---

graduated scale of proximity [...] pertain[ing] less to the things themselves than to the world in which they exist' (p. 21).

[28] Florike Egmond, 'Pain, Punishment, Dissection and Infamy: A Morphological Investigation', in *Bodily Extremities: Preoccupations with the Human Body in Early Modern European Culture*, ed. Florike Egmond and Robert Zwijnenberg (Burlington, VT: Ashgate, 2003), pp. 92–128 at p. 101. Mitchell B. Merback analyses the specific spectacle of breaking on the wheel in regard to images of the Crucifixion, and discusses the wheel's use, particularly in Germany: Merback outlines the debate among historians about the proliferation of the wheel as an instrument of both torture and punishment: 'while some go so far as to declare it practically a daily occurrence in parts of Europe, others give a more modest accounting. In the records published by Richard van Dülmen for the city of Nuremberg, we find that between 1503 and 1743 only 55 out of a total of 939 executions were performed with the wheel. However, the ratio of wheelings to total executions in those German cities for which records exist appears to have been much greater in the late Middle Ages than in the following centuries. Its heyday was most likely the second half of the fifteenth century through to about 1600, when execution rates overall began to decline in Germany

documentary evidence, it is simply not possible to determine the precise relationship between the nature of Stubbe's crimes and the forms of his torture and execution. It is, however, possible to suggest that, in accordance with the 'caractère "réfléchissant"'[29] of medieval and early modern corporal punishment, such a relationship did exist, and, furthermore, that it was predicated on a sixteenth-century similarity model. For Stubbe's were corporal punishments and his were carnal crimes. As the London account puts it, he 'gaue both soule and body to the deuil for euer, for small carnall pleasure in this life' (p. 3). His rapacious 'stripping naked' was not only what Georges Bataille terms a 'simulacrum of killing',[30] it was also its locus and thrust. And if the early modern magistrates who handed down Stubbe's sentence did not leave a document explaining precisely why they ordered that he be broken on the wheel rather than hanged, or burned at the stake rather than drowned, they did leave a compelling example of *convenientia* in the structure they had erected after his death:

> After the execution, there was by the aduice of the Maiestrates of the town of *Bedbur* a high pole set vp and stronglye framed, which first went through yᵉ wheele wheron he was broken, whereunto also it was fastened, after that a little aboue the Wheele the likenes of a Woolfe was fra|med in wood, to shewe vnto all men the shape wherein he executed those cruelties. Ouer that on the top of the stake the sorce|rers head it selfe was set vp.   (pp. 18–19)

The explicit spatiality of this order – that Stubbe's severed head be mounted above the body of a wolf, itself mounted above the 'wheel whereon he was broken', and that his flayed, broken, headless body be burned to ashes beside it – not only formalizes the relationship between

---

and most of Europe.' Mitchell B. Merback, *The Thief, the Cross, and the Wheel* (London: Reaktion, 1999), p. 158. However frequently it was used, a large proportion of accounts recording the wheel's use are German sources that date from the end of the fifteenth century.

[29] Toureille, *Crime et châtiment*, p. 260. 'Le choix de la partie du corps à meurtrir', explains Toureille, 'répond souvent au crime lui-même' [The choice of the body part to hurt ... often reflects the crime itself] (p. 260). Foucault writes, 'Torture correlates the type of corporal effect, the quality, intensity, duration of pain, with the gravity of the crime, the person of the criminal, the rank of his victims.' Michel Foucault, *The Spectacle of the Scaffold*, trans. Alan Sheridan (London: Penguin, 2008), p. 34.

[30] Georges Bataille, *Eroticism: Death and Sensuality*, trans. Mary Dalwood (London: Penguin, 2001), p. 18. The Latin word for 'werewolf', *ver-sïpellis, is*, m., is related to the adjective *versïpellis* (vorsïp-), e, adj. *vertopellis*, 'that changes its skin'. The adjective *versïpellis* has, as well, the sense of 'skilled in dissimulation, sly, cunning, crafty, subtle'. Definitions from Charlton T. Lewis and Charles Short, *A Latin Dictionary*, accessible online through the *Perseus Digital Library*: http://www.perseus.tufts.edu (accessed 14 Jun. 2015). Cf. Small, 'The Medieval Werewolf Model', p. 83.

self and simulacrum, it surely also forces the public's hand in this deadly game of 'Exquisite Cadaver'. For the obliteration of Stubbe's body and the simultaneous juxtaposition of his severed head and the body of a wolf leave no doubt as to their fractured and incongruous but unmistakable ontological contiguity.[31]

In *The Modulated Scream: Pain in Late Medieval Culture*, Esther Cohen observes that 'Outside Germany, there is little evidence of pre-execution torture before the sixteenth century. What appears in German illuminations is usually pinching with hot pincers, but these illuminations usually accompany general texts like the *Sachsenspiegel* or later the *Constitutio Carolina*, and there is no evidence that they mirror actual practice.'[32] There is, however, ample evidence that 'pinching with hot pincers' did 'mirror actual practice' in sixteenth-century Germany itself – either as a form of interrogatory torture in the interests of extracting a confession, or as punishment once the sentence had been handed down. Statistics for the period 1581–1600 – Stubbe was executed in 1589 – indicate fifteen instances of execution by 'sword with intensifying additional punishments' (out of a total of eighty-one executions) in the city of Nuremberg, and six instances (out of a total of 102 executions) in Frankfurt. An exceptional practice, then, perhaps, but not a rare or an insignificant one. Records for the cities of Augsburg and Würtzburg in Germany, and Zürich in nearby Switzerland, present similar statistics for the same period.[33] Moreover, among the twenty-three paid duties of the executioner for the city of Kaufbeuren, for example, there appears a one Florin stipend

---

[31] The gesture might, however, prove futile: 'The animal-man and the man-animal', says philosopher Giorgio Agamben, 'are the two sides of a single fracture, which cannot be mended from either side'. Giorgio Agamben, *The Open: Man and Animal*, trans. Kevin Attell (Stanford: Stanford University Press, 2004), p. 36.

[32] Esther Cohen, *The Modulated Scream: Pain in Late Medieval Culture* (Chicago: University of Chicago Press, 2010), p. 46. See also: Maria R. Boes, *Crime and Punishment in Early Modern Germany: Courts and Adjudicatory Practices in Frankfurt am Main, 1562–1696* (Burlington, VT: Ashgate, 2013); and Larissa Tracy, *Torture and Brutality in Medieval Literature: Negotiations of National Identity* (Cambridge: D. S. Brewer, 2012), esp. p. 16. In *Suspended Animation: Pain, Pleasure and Punishment in Medieval Culture* (London: Reaktion, 2005), Robert Mills discusses 'the place of flaying in what [he] call[s] the medieval penal imaginary – the network of visual and textual significations that transform the violated bodies of executed criminals into discourse and fantasy' (pp. 65–6). Mills, like Cohen, Boes and Tracy, argues that, in contrast to their pronounced presence in the art and literature of the period, actual cases of flaying as torture in the later Middle Ages were 'exceptional' (p. 65).

[33] See: Richard van Dülmen, *Theatre of Horror: Crime and Punishment in Early Modern Germany*, trans. Elisabeth Neu (Cambridge: Polity Press, 1990), p. 85, table 5.5.

'[f]or each pinching with tongs'.[34] Documented cases of this punitive practice include those of criminals in Frankfurt (1600): 'pinched in each arm twice with red-hot tongs';[35] St Gallen, Switzerland (1600): 'pinched with red-hot tongs once on his chest and six times on each arm', then later, six times on each thigh;[36] Memmingen (1588): 'pinched once in each arm with red-hot tongs, and once again in his chest';[37] Rottenburg am Neckar (1527): 'twice with red-hot tongs tear out pieces of flesh from his body', the process 'to be repeated five times';[38] Nüremberg (1522): 'pinched with red-hot tongs'.[39] These statistics are, furthermore, supported by the evidence presented in the woodcuts of the period. A broadsheet by Leonhart Gerhart entitled 'Murder Committed in Halle, Saxony, and the Torture of the Culprit in Mainz, 30 July 1572',[40] the two Stubbe woodcuts, and a second woodcut by Lucas Mayer depicting the 1589 torture and execution of the murderer Franz Seubold at Gräfenberg,[41] attest to the active use of this very specific type of punishment in Germany and Switzerland at least until the end of the sixteenth century.

The term 'pinching', which could conceivably involve piercing, puncturing, searing, scarring and even tattooing the skin, may be somewhat misleading; only the Rottenburg am Neckar order to 'with red-hot tongs tear out pieces of flesh from his body' expresses the violent rupture that the term actually represents. Moreover, it is this formulation which is used in the London account: 'with red-hot burning pincers in ten several places to have the flesh pulled off from the bones'; similarly, in Verstegan, '[t]he flesh of divers parts of his body [...] pulled out with hot iron tongs'.[42] The verb-particle constructions 'plukt from', 'pulled off from' and 'pulled out' add to the act of punishment a gestural force and immediacy that the simple verb 'pinching' does not, in that they attach to the action of each verb a tangible object, a specific body part, the viscerally suggestive/reactive

---

[34] van Dülmen, *Theatre of Horror*, p. 163 n. 29.

[35] Ibid., p. 78.

[36] Ibid., p. 96.

[37] Ibid., pp. 77–8.

[38] Ibid., p. 78.

[39] Ibid., p. 89.

[40] The top right-hand panel of this four-panel woodcut by Magdeburg, *Briefmaler*, Leonhard Gerhart clearly depicts an official torturing the culprit with a pair of pincers. Reproduced in Strauss, *Single-Leaf Woodcut*, 1:246.

[41] See n. 19 above. Mayer's woodcut is also reproduced in Merback, *The Thief, the Cross, and the Wheel*, p. 214, fig. 86.

[42] Verstegan, *Restitution*, p. 237. Roman Jakobson notes that the Russian infinitives *drat'* (to skin), *žrat'* (to devour), and *rvat'* (to tear away), among others, are distinguished by a single phonetic feature. Roman Jakobson, *Six Lectures on Sound and Meaning*, trans. John Mepham (Sussex: Harvester Press, 1978), Lecture III, p. 62.

(soft) 'flesh' and (hard) 'bones'. Flesh, like the head, has an 'unnerving severability'.[43]

After restraint, then, flaying is the next logical step towards Stubbe's corporeal disintegration, as it tears open the skin envelope and pulls out its fleshy contents. As the woodcuts illustrate, the 'red-hot burning pincers' are not only searing instruments of pain; they are also razor-sharp writing implements, branding Stubbe's story into his skin and flesh, and foretelling the flames in which it will end.[44] Taking red-hot tongs and opening up Peter Stubbe's skin might therefore be seen as an attempt to let out the incubus, the rapist, the predator and the cannibal who crawled around in the furry and corroded skin of the werewolf that lived beneath it.

Flaying – piercing Stubbe's skin and pulling his flesh away from his bones – having failed to rout the werewolf out of his subcutaneous den, taking an axe or a wooden hatchet and smashing those bones might seem the next logical step. An additional punishment, not mentioned in the London account but documented in the woodcut attached to it, was hacking off Stubbe's hands and feet. Moreover, the relationship of analogy that obtained between human skin and wolf fur extended to other body parts, most notably limbs, a hand being to a front paw what a foot was to a back one. Foucault, who observes that in the sixteenth century, '[m]an's body is always the possible half of a universal atlas',[45] gives as an example Pierre Belon's comparative mapping of human and bird skeletons, but the animal half of the universal atlas has also long been populated by wolves. Perhaps the most vivid of these is Lycaon in Ovid's *Metamorphoses*: 'His clothes became bristling hair, his arms became legs. He was a wolf, but kept some vestige of his former shape' (1:199–243).

The relationship between Stubbe's 'all too solid flesh' (now melting in the flames) and its furry wolfish simulacrum is a complex one, for if flesh and fur are analogous (flesh is to man as fur is to wolf),[46] a severed human

---

[43] See: Asa Simon Mittman's analysis of what William Ian Miller calls the human body's 'unnerving severability' and 'unnerving and disgust evoking [...] partability', in 'Answering the Call of the Severed Head', in *Heads Will Roll: Decapitation in the Medieval and Early Modern Imagination*, ed. Larissa Tracy and Jeff Massey (Leiden: Brill, 2012), pp. 311–27 at p. 311. For a fascinating discussion of other flaying instruments and of the many ways in which 'metal sliced through skin to meet bone' in medieval and early modern Europe, see: Jack Hartnell, 'Tools of the Puncture: Skin, Knife, Bone, Hand', in this volume.

[44] Similarly, 'the pen is to the writer of the pamphlet what the knife is to the physician, namely, a surgical, analytical instrument that can probe the cause of an infection in order to expose an inner corruption or depravity.' Goth, 'Killing, Hewing', pp. 11–12.

[45] Foucault, *The Order of Things*, p. 25.

[46] See: ibid., pp. 23–6, for a discussion of analogy as a similarity relation in the sixteenth century.

head and a fake wolf are not. This is a construct that would, then, fall under the same rubric of *convenientia* that connects, for example, flesh with 'red hot burning tongs'. Foucault further explains:

> Those things that are 'convenient' come sufficiently close to one another to be in juxtaposition; their edges touch, their fringes intermingle, the extremity of one also denotes the beginning of the other. In this way, movement, influences, passions, and properties, too, are communicated. So that in this hinge between two things a resemblance appears.[47]

In Stubbe's story, 'this hinge between two things' is reified in the girdle that functions as the mechanism of his transformation, creating a simulacrum that makes man and wolf appear 'as if they were not contiguous, but continuous',[48] and is conceptualized in the notion of time. Time constitutes the 'hinge' between the atemporal 'man is a wolf' metaphor,[49] based on a figurative feature-mapping between the two elements (Stubbe and the wolf), and the man–wolf metamorphosis in which Stubbe assumes the 'wolfish likeness' which literalizes it. Michel Le Guern, philosopher and linguist, explains: 'Si je dis 'A est B' alors que chacun sait que le fait d'être A exclut la possibilité d'être B, j'impose de comprendre B [...] comme une métaphore. Mais je peux dire que A au moment t_1 est le même être que B au moment t_2.' [If I say that 'A is B' when everyone knows that the fact of being A excludes the possibility of being B, I impose a metaphorical interpretation of B [...]. But I can say that A at moment t_1 is the same being as B at moment t_2.][50] For the girdle activated a time warp in which

---

[47] Ibid., p. 20.

[48] 'quasi non sint / Contiguae, sic continuae' [as if they were not / Contiguous, but continuous]. Geoffrey of Vinsauf, *Poetria nova*, trans. Margaret F. Nims (Toronto: Pontifical Institute of Mediaeval Studies, 2010), p. 25. Qtd. in Vincent Rockwell, *Rewriting Resemblance in Medieval French Romance: Ceci n'est pas un graal* (New York: Garland, 1995), pp. 6, 77. For the distinction between 'contiguous' and 'continuous', see also: Aristotle, *Physics*, Book 8, Part viii. http://classics.mit.edu/Aristotle/physics.8.viii.html (accessed 14 Nov. 2014). Referenced in Guy Achard-Bayle, *Grammaire des métamorphoses: référence, identité, changement, fiction* (Brussels: Duculot, 2001), p. 77.

[49] See: Max Black, 'Metaphor', in his *Models and Metaphors: Studies in Language and Philosophy* (Ithaca, NY: Cornell University Press, 1962), pp. 25–47, for a superb analysis of the 'man is a wolf' metaphor in terms of metaphor interaction theory.

[50] Or, in other words: 'Pour qu'il y ait métamorphose, il faut faire intervenir le temps. Il faut un *avant* et un *après*. La relation métaphorique est intemporelle,' [In order for there to be metamorphosis, time must be involved. There must be a *before* and an *after*. The metaphorical relation is timeless.] Michel Le Guern, 'La métamorphose poétique: essai de définition', in *Poétiques de la métamorphose*, ed. Guy Demerson *et al.*

the hunters who cornered and captured the wolf in the woods claim they saw 'him in the same place metamorphosed', i.e. saw that A (the wolf) at moment t_1 was the same being as B (Peter Stubbe) at moment t_2. And it is on this fact – and the relationship between these two moments – that the entire case against Peter Stubbe 'hinges', for, continues the narrative, 'finding him to be the man indeede, and no delusion or phanta|sticall motion, they had him incontinent before the Maiestrates to be examined' (p. 16).

In the melee of the pre-capture scuffle, Stubbe slipped off the girdle. There being no physical similarity between his human and his wolfish shapes – an *écart* which had enabled him to escape capture for over twenty-five years – there was also no image that would have allowed the hunters to identify him. Nevertheless, slipping off the girdle proved to be a highly problematic act since it also activated the mechanism that restored Stubbe to his full human sartorial glory (including walking stick accessory), and it did so right in front of the hapless hunters, who, 'seeing him in the same place metamorphosed contrary to their ex|pectation' (p. 16), superimposed the human transparency on the wolfish one – they saw 'him *in the same place* metamorphosed' – and found proof of their culpable and criminal identity.

There is yet another sixteenth-century similarity model operating in this metamorphosis, one which informs the relationship of similarity between the 'likeness of a wolf' and a real wolf. That model is *aemulatio*, for '[t]here is something in emulation', explains Foucault, 'of the reflection and the mirror'; and, perhaps more significantly, there is also something of the duplicitous and the illusory: 'Which is the reality', one might, with Foucault, ask, 'and which is the projection?'[51] For, just as the act of taking off the girdle removed the wolf skin that had masked Stubbe's 'fleshy, furred, corroded underside',[52] the act of donning it painted on the surface of his human skin a 'likeness', a simulacrum, of what Gilles Deleuze terms 'transformational decors, painted skies, all kinds of *trompe l'oeil*'[53] that actualize, literalize and exteriorize the various descriptors (cruel, savage, lawless, rapacious etc.) that project the animal onto the human.

(Saint-Étienne: Publications de l'Université Saint-Étienne, 1981), pp. 27–36 at p. 31.

[51] Foucault, *The Order of Things*, p. 22.

[52] 'Both [the vampire and the werewolf]', says Patricia MacCormack, 'are fleshy, furred, corroded, showing different conditions of the smooth, hard flesh of normal humanity'. Patricia MacCormack, 'Posthuman Teratology', in *The Ashgate Research Companion to Monsters and the Monstrous*, ed. Asa Simon Mittman with Peter Dendle (Burlington, VT: Ashgate, 2013), pp. 293–310 at p. 305.

[53] Gilles Deleuze, *The Fold*, trans. Tom Conley (New York: Bloomsbury Academic, 1993), p. 31.

This portrayal of the werewolf as *versipellis*, or skin-changer,[54] was famously depicted in John Webster's *The Dutchesse of Malfy* (1612–13), when it was reported that the incestuous werewolf Duke Ferdinand had '[s]aid he was a Woolffe: onely the difference / Was, a Woolffes skinne was hairy on the out-side, / His on the In-side' (V.ii.19–20)'.[55] This formulation finds a mid-fifteenth-century historical precedent in the report of a murderer in Pavia who 'did constantly affirme that hee was a Wolfe, and that there was no other difference, but that Wolves were commonly hayrie without, and hee was betwixt the skinne and the flesh'.[56] Wolves and flesh, particularly wolf-flesh – wearing and removing, fleshing out and flaying – were inextricably linked. Situating the wolf beneath the skin of the werewolf provides the hunter, the magistrate and the executioner with an ironclad argument for flaying. Indeed, following Ferdinand's explanation is a rarely-quoted exhortation in which he 'bade them take their swords, Rip up his flesh, and try' (V.ii.21–2). The Pavia werewolf was, moreover, put to the same test, as '[s]ome (too barbarous and cruell Wolues in effect) desiring to trie the truth thereof, gaue him manie wounds vpon the armes and legges'.[57]

This flayed skin, like Stubbe's, 'riddled with holes', is not a façade in the Deleuzian sense, i.e. it is not 'an outside without an inside';[58] rather, it is an interior exteriorized. Pinned to the wheel, it is no more than a racked animal hide,[59] the imprint of the corroded werewolf skin scraped out from its underside now clearly visible on its surface. The 'wolfish

[54] See n. 52 above.

[55] John Webster, *The Tragedy of the Dutchesse of Malfy* (Menston, UK: The Scolar Press, 1968) [facsimile edn].

[56] Job Fincel, *De mirabilibus*, lib. xi, in Simon Goulart, *Admirable and memorable histories containing the wonders of our time. Collected into French out of the best authors. By I. [sic] Goulart. And out of French into English. By Ed. Grimeston* (London: George Eld, 1607), p. 387. Also reproduced in Charlotte Otten, ed., *A Lycanthropy Reader: Werewolves in Western Culture* (Syracuse, NY: Syracuse University Press, 1986), pp. 41–4 at p 42.

[57] Fincel, *De mirabilibus*, lib. xi. The historian David Cressy tells the story of a woman named Agnes Bowker, in 1560s London, who claimed that she had sex with the Devil in the form of a cat, became pregnant, and gave birth to a creature which was described by a midwife as 'resembling nothing so much as a skinned cat'. A commissary who tested her claim by flaying both this creature and a real cat, and determined that they were both the same under the skin, later explained, 'If it had been a monster, then it should haue had somewhat more or els lesse; But an other Catte was flaied in the same sorte, and in all poinctes like, or, as it were, the self same'. David Cressy, 'Agnes Bowker's Cat: Childbirth, Seduction, Bestiality, and Lies', in his *Travesties and Transgressions in Tudor and Stewart England: Tales of Discord and Dissension* (Oxford: Oxford University Press), pp. 9–28.

[58] Deleuze, *The Fold*, p. 31.

[59] To 'rack a hide' is to bore holes into it so that it can be tied to a rack in preparation for tanning.

likeness' which roamed the early modern German forests was what Stubbe's hunters would later call a 'delusion or fantastical motion', the projection of the private man onto a public screen, but it was this corrosion – the physical representation of Stubbe's moral corruption – which blurred the border between inner and outer, public and private, making the creature's forays both bolder and more difficult to pin down. For Stubbe was a predator who appeared 'sometime in the likenes of a Woolfe, sometime in the habit of a man' (p. 10), and it was perhaps when he took on the shape of a man that he was most dangerous, for it was then that there was a gap, a hidden fissure, between who he was and who he appeared to be, and it was this gap that tricked, lured and seduced. It forced a fatal misreading of Stubbe's appearance as he walked through the streets in his bourgeois Sunday best, smiling at friends whose children he had slaughtered, choosing his next victim. S. J. Wiseman's comment that he was 'rubbing neighborly shoulders with those who were to fuel his solitary cannibal feasts'[60] neatly expresses the threat inherent in this unfettered Jeckyllian adjacency.[61] He wore respectability like a second skin, hiding his wolfish nature under the human façade and, in his execution, he would be stripped bare of the trappings of humanity as his flesh was stripped from his body.

For Stubbe's daughter, Beell, the danger was immediate and inescapable, for when her bedroom door closed, so did the gap in this already dangerous proximity. Casting off both his wolfish sheath and his social skin,

---

[60] Susan J. Wiseman, 'Hairy on the Inside: Metamorphosis and Civility in English Werewolf Texts', in *Renaissance Beasts: Of Animals, Humans, and other Wonderful Creatures*, ed. Erica Fudge (Urbana: University of Illinois Press, 2004), pp. 50–69 at p. 54.

[61] A psychoanalytic reading might find in Stubbe's flaying the physical equivalent of psychoanalysis itself, defined as a process of 'stripping away layers of strategic displacement that obscure the self's underlying drives': Stephen Greenblatt, 'Psychoanalysis and Renaissance Culture', in *Literary Theory/Renaissance Texts*, ed. Patricia Parker and David Quint (Baltimore: The Johns Hopkins University Press, 1986), pp. 210–24 at p. 222. Indeed, it was a conscious displacement strategy that enabled Stubbe, in a reversal of the flaying process, to evade capture for over twenty-five years by inserting what Stéphane Dumas calls a 'thickness which exudes legibility' – here, a consciously specious legibility – between his real and apparent selves. Stéphane Dumas, 'The Return of Marsyas: Creative Skin', trans. John Lee, in *SK-Interfaces*, ed. Jens Hauser (Liverpool: Liverpool University Press-FACT, 2008), pp. 18–31. In essence, this is the argument presented in the most persuasive theological tracts and treatises of the period, such as Jean Beauvoys de Chauvincourt's *Discours de la lycantropie, ou De la transmutation des hommes en loups* (Paris: J. Rezé, 1599), which present metamorphosis as a glamour or illusion by means of which the Devil misdirects and reprogrammes human perception in order that abnormal or perverted human drives be misinterpreted as normal (albeit savage) animal ones.

her father penetrated her like the animal he really was.[62] It was a solitary act of repeated predation, re-enacted in the countless rapes Stubbe committed over the course of twenty-five years as he stalked his female prey. Some 'if he could by any meanes get them alone, he would in the feeldes rauishe them, and af|ter in his Wooluish likenes cruelly murder them' (p. 6), others, 'when he had first deflowred, he after most cruelly murdered' (p. 11). In a twisted act of inversion, the violence of this penetration found its mirror-image in a savage parody of withdrawal when he murdered 'two goodly yong women bigge with Child, tearing the Children out of their wombes, in most bloody and sauedge sorte, and after eate their hartes panting hotte and rawe' (p. 7). It was this same push in / pull out binary which operated in the second stage of Stubbe's pre-execution punishment, when the executioner plunged 'red-hot burning pincers' into his skin and tore his flesh away from his bones. This was the third sixteenth-century similarity structure, *analogia*, operating at its retributive best: the executioner was to the murderer what the murderer was to his victim.

If 'death-torture' is what Foucault terms 'the art of maintaining life in pain, by subdividing it into a "thousand deaths"',[63] decapitation is, he argues, 'the zero-degree of torture', an act 'which reduces all pain to a single gesture, performed in a single moment'.[64] It is a gesture and a moment that was repeated time and time again in early modern Germany. As previously noted, the Nuremberg and Frankfurt execution statistics record a total of 183 executions in Nuremberg and Frankfurt for the period 1581–1600, twenty-one falling under the category 'S*' ('Sword with intensifying additional punishments'), which Richard Van Dülmen describes as 'cases of beheading with such severe refinements of punishment that they can no longer be compared with a simple execution by sword'.[65]

The phenomenology rather than the function of pain is instructive in Stubbe's case. For pain, as Scarry puts it, 'is devoid of

---

[62] It is in this sense that Stubbe embodied what Julia Kristeva terms 'the abject: "what disturbs identity, system, order. What does not respect borders, positions, rules. The in-between, the ambiguous, the composite"'. Kristeva, *The Powers of Horror: An Essay on Abjection*, trans. Leon S. Roudiez (New York: Columbia University Press, 1982), p. 4. Stubbe's incestuous sexuality was recast in a cannibalistic mode when 'incontinent in the shape and likeness of a wolf he encountered his own son and there most cruelly slew him, which done, he presently ate the brains out of his head as a most-savory and dainty delicious meal to staunch his greedy appetite: the most monstrous act that ever man heard of, for never was known a wretch from nature so far degenerate'. Prieur's *Dialogue de la lycanthropie* includes an embedded quote from the Venerable Bede claiming that 'Homo bestialiter vivens est centies millesies bestia peior' (p. 17).

[63] Foucault, *The Spectacle of the Scaffold*, p. 41.

[64] Ibid.

[65] van Dülmen, *Theatre of Horror*, p. 86.

self-extension'.[66] That is to say that inflicting pain renders the body incapable of the desire or hunger for objects outside the boundaries of the body, and, more importantly, of the search for the satisfaction of those needs.[67] For it was the pulsion of that desire that sent Stubbe, in a twisted and toxic need for self-extension, out in search of his prey. This was a man whose whole life was predicated on ruinous appetite, on a predatory hunger for bodies outside his own. It was an insatiable, transgressive hunger that penetrated, consumed, cannibalized, invaded, fed upon, ruined and laid waste to the bodies of others in order to satisfy its own appetites. In Scarry's words, 'desire is desire of *x*, fear is fear of *y*, hunger is hunger for *z*; but pain is not "of" or "for" anything – it is itself alone'.[68] Inflicting pain on Stubbe deprived him of the ability to escape from the boundaries of his own body even as it pierced, peeled back, fractured, smashed, severed and torched those very boundaries. It set up the same ineluctable double bind that had ensnared Stubbe's victims as he captured them and violated them, pinned them down and dismembered them, seized them and slit their throats. Their bodies were the surface on which the weapon of his desire fell, trapping them inside. And what tied them to him, as he was tied to his executioner, was the inescapable physical contact of one body (or weapon as an extension of that body) with another.

Foucault saw in *convenientia* a 'mingling of fringes, the extremity of one also denot[ing] the beginning of the other'.[69] Gilles Deleuze and Félix Guattari spoke of metamorphosis as 'threshold and fiber, symbiosis of or passage between heterogeneities'.[70] And Stéphane Dumas locates flaying in a 'topography of the border, where extension is reduced to a fringe, a line of friction, or even a point of contact'.[71] For the hybrid Marsyas, as for the *versïpellis* Stubbe, that fringe, that fibre, is the skin. As he is being

---

[66] Scarry, *The Body in Pain*, pp. 161–2.

[67] Modern psychoanalytic psychology defines 'self-extension' as a construct 'in which others are experienced symbiotically as part of one's self, vis-á-vis [*sic*] Kohut's concept of the self-object'. John Fiscalini and Alan L. Grey, eds., *Narcissism and the Interpersonal Self* (New York: Columbia University Press, 1993), p. 61. Stubbe's personality would, for Heinz Kohut, be one that was marked by a 'chronic, archaic "hunger" for self-object experiences, and his [...] behaviour characterized by a continuing search for satisfaction of self-object needs'. Erez Banai, Mario Mikulincer and Phillip R. Shaver, '"Self object" Needs in Kohut's Self Psychology: Links with Attachment, Self-Cohesion, Affect Regulation, and Adjustment Needs', *Psychoanalytic Psychology* 22.2 (2005): 224–60 at p. 228.

[68] Scarry, *The Body in Pain*, pp. 161–2.

[69] Foucault, *The Order of Things*, p. 20.

[70] Gilles Deleuze and Felix Guattari, *A Thousand Plateaus: Capitalism and Schizophrenia*, trans. Brian Massumi (Minneapolis: University of Minnesota Press, 1987), p. 272.

[71] Dumas, 'The Return of Marsyas'.

flayed, Marsyas cries, 'quid me mihi detrahis?' [Why are you tearing me from myself?][72], and it is this same act of *detraho* which is recorded in the account of Stubbe's flaying, when he is condemned 'with red hotte burning pincers in ten seue|ral places to haue the flesh puld off from the bones' (p. 17).

Now trapped in a human body and abandoned by the Devil 'to indure the torments which his deedes deserued' (p. 17), Stubbe found himself prey to the annihilistic agenda of a judicial system bent on proving to a public mesmerized and terrorized in equal measure by this monster that it could wield the weapons of destruction with the same brutal finesse that had marked his own murderous campaign. Moreover, unlike Stubbe, it could do so with the full assent and approval of its magistrates, and 'in the presence of many peeres & princes of Germany' (p. 18).

Therefore, abandoned by the Prince of Darkness, Stubbe 'was short|ly after put to the racke in the Towne of Bedbur, but fearing the torture, he vollun|tarilye confessed his whole life, and made knowen the villanies which he had com|mitted for the space of xxv. yeeres, also he cōfessed how by Sorcery he procured of the Deuill a Girdle, which beeing put on, he forthwith became a Woolfe' (pp. 16–17). Stubbe's confession did, in fact, allow him to escape torture, defined as 'a legal means of painfully extracting truth, specifically a confession, from a criminal who already had a "so-called half-proof" against him',[73] but it did not, as he had perhaps hoped, allow him to escape punishment, for his execution was staged as a slow, inexorable series of punishments, systematically slicing to pieces the veil that black magic had thrown over the public eye. In flaying, crushing, dismembering and decapitating Stubbe, and burning his headless body to ashes, the authorities annihilated the argument that magic was more powerful than pain, and, even more importantly, more powerful than they were. In mounting Stubbe's head above 'the likenes of a Woolfe' (p. 19) as 'a warning to all Sorcerers and Witches, which vnlaw|fully followe their owne diuelish imagina|tion to the vtter ruine and destruction of their soules eternally' (p. 18), they simultaneously mimicked and mocked the contiguity inherent in the man–beast continuum that had marked the trajectory of Stubbe's life and that, once severed, led him to his death.

---

[72] Ovid, *Metamorphoses*, 6.385. The Lewis and Short Latin dictionary translates *detraho* as 'to draw off, take down, pull down, take away, remove, withdraw, drag, bring'.

[73] Tracy, *Torture and Brutality*, p. 22.

4

Medievalism and the 'Flayed-Dane' Myth: English Perspectives between the Seventeenth and Nineteenth Centuries

Mary Rambaran-Olm

THE fascination with the Middle Ages has a lengthy tradition which, arguably, began shortly after the period ended. For centuries the popular view of the age was based on the claim of the fourteenth-century Italian scholar Francesco Petrarch (1304–74) that the medieval period was one of literary and cultural 'darkness'.[1] Whereas the terms 'medieval' and 'medievalism' were first used in the nineteenth century to denote the intermediate period between the 'classical' and 'modern' eras of history, for centuries the post-medieval English fostered images of a 'dark' and 'savage' past to support the Petrarchan view of pre-Conquest England and the Continent.[2] This anachronistic view has long been abandoned by scholars; however, the concept of the 'Dark Ages' became firmly established among English dilettanti and scholars alike, beginning in the Renaissance and

---

[1] Writing of the period after the fall of the Roman Empire, Petrarch explained that: 'Nullo enim modo divinarum rerum veritas apparere illis poterat, quibus nondum verus sol iustitie illuxerat. Elucebant tamen inter errores ingenia, neque ideo minus vivaces erant oculi, quamvis tenebris et densa caligine circumsepti, ut eis non errati odium, sed indigne sortis miseratio deberetur' [Amidst the errors there shone forth men of genius; no less keen were their eyes, although they were surrounded by *darkness* and dense gloom; therefore they ought not so much to be hated for their erring but pitied for their ill fate]. See: Francesco Petrarch, *Apologia cuiusdam anonymi Galli calumnias* (*Defence Against the Calumnies of an Anonymous Frenchman*) in his *Opera Omnia* (Basileæ: Execudebat Henrichus Petri, 1554) p. 1195. Translation from Theodore Mommsen, 'Petrarch's Conception of the "Dark Ages"', *Speculum* 17 (1942): 226–42 at p. 227, n. 9.

[2] The broad term 'post-medieval' is used interchangeably with any subsequent period in English history after the Middle Ages. The *OED* states that 'medieval' was first used by T. D. Fosbroke in 1817, and 'medievalism' was coined by John Ruskin in 1853. 'Medievalism' has become identified with the study of the on-going construction of the idea of the Middle Ages. See, for example: David Matthews, *Medievalism: A Critical History* (Cambridge: D. S. Brewer, 2015); Clare A. Simmons, *Popular Medievalism in Romantic-Era Britain* (New York: Palgrave, 2011); Karl Fugelso, ed., *Studies in Medievalism XVII: Defining Medievalism(s)* (Cambridge: D. S. Brewer, 2009); and Michael Alexander, *Medievalism: The Middle Ages in Modern England* (New Haven: Yale University Press, 2007).

reaching its height in nineteenth-century England, with some residual traces in the early twentieth century.[3] This (often inaccurate) vision included a presumption of brutality and violent punishment meted out by a lawless populace. Early modern society, in particular, was convinced of medieval savagery, which they believed included flaying, castration and frequent use of torture.[4] In the seventeenth century a myth involving a 'flayed Dane' – a pillaging Viking skinned by Anglo-Saxons – captured the attention of the English diarist Samuel Pepys, who first recorded it; from that point until the twentieth century, the legend of the 'Dane-skin' tacked to the doors of early medieval English churches persisted. The 'historical reality' of the myth is loosely rooted in an actual episode during the reign of King Æthelred II (r. 978–1013 and 1014–16), but the myth itself is a chimera constructed through the conflation of events and the invention of 'material evidence' to support early modern claims of the barbaric and uncultured 'Dark Ages'. Rather than providing evidence of an actual Anglo-Saxon practice of flaying sacrilegious Danes, or of displaying the flayed remains of hapless, massacred Danes, this myth perpetuates an early modern perception of medieval brutality and acts as nothing more than sensational modern nationalist propaganda.

In 1002 CE the Anglo-Saxons had for a decade been making regular payments called the *Danegeld*, while still living under the constant threat of attack from Vikings.[5] Hatred for the Vikings was already seething

---

[3] Johan Huizinga, in particular, perpetuated this idea in his work. His perspective was furthered by popular scholars like Barbara Tuchman, who fostered this image well into the twentieth century. It is only in the last thirty years that medieval scholars have aggressively challenged this idea of a sweeping 'Dark Age'. See: Johan Huizinga, *The Waning of the Middle Ages*, trans. Federick Jan Hopman (London: Penguin Books, 1924, repr. 1990) and Barbara W. Tuchman, *A Distant Mirror: The Calamitous Fourteenth Century* (New York: Ballantine Books, 1978).

[4] For a discussion of early modern and modern misconceptions about medieval torture, punishment and brutality, see: Larissa Tracy, *Torture and Brutality in Medieval Literature: Negotiations of National Identity* (Cambridge: D. S. Brewer, 2012).

[5] Literally translated to 'Dane tribute', *Danegeld* was first implemented in 991 by Æthelred II in order to make payments of *gafol* (as some sources referred to the payment) to the Danes to avoid further combat. Although there were other measures adopted during the 990s to defend the Anglo-Saxon kingdom, the specific policy that allowed for payments of *gafol* to the Vikings during difficult episodes of unrest and conflict was officially adopted by Æthelred in 994. It is said that over the course of the next two decades an estimated six million pence was paid by the Anglo-Saxons. For further information on *gafol* payments see: Sven Jansson, *Runstenar* (Stockholm: Svenska turisföreningen, 1980), p. 35; Simon Keynes, *The Diplomas of King Æthelred 'The Unready', 978–1016* (Cambridge: Cambridge University Press, 1980), pp. 176–85; Simon Keynes, 'A Tale of Two Kings', *Transactions of*

when Æthelred II learned of a supposed assassination plot by the Danes living in England.[6] With the possibility of usurpation, combined with the understanding that his people loathed those who had been pillaging the kingdom for a decade, Æthelred II allegedly ordered the killing of Danes in Anglo-Saxon England – the St Brice's Day massacre.[7] The supposed flayed human skin displayed on the eleventh-century door of a church in Hadstock, Essex, was said to have been that of one of those Danes slaughtered in the massacre – a real atrocity gave way to post-medieval legends that conflated fact, fiction and pure fantasy with a desire to sensationalize the past. Various

the Royal Historical Society 36 (1986): 195–217 at p. 201; and Ryan Lavelle, *Aethelred II, King of England* (Stroud: The History Press, 2008), pp. 68, 78–9.

[6] This particular account is provided by, arguably, one of the more notorious medieval historiographers, the twelfth-century historian William of Malmesbury, in the *Gesta Regum* ii.177. Some scholars argue that William was subjective and thus exaggerated the event to suit his agenda. Twelfth-century historiographers such as Henry, Archdeacon of Huntingdon, offer a similar impression. See: Henry of Huntingdon, *Historia Anglorum*, ed. and trans. Diana Greenway (Oxford: Clarendon Press, 1996), p. 341. Additionally, the ideas of twelfth-century monks, especially William of Malmesbury, were of interest to seventeenth-century English reformers for reasons relating to religious and political restructuring; it is therefore possible that the credibility of William's accounts was not subjected to widespread criticism, because many medieval accounts of events were reused and reinterpreted during the seventeenth century to support socio-political and religious agendas. For further discussion of the issue of William of Malmesbury's credibility, see: Jay Paul Gates, 'Imagining Justice in the Anglo-Saxon Past: Eadric Streona, Kingship, and the Search for Community', *The Haskins Society Journal* 25 (2013): 125–46; and Jay Paul Gates and Nicole Marafioti, eds., *Capital and Corporal Punishment in Anglo-Saxon England* (Woodbridge: Boydell Press, 2014). See also: Elaine Treharne, *Living through Conquest: The Politics of Early English, 1020–1220* (Oxford: Oxford University Press, 2012).

[7] See: *Anglo-Saxon Chronicle*, vol. 5: *MS C*, ed. Katherine O'Brien O'Keeffe (Cambridge: D. S. Brewer, 2001). This 'so called' massacre suggests that the English had finally lost patience with financial extortion that failed to end episodes of Viking raids and violence, but Simon Keynes argues that the specific targets of the slaughter were actually recently employed mercenaries who had turned against their employers. The circumstances surrounding the St Brice's Day massacre are also hotly contested by other critics, as are the motivations for the subsequent Danish invasion and conquest of England by both Svein Forkbeard and his son Cnut. See: Simon Keynes, *Æthelred II*, ODNB online (2004; accessed 3 Jan. 2016); and Lavelle, *Aethelred II*, p. 104. See also: Helen Damico, 'Grendel's Reign of Terror: From History to Vernacular Epic', in *Myths, Legends, and Heroes: Essays on Old Norse and Old English Literature in Honour of John McKinnell*, ed. Daniel Anlezark (Toronto: University of Toronto Press, 2011), pp. 148–66 at p. 161.

other churches boasted their own 'Dane-skins' that were also said to be the flayed skins of victims of the massacre.[8] However, evidence of flaying in Anglo-Saxon England points only to practical uses for animal skins in book-production and leather-making, *not* to the punishment of human beings (except in a few references to scalping); literary references are most often associated with hagiography or, in rare instances, appear in medical texts, where flaying is used as part of a cure.

The custom of flaying the impious and tanning their hides has roots in Greek antiquity;[9] however, in the corpus of Old English, the verb *flēan* (to flay) and its variants *a-flēan* and *be-flēan* are found in only a handful of references. According to the *Dictionary of Old English*, the verb *flēan* is related to the Old Norse *flā*. *Flēan* is found twice in the corpus of Old English in Latin–Old English glossaries. This is not to suggest that *flēan* is the only word used in reference to flaying, but there are only a scattered number of surviving references specifically relating to human skin. Excoriation and its various Latin cognates – *decoriare, decorticare, deglubere, eviscerare, excoriare* and *viscera* – are mentioned sporadically in Anglo-Saxon glosses of Latin dictionaries, and are used to describe the deaths of flayed saints, most notably St Bartholomew.[10] *Beflēan* appears on ten occasions, again mostly in Latin–Old English glossaries, but two instances are cited in the Old English Martyrology for Bartholomew. *Aflēan* is cited in Gregory the Great's *Dialogues* in his telling of the flaying of Herculanus of Perugia (d. 549), Bishop of Perusium, at the hands of the king of the Ostrogoths, Totila (d. 552).[11] None of the Old English variants are used

---

[8] The door in Hadstock had the earliest evidence of the 'Dane-skin'. Other church doors that were said to include skins were found in Rochester, Worcester, Copford, East Thurrock, Southwark and Westminster Abbey.

[9] According to the Phrygian legend the river-god, Silenus Marsyas, challenged Apollo to a contest with a lyre. Upon losing, Silenus Marsyas was flayed. See: Harry Thurston Peck, ed., *Harper's Dictionary of Classical Literature and Antiquities* (New York: American Book Company, 1896), pp. 1009–10.

[10] Christian tradition contains three versions of Bartholomew's death, one of which involves the apostle being skinned alive and beheaded. The other two versions involve him being kidnapped, beaten and drowned, or being crucified upside-down. According to the *Dictionary of Old English Corpus* online (http://doe.utoronto.ca/pages/index.html) there are some sixty-three references to St Bartholomew's flaying; however, the references associated with the saint are used in conjunction with retellings of his legendary execution. Thus, the references to flaying in these cases cannot be considered as evidence of the practice within the Anglo-Saxon period. See: Asa Simon Mittman and Christine Sciacca, 'Robed in Martyrdom: The Flaying of St Bartholomew in the Laudario of Sant'Agnese', pp. 140–72, in this volume.

[11] See: Gregory the Great, *Dialogues* III.13.198.6, and 199.2, I.77. *Dialogorum Libri IV*, in *Patrologia Latina* 77, *S. Gregorii Papaei III* (Paris: Migne, 1862).

in conjunction with instances of flaying during the Anglo-Saxon period; they appear only in reference to flaying as a motif in Christian history. Synonyms for *flēan* in the Old English corpus generally refer to ripping as a result of animal attacks, such as scratching, tearing, lacerating, clawing and biting; the verbs *be-hyldan* and *hyldan* refer specifically to skin flaying, while *hættian* and its variant *behættian* refer to scalping. *Be-hyldan* and *hyldan* are cited in connection with Christian martyrs of the early Church, or used in conjunction with Latin–Old English glossaries. Like *flēan*, all instances of *hættian* and *behættian* refer to Christian martyrs in Ælfric's *Lives of the Saints*.

Hagiographical references to flaying suggest a didactic function, much like other kinds of torment to which a saint might have been subjected. Emphasis on a martyr's painful execution by flaying would evoke a sympathetic response from audiences while further highlighting the unjust and inhumane manner of punishment. Larissa Tracy notes that 'flaying is a symbolic and largely literary punishment', and there is much more significance in visualizing the punishment of flaying through oral or literary tradition, to instil fear, than there is in actually performing it.[12] Descriptions of flaying as a punishment or execution for saints call attention to a martyr's faithfulness in the face of adversity, while also reinforcing the legitimacy of his/her sainthood through the extreme manner of suffering death for his/her faith. This message of loyalty is conveyed 'by looking past the skin to [the] inner truth'.[13] References to flaying within the corpus of Old English appear to function on a purely literary level to emphasize the sacral, rather than suggesting that Anglo-Saxons actually practised human excoriation.

However, despite the lack of material or literary evidence for flaying as punishment in Anglo-Saxon tradition, Lawrence Thompson contends that, throughout the centuries in English history, 'the notion of completely tanned human skins has kept a firm hold on the medical as well as the lay mind'.[14] The corpus of Old English offers some evidence of practical uses for flaying, most specifically as medical treatment. Skin – usually animal skin – was thought to have curative properties. The *Anglo-Saxon Leechbook* recommends porpoise skin as a cure for lunacy. The medical procedure advises: 'Wiþ þon þe mon sie monaþ seoc nim mere swines fel wyrc to swipan swing mid þone man sona bið sel. Amen.' [In case a man be lunatic; take the skin of mereswine *or porpoise*; work it into a whip, swinge the man

---

[12] Tracy, *Torture and Brutality*, p. 164.

[13] Karl Steel, 'Touching Back: Responding to Reading Skin', in *Reading Skin in Medieval Literature and Culture*, ed. Katie L. Walter (New York: Palgrave, 2012), pp. 183–95.

[14] Lawrence S. Thompson, 'Religatum de Pelle Humana', in his *Bibliologia comica; or, Humorous Aspects of the Caparisoning and Conservation of Books* (Hamden, CT: Archon Books, 1968), pp. 119–60 at p. 123.

therewith, soon he will be well. Amen.][15] The skinning of the porpoise is not outlined in detail, but the skin or flesh of mammals was thought to be a potent cure.

The *Leech Book* describes flaying as a means of slicing away 'dead' flesh when a patient's wound develops necrosis:

> ʒif þæt asweartode lic to þon swiþe adeadige þæt þær nan gefelnes on ne sie þonne scealt þu sona eal þæt deade ⁊ þæt ungefelde of asniþan oþ þæt cwice lic. þæt þær na miht þær deadan lices to lafe ne sie þær þe ær ne iren ne fyr gefelde.

> [If the swarthened body be to that high degree deadened that no feeling be thereon, then must thou soon cut away all the dead and the unfeeling *flesh*, as far as the quick, so that there be nought remaining of the dead flesh, which ere felt neither iron nor fire.][16]

On a purely technical level, skin removal in cases of necrosis is 'flaying', although in these instances it carries little symbolism beyond medical necessity. However, the procedure might certainly have involved a technique similar to removing 'live' skin.[17] In most cases, medieval medical discourses of skin and surgery point to established techniques and surgical knowledge passed down from earlier medical practitioners from the

---

[15] *Anglo-Saxon Leechbook*, III.xl, in *Leechdoms, Wortcunning, and Starcraft of Early England: Being a Collection of Documents Illustrating the History of Science in this Country Before the Norman Conquest*, ed. and trans. T. O. Cockayne, 3 vols. (London: Longman, Green, Longman, Roberts & Green, 1864–6; repr. Cambridge: Cambridge University Press, 2012), 2:334. The *Leech Book* is the oldest extant book of medicine in Old English; it survives in London, British Library, MS Royal 12. D. xvii. The manuscript contains three sections: the first two are commonly referred to as *Bald's Leechbook*, and the much shorter third section is called *Leech Book III*. For further information, see: *Bald's Leechbook*, ed. C. E. Wright and R. Quirk (Baltimore: The John Hopkins Press, 1955); and M. L. Cameron, *Anglo-Saxon Medicine* (Cambridge: Cambridge University Press, 1993), pp. 30–5. Apart from a few glimpses into Anglo-Saxon medical practice in the works of Aldhelm of Malmesbury (*c.* 639–709) and the Venerable Bede (*c.* 672/3–735), all surviving Anglo-Saxon medical texts can be dated to the last two centuries of the period. See: Aldhelm, *Enigma xliii*, in *Aldhelmi Opera*, ed. R. Ehwald (Berlin: Apud Weidmannos, 1919), pp. 97–149, and a description of a surgical procedure in Bede's *Historia ecclesiastica gentis Anglorum*, in *Patrologia Latina* 95 (Paris: Migne, 1815–75), 4:19. For an in-depth study of medical texts of the Anglo-Saxon period see: Cameron, *Anglo-Saxon Medicine*; and Stephen Pollington, *Leechcraft: Early English Charms, Plantlore and Healing* (Hockwold-cum-Wilton: Anglo-Saxon Books, 2003).

[16] *Leechdoms*, ed. Cockayne, 2:82–3.

[17] Most notably, see in this volume: Valerie Gramling's '"Flesche withowtyn hyde": The Removal and Transformation of Jesus' Skin in the English Cycle Passion Plays', pp. 240–60.

classical period, but descriptions of the procedures of flaying in Anglo-Saxon medical texts are still relatively rare.[18]

Cutting away rotting skin or tissue was connected with a physical process of cleansing; however, the spiritual purification of an individual could also be inferred from the specific act of removing flesh, thus leaving an individual clean and transparent. The Old English *Blickling Homily* 10 describes the transparency of bodies at the Last Judgement as being almost like that of a looking glass or window: 'þe deadan upstandaþ, biþ þonne se flæschoma ascyred swa glæs, ne mæg ðæs unrihtes beon awiht bedigled' [the dead shall stand up, then shall the body (flesh-garb) be as transparent as glass, nought of its nakedness may be concealed].[19] Jack

---

[18] According to C. Roberts, documentary evidence of surgery suggests that it was used infrequently in Anglo-Saxon England. See: 'Surgery', in *The Blackwell Encyclopeadia of Anglo-Saxon England*, ed. Michael Lapidge *et al.* (Oxford: Wiley, 2001), p. 431. Faye Getz's extensive work on medicine and medical procedures throughout the Middle Ages in England offers no evidence of surgical procedures in the Anglo-Saxon period. See: Faye Getz, *Medicine in the English Middle Ages* (Princeton: Princeton University Press, 1998), p. 47; and Virginia Langum, 'Discerning Skin: Complexion, Surgery and Language in Medieval Confession', in *Reading Skin*, ed. Walter, pp. 141–61. On surgical procedures for head wounds, see: Lisi Oliver's *The Body Legal in Barbarian Law* (Toronto: Toronto University Press, 2011), pp. 84–91. Although surgical techniques are not discussed in Old English literature, surgeons would have practised known surgical procedures, and perhaps new techniques would have developed for those working close to battlefields. Hunters and *flæsc-mangeres* [butchers] would also have had experience with flaying animal skins. On surgical references in Anglo-Saxon medical texts, see: Debby Banham and Christine Voth, 'The Diagnosis and Treatment of Wounds in the Old English Medical Collections: Anglo-Saxon Surgery?' in *Wounds and Wound Repair in Medieval Culture*, ed. Larissa Tracy and Kelly DeVries (Leiden: Brill, 2015), pp. 153–74. For a further discussion of skin removal in medical practice, see in this volume: Jack Hartnell, 'Tools of the Puncture: Skin, Knife, Bone, Hand', pp. 20–50. The most concrete evidence for skin removal of animals in the Anglo-Saxon period comes from manuscript production, although there is some material evidence of deer-skinning after hunting expeditions. See: Eltjo Bu, *Medieval Manuscript Production in the Latin West: Explorations with a Global Database* (Leiden: Brill, 2011); Laurel N. Braswell, *Western Manuscripts from Classical Antiquity to the Renaissance: A Handbook* (New York: Garland, 1981); and Malcolm Beckwith Parkes and Andrew G. Watson, eds., *Medieval Scribes, Manuscripts, and Libraries: Essays Presented to N. R. Ker* (London: Scolar Press, 1978).

[19] *Blickling Homily X*, in *The Blickling Homilies of the Tenth Century*, ed. and trans. Richard Morris, EETS o.s. 58, 63 and 73 (London: N Trübner & Co., 1880; repr. in 1 vol., 1967), pp. 108–11. The concept of skin reflecting a looking glass in Old English poetry is identified and discussed in Jacqueline A. Stodnick and Renée Trilling, 'Before and After Theory: Seeing Through

Hartnell argues that 'like many diagnostic tools in medieval medicine, examination of the skin was as likely to highlight defects in the patient's moral or spiritual integrity as it was to expose more corporeal flaws in the patient's humoral balance or diet'.[20] Thus, peeling away the skin of martyrs reveals their internal goodness and, similarly, eliminating dead skin could remove any spiritual defects. For Anglo-Saxons, then, human flaying was most commonly articulated in hagiographical and liturgical texts that encouraged spiritual contemplation of the inhumane act; it was not carried out as a form of corporal punishment on criminals or enemies, even if they were supposedly guilty of sacrilege.

Continued widespread rebellion brought about the end of Æthelred's reign, and perhaps the fall of the entire kingdom. The king's attention was spread thin as he was forced not only to focus on domestic affairs but on international relations as well. Among the many other issues that plagued his reign were the sometimes volatile relationship with the Danes and the occasional international threat posed by late tenth-century Viking invaders. With the kingdom in disarray by the beginning of the eleventh century, Archbishop Wulfstan (d. 1023) urged that:

> Cristenum cyninge gebyreð on cristenre þeode þat he sy ealswa hit riht is, folces frofer ⁊ rihtwis hyrde ofer cristene heorde [...] ⁊ he sceal mandæde men þreagan þearle [...] ⁊ ægðer he sceal beon mid rihte, ge milde ge reðe [...] Ðæt bið cyninges riht ⁊ cynelic gewuna ⁊ þæt sceal on þeode swyþost gefremian.

> [It is befitting for a Christian king in a Christian nation to be, as is right, the people's comfort and a righteous shepherd over the Christian flock [...] he shall severely punish evil-doing men [...] and according to justice he is to be either merciful or severe. That is the king's right and a kingly practice, and that in a nation shall be most effective.][21]

This is not to suggest, however, that violent corporal punishment was the norm – just the opposite. Nicole Marafioti and Jay Paul Gates argue that 'in the early eleventh century Archbishop Wulfstan of York was confronted with the problem of reconciling principles of Christian mercy with the earthly obligation to punish criminals'.[22] Certainly, Wulfstan endorsed

---

the Body in Early Medieval England', *postmedieval: a journal of medieval cultural studies* 1 (2010): 347–53.

[20] Hartnell, 'Tools of the Puncture', p. 23.

[21] Karl Jost, *Die 'Institutes of Polity, Civil and Ecclesiastical'. Ein Werk Erzbischof Wulfstans von York.* Schweizer anglistische Arbeiten 47 (Bern: Francke Verlag, 1959). I Polity 'Be cynge' 1–9, text G1, pp. 41–6. My translation.

[22] Nicole Marafioti and Jay Paul Gates, Introduction to *Capital and Corporal Punishment*, ed. Gates and Marafioti, p. 1.

punishments for crimes in order to maintain order within the kingdom, but 'in contrast to the laws of previous Anglo-Saxon kings, which required capital punishment for a range of offences, Wulfstan's legislation prescribed non-lethal penalties'.[23] In an attempt to maintain Christian themes of mercy and fairness when dealing with punishable offences, Wulfstan proposed that the penalties should reflect the severity of the crime, so that 'ne forspille for lytlum Godes handgeweorc 7 his agenne ceap, þe he deore geboht' [God's handiwork and his own purchase, which he dearly bought, not be destroyed for small offences].[24] Some surviving Anglo-Saxon records do highlight harsh punishments such as body mutilation and amputating limbs or appendages, but, as Wulfstan's legislation reveals, there was an explicit attempt to balance spiritual and secular priorities when passing sentence.[25] Kathleen Casey explains:

> kings continued to resurrect the good old law that made amends by setting a community back on an even keel. At the same time, as representatives of divine justice, those same kings sought to create a moral climate in which customary law and the Christian faith might coexist in a shared aversion to bloodshed.[26]

Wulfstan's just and objective legislation would most certainly have come as a shock to post-medieval English historians who had constructed an image

---

[23] Ibid.

[24] Æthelred V.3.1, in Felix Liebermann, *Die Gesetze der Angelsachsen*, 3 vols. (Halle, 1903–16). Translation from Marafioti and Gates, Introduction to *Capital and Corporal Punishment*, p. 1.

[25] Penalties and punishment within the Anglo-Saxon period have been the subject of many historical studies, though most studies focus on the late Anglo-Saxon period. Discussion of various crimes and associated punishments involving body mutilation during the later Anglo-Saxon period is found in: T. B. Lambert, 'Theft, Homicide and Crime in Late Anglo-Saxon Law', *Past & Present* 214 (2012): 3–43; Frederick Pollock, 'Anglo-Saxon Law', *English Historical Review* 8 (1893): 239–71; Kathleen Casey, 'Crime and Punishment: Anglo-Saxon Law Codes', in *The Middle Ages in Texts and Texture: Reflections on Medieval Sources*, ed. Jason Glenn (Toronto: University of Toronto Press, 2011), pp. 85–92; Don Brothwell and V. Møller-Christensen, 'Medico-historical Aspects of a Very Early Case of Mutilation', *Danish Medical Bulletin* 10 (1963): 21–7; and Lisi Oliver, 'Genital Mutilation in Medieval Germanic Law', in *Capital and Corporal Punishment*, ed. Gates and Marafioti, pp. 48–73. The promotion of salvation amongst lawmakers prior to Wulfstan is highlighted in Patrick Wormald, 'Archbishop Wulfstan and the Holiness of Society', in his *Legal Culture in the Early Medieval West: Law as Text, Image and Experience* (London: Hambledon Press, 1999), pp. 225–51. For discussion of the theme of Christianity and early Anglo-Saxon law, see: Lisi Oliver, *The Beginnings of English Law* (Toronto: Toronto University Press, 2002), pp. 14–20.

[26] Casey, 'Crime and Punishment', p. 91.

of the pre-Conquest period as one in which merciless punishments were routinely exacted upon criminals. Reformers and Victorians alike believed that this was a brutal and primitive period in English history – a belief that was partly fed by later assumptions of brutality introduced with the Danish conquest of Svein Forkbeard (1013) and his son Cnut (1016), in whose laws *hættian* [scalping] does occur.

Scalping and flaying are separate practices, but both involve the removal of skin in a painful manner, where an individual is alive and feels his skin being removed. W. R. J. Barron explains that scalping was considered an appropriate punishment for a variety of crimes in Anglo-Saxon England.[27] In the laws of King Edmund (r. 939–46) scalp removal is recommended for slaves who commit theft. The code states: 'Et dictum est de seruis: si qui furentur simul, ut senior ex eis capiatur et occidatur uel suspendatur, et aliorum singuli uerberentur ter et excorientur, et truncetur minimus digitus in signum.' [And we have declared with regard to slaves, if a number of them commit theft, their leader shall be captured and slain, or hanged, and each of the others may be scourged three times and have his scalp removed, and his little finger mutilated as a token of his guilt.][28] Additionally, amongst the laws of King Cnut (r. 1016–35), specifically I–II Cnut written by Wulfstan, mutilations are suggested as alternatives to executions for repeated law-breaking. Cnut's lawcode states:

> ⁊ gyf hit ðonne gyt mare weorc geweorht hæbbe, ðonne do man ut his eagan, ⁊ ceorfan of his nose ⁊ earan ⁊ ða uferan lippan oððe hine hættian, swylc ðisra swa man wyle oððe ðonne geræde, ða ðe ðærto rædan sceolon: swa man [sceal] steoran ⁊ eac ðære saule beorgan.

> [And if he has wrought still greater crime, he shall have his eyes put out and his nose and ears and upper lip cut off or his scalp removed, whichever of these penalties is desired or determined upon by those with whom rests the decision of the case; and thus punishment shall be inflicted, while, at the same time, the soul is preserved from injury.][29]

---

[27] W. R. J. Barron, 'The Penalties for Treason in Medieval Life and Literature', *Journal of Medieval History* 7 (1981): 187–202 at p. 190. Barron argues that scalping was a Germanic inheritance. On the Germanic origins of scalping, see: Floyd S. Lear, *Treason in Roman and Germanic Law* (Houston: University of Texas Press, 1965), pp. 159–61; and Jean Hoyoux, 'Reges criniti: chevelures, tonsures et scalps chez les Merovingiens', *Revue belge de philologie et d'histoire* 26 (1948): 479–508.

[28] III Edmund 4, in Liebermann, *Die Gesetze*, 1:191. Trans. A. J. Robertson, *The Laws of the Kings of England from Edmund to Henry I* (Cambridge: Cambridge University Press, 1925), p. 15.

[29] II Cnut 30.5, Liebermann, *Die Gesetze*, 3:334–5. Trans. Robertson, *The Laws of the Kings*, p. 191.

Among the accepted mutilation-punishments a mere fifty years after the Norman Conquest, scalping still appears in the law codes of King Henry I (r. 1068–1135), the *Leges Henrici Primi*, which assert:

> Si quis dominum suum occidat, si capiatur, nullo modo se redimat, set decomatione uel e[uiscer]atione uel ita postremo seuera gentium animaduersione dampnetur, ut diris tormentorum cruciatibus et male mortis infortuniis infelicem prius animam exalasse quam finem doloribus excepisse uideatur et, si posset fieri, remissionis amplius apud inferos inuenisse quam in terra reliquisse protestetur.

> [If anyone kills his lord, then if in his guilt he is seized, he shall in no manner redeem himself but shall be condemned to scalping or disembowelling or to human punishment which in the end is so harsh that while enduring the dreadful agonies of his tortures and the miseries of his vile manner of death he may appear to have yielded up his wretched life before in fact he has won an end to his sufferings, and so that he may declare, if it were possible, that he had found more mercy in hell than had been shown to him on earth.][30]

There are no other references to flaying in surviving Anglo-Saxon law codes, and so scalping in lieu of death seems to have been the only punishment involving skin removal in the latter Anglo-Saxon period. There is also no indication that this punishment was associated with massacre; scalp removal and other mutilations were decreed by the king, so scalping does not seem to offer a sensible narrative connection with the 'Dane-skin' legend, other than to suggest that governing Anglo-Saxon kings sometimes implemented painful penalties involving skin.

The scattered references to flaying in Old English literature speak much less of a gruesome culture, and more of a kingdom attempting to balance secular priorities with religious principles. The 'art' of flaying was a familiar surgical procedure to Anglo-Saxon leeches, or medical practitioners, and the flayed skins themselves carried significance in terms of diagnosis, prognosis and healing. Animal skins were flayed after hunting, as was the custom in neighbouring cultures and beyond; animal skins had practical uses, including vellum production and medicine. Surviving literature suggests that the Anglo-Saxons did not rely on flaying as a type of execution but that, as in most liturgical texts from the period, references to it demonstrate a cruel and sadistic manner of death inflicted on the

---

[30] L. J. Downer, ed. and trans., *Leges Henrici Primi* (Oxford: Clarendon Press, 1972), 75.1 at pp. 232–3. A now-lost code of Edgar recorded by Lantfred in *Translatio et miracula de S. Swithuni* alludes to scalping as a punishment as well. Patrick Wormald, *The Making of English Law: King Alfred to the Twelfth Century*, vol. 1: *Legislation and its Limits* (Oxford: Blackwell, 2001), pp. 125–6. Cf. Valerie Allen, 'When Compensation Costs an Arm and a Leg', in *Capital and Corporal Punishment*, ed. Gates and Marafioti, pp. 17–33 at p. 18.

godly. Nevertheless, these references likely played little part in shaping the conclusions drawn by historians between the seventeenth and nineteenth centuries regarding Anglo-Saxon England; rather, there was often a vested interest in bolstering the Petrarchan view of the period as dark and savage.

Despite the lack of literary and material evidence to suggest any verifiable practice of human flaying during the period, the 'Dane-skin' legend persisted throughout post-medieval England up until the early twentieth century. Examining the legend's continuity, from its first written occurrence in the seventeenth century until the height of 'medievalism' in England in the mid-nineteenth century, reveals how the anachronistic view of the Anglo-Saxon period and the accompanying 'Dane-skin' myth was used in a variety of ways to promote different ideals. The myth was malleable; it was used in some instances throughout the seventeenth, eighteenth and nineteenth centuries to perpetuate the narrative of a savage past, while at other times it was used to promote an English nationalist agenda serving as a model for nationalist sentiments of later centuries.

Seventeenth- and eighteenth-century antiquarians collected some of the surviving leather fragments of the skins fastened to a number of church doors across England, investigating the 'Dane-skin' myth and developing theories about the skins' origins. Over the next few centuries in post-medieval England, a legend emerged suggesting that these fragments were from Danes apprehended before the Norman Conquest.[31] According to Michael Swanton, leather lining on wooden doors was a common practice in medieval England; however, seventeenth- and eighteenth-century antiquarians who discovered the remains posited that it was human skin beneath the hinges, locks and strap-work of some church doors.[32] The mythology of the door-skins cultivated an image of England's dark and

---

[31] There are other instances of human skins nailed to doors, most notably Julian the Apostate, who was flayed for spiritual treason. Legend has it that he was flayed post-mortem on the order of the Persian king Sapor, and his skin was then nailed to the palace door. See: John Lydgate, *Fall of Princes*, ed. Henry Bergen. EETS e.s. 121–4 (London: Oxford University Press, 1918–19), ll. 1632–8.

[32] See: Michael Swanton, '"Dane-Skins": Excoriation in Early England', *Folklore* 87 (1976): 21–8. On the history of bookbinding and leather-making from human skin, see: Thompson, 'Religatum de Pelle Humana'. In this volume, see: Perry Neil Harrison, 'Anthropodermic Bibliopegy in the Early Modern Period', pp. 366–83. For a discussion on the various functions of skin throughout Western history and culture, see: Steven Connor, *The Book of Skin* (Ithaca, NY: Cornell University Press, 2004). The pseudonymous author or compiler, known as Theophilus Presbyter (*c.* 1070–1125), of a Latin text detailing the medieval arts including door-coverings describes wooden doors being covered with untanned hide. Theophilus mentions that leather covered all manner of objects in the Middle Ages, from altar panels and shields to doors and furniture. See: Theophilus, *De diversis artibus*, ed. C. R. Dodwell (Oxford: Clarendon Press, 1961), pp. 17–19.

violent past, which, by the latter half of the eighteenth century, played into romanticized accounts of Anglo-Saxon social and political structures that historians were beginning to document.[33] Between the seventeenth and nineteenth centuries, the English responses to the skins on the church doors reflect developing or changing socio-political ideologies concerning national liberty, and reveal a nationalizing agenda centred on an English 'race' and dependent upon an appropriation and refashioning of the past.

Although the legend may have passed down orally for centuries, Pepys provides the earliest written record of the story about the skin on one of the doors. On 10 April 1661 he wrote: 'To Rochester, and there saw the Cathedral; then away thence observing the great doors of the church, which *they say* was covered with the skins of the Danes.'[34] Pepys' account reveals that 'they' (presumably the English residents in Rochester) had an established lore that the skin was not just human, but specifically Danish. Although the oral origin of the myth is lost, Pepys' early record reflects a continuing belief that corporal punishment and torture were inflicted regularly on enemies of the Anglo-Saxons. These ideas are entirely unfounded; however, seventeenth-century views of the Anglo-Saxon

---

[33] For example, see: Catherine Macaulay's *History of England*, written 1763–83, and Gilbert Stuart's *View of Society in Europe*, written in 1782. See: Macaulay, *The History of England from the Accession of James the Second, 'Before the Restoration'* (London: Printed for J. Nourse, R. and J. Dodsley and W. Johnston, 1763–83); and Stuart, *A View of Society in Europe, in its Progress from Rudeness to Refinement* (London: Printed for J. Murray, 1782). The growing popularity of 'historical fiction' about pre-Conquest England and the Conquest itself roughly coincided with the revival of antiquarian and historical interest in Saxon England. Billie Melman argues that 'novelists could make use of translated chronicles and poetry (both Anglo-Saxon and Nordic), and legal documents, which poured from the presses of the antiquarian and ecclesiological societies, and later, the Rolls Series'. Billie Melman, 'Claiming the Nation's Past: The Invention of an Anglo-Saxon Tradition', *Journal of Contemporary History* 26 (1991): 575–95 at p. 580. This revival of interest coincided with there being an increasing number of materials collected by antiquarians, growing access to the surviving Anglo-Saxon texts, and expanding knowledge of Old English. Still, antiquarians, especially in the eighteenth century, 'valued manuscripts for their aesthetic rather than historical value'. Elizabeth Fay, *Romantic Medievalism* (New York: Palgrave, 2002), p. 12. See also: Laura Kendrick, 'The Science of Imposture and the Professionalization of Medieval Occitan Literary Studies', in *Medievalism and the Modernist Temper*, ed. R. Howard Bloch and Stephen G. Nichols (Baltimore: Johns Hopkins University Press, 1996), pp. 95–126 at p. 101.

[34] *The Diary of Samuel Pepys*, ed. Robert Latham *et al.* (London: G. Bell and Sons, 1970), p. 70. Emphasis added. The skin on the Rochester Cathedral door was gone by the time Pepys viewed the church, as he only refers to previous viewing of the actual skin.

period suggest a reimagining of the past to suit contemporary political
agendas. Sir James Holt highlights the endeavours of seventeenth-century
political reformers to connect English constitutional liberties to *Magna
Carta*. This interest in employing the past to reform the nation was further
emphasized in what Holt describes as 'an earlier antiquarian movement
in the late twelfth century [where] monks were developing a new interest
in the English past to replace the wary hostility with which they had
regarded the traditions of the conquered English hitherto'.[35] Julia Crick
notes that 'from at least the seventeenth century to the twentieth historians,
politicians and polemicists sought and found liberty in the pre-Conquest
past'.[36]

Reformers were not only concerned with religious restructuring, and
did not simply select negative examples to bolster a religious agenda. In an
address to parliament in June 1610, Thomas Hedley (*c.* 1569–1637) defended
the ancient freedom of the subjects of England, praising pre-Conquest
England for establishing national liberty. He remarked that he did 'not take
Magna Carta to be a new grant or statute, but a restoring and confirming
of the ancient laws and liberties of the kingdom, which by the conquest
before had been much impeached or obscured'.[37] There are few, if any,
seventeenth- or eighteenth-century monographs highlighting Anglo-Saxon
development, yet the English in these centuries constructed their own
narrative of the earlier period. Reformers like Hedley hastened away from
the 'Dark Ages' narrative and constructed idealized views of the Anglo-
Saxon period to connect contemporary English identity with its Anglo-
Saxon roots. However, these seventeenth-century connections based on
'liberty' were entirely superficial. Crick argues:

> This kind of liberty belongs to a cultural and conceptual universe
> remote from those of later constructions of personal and
> constitutional liberty. It embraces privilege licensed by kings, a
> right claimed for institutions, an abstraction of a sort but more
> circumscribed and concrete in nature than the freedoms later
> claimed. But Anglo-Saxon liberty in its medieval guise resembles the
> later manifestations of liberty claims in one particular: it appears to
> function as an origin myth, a sought-after quality anachronistically
> attributed to pre-Conquest origins.[38]

---

[35] James Clarke Holt, 'The Origins of the Constitutional Tradition in England',
in *Magna Carta and Medieval Government* (London: Hambledon Press,
1985), pp. 1–22 at p. 8.

[36] Julia Crick, '"Pristina Libertas": Liberty and the Anglo-Saxons Revisited',
Transactions of the Royal Historical Society 14 (2004): 47–71 at p. 47.

[37] Thomas Hedley, *Parliament of 1610, Proceedings in Parliament 1610*, ed.
Elizabeth Reed Foster (New Haven: Yale University Press, 1966), p. 190.

[38] Crick, 'Pristina Libertas', p. 49.

The evolution of the English judicial system and the formation of laws of government were often inspired by retrospective analysis, not only by looking back to Roman law, but also by seeking examples from various episodes in the pre-Norman era. This emphasis on the past was often ideologically motivated. While reflection on negative episodes of governance during the Anglo-Saxon period could bolster a current political agenda, individuals and groups could also choose from a myriad of examples where the Anglo-Saxons exemplified good governance. Billie Melman contends:

> The notion of an 'ancient' national constitution loomed large in discussions on the modern one even before the seventeenth century. The Saxon character of representative government, of English freedoms and of the limited monarchy, are motifs which recur in the writings of constitutionalists – Whig and radical alike.[39]

Analysing Anglo-Saxon England for what it was, instead of reimagining it anachronistically, would not have suited the frame of mind of a seventeenth-century Englishman searching for connections and links between his present day and the pre-Conquest era. This comparative historical consciousness is what Jerome McGann calls 'double perspectivism' and involves making the past a living presence.[40] For seventeenth-century viewers of the skin fragments on the doors, the presence of the fragments and any subsequent acceptance of them as human skin were material evidence of Anglo-Saxon fortitude and moral justice in punishing invaders for crimes against their community and Church. This tangible evidence was a visual reminder of early English defenders of the state and faith, to which seventeenth-century reformers could look for inspiration. The belief that the skin fragments were from pagan Danes symbolized the living qualities of the past and spoke to the narrative of seventeenth-century reformers, who could use the material evidence to promote concepts of liberty and racial purity by emphasizing Anglo-Saxon justice against foreign marauders.

Historians and antiquarians in the subsequent two centuries who were aware of other tales of skins on church doors throughout southern England embraced Pepys' description of the skin fragments on the door of Rochester Cathedral, which seemed to validate the legitimacy of the legend. Verification of the skins as human reaffirmed this anachronistic image of the Anglo-Saxon period, and many nineteenth-century antiquarians and historians documented their findings or reiterated the legend in the

---

[39] Melman, 'Claiming the Nation's Past', p. 578.

[40] Jerome McGann, *The Beauty of Inflections: Literary Investigations in Historical Method and Theory* (Oxford: Clarendon Press, 1988), p. 266.

early volumes of *Notes & Queries*.[41] One particularly detailed account comes from Duffield William Coller's 1861 *People's History of Essex*, which describes the origin of the skin on the door of a church in Copford as follows:

> Some Danes, saith this authority, robbed the church – considered one of the most heinous of crimes in the mediaeval ages – and were subjected to the fearful process of flaying alive, their skins, carefully preserved, being thus affixed to the door as a terrible memento of the wretches who had dared to raise their sacrilegious hands against the house of God.[42]

[41] See: *Notes & Queries*, 2nd series 2 (1856): 119, 157, 250–2, 299, 419; 3rd series 8 (1865): 463, 524; 9 (1866): 309, 422; 10 (1866): 277, 341; 4th series 11 (1873): 138–9, 292, 373; 4th S. VII (1899): 246. All the churches cited in the *N&Q* excerpts have some architectural origins in the Anglo-Saxon period or shortly thereafter, although the churches have undergone massive reconstruction and many of them were re-established centuries later. Further still, many of the doors were dilapidated and, thus, replaced. Dendrochronology tests on the tree ring of the wooden door of Hadstock church conducted by D. Miles and M. Bridge revealed that the most recent ring dated to 1025. The scientists estimated that construction for the church door ranged between the years 1044 and 1067. See: M. C. Bridge and D. H. Miles, 'The Tree-Ring Dating of the North Door, St Botolph's Church, Hadstock, Essex', *Oxford Dendrochronology Lab Rep* 30 (unpublished 2003). The door of the church of Rochester dates to the Anglo-Saxon period, but it deteriorated and was replaced in the Anglo-Norman period. Worcester Cathedral was founded in the seventh century and the present building was begun in 1084; however, the doors were replaced in the fourteenth century, so any skin samples attached to the door were newer, some three-hundred years after the Anglo-Saxon period and, thus, could not validate the myths. Architectural evidence indicates that the church in Copford was founded *c.* 1100. The church door at East Thurrock was built some time in the eleventh century, possibly before 1066. Southwark Cathedral was first built in the early seventh century, but the church was later refounded in 1106 by two Norman knights. Westminster Abbey first opened in 1090. See also: Albert Way, 'Some Notes on the Tradition of Flaying, Inflicted in Punishment of Sacrilege: The Skin of the Offender being Affixed to the Church-Doors', *Archaeological Journal* 5 (1848): 185–92.

[42] Duffield William Coller, *The People's History of Essex: Comprising A Narrative Of Public And Political Events In The County, From The Earliest Ages To The Present Time* (Chelmsford: Meggy and Chalk, 1861), p. 555. Other early records containing slightly altered versions of the legend were mentioned in: John Dart, *Westmonasterium Or The History and Antiquities of the Abbey Church of St. Peters Westminster* (London: Carington Bowles, 1723) 1:64; William Stukeley, *Itinerarium Curiosum* (London: Messrs. Baker and Leigh, 1724), p. 75; Richard Newcourt, *Repertorium Ecclesiasticum Parochiale Londinense* (London: Benj. Motte, 1708), p. 191; and Alfred H. Burne, *The Battlefields of England* (London: Methuen, 1973), p. 97.

Neither Anglo-Saxon nor Norse sources verify Coller's claim; however, this excerpt precisely articulates the persistence of the legend that had first been reported 200 years before, in Pepys' diary.[43] By the time Coller wrote his account, in the inaugural years of the Victorian period, the Viking raid narrative, telling of Danes ravaging Æthelred II's kingdom and his people, had strong significance in the English psyche.[44] By suggesting that the skins on the doors were not simply human but, more specifically, 'Danish-skins', Coller implies that the English were able to punish some Danes for attacking the English coast. Coller and other historians of his generation who continued to claim that the church doors bore 'flayed Danes' were, in a sense, exacting revenge on behalf of the Anglo-Saxons through the continued use of the legend. The sustained belief in the legend was useful, as Elizabeth Fay argues, because it allowed the English 'to view history as a pastness that orients the future'.[45] Essentially, the legend offered the English, between the seventeenth and nineteenth centuries, some level of justice against the tenth-century marauding Danes, thus further emphasizing a sense of continued and unmixed, or 'pure', 'English' identity rooted in Anglo-Saxon England, rather than an imperial 'Britishness' that extended across the globe. The late nineteenth-century English prime minister Benjamin Disraeli noted how the past alone could energize an atrophied nation; a cleverly manipulated version of the past, or even an entirely invented past, 'explains the present' and 'moulds the future'.[46] By the nineteenth century, and certainly in the previous two centuries, dilettanti and scholars alike were keen to believe the myth of Danish captives being tortured and publicly displayed because it helped reaffirm their national identity as ancestrally 'English', denying any affinity with the marauding Vikings. Moreover, the flayed 'Dane' allowed the English

[43] It should be noted that not all nineteenth-century antiquarians took the story of Dane-skins as fact. The local Hadstock antiquarian R. C. Neville maintained measured scepticism of the theory. In his book *Antiqua Explorata* (London, 1847), he commented: 'Of course so pretty a tale finds ready credence, and not for worlds would we bring it into disrepute, merely insinuating that on the fragment of the ancient portal, removed last year to make way for one at least weather tight, there is certainly something tawny in hue and coarse in substance; but whether the parentage so flattering to human vanity derives thence confirmation, we will not determine', pp. 34–5.

[44] For a thorough historical examination of Victorian views of the Middle Ages see: Alice Chandler's *A Dream of Order: The Medieval Ideal in Nineteenth-Century Literature* (Lincoln: University of Nebraska Press, 1970); and Matthews, *Medievalism*, pp. 13–45.

[45] Fay, *Romantic Medievalism*, p. 8.

[46] Benjamin Disraeli, *Sybil, or the Two Nations* (London: Henry Colburn Publisher, 1845), p. 496.

historians in those post-medieval centuries to continue the false narrative that portrayed the Danes as violent raiders who deserved an equally violent punishment during the 'Dark Ages'.[47]

With the post-medieval belief that the skins and their fragments were genuine 'Dane-skins', the English could continue a historical narrative about national character and race as unifying elements in English history, even if those hides *actually* belonged to cattle. The bovine skins were placed on the church doors much later than people throughout the seventeenth to nineteenth centuries believed; however, the exposed skin on the cathedral doors, or the fragments beneath the hinges, allowed the English to develop and continue a story that promoted an image of their own remote past. This reifying exercise in English identity politics is a retrospective act of defiance against the Danes who ruled England for nearly fifty years. The skin narratives functioned as flags of resistance to colonial domination – an idea that persisted post-Conquest when the invaders were no longer Danes, but Norman French who had their own origins in the Viking past. This ethnic association was poignant and pressing in nineteenth-century England as the English searched to identify their roots as purely 'English' in opposition to France, with which it was once again at war. The study of race and racial differences was a fascination for scientists and ethnographers throughout the eighteenth and nineteenth centuries, and so the mere 'fact' that the skin was from a Dane emphasized 'Otherness' to those viewing the skins or hearing the legend. As long as there was an assertion of Vikings as barbaric, pagan raiders, the fantasy that the skins on the doors were both human and foreign could persist. This anachronistic medievalism offered a way of evading a more factual image of 'Others' in England who had ancestral ties to the country.[48] Despite the long history of invasion and

---

[47] Romantic interest in Anglo-Saxon England was coupled with rediscoveries of Scandinavian artifacts and treasures in Iceland by Scandinavian scholars beginning in the seventeenth century. English historians, too, took interest in the Nordic sagas and undoubtedly constructed ideas of the 'Viking' past as a result of reading Norse tales. Although there is no recorded evidence that the Danes practised the punishment of flaying, there are punishments in the Norse sagas that feed into this perception; one highly contested example is the 'blood-eagle'. However, it seems likely that the antiquarians and historians in the Reformation and Romantic periods in England took the blood eagle and other violent acts described in Norse sagas more literally, as these images reinforced the portrayal of the Vikings as aggressively violent pagans. See: Roberta Frank, 'Viking Atrocity and Skaldic Verse: The Rite of the Blood-Eagle', *English Historical Review* 99 (1984): 332–43; and Susanne Kries, 'English: Danish Rivalry and the Mutilation of Alfred in the Eleventh-Century "Chronicle" Poem "The Death of Alfred"', *Journal of English and Germanic Philology* 104 (2005): 31–53. See also: Tracy, *Torture and Brutality*, pp. 70–131.

[48] The nineteenth-century historians Edward A. Freeman and William Stubbs pursued a romantic quality intrinsic to the national character since the

integration in England, imagining a direct connection to the Anglo-Saxon past free from alien associations cleansed the English psyche of the 'foreign' elements that, in fact, constituted the English population.

In addition to the continued portrayal of both the Anglo-Saxons and the Norsemen in ways that promoted English identity and national sociopolitical progress, the persistent Dane-skin myth also reflects the post-medieval fascination with skin. There is no physical evidence to support Coller's description of flayed Danes; however, his account reflects a nineteenth-century reimagining of an episode within the St Brice's Day massacre and draws on this fictitious narrative to reassert a strong interest in ideas about flaying in general. Certainly, an interest in skin and the body was most commonly connected with early medicine and dissection, but the eighteenth-century Anglo-Irish satirist Jonathan Swift's *A Modest Proposal* suggests human flaying as a means of social commentary. Swift's essay proposes that the impoverished Irish reduce famine by offering fattened Catholic children as food and clothing to the wealthy. He remarks, hyperbolically, that the bodies could be sold at English meat markets where the skins 'artificially dressed will make admirable gloves for ladies and summer boots for fine gentlemen'.[49] Swift's satire is meant to repulse his readership; he specifically targets the Anglo-Irish upper-classes as vampires who consumed the bodies of the poor through extortionate rents and discrimination, suggesting that they may as well do it literally as a means of employment and to bolster their sense of self-worth. But some scholars argue that Swift was merely drawing upon common practice. According to Swanton, 'the use of human skin for such purposes as proposed in his essay is well documented in Swift's England'.[50] In fact, there is a record of the flaying of a peasant boy in Leicestershire *c.* 1700; however, this type of judicial sentence seems remarkable.[51] Still, innumerable reports in *Notes & Queries* confirm that the skin of notorious malefactors – removed post mortem – was tanned and sold to the public throughout the 1700s.[52] As Perry Harrison explains, anthropodermic bibliopedigy –

establishment of the English as a nation. This idea of 'Englishness' as a race is discussed in: Hugh A. MacDougall, *Racial Myth in English History: Trojans, Teutons and Anglo-Saxons* (Montreal: Harvest House, 1982).

[49] Jonathan Swift, *Prose Works*, ed. Herbert Davis (Oxford: Blackwell, 1955) p. 112.

[50] Swanton, ' "Dane-Skins" ', p. 23.

[51] In ordinary judicial contexts, executed felons traditionally were left to the disposal of the executioner.

[52] The process of skinning humans and using the tanned skin to make various items, including wallets and book covers, in the West as late as the early twentieth century is discussed in detail in Thompson, 'Religatum de Pelle Humana', pp. 131–4. The pieces of skin were sold in small portions as souvenirs, or in larger pieces suitable for book-binding or making clothing accessories like belts, gloves and shoes. This phenomenon was

binding books in human skin – was a morbid novelty in the eighteenth century and a few examples still survive.[53] The practice of flaying human skin in Enlightenment-era England further demonstrates this 'double-perspectivism', as the Dane-skin narrative validated, through the skin-fragments themselves, an eighteenth-century fascination with skin. The eighteenth-century English misperception that the Anglo-Saxon period was fraught with violence and savage punishments is reflected in the legend of the door-skins, and the material evidence (scant as it was) apparently reaffirmed age-old misconceptions of pre-Conquest England.

Having the actual 'evidence' on the doors during the eighteenth century was significant for early scholars, and, with the development of microscopy in the early nineteenth century, several surviving skin samples were procured for testing. In 1848 fragments of skin taken from beneath the strap-work of Worcester Cathedral's north door were examined by the pioneer histologist John Quekett (1815–61), conservator at the Royal College of Surgeons, at the request of antiquarian Albert Way (1805–74). Upon observation, Quekett concluded that the skin was human and most likely 'taken from some part of the body of a light-haired person, where little hair grows'.[54] With no sound method of scientific analysis to completely verify the skins' origins, the histologist relied most heavily on microscopic analysis of surviving hairs on the surface. In the excitement of the revelation, Quekett and Way overlooked a chronological discrepancy in their argument: they failed to consider that the cathedral's north door dates to the fourteenth century.[55]

As material evidence continued to deteriorate and/or disappear, confirming whether the skins were human or not became more difficult. Quekett examined additional skin fragments from the north door of Hadstock church and the south door of the nearby church in Copford. In both cases Quekett concluded the fragments were human skin. He reported that the skin from Hadstock was 'in all probability from the

---

not restricted to England. Other countries, including France, also practised human flaying, and one such episode is graphically recounted in the first chapter of Michel Foucault's *Discipline and Punish: The Birth of the Prison*, trans. Alan Sheridan (Harmondsworth: Penguin, 1979).

[53] Harrison, 'Anthropodermic Bibliopegy', p. 367.

[54] John Quekett, 'On the Value of the Microscope in the Determination of Minute Structures of a Doubtful Nature', *Trans. of the Microscopical Society of London* 2 (1849): 152–3.

[55] Swanton argues that all the church doors can be dated to centuries following the Anglo-Saxon period. Structural evidence in Rochester and Hadstock offer the only possibility that the doors may have been cut down or re-inserted from previous Saxon buildings; however, Swanton notes that there is historical documentation stating that the building was in a state of considerable disrepair by the time of the Norman rebuilding. See '"Dane-Skins"', pp. 23–4 n. 28.

back of the Dane, and that he was a fair-haired person', and that the Copford fragment was similar except the hairs on the fragment were 'more numerous, larger and darker than before'.[56] As a result of these claims, many other unsolicited skin fragments were sent to Quekett, such as a piece from the door of the church at East Thurrock, Essex. Subsequently, Quekett identified each fragment as human skin; however, further research on the surviving fragments debunked his claim. As founder of the Royal Microscopical Society (1839), Quekett seems to have been a formidable histologist in his day. It is difficult to determine whether previous knowledge of the myth led him to conclude that the fragments were human; however, given that more modern results have also been inconclusive, it is clearly difficult to acquire concrete evidence from microscopy alone. Considering his detailed research, Quekett seems to base his findings on the scientific evidence available to him rather than searching for evidence to suit the claim that the fragments were human.[57]

Since the time of Quekett's preliminary study, there has been a proliferation of scientific analyses relating to archaeological material evidence, though the skin fragments in question have deteriorated a great deal since the early investigations in the mid-nineteenth century. While some early twentieth-century historians accepted Quekett's conclusion, most of the material evidence that Quekett initially examined is gone; his collection was destroyed by German bombing raids during World War II.[58] This effort to validate the 'Dane-skin' myth suggests a deep-rooted desire to create another link between the remote past and post-medieval England, revealing, as Melman argues, an early English historian and antiquarian 'obsess[ion] with unities and with [enforcing] the "great lines" in British history'.[59]

---

[56] Ibid., p. 24. King Cnut (*c.* 985–1035), who governed Denmark, England, Norway and parts of Sweden, was said to have founded the church in Hadstock in 1020. As a Dane, it seems unlikely that Cnut would have left the skin of one of his compatriots on the door. See: Burne, *The Battlefields of England*, p. 97.

[57] William Quekett, *My Sayings and Doings, with Reminiscences of my Life* (London: K. Paul, Trench, 1888), p. 117. There is at least one other report on a skin fragment that was determined to be human at Pembridge in Herefordshire. The record reveals the conclusion of the investigation, but does not identify the histologist who conducted the examination. Swanton queries whether the 'expert' might have been Quekett. Swanton, '"Dane-Skins"', n. 38. See also: *Transcript of the Woolhope Naturalists Field Club* 1 (1901–2), p. 142.

[58] The cataloguer of the collection of the Royal College of Surgeons in 1923, Sir Arthur Keith, accepted Quekett's identifications without reservation. See: *Catalogue of the Hunterian Collection in the Museum of the Royal College of Surgeons* (London: Livingstone, 1923).

[59] Melman, 'Claiming the Nation's Past', p. 576.

Other fragments besides those owned by Quekett are still available and were examined in the latter half of the twentieth century. As Swanton explains, there have been considerable developments in analytical techniques since Quekett's pioneering investigations. Particularly, 'with respect to skin identifications, modern diagnosis would place emphasis less on the character of individual hairs than on the grouping of follicles – the hair of human skin being placed at random and at considerably lower density than that of other animals'.[60] M. L. Ryder of the Animal Breeding Research Organization at Roslin examined a skin fragment in 1959, concluding that the follicles completely lacked pigment and were arranged more densely than could be expected for a human scalp.[61] Considering that the original account claims that the skin was from the 'back of a Dane', it is fair to say that skin from the scalp would have hardly covered a large medieval church door. Ryder's findings provided further scientific evidence debunking the 'Dane-skin' myth. In 1970, Ronald Reed, a researcher from the Department of Food and Leather Science at Leeds University, examined a second piece from the former vestry door at Westminster. In both instances the skin was determined to be most likely cowhide. However, Reed also examined additional fragments from Copford, and his conclusion that *some* may indeed be human gave weight to earlier claims.[62] Reed reported that 'the grain pattern and the hair distribution

---

[60] Swanton, '"Dane-Skins"', p. 25. Twentieth-century methods of ancient skin analysis are further explored in Don Brothwell and E. Higgs, eds., *Science in Archaeology*, 2nd edn (New York: Thames & Hudson, 1969), pp. 539ff. For discussions on a range of newer methods for analysing ancient skin, including biomolecular, isotopic and laser ablation-inductively coupled plasma-mass spectronometry, see: Michael Glascock, Robert J. Speakman and Rachel Popelka-Filcoff, eds., *Archaeological Chemistry: Analytical Techniques and Archaeological Interpretation* (Washington, DC: American Chemical Society, 2007); and Joseph Lambert, *Traces of the Past: Unraveling the Secrets of Archaeology through Chemistry* (Reading: Helix Books, 1977), pp. 214–58. For select studies relating to DNA sequencing on archaeological finds, see: Brian Kemp, Cara Munroe and David Glenn Smith, 'Extraction and Analysis of DNA from Archaeological Specimens', in *Archaeological Chemistry*, ed. Glascock *et al.*, pp. 78–98; A. M. Pollard *et al.*, 'Sprouting Like Cockle amongst the Wheat: The St Brice's Day Massacre and the Isotopic Analysis of Human Bones From St John's College, Oxford', *Oxford Journal of Archaeology* 31 (2012): 83–102; Martin Jones, *The Molecule Hunt: Archaeology and the Hunt for Ancient DNA* (London: Allen Lane, 2001); and Els Jehaes, *Optimisation of Methods and Procedures for the Analysis of mtDNA Sequences and their Applications in Molecular Archaeological and Historical Finds* (Leuven: Leuven University Press, 1998).

[61] Ryder reported his findings in personal communication with Swanton. See: Swanton, '"Dane-Skins"', p. 25 and n. 43.

[62] Ronald Reed, *Ancient Skins, Parchments and Leathers* (London: Seminar Press, 1972), pp. 285–7. It should be noted that analysing the size of human

corresponds closely to human skin, for cattle, sheep, goat and pig are of a different character'.[63] He concluded that the thickness of the fragment was correct for human skin, most likely from a man with light or greying hair.[64] Reed's final conclusion was that the majority of the fragments were bovine, but that some of the Copford fragments were 'likely to be of human origin'.[65] Although each observation of the skin through a microscopic lens might have been as thorough as possible in 1970, there was still no way of establishing with complete certainty that any of the fragments were human skin because further tests involving chemical analysis were not undertaken. In the late 1970s, Swanton called for a re-evaluation of the surviving evidence using modern scientific methods and argued that the concept of excoriated human remains displayed on church doors during the early medieval period could not be dismissed.[66]

Since Swanton's appeal, DNA testing has come to the forefront of investigative research and has become an invaluable tool of analysis in areas of forensic studies, nanotechnology, history and anthropology. In 2001, DNA testing was carried out on the Hadstock skin fragment by Alan Cooper, an expert in ancient DNA. Cooper ran a number of tests in an attempt to isolate any identifiable human markers.[67] There was no trace of human DNA and further testing established that the skin was, in fact, cowhide. This DNA test definitively proved the skin's origin and ended a nearly millennium-old legend that may have persisted at length because of an anachronistic view of the Anglo-Saxon period and a misunderstanding

---

hair on the skin is not necessarily a straightforward matter, because there is variation of hair-follicle size and distribution in different areas of the body, and without the proper investigative tools or experience hairs from other land mammals such as cows could be mistaken for human hairs (as was the case with the Dane-skins). For an evaluation and quantification of follicular variations on different areas of the body, see: Nina Otberg *et al.*, 'Variations of Hair Follicle Size and Distribution in Different Body Sites', *Journal of Investigative Dermatology* 112 (2004): 14–19.

[63] Reed, *Ancient Skins*, p. 286.

[64] Reed confirmed his findings in personal communications with Swanton. Swanton '"Dane-Skins"', describes the Copford skin as being relatively thick, which indicated 'a reasonably mature as distinct from a young person; and traces of pigment confirmed that he had in fact been fair-haired as Quekett supposed' (p. 26).

[65] Reed, *Ancient Skins*, p. 286.

[66] The chemical legacy of humans is present in bodily remains. Perhaps the skins could have undergone archaeological chemistry investigations used by anthropologists to determine whether there were human markers in the skin. See: Lambert, *Traces of the Past*, esp. chap. 8.

[67] The DNA test, conducted at the University of Oxford, was done in connection with the 2001 BBC documentary series entitled *Blood of the Vikings*.

of the complex relationship and interactions between the Anglo-Saxons and the Scandinavians throughout the tenth and eleventh centuries.[68]

This persistent mythology highlights a desire for retrospective vengeance on the part of the post-medieval English as they re-imagined Anglo-Saxon retribution for Danish invasion and sacrilege in the supposed skins of flayed Danes nailed to church doors. At times the skins and fragments were used to bolster a narrative of savagery and violence, but between the seventeenth and nineteenth centuries the 'Dane skins' served as tangible evidence of a connection between the English and their distant Anglo-Saxon ancestors.[69] Modern Englishmen could see in this reimagined past an adherence to justice, law and Christianity that mirrored their perception of themselves. However, while the doors could be traced to the medieval period, there is no way to confirm the function of the door-skins. They could simply have been fastened on the doors to provide insulation, with no didactic function for medieval onlookers. This is not the case in the subsequent centuries, when the fictitious story, interwoven with the displayed skins, symbolized the sobering reality of that brutal episode in English history, the St Brice's Day massacre. There is no evidence to support the myth of human skins on the medieval church doors; however, the symbolism and shock value of those skins made them a powerful propaganda tool over the centuries, satisfying various cultural, political and religious agendas.

The 'Dane-skin' myth promoted a false perspective of the Anglo-Saxon period, but one that was certainly appealing because it aroused the imaginations of the post-medieval English. The absence of much surviving material from the Anglo-Saxon period presents a sense of remoteness, and this lack of sources (as opposed to the substantial amount of surviving post-Conquest medieval literature) is what allowed for the historical narrative of the pre-Norman era to be rewritten with imaginative vivacity by later historiographers. What complicated the post-medieval view of the Anglo-Saxon period was the changing socio-political and religious landscape during the seventeenth, eighteenth and

---

[68] Though our scientific methods of analysis may ultimately prove no more definitive than were those of the nineteenth century, it does seem unlikely that DNA sequencing showing evidence of cowhide will some day prove to be human DNA.

[69] This is not to suggest that the image of the pre-Conquest era as a violent and dark part in English history began in the mid-seventeenth century. As previously mentioned, the image was already well established through Petrarch's influential view. The Elizabethans further established Petrarch's view of the Anglo-Saxon period. See: Rebecca Brackmann, *The Elizabethan Invention of Anglo-Saxon England: Laurence Nowell, William Lambarde, and the Study of Old English* (Cambridge: D. S. Brewer, 2012); and Robert Allen Rouse, *The Idea of Anglo-Saxon England in Middle English Romance* (Cambridge: D. S. Brewer, 2005).

nineteenth centuries in England, and a desire to either connect with, or disconnect from, the Anglo-Saxon historical narrative. The skins on the doors were transformed into a historical fiction not unlike any other of the remote past that reconstructs the lives of ordinary people. The post-medieval English were preoccupied with definitions of what it meant to be 'English'. Persistent belief in the 'skinned Dane' contributed to that debate, and partially countered what the English acknowledged to be the realities of Æthelred's shortcomings against foreign aggressors, as it pointed to a fictitious moment of victory and justice for the early 'English' people. The 'flayed Dane' myth spoke to the spirit of the English in post-medieval England, reminding them that their Anglo-Saxon forefathers were at times much akin to themselves. The image of the 'Dane-skin' myth supplemented a 'nationalist' or 'patriotic' agenda, while the belief that the skins were those of flayed Danes added to a growing fascination with race. Thus, the 'Dane-skin' legend contributed to the origin myth of the English. The Anglo-Saxons as a nation and 'race' played heavily in political discourse throughout the post-medieval centuries, and the remoteness of the pre-Norman era was often reconstructed to include fictitious narratives to promote political messages, whether they be ones of patriotism, imperialism or something else. Such is the case of the 'Dane-skin' myth, which would have undoubtedly appealed on account of its national sentiment.

How the legend of the 'flayed Dane' became attached to the skin fragments is unknown, but the myth's endurance throughout the centuries was associated with antiquated notions of the Anglo-Saxons and Vikings. The lack of evidence of flaying as a form of punishment in Anglo-Saxon England is striking, and there seems to have been a genuine effort to create a humane government in the late Anglo-Saxon period. Early spectators of the 'Dane-skins' in post-medieval England might have endeavoured to construct the legend to reflect their misguided understanding of the Anglo-Saxon period and emphasize the cruelty associated with Anglo-Saxon punishments, or their strength of law; however, the actual evidence provides a salutary warning against having a patronizing attitude to the people of the past, whether that be a view of the English throughout the seventeenth and nineteenth centuries, or the assumption that Anglo-Saxon judiciary procedures were more cruel, or less civilized, than those of the centuries that followed.

5

Skin on Skin: Wearing Flayed Remains

Frederika Bain

[T]he skin is the sign of our transformability, our [...] ability to become other.[1]

IN the *Florentine Codex* (*c.* 1588), Spanish chronicler Bernardino de Sahagún describes the Aztec festival of Tlacaxipehualiztli. In this celebration honouring the skin-garbed god Xipe Totec, elite captives of war were flayed and their removed skins worn for twenty days by priests,[2] a practice called *neteotquiliztli*, 'impersonating a god'. Jill Furst observes, 'The prisoner became Xipe and died, but his skin retained the god's life force', and the two were taken on together by the second wearers.[3] Though dramatic, *neteotquiliztli* is only one example among many in which skin-wearing is assumed to facilitate passage to an alternative state of being. Practices and representations of wearing skin – recognizably animal as well as human – cover a wide generic, geographic and temporal range[4] but follow a similar logic. In the Middle High German verse narrative *Salman und Morolf*,[5] historical accounts of punitive and prophylactic skin-wearing in Germany and Italy, early modern Icelandic folk traditions and the

[1] Steven Connor, *The Book of Skin* (Ithaca, NY: Cornell University Press, 2003), p. 32.

[2] Bernardino de Sahagún, *Florentine Codex: A General History of the Things of New Spain*, book 2, trans. Arthur J. O. Anderson and Charles E. Dibble (Santa Fe, NM: School of American Research, 1970), 3:3–4, 47–60.

[3] Jill Leslie Furst, 'Flaying, Curing, and Shedding: Some Thoughts on the Aztec God Xipe Totec', in *Painted Books and Indigenous Knowledge in Mesoamerica: Manuscript Studies in Honor of Mary Elizabeth Smith*, ed. Elizabeth Hill Boone (New Orleans: Tulane University, 2005), p. 66. See also: Franke Neumann, 'The Flayed God and his Rattle-Stick: A Shamanic Element in Pre-Hispanic Mesoamerican Religion', *History of Religions* 15.3 (Feb. 1976): 251–63.

[4] They include not only early modern Mexican examples, but also eighteenth-century Afghan, medieval and early modern Scandinavian, and pre-contact Native American and Ainu cultural traditions and stories, as well as modern American novels and films.

[5] Dates offered for the composition of *Salman und Morolf* range between the late twelfth and the fifteenth century, according to Joseph H. Magedanz, who provides a section on dating in the introduction to his '*Salman und Morolf*: An English Translation with Introduction', PhD dissertation (University of Nebraska-Lincoln, 1994), pp. 10–19. The question is also discussed in Sara S. Poor, 'Why Surface Reading is not Enough: Morolf,

sixteenth-century English *Merry Ieste of a Shrewde and Curst Wyfe Lapped in Morrelles Skin for Her Good Behauyour*, the removed and re-donned skin, detached from that which originally gave it meaning, initiates a mode of border-crossing, becoming a floating threshold between one form of the self and another.

Much of the burgeoning scholarship on the skin recognizes its literal and metaphorical function as *limen*, a space that Victor Turner describes as 'represent[ing] the midpoint of transition'.[6] The skin, says Steven Connor in his wide-ranging *Book of Skin*, is a 'milieu' that he explains as a 'midplace [...] where inside and outside meet and meld'.[7] In her discussion of practices of bodily inscription that take place on and through the skin, such as branding and tattooing, the anthropologist Enid Schildkrout also emphasizes the 'liminal quality of skin', arguing that the integument constitutes an 'ambiguous terrain at the boundary between self and society'.[8] The skin as *limen* may be read as threshold or barrier: as the former, it allows controlled entry; as the latter, it separates and individuates, distinguishing self from what is outside itself. As Judith Halberstam comments, 'skin is at once the most fragile of boundaries and the most stable of signifiers'.[9] It is, however, only stable as a signifier so long as it is attached. Before being removed from the body it acts as a powerful marker of identity, displaying race, age, gender and other identifiers, but it loses this function after it is flayed off. Connor notes that 'the skin is not detachable in such a way that the detached part would remain recognizable [...] by being peeled away from the body, it has ceased to be itself'.[10] Instead, it becomes a literally unanchored signifier, both unstable and multipotent,[11] that serves as a moveable, transferrable site of possibility.

Medieval and early modern European representations of those who don the skin of animals and, even more potently, of humans show that it is specifically wearing that allows them to access the possibility-space created by the detached integument. Wearing is a powerful act. A recurrent belief surfaces that what is worn filters into and alters the nature of the wearer, an understanding that can be seen in terms of clothing as well as skin. E. Jane

the Skin of the Jew, and German Medieval Studies', *Exemplaria* 26.2–3 (Summer/Fall 2014): 148–62 at pp. 149–50.

[6] Victor Turner, *Dramas, Fields, and Metaphors* (Ithaca, NY: Cornell University Press, 1974), p. 237.

[7] Connor, *Book of Skin*, p. 27.

[8] Enid Schildkrout, 'Inscribing the Body', *Annual Review of Anthropology* 33 (2004): 319–44 at p. 321.

[9] Judith Halberstam, *Skin Shows: Gothic Horror and the Technology of Monsters* (Durham, NC: Duke University Press, 1995), p. 163.

[10] Connor, *Book of Skin*, p. 29.

[11] In physiological terms, the skin is an available source of stem cells, whose defining characteristic is their multipotency.

Burns argues in *Medieval Fabrications* for a mode of 'read[ing] clothing [...] as forging sartorial bodies derived equally from fabric and from flesh, bodies that erode the ostensible line between artifice and nature', adding that 'clothes and representations of them can be active agents in constructing social bodies'.[12]

This construction also extends past the 'social' and into the physical body. Most commonly, the transformation assumed to be effected by wearing is the relatively straightforward one at the heart of sympathetic magic: taking on others' appearance by dressing in the clothing they favour brings the wearer's nature closer to theirs. An example is Philip Massinger's *The Renegado* (1630), in which clothing not only signals but may potentially alter its wearer's religious or ethnic identity. When the Italian Vitelli dresses in the rich garments given to him by his Saracen lover Donousa, he not only illustrates but also increases his danger of 'turning Turk', or converting to Islam.[13] Nor is he fully recuperated back into the Catholic Church until he throws off the Saracen-infected jewels and clothing, which he terms 'sin's gay trappings, the proud livery / Of wicked pleasure', tellingly comparing them to 'Alcides' fatal shirt, [which] tears off / Our flesh and reputation both together' (3.5.49–51, 53–4). Alcides' shirt is the poisoned garment, described in Ovid's *Metamorphoses*, that killed Hercules by burning into and adhering to his body, so that he was forced to rip off his own skin and flesh in order to divest himself of it.[14] Vitelli's comparison, which envisions this disrobing as a form of flaying, illustrates the potentially profound effects on the body of what is laid on the skin.[15]

To an even greater extent, many practices and representations of

---

[12] E. Jane Burns, ed., *Medieval Fabrications: Dress, Textiles, Clothwork, and other Cultural Imaginings* (New York: Palgrave, 2004), pp. 10, 11.

[13] Philip Massinger, *The Renegado*, ed. Michael Neill (London: Methuen, 2010).

[14] *Ovid's Metamorphoses*, trans. Arthur Golding, ed. John Frederick Nims (Philadelphia: Paul Dry Books, 2000), 9:190–214.

[15] The effect of clothing on physical self can also be seen in accounts of cross-dressing. The mid-thirteenth-century Anglo-Norman *Roman de Silence*, which tells the story of a girl who is dressed as a male from infancy through young adulthood, assumes that her masculine garb has affected her nature to the extent that when she adopts feminine dress, she must undergo over several days what amounts to a purging process to remove the maleness from her body and character and replace it with female characteristics. Heldris de Cornualle, *Roman de Silence*, ed. Regina Psaki (New York: Garland, 1991). Likewise, the early seventeenth-century pamphlet *Hic Mulier*, which is concerned with the contemporary women's fashion of wearing masculine clothing, betrays significant anxiety surrounding the possibility that such women will become, rather than merely appear, mannish by virtue of their dress. *Hic Mulier*, in *'Custome Is an Idiot': Jacobean Pamphlet Literature on Women*, ed. Susan Gushee O'Malley (Champaign: University of Illinois Press, 2004), pp. 263–84.

wearing animal skins assume the wearer takes on the qualities of the animal.[16] Shamanic rites in Native American, Norse, Saami and other traditions incorporate the donning of animal hides and other body parts to access powers or attributes of the animal for protection, success in the hunt or spiritual insight. Folktales of shape-changing animal/human beings may also stipulate that the change be effected by dressing in the physical skin of the animal into which the human is to turn; Scandinavian, Irish and Orkney selkies and swan-maidens put on a sealskin or a feather shirt or cape to complete their metamorphosis. This is also a common transformative motif of lycanthropy: donning a wolfskin creates the wolf. Jean Grenier, a French *loup-garou* described by Pierre de Lancre in his *Tableau de l'inconstance des mauvais anges et demons* (1612), is given a wolfskin by the Devil that has the power to transform him into a ravening wolf when he wears it,[17] while Sigmund and Sinfjötli in the late thirteenth-century *Völsunga saga* are endued with a similar power by the wolfskins they find hanging in a building in the forest.[18]

In as many instances, however, skins are not assumed to endow their second wearers specifically with the characteristics of the first. All leather begins as skin, as Sarah Kay and other scholars have discussed in reference to parchment.[19] Yet, turned into leather, hides may be utilized as though purified, scraped clean, of animal signification; through the process of tanning, the raw beast hide is refined, civilized and preserved. The process alters it from body part to artefact, as the encapsulation of saints' relics in reliquaries turned them into, or allowed them to be seen as, *memento sanctitate* rather than unidentifiable bones or bodily fluids. Animal skins that have not undergone this refining process, conversely, retain and continue to manifest the characteristics of the creatures from whom they have been flayed.

However, wearers of animal as well as human skin often seek not the

---

[16] For an illuminating discussion of the wearing of animal skins and the implications of such wearing, see, in this volume: Renée Ward, ' " Thou shalt have the better cloathe": Reading Second Skins in *Robin Hood and Guy of Gisborne*', pp. 349–65.

[17] *On the Inconstancy of Witches: Pierre de Lancre's Tableau de l'inconstance des mauvais anges et demons (1612)*, ed. and trans. G. S. Williams (Turnhout: Brepols, 2006), pp. 270, 272. On the associations of wolfskins, lycanthropy and witchcraft, see: Susan Small, 'Flesh and Death in Early Modern Bedburg', pp. 71–90, in this volume.

[18] *Saga of the Volsungs: The Norse Epic of Sigurd the Dragon Slayer*, trans. Jesse Byock (Berkeley: University of California Press, 1990), pp. 44–5.

[19] See: Sarah Kay, 'Legible Skins: Animals and the Ethics of Medieval Reading', *postmedieval: a journal of medieval cultural studies* 2.1 (2011): 13–32, and 'Original Skin: Flaying, Reading, and Thinking in the Legend of Saint Bartholomew and other Works', *Journal of Medieval and Early Modern Studies* 36.1 (2006): 35–74.

characteristics of the one whose skin they wear but rather the property of traversing other borders. While some folk traditions of therianthropy (human/animal metamorphosis) prescribe an animal skin as the agent of change, others specify a girdle of *human* skin as the means of transformation *into an animal*, as described in Jacob Grimm's *Deutsche Mythologie* (1835). Regarding the metamorphosis of a werewolf, Grimm comments, 'this is a common belief among us, that the transformation is effected by tying a strap round the body [...] [that] is cut out of human skin'.[20] Sabine Baring-Gould identifies the same transformative agent in German tradition,[21] as well as a related Polish belief that a girdle of human skin laid across the threshold of a room causes those who step over it to become werewolves.[22] In these traditions the wearers do not wish to take on the characteristics of the humans whose skin they use, but rather to attain other forms of being that are opened into possibility by skin-wearing.

Two early modern descriptions of animal-skin-wearing invoke the act's power to facilitate the crossing of a range of metaphoric boundaries. In these accounts, one ostensibly historical and one literary, skin-wearing is imposed on another to force a form of transition. While an association with the skin's original animal wearer informs these incidents, the alteration is not a simple one-to-one transferal of attributes. In a German chronicle's description of a poacher punished by being sewn into a deer hide, forced skin-wearing vengefully enacts the same boundary permeability assumed to be illustrated in the original offence. The *Historia ecclesiastica isenacensis* (1621) by the General Superintendent of Eisenach, Nikolaus Rebhan, describes a violent punishment meted out in 1537 by 'einem Erzbischof oder vielmehr greulichen Unmenschen, Wüterichen und Thyrannen "Michael" gennant, zu Salzburg' [an archbishop or rather a horrible monster, a savage and cruel tyrant, called Michael of Salzburg].[23] When the judge charged with sentencing the man refuses to 'pronounce the death verdict'

---

[20] Jacob Grimm, *Teutonic Mythology*, trans. James Steven Stallybrass (London: George Bell and Sons, 1883). Grimm also describes the converse case of a metamorphosis from werewolf back into human effected by throwing a *fur* pelisse over the beast (p. 1096).

[21] Sabine Baring-Gould, *The Book of Were-Wolves, Being an Account of a Terrible Superstition* (London: Smith, Elder and Co., 1865), pp. 112–3.

[22] Ibid., p. 116. Cf. Small, 'Flesh and Death', p. 74. As Small explains, the notorious werewolf/murderer Peter Stubbe was also said to achieve his transformation by wearing a magic girdle.

[23] Qtd. in Erich Hobusch, *Von der edlen Kunst des Jagens: Eine Kulturgeschichte der Jagd und der Hege der Tierwelt* (Innsbruck: Pinguin-Verlag, 1978), p. 119. English translation qtd. in Erich Hobusch, *Fair Game: A History of Hunting, Shooting and Animal Conservation*, trans. Ruth Michaelis-Jena and Patrick Murray (New York: Arco Publishing, 1980), pp. 117–18. Hereafter, page numbers are given in parentheses.

that the archbishop demands, the latter usurps the judge's prerogative, substituting an even harsher doom: the man accused of hunting illegally

> solle ihn in des gefundenen Hirsches Haut einnähen mit Hunden hetzen, doch mit der Bedingung oder vielmehr giftigen Gespött, wenn er den Hunden entrinnen könne, wie ein Hirsch, so soll er frei sein. [...] Hat auf offenem Marktplatz eine Jagd angestellt, den armen in die Hirschhaut genähten Menschen, der seine Seele Gott befohlen, vorführen lassen. Selbst in das Jagdhorn gestoßen, die englischen Hunde angehetzt und laufen lassen, welche den jammervollen Mann für ein Wildtier erbärmlich zerfleischt und zerrissen haben, welches alles der Tyrann mit Lust angeschaut.   (p. 119)

> [was to be sewn into a stag's skin, coursed by hounds, and then be exposed to wicked mockery, saying that on condition he could escape from the hounds, he would be free. [...] The hunt was held in the market place for everyone to see, and the man sewn into the stag's skin, commanded [sic] his soul to God, as he was brought along. The horn was sounded, English hounds were then let loose, and, taking the poor man for game, they mauled him cruelly and tore him to pieces, all of which the brutal tyrant watched with pleasure.]
>   (p. 117)

Poaching was a vexed subject in medieval and early modern Europe. The hunt was a significant arena in which to contest and reify status, one of the most jealously guarded barriers associated with it being that between those who were and were not permitted to take part in this elite activity. Because the poacher dared to cross what the archbishop sees as the inviolable boundary between commoner and noble, between one forbidden and one empowered to hunt, the archbishop illustrates this barrier-breach by symbolically making him a hybrid being: a man who looks like a deer, who is treated worse than either. Wearing a deerskin is not assumed – by the humans – to bring the man closer to deer nature, though the dogs are represented as believing that it has, with tragic results. Theirs is the simpler misprision: the man has become (equivalent to) their usual quarry because by wearing its skin he is associated with the characteristics on which they depend for identification: smell, general shape, external attributes such as antlers.

By contrast, Archbishop Michael implicitly accepts the literal limits of the condemned man's deerskin-wearing; he does not treat him as a deer under the terms of the ornate ceremony of the hunt. Comprised of a series of elaborate rituals outlined in medieval German, French and English hunting manuals and romances,[24] hunt protocol makes no provision

---

[24] See, for example: *Sir Gawain and the Green Knight*, ed. J. R. R. Tolkien and E. V. Gordon (Oxford: Oxford University Press, 1967); Juliana Berners, *The Boke of St. Albans: Containing Treatises of Hawking, Hunting,*

for the dogs to kill and tear to pieces the deer they have chased. Rather, the 'breaking' or dismembering of the deer is one of the activity's most complex and precise episodes, performed by skilled huntsmen. The dogs, meanwhile, are only permitted to eat bits of offal and blood-soaked bread that are presented to them on the eviscerated and flayed deer hide – at the appropriate point in the process, and at the express command of the huntsman. Interpretations of the story of Actaeon, in which the doomed hunter is transformed into a deer as punishment by the goddess Diana and is likewise torn apart by his dogs, occasionally focus on the ill-training of these dogs evidenced by their mauling him, implying that Actaeon's fate is deserved because he must have been a poor hunter and dog-keeper. John of Salisbury is one such critic, arguing in *Policraticus* (*c.* 1159) that the attack by Actaeon's dogs is 'a deplorable result of the type of training they had received',[25] an attitude echoed by Henry Cornelius Agrippa in *Vanite and Uncertaintie of the Artes and Sciences* (1530).[26] Nor was the hunter's attitude towards his prey vindictive or denigratory: the deer was honoured and lauded as a noble beast of venery and the king of the forest, not exterminated sadistically like the condemned man in Rebhan's account.

While the physical import of the doom is inescapable – the poacher is killed by being torn apart – so too is its symbolic valence; it is his horror at the symbolism, not merely at the death of the man, that emerges so clearly in Rebhan's denunciation. The system of capital punishment was well established in early modern Germany;[27] it is not merely that the

---

and Cote-Armour (1486; London: Elliot Stock, 1901); Johannes Caius, *Of Englishe Dogges*, 1576 (1576; New York: Da Capo, 1969); Jaques Du Fouilloux, *La Venerie* (1561; RenTexte, online at http://homes.chass. utoronto.ca/~wulfric/rentexte/fouillou/fou_chiens.htm [accessed 14 Jun. 2015]); George Gascoigne, *Noble Arte of Venerie* (1575; Text Creation Partnership digital edition, availabe through *Early English Books Online* [http://eebo.chadwyck.com/home]); Alan Lupack, ed., *Sir Tristrem*, in *Lancelot of the Laik and Sir Tristrem* (Kalamazoo, MI: Medieval Institute Publications, 1994); Gaston Phoebus, *Livre de chasse*, ed. Gunnar Tilander, Cynegetica 18 (Sweden: Karlshamn, 1971); George Turbervile, *Turbervile's Booke of Hunting* (1576; Oxford: Clarendon, 1908).

[25] John of Salisbury, *Frivolities of Courtiers and Footprints of Philosophers: Being a Translation of the First, Second, and Third Books and Selections from the Seventh and Eighth Books of the 'Policraticus' of John of Salisbury*, trans. Joseph B. Pike (New York: Octagon, 1938, repr. 1972), p. 14.

[26] Henry Cornelius Agrippa, *Vanite and Uncertaintie of the Artes and Sciences*, ed. Catherine M. Dunn (Northridge: California State University, 1974), pp. 260–3.

[27] See: Joel F. Harrington, *The Faithful Executioner: Life and Death, Honor and Shame in the Turbulent Sixteenth Century* (New York: Farrar, Straus and Giroux, 2013); Kathy Stuart, *Defiled Trades and Social Outcasts: Honor and Ritual Pollution in Early Modern Germany* (Cambridge: Cambridge University Press, 1999), pp. 69–93; and Petrus Spierenburg, *The Spectacle*

poacher has been sentenced to die that prompts this strong censure, but rather the manner in which the death takes place. The condemned man is forced into the space between animal and human. The archbishop, for his part, not only usurps a secular matter of punishment, sentencing him to death although the Church forbade ecclesiastics to either pronounce death sentences or perform executions; he also participates in an act associated, if grotesquely, with the hunt at a time when religious in Germany were forbidden from bloodsport.[28] It is the archbishop's own transgressing of boundaries – between secular and ecclesiastical and between human and non-human – by mandating this punishment that prompts Rebhan's disgust and outrage. For while not considering him a deer, Michael treats the poacher as one, in a vicious parody of a true huntsman's conduct towards his quarry. In this way he shows his estimation of those unlearned in – and unfit to learn – hunt protocol, as desecrating the sport of kings. At the same time, he uses the possibility-space opened by the wearing of the skin to illuminate the grotesque being he sees the poacher as having become in attempting to hunt. He illustrates the transgression of one boundary, between commoner and nobleman, by forcing the condemned to traverse another, between human and non-human. Thus, the skin-wearing acts as a mimetic punishment, a form of talion: an eye for an eye, a hunt for a hunt, a crossing of boundaries for a crossing of boundaries.

Forced border-rupture is also at play in the verse narrative *A Merry Ieste of a Shrewde and Curst Wyfe Lapped in Morrelles Skin for Her Good Behauyour* (*c.* 1580).[29] Here the skin of the black horse Morel[30] is used both to punish a too-independent woman's transgression and to force her transformation: not into a horse, but into a meek and submissive wife. Its tone, unlike that of Rebhan's *Historia ecclesiastica*, approves of the punishment, the wife's defeat and subsequent alteration. Refusing to treat her husband with the respect he deserves, or his employees with the decency demanded by *noblesse oblige*, she is framed as a transgressor of society's norms and standards. She must therefore 'turne and change her minde' (l. 767), a feat accomplished with the touch of the horse's skin against her own. The *Merry Ieste* is generally accepted as one of the sources

of *Suffering: Executions and the Evolution of Repression* (Cambridge: Cambridge University Press, 1984). Cf. Small, 'Flesh and Death'.

[28] Hobusch explains this ban was in effect, though not universally upheld, through the sixteenth century (*Fair Game*, p. 74).

[29] 'Here Begynneth a Merry Ieste of a Shrewde and Curst Wyfe Lapped in Morrelles Skin for Her Good Behauyour', in *Remains of the Early Popular Poetry of England*, ed. W. Carew Hazlitt, vol. 4 (London: John Russell Smith, 1866). Hereafter, line numbers are given in parentheses.

[30] For 'morel', the *OED* n. 1b gives the definition 'A dark-coloured horse. Also used as a proper name for a horse of this kind.' There may also be a punning reference to 'moral skin', a skin that causes the one who wears it to act in a morally righteous manner.

for the *Taming of the Shrew*, frequently given as an example of a 'brutal' shrew-taming account in comparison to Kate's less physical and violent, more humanistic, taming at the hands of Petrucchio.[31] Here a husband attempts to establish his domestic dominance by tearing off his new wife's clothing and beating her severely after he has killed and skinned his horse; he then swathes her in the hide, keeping her thus in the cellar until she submits to his rule.[32] While most critics focus on the beating and physical chastisement in the account, the skin-wearing aspect of the punishment is markedly significant in bringing about the wife's dramatic taming.

The beginning of the *Ieste* introduces a meek man, his shrewish wife and their two daughters, one of them as rebellious as her mother. An unnamed suitor, focused on the rich dowry he will gain, weds Jone, the shrewish daughter, and after the wedding immediately sets about taming her. He exhausts her with physically painful sexual pursuit: 'They dallyed togither, and had good game; / He hit her awry; she cryed, alas' (ll. 512–13), as he chases her up and down the bed, preventing her from sleeping. She complains to her mother that he has torn her smock as well as her skin: 'I will no more lye by this man, / For he doth me brast both vayne and sinew' (ll. 529–30). This prefigures his later and fuller rupture of her skin's integrity: 'Thou hast my white skin, and my body all to torne' (l. 970). The centrepiece of his efforts, however, is his determination to wrap her in Morel's skin.

Though this is a corporal as well as a symbolic punishment – Jone is beaten bloody before being wrapped in the skin, which has been salted to preserve it and so makes her wounds 'smarte' (l. 988) – the hide's presence and powers extend far beyond the material. In a poem of just over 130 stanzas, the skin and Jone's encasement appear in almost a fifth, exceeding the physically painful beating and salting adjuncts. The husband even addresses the skin as though it were a separate and sentient being: 'Now good Morels skin, / Receiue my curst wife in' (after l. 918). And after she is brought to submission, the skin is kept in the cellar in case it should be needed again, lurking there waiting to envelop her like a dark, chthonic creature – the 'deuill' (l. 1075), the wife's mother terms it – a 'fell' (skin) with fell (menacing) import. There it is also exhibited to others, such as Jone's mother; as Lesley Ferris notes, along with the rods used for

---

[31] Linda Woodbridge, 'New Light on "The Wife Lapped in Morel's Skin" and "The Proud Wife's Paternoster"', *English Literary Renaissance* 13.1 (1983): 3–35 at p. 3.

[32] Valerie Wayne traces earlier variants of the situation in which a wife is 'tamed' by being beaten and wrapped in a horse's skin, showing that the trope first appeared in the early fifteenth-century *Historia Regis Waldei*, and then in four sixteenth-century plays: *Andrisca* (1537), *Bosen Frauen* (1540–50), *Das New Morgens Fell* (1582) and *Moorkensvel* (c. 1600). See: 'The Compliant Shrew in Shakespearean Comedy and Romance', PhD dissertation (University of Chicago, 1978), pp. 117–8.

the beating, it is 'proudly displayed as [a] sign […] of the husband's triumphant success and the wife's humiliating defeat'.[33] There is also an extra-physical significance to her beating: the husband alludes to the depth that the skin's touch will penetrate into her body at the same time that he threatens to beat her when he warns, 'Thy bones will I swaddle' (l. 846), where 'swaddle' means both to thrash and to wrap closely.[34] The rupture of her skin makes her susceptible to the touch of the horse's: her own skin is made permeable before being pressed against the inner surface of the skin of Morel, allowing it to touch her more intimately and transformatively and thus 'turne and change her'.

There is a long tradition of correspondence between horses and women, though little in the poem indicates that wrapping in the skin is intended to turn Jone into a horse, even metaphorically, or to illustrate any horse-like characteristics she might already possess. The poem includes no bawdy jokes about riding or bearing, such as appear in the *Taming of the Shrew*, while repeated references to Morel as male and aged underscore their difference. Yet being wrapped in his skin is intended to, and does, effect a transformation: not to a more bestial but to a more civilized frame of mind. The role played by Morel's hide is explicit, though the process by which it converts her (or seems to) is understood as magical rather than logical; the poem offers no explanation for its effect. Planning the flaying and wrapping, the husband muses that Morel is old and can no longer work, but that he understands now why he has kept him on past his usefulness: 'I trowe I haue kept him thus long in store / To worke a charme that shall be feate' (ll. 793–4). He then resolves, 'I thinke that Morels fell / Must mend all thing that is amis' (ll. 813–14), tendering it the role of all-curing talisman. And just before placing his wife in the skin, he announces, 'For now I am set thee for to charme, / And make thee meeke, by Gods might' (ll. 915–16).

It is not God's might, however, but the supposed properties of the skin that effect the change. Throughout the beating Jone continues defiant, insulting and rebuking her husband; however, when she awakens from a swoon to discover herself wrapped in Morel's fell she undergoes an immediate reversal. She fears she cannot continue to live and begins to lose her mind: 'When she did spy that therein she lay, / Out of her wit she was full nye' (ll. 991–2). And after the husband tells her he will keep her swathed for the rest of her life, if necessary, she immediately begs his love and promises never to offend him again. She also credits the skin as the agent of her alteration, telling her mother that if the mother herself 'had bene in Morels fell' (l. 1073), she would understand her daughter's sudden submissiveness.

---

[33] Lesley Ferris, 'Staging Violence against Women: A Long Series of Replays', *Theatre Symposium: Theatre and Violence* 7 (2006): 31–40 at pp. 34–5.

[34] The *OED* gives this quotation as an example of its definition '[t]o beat soundly' (n. 3), but a definition more familiar to present-day readers, 'to envelop with wrappings, to swathe' (n. 2), was recorded as early as 1522 and is directly relevant to this passage as well.

Having crossed the line between appropriate and inappropriate behaviour by her shrewishness, she is now repositioned on the appropriate side by being 'lapped in Morrelles skin, for her good behauyour'. Wearing the skin has changed her, or she performs this change – if not into a similarly esteemed and valued steed, at least into a good wife.

The *Merry Ieste* and the passage from the *Historia ecclesiastica* specify animal skins as the agents of supposed transformation and, in each, the original animal is in some sense valued above the human wrapped in its hide: the deer that must be protected from illicit hunters, the faithful horse juxtaposed with the disobedient wife. At the same time, the flaying of an animal is a common act, one that would occasion little comment without the skin-wearing adjunct. In the *Spielmannsepik* [minstrel epic] *Salman und Morolf*,[35] the skin worn is that not of an animal but of a Jew, a member of a group so denigrated that the narrative occludes his death with the same ease as an animal's, without any amending valuation of his positive qualities.[36] In this text skin is the means by which the protagonist can cross physical as well as cultural barriers, at the same time that the extent and mode of its transformative power is in question. The story recounts the adventures of Morolf, brother to King Salman, on his two quests to find and retrieve Salman's bride, Salme, who is stolen away by the Saracen kings Fore and then Princian. As well as occluding the flayed man, the narrator associates a continual series of praises and positive epithets with Morolf, as though to emphasize the rightness of his actions, including flaying. A salient aspect of his cleverness is his skill at creating and employing material artefacts, primarily disguises, on his long and difficult quests.

Morolf's first disguise, most disturbing to modern sensibilities, is also presented as his most successful: the skin of Berman, an elderly Jew. Charged by Salman to find Salme, Morolf first visits Berman to ask his advice, as he tells him, on the matter. Berman accordingly invites him into his inner rooms to talk, whereupon Morolf stabs and kills Berman, then flays the top half of his body, including his face and scalp: 'Morolff zoch uß ein messer scharff und lang, er stach es dem juden durch sin hertz, das es im an der hende wider want. Morolff Salmons drut oberthalb dem gurtel loste er dem juden abe die hut. er balsamte sie und leite sie an sinen lip.' [But Morolf drew a long, sharp knife and thrust it up to the hilt through the Jew's heart. Salman's favourite then skinned the man from the waist up,

[35] The story has been translated into English by Magedanz, '*Salman und Morolf*'. Both German and English quotations are drawn from this facing-column edition. Stanza and line numbers are given in parentheses.

[36] On the association of Jews with animals, see: Claudine Fabre-Vassas, *The Singular Beast: Jews, Christians, and the Pig*, trans. Carol Volk (New York: Columbia University Press, 1997); on medieval anti-Judaism, see: Irven Resnick, *Marks of Distinction: Christian Perceptions of Jews in the High Middle Ages* (Washington, D.C.: Catholic University of America Press, 2012).

cured the skin and dressed himself in it.] (161:4–162:5).[37] Berman is not killed by flaying; he is killed in order that he may be flayed. This is not a punishment for any misdeed but is equated with killing an animal for its hide or meat: the Jew as disposable person.

Of far greater interest to the narrator than Berman's fate is Morolf's skill at flaying, preserving and utilizing Berman's skin, feats presented as worthy of praise: 'Der vil listige man, er hette der lande vil erfarn. inn der hute ging der ritter lobesan in alien den geberden, als were sie im gewachssen an.' [This most clever man had become acquainted with many lands and was able to wear Berman's skin as if it had become a part of his own body.] (163:1–6). The skin disguise allows him to travel to Wendlese, the site of Fore's court, and, thus, is a correlative of Morolf's other skin object, his leather boat. This he also makes with his own hands, sewing it together and covering it with pitch, in the same way that he prepares Berman's skin for its protection and preservation. Morolf carries the boat by his side, the narrator explains, and it has saved his life many times, in the same way that the Berman-skin disguise preserves his life throughout his lengthy journey. The wearing of skin likewise bestows upon Morolf the property of traversing religious and cultural barriers and of restoring, if temporarily, the similarly border-crossing Salme to her legal husband. This focus away from the killing, on skin as object rather than body part, reinforces the anti-Jewish stance of the text and the markedly abjected status of Berman, as a Jew, but it also underscores the point that Morolf does not appear to take on the deeper characteristics of this denigrated person with his skin and his appearance. He is 'untainted' by his time in the skin of the Jew; his transformation is temporary and only skin deep.

After flaying and putting on the skin, Morolf signals that he has performed a momentous act, saying, 'nu wil ich nimmer erwinden, ich finde dann das wunder schone wip' [[Now] I will not return until I find the marvellously beautiful woman] (162:6–9); the vow, or prophecy, marks the profound and fateful nature of what he has just done. It is not, however, his murder of another human being to which he alludes; rather, the significance is in his acquisition and donning of the skin. Connor argues, 'so many figurings of the skin emphasize [...] passage, from hand to hand, body to body, time to time and state to state', a point which is truer still of figurings of skin-wearing.[38] By putting on Berman's skin, Morolf has taken an irreversible step away from his life at Salman's court and into his life as wanderer – if not precisely outcast, at least displaced.[39] His actions take on

---

[37] At precisely the point when Morolf undertakes this violent deed, the narrator notes that he is 'Salman's favourite', beloved of an unquestionably positively coded character; this implicitly conveys the narrator's approval of Morolf's action.

[38] Connor, *Book of Skin*, p. 30.

[39] Because Morolf is dressed as/in a Jew, there may be overtones here of the Wandering Jew, who is compelled to stay continually in motion through the

the 'transition' and '*passage*' quality of liminality identified by Turner in *The Ritual Process*;[40] wearing the skin, he changes from Morolf-the-courtier to Morolf-the-traveller.[41] His vow not to return, thus, refers not only to his absence from Salman's court but also perhaps to the subsuming of his own identity, which does not resurface until after he has found Salme, seven years later.

Sara Poor has argued that the guise of a Jewish pilgrim would not be a safe one in which to travel, owing to the periodically violent anti-Judaism extant in Europe during the time the poem may have been written.[42] Poor implicitly assumes that Morolf looks Jewish, a reasonable assumption considering the medieval view of Jews as instantly recognizable by physical characteristics, as well as the emphasis on Morolf's skill at removing the skin from the complicated surfaces of the face such that it retains its shape completely. However, the skin is not described as having any specifically Jewish characteristics; the only way it is marked as different from Morolf's is that the flayed scalp has grey hair, while Morolf's is blond. Other characters' reactions make it unclear whether he appears to them as a Jew; when he arrives at Wendelse, he is described as both wearing Berman's skin and carrying a palm frond and a staff, accoutrements of a (Christian) pilgrim, but his supposed religious identity is never discussed by those he meets. His aim, indeed, may not be to look Jewish but merely to look Other, and taking a Jew's skin would have seemed less repugnant to the audience than taking a Christian's. For whether or not Morolf looks Jewish, he does not look like he did originally: in the Berman-skin disguise he fools all beholders, including Salman, on whom he tests the costume before setting out. When he afterwards reveals the imposture, Salman expresses pleasure and admiration: 'Von freuden kuste ine der kunig rich. er sprach: "lieber Morolff, din liste sint wunderlich. vor den kan sich nieman wol bewarn in aller dirre welte, wo du wilt in dem lande varn."' [The noble king joyfully kissed him and said, 'Morolf, your skills are truly marvellous. No one can protect himself from them, wherever in the whole world you might want to go.'] (172:3–8).[43]

---

ages after mocking Christ – a legend popular in the medieval period.

[40] Victor Turner, *The Ritual Process: Structure and Anti-structure* (Chicago: Aldine Publishing, 1969), p. 107, emphasis in original.

[41] In the Norse romance *Örvar-Odds saga*, the protagonist undergoes a similar transformation as he wanders and adopts a new identity, but he is wrapped in a bark skin, not the flayed skin of another human being. See in this volume: Larissa Tracy, 'Face Off: Flaying and Identity in Medieval Romance', pp. 322–48.

[42] Poor, 'Surface Reading', p. 155.

[43] Salman here confesses himself unable to 'protect himself from' being fooled by the disguise, further emphasizing Morolf's skill in creating it, but behind the compliment floats the understanding that Berman, too, had not been able to 'protect himself from' becoming that disguise.

Even if he is assumed to look Jewish, it is clear that wearing Berman's skin has no effect on Morolf's nature. It is rather his likeness to a poor, elderly wanderer that disarms both Salman, before the journey, and Salme, at his journey's end; and the virtuous king and his wicked wife[44] each read him in terms of their own status. Salman yields to the disguised Morolf's requests for money and a gold ring because of the apparent piety of the pilgrim petitioner, while Salme, herself a foreigner in Wendlese, identifies with the disguised man's liminal, outsider status, referring to him as *wal(le) bruder* [fellow wanderer] (206:3, 208:2) when she invites him to sit and converse with her. Indeed, Salme emphatically prefers him in this guise, reacting angrily when she realizes the deception. She accepts him more readily when he seems akin to her in this respect than when she realizes he is an emissary of the life and husband she has left behind, come to take her back. In each case, the skin has multipotent significations, dependent on its wearer and viewer.

Unlike Salman, who must have the masquerade revealed to him, Salme soon apprehends Morolf's true identity after his passing reference to the 'schone und wunnesam' [handsome and magnificent] (257:7–8) Duke Morolf, whom he says he has recently met. Fore, too, may see through the Berman-skin disguise, commenting that he can tell by the visitor's appearance that he is 'von hoher art geborn' [highborn] (195:6). This may also, however, be a humorous reminder of Fore's own status: a king in his own land but a heathen according to the narrator and audience, he is, thus, in Christian estimation even lower than a Jew and consequently regards one who looks like a Jew as noble. But the text's stance as to the nature of the integument is demonstrated by the circumstance that two characters coded as wicked may be able to see beneath the skin while the most virtuous cannot: only those who are duplicitous themselves recognize duplicity, or skin-layering, in others, while the pious expect the surface candidly to reflect inner nature. Morolf himself, whom Maria Dobozy calls an 'ambiguous character having both [...] positive and negative potential',[45] thus understands the limits of his disguises as well as the benefits they can confer. He is perfectly positioned to take advantage of wearing skin. In the end, his disguise does fully reflect his inner self, his liminality and doubled nature.

While Berman's personhood is only marked through the practical consideration that Morolf continues to look human while wearing his skin,

---

[44] Salme, who consents to flee with Fore only after being ensorcelled by a magic ring into believing herself in love with him, is nevertheless treated by the narrator – and Morolf – as culpable and faithless for her part in the flight.

[45] Maria Dobozy, 'The Function of Knowledge and Skill in *Salman and Morolf*', in *The Dark Figure in Medieval German and Germanic Literature*, ed. Edward Haymes and Stephanie Cain Van D'Elden (Göppingen: Kümmerle Verlag, 1986), pp. 27–41 at p. 28.

other representations of skin-wearing recognize, to a greater or lesser extent, the significance of the human source. Rikke Hansen suggests that animal skins tend to retain the characteristics of their first wearers, the animals, far more than do the skins of humans: 'Where human skin appears to cling to the body, becoming *formless* once detached, animal skin seems to "travel" easily beyond the boundaries of the animal corpus'.[46] Susan Small goes further, arguing that 'the ineffable, irradicable difference between man and animals is written on his skin'.[47] Flaying often presupposes or causes death, and the death of a human is generally assumed to be of greater moment than that of an animal, the power released by that death consequently greater. While animals are accepted as sources for material objects such as meat, horns and hides, it is from human beings that some of the most potent religious, magical and medicinal objects were assumed to derive.[48]

The specific significance of human skin is a contested question in Giorgio Vasari's account of skin-wearing in *Le vite de' più eccellenti pittori, scultori, ed architettori* (1568). Vasari describes the sculptor Silvio Cosini, who worked in the early to mid-sixteenth century, as having succumbed to 'una volta capriccio [...] della più strana cosa del mondo' [the strangest caprice in the world].[49] Cosini, having dissected the body of an executed criminal[50] 'per conto della'arte' [for the purposes of his art], then flayed it and, 'acconciate la pelle, secondo che gli era stato insegnato, se ne fece, pensando che avesse qualche gran virtù, un coietto, e quello portò per alcun tempo' [with the skin, prepared after a method that he had been taught, he made a jerkin which he wore for some time [...] believing that it had some great virtue], until rebuked by a monk and told to bury

---

[46] Rikke Hansen, 'Travelling Skins: Hides, Furs and other Animal Surfaces in Art', presentation given at the Meet Animal Meat conference, Uppsala University, Sweden (2009), p. 3, emphasis in original.

[47] Susan Small, 'The Medieval Werewolf Model of Reading Skin', in *Reading Skin in Medieval Literature and Culture*, ed. Katie L. Walter (New York: Palgrave, 2013), pp. 81–97 at p. 83.

[48] See: Louise Noble, *Medicinal Cannibalism in Early Modern English Literature and Culture* (New York: Palgrave, 2011), for an extensive discussion of the assumed medical uses of the human body. Body parts of saints, of course, were also used for many purposes, including their protective effects.

[49] Quotations in Italian drawn from Giorgio Vasari, *Le vite de' più eccellenti pittori, scultori, ed architettori*, ed. Gaetano Milanesi (Florence, 1879), 4:483. English translation from Gaston du C. De Vere, trans., *Lives of the Most Eminent Painters, Sculptors, and Architects, Andrea da Fiesole to Lorenzo Lotto* (London: Philip Lee Warner, 1913), 5: 7.

[50] Historically, the easiest method of obtaining bodies or body parts was to get them from those who had no rights, particularly executed criminals or vanquished enemies; see: Stuart, *Defiled Trades and Social Outcasts*, pp. 157–60, and Mabel Peacock, 'Executed Criminals and Folk-Medicine', *Folklore* 27.7 (1896): 268–83 at pp. 270–1.

it. The jerkin itself occupies an unstable position, shifting in significance between a raw material, a constructed article of clothing and a body part, as well as between a waste product with no significance, an object imbued with magical power by virtue of its physical origin and a portion of the body deserving of burial like the rest due to its association with the soul but with no specific importance beyond that.[51] Katherine Park explains the desirable quality of the skin garment as 'its magical and protective powers',[52] a conjecture that may be intuitive to the modern mind but is not confirmed in the text. Vasari does not identify what Cosini believes to be the skin's 'great virtue', if indeed he knows it.[53]

It is clear, however, that whatever his motivation, the significance of the skin jerkin to Cosini is extra-rational. The artist created and wore it, says Vasari, 'come capriccioso e forse maliastro, e person che prestava fede agl'incanti e simili sciocchezze'[54] [being a whimsical fellow, and perhaps a wizard, and ready to believe in enchantments and suchlike follies].[55] While the term 'wizard' has overtones of evil, especially evident in the Italian *maliastro*, the predominant tone of Vasari's account is not moral condemnation, such as is evinced by the monk, but amused contempt at the artist's foolishness. Vasari sees the skin as essentially a by-product, without its own import, of the flaying necessary 'for the purposes of his art'. It is not, in his view, an object with symbolic significance that might lend it extraordinary powers.[56] Cosini, meanwhile, does not wish to become, or to disguise himself as, a criminal, but he understands human skin as

---

[51] In Italy, to a greater extent than in some other countries, executed criminals were often buried, owing to the existence of confraternities associated with the comforting and sepulture of the condemned, though burial was by no means a universal practice. See: Trevor Dean, *Crime and Justice in Late Medieval Italy* (Cambridge: Cambridge University Press, 2007), pp. 62–3.

[52] Katherine Park, 'The Criminal and the Saintly Body: Autopsy and Dissection in Renaissance Italy', *Renaissance Quarterly* 47.1 (Spring 1994): 1–33 at p. 26.

[53] Vasari may have considered that the belief would have been familiar to his audience, or that it would be inappropriate to expand on such wrongheadedness.

[54] Vasari, *Le vite*, p. 483.

[55] De Vere, trans., *Lives*, p. 7.

[56] Modes of understanding that prize the flayed body over the skin that had covered it may have little use for the skin as a symbolic object. A similar emphasis can be seen in Renaissance artists' and anatomists' growing fascination with laying bare the inner human body, a focus that often relegated the skin to the status of hindrance, even waste product, to be torn off or held aside to reveal the body's musculature, articulation and inner organs. See: Claudia Benthien, *Skin: On the Cultural Barrier between Self and the World*, trans. Thomas Dunlap (New York: Columbia University Press, 1999), pp. 64–8.

having magical properties that it is possible to access by wearing it. Its significance likely relates to its purpose in the living body: he ascribes no extraordinary powers to the rest of the condemned man's corpse beyond its utility in showing him correct conjunctions and proportions, helping him to depict living bodies more accurately. He does not choose to eat a piece of flesh as a medicine, nor drink the blood as a tonic, nor carry a tuft of hair as a talisman, nor wear a tooth as a pendant – all uses for body parts that are recorded in medieval and early modern texts.[57] It is the skin, and the wearing of it, that is meaningful to him. And though Cosini's act of creating and using the skin garment appears to the monk as highly degrading to the skin's previous owner, even blasphemous, it illustrates a far greater respect for the integument itself than that evinced by Vasari, a respect informed by Cosini's understanding of its literal and magical function.

The wearing of human skin is shown as unquestionably potent yet simultaneously sacrilegious in several Icelandic folk traditions collected by Jón Árnason in *Íslenzkar þjóðsögur og ævintýri* (1864), many of which have medieval and early modern origins.[58] By means of the act, wearers are transformed into sorcerers and thereby excluded from their former society.[59] Shoes made of human-skin leather, explains Árnason, will potentially last forever, never wearing out, unless they are worn over consecrated ground, whereupon they fall to pieces.[60] Human-skin gloves

[57] See: Noble, *Medicinal Cannibalism*, and Richard Sugg, *Mummies, Cannibals and Vampires: Corpse Medicine from the Renaissance to the Victorians* (Oxford: Routledge, 2011).

[58] Quotations from the Icelandic original are drawn from Jón Árnason, *Íslenzkar þjóðsögur og ævintýri* (Leipzig: J. C. Hinrichs's Bókaverzlunar, 1862); English translation and commentary from Jacqueline Simpson, trans., *Icelandic Folktales & Legends* (Stroud: Tempus, 1972, repr. 2004, 2009). Hereafter, page numbers will be given in parentheses. Simpson notes that 'one can often trace the existence of various stories, motifs, and beliefs [in the book] back to the twelfth, thirteenth and fourteenth centuries' (p. 12).

[59] Michael Fell notes that while malicious magic was penalized and stigmatized more harshly than beneficial or protective spells through much of Iceland's medieval period, pronouncements by both ecclesiastical and secular authorities in 1592, 1617 and 1630 assured that 'by the middle of the seventeenth century it seems to have been generally agreed by the ruling classes in Iceland that all practice of magic […] white and black alike, was criminal and deserved the harshest punishment.' His stipulation that this was the view of 'the ruling classes' suggests the possibility that magic was viewed differently by the common people; however, the majority of the accusations of sorcery that led to more than twenty witch-burnings between 1625 and 1683 originated from the accused witches' fellow villagers, implying *galdramenn*, or wizards, were not necessarily regarded with complaisance. Jon Magnússon, *And Though This World With Devils Filled*, ed. and trans. Michael Fell (New York: Peter Lang, 2007), pp. 14–17.

[60] Simpson, *Icelandic Folktales*, p. 183.

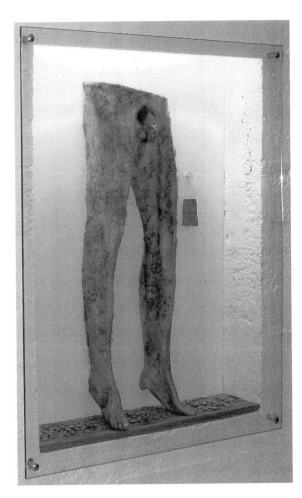

Fig. 5.1
Reproduction
of *nábuxur*,
popularly known
as 'necropants', in
The Museum of
Icelandic Sorcery
and Witchcraft

are associated with similarly durable and magical properties and taboos, augmented by demonic power until that power is destroyed by physical contact with material associated with the divine. Jacqueline Simpson, Árnason's translator, notes that a person may also be ridden through the air and the water by means of a 'witch bridle', a strip of human skin,[61] the skin object placed upon the living skin allowing for levitation and strength yet contravening the human steed's free will.

The association of demonic powers with skin-wearing, and the isolation of the wearer, are emphasized in the Icelandic skin-wearing tradition that has garnered the most horrified fascination, that of the *nábuxur* (Fig. 5.1). These 'wealth-breeches',[62] consisting of leg-skin flayed off from the waist down and kept anatomically intact, act as a source of unending wealth to

[61] Ibid., pp. 194–5.
[62] They are also known as *nábrók*, which has a similar connotation.

their wearer while binding him by the taboos and complications attendant on their sorcerous nature, forcing him away from his former mode of existence and into an alternative state of being. Árnason makes clear their association with sorcery and the Devil, which is signalled by another name: *Skollabrækur*, or 'Old Nick's breeches'.[63] Their *djöfullegt* [diabolical][64] association is independent of the method of obtaining the breeches; they are evil even though they are not acquired cruelly. Árnason emphasizes that they may only be obtained through a pact entered into between two men, who agree that whoever dies first shall yield his skin to the other; the flaying is both post-mortem (therefore painless) and consensual. Nevertheless, the act is coded as illicit; the survivor must go to the graveyard in the night and dig up the corpse to take its skin, a procedure not to be performed in the presence, or with the knowledge, of others.[65] After flaying the skin from the corpse's legs – all in one piece, without any holes – the survivor draws it over his own bare legs, whereupon it immediately adheres to them. It does this so quickly, Árnason explains, that even if the wearer should change his mind after donning one leg's worth of skin and attempt to draw out his leg from it, he would find himself instead pulling on the other leg, as though the alien, yet integrated, skin was providing the motive power for his movements, having already begun transforming him.

In one area the skin does not adhere. Árnason specifies the *pung*, a word translated by Simpson as 'pocket' but which rather means 'scrotum', as the location in which a coin must be placed, along with a specific stave or magical rune.[66] There the coin immediately begins to proliferate, providing an unending source of wealth to the wearer as long as the original stolen coin is never removed. If the desecration of the corpse in the churchyard and the location in which the coin is kept associate the *nábuxur* with illicit forces, so too does the coin's provenance. It must be stolen from a 'bláfátækri ekkju' [wretchedly poor widow] during a particular period in the Church calendar, 'á einhverri hinna þriggja stórhátíða ársins á milli pistils og guðspjalls' (p. 428) [at the moment between the reading of the Epistle and the Gospel on one of the three major church festivals of the year] (p. 182). This procedure couples antisocial and sacrilegious acts that

---

[63] Simpson, *Icelandic Folktales*, p. 181.

[64] Árnason, *Íslenzkar þjóðsögur*, p. 429.

[65] Icelandic sorcery was an activity to be undertaken in secret; Fell emphasizes this in his speculation as to why so few witches and sorcerers accused and convicted in early modern Iceland were female: women were rarely alone. See Fell's commentary in Magnússon, *Though This World*, p. 48 n. 36.

[66] The stave was also a marker of the infernal. The sixteenth-/seventeenth-century scholar Arngrímur Jónsson argued that runes, extensively used in Icelandic sorcery, 'have no magical power in and of themselves, but only in so far as the sorcerer [...] has fellowship with the devil' (qtd. in Magnússon, *Through This World*, p. 23).

isolate the wearer from both the Christian and the sorceric community, theft being deeply problematic and deserving of retribution among magic users as well as being forbidden by the tenets of Christianity.[67] Extrapolating from Árnason's account of the shoes made from human skin that cannot touch consecrated ground, it seems likely that the wearer of the *nábuxur* would be unable to enter a church – or at least to sit down in one – for fear that his skin-pants would disintegrate off him at the touch of the consecrated bench. Both creating and wearing the skin-pants, then, abstract the wearer from his surrounding community, situating him at the margins of his society.

This occurs in ways beyond the religious as well. Another of the names of the artefact, *finnabrækur* [Finnish or Lappish breeches], not only relates to the Icelandic understanding of the Lappish people as being *galdramenn* (p. 429) [wizards], and therefore more prone to manipulating demonic objects; it also associates the wearer with outlanders. The possession of wealth in and of itself seems to have been so comparatively rare as to excite rumours involving necromantic schemes, a form of isolation alluded to in Árnason's account of a Papey Island resident in the late eighteenth century who was assumed to have acquired such pants on account of his otherwise inexplicable riches.[68] Finally, the trousers probably would also have kept the wearer from sexual relations, imprisoning his genitals behind a barrier of acquired skin and interposing a cumbersome load of coins, one that moreover must be kept secret, between himself and his potential partner.[69] Wearing the skin alienates him by multiple means, trapping him behind not just physical, but social, sexual and religious barriers too.

The removal of the *nábuxur* is a far more difficult proposition than the taking off of Cosini's jerkin or Morolf's disguise, owing to the far deeper transformation they work on their wearer. They must be removed, however; if they are still in place at the wearer's death, Árnason warns, they become infested with lice, making visible on the skin's surface his moral lapse in the same way that pox and leprous lesions were assumed to act as outward and visible signs of an inward, invisible fall from grace.[70] Far more dreadfully, the wearer forfeits his soul to the Devil,[71] alienating him

---

[67] Stephen Flowers notes that in the *Galdrabók*, the most comprehensive early modern Icelandic grimoire extant, spells to find and punish thieves are disproportionately represented. *The Galdrabók: An Icelandic Grimoire* (York Beach: Samuel Weiser, 1989), p. 32.

[68] Simpson, *Icelandic Folktales*, p. 182.

[69] Celibacy was not required of Icelandic wizards in general; the *Galdrabók* and other Icelandic grimoires include several spells to win the love (or lust) of both women and men, and those who were historically burned as witches included married men and fathers.

[70] See: Julie Orlemanski, 'Desire and Defacement in *The Testament of Cresseid*', in *Reading Skin*, ed. Walter, pp. 161–81 at pp. 162–3.

[71] Simpson, *Icelandic Folktales*, p. 182.

from the community of Christendom not only in this world but also in the world to come. The effects of the surface skin can be kept from reaching the soul while the wearer is alive; he can be redeemed by sloughing it in time. However, beside the assumed disinclination to remove so miraculous a source of wealth, the pants may only be yielded to a new bearer. One leg must be peeled off the previous wearer and immediately donned by the next one before the second leg may be removed. This deeply intimate physical conjunction with another – each standing with one leg encased, joined at the crotch of the skin breeches – emblematizes the beginning of the former wearer's integration back into the community; he is only saved and transformed back into his former self by his return to contact with another. At the same time, however, the new wearer is leaving his community; for, as before, having put on the first leg, he too will find himself unable not to follow it with the second and will then be subject to the same constraints and taboos. This cycle may potentially be continued forever; like the human-skin shoes, the corpse-breeches are said never to wear out: a promise or a doom.

Instances of skin-wearing recurrently enact – or provoke – trans-formation, the breaking of barriers between states. The poacher is forced into a deer hide to illustrate the wrongful crossing of boundaries, while Jone's wrapping in Morel's skin not only demonstrates but also appears to correct her transgression. Morolf crosses physical as well as metaphoric borders by his use of a skin disguise that is not, in the end, a disguise, but rather an illustration of his essentially border-crossing and duplicitous nature. Cosini's jerkin shows that beliefs about the magical powers of human skin relate to its physical function as limen as much as to its provenance. And the *nábuxur* demonstrate the soul-deep alteration to be feared from wearing surface skin. The very possibility of these alterations may stem from the medieval and early modern understanding of the skin itself as partially penetrable. Poultices, washes and salves were understood to effect cures within, not merely at the surface, of the body; sorcerous ointments rubbed into the skin were understood to allow witches to fly[72] or werewolves to shift to their animal form.[73] The worn skin, and its powers, could touch the wearer through her or his own integument.

Yet in all these instances, the crossing of boundaries effected by

---

[72] This is described in Thomas Middleton, *The Witch*, ed. Marion O'Connor, in *Thomas Middleton: The Collected Works*, ed. Gary Taylor and John Lavagnino (Oxford: Oxford University Press, 2010), 1.2.15–18. The note to these lines, pp. 1133–4, references Reginald Scot's *The Discoverie of Witchcraft*; the *Malleus Maleficarum* also promulgates this belief.

[73] This is the cause of the werewolf Alphonse's transformation in the Old French romance *Guillaume de Palerne* and its Middle English translation *William of Palerne*. Conversely, Gorlagon in *Arthur and Gorlagon* is transformed by a verbal spell and the touch of a magic sapling. See: Tracy, 'Face Off', p. 344.

skin-wearing is necessarily partial, incomplete or limited. In her analysis of medieval werewolf transformations, Small argues for a distinction between the '"overlay model" of reading skin', in which 'animal skin [is] presented as an adjunct to human skin […] and the "fusion model": those texts in which human skin and animal […] skin constitute the verso and recto of the same organic surface'.[74] Under the terms of the latter model, Small explains, 'nakedness is a necessary condition for the metamorphic process by means of which the threshold between human and animal skin is breached and overturned';[75] those who attempt to turn lycanthrope must first remove their clothing.[76] The instances of skin-wearing discussed here merge and extend these models: the skin, overlaid on the skin, then fuses with the wearer's nature. A far greater dislocative effect is created by the flaying of the first wearer's skin before its placement on the second wearer's; the skin-garment does not magically appear but is torn off one being and placed on another. More transformative still, however, are those instances in which the second wearer's own skin wall, however originally porous, is breached. In Jone's punishment in the *Merry Ieste*, the wounds of the beating render her beyond naked in places, naked even of her skin, such that she takes on Morel's fell as her own. And the powers of the *nábuxur* are so much greater and more dangerous than those of other skin-garments discussed because they originate within the possibility-space that either member of the pact may be required to yield his skin. The two episodes showing the greatest transformative power come closest to realizing the full abdication of the barrier function of the wearer's original skin, a process required for complete alteration: full transformation through skin-wearing, that is, would require that the new wearer first be flayed.

[74] Small, 'The Medieval Werewolf Model', p. 86.

[75] Ibid., p. 83.

[76] This is how the werewolf in Marie de France's twelfth-century lai *Bisclavret* effects his transformation.

II
REPRESENTATIONS
OF FLAYING

Fig. 6.1 Pacino di Bonaguida, folio from the Laudario of Sant'Agnese, showing five scenes from the flaying of St Bartholomew, c. 1340 (New York, The Metropolitan Museum of Art, The Cloisters Collection, 2006.250)

6

Robed in Martyrdom:
The Flaying of St Bartholomew
in the Laudario of Sant'Agnese

Asa Simon Mittman and Christine Sciacca

S T B A R T H O L O M E W is the most prominent flayed Christian martyr, perhaps best known in Michelangelo's rendition on the Last Judgement wall of the Sistine Chapel (1534–41). In this High Renaissance work, the saint holds the instrument of his martyrdom – a knife – in his right hand and his flayed skin, draped like an old coat, in his left. The figure holding his skin is, inexplicably, *also* wearing his skin.[1] That is, he demonstrates his grisly martyrdom and simultaneously defies both its gore and its finality. Such a presentation of Bartholomew is common, particularly in iconic, rather than narrative, images, where the clothed saint holds his attribute and yet his skin remains intact.[2] Two hundred years before this, the Florentine artist Pacino di Bonaguida (active *c*. 1303–*c*. 1347) created a complex composition to present this unsettling figure and his martyrdom. His strikingly different Bartholomew appears on a folio of the fragmentary Laudario of Sant'Agnese, a book of Italian hymns produced for the Compagnia di Sant'Agnese (Confraternity of St Agnes) (*c*. 1340, Fig. 6.1).[3] The manuscript was disbound in the nineteenth century and only

---

[1] Sarah Kay, 'Original Skin: Flaying, Reading, and Thinking in the Legend of Saint Bartholomew and other Works', *Journal of Medieval and Early Modern Studies* 36.1 (2006): 35–73 at p. 42. In this volume, Jack Hartnell discusses the imagery of knives in representations of flaying. See: 'Tools of the Puncture: Skin, Knife, Bone, Hand', pp. 20–50.

[2] One such example from early fourteenth-century Florence by Jacopo del Casentino depicts St Bartholomew seated and surrounded by angels and holding a book and a knife in his left hand (Florence, Galleria dell'Accademia, No. 440). This panel likely formed a portion of an altarpiece from the church of San Bartolommeo dei Pittori, now destroyed, the only church in Florence dedicated to St Bartholomew. See: Walter Paatz and Elisabeth Paatz, *Die Kirchen von Florenz: Ein kunstgeschichtliches Handbuch* (Frankfurt: Vittorio Klostermann, 1955), pp. 333–6. Roughly two decades before the Laudario, Pacino di Bonaguida painted an iconic, half-length figure of St Bartholomew on panel, in which the saint holds a book and the knife of his martyrdom (Philadelphia, The Barnes Foundation, BF 833).

[3] On the St Bartholomew leaf, see: Miklós Boskovits, *A Critical and Historical Corpus of Florentine Painting*, sect. 3, vol. 9: *The Fourteenth Century: The Painters of the Miniaturist Tendency* (Florence: Giunti, 1984), p. 53 n. 179, 268, pl. CXa; Richard Offner, with Karla Steinweg, *A Critical and Historical*

thirty-one illuminated leaves and fragments now survive, some by Pacino and others by the Master of the Dominican Effigies.[4]

The Bartholomew folio, housed in the collection of the Cloisters Museum, New York, presents five moments within (and bursting out of) three frames. Three scenes are contained within the central frame, divided into two conjoined rectangular panels that occupy the upper half of the text block. The opening of the *lauda* for Bartholomew is below: 'Appostolo beato da gesu cristo amato. Bartholomeo te laudiam diboncore' [Blessed Apostle, loved by Jesus Christ, Bartholomew we praise you whole-heartedly].[5] In the left margin, which was the outer margin when this folio was bound, there are two small roundels, connected by delicate, multicoloured leafy decoration that then spills downward and unfurls into the lower margin. The beauty and elegance of the foliate work, dominated by pinks and blues and highlighted with spots and points of gold, stand in sharp contrast with the horrific acts occurring in the images it frames.

Corpus of Florentine Painting, sect. 3, vol. 2: *The Fourteenth Century: Elder Contemporaries of Bernardo Daddi*, ed. Miklós Boskovits, with Mina Gregori (Florence: Giunti, 1987), p. 71; Barbara Drake Boehm, 'The Laudario of the Compagnia di Sant'Agnese', in *Painting and Illumination in Early Renaissance Florence, 1300–1450*, exhibition catalogue, ed. Laurence B. Kanter *et al.* (New York: Metropolitan Museum of Art, 1994), pp. 62, 77, fig. 30; Pia Palladino, *Treasures of a Lost Art: Italian Manuscript Painting of the Middle Ages and Renaissance*, exhibition catalogue (New York: Metropolitan Museum of Art, 2003), cat. 21b, pp. 40–1; Stella Panayotova, 'New Miniatures by Pacino di Bonaguida in Cambridge', *Burlington Magazine* 151.1272 (Mar. 2009): 144–8 at p. 148, appendix no. 24; Christine Sciacca, ed., *Florence at the Dawn of the Renaissance: Painting and Illumination, 1300–1350* (Los Angeles: J. Paul Getty Museum, 2012), cat. 45.23, pp. 275–7 (entry by Christine Sciacca).

[4] On the Laudario di Sant'Agnese, see: Boehm, 'The Laudario of the Compagnia di Sant'Agnese', pp. 58–80; Panayotova, 'New Miniatures by Pacino di Bonaguida', pp. 144–8; Christine Sciacca, 'Reconstructing the Laudario of Sant'Agnese', in *Florence at the Dawn of the Renaissance*, ed. Sciacca, pp. 219–35. Three of these Laudario leaves were recently identified in the collection of the Musée Antoine Vivenel in Compiègne. We thank Roberta Bosi for bringing our attention to her entry on these leaves in *Jan Fabre: Illuminations, enluminures, trésors enluminés de France: Chalcosoma, 2006–2012, hommage à Jérôme Bosch au Congo, 2011–2013* [exhibition catalogue] (Ennetières-en-Weppes: Invenit, 2013), pp. 222–3, cat. 34, fig. 27. See also: François Avril, 'À la [Re]découverte des manuscrits et enluminures des Musées de France', in *Trésors enluminés des musées de France: pays de la Loire et Centre*, ed. Pascale Charron, Marc-Édouard Gautier and Pierre-Gilles Girault (Angers: Musées d'Angers and INHA, 2013), pp. 15–22 at pp. 18–19.

[5] For a corpus of Florentine *laude*, and English translations, see: Blake Wilson, *The Florence Laudario: An Edition of Florence, Biblioteca Nazionale Centrale, Banco Rari 18* (Madison, WI: A-R Editions, 1995), esp. p. lxxvii.

Fig. 6.2 The folio
in Fig. 6.1, with the
sequence of the
scenes marked
(New York, The
Metropolitan
Museum of Art, The
Cloisters Collection,
2006.250)

The images depict: the flaying of Bartholomew, his *subsequent* preaching, his beheading, the elevation of his soul to Heaven and the lowering of his body into his sarcophagus. The sequence is somewhat convoluted, since following it in chronological order according to the saint's *vita* means starting at the left rectangular panel, descending to the lower roundel, crossing over to the lower scene within the right rectangular panel, moving upward to the top-right corner of the same panel for the elevation and then crossing from far right to far left for the burial scene in the upper roundel (Fig. 6.2). This produces a disjointed and unnatural mode of viewing and requires visually traversing numerous layers of framing. The central panel is circumscribed by multiple nested frames, most of which join the two panels like the frames of a diptych, and is further strengthened by the delicate white linework against the rich blue skies just within the images, and the grey shadow that the lower member of the frame seems to cast on the stylised landscape it encloses. In the first scene Bartholomew is nude and, as he is in the process of being flayed, also seems as if he is being stripped yet further, with his pale skin being pulled off to reveal another form beneath. In the two final episodes, in which Bartholomew appears as a soul and as a corpse, he is wrapped in ochre garments meant to suggest golden robes of cloth. Of particular significance, though, are the two scenes in the second and third episodes, those scenes in which Bartholomew, already flayed but apparently not quite dead, wears his own light-greenish skin – substantially less ruddy than it appears in the first scene and therefore intended to signify its status as removed, flayed skin – draped around his shoulders and tied at his neck like a cape; this loose garment of skin recalls the white robes that 'nec veterascunt nec sordidantur' [neither wear out nor become dirty] by which he is recognized in the account of his life in the *Legenda aurea* (*Golden Legend*).[6]

In the lower roundel, one of Bartholomew's flayed hands is clearly visible, painted an eye-catching white, dangling from the lower hem of his skin-robe.[7] The artist added the hand to the skin as a final detail, painted in five simple strokes of white pigment. In the main scene, however, both hands are clearly visible, tied at the base of the beheaded figure's severed neck. This shift in a rather minor detail necessitates that the viewer imagine the grotesque, if ordinary, act of the skinless figure untying and retying his cloak, or, perhaps, its loosening and falling to the barren, rocky ground, only to be retrieved and retied more securely at the wrists. The Laudario's images contain a tension in the representation of this slow-motion martyrdom: they are at once remarkably explicit, given time and place, and suffused with a calmness and confidence centred on the repeated figure of Bartholomew. The gruesome figure we see in the roundel, viewed by the lay confraternity that sang from the Laudario nightly, is skinless but not yet dead, martyred but still animate on earth. This is an early example of the tradition of presenting the saint *wearing his own skin* as a cloak, a device that visually transforms the figure from preacher to saint, human to posthuman. Indeed, the very transformative nature of the figure of Bartholomew, presented in iterations throughout the Laudario folio, embodies his posthumanism, in which 'plethora replaces persona and being becomes becoming'.[8]

---

[6] Jacobus de Voragine, *Legenda aurea, vulgo Historia Lombardica dicta*, ed. Th. Graesse, 2nd edn (Leipzig: Impensis Librariae Arnoldianae, 1850), p. 541. Hereafter, page numbers are given in parentheses. This and all other translations, unless otherwise noted, are our own. For a recent discussion of the history of *The Golden Legend*, see: Jacques Le Goff, *In Search of Sacred Time: Jacobus de Voragine and 'The Golden Legend'*, trans. Lydia G. Cochrane (Princeton: Princeton University Press, 2014). In this volume, William Sayers frames the absence of flaying in Irish epic and law with a unique account of Bartholomew wrapped in his skin like a cloak. See: 'No Skin in the Game: Flaying and Early Irish Law and Epic', pp. 261–84.

[7] We thank Andrew Winslow of the Cloisters Museum for directing our attention to this, and for his assistance in a close examination of the St Bartholomew leaf.

[8] Patricia MacCormack, 'Posthuman Teratology', in *Research Companion to Monsters and the Monstrous*, ed. Asa Simon Mittman with Peter Dendle (London: Ashgate, 2012), pp. 293–309 at p. 297. Indeed, MacCormack's

The most popular account of Bartholomew's life and death is in Jacobus de Voragine's *Legenda aurea* [hereafter *LgA*], compiled in the later thirteenth century. The text was in wide circulation in Italy by the mid-fourteenth century, when the Laudario was created. The account records the apostle's travels to India, 'quae est in fine orbis' [which is at the end of the earth] (p. 540), where he topples the idol of Astaroth, inhabited by a demon. The man of God then takes up residence in the temple that was formerly occupied by the demon. Those who were used to appealing to the idol for cures flee to the idol of Berith in a nearby city, and the demon in this idol tells them how to recognize Bartholomew:

> [C]apilli ejus crispi et nigri, caro candida, oculi grandes, nares aequales et directae, barba prolixa habens paucos canos, statura aequalis, *collobio* albo clavato purpura vestitur, induitur *pallio* albo, quod per singulos angulos gemmas habet purpureas. Viginti sex anni sunt, ex quo vestes et sandalia ejus nec veterascunt nec sordidantur.
>
> (p. 541, emphasis added)

> [His hair is curly and black, his skin white, his eyes large, his nose even and straight, his long beard has a few grey hairs. His stature is even. He is dressed in a white *collobio* trimmed in purple, and clothed in a white *pallio* that has purple gems at each corner. He has worn these garments and sandals for twenty-six years, and they neither wear out nor become dirty.]

The attention to details of features and clothing is unusual, and the focus on richness, beauty and spotlessness is transparently metaphorical, standing in for Bartholomew's perpetually unstained soul. The particular vocabulary is important here. *Collobio* is a declined variant of *colobium*, which is a short tunic with short sleeves worn by deacons.[9] The *pallium* is a long cloak of the sort worn by classical philosophers and contemporaries of Bartholomew.[10] In the Middle Ages the term *pallium* referred to a kind of scarf, and eventually a circle of fabric with long tails, arranged around the neck of a pope or bishop. While Pacino depicts the long robe of Bartholomew's time, for the medieval reader of the *LgA* the sartorial term would have signified episcopal authority, which itself was based on the apostolic authority bestowed upon Bartholomew and his fellow disciples. In addition to the images that accompany the *lauda* for Bartholomew,

---

characterization of the posthuman reads like a description of the Bartholomew folio: 'the multiple, the transformative, the space between, the manifold, the other' (p. 296).

[9] Alexius Aurelius Pelliccia, *The Polity of the Christian Church of Early, Medieval, and Modern Times*, trans. J. C. Bellett (London: J. Masters, 1883), p. 181.

[10] Maureen C. Miller, *Clothing the Clergy: Virtue and Power in Medieval Europe, c. 800–1200* (Ithaca, NY: Cornell University Press, 2014), pp. 250–1.

the saint is identifiable in three other miniatures from the Laudario of Sant'Agnese, primarily in the company of the twelve apostles.[11] In *Christ in Majesty* and *The Last Supper* he is the only figure who wears a white robe (besides Christ), and in *Christ in Majesty* and *The Ascension of Christ* his robe is covered with a rich pattern of cross-shaped motifs and is the only one decorated in any way. In each case, therefore, Bartholomew is set apart by means of his resplendent clothing that, in the textual and visual narratives, foreshadows his more glorious, miraculous clothing of skin.

Of course, the real meat of the *vita* comes a bit later. After Bartholomew casts out another demon[12] and converts King Polemius, his family and subjects, the king's brother, King Astyages, has the apostle brought before him. It seems that Bartholomew's mere presence in the kingdom is sufficient to topple the idol to Baldach, thereby enraging the king. In this first account in the *LgA*, Astyages orders Bartholomew to be beaten and flayed alive: 'Quod rex audiens purpuram scidit, qua indutus erat, et apsotolum fustibus caedi jussit et caesum vivum excoriari mandavit.' [When the king heard, he rent the purple in which he was clothed, and ordered the apostle beaten with clubs and commanded that he be flayed alive.] (p. 543). This is the first account of Bartholomew's martyrdom in the *LgA*, but not the only one. Jacobus proceeds to provide other competing accounts, often with attributions of source. St Dorotheus claims Bartholomew was crucified head downward, but St Theodore says he was flayed; unnamed others say he was beheaded. Ambrose also has him beaten and flayed: 'caesum atque excoriatum acerrimam fecit suscipere mortem' [beaten and flayed, he did accept the bitterest death] (p. 546). Theodore places him in Albania, where 'primo excoriatus, tandem capite

---

[11] Bartholomew, with his short, curly, reddish hair and long beard, appears in the following miniatures: *Christ in Majesty*, Washington, DC, National Gallery of Art (Rosenwald Collection, 1952.8.277); *The Ascension of Christ*, Los Angeles, The J. Paul Getty Museum (MS 80a; 2005.26); *The Last Supper*, Antwerp, Museum Mayer van den Bergh (Ms. 303).

[12] This demon is described as 'Aethiopem nigriorem fuligine, facie acuta, barba prolixa, crinibus usque ad pedes protensis, oculis igneis ut ferrum ignitum scintillas emittentibus, flammas sulphureas ex re et oculis spirantem, catenis igneis vinctum retro minibus' [An Ethiopian more black than soot, with a sharp face, thick beard, and hair stretched down to his feet, with fiery eyes emitting sparks like red hot iron, breathing flames of sulfur out of the thing and its eyes, his hands bound behind him with fiery chains]. This passage merits an essay of its own, given the Othering of the demon via 'proto-racial' terminology, but also because saint and demon are twinned, such that the latter becomes the doppelgänger of the former. Both are described with the same phrase, as both bear 'barba prolixa'. See: Peter Biller, 'Proto-Racial Thought in Medieval Science', in *The Origins of Racism in the West*, ed. Miriam Eliav-Feldon, Benjamin Isaac and Joseph Ziegler (Cambridge: Cambridge University Press, 2009), pp. 157–80.

plexus, ibidem sepultus est' [he was first flayed, and then beheaded, and in the same place buried] (p. 546), and, a bit further on, 'postquam vivus excoriatus est, capite plectitur' [after he was flayed alive, he was beheaded] (p. 547). Jacobus reconciles the accounts by helpfully suggesting that Bartholomew could have been pulled down from the cross before death in order to be flayed and then ultimately beheaded (pp. 543–4). In the text, then, the apostle is subjected to repeated punishment and execution. Within a half-dozen pages (in the modern print edition), Bartholomew is beaten, flayed, crucified, flayed, beheaded, beaten, flayed, flayed, beheaded, flayed and beheaded. His torment and death seem never-ending, or endlessly repeating, albeit with variation from one horror to another.[13]

The image of Bartholomew from the Laudario presents two of the three martyrdom scenes mentioned in the *LgA*, excluding the inverted crucifixion. However, it contains another scene from Bartholomew's passion, which is perhaps the most puzzling element of this folio: in the lower roundel, Bartholomew preaches to a rapt audience of seated figures. He is haloed, his hands raised in oratory gestures. Although he has been divested of his skin, he wears it as if a garment.[14] In this scene of preaching, Bartholomew has *already been flayed* but is not yet dead. This miracle is mentioned in the *Acta sanctorum*, where the notable eighteenth-century Bollandist Jean Stiltingh[15] (aka Joanne Stiltingo) writes:

> addit Equilinus: Cumque pelle nudatus adhuc vivus permansisset: & excoriatus Dominum prædicaret: & multos tantum cernentes

---

[13] For a related discussion of visual and textual repetition, see: Asa Simon Mittman and Susan M. Kim, 'Locating the Devil "*Her*" in MS Junius 11', *Gesta* 54.1 (Apr. 2015): 3–25.

[14] The *LgA* cites a *vita* by St Theodore Studita as saying of Bartholomew that 'postquam intolerabilia tormenta subiit, ab iis decoriatus in morem follis fuit' [after unbearable torture, he was flayed by them like a leather bag] (p. 547). Theodore's text is documented in the *Acta sanctorum* as St Theodore Studita, *Bartholomæus apostolus, Albanopoli in Armenia vel Albania*, Bibliotheca Hagiographica Latina 1005, col. 0039A. This version reads, at slightly greater length, 'postquam multa & intolerabilia tormenta subiit, decoriatus ab impiis, in morem follis, fuerit' [after he had to be in such great and intolerable pain, he had been flayed by the wicked [one], in the manner of a leather bag].

[15] Louis J. Swift, 'The Bollandists', *Encyclopedia of Library and Information Science*, vol. 38, ed. Allen Kent (New York: Marcel Dekker, 1985): 'Undoubtedly the most versatile Bollandist of this period was Jean Stiltingh (1703–62), a prodigious worker with an almost unbounded capacity for assimilating and ordering knowledge. Although the long historical commentaries which had become typical of the *Acta* by this time tended to get out of hand under his leadership, his distinguished reputation among contemporaries won for the society both the support of the Empress Maria Theresa and the affection of Pope Benedict XIV' (p. 42).

miraculum convertisset: jussu regis decollatus est die sequenti videlicet VIII Calend. prædicti mensis (Septembris).[16]

[Equilinus adds, when [Bartholomew] was stripped of his skin, he still remained alive, and after flaying, preached of the Lord, and only seeing the miracle, many converted; thus he was beheaded by order of the king on the day following 8 Kalends of the aforesaid month (September).]

'Equilinus' is Petrus de Natalibus, a canon in Equilio (present-day Jesolo, just north of Venice), author of the fourteenth-century *Catalogus sanctorum et gestorum eorum*. Little is known about Petrus' life, but his text, which may, perhaps, be a few decades later than the Laudario, and written not far from Florence, was widely disseminated and was published in several early modern editions. In it, we find the portion of the narrative referenced by Stiltingh, which is apparently not present in other extant *vitae*. This miracle must have been known at the time the Laudario was made. The passage reads:

quod rex audines purpuras: qua indutus erat: scidit: & apostolu[m] fustibus cedi iussit: deinde in cruce ipsum extensum viuum excoriari mandavit: qui excoriatus est .ix. kalendas septe[m]bris. Cunq[ue] pelle nudatus ad huc viuus permansisset: et excortiatus d[omi]n[u]m predicaret: et multos tantum cernentes miraculum convertisset: iussu regis decollatus est die sequenti videlicet .vii. kalen pererdicti mensis. Propter hoc quida[m] eius festum celebrant die precedenti: agentes memoria[m] martyrii excoriationies: quida[rum] die sequenti agentes memoria[m] decollationis.[17]

[When the king heard, he rent the purple in which he was clothed, and ordered the apostle to submit to clubs; and thence for his life to be extended, he commanded that he be [taken] off from the cross and flayed; and he was flayed on 9 Kalends of September. When

---

[16] Jean Stiltingh (Joanne Stiltingo), 'Bartholomæus apostolus, Albanopoli in Armenia vel Albania (S.)', August V, De S. Bartholomæo Apostolo, Albanopoli in Armenia vel Albania, Seculo I, Commentarius Prævius, in *Acta Sanctorum Augusti, ex Latinis & Graecis ...* (Antwerp: Bernardus Albertus vander Plassche, 1741), col. 0007A. Digitized edn, Cambridge: Chadwyck-Healey, 2001. For a curious Irish variant on this narrative, in which Bartholomew is made to carry his own skin through town to sell it, see: Sayers, 'No Skin in the Game', p. 262.

[17] Petrus de Natalibus, *Catalogus sanctorum et gestorum eorum* (Lugdunum: Thomas, 1514). The work is not paginated, but the relevant section can be found on pp. 399–401 of the digital version accessible through the website of the Bayerische Staatsbibliothek. Go to https://www.bsb-muenchen. de, and search the catalogue for 'Catalogus sanctorum et gestorum eorum' (accessed Sept. 2014).

stripped of his skin, he remained alive. And flayed, he preached, and converted many who saw the miracle. The king ordered him beheaded the next day, 7 Kalends of the aforesaid month. Because of this, some celebrate his feast a day earlier, in memory of the flaying of the martyr; others celebrate the next day in memory of his beheading.]

Thus, while previous scholarship has cited Pacino's indebtedness to the texts of the *LgA* for the subjects and details of his illuminations in the Laudario,[18] the above selection of Bartholomew's various *vitae* suggests that the artist drew instead from a variety of sources, both written and visual.

The apparent increase in interest in the subject of Bartholomew displayed in the Laudario may result from local concerns. Some of the leaves from the Laudario display images of the patrons of the manuscript in the lower margin. The figures appear in the dress of middle-class Florentine laypeople, reflecting the male merchants and shopkeepers who formed the confraternity's membership, and their wives and sisters, who were able to join the group as secondary members with minor roles in its religious and social life.[19] Because these images of patrons vary from one to two per page and appear in various gender combinations (one man, a man and a woman, two men) it is possible that individual members of the confraternity, or small groups within it, sponsored particular leaves in the manuscript according to their personal devotional attentions and patron saints.[20] The Bartholomew leaf, however, displays no donor figures. While only the main miniatures survive from the other martyrdom leaves mentioned above, they are of similar dimensions to the Bartholomew miniature, so it seems likely those leaves displayed a *mise-en-page* similar to the Bartholomew leaf. The surviving images of the patrons appear mostly on the pages devoted to temporal feasts, and where they do appear on pages for sanctoral feasts the accompanying images focus on saintly miracles and do not display bloody martyrdoms. It seems, then, that St Bartholomew's martyrdom may have had more general significance for the confraternity. While records describing the membership of the Compagnia di Sant'Agnese from the time of the Laudario do not survive, later rolls listing the occupations of the members who joined the confraternity from 1485–93

[18] See: Boehm, 'The Laudario of the Compagnia di Sant'Agnese'; Panayotova, 'New Miniatures by Pacino'; and Sciacca, *Florence at the Dawn of the Renaissance*.

[19] Sciacca, 'Reconstructing the Laudario', p. 220; Blake Wilson, *Music and Merchants: The Laudesi Companies of Republican Florence* (Oxford: Oxford University Press, 1992), p. 46; Ronald E. Weissman, *Ritual Brotherhood in Renaissance Florence* (New York: Academic Press, 1982), pp. 212–13.

[20] Panayotova, 'New Miniatures by Pacino', pp. 144–8.

cite a leather dealer among their ranks.[21] This craft of leather-working, with which modern-day Florence is so intimately associated, is also closely allied with the related fields of book-binding and parchment-making. St Bartholomew's role as the patron saint of book-binders and parchment makers,[22] and the membership of merchants and shopkeepers involved in this trade in the Compagnia di Sant'Agnese, may have sparked the inclusion of the striking visual celebration of his martyrdom in the confraternity's Laudario.

On the St Bartholomew leaf from the Cloisters Museum, the first event depicted from the martyrdom, namely Bartholomew's flaying at the left in the central miniature, is perhaps the most gruesome. While certainly not the earliest instance of this scene in painting, Pacino's rendition displays an unusual approach. In scenes of his flaying, Bartholomew is typically stretched out horizontally on a table or the ground while his tormentors begin their surgical work, as in the upper right quadrant of the late-thirteenth-century Sienese *Diptych of Saint Clare* (Fig. 6.3).[23] Similarly, in the mid-fourteenth-century fresco depicting the Last Judgement and Hell in the Camposanto in Pisa, a figure wearing a papal tiara and labelled as 'Antichrist' lies on his back as his skin is torn away by devils.[24] This scene

---

[21] Weissman, *Ritual Brotherhood*, pp. 76–7. For more on the membership of confraternities in Florence, see: Wilson, *Music and Merchants*.

[22] Kay, 'Original Skin', p. 37.

[23] We thank Ada Labriola for bringing this image to our attention. See: Piero Torriti, *La Pinacoteca Nazionale di Siena: I dipinti* (Genoa: Sagep, 1990), p. 18, fig. 15. A similar composition also appears in a Tuscan fresco from the first decade of the fourteenth century found in the San Niccolò chapel in the Palazzo dei Vescovi in Pistoia. See: Ada Labriola, 'Gli affreschi della cappella di San Niccolò nell'Antico Palazzo dei Vescovi a Pistoia', *Arte Cristiana* 727 (1988): 247–66, esp. pp. 247–8, fig. 1. In addition, one twelfth-century example is found on a portable altar from Stavelot in Brussels, Musées royaux d'Art et d'Histoire, Musées Cinquantenaire (no. 1590). See: Louis Réau, *Iconographie de l'art chrétien* (Paris: Presses Universitaires de France, 1958), 1:183. In a French copy of the *LgA* from 1348, illuminated by Richard de Montbaston, St Bartholomew is laid out on a trestle table (Paris, Bibliothèque nationale de France, MS Fr. 241, fol. 219r). On this manuscript, see: Kay, 'Original Skin', pp. 50–2. See also Jack Hartnell, 'Tools of the Puncture. Skin, Knife, Bone, Hand', in this volume, p. 25, for discussion of the relation of images of Bartholomew's flaying to medieval medical images.

[24] Robert Mills, 'Havelok's Bare Life and the Significance of Skin', in *Reading Skin in Medieval Literature and Culture*, ed. Katie L. Walter (New York: Palgrave, 2013), pp. 57–80 at p. 63; Jérôme Baschet, *Les Justices de l'au-delà: les représentations de l'enfer en France et en Italie, XIIe–XVe siècle* (Rome: École française de Rome / Paris: Diffusion De Boccard, 1993), pp. 294–6; Giuseppe Rossi, *Pitture a fresco del Camposanto di Pisa* (Florence: Tipografia all'Insegna di Dante, 1832; repr. Florence: Cassa di Risparmio di

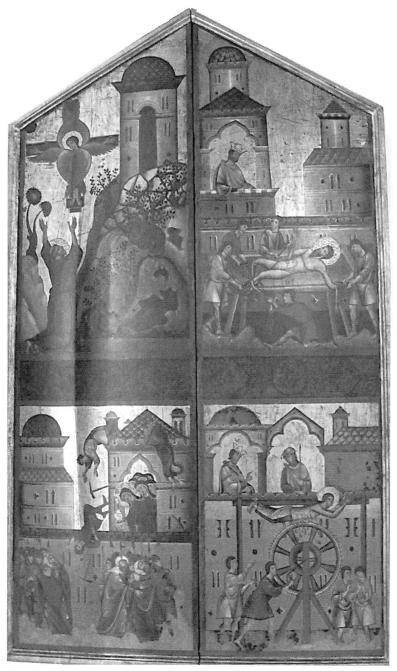

Fig. 6.3 Diptych of St Clare, from the workshop of Guido da Siena, late thirteenth century (Siena, Pinacoteca Nazionale, Inv. no. 4)

may directly relate back to the flayed saint, as the Camposanto received the relics of Bartholomew's skin, though it is unclear when these relics arrived in Pisa. This arrangement of the body recalls scenes of animals flayed as part of the medieval hunt, where the animal is tracked, killed, skinned, cooked and then feasted upon.[25] The typological connection between animal sacrifice and martyr sacrifice was laid out clearly in the medieval *Bible moralisée*, including one roughly contemporary example from Naples (Fig. 6.4). The double-register miniature juxtaposes scenes of sacrificial offerings made to God (Leviticus 1.3–13) with the stages of a Christian saint's martyrdom. Above, the animal is flayed, butchered and then washed, while below, the similarly supine saint is flayed, beaten and then blessed and cleansed through confession and penance.[26]

Pacino, however, avoids all the associations with victimhood in his treatment of Bartholomew. The martyr stands chained to the building behind him, gazing outward confrontationally, while three grim-faced men concentrate intently on the grisly task at hand. In one of the earliest Western stories of flaying, Marsyas loses to Apollo in a contest of musical skill and is condemned to be flayed as punishment. This story survives in visual form through classical sculpture, wherein the body of Marsyas typically appears strung up to a tree with his arms tied above his head as he awaits his punishment. In several surviving examples the satyr seems compromised and helpless, trapped into suffering his fate, strung up like the animal he in part is.[27] In one of the earliest surviving scenes of Bartholomew's martyrdom, found on the eleventh-century Byzantine bronze doors of San Paolo fuori le Mura in Rome, the saint stands fixed to a truncated cross with his arms raised above his head, while a man approaches his feet with what appear to be a set of pincers, which would be used to rip the skin off of a person being flayed (Fig. 6.5).[28] The pincers are

Firenze, 1976), p. 17; Joseph Polzer, 'Aristotle, Mohammed and Nicholas V in Hell', *Art Bulletin* 46.4 (Dec. 1964): 457–69 at pp. 463–4.

[25] See, for example: *Hunters Flaying a Deer's Carcass*, from Gaston Phébus, *Livre de la Chasse*, about 1430–40, Los Angeles, J. Paul Getty Museum, MS 27, fol. 64. Cf. Hartnell, 'Tools of the Puncture', p. 44, and Frederika Bain, 'Skin on Skin: Wearing Flayed Remains', pp. 116–37, both in this volume.

[26] We thank Martin Schwarz for bringing our attention to this image.

[27] *The Flaying of Marsyas*, Roman, 1st–2nd c. CE, Paris, Musée du Louvre (MR 267); Istanbul, Archaeological Museums, Roman, copy of a 3rd c. BC original (inv. no. 400 T).

[28] For a discussion of the full visual programme of the doors, see: Guglielmo Matthiae, *Le porte bronzee bizantine in Italia* (Rome: Officina, 1971), pp. 73–81. For more on pincers and flagellation as a form of flaying, see, in this volume: Susan Small, 'Flesh and Death in Early Modern Bedburg', pp. 71–90; Sherry C. M. Lindquist, 'Masculinist Devotion: Flaying and Flagellation in the *Belles Heures*', pp. 173–207; Peter Dent, 'A Window for the Pain: Surface, Interiority and Christ's Flagellated Skin in Late Medieval

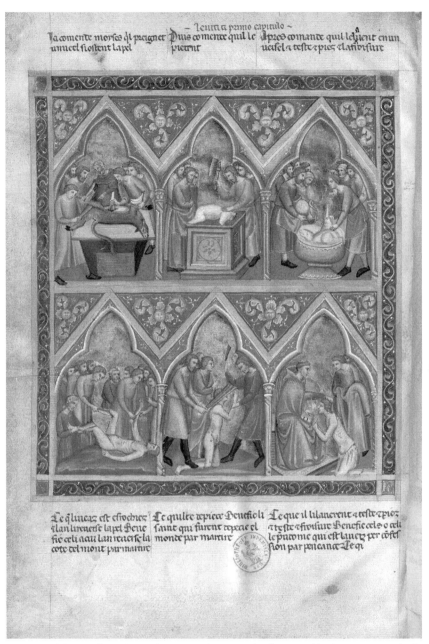

Fig. 6.4 Bible moralisée de Naples, 1350 or later, Naples (Paris, Bibliothèque nationale de France, MS Fr. 9561, fol. 78v)

Fig. 6.5 Martyrdom
of St Bartholomew,
bronze carving on
the door of San Paolo
fuori le Mura, Rome,
eleventh-century

the only visual indication of flaying and the inscription, as transcribed and
translated by Thomas Jex Preston, reads 'Saint Bartholomew dies hanged
upon a cross';[29] the depiction is quite abstract, so the figure crouching
at the base of the cross could easily be misread as removing a nail from
Bartholomew's feet, evoking Nicodemus' action after Christ's crucifixion.
As in the Laudario, the scene seems to be 'occurring in an inhabited
place [...] On either side of the picture is a house capped by a small
cross'.[30] While these Roman copies and Byzantine examples may well
have provided models for Pacino's unusual presentation of Bartholomew's
stance, the Laudario leaf shows the saint as anything but helpless. Even
though he is shackled by one wrist to an edifice, he leans toward the knife-
wielding men on the left, offering his free limbs to them. His steady gaze

Sculpture', pp. 208–39; and Valerie Gramling, '"Flesche withowtyn hyde":
The Removal and Transformation of Jesus' Skin in the English Cycle
Passion Plays', pp. 240–60.

[29] Thomas Jex Preston, Jr., *The Bronze Doors of the Abbey of Monte Cassino
and of Saint Paul's, Rome* (Princeton: Princeton University Press, 1915),
p. 48, available online via the Hathi Trust at <http://hdl.handle.net/2027/
wu.89054765094> (accessed Sept. 2016).

[30] Ibid., p. 48.

confronts the viewer and reveals his lack of anguish at the torment he endures, as well as his seeming control of his circumstances.[31]

Beyond the examples found in textual and visual sources, the actual practice of human flaying loomed large in the collective medieval imagination. Several scholars have noted that flaying, and anxiety about flaying, is much more frequent in literature than it was in actual custom.[32] While rare, several cases were documented as having taken place, and in each one this extreme act was used as a punishment for treason.[33] As

---

[31] One other early example of Bartholomew flayed while standing appears in a fresco cycle that originally decorated the now-destroyed Covoni chapel in the Badia Fiorentina. In this image, most recently attributed to Maso di Banco and therefore roughly contemporary with (or a bit earlier than) the Laudario, the saint appears similarly affixed by one arm as his tormentors remove his skin; however, Bartholomew's head is inclined downward and his gaze averted from the viewer. We thank Anne Leader for her photos and insights on the original location of this now-removed fresco. See also: Anne Leader, *The Badia of Florence: Art and Observance in a Renaissance Monastery* (Bloomington: Indiana University Press, 2012), p. 72. Although the significance of St Bartholomew for the Covoni has yet to be confirmed, the location of the Badia, directly across the Via del Proconsolo from the Bargello, suggests a connection with the punishment theme of the fresco and the function of the Bargello as the Palace of Justice. See: Allie Terry, 'Criminal Vision in Early Modern Florence: Fra Angelico's Altarpiece for Il Tempio and the Magdalenian Gaze', in *Renaissance Theories of Vision*, ed. John Hendrix and Charles Carmen (Aldershot: Ashgate Press, 2010), pp. 45–62, esp. p. 47; and Gabriele Taddei and Matteo Ferrari, 'Palazzo del Bargello', in *I luoghi dell'arte civica a Firenze*, ed. Daniela Parenti and Maria Monica Donato (Florence: Giunti, 2013), pp. 24–31.

[32] Mills, 'Havelok's Bare Life', p. 62; Kay, 'Original Skin', p. 39; W. R. J. Barron, 'The Penalties for Treason in Medieval Life and Literature', *Journal of Medieval History* 7 (1981): 187–202 at p. 188; Larissa Tracy, *Torture and Brutality in Medieval Literature: Negotiations of National Identity* (Cambridge: D. S. Brewer, 2012), pp. 16, 62–3, 74, 92–3, 147–55.

[33] Among the more well-known images of flaying is the Judgement of Cambyses, recorded by Herodotus, fifth-century BC Greek historian, and Valerius Maximus, first-century CE Roman historian. Cambyses is a king of 'extraordinary severity' who has a corrupt judge flayed and then appoints the judge's son to serve in the same office, while seated on a chair covered in his father's skin, which Valerius describes as an 'outrageous and unprecedented punishment of the corrupt judge': 'Iam Cambyses inusitatae seueritatis, qui mali cuiusdam iudicis e corpore pellem detractam sellae intendi in eaque filium eius iudicaturum considere iussit. ceterum et rex et barbarus atroci ac noua poena iudicis ne quis postea corrumpi iudex posset prouidit.' Valerius Maximus, *Factorum et dictorum memorabilium libri novem*, 6.3.ext.3; online at *The Latin Library* (no date), http://www.thelatinlibrary.com/valmax.html (accessed Sept. 2016). Gerard David's 1498 painting is the best-known image of the subject. Cf. n. 63. For more on

W. R. J. Barron notes, this offence was a felony and defined as 'a crime involving some breach of the feudal bond between lord and man, meriting forfeiture of his *fief* by the dependent, if he were the guilty party, or, if the superior were at fault, the loss of his lordship'.[34] Aspects of the Camposanto fresco are based upon Dante's *Inferno*,[35] where the Florentine author describes the final circle of Hell as devoted to the punishments for this most serious offence. This section contains Dante's single reference to flaying, specifically as Lucifer tears at the skin of Judas, the quintessential traitor:

> For the one who was in front, the biting was nothing
> Compared with the clawing, so that at times his spine
> Was left stripped of every scrap of skin.

> 'That soul there, which has the worst punishment,
> Is Judas Iscariot', my master said
> 'With his head inside and kicking his legs.'[36]

Dante completed his text in 1321, and it gained rapid popularity in the author's birthplace. In addition to its production of liturgical manuscripts and devotional panel paintings, Pacino di Bonaguida's workshop was the primary producer of illuminated copies of the *Divine Comedy* in the early decades of its circulation in Florence.[37] While the so-called Dante Poggiali, the only surviving copy of the text from Pacino's workshop that contains narrative images, illustrates only the previous two cantos (31–3) about the punishments for traitors, Pacino's likely familiarity with the text and Dante's association of treason with flaying may have helped form the foundation for the later St Bartholomew excoriation scene in the Laudario.[38] Moreover, Florentine confraternities, including the *laudesi*,

---

the Judgement of Cambyses, see: Valerie Gramling, '"Flesche withowtyn hyde"', p. 251.

[34] Barron, 'Penalties for Treason', p. 188.

[35] Joachim Poeschke, *Italian Frescoes: The Age of Giotto, 1280–1400* (New York: Abbeville Press, 2005), p. 321; Lina Bolzoni, 'La predica dipinta: gli affreschi del "Trionfo della Morte" e la predicazione domenicana', in *Il Camposanto di Pisa*, ed. Clara Baracchini and Enrico Castelnuovo (Turin: Giulio Einaudi, 1996), p. 110.

[36] *Inferno* 34.58–63. Dante Alighieri, *The Divine Comedy*, trans. C. H. Sisson (Oxford: Oxford University Press, 1998), p. 192. Cf. Dent, 'A Window for the Pain', p. 208.

[37] On this tradition, see: Francesca Pasut, 'Florentine Illuminations for Dante's *Divine Comedy*: A Critical Assessment', in *Florence at the Dawn of the Renaissance*, ed. Sciacca, pp. 155–69.

[38] On the Dante Poggiali (Florence, Biblioteca Nazionale Centrale, Pal. 313), see: Rudy Abardo, *Chiose Palatine: Ms. Pal. 313 della Biblioteca Nazionale Centrale di Firenze* (Rome: Salerno, 2005); Sciacca, *Florence at the Dawn of the Renaissance*, pp. 210–13, cat. 43 (entry by Pasut).

habitually confronted sin, specifically the sin of treason, in their rituals and ceremonies. As Ronald Weissman points out, infractions, including arguing with fellow brothers or creating discord within the community, were punished swiftly since, '[o]ne must not ruin one's own reputation, for that would stain the reputation of the brotherhood'.[39] For most confraternities in Florence, the major corporate celebration was held annually on Maundy Thursday, when the members would re-enact three events: the betrayal of Christ by Judas, the Last Supper and the Washing of the Feet.[40] In this pursuit, Weissman states, '[t]hey experienced the symbolic passage from traitor to brother'.[41] Although Bartholomew's gruesome demise as a result of defending his faith was meant to be a model for medieval Christians, Pacino's graphic visualization of the saint's punishment must have recalled for the confraternity members the confession required of them before the brotherhood and the public penance they subsequently had to endure; it is simultaneously an aspirational and cautionary tale.

At first sight Bartholomew seems hardly guilty of treason. However, the crime that precipitates his punishment by flaying, namely his conversion of King Astyages to Christianity, would have been viewed by the king's brother as a crime against the regent and, therefore, as treason. A similar fate befalls the prophet Mani, as related in the *Shāhnāma*, when, unlike Bartholomew, he fails to convince King Shapur of the merits of a new religion and Shapur has him flayed and his skin stuffed – not unlike the skin of Marcantonio Bragadin, as discussed in this volume by Kelly DeVries.[42] In a rare sixteenth-century Persian depiction of this event, the raw, skinless and faceless body of Mani lies on the ground, and his skin hangs from a gibbet above on display before the assembled court (Fig. 6.6).[43] Barron cites the often public nature of flaying as a key element of the penalty: 'Flaying [...] no matter how ritualized, could never be anything but a horrifying spectacle; a slow and hideous torture under which no nobleman could maintain his *sang froid*, but must die inch by inch, shrieking in agony, amidst the contempt and derision of ordinary men.'[44] Bartholomew's remarkable composure in the Laudario image must be understood in the context of the brutal reality of flaying, as evoked in Barron's description. In the Laudario image he withstands the most torturous of martyrdoms with superhuman calm.

[39] Weissman, *Ritual Brotherhood*, p. 88.

[40] Ibid., p. 99.

[41] Ibid., p. 104.

[42] Kelly DeVries, 'A Tale of Venetian Skin: The Flaying of Marcantonio Bragadin', pp. 51–70, in this volume.

[43] This leaf from Shiraz, *c.* 1570, is in the collection of William M. Voelkle, New York. <http://www.themorgan.org/collection/treasures-of-islamic-manuscript-painting/90?page=90> (accessed Sept. 2016).

[44] Barron, 'Penalties for Treason', p. 199.

Fig. 6.6 King Shapur Zu'l Aktaf observes Mani's flayed body, from Abu 'l-Qasim Ab Ferdowsi Tusi, *Shāhnāma* (*Book of Kings*), *c.* 1570, Persia, Shiraz (New York, Morgan Library & Museum, promised gift of William M. Voelkle)

Fig. 6.7 Façade of the church of St Bartholomew in Logroño, Spain, showing Bartholomew preaching, thirteenth century

From the scene of Bartholomew's flaying, the narrative thread of the Laudario images moves to the margin of the Cloisters leaf and into the lower roundel depicting Bartholomew preaching to a group of followers after being flayed. While not part of the *LgA*, Pacino picked up on this detail from other versions of the saint's *vita*, as described above. One of the rare early images of Bartholomew wearing his skin while preaching is found on the thirteenth-century façade of the church of St Bartholomew in Logroño in northern Spain (Fig. 6.7).[45] Despite some losses to the sculptural relief, Bartholomew's skin is clearly draped over his right shoulder so that one or perhaps both hands hang down and clutch at his knees as the figure strides forward towards his audience. Louis Réau states that the early iconography of Bartholomew preaching while wearing his flayed skin is particular to Spanish art and, indeed, Spanish artists were

---

[45] For more on the church and its sculptural programme, see: Adolfo López Fernández, *La iglesia de San Bartolomé de Logroño: historia de la conservación del monumento en el siglo XIX* (Logroño: Instituto de Estudios Riojanos, 2013).

granted commissions in Italy in the thirteenth and fourteenth centuries. For example, the Catalonian artist Guerau Gener (1369–*c.* 1410) produced an altarpiece for the cathedral of Monreale in 1401 and also in the same year painted a retable for Barcelona Cathedral that features a horrifying image of St Bartholomew flayed from head to toe and preaching while wearing his skin draped over one shoulder.[46] Indeed, while Pacino's images of Bartholomew were unusually brutal for their historical moment, increasingly graphic images of Bartholomew do begin to appear in late fourteenth-century Italy. Around the year 1400 visual representations of Bartholomew's suffering proliferate in Tuscany, as they do in the work of Gener.[47] Many of these repeated motifs, such as the martyr's arm raised by a pulley attached to a building, were first laid down on parchment by Pacino.

In contrast to these images, in rendering the same scene Pacino depicts Bartholomew's skin tied about his neck and then wound under his right arm and across his body. From where the skin gathers under his left arm, a single brachial appendage hangs down in front of his body in the same

---

[46] Réau, *Iconographie*, p. 184; Margaret Lindsey, 'The Iconography of St Paul in Medieval Malta', in *Insights and Interpretations: Studies in Celebration of the Eighty-Fifth Anniversary of the Index of Christian Art*, ed. Colum Hourihane (Princeton: Index of Christian Art in Association with Princeton University Press, 2002), pp. 140–55 at p. 147. On Guerau Gener, see: Rosa Alcoy i Pedrós, 'La pintura gòtica', in *Art de Catalunya: Ars Cataloniae*, vol. 8: *Pintura antiga i medieval* (Barcelona: Edicions L'isard, 1998), pp. 234–6; Frick Art Reference Library, *Spanish Artists from the Fourth to the Twentieth Century: A Critical Dictionary* (New York: G. K. Hall, 1993–6), p. 47; Josep Gudiol and Santiago Alcolea i Blanch, *Pintura gótica Catalana* (Barcelona: Polígrafa, 1986), pp. 86–7. For more on the connections between Italian and Spanish art at the time of Giotto, see: Rosa Alcoy i Pedrós, 'La ricenzione della pittura giottesca in Spagna, dai Bassa a Starnina', in *Giotto e il Trecento: 'Il più Sovrano Maestro stato in dipintura'*, ed. Alessandro Tomei (Milan: Skira, 2009), pp. 321–35.

[47] Sciacca, 'Reconstructing the Laudario', p. 277. The Tuscan examples include a predella panel by Cenni di Francesco, *c.* 1385, in the Philadelphia Museum of Art (Johnson Collection, inv. 1292), a fresco by Spinello Aretino in the chapel to the right of the high altar in San Michele Visdomini in Florence, and two panel paintings by Lorenzo di Niccolò, one signed and dated to 1401 in San Gimignano at the Museo Civico, and a second in the Museum of Fine Arts, Boston (04.237). On the Philadelphia panel, see: Carl B. Strehlke, *Italian Paintings 1250–1450 in the John G. Johnson Collection and the Philadelphia Museum of Art* (Philadelphia: Philadelphia Museum of Art, 2004), pp. 94–5; on the San Michele Visdomini fresco, see: Angelo Tartuferi, 'Spinello Aretino in San Michele Visdomini a Firenze (e alcune osservazioni su Lorenzo di Niccolò)', *Paragone. Arte.* 34 (1983): 3–18; and on the San Gimignano and Boston paintings, see: Laurence B. Kanter, *Italian Paintings in the Museum of Fine Arts, Boston*, vol. 1: *13th–15th Centuries* (Boston: Museum of Fine Arts, 1994), pp. 129–30.

limp, lifeless fashion as the right arm of Bartholomew's skin in the flaying scene above, which provides a vivid reminder of the punishment he endured before he calmly proceeded to convey Christ's teachings. Thus, in the preaching scene Bartholomew's skin is wound around him in a manner that suggests the styling of the togas worn by classical orators. In this scene, his skin and the way in which he wears it continue to express his identity: namely, that of a preacher who utilized the power of his words to convince people far and wide to follow Christ. Kay argues that, in other contexts, Bartholomew's giving up of his skin may be equated to the sacrifice of his 'human identity which resides in the skin'.[48] However, in this image, supplanting a toga with Bartholomew's skin instead emphasizes that his role as preacher is not merely a profession, but his essential identity. There is no 'sacrifice' here, since the identity given up is both illusory – his true self is uncovered through his flaying – and inferior to his revealed saintly identity.[49]

An actual act of flaying would almost certainly result in immediate death.[50] Like other saints, though, Bartholomew survives this process long enough to undergo additional violence. In this case, Bartholomew's continued proselytizing forces his tormentors to resort to even more extreme measures.[51] In the right half of the main miniature, Bartholomew meets his ultimate death via that most reliable method for the killing of obstinately alive saints: beheading. While relying on earlier compositional conventions for depicting martyrdom by beheading – including the sword-bearing figure, the saint kneeling in prayer and the outdoor setting – Pacino takes the unusual step of perpetuating the motif of the flayed skin,

---

[48] Kay, 'Original Skin', p. 44.

[49] See: Small, 'Flesh and Death', p. 80, for a related, if converse, notion, wherein the flaying of a purported werewolf reveals the true nature of the creature.

[50] As Sarah Kay has noted, '[o]nce your skin is off you are dead, and what happens then depends on the capacity to sublimate death as its contrary, immortality'. Sarah Kay, 'Flayed Skin as *objet a*: Representation and Materiality in Guillaume de Deguileville's *Pèlerinage de vie humaine*', in *Medieval Fabrications: Dress, Textiles, Clothwork, and Other Cultural Imaginings*, ed. E. Jane Burns (New York: Palgrave, 2004), pp. 193–251 at p. 205; Kay, 'Original Skin', p. 36.

[51] St Christina similarly continues preaching despite an act of violence that should have stopped her: her tongue is cut out, which ought to have left her mute, setting up a pointed contrast with her continued acts of speech. Jacobus, *LgA*, p. 421: 'Deinde linguam ejus praecidi fecit, Christina vero nequaquam loquelam amittens praescissuram linguae accipiens in faciem Juliani projecit et oculum ejus item percutiens eum excaecavit' [Then he cut out her tongue, but Christina never lost the power of speech; taking up her severed tongue, she threw it in the face of Julian and indeed hit his eye, striking him blind]. See also: Tracy, *Torture and Brutality*, pp. 41–5.

and foregrounding it not merely as an iconographical device, but as a prominent element in the narrative.[52] The emphasis on the flayed skin is intensified by the overall composition of the page and its central images. The two panels within the rectangular miniature contain a curious array of loose echoes and mirrorings, creating a pair that is neither duplicative nor symmetrical, but a hybrid of these compositional devices.[53] The main figures, for example – Bartholomew on the left and the executioner on the right – stand with their legs similarly posed and angled, but their torsos diverge in opposing directions. Likewise, each scene contains a kneeling figure, but, while they both face to the right, one is at the lower left corner and the other at the lower right. The result is a sense of deep and dynamic interaction between these conjoined scenes, bound within a single frame. They are not narratively contiguous, but are presented as the central visual and hermeneutic element of the page.

In the centre panels Pacino presents each image of Bartholomew's skin not only as a repetition of the other, but also as uncanny doubles of his body. In the flaying scene the skin of Bartholomew's right arm and right leg fall in concert with the limbs they once covered. The beheading scene reiterates this doubling, with the flayed skin of his right leg falling in an echo of the skinless leg beside it and the skin of his foot dangling over the frame, into the viewer's space. Significantly, between the preaching roundel and the beheading scene, the skin has been re-arranged, with the hands tied about his neck in a knot situated where one would typically expect a metalwork clasp, so that the skin hangs over both of his shoulders, down his back, and his leg skin trails over the raw, exposed flesh of his limbs. In the Laudario's image *The Martyrdom of Saint Christopher*, the martyr kneels in an analogous pose, wearing the rose-coloured textile equivalent of this garment secured about his neck. The same type of mantle, now affixed with the more typical and ostentatious gold brooch, appears in several other scenes from the Laudario, most notably adorning the figures of the three Magi in *The Adoration of the Magi*, the emperor Decius and his prefect Valerian in *The Martyrdom of Saint Lawrence*, and the capes of the angels in

[52] One contemporary French image from a copy of the *Vie de saints* depicts Bartholomew kneeling in prayer while two tormentors simultaneously behead him and slice his skin with a knife (Cambridge, St John's College, MS B.9, fol. 102v). Since Bartholomew's skin appears damaged but still intact, the conflation of these two events is likely in an effort to compress the narrative into the relatively limited space afforded by the two-column format of the text, rather than to grant the moment of flaying, and therefore the removed skin, the degree of focus afforded it by Pacino.

[53] The care with which these panels were planned is evinced in the way that Pacino varies the teal rectangles at the corners of the central frame. They are quite similar, so do not catch the viewer's attention, but each is subtly different, furthering the effect of the images they contain as both consistent and varied.

the margins of *The Trinity*.[54] This type of garment also recalls the outermost robe worn by a pope or bishop, known as a cope, or *capa* – a semicircle of fabric draped over the shoulders, left open at the front and often fastened with a decorative clasp or band of fabric.[55] As Gaston Duchet-Suchaux and Michel Pastoureau state, '[f]or a long time, the mantle was one of the most important attributes of sovereign power and, as such, was worn by both gods and kings. In the Bible, many representations of authority wear one, and it becomes an insignia of status, participating in its owner's power.'[56] Therefore, at the moment of his final demise, Bartholomew's skin-cape – like the opulent garments it replaces in the narrative – reflects the dress of high-ranking officials in both the ecclesiastical and royal spheres. At the same time, this arrangement of his skin makes the four dangling appendages all the more apparent, and a garment that initially recalls that worn by men of stature becomes unmistakable – horrifyingly so – as the saint's own hide. The appearance of his now cape-like skin is the first indication to the viewer of a distinct shift in Bartholomew's identity from a follower of Christ and a preacher to a martyr who will receive his final reward by becoming one of the elect in Heaven. As Robert Mills states regarding the saint's legend, 'Bartholomew's flaying forces him to renounce his earthly life, but this enables him to deck himself out in a far more distinguished garment, the cloak of sanctity, which testifies to the existence of a heavenly body independent of his mortal skin.'[57]

Bartholomew's pristine skin-robes in the Laudario recall again the *LgA* passage cited above, in which we learn that the preacher wears white robes that remain enduringly clean: 'Viginti sex anni sunt, ex quo vestes et sandalia ejus nec veterascunt nec sordidantur' (p. 541) [He has worn these garments and sandals for twenty-six years, and they neither wear out nor become dirty]. Here his unsoiled clothing is a thinly veiled allusion to the spotlessness of his soul. In contrast, the image of Bartholomew's flaying is bloody – blood rains down from where the skin is pared away from the flesh on his arms and legs. It falls in thick, heavy drops and splatters the ground. Similarly, in the adjacent beheading scene, blood spurts from his sundered neck and pours from his severed head onto the craggy rocks below. The brushstrokes with which Pacino rendered all of this blood

---

[54] Switzerland, private collection; Los Angeles, The J. Paul Getty Museum (MS 80b; 2006.13); and New York, The Morgan Library & Museum (MS M.742), respectively.

[55] Miller, *Clothing the Clergy*, p. 249. For the symbolism of the *capa*, see: Andrea Denny-Brown, 'The Case of the Bishop's Capa: Vestimentary Change and Divine Law in the Thirteenth Century', in her *Fashioning Change: The Trope of Clothing in High- and Late-Medieval England* (Columbus: The Ohio State University Press, 2012), pp. 82–113, 202–9.

[56] Gaston Duchet-Suchaux and Michel Pastoureau, *The Bible and the Saints*, trans. David Radzinowicz Howell (New York: Flammarion, 1994), p. 227.

[57] Mills, 'Havelok's Bare Life', p. 62.

are the most active and energetic on the page. The rest is painted with painstaking care, as in the figures' shining curls of hair and the delicate hatching and crosshatching used to modulate and highlight Bartholomew's as-yet-still-attached skin in the flaying scene. The drops of blood, though, are rapid strokes, slashed along the surface. They are perhaps most surprising – and therefore effective – streaming down from the severed head, across the gold of the halo. Through all of this bloodshed, as well as through his life as an itinerant preacher, his imprisonment and abuse, his subsequent use of his skin as a robe and his kneeling on it on the ground, Bartholomew's skin remains as pristine as the garments it replaces. Looking at the rhetoric around the production of vellum, Bruce Holsinger finds evidence that medieval authors saw the flaying of animals as a process of purification, such that:

> in a twelfth-century sermon by Peter Comestor, our hearts follow a grisly path of salvation into parchment, leaving the 'filth' of the pre-scraped animal hide behind: 'You know the scribe's work. First, with the knife he cleans the parchment of fat and removes all filth.' [58]

This discussion of the purification of the form through flaying, though, should draw attention to Bartholomew's exposed red flesh. It is painted with faint striations, as if to convey the presence of revealed musculature, though this is not nearly as prominent as on several later sculptures of the figure, from Marco d'Agrate's work in Milan Cathedral (1562) to Damien Hirst's *Saint Bartholomew, Exquisite Pain* (2006).[59] Similarly, there are other early fourteenth-century illuminations of Bartholomew flayed that stress the revealed flesh and are far more graphic than Pacino's image. For example, Morgan Library & Museum, M.360, a Legendary perhaps produced in Bologna, Italy (*c.* 1325–1335), presents an image of abject horror (Fig. 6.8).[60] The exposed flesh looks slick with the blood that runs in rivulets down Bartholomew's body. The bloody inner side of his arm skin is visible where it hangs limp from his side. Most powerfully, though, Bartholomew's flayed face confronts the viewer, grimacing out in a terrifying fashion, offset by the rich, radiant gold of his halo. This same horrific visage emerges from the saint's gold-patterned burial wrappings in the scene of his entombment to the right. In comparison, the Laudario's image is tame, both suggesting Bartholomew's transcendence of the

---

[58] Bruce Holsinger, 'Of Pigs and Parchment, Medieval Studies and the Coming of the Animal', *PMLA* 124.2 (2009): 616–23 at p. 621, with interior quotation from Eric Jager, 'The Book of the Heart: Reading and Writing the Medieval Subject', *Speculum* 71.1 (1996): 1–26 at pp. 11–12.

[59] For an image of Hirst's sculpture, see <http://www.damienhirst.com/saint-bartholomew-exquisite-p> (accessed Sept. 2016).

[60] For more on the Legendary and the complicated history of its dismemberment, see: Levárdy Ferenc, *Magyar Anjou Legendárium* (Budapest: Magyar Helikon, 1973).

Fig. 6.8 Hungarian Master and workshop, the apostle Bartholomew's martyrdom and burial, Hungarian Anjou Legendary, *c.* 1325–1335 (New York, The Morgan Library & Museum, MS M.360.21r)

violence perpetrated against him and also allowing us to gaze upon the scene unflinchingly. The exposed flesh is more of a dusty rose or puce and seems clean and dry, as if the removal of the outer skin has revealed a second surface rather than an uncontained interior. Bartholomew's face retains its skin, both in the preaching roundel and the beheading panel. It is hard to envision a roundel wherein a faceless horror like that of the Morgan manuscript preached to a cheerfully enrapt audience. In the gory Barcelona preaching panel by Gener, for example, the audience looks distraught and horrified, as surely do many of the people who stand before the altarpiece. Bartholomew's audience in the Laudario's roundel again provides response cues for members of the confraternity (as well as modern viewers). While Gener's image repels, Pacino's suggests that the proper response is awe.

The Laudario has another image of a red figure: in *The Resurrection and the Three Marys at the Tomb*, the angel, clothed in a white robe with gold trim, blazes red.[61] The Vulgate Gospel of Mark (16.5) describes the figure as 'coopertum stola candida' [clothed in a white robe]. Matthew 28.3 mentions the white robe, but also the appearance of the figure (now a *magnus angelus* [great angel] rather than a *iuvenem* [young man]): 'erat autem aspectus eius sicut fulgur et vestimentum eius sicut nix' [his countenance was like lightning, and his clothing white as snow].[62] It is far from obvious how one would render a 'countenance [...] like lightning'. Pacino chooses a bright vermillion. The effect is otherworldly, ethereal, distinctly non-human. Kay notes:

> [T]he idea that the 'skin of mortality' is an outer garment over an inner, immortal being can be traced through Augustine to the earliest church fathers. The hagiographer is persuaded that there is an individual called 'Bartholomew' who exists independently of his skin, survives death, and retains all the human powers of speech, agency, and miracle-working that he possessed in life. Some depictions of Bartholomew render this idea graphically by representing him carrying his skin over his arm as if he himself were none the worse for wear, safe and sound inside where his skin used to be.[63]

This implies, though, that there is a permanent, fixed state in which Bartholomew exists. The angel who addresses the Three Marys is fundamentally and ontologically inhuman; Bartholomew, in contrast, begins as a human being of flesh and blood. However, at the moment when, flayed, he walks off, presumably leaving his would-be executioners stunned in his wake, Bartholomew transcends his humanity. As he wraps himself in his former skin, he either *becomes* or *reveals himself to be* something new and miraculous, something posthuman.

---

[61] Cambridge, The Fitzwilliam Museum, MS 194.

[62] *Biblia sacra: iuxta vulgatam versionem*, ed. Bonifatius Fischer, Robert Weber and Roger Gryson, 4th edn (Stuttgart: Deutsche Bibelgesellschaft, 1994).

[63] Kay, 'Original Skin', p. 42.

As constructed by Patricia MacCormack, the posthuman is not a state of being, but a process and an encounter with difference, 'an event of perception' that destabilizes the viewer's understanding of the 'base level zero, normal human'.[64] The posthuman is the space where the monstrous and wondrous collide and generate new interactions. In MacCormack's words, '[t]he posthuman does not therefore depose the human, nor come after it, but allows access to and celebrates the excesses, conundrums [...] and disruptive events which are already inherent in any possibility of contemplation'.[65] The experience of viewing the Bartholomew folio of the Laudario is compelling, disturbing and fascinating. The figure of Bartholomew transforms from image to image, so that he is fundamentally unstable and ultimately incomprehensible as a 'normal' human form. Even in his most understandable presentation, the flaying scene, he stands upright, alert and calm, as the skin is being sliced from his flesh with knives and yanked vigorously downward. It is not only his giant stature – his hand reaches toward the top of the tower to which he is chained – nor the halo that signals his sanctity, but his demeanour amidst the most brutal of torments that estranges us from him, and him from his apparent humanity. Kay asserts that 'since sacrifice requires that what is given up be what is valued [...] what is sacrificed is human identity which resides in the skin'.[66] Kay is describing the internal dynamics of the Judgement of Cambyses, as recounted in the *Gesta Romanorum*, a popular text contemporary with Pacino's work. She describes the flaying of a corrupt judge, but immediately pivots to Bartholomew, arguing that there, too, 'the "inside" can be depreciated' in favour of an identity residing in the skin.[67] Similarly, in Irish narratives, flaying would represent a wholesale denial of humanity.[68] While some might argue that it is Bartholomew's worldly or mundane identity that is lodged in his skin, and that his human identity is preserved throughout the narrative, Bartholomew's survival of his flaying presses well beyond the capacity of a human and renders him something else – posthuman: neither quite human, nor fully non-human, exceeding the bounds of the mundane and mortal and thereby challenging and expanding our notion of humanity. Bartholomew is not reduced, not destroyed, by the transformation, but elevated by it. Further, the idea that the shedding of 'human identity' is an act of sacrifice is embedded in humanist notions emerging just at the time Pacino was active, and this image seems ambivalent about their value. Most of the source texts were produced in earlier moments when humanity was viewed askance and exiting it could be the highest elevation. In later flaying scenes, such as

[64] MacCormack, 'Posthuman Teratology', pp. 293–4.

[65] Ibid., pp. 295.

[66] Kay, 'Original Skin', p. 44.

[67] Ibid., p. 45.

[68] Sayers, 'No Skin in the Game', p. 280.

Gerard David's *The Judgement of Cambyses* (1498) – 'one of the earliest surviving depictions of this theme' – and, yet more vividly, Jusepe de Ribera's *Apollo Flaying Marsyas* (1637), the victims exhibit varying degrees of emotion, with artists lavishing great care on the presentation of pain.[69] But the Laudario's figure does not elicit the sort of 'sado-erotic gaze' encouraged by the Limbourg brothers' image of the flaying of Bartholomew, as described by Sherry C. M. Lindquist in this volume, building on the work of Martha Easton.[70] In comparison, the composure of Pacino's figure – a hallmark not of humanity but of sanctity – is at once inspiring and strikingly alienating.

Bartholomew, though, is not fixed in this state. From image to image, he metamorphoses, first to the profoundly disturbing figure preaching, alive without his skin, then to the headless figure that *still* seems alive, now without his head. This scene recalls James Elkins' description of a photograph of an execution. He writes:

> The photograph was taken a half second after the decapitation; I know because the blood is still on its way up into the air and the hair on the man's head is still blown back by the fall [...] The body, it seems, is still living, hanging in the position it had before the executioner struck.[71]

Elkins even compares this image to 'medieval illuminated manuscripts' like that under discussion here, in which 'decollated trunks spurting blood can be found'.[72] The photograph and the illumination are strikingly similar. Both feature an executioner with a sword, standing over a headless body that still kneels upright while the body's head lies on the ground. However, there are substantial gaps in the Laudario image's realism: as Elkins notes, in the photograph the executioner's sword is still in mid-swing. The decapitation has *just* occurred, the instant before. In the illumination, though, the executioner is standing back, sheathing his sword and gazing with some confusion or concern at the neck he has severed. Time has passed, but this posthuman body will not stop. It should have lain down dead after – or even *during* – the flaying, but did not. It carried on, calmly preaching, and without the horrifying gore of the Barcelona version of the scene. And then it should have collapsed seconds after the beheading,

---

[69] Robert Mills, *Suspended Animation: Pain, Pleasure and Punishment in Medieval Culture* (London: Reaktion, 2005), p. 60. For an extended and insightful discussion of the David painting, see: chap. 2, 'Skin Show'.

[70] Lindquist, 'Masculinist Devotion', pp. 174, 187; and Martha Easton, 'Uncovering the Meanings of Nudity in the *Belles Heures* of Jean, Duke of Berry', in *The Meanings of Nudity in Medieval Art*, ed. Sherry C. M. Lindquist (Burlington, VT: Ashgate, 2012), pp. 149–81 at p. 166.

[71] James Elkins, *The Object Stares Back: On the Nature of Seeing* (New York: Harvest, 1996), p. 108.

[72] Ibid.

long before the soldier had sheathed his sword. His discomfiture is understandable; surely, he would be wondering if anything could kill this man. In addition, the head in Elkins' illustration has landed on the ground in the heartbeat of time between its decollation and the snap of the camera's shutter. Bartholomew's head, in contrast, seems oddly suspended in space as in time. It does not seem to rest securely on the sharply sloping hillside – how could it? – and so instead appears to hover in the space between the hill and the still-erect, truncated torso, as it floats in the gap between life and death, between humanity and posthumanity.

Elina Gerstman, writing of the space between life and death in images of the Three Dead and the Three Living, argues that the moment of death is not – cannot be – represented, that instead it is the viewer who must step into the gap and thereby create the death within the narrative:

> Mindful of the fecund implications of the void, the viewers here are invited to fill it by crafting their own cognitive creation: the imaginary, here invisible, processes of death. The conjuring of this fictive vision casts the viewers as witnesses and creators of the inevitable progress of death: in imagining and therefore imaging it in their minds, they themselves perpetrate its violence.[73]

The viewer generates this unseen moment by enacting what Scott McCloud has termed 'closure'.[74] That is, if Bartholomew dies in this sequence, he does so because the viewer fills in the gaps. Bartholomew, though, transforms again: his skin seems reattached as a pair of angels carry his soul aloft. Of course, this is his soul, now apparently severed from his body, but presented as a largely intact form – though it is worth noting that it too is truncated, cut off at the waist. In the final scene Bartholomew has transformed again, and without explanation in the various *vitae* discussed above. Instead, like the English king and martyr St Edmund (who was known in Italy through an account of the miraculous healing of a boy in Lucca, 50 miles west of Florence),[75] in the burial scene Bartholomew's head seems to be reattached:

---

[73] Elina Gertsman, 'The Gap of Death: Passive Violence in the Encounter between the Three Dead and the Three Living', in *Beholding Violence in Medieval and Early Modern Europe*, ed. Erin Felicia Labbie and Allie Terry-Fritsch (Burlington, VT: Ashgate, 2012), pp. 85–104 at p. 98.

[74] Scott McCloud, *Understanding Comics: The Invisible Art* (New York: Harper Perennial, 1994), p. 65: 'the audience is a willing and conscious *collaborator* and closure is the agent of *change, time* and *motion*'.

[75] *The Memorials of St Edmund's Abbey*, ed. T. Arnold, Rolls Series 96, vol. 1 (London, 1890–6), pp. 68–74, available online at https://archive.org/details/memorialsofstedm01arno (accessed Sept. 2016). See also: Emma Cownie, 'The Cult of St Edmund in the Eleventh and Twelfth Centuries: The Language and Communication of a Medieval Saint's Cult', *Neuphilologische Mitteilungen* 99.2 (1998): 177–97 at pp. 181 and 185.

When they exhumed Edmund's body preparatory to translating it
to the new building, they find – *mirabile dictu* – the body 'sanum et
incolume' [sound and whole] (14/3), unwounded and with only 'una
tenuissima riga in modum fili coccinei' [an extremely thin red crease,
like a scarlet thread] (14/10) to mark the former separation of his
head from his body (*ob signum martyrii*, 14/9).[76]

In the beheading scene Bartholomew's head is very clearly detached from
his body, but then his soul flies off to the right – following an upward
trajectory through the verdant tree springing from the barren rock – while
his body is being buried on the far left. The rugged, sloping rock recalls
that of Giotto's *Lamentation* from the Scrovegni (or Arena) Chapel in
Padua, painted some three or four decades earlier. In Giotto's famous
image the tree that emerges is dead, emblematizing the death of Christ,
whereas in Pacino's image the tree seems burgeoning, suggesting the new
life, glorious and eternal, into which Bartholomew is being ushered above.
In the roundel to the left, where the mortal remains of Bartholomew are
being buried, his body is now 'sound and whole', like that of Edmund,
and without even the 'thin red crease' on his neck, which would perhaps
be covered by his long beard. The head, though, is certainly attached:
it is tilted forward, though there seems to be no hand holding it up from
behind. The body is rendered undivided, but the soul is now sundered
from it. The figure is, again, transformed until the moment when soul and
body will be reunited at the end of days.[77]

The small but shocking preaching roundel, below this scene of burial, is
only about two inches in diameter, but is the pin around which the rest of
the images turn; it is the portion of the narrative that presses most urgently

---

[76] Mark Faulkner, '"Like a Virgin": The Reheading of St Edmund and
Monastic Reform in Late-Tenth-Century England', in *Heads Will Roll:
Decapitation in the Medieval and Early Modern Imagination*, ed. Larissa Tracy
and Jeff Massey (Leiden: Brill, 2012), pp. 39–52 at pp. 45–6, with internal
quotations from Abbo of Fleury's *Passio sancti Eadmundi* (*c.* 987), as found
in Michael Winterbottom, ed., *Three Lives of English Saints* (Toronto:
Pontifical Institute of Medieval Studies, 1972), pp. 67–87, by chapter
and line number. Ælfric's Anglo-Saxon *vita* also notes this miraculous
reattachment: 'and his neck was healed which before was cut through'.
*Ælfric's Lives of Saints: Being a Set of Sermons on Saints' Days Formerly
Observed by the English Church*, ed. Walter W. Skeat, 4 vols., EETS o.s. 76, 82,
94 and 114 (London: N. Trübner & Co., 1900), 3:329. See also: Asa Simon
Mittman, 'Answering the Call of the Severed Head', in *Heads Will Roll*, ed.
Tracy and Massey, pp. 311–28.

[77] As Caroline Walker Bynum has pointed out, in the thirteenth and
fourteenth centuries the mendicant orders of Franciscans and Dominicans
emphasized 'the yearning of soul and body for each other after death'.
*Fragmentation and Redemption: Essays on Gender and the Human Body in
Medieval Religion* (New York: Zone, 1991), p. 229.

on our understanding of the figure of Bartholomew and the nature of his being. A very close examination of the process of painting here generates further implications about his flaying and about his body. The paint on his legs is somewhat abraded, following a series of vertical cracks that can be seen through this roundel, particularly on the gold halo, as well as on the burial roundel above. These fissures in the surface of the image allow us to see the layer beneath, and what is revealed is somewhat surprising. Beneath the raw red is the greenish shade used by Pacino as the underpainting for skin. When Pacino painted figures, he blocked in the flesh areas in green first, then laid pink over the top and then modelled in white as the final layer.[78] In painting the exposed flesh in the preaching and beheading images, then, the illuminator treated the areas as if they were meant to become flesh areas; he then left the epidermis off. That is, in the *narrative*, Bartholomew's skin is removed to reveal his raw flesh beneath, and in the *image* depicting this narrative, the image of his flesh is produced by leaving off the skin. The image, then, becomes something of an artistic flaying, a surrogate or proxy for the flaying of the actual saint.

Kay asks the central question, obvious but often overlooked: 'Why is Bartholomew flayed? He isn't guilty of treason or envy […] [I]n literary texts flaying may be envisaged as a means of destroying what is so different as to be incapable of assimilation.'[79] Nicola Masciandaro makes a similar argument regarding beheading as the annihilation of the identity of the beheaded, '[g]rounded in the inevitable and impossible identification of human person and head'.[80] That is, a person without a head is not a person, since identity is largely lodged within the missing head. So too, without the skin, the identity is surely ruptured in a fundamental way. The retention of the skin of the head and face in the Laudario image, though, presses back against these readings. Bartholomew remains Bartholomew in the preaching roundel, in a way that he does not in the Morgan Legendary or Barcelona retable. The removal of Bartholomew's skin does not obliterate his identity; rather, it forges it. It is the act of flaying that transforms him from mortal preacher to immortal saint, as emblematized by his refusal to lie down dead during and after flaying, and again after beheading. In most cases the removal of skin and of head would surely obscure or even expunge the identity of the victim, but in Bartholomew's case these are the processes by which his new posthuman identity is forged.

The repetition is not confined to this leaf, but also occurs throughout the manuscript's images. The Bartholomew miniature is one among

---

[78] For more on Pacino's painting technique, see: Yvonne Szafran and Nancy Turner, 'Techniques of Pacino di Bonaguida, Illuminator and Panel Painter', in *Florence at the Dawn of the Renaissance*, ed. Sciacca, pp. 335–55, esp. 342.

[79] Kay, 'Original Skin,' p. 40. See p. 157 above, for discussion of Bartholomew's potential treason against King Astyages.

[80] Nicola Masciandaro, 'Non potest hoc corpus decollari: Beheading and the Impossible', in *Heads Will Roll*, ed. Tracy and Massey, pp. 15–36 at p. 24.

several surviving scenes of graphic saintly martyrdom in the Laudario of Sant'Agnese, the majority of which appear towards the end of the manuscript. Beginning with *The Martyrdom of Saints Peter and Paul* and ending with *The Martyrdom of Saint Bartholomew*, several of the leaves display a male martyr kneeling in prayer in the lower right-hand corner of the miniature as he is beheaded, or about to be beheaded, by a figure either sheathing or raising his sword.[81] This creates a certain repetitive gruesomeness when scanning through them, much in the way Bartholomew is beaten, flayed, crucified and beheaded repeatedly and in rapid succession through his vita in the *LgA*. From this collection of martyrdoms, the audience sees enacted what its members surely already knew: that martyrdom is central to the experience of the saint. For Bartholomew, who carries on *after* his initial martyrdom, the finality of beheading is diminished. If he carried on preaching after flaying, then surely he is *still*, in a sense, preaching at present. Beheading is just another moment of transformation for this apparently unstoppable body.

Holsinger, writing about the famous Book Riddle, argues that, 'The riddle's pat "solution" cannot simply be "Bible" or "book", for a Bible never had an enemy end its life, rip off its flesh, and leave its skin, dipping it in water and stretching it: these things happened to the body of an animal in the process of becoming parchment.'[82] The book is not the animal – really, the many animals – from which it was made. So too, the posthuman Bartholomew is not the same man as he was before flaying, not the same sort of being at all.

---

[81] The miniatures include: *The Martyrdom of Saints Peter and Paul*, Cambridge, The Fitzwilliam Museum (Marlay cutting It. 83); *The Martyrdom of Saint James the Greater*, Cambridge, Queens' College (MS 77d); *The Martyrdom of Saint Christopher*, Cambridge, Queens' College (MS 77b); and *The Martyrdom of Saint Bartholomew*. Of the surviving Laudario leaves, the only female martyr who is shown to meet her demise by beheading (St Catherine) appears twenty-seven folios after this cluster of images, and sixteen folios after the Bartholomew leaf. See: Bosi in *Jan Fabre*, p. 222.

[82] Holsinger, 'Pigs and Parchment', pp. 621–2.

7

Masculinist Devotion:
Flaying and Flagellation in the *Belles Heures*

Sherry C. M. Lindquist

THE *Belles Heures* (1408–9) is the first Book of Hours that the noted bibliophile Jean, duc de Berry (d. 1416), commissioned from the gifted Limbourg brothers: Herman, Jean and Pol (all d. 1416).[1] It is acknowledged in the history of art as a step on the way to the illuminators' realization of their artistic powers, thought to culminate in their celebrated final work, the *Très Riches Heures* of Jean, duc de Berry (1413–16).[2] The *Très Riches Heures* is among the most famous manuscripts in the world not only because of the degree of luxury it represents, but also because it fits a traditional art-historical narrative that privileges aesthetic preferences associated with the Italian Renaissance, such as the heroic nude and the Albertian window. When the *Belles Heures* is compared to the *Très Riches Heures* on these terms, it seems embryonic, experimental and eccentric.[3]

Many thanks are owed to an anonymous reviewer, and especially Larissa Tracy, for their perceptive comments on an earlier version.

---

[1] New York City, Metropolitan Museum of Art, The Cloisters, New York, acc. no. 54.1.1. Timothy Husband, *The Art of Illumination: The Limbourg Brothers and the Belles Heures of Jean de France, Duc de Berry* (New York: Metropolitan Museum of Art / New Haven: Yale University Press, 2008) is now the standard reference on the *Belles Heures*. The Limbourg brothers' career has received a thorough reassessment following an exhibition of their work in Nijmegen in 2005. See the catalogue accompanied by a series of essays updating much of the scholarship on the artists, Rob Dückers and Pieter Roelofs, *The Limbourg Brothers: Nijmegen Masters at the French Court, 1400–1416* (Nijmegen, Holland: Ludion, 2005). See also the essays in Rob Dückers and Pieter Roelofs, eds., *The Limbourg Brothers: Reflections on the Origins and the Legacy of Three Illuminators from Nijmegen* (Leiden: Brill, 2009). Still essential is the magisterial work by Millard Meiss, with the assistance of Sharon Off Dunlap Smith and Elizabeth Home Beatson, *French Painting in the Time of Jean de Berry: The Limbourgs and their Contemporaries*, 2 vols. (London: Thames & Hudson, 1974). There are two other useful facsimile volumes: Millard Meiss and Elizabeth H. Beatson, *The Belles Heures of Jean, Duke of Berry* (New York: G. Braziller, 1974); and Eberhard König, *Die Belles Heures des Duc de Berry: Sternstunden der Buchkunst* (Stuttgart: K. Theiss, 2004).

[2] Husband, *Art of Illumination*, p. xii. The *Très Riches Heures* is Chantilly, Musée Condé, MS 6.

[3] Husband calls it a 'laboratory' (*Art of Illumination*, p. xii).

This bias in the art-historical narrative impedes interpretations that consider the powers and purposes of alternative aesthetics exemplified by the *Belles Heures*. The pictorial programme of this manuscript mingles beautiful martyrs that Martha Easton suggests 'enable a transgressive sado-erotic response', with bodies that do not seem to anticipate the idealized nudes inspired by Classical Greece: broken, bleeding, diseased and contorted bodies, strangely animated corpses and – a quality that has not been recognized in previous literature – the monstrous merging of humans with other people, animals and things.[4] Such an affective aesthetic suits the purpose of a Book of Hours, which was to craft a better soul.

This extraordinary personal prayer book thus testified to the duke's piety at a time when claims of divine approval played a role in the violent civil wars – in which Jean, duc de Berry, was a key player – that rocked France in the period in which the book was made. Jean de Berry needed to shore up his reputation in response to his enemies' frequent attacks, which (among other things) targeted his sexual behaviour, specifically his liaisons with young men of lower social status.[5] Robert Mills suggests that an unusual miniature depicting a scene from the life of St Jerome where the blameless saint is tricked into wearing a woman's dress (fol. 184v) is a representation of sexual slander that would resonate with the duke under the circumstances.[6] Even though we cannot know the exact nature of the duke's sexuality, or, indeed, his relationship to the Limbourg brothers, consideration of evidence for the sexual sensibilities of duke and artists offers insight into how distinctive aspects of the prayer book provided opportunities for identity construction for both.[7]

[4] Martha Easton, 'Uncovering the Meanings of Nudity in the *Belles Heures* of Jean, Duke of Berry', in *The Meanings of Nudity in Medieval Art*, ed. Sherry C. M. Lindquist (Burlington, VT: Ashgate, 2012), pp. 149–81 at p. 175; for further discussion of the objectified female nudes in this book, see: Brigitte Buettner, 'Dressing and Undressing Bodies in Medieval Images', in *Künstlerischer Austausch. Akten des XXVIII. Internationalen Kongresses für Kunstgeschichte, Berlin 15–20 July 1992* (Berlin: Akademie Verlag, 1993), pp. 383–92.

[5] Michael Camille examines evidence concerning Jean, duc de Berry's sexuality in his '"For our Devotion and Pleasure": The Sexual Objects of Jean, Duc de Berry', *Art History* 24.2 (2001): 169–94. Contemporary accounts include the *Songe véritable*, a work of Burgundian propaganda in 3,174 allegorical verses that attacks Jean de Berry on multiple grounds and alludes to his purported homosexual liaisons by transforming the duke's 'gentle' servants into demons who sodomize him in Hell for eternity. The relevant lines are in Henri Moranvillé, *Le Songe véritable; pamphlet politique d'un parisien du XVᵉ siècle* (Paris, 1891), ll. 3050–79.

[6] Robert Mills, *Seeing Sodomy in the Middle Ages* (Chicago: University of Chicago Press, 2014), p. 10.

[7] Perhaps because the *Belles Heures* already addressed the pressing issue of the duke's sexual sins, the Limbourgs' next project for the duke, the

The unusual suite of images of flaying and flagellation in the *Belles Heures*, for example, calls attention to skin as barrier between inside and out, between self and other – as a primary marker of identity; skin, as Mills put it, is a 'surface with deep meditative possibilities'.[8] The peeling back of this surface, especially evoked by the Limbourgs' representations of flagellation and flaying, is a powerful intervisual motif in this manuscript that operated in constructing models of masculinist devotion and artistic identity.

The relationship between the Limbourg brothers, particularly Pol, and Jean, duc de Berry, seems to have been exceptionally familiar. Not only did the duke number the artists among his *varlets de chambre* (household officials with special status), but he also gave Pol clothes, jewels and a grand townhouse in Bourges.[9] Furthermore, in an extraordinary turn of events, Jean de Berry appears to have abducted a nine-year-old heiress to be Pol's bride; the duke only reluctantly relinquished the girl when her mother complained to the king – though she appears to have ended up married to Pol nonetheless.[10] Millard Meiss assumes that 'the brother to whom he [the duke] gave such exceptional gifts was the best artist', and used this as a premise to attribute what he considered the most accomplished miniatures

Très Riches Heures, shifted the emphasis to different ideological needs. A number of studies explore the political implications of imagery in the later manuscript. See: Herman Colenbrander, 'The Limbourg Brothers, the Joyaux of Constantine and Heraclius, the *Très Riches Heures* and the Visit of the Byzantine Emperor Manuel II Palaeologus to Paris in 1400–1402', in *Flanders in a European Perspective: Manuscript Illumination around 1400 in Flanders and Abroad: Proceedings of the International Colloquium, Leuven, 7–10 September 1993*, ed. Maurits Smeyers and Bert Cardon (Leuven: Peeters, 1995), pp. 171–84; Michael Bath, 'Imperial renovatio symbolism in the *Très Riches Heures*', *Simiolus* 17.1 (1987): 5–22.

[8] Robert Mills, *Suspended Animation: Pain, Pleasure and Punishment in Medieval Culture* (London: Reaktion, 2005), pp. 67–8. For the relationship between skin and identity in the early modern period, see: Daniela Bohde, 'Skin and the Search for the Interior: The Representation of Flaying in the Art and Anatomy of the Cinquecento', in *Bodily Extremities: Preoccupations with the Human Body in Early Modern European Culture*, ed. Florike Egmond and Robert Zwijnenberg (Burlington, VT: Ashgate, 2003), pp. 10–47.

[9] See: Husband, *Art of Illumination*, pp. 34–5. For the transcription of the document relevant to the house in Bourges, see: Meiss, *French Painting*, I:81.

[10] As discussed in Meiss, *French Painting*, I:69; Husband, *Art of Illumination*, p. 35; Camille, 'For our Devotion and Pleasure', p. 180; Willy Niessen, Pieter Roelofs and Mieke van Veen-Liefrink, 'The Limbourg Brothers in Nijmegen, Bourges, and Paris', in *Limbourg Brothers: Nijmegen Masters*, ed. Dückers and Roelofs, pp. 13–27 at p. 22. For transcriptions and translations from the archival documents regarding this affair, see: Meiss, *French Painting*, I:74–5.

and passages to Pol.[11] But it may be that the duke's evident favour (also or instead) reflects a sexual relationship between Pol and his master, which is not easily definable.[12] Michael Camille has stressed the need for caution in applying anachronistic notions of sexual propriety and identity to the duke. He writes that, 'In a society controlled by a male elite in which women, children and social inferiors were treated as political pawns as well as easily obtainable sexual objects, twentieth-century terms like "child abuse", "lover", or even "homosexuality" are misleading.'[13] As Timothy Husband tentatively comments, 'If indeed, the duke admired Pol de Limbourg as much for his artistry as his person, the painter assuredly was charged with a delicate balancing act.'[14] Familiarity with great princes brought both risks and rewards, and it appears that the *Belles Heures* played a role in the artists' attempt to leverage their relationship with their powerful patron. According to Werner Paravicini, in court culture of this era, 'intimacy with the prince was a sign of social status and for everyone, whether of high or low ranking, it represented a source of informal power, which aroused jealousy and was constantly under threat'.[15]

That the Limbourg brothers had unusual control over the *Belles Heures* strengthens the case that these complicated dynamics are manifest in the pictorial programme they created for the duke. Husband's examination of the relevant documents indicates that Jean de Berry's *libraires* seem not to have been involved in overseeing the commission.[16] Undoubtedly, the duke supervised aspects of the programme, and it may be that a spiritual advisor was consulted; nevertheless, considering the duke's frequent travels and preoccupation with complicated negotiations and entangled intrigues of the French court in politically tumultuous times, it seems unlikely that he was involved in the day-to-day decisions in what was a full-time job for three illuminators for several years. Rather, the illuminators drew on inside knowledge gained from an unusually close relationship with their patron to create a customized book tailored to his tastes and concerns.[17]

[11] Meiss, *French Painting*, I:110.

[12] Camille, 'For our Devotion and Pleasure', esp. pp. 177–9.

[13] Ibid., p. 174.

[14] Husband, *Art of Illumination*, p. 35.

[15] Werner Paravicini, 'The Court of the Dukes of Burgundy: A Model for Europe?', in *Princes, Patronage, and the Nobility: The Court at the Beginning of the Modern Age, c. 1450–1650*, ed. Ronald Asch and Adolf M. Birke (Oxford: Oxford University Press, 1991), pp. 69–102. See also: Sherry C. M. Lindquist, 'The Will of a Princely Patron and Artists at the Burgundian Court', in *The Artist at Court*, ed. Stephen Campbell (Chicago: University of Chicago Press for the Isabella Stewart Gardner Museum, 2004), pp. 46–56 esp. p. 52.

[16] Husband, *Art of Illumination*, p. 59.

[17] For discussion of the complexities of artistic agency in the context of the Valois courts, see: Sherry C. M. Lindquist, *Agency, Visuality and Society at*

Camille was the first to suggest the Limbourg brothers provided Jean de Berry with visual jokes to appeal to the duke's sexual appetites in the manuscripts they made for him. For, example, the famous January page of the *Très Riches Heures* depicts the duke at a feast surrounded by the things that give him pleasure, including the elegant young men of the court, sexualized especially through their phallic purses, and a cupbearer and water-bearer whom Camille interprets as allusions to Ganymede, 'a common Classical allusion to a male sex-slave' (fol. 2r; Fig. 7.1a).[18] He even proposes '"hidden" portraits of the three brothers, whose faces are covered by hats as though they were picture-puzzles for their patron to find below the surface of the picture. Pol himself is probably the third figure on the left from the duke's fool whose profile is occluded.'[19] Perhaps the duke may have associated and/or been meant to associate the Limbourg brothers with the generic courtiers represented in the miniature, but there is no hard proof that the Limbourgs represented themselves.[20] In addition, Camille sees the unique full-page miniature of a smooth-bodied youth pictured as a 'Zodiac Boy' shown twice, from both front and back, as the artists' acknowledgement of the duke's voracious gaze, a feast for the eyes that the duke could 'relish in his private prayer book' (fol. 14v; Fig. 7.1b).[21] The doubling of the figure, Camille contends, 'sets up a powerful image of masculinity divided against itself, a repetition – a need for more than one', he argues, that lies 'at the very centre of Jean de Berry's duplicative model of desire'.[22] As Camille astutely recognizes, one way that Jean de Berry constructed his masculinity was by acquiring rare and beautiful objects, particularly those with religious significance: 'We should not be surprised to see', he writes, 'this alignment of the sacred and the sexual in Jean's tastes.'[23] The Limbourg brothers show themselves to be sensitive to the duke's double preferences not only in the *Très Riches Heures*, but also the *Belles Heures*, in which eroticism and devotion are also intimately imbricated.

In the *Belles Heures* the Limbourg brothers offer a daring pictorial sequence that uses the theme of flagellation and the more extreme form of skin removal, flaying, to create a programme of penitential devotion

---

the *Chartreuse de Champmol* (Burlington, VT: Ashgate, 2008), pp. 85–120.

[18] Camille, 'For our Devotion and Pleasure', p. 177.

[19] Ibid., p. 181.

[20] On the difficulties of identifying contemporary figures in the calendar pages of the *Très Riches Heures*, see: Stephen Perkinson, 'Likeness, Loyalty, and the Life of the Court Artist: Portraiture in the Calendar Scenes of the *Très Riches Heures*', *Quaerendo* 38 (2008): 142–74 (also published in *Limbourg Brothers: Reflections*, ed. Dückers and Roelofs, pp. 51–83).

[21] Camille, 'For our Devotion and Pleasure', p. 177.

[22] Ibid., p. 179.

[23] Ibid., p. 185.

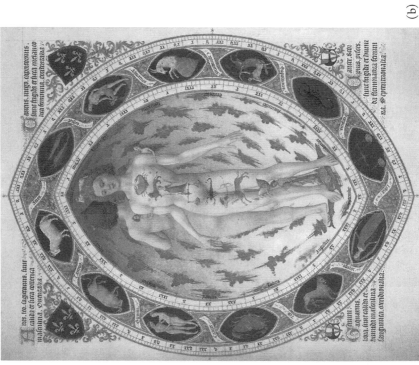

Fig. 7.1 Jean Herman and Paul de Limbourg, (a) 'January', (b) 'Zodiac Boy',
Très Riches Heures of John, Duke of Berry, 1411/12–1416 (Chantilly, Musée Condé, MS 5, fols. 2r, 14v)

Fig. 7.2 Jean Herman
and Paul de Limbourg,
'Flagellants', *Belles
Heures* of John, Duke
of Berry, 1405–1408/9
(New York, The
Cloisters Collection
1954, MS. 54.1.1,
fol. 74v)

alluding to Jean de Berry's sexual sins, and offering him an empowering
redemptive narrative. The key miniature in this pictorial thread is the first
instance of flogging in the manuscript, a unique miniature that depicts the
controversial practice of public self-flagellation in penitential processions
(fol. 74v; Fig. 7.2). The central drama of the scene focuses on two of the
party who subject their bare backs to the ministrations of their brethren.
Thus, the Limbourgs offered the duke a composition that allowed him a
prolonged gaze on submissive men presenting themselves to dominating
companions; the central hooded figure, who makes a show of clutching
the fabric of his robe in front of his groin, gives the scene even more of an
erotic charge. In fact, flagellation was associated with inappropriate sexual
feelings, as it was the recommended treatment for these prescribed by
Albert the Great and others.[24] This remedy is illustrated for the duke by
the image of St Jerome in the manuscript (fol. 183v; Fig. 7.3a); according
to Jerome's *vita*, he suffered terribly from the pains of sexual temptation –
his temptation by sexy demonesses is also represented in the *Belles
Heures* (fol. 186r; Fig. 7.3b).[25] One point that might be taken from this
representation of St Jerome being flogged in his dream is that one can
atone for thought sins with thought penance.

[24] Danielle Jacquart and Claude Alexandre Thomasset, *Sexuality and Medicine
in the Middle Ages* (Princeton: Princeton University Press, 1988), p. 150,
citing *De Bono* in *Alberti Magni Opera Omnia* (Monasterii Westfalorum:
Aschendorff, 1951), 28:160–3.

[25] On this scene, see: Easton, 'Uncovering the Meanings of Nudity', p. 163.

Fig. 7.3 Jean Herman and Paul de Limbourg, (a) 'St Jerome's Dream'; (b) 'Temptation of St Jerome', *Belles Heures* of John, Duke of Berry, 1405–1408/9 (New York, The Cloisters Collection 1954, MS. 54.1.1, fols. 183v, 186r)

Indeed, one of the reasons that influential contemporary clerics like Jean Gerson (1363–1429) objected to self-flagellation was that lay people might thereby seek to avoid the sacrament of confession and the penance prescribed by a qualified confessor – that they might attempt to determine and mete out their own penance.[26] The priest-like power claimed by the flagellants extended beyond the individual to the larger Christian community, and it was for this reason that Clement VI issued a bull to suppress these movements.[27] The first flagellants gathered in response to crises: war in Perugia inspired movements in Northern Italy in 1260–1, as did the spread of the plague across Europe in 1348–9.[28] In spite of the papal ban, such movements continued to flare up sporadically, and a third wave of flagellants at the end of the fourteenth century may have reflected public anxiety about papal schism in conjunction with outbreaks of plague and apocalyptic expectations associated with the jubilees of 1390 and 1400.[29] The spectacles staged by the flagellants, spurred on by the star power of the charismatic future saint Vincent Ferrer – who travelled with a company of self-scourging followers – captured the public imagination. In fact, Mitchell Merback has argued that these peregrinating groups of penitents performed in an intervisual dialogue with the affective devotional imagery that characterizes the art of the later Middle Ages, what he calls 'experiential transfers between visual art and spectacle'.[30]

[26] Jean Gerson, '*Contra sectam flagellantium*', *Œuvres complètes*, ed. Palàemon Glorieux, 10 vols. (Paris, New York: Desclée, 1973), 10:47.

[27] *Inter sollicitudines* (20 Oct. 1349), reproduced in Shlomo Simonsohn, *The Apostolic See and the Jews: Documents 492–1404*, Studies and Texts 94 (Toronto: Pontifical Institute of Mediaeval Studies, 1988), pp. 399–401.

[28] For a history of flagellation, including the movements of 1260 and 1348, with additional bibliography, see: Niklaus Largier, *In Praise of the Whip: A Cultural History of Arousal*, trans. Graham Harman (New York: Zone, 2007). See also: Gordon Leff, who connects the first movement in Perugia to Joachite prophesies, *Heresy in the Later Middle Ages: The Relation of Heterodoxy to Dissent, c. 1250–c. 1450*, 2 vols. (Manchester: Manchester University Press, 1967), p. 1: 485–93; and Richard Kieckhefer, 'Radical Tendencies in the Flagellant Movement of the Mid-Fourteenth Century', *Journal of Medieval and Renaissance Studies* 4 (1974): 157–76. In this volume, see: Susan Small, 'Flesh and Death in Early Modern Bedburg', pp. 71–90; Peter Dent, 'A Window for the Pain: Surface, Interiority and Christ's Flagellated Skin in Late Medieval Sculpture', pp. 208–39; and Valerie Gramling, '"Flesche withowtyn hyde": The Removal and Transformation of Jesus' Skin in the English Cycle Passion Plays', pp. 240–60.

[29] The term 'third wave' belongs to Catherine Vincent, 'Discipline du corps et de l'esprit chez les Flagellants au Moyen Âge', *Revue historique* 302.3 (2000): 593–614 at p. 596. For reports of flagellants in Northern Europe between 1370 and 1400, see: Largier, *In Praise of the Whip*, p. 12.

[30] Mitchell B. Merback, 'Living Image of Pity: Mimetic Violence, Peacemaking and Salvific Spectacle in the Flagellant Processions of the

The miniature of flagellants in the *Belles Heures* bears witness to this interchange (fol. 74v; Fig. 7.2). Here, the Limbourg brothers linked the duke's personal devotional exercise to the public practices of flagellant groups by reproducing many of the elements of contemporary accounts, including the hats, hoods and white garments worn by lay societies like the aptly named *bianchi*, the raised cross and banner, and the formation in which flagellants scourged the bare backs of their prostrate brethren.[31] The prayers that the duke recited with the aid of his prayer book recalled the hymns, chants of absolution, sermons and benedictions that were part of the flagellants' rituals. The miniature, thus, offered an opportunity for a kind of vicarious participation on the part of the duke – with the implication that he might receive the spiritual benefits, and indeed authority, that the practices of the flagellants were thought to accrue. In fact, the ecclesiastical establishment objected to these public paraliturgical demonstrations precisely because they seemed to usurp the Church's place. Critics like Gerson complained that the stripping, flagellation and sometime posture of crucifixion all enabled witnesses to identify the flagellant's tormented body with Christ's – his blood with the blood of Christ – an *imitatio Christi* that had the potential to short-circuit priests' exclusive role in channelling Christ's salvific body and blood in the performance of Mass.[32] As noted by Merback and others, the flagellant movement consisted almost entirely of men, and, furthermore, this public, voluntary flogging was a male prerogative precisely because it was self-directed, public and meant to make a difference in the world.[33] Scholars propose several reasons for the absence of women among the flagellants, including concerns with sexual modesty, but especially the prevalent notion that the pain of women was less able to be a voluntary, Christ-like action with exculpatory implications, since women were already condemned to suffer pain for their part in original

---

Later Middle Ages', in *Images of Medieval Sanctity: Essays in Honour of Gary Dickson*, ed. Debra Higgs Strickland (Leiden: Brill, 2007), pp. 135–80 at p. 159. He makes a related argument in his brilliant study of the connections between late medieval public spectacles of corporal punishment and painted Crucifixion scenes in *The Thief, the Cross, and the Wheel: Pain and the Spectacle of Punishment in Medieval and Renaissance Europe* (Chicago: University of Chicago Press, 1999), esp. pp. 28–32.

[31] For descriptions, see: Largier, 'The Theater of the Flagellants', in *In Praise of the Whip*, pp. 101–74.

[32] Gerson, '*Contra sectam flagellantium*', 10:46–51.

[33] See: Lisa Silverman, *Tortured Subjects: Pain, Truth, and the Body in Early Modern France* (Chicago: University of Chicago Press, 2001), pp. 126–9; Merback, 'Living Image of Pity', pp. 154–5; and Marla Carlson, *Performing Bodies in Pain: Medieval and Post-Modern Martyrs, Mystics, and Artists*, Palgrave Studies in Theatre and Performance History (New York: Palgrave, 2010), pp. 112–13.

sin.[34] Female exclusion from flagellant groups implied that, like priests, only men – thought to be made more perfectly in the image of Christ – could emulate his sacrificial interventions. The flagellants in the *Belles Heures*, thus, provided the duke with a model of heroic masculine piety grounded in the *imitatio Christi*, and so potent in its potential impact on earthly affairs that it threatened ecclesiastical authorities.

One way in which flagellant processions were meant to intervene in the world was as action against plague. Plague is a worry that permeates the *Belles Heures*, not only by attention to plague saints like Sebastian (fol. 165v) and Anthony (fols. 191v–194v), but also by the expansive treatment of the procession of St Gregory. This is the event in which the saint inaugurated the litany, his pleas to heaven finally persuading God to send St Michael to signal the end of the epidemic by sheathing his bloody sword (fols. 73v [Fig. 7.4a], 73r [Fig. 7.4b], 74r).[35] In this sequence, the Limbourg brothers produced extraordinarily affective plague victims, whose agonized expressions and convulsing bodies contrast with both the flagellants and the saintly martyrs in the manuscripts, who face pain with pious equanimity. By directly following the Procession of St Gregory with their unique image of flagellants (fol. 74v; Fig. 7.2), the Limbourgs connected the two. The caption under the miniature of the flagellants explicitly encourages the reader to make this link between present and past, historical illustration and lived experience: 'Servaturque hec consuetudo usque in hodiernum diem quod homines vadunt nudi in aliquibus locis, verberantes se et macerando carnem in jejunio et oracione et planctu processionaliter omnium sanctorum patrocinia implorantes.' [This practice is maintained until the present day when, in certain places, men go nude, flogging themselves, and laying waste to their flesh through fasting, prayer, and mourning, and thus through these processions imploring the protection of all the

---

[34] The gendered differences in historical attitudes about pain even extend to the lives of the saints. When pain was a feature of hagiographical emphasis, it was more likely that female saints would be praised for enduring pain, while male saints effected and benefited from miraculous cures. The pain of male saints was more often a mechanism of power in the world, while the suffering of female saints was an aspect of mystical interiority. On these points, see: Caroline Walker Bynum, *Fragmentation and Redemption: Essays on Gender and the Human Body in Medieval Religion* (New York: Zone, 1991), esp. pp. 36–7, 154, 188–90, 231; and Larissa Tracy, *Torture and Brutality in Medieval Literature: Negotiations of National Identity* (Cambridge: D. S. Brewer, 2012), pp. 31–69.

[35] Plague, though a serious concern for everyone at the time, may have been particularly terrifying to Berry, who lost his mother to it at age nine. Françoise Lehoux, *Jean de France, duc de Berri: sa vie, son action politique (1340–1416)*, 4 vols. (Paris: A. et J. Picard et Cie, 1966), 1:13.

Fig. 7.4 Jean Herman and Paul de Limbourg, (a) 'Procession of St Gregory,' (b) 'Procession of St Gregory,' *Belles Heures of John, Duke of Berry,* 1405–1408/9. (New York, The Cloisters Collection 1954, MS. 54.1.1, fols. 73v, 73r)

Fig. 7.5 Jean Herman and Paul de Limbourg, 'Flagellation of Christ', *Belles Heures* of John, Duke of Berry, 1405–1408/9 (New York, The Cloisters Collection 1954, MS. 54.1.1, fol. 132r)

saints.][36] The dragon banner that follows the cross in the miniature further testifies to both the sanctity and efficacy claimed for flagellants. The popular compilation of saints' lives the *Legenda aurea* – the major source for the text of the suffrages in the *Belles Heures* – mentions that in some rogation processions in Gaul, such a banner precedes the cross for two days, symbolizing the rule under the law, before being moved, on the third day, to a position behind the cross, indicating the rule of grace ushered in by Christ's sacrifice.[37] Thus, the flagellants are shown performing their ritual under the auspices of God's grace, and the crown of thorns and *flagellum* that hang from the processional cross encourage the reader to relate this image to the Flagellation of Christ later in the manuscript (fol. 132r; Fig. 7.5). This representation of the crown of thorns links the devotional aspirations activated by the miniature to the relics of the Passion that Louis IX brought to Paris, which are pictured three times in this manuscript (fols. 93r, 157r, 207v). The intervisual links among these miniatures suggest that engaging in the proper penitential practices encouraged by the miniature of

[36] Husband, *Art of Illumination*, p. 141. This and all subsequent translations from the *Belles Heures* are from Husband.

[37] Husband, *Art of Illumination*, p. 141. See: Jacobus de Voragine, *The Golden Legend: Readings on the Saints*, trans. William Granger Ryan (Princeton: Princeton University Press, 1993), p. 288.

the flagellants makes the duke a worthy beneficiary of the powers inherent in Christ's relics, a source of French royal authority.[38]

The Limbourgs' representation of flagellants creates a psychologically challenging tension because it is both an argument that such displays of male devotion were a kind of *imitatio Christi* enabling effective intervention in world affairs, *and* an acknowledgment that the devotees are sinners receiving just – even if self-inflicted – penance. For Jean de Berry, a particularly important model of a powerful ruler whose devotional exercises were thought to increase his influence in the world was St Louis, as illustrated in the *Hours of Jeanne d'Evreux*, a tiny prayer-book in Jean de Berry's collection, which pictured the duke's royal progenitor, St Louis, submitting to scourging by his confessor (fol. 103r).[39] In the *Belles Heures* the intervisual relationship between the flagellants (fol. 74vr; Fig. 7.2), the Flagellation of Christ (fol. 132r; Fig. 7.5) and St Jerome's dream (fol. 183v; Fig. 7.3a) reminds the duke to engage, like saints Louis or Jerome, in a heroic spiritual struggle to overcome the desire that the illuminations in the book are in danger of provoking. In this respect, the images in the *Belles Heures* can be compared to the way that, according to Thomas Dale, the combination of monstrous and sexualized images functioned for monastic viewers of Romanesque sculpture: both encouraged prolonged meditation on sexualized images in the context of images of abjection, penance and judgement, so that viewers might 'sublimate sexual, fleshly desire in favour of its spiritual counterpart'.[40] In the procession of the flagellants, the Limbourgs offered the duke a mechanism by which he could triumph over his transgressions and accumulate virtue and divine approval to leverage

[38] For the politically tinged devotion to these relics among nobles closely linked to the French royal house, see: Elizabeth L'Estrange, *Holy Motherhood: Gender, Dynasty and Visual Culture in the Later Middle Ages* (Manchester: Manchester University Press, 2008), pp. 183–6.

[39] Scholars generally agree that three entries in Jean de Berry's inventories refer to this book; the documents are published in Kathleen Morand, *Jean Pucelle* (Oxford: Clarendon Press, 1962), p. 31, and discussed at greater length in the facsimile edition by Barbara Boehm, Abigail Quandt and William Wixom, *The Hours of Jeanne d'Evreux, Acc. No. 54.1.2, The Metropolitan Museum of Art, the Cloisters Collection, New York* (New York: Verlag Luzern, 2000), pp. 89–94. On St Louis' ideological importance as a model to the French kings, see: Anne Dawson Hedeman, *The Royal Image: Illustrations of the Grandes Chroniques de France, 1274–1422* (Berkeley: University of California Press, 1991); and Paula Mae Carns, 'The Cult of Saint Louis and Capetian Interests in the Hours of Jeanne d'Evreux', *Peregrinations* 2.1 (2009): 1–32.

[40] Thomas Dale, 'The Nude at Moissac: Vision, Phantasia, and the Experience of Romanesque Sculpture', in *Current Perspectives in Romanesque Sculpture Studies*, ed. Kirk Ambrose and Robert Maxwell (Turnhout: Brepols, 2011), pp. 61–76 at p. 74; and his 'Monsters, Corporeal Deformities and Phantasms in the Cloister of Saint-Michel de Cuxa', *Art Bulletin* 83.3 (2001): 402–36.

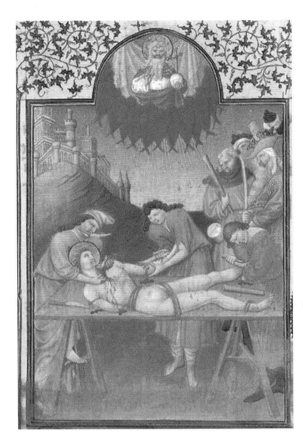

Fig. 7.6 Jean Herman and Paul de Limbourg, 'Martyrdom of St Bartholomew', *Belles Heures* of John, Duke of Berry, 1405–1408/9 (New York, The Cloisters Collection 1954, MS. 54.1.1, fol. 161r)

in the public sphere. In a complete circuit of potential sin and redemption, the manuscript pictured beautiful, penetrable bodies that might stimulate pleasurable fantasies, appealing flesh ruptured as a reminder of the penance due for sinful thoughts, and bleeding that recalled the salvific blood of Christ.

The representation of lacerated skin in this manuscript finds an extreme expression in the miniature of the flaying of St Bartholomew, which similarly presents the bleeding body in ways that, at once, titillate, accuse, reassure and redeem (fol. 161r; Fig. 7.6). The emotive charge in this miniature is ratcheted up by images of pools of blood, and by the punishers' being particularly intent on their work. One momentarily holds his knife in his mouth so that he can use both hands to rip off a hunk of flesh; he has taken off his shoe in order to better brace himself against the trestle table for this operation. Bartholomew is one among several beautiful martyrs in the *Belles Heures* whose undressed bodies are available to the viewer's sado-erotic gaze, as described by Martha Easton.[41] It is worth remarking, however, that, with the exception of St Ursula and the 11,000 Virgins

---

[41] See: Easton, 'Uncovering the Meanings of Nudity', esp. p. 166.

(fol. 178v), a dramatic massacre scene that the artists evidently thought could not be portrayed without bloodshed, the bodies that bleed in the *Belles Heures* are male. As Caroline Walker Bynum writes, '[b]lood – spilled and sacrificial – was both closely connected to the Eucharist and yet had a devotional life of its own as stimulator of guilt and penitence, frenzy and love.' [42] At a time when the Eucharistic chalice was reserved to the clergy, the laity found other ways of accessing the saving blood of Christ and the martyrs: the *Belles Heures* provided Jean de Berry with his own simulated supply. The bloody male martyrs and Christ, unlike St Ursula and the virgin martyrs, are mostly presented to the duke's gaze as large-scale nudes, whose bodies dominate the composition at the front of the picture plane: vertically (Christ, fols. 80r, 132r [Fig. 7.5], 142r, 145r, 145v, 149r; Sebastian, fol. 165v), diagonally (Christ, fols. 141v, 152r; Lawrence, fol. 162v), or horizontally (Christ, fol. 149v; Bartholomew, fol. 161r [Fig. 7.6]). The compositional emphasis forced the duke to confront alluring male flesh and sacrificial blood at the same time. His potentially transgressive gaze on the saint's body is tantamount to torture, the miniature of St Bartholomew implies, since it gives the viewer a place at the table and even makes available to him a knife unused by the saint's tormenters. The disquieting implication of complicity on the part of the viewer was balanced, or perhaps even overbalanced, with the heartening presence of God the Father surrounded by his angels, offering a gesture of blessing available to be intercepted by the viewer. The only other place in the manuscript in which God appears in a similar way is to supervise the oneiric flogging of St Jerome (fol. 183v; Fig. 7.3a). In both cases the striking orange of God's angelic entourage is highlighted against a clear blue sky, different from the decorative patterned backgrounds of the majority of other scenes in the manuscript. In both, a single unobstructed figure is positioned horizontally across the picture plane. The duke can take comfort, the Limbourgs imply, through this intervisual connection, that even the saints must resist temptation and serve penance for impure thoughts. They appear to take this a step further in their magnificent rendering of the Temptation of Christ in the *Très Riches Heures*, which they locate over an architectural portrait of one of the duke's luxurious castles, Mehun-sur-Yèvre (fol. 161v) – implicitly inviting the duke to identify with Christ himself. [43]

An examination of a later artist's selective borrowing from the

---

[42] Caroline Walker Bynum, 'The Blood of Christ in the Later Middle Ages', *Church History* 71.4 (2002): 685–714 at p. 712. See also her *Wonderful Blood: Theology and Practice in Late Medieval Northern Germany and Beyond* (Philadelphia: University of Pennsylvania Press, 2007).

[43] For the identification of the castle, see: Perkinson, 'Likeness, Loyalty, and the Life of the Court Artist', p. 153, citing Raymond Cazelles, *Illuminations of Heaven and Earth: The Glories of the Très Riches Heures du duc de Berry* (New York: H. N. Abrams, 1988), p. 188.

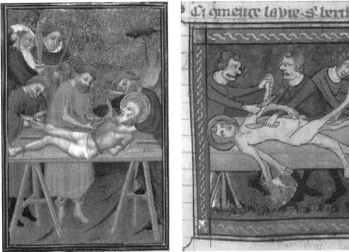
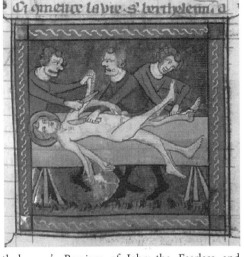

(a)   (b)

Fig. 7.7 (a) Breviary Master, 'St Bartholomew', Breviary of John the Fearless and Margaret of Bavaria, 1410–19 (London, British Library, MS Harley, 2897, fol. 379r); (b) 'St Bartholomew', from Jacobus de Voragine, *Legenda aurea*, 1348 (Paris, Bibliothèque nationale de France, MS Fr. 241, fol. 219r)

Limbourgs' composition for the martyrdom of St Bartholomew suggests that the penitential themes they directed to the duke were so embedded in the intervisual programme that they were not legible outside of the manuscript context of the *Belles Heures*. The *Belles Heures* is an established source of the Breviary of John the Fearless (London, British Library, MS Harley 2897, *c.* 1410–1419), the eponymous work of the Breviary Master.[44] This artist clearly had access to the *Belles Heures*, or drawings from it, and he employed mirror images of the Limbourg brothers' compositions, which suggests that tracing was one stage in the transfer. Nevertheless, in the case of the scene with St Bartholomew, the Breviary Master made some significant changes (fol. 379r; Fig. 7.7a). The young aristocratic Bartholomew has been turned into a greybeard covered with a pair of prosaic underpants. The tormentor's bare foot is shod and the pools of blood cleaned up, and two of them illogically clench knives in their teeth

---

[44] London, British Library, MS Harley 2897 is the summer portion of the breviary; the winter portion is London, British Library, Add. MS 35311. On this manuscript, see: Gregory Clark, 'The Master of Guillebert de Mets, Philip the Good and the Breviary of John the Fearless', in *The Limbourg Brothers: Reflections*, ed. Dückers and Roelofs, pp. 191–210. The role of the *Belles Heures* as artistic source of the breviary is discussed in Jean Porcher, *Les Belles Heures de Jean de France, duc de Berry* (Paris: Bibliothèque nationale de France, 1953), p. 25; Meiss, *French Painting*, I:232–7; and Gregory Clark, 'The Influence of the Limbourg Brothers in France and the Southern Netherlands, 1400–1460', in *Limbourg Brothers: Nijmegen Masters*, ed. Dückers and Roelofs, pp. 208–35; esp. pp. 209–14.

even though they already have knives in their hands. The haunting idea that a single extra blade is offered to the viewer is lost in a general surfeit of weaponry. In a miniature where the focus is St Bartholomew's martyrdom rather than the viewer's spiritual struggle, God's dramatic appearance against a clear blue sky apparently seemed superfluous. The Master of the Breviary of John the Fearless took out all of the innovative aspects that seem tailored to Jean de Berry, as reinforced by intervisual elements in the *Belles Heures*.

The kind of identification that the Limbourgs' image of Bartholomew offers is novel, nuanced and flexible. It is different from other medieval treatments that focus on the sensational aspects of St Bartholomew's martyrdom, which sometimes depicted the saint as a kind of monster, where his partially peeled skin gives the impression of multiple arms and legs – as illustrated, for example, in a fourteenth-century *Legenda aurea* in the Bibliothèque nationale de France (MS Fr. 241, fol. 219r; Fig. 7.7b) associated with the illuminators Richard and Jeanne Monbaston.[45] Alternatively, Bartholomew might be shown 'completely skinned like a monster', as the post-Tridentine theologian Molanus complained in his encyclopaedic treatise on sacred images.[46] The Limbourg brothers offered a more appealing, idealized Bartholomew, who enabled a degree of identification that the monstrous Bartholomew did not. But the sensualized body of the saint also presented a danger of engendering impure thoughts, which must be overcome in order not to assault the saint with an inappropriate gaze that injured the sacred body, as much, medieval writers such as St Birgitta of Sweden insisted, as physical instruments of torture.[47] The miniature introduces the disturbing prospect that the viewer might be metaphorically joined to the tormenters via his own gaze.

The powerful notion that sinner and sacred figure are intimately united

---

[45] On these illuminators, see: Richard H. Rouse and Mary A. Rouse, *Manuscripts and their Makers: Commercial Book Producers in Medieval Paris, 1200–1500*, 2 vols. (Turnhout: Harvey Miller, 2000), 1:235–60. Other examples of the type include a miniature in a thirteenth-century psalter from Ghent associated with the artist Tweede Groep, now in the Morgan Library, New York (MS M. 72, fol. 76r); and a *bas-de-page* illustration in the Luttrell Psalter, *c.*1325–1335 (London, British Library, Add. MS 42130, fol. 103v). Also see: Asa Simon Mittman and Christine Sciacca, 'Robed in Martyrdom: The Flaying of St Bartholomew in the Laudario of Sant'Agnese', pp. 140–72, in this volume.

[46] Johannes Molanus, *Traité des saintes images*, 2 vols. (Paris: Cerf, 1996), 1:426. On the 'completely skinned' type of Bartholomew, see the chapter in this volume by Mittman and Sciacca.

[47] For discussion, see: Corine Schleif, 'Christ Bared: Problems of Viewing and Powers of Exposing', in *The Meanings of Nudity*, ed. Lindquist, pp. 251–78 esp. pp. 263–4; and Susan Smith, 'Bride Stripped Bare: A Rare Type of the Disrobing of Christ', *Gesta* 34.2 (1995): 126–46.

Fig. 7.8 Master
of the Parement
of Narbonne
(Jean d'Orléans?),
'Flagellation of Christ',
*Très Belles Heures de
Notre Dame*, 1382–4
(Paris, Bibliothèque
nationale de France,
MS nouv. acq. Lat.
3093, fol. 197r)

is strengthened and justified intervisually in the Flagellation of Christ
miniature in the *Belles Heures* by showing Christ himself appearing to
merge with one of his attackers, so much so that, at first glance, he seems
to be a monstrous three-legged being with one pink boot (fol. 132r;
Fig. 7.5). Union with Christ, in fact, is understood to be the primary goal
for the devout, but one which was difficult for humans to negotiate. As
Corine Schleif observes, 'all Christians shared in the guilt of Christ's
Passion, and this guilt was one of the emotions that images of Christ's
Passion were to engender'.[48] Sarah Salih, too, notes that the position of
witnesses of Passion imagery 'could easily slip into that of the torturer'.[49]
The deliberate merging of tormenter and Christ was a 'strange' departure
from the miniature's source, an illumination of the Flagellation of Christ
in Jean de Berry's *Très Belles Heures de Notre Dame* by the Master of the
Parement of Narbonne (begun *c.* 1390) (fol. 197r; Fig. 7.8).[50] 'Strangeness'

---

[48] Schleif, 'Christ Bared', p. 264.

[49] Sarah Salih, 'The Medieval Looks Back', in *Troubled Vision: Gender,
Sexuality, and Sight in Medieval Text and Image*, ed. Emma Campbell and
Robert Mills (New York: Palgrave, 2004), pp. 223–31 at p. 224; as cited by
Schleif, 'Christ Bared', p. 264.

[50] This original manuscript was divided into three parts: Paris, Bibliothèque
nationale de France MS nouv. acq. Lat. 3093; Turin, Museo Civico
d'Arte, MS inv. no. 47; and Turin, Biblioteca Nazionale, MS K.IV.29 (now
destroyed). For the Limbourgs' use of the *Très Belles Heures de Notre Dame*
as a source for the *Belles Heures*, see: Husband, *Art of Illumination*, p. 282.

was a desirable quality thought to convey ideas effectively and memorably, and 'strange' and novel objects were particularly admired in late medieval court culture.[51] In the *Belles Heures,* the Limbourg brothers changed a version of the Flagellation familiar to the duke, and made it strange and newly effective for him. Several studies suggest that looking for quotations and meaningful adaptions from prestigious books was a habit of viewing among the elite bibliophiles of fifteenth-century court culture.[52] No doubt the duke would have noticed evident changes: how the Limbourgs simplified the Parement Master's stage-like space and moved Christ in front of the column so that the spectator has an unobstructed view of his tortured flesh; how they elongated his body while making his loincloth smaller and slung lower on his hips. Christ's hands are no longer tied in an elegant chiastic position that recalls what was recognized as a particularly expressive gesture of prayer. Instead, his arms seem truncated at the elbows, evoking the spectre of dismemberment as they are pulled tightly behind his back. The Limbourgs amplified Jesus' humiliation by having one of the tormenters reach forward to pull his hair, and further intensified the violence by having five, rather than three, attackers; one kneels at his feet to secure him to the column with a rope, while four more assault him, not only with *flagella* (whips with knotted cords), but also birches (bundles of flexible rods). They raise their weapons high above their heads, and one even lifts his knee in order to put more of his weight behind the blow. In the Limbourg's version, a *flagellum* actually makes contact with the sacred flesh, unleashing streams of blood that flow down Jesus' body towards his pristine white *perizonium.* Pilate, who in the Parement Master's composition is a regal authority positioned to Christ's right, is relegated to the upper left background in the Limbourgs' revision, half cut-off by the frame and conferring with a figure wearing an oversized version of the *pileum cornutum,* the conical hat medieval viewers associated with Jews. Their conspiratorial tête-à-tête, juxtaposed with the brutal attack taking place in the foreground, might, in fact, have been a strong emotional trigger of hateful feelings in this context, since Jews were commonly blamed for

---

[51] For the quality of 'strangeness' (*l'étrangeté*) in Valois court culture, see: Brigitte Buettner, 'Past Presents: New Year's Gifts at the Valois Courts, ca. 1400', *Art Bulletin* 83.4 (2002): 598–625; Stephen Perkinson, *The Likeness of the King: A Prehistory of Portraiture in Late Medieval France* (Chicago: University of Chicago Press, 2009), pp. 238–44; and my discussion of 'Innovation and Strangeness', in *Agency, Visuality and Society*, pp. 122–38. Also see: Perkinson, 'Likeness, Loyalty, and the Life of the Court Artist', in *Limbourg Brothers: Reflections*, ed. Dückers and Roelofs, pp. 51–83 esp. pp. 71–2 and 81–3.

[52] See: James H. Marrow, 'History, Historiography, and Pictorial Invention in the *Turin-Milan Hours*', in *In Detail: New Studies of Northern Renaissance Art in Honor of Walter S. Gibson*, ed. Laurinda S. Dixon (Turnhout: Brepols, 1998), pp. 1–14; and L'Estrange, *Holy Motherhood*, pp. 113–98 esp. 151.

Christ's Crucifixion.[53] The result of these changes – adding more figures, including a recognizably Jewish scapegoat, perpetrating greater violence against a more vulnerable Christ – made what was already an affecting scene even more unsettling. The heightened violence and emotion of this scene intensify the impact of the unexpected assimilation of Christ and tormentor, a deliberate departure from the Limbourgs' model in the *Très Belles Heures de Notre Dame*. In the Limbourgs' version, Christ's right leg crosses behind, instead of in front of, his left leg, creating the illusion that the tormentor's pink boot extends from Christ's knee – a merging that evokes the prospect of a sinner's union with the divine.[54]

Such 'strange' mergings are repeated throughout the *Belles Heures*; their effects are akin to the skin removal featured in the images of flagellation and flaying. These are visual strategies that reinforce each other: both are part of an aesthetic meant to destabilize the viewer as part of a process of making a better, more devout and virtuous, version of the self. Not only do these strategies unnervingly breach the integrity of individual bodies, they also collapse roles and identities: saint and sinner, witness and participant, layman and cleric. For example, in the Limbourgs' scene of Christ before Caiaphas, the two soldiers escorting Christ look as though they share three legs, while Christ's shoulder merges with that of the yellow-clad centurion in front (fol. 124r; Fig. 7.9a). At the Burial of Diocrès, a gravedigger in blue bends down so that the torso of the man behind him appears to extend from the first figure's hips (fol. 95r; Fig. 7.9b). A Carthusian entering the Grande Chartreuse pulls his habit over his head so that the heads of the two monks behind him seem to emerge, Janus-like, from his cowl; one of them joins heads with another figure in blue, probably a novice who had not yet attained the status of monk (fol. 97r; Fig. 7.10a). In the vision of Bishop Hugh, the tonsured figure in green on the left seems to have a third foot – which must, on a second look, belong to the student behind him (fol. 95v; Fig. 7.10b). A *pentimento* of a similar 'third foot' in the miniature of the Flaying of St Bartholomew must have been intended to belong to the sword-bearing king overseeing the man bent over his work of removing skin from Bartholomew's left leg (fol. 161r; Fig. 7.6). The king

---

[53] By contrast, the Parement Master's black-skinned 'Ethiopian' attacker, though exotic, was less provocative than the Limbourgs' Jewish conspirator. Featured alongside bearded and unbearded compatriots, they may have been meant to work like some representations of the three Magi, in which the men's diverse ages and ethnicities indicate the universal scope of Christianity. See: Paul H. D. Kaplan, *The Rise of the Black Magus in Western Art* (Ann Arbor: University of Michigan Press, 1985); and in this volume, Frederika Bain, 'Skin on Skin: Wearing Flayed Remains', pp. 116–37.

[54] In this case, the Limbourg brothers may have been inspired by Jean Pucelle's version of the Flagellation in the *Hours of Jeanne d'Evreux*, which was in Jean de Berry's possession (fol. 54v). Here the right leg of Christ's tormentor seems to merge with Christ's left hip.

(b)

(a)

Fig. 7.9 Jean Herman and Paul de Limbourg, (a) 'Christ before Caiaphas', (b) 'Burial of Diocrès', *Belles Heures* of John, Duke of Berry, 1405–1408/9 (New York, The Cloisters Collection 1954, MS. 54.1.1, fols. 124r, 95r)

Fig. 7.10   Jean Herman and Paul de Limbourg, (a) 'Entering the Grande Chartreuse', (b) 'Vision of Bishop Hugh', 1405–1408/9; *Belles Heures* of John, Duke of Berry (New York, The Cloisters Collection 1954, MS. 54.1.1, fols. 97r, 95v)

Fig. 7.11 Jean Herman and Paul de Limbourg, 'Pilate Washes his Hands', *Belles Heures* of John, Duke of Berry, 1405–1408/9 (New York, The Cloisters Collection 1954, MS. 54.1.1, fol. 138r)

places a familiar hand on the shoulder of the flayer; he is dressed in the type of deep blue garment associated with the French royals, such as the duke wears in the January page of the *Très Riches Heures* (fol. 2r; Fig. 7.1a). The king's position behind the torturer, and the prodigious phallic sword that he holds erect above the figure's head, are suggestive enough; perhaps the Limbourgs thought that blending the feet of these figures was a bridge too far (still, they left the sketched-in foot for the alert viewer to find). This merging between king and commoner might have been just too provocative to illustrate, especially considering the unconventional relationship between the Limbourgs and the duke.

Indeed, when it comes to figures from the underclass depicted in the manuscript, the Limbourg brothers turned this unsettling aesthetic of hybrid monstrosity into a broad joke, merging peasants with things and animals in a way that precluded identification by the aristocratic viewer. A ewer-headed servant helps Pilate wash his hands (fol. 138r; Fig. 7.11). Labourers in the calendars seem to sprout grapes (fol. 10r; Fig. 7.12a) and jugs from their necks (fol. 2r; Fig. 7.12b). St Martin's abject beggar has a stump and a staff that suggests a third leg, and his head seems to be merging with or swallowed by the head of the horse (fol. 169r; Fig. 7.13a). The second beggar is coextensive with the horse's rear end, and his legs are splayed in imitation of the animal's back hooves. His position vis-à-vis the horse suggests that he may be engaged in dehumanizing bestiality. In spite of all of the nudity in the manuscript, a disabled beggar in the scene of the death of St Jerome is the only one shown with prominent genitals (fol. 189v; Fig. 7.13b) – another way of emphasizing Otherness and

Fig. 7.12 Jean Herman and Paul de Limbourg, (a) 'September: Treading Grapes – Libra', (b) 'January: Youth and Old Age – Aquarius', *Belles Heures* of John, Duke of Berry, 1405–1408/9 (New York, The Cloisters Collection 1954, MS. 54.1.1, fols. 2r, 10r)

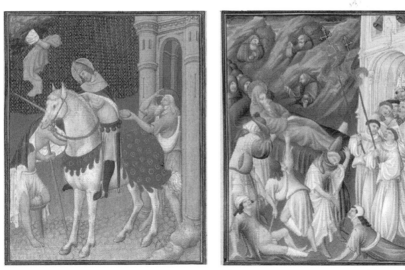

Fig. 7.13 Jean Herman and Paul de Limbourg, (a) 'St Martin and the Beggar', (b) 'The Sick Attending the Funeral of St Jerome', *Belles Heures* of John, Duke of Berry, 1405–1408/9 (New York, The Cloisters Collection 1954, MS. 54.1.1, fols. 169r, 189v)

monstrosity, as Salih and others have discussed.[55] Easton has observed that the Limbourg brothers emphasize swelling genitals beneath the undergarments of several of the semi-nude torturers and executioners (e.g. fols. 19r & 19v), as well as the labourers shown in the calendar (fols. 8r, 9r, and 10r [Fig. 7.12a]) – demeaning treatment that underscores

[55] Salih, 'The Medieval Looks Back', pp. 223–31.

class hierarchies at a time of increasing peasant unrest.[56] Undignified representation of the bodies of lower-status figures further suggests that 'conversion journeys' from sexual to spiritual stimulation were not available to men of the labouring classes, whom, as Sharon Farmer has shown, were thought to embody an inferior brand of masculinity.[57] Through denigrating representations of labourers and beggars, the Limbourg brothers reassured the duke of his superior status and provided some relief from the discomfiting identifications encouraged in the flaying and flagellation scenes.

By crafting themes tailored to the duke's tastes, especially those emphasizing penance that culminated in the interrelated flagellation and flaying scenes, the Limbourg brothers not only created a book to be used in shaping Jean de Berry's identity, but also, in constructing their own relationship to the duke and their status as court artists, which hinged on the duke's favour. One way they did this was by linking the personalized theme of effective penance in the *Belles Heures* to portraits of Jean de Berry in the manuscript. The ability to render a recognizable likeness underscored the artists' access to and intimacy with the figure portrayed; according to Stephen Perkinson, this was a novel strategy that late-medieval artists used to elevate their status in court contexts.[58] Medieval manuscripts – even the most customized – were made to be seen by a viewing community including family members and other familiars, imagined viewers-to-be-impressed, future owners (who might be destined to receive 'pre-owned' manuscripts as gifts upon important occasions such as marriage or birth) and posterity. These objects are semi-public things that not only express the concerns of a particular person, but also embed information about the relationships that characterized their viewing community. In this context, the Limbourgs' status-elevating claims of intimacy with the duke would be all the more effective.[59]

---

[56] Easton, 'Uncovering the Meanings of Nudity', p. 166. On the peasants as objects of the aristocratic gaze in Jean de Berry's manuscripts, see also: J. J. G. Alexander, '*Labeur* and *Paresse*: Ideological Representation of Medieval Peasant Labor', *Art Bulletin* 72.3 (1990): 436–52; and Camille, 'For our Devotion and Pleasure'.

[57] Sharon A. Farmer, 'The Beggar's Body: Intersections of Gender and Social Status in High Medieval Paris', in *Monks and Nuns, Saints and Outcasts: Religion in Medieval Society: Essays in Honor of Lester K. Little*, ed. Lester K. Little, Sharon A. Farmer and Barbara H. Rosenwein (Ithaca, NY: Cornell University Press, 2000), pp. 153–71 at p. 159. On the role of medieval art in 'conversion journeys' influenced by St Bernard's sermons on conversion, see: Dale, 'Nude at Moissac', pp. 72–4.

[58] Perkinson, *Likeness of the King*; for his discussion on the Limbourgs and Jean de Berry see, pp. 258–71.

[59] For discussion of the 'public' implications of Books of Hours, see: Andrea G. Pearson, *Envisioning Gender in Burgundian Devotional Art, 1350–1530*:

The wider constituency of the manuscript helps to explain the presence of the portraits of both the duke, Jean de Berry, and the duchess, Jeanne of Boulogne. In her exploration of the meanings of nudity in the *Belles Heures*, Easton rightly draws attention to Jeanne's status as possible patron and/or reader.[60] Even so, a comparison of the portraits of Jean and Jeanne demonstrates the extent to which the devotional programme of the manuscript was designed to privilege the duke's particular concerns, rather than the duchess's. Jeanne of Boulogne's features are generic and her pose stiff and conventional; an attendant pulls back the curtain of her private chapel, where we see her praying to the Trinity presiding from a second columnar miniature (fol. 91v; Fig. 7.14a).[61] The prayer, in French, that accompanies the duchess's portrait beseeches the Trinity to take pity on her, 'en l'onneur et a la remembrance de celui hautisme conseil que vous preinstes de vostre propre sapience quant // vous envoiastes vostre saint angle Gabriel a la Vierge Marie' [in honour and remembrance of the highest advice you took from your own wisdom when you sent your blessed angel Gabriel to the Virgin Mary].[62] The prayer on this folio invokes the Annunciation, thus anticipating that the duchess would be most concerned with matters of conception and birth. It points her to the Hours of the Virgin, an accomplished and appealing section of the manuscript, to be sure, but not one in which the strange, often gory corporeal aesthetic that sets the manuscript apart is on display.

In contrast, the duke appears in a rare one-column miniature, one of only two in the book (fol. 91r; Fig. 7.14b). The other occurs on the very next illuminated folio, illustrating the Hours of the Cross, in which two unidentified figures adore the crown of thorns standing in for a crucifix (fol. 93r). It makes sense that the Limbourgs would flatter the duke with this intervisual connection, since he was the owner of one of the thorns, which he had had encased in a sumptuous reliquary.[63] Both the duke and duchess are depicted royally: she with a crown and he in an ermine robe

---

Experience, Authority, Resistance (Burlington, VT: Ashgate, 2005), pp. 70–8. Cf. Myra Orth, 'Family Values: Manuscripts as Gifts and Legacies among French Renaissance Women', *Journal of the Early Book Society* 4 (2001): 88–111; Marrow, 'History, Historiography, and Pictorial Invention'.

[60] Easton, 'Uncovering the Meanings of Nudity', pp. 151, 171–5.

[61] Stephen Perkinson contrasts the duchess's 'bland' portrait to the individualized features and physical presence of the duke on the recto of the same folio (*Likeness of the King*, p. 263).

[62] Easton discusses the portrait in light of the duchess's likely concern to produce a legitimate heir – an urgent matter for the ducal couple since the duke's sons from his previous marriage had predeceased him, 'Uncovering the Meanings of Nudity', p. 173. Cf. Husband, *Art of Illumination*, p. 151.

[63] On this object, now in the British Museum, see: John Cherry, *The Holy Thorn Reliquary* (London: British Museum Press, 2010).

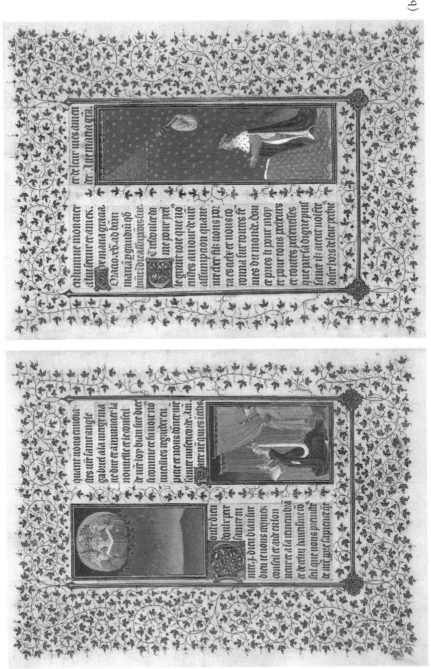

Fig. 7.14 Jean Herman and Paul de Limbourg, (a) 'The Duchess of Berry in Prayer to the Trinity', (b) 'The Duke of Berry in Prayer', *Belles Heures* of John, Duke of Berry, 1405–1408/9 (New York, The Cloisters Collection 1954, MS. 54.1.1, fols. 91v, 91r)

and golden coronet. The duke is shown anachronistically young – he was in his sixties at the time – but his features are still more individualized than those of the duchess. Examination of the disturbed paint surface indicates that the Limbourgs altered the image – the duke originally turned toward the viewer and wore a turban-like hat.[64] The other portrait of the duke, on the final folio of the manuscript, also suggests that the Limbourgs were inclined to experiment with their patron's image; in order to portray him riding into the scene, they daringly cut off the left side of his body (fol. 223v; Fig. 7.15a).[65] It is impossible to know if and who decided the portrait of the duke at prayer should match that of the duchess with a more formal headdress and profile, but, even so, the portrait still singles him out by deviating from iconographic expectations. For, unlike the duchess and other petitioners in the manuscript (fols. 18v, 26v, 66v, 67v, 70r, 71v, 73v–74r, 88v, 172v), the duke is not rewarded with a rendering of the heavenly recipient of his prayer. It may be that this portrait shows the duke engaging in an elite form of imageless devotion, even though this would belie the purpose of the richly illustrated *Belles Heures*. Perhaps Jean de Berry was meant to interpret his painted alter ego as reading the actual words in the opposite column rather than the book pictured in front of him, which would animate his portrait in a novel way. The prayer accompanying the duke's portrait invokes the Virgin on her Assumption and beseeches her to intercede for him with Christ: 'pries li pour moy et pour tous pecheurs et toute pecherresses que par sa digne puissance, ilz aient volent d'isir hors de leur pechies // et de leur vies amender' [pray to him for me and for all sinners, so that by his worthy power they may be willing to forgo their sins and improve their lives].[66] This invocation encourages the duke to page back several folios to find the Assumption of the Virgin (fol. 88r) appearing to an unnamed king – a logical candidate for the duke's identification – who also asks the Virgin to intercede for him and to grant him 'vraye confession et repetance de tous les peches que je fis oncques' [true confession and contrition for all the sins I have committed in the past].[67] Thus, the portraits of duke and duchess instruct them on how to use the manuscript: she was to pray for a successful pregnancy, and he was to pray for self-control and forgiveness. The greater emphasis in the manuscript is on penitential themes directed to the duke: uncommonly, the seven penitential Psalms include a miniature for each Psalm rather than

---

[64] Husband, *Art of Illumination*, p. 148.

[65] The Limbourg brothers were not alone in appealing to the duke through innovative portraits, see: Pearson's discussion of the portraits of Jean de Berry by André Beauneveu in the *Brussels Hours* in *Envisioning Gender*, pp. 65–7; and Carol J. Purtle, 'The Iconography of Prayer, Jean de Berry, and the Origin of the Annunciation in a Church', *Simiolus* 20.4 (1990): 227–39.

[66] Husband, *Art of Illumination*, p. 148.

[67] Ibid., p. 146.

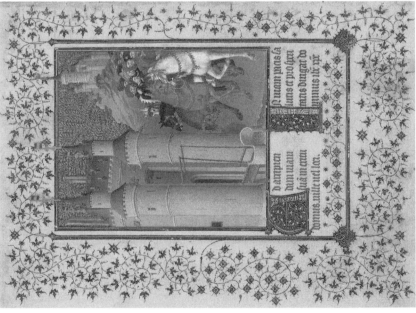

Fig. 7.15 Jean Herman and Paul de Limbourg, (a) 'The Duke of Berry on a Journey',
(b) detail of (a), showing letter 'P' (for Paul de Limbourg?) on the castle turret,
Belles Heures of Jean, Duke of Berry, 1405–1408/9 (New York, The Cloisters Collection 1954, MS 54.1.1, fol. 223v)

a single frontispiece (fols. 66r–72v), and the Presentation in the Temple (fol. 57r) is bordered by a scroll inscribed with a penitential plea for mercy: 'secundum multitudinem miserationum tuarum dele iniquitatem meam' [according to the multitude of thy mercy, blot out my iniquity].[68] There is unusual emphasis on the regretful sinner Diocrès (fols. 94r, 95r [Fig. 7.9b], 95v), on struggles against temptation in the legends of saints such as Jerome (fol. 186r; Fig. 7.3), Paul (fol. 191v) and Anthony (fol. 194r), and finally the unique intervisual thread dedicated to flagellation and flaying (fols. 74v [Fig. 7.2]; 132r [Fig. 7.5]; 161r [Fig. 7.6]; 183v [Fig. 7.3]).

If the duke's first portrait affirms the relevance of the manuscript's penitential theme for him, the second portrait predicts his success and its positive consequences in the world (fol. 223v; Fig. 7.15a). Merback argues that 'self-scourging served as a kind of magical technique for defusing and controlling unwanted violences', and that public spectacles of flagellation drew strength from affective visual images and vice-versa.[69] The peacemaking function of the flagellants pictured in his manuscript would certainly have been germane to Jean de Berry's interests, considering the simmering civil war between the Burgundians and Armagnacs that he repeatedly attempted to arbitrate. It has been argued that the narrative of this folio refers to the duke's efforts to treat with the Burgundians following the murder in 1407 of one of his nephews, Louis of Orléans, by another of his nephews, John the Fearless, the duke of Burgundy.[70] The rubric beneath the miniature makes explicit its purpose, as it asks for angelic help 'ad dirigendos pedes nostros in viam paces' [to guide our feet towards the way of peace].[71] The disturbing bloody bodies, the strange relationships and elisions among subjects and objects, the sacred sado-erotic aesthetic, all of which are foregrounded in representations of flaying and flagellation in the *Belles Heures*, offered opportunities for self-guided penance. If properly pursued, the final portrait implies, the duke will be empowered with the sacred and political authority needed to achieve the peace alluded to in the diplomatic venture pictured on the final folio of the book. The Limbourg brothers seem to have struck a chord with this portrait, since Jean de Berry had versions of it added to two of his other Books of Hours: the *Très Belles Heures de Notre Dame* and the *Petites Heures*.[72]

It was on this favoured folio that the duke's favourite, Pol, may have chosen to call attention to his role in creating this extraordinary customized book. A tiny 'P' appears on a turret of the castle in the background (fol. 223v; Fig. 7.15b). Margaret Lawson, whose technical analysis of the

---

[68] Ibid., p. 67.

[69] Merback, 'Living Image of Pity', pp. 145, 159.

[70] The political import of this miniature was first proposed by Meiss, *French Painting*, I:108–9, and is endorsed by Husband, *Art of Illumination*, p. 263.

[71] Husband, *Art of Illumination*, p. 263.

[72] For discussion, see: ibid., p. 41, and Perkinson, *Likeness of the King*, p. 268.

manuscript brought it to light, wonders if this is testimony that painters could be 'secretly playful' – implying that the 'P' might stand for 'Pol'.[73] If this were a tiny artist signature, its location does not seem haphazard. The turret stands out, implausibly perched as it is on the very point of the second-largest tower of the castle. This castle is more prominent than the corresponding motif in the other two versions: it is bigger and its highest, flag-bearing, roof breaches the frame of the miniature, just like the two recognizably Burgundian flags waving from the turrets of the castle in the foreground. It is hard to fathom why the castle on the hill is not identified, given the prominence of the Burgundian banners; but it does line up over the duke's entourage and may have been meant to suggest that one of his properties was the point of departure for his journey, especially since the rubric refers to departing from and returning home.[74] Perkinson notes that the system of signs employed in the duke's manuscripts was sometimes intentionally obscure, that it 'served as a test of iconographic knowledge, allowing members of the court to gauge each other's degree of access to their lord's identity'.[75] The tiny grey flag surmounting the principal tower matches the tinier grey flag on the turret with the 'P'. It has some possibilities as an inside joke: Pol represents himself as an inscription on the duke's turret; the banner over his initial is next to the principal banner of the duke's castle and on a shorter pole.

If, as Perkinson suggests, the insertion of portraits and other clever references to the patron's identity that exceeded the terms of commission might be interpreted as a form of gift-giving, then perhaps the manuscript operated in an additional way to build the relationship between artists and patron.[76] Scholarship is increasingly revealing the profound social and political implications of gift-giving in late medieval court culture.[77] Modest gifts were offered to individuals of lower rank by those of higher rank; more extravagant ones, infused with complex personal and political

---

[73] Margaret Lawson, 'Technical Observations: Materials, Techniques, and Conservation of the *Belles Heures* Manuscript', in Husband, *The Art of Illumination*, pp. 325–36 at p. 327.

[74] Husband, *Art of Illumination*, p. 263. On the Limbourg brothers' 'architectural portraits', see: Perkinson, 'Likeness, Loyalty, and the Life of the Court Artist', pp. 152–5.

[75] Perkinson, 'Likeness, Loyalty, and the Life of the Court Artist', pp. 158–9.

[76] Perkinson, *Likeness of King*, p. 272.

[77] For an overview, see: Jan Hirschbiegel, *Étrennes: Untersuchungen zum höfischen Geschenkverkehr im spätmittelalterlichen Frankreich der Zeit König Karls VI. (1380–1422)* (München: Oldenbourg, 2003). See also: A. J. Bijsterveld, *Do ut des: Gift Giving, 'Memoria', and Conflict Management in the Medieval Low Countries* (Hilversum: Verloren, 2007); Carol M. Chattaway, *The Order of the Golden Tree: The Gift-Giving Objectives of Duke Philip the Bold of Burgundy* (Turnhout: Brepols, 2006); and Buettner, 'Past Presents'.

significance, were exchanged among equals or near equals. The Limbourgs clearly aspired to participate in this symbolic discourse with their patron; in 1411, not long after they completed the *Belles Heures*, they offered the duke a block of wood tricked out to look like a luxury manuscript as a New Year's gift.[78] This was a bold gesture that pushed the normative etiquette of the exchange of these *étrennes*. The counterfeit book, and perhaps luxurious additions to the *Belles Heures*, may represent a clever compromise, a way of acknowledging the duke's own (possibly inappropriate) gifts to the artists without being perceived as taking liberties. The positive reception of the fake book, as indicated by its entry into the duke's official inventories, may have encouraged Pol to proffer a true *étrenne* in 1415: a bejewelled salt cellar of agate and gold.[79]

Like the fake book, the real book – the *Belles Heures* – was semi-public, made to be displayed, shared and talked about. The awareness that it was part of a larger network of relationships surely shaped the decision to include at least limited pictorial acknowledgment of the duchess's preferences and concerns, including a respectful, if generic, portrait. Perhaps the bodies in the manuscript provided female viewers with opportunities for identification and pleasure, as Easton suggests.[80] But given the artists' exceptional and, no doubt to many contemporaries, unseemly familiarity with the duke, it may be that the female nudes such as saints Catherine and Agatha (fols. 17r–v, 179r) and the tempting women illustrated in the legends of saints Jerome and Paul (fols. 186r, 191r) were meant to reinforce the duke's possibly contested masculinity, given the rumours of his homosexual liaisons. Representing the duchess praying for children in his prayer book, too, might have projected a socially expected claim to heterosexual potency, underscoring his desire to become the patriarch of a strong and enduring dynastic line. These aspects of the pictorial programme counter others that seem to address the duke's homosexual predilection – by providing sensualized male nudes for the

---

[78] The inventory entry describing the trick book is transcribed in Jules Guiffrey, *Inventaires de Jean duc de Berry (1401–1416)*, 2 vols. (Paris: E. Leroux, 1894), 1:265; and Meiss, *French Painting*, I:76. On this object, see also: Husband, *Art of Illumination*, pp. 22, 35; and Perkinson, *Likeness of the King*, pp. 259–60.

[79] Guiffrey, *Inventaires*, 1:323; Meiss, *French Painting*, I:78.

[80] Easton identifies opportunities in the manuscript for an active female gaze, especially instances in which women might be admiring other women's bodies, such as when the Empress Faustina approaches the semi-nude St Catherine (fol. 17v), and when two demonic temptresses appear to be eyeing each other's breasts (fol. 186r, fig. 7.6): 'Uncovering the Meanings of Nudity', pp. 163–4, 173. She also suggests that the beautiful male bodies in the manuscript may have provided visual pleasure to female viewers (p. 166).

duke's pleasure, even while encouraging him to repent his sexual sins so that he could better exert authority on the world stage.

The images of flaying and flagellation in the *Belles Heures*, when understood in the context of their intervisual relationship to each other and to other elements of the pictorial programme, affirm that the manuscript was a book by men for men. The Limbourg brothers created a manuscript customized to Jean de Berry's desires and devotional needs by capitalizing on their intimate knowledge of the duke. They devised an aesthetic of sensualized violence, of stripped bodies, skin removal and startling hybrids, which had the potential to please and disturb. The beautiful, suffering, permeable bodies in the *Belles Heures* encouraged the duke to meditate on sexual desires construed at the time as unnatural and sinful, on homosexual unions that crossed class barriers and transgressed socially accepted limits. The Limbourg brothers' miniature of the flagellants (fol. 74v; Fig. 7.2), which positioned a traditional punishment for sinful sexual desire within a narrative that empowered male sinners by likening them to Christ and the saints, encapsulates the complex double message of the entire book. This miniature of the flagellants seems never to have been imitated, and when an illuminator, the Breviary Master, did copy the related scene of the flaying of St Bartholomew (fol. 161r; Fig. 7.6), he toned down its most provocative qualities (Fig. 7.7a). The Breviary Master's alterations show that the book was thought worthy of imitation, but also that it was confounding, that its message did not transfer easily across time and space. This seems to hold true to this day: for while the *Belles Heures* is considered an uncontested masterpiece from illuminators thought to be among the best of all time, it is still also characterized as a fledgling work, a stop on the way to the less discomfiting and (therefore) more admired *Très Riches Heures*.[81] And yet, there is every reason to think that it was with the *Belles Heures* that the Limbourg brothers established their artistic reputation; where they devised their signature self-referential motifs and daringly integrated them into a picture programme that provided for the duke's particular penitential requirements. Their success in garnering and keeping the duke's favour is reflected in the extravagant gifts he bestowed on them, and in their continued employment with a grand new commission. Given the psychologically demanding and potentially incriminating implications of the *Belles Heures*, it is perhaps not surprising that the duke wished to have an alternative book by his

---

[81] The impression that the *Belles Heures* contains considerably more – and more dramatic – violence than the *Très Riches Heures* is confirmed statistically: twenty-four versus two notably bloody scenes. The forceful knee-lifting attack of many perpetrators that appears nine times in the earlier book is absent from the *Très Riches Heures*, as is the distinctive blending of bodies that is repeated in the *Belles Heures*. Gratuitous nudity, also, is reduced in the *Très Riches Heures*, and nudes in the later book are mostly idealized beauties.

favoured artists. Rather than see one manuscript as leading to another in a teleological stylistic trajectory, it makes sense to view the differing character of these books as intentional attempts to accommodate different moods, ideological needs, audiences and occasions. The *Belles Heures* emerged from a complex and unique constellation of personalities and circumstances, where remarkably skilled artists cultivated an unusually intimate relationship to a patron who was at the centre of a tumultuous history-altering crisis. The resulting aesthetic engenders a range of possible viewing responses – both medieval and modern – that include wonder, discomfort, awe, pride, delight, curiosity, distaste and transgressive pleasure.

8

A Window for the Pain:
Surface, Interiority and Christ's Flagellated Skin in Late Medieval Sculpture

Peter Dent

O NE of the most striking developments in late medieval visual culture concerns the emergence of a new type of sculpted image of Christ Crucified towards the beginning of the fourteenth century. Known to modern scholarship as the *crucifixus dolorosus*, these objects display an obsessive and extreme attention to the wounding of Christ's body, almost to the point where the sheer number and variety of wounds threaten to overwhelm the surface and obliterate the skin, in other words, almost to the point at which the body is flayed. Such images appear to have enjoyed something approaching universal popularity throughout Europe, even though they sometimes met with official disapproval.[1] In modern scholarship they have generally been marginalized because of the lack of secure information about their authorship and dating, although recent technical analysis has made significant contributions to our knowledge. Their reception has also been dogged by a tendency to interpret their remarkable features as a simple piling-up of gore. Again, recent analysis suggests a much greater level of sophistication, not only in their facture but also in their consumption by late medieval beholders. The multi-layered and highly articulate surfaces of these works encourage the viewer to read through that surface, stripping off Christ's skin and flesh as though visually flaying his body in the process of devotional adoration. Indeed, flaying – mediated through the metaphors of the body as book and the flesh as fabric – offers a powerful framework through which to interpret the significance of these sculptures. Before applying that framework, however, we must begin by stepping back from the sculptures in order to address the meaning of wounding itself at the beginning of the fourteenth century.

We are in the pit of Hell, following as Dante the pilgrim descends through the infernal kingdom with his guide, the classical poet Virgil. He is making his way across the seventh circle, where the sin of violence is punished. The two men have just forded a river of blood, thick with boiling sinners, and they stand on the fringe of a trackless wood. The pilgrim is puzzled. The place echoes to cries of distress, but the source

---

[1] For a discussion of an episode in London involving the official condemnation of a sculpture of this type in 1305/6, see: Paul Binski, *Becket's Crown: Art and Imagination in Gothic England, 1170–1300* (New Haven: Yale University Press, 2004), pp. 201–5.

of these laments is nowhere to be seen. Virgil encourages him to reach out and pluck a branch from a thorn bush. In a poem full of shocking scenes, what follows is among the most disturbing and uncanny. The broken branch begins to bleed, and through the flow of blood it starts to speak. Dante fashions a particularly vivid metaphor for this unnatural wound: 'Come d'un stizzo verde ch'arso sia / da l'un de' capi, che da l'altro geme / e cigola per vento che va via: / sì de la scheggia rotta usciva insieme / parole e sangue' [As when a green log is burnt at one end, from the other it drips and sputters as air escapes: so from the broken stump came forth words and blood together] (*Inferno*, 13.40–4).[2] In this episode

[2] All quotations are from *The Divine Comedy of Dante Alighieri*, vol. 1: *Inferno*, ed. and trans. Robert M. Durling (Oxford: Oxford University Press, 1996). Canto and line numbers are given in parentheses. The following studies have been consulted for the summary interpretation offered here: Patrick Boyde, '*Inferno* XIII', in *Cambridge Readings in Dante's Comedy*, ed. K. Foster (Cambridge: Cambridge University Press, 1981), pp. 1–22; Antonio Marzo, 'I violenti contro sé e le proprie cose: lettura del canto XIII dell'*Inferno*', in *Lectura Dantis Lupiensis*, ed. Valerio Marucci and Valter Leonardo Puccetti (Ravenna: Longo, 2012), 1:39–72; Kurt Ringger, 'Pier della Vigna o la poesia del segno: per una rilettura del canto XIII dell'*Inferno*', *Medioevo Romanzo* 5.1 (1978): 85–99; Giorgio Petrocchi, 'Canto XIII', in *Lectura Dantis Neapolitana: Inferno*, ed. Pompeo Giannantonio (Naples: Loffredo, 1986), pp. 231–42; Leo Spitzer, 'Speech and Language in "Inferno" XIII', in *Representative Essays*, ed. A. K. Forcione, H. Lindenberger and M. Sutherland (Stanford: Stanford University Press, 1988), pp. 143–71; Martin McLaughlin, 'The Rock and the Vine: Pier della Vigna, Dante, and the Imagery of Empire', in *Dante and Governance*, ed. John R. Woodhouse (Oxford: Clarendon, 1997), pp. 121–36; Rebecca S. Beal, 'Ending in the Middle: Closure, Openness, and Significance in Embedded Medieval Narratives', *Annali d'Italianistica* 18 (2000): 175–98; Anthony K. Cassell, 'Pier della Vigna's Metamorphosis: Iconography and History', in *Dante, Petrarch, Boccaccio: Studies in the Italian Trecento in Honor of Charles S. Singleton*, ed. Aldo S. Bernardo and Anthony L. Pellegrini (Binghamton, NY: Center for Medieval & Early Renaissance Studies, 1983), pp. 31–76; James T. Chiampi, '*Consequentia rerum*: Dante's Pier della Vigna and the Vine of Israel', *The Romanic Review* 75.4 (1984): 162–75; Gianni Oliva, 'Pier delle Vigne: l'uomo pianta', in *Inferno: Dante personaggio, Francesca, Farinata, Pier delle Vigne, Ulisse, Ugolino* (Rome: Bulzoni, 2006), pp. 63–85; Stefania Benini, '"Parole e sangue": parola, fede e retorica in *Inferno XIII*', *L'Alighieri* 22 (2003): 69–82; Gabriele Muresu, 'La selva dei disperati ("Inferno" XIII)', and 'VINEA VS SILVA? (sulla pena dei suicidi)', both in Gabriele Muresu, *Il richiamo dell'antica strega: altri saggi semantica dantesca* (Rome: Bulzoni, 1997), pp. 11–71 and pp. 73–84 respectively; Christie K. Fengler and William A. Stephany, 'The Capuan Gate and Pier della Vigna', *Dante Studies* 99 (1981): 145–57; Claudia Villa, 'Canto XIII', in *Lectura Dantis Turicensis: Inferno*, ed. Georges Güntert and Michelangelo Picone (Florence: F. Cesati, 2000), pp. 183–91.

wounding is deployed as a medium of communication. The wounded body is potentially an articulate body that can speak precisely because it is wounded. From this perspective, the flayed body – all wound – would be the most eloquent of all. The bodies encountered in Dante's Hell are all, in some respect, parodic images of Christ. The obscene spurt of indistinct words released from the broken branch stands at the opposite extreme from Christ, the Word incarnate. Christ's body is not flayed, but as the source of all meaning, it logically occupies the location where we might expect to find the flayed body in this bloody spectrum. If the bark surface must be stripped away to release meaning from within, and if that meaning is liberated through a flow of blood, then the more surface that is stripped away and the more powerful the outpouring of blood, the more expressive the body can be. In the economy of Christian salvation, there can be no more meaningful flow of blood than that shed by Christ. And yet, the positioning of Christ's body as a flayed body in this sense is problematic, not only because it was not flayed, but also because without any framing skin the wound almost ceases to be legible as a wound, and the wound-mouth loses the lips that shape and direct its words. Nevertheless, in this context, the late medieval fascination with Christ's wounded skin conceals an overwhelming desire for communication with divinity. That desire creates so much pressure that the flagellation is reimagined almost as a flaying; the hypothetical excoriation of Christ's skin offers a fantasy of absolute and unmediated access to the Word.

Each of the trees in the infernal wood was once human. They are being punished here in the seventh circle of Hell for violence against the self, for committing suicide. In voluntarily dissolving the bond between body and soul, they have rejected the essence of their humanity and so are doomed to spend eternity as sub-human, sub-animal vegetation, a parodic expression of the rational, animal and vegetative powers of the human soul. Even at the Resurrection, they will not resume their bodies, but hang them, spread-eagled from their branches.

Transformation into a tree is a particularly ironic punishment for the damned soul who speaks to Dante and Virgil in this canto. Although he never reveals his name, he implicitly identifies himself as Pier della Vigna, official spokesman and advisor to Frederick II, whose fall from grace on charges of conspiracy in 1249 led him to take his own life. Names have power in Dante's world and the poet plays on their associations. Pier sets himself up as a second St Peter, holding the keys to the emperor's heart, yet Peter's keys now shut him out of Heaven. Moreover, his surname, della Vigna, contains a plant, the vine, traditionally invoked as an image of Christ and of the righteous. Suicide is a rejection of Christ, and by rejecting the true vine, Pier has become its terrible shadow, a barren thorn bush.

But there is a further irony to this unusual punishment. In life Pier was celebrated as a great rhetorician, and Dante has him speak in carefully crafted phrases that echo his official letters and speeches. The disjunction between this rhetorical eloquence and the metaphor of the sputtering stump enhances the image of words being forced through a stream of blood. In fact, the whole episode is a meditation on the power of language. The image of a bleeding, speaking tree is an elaboration on Virgil's description in the *Aeneid* of Polydorus' disembodied voice emerging from deep beneath the bloody roots of a grove growing over his corpse. Within his own poem, Dante even has Virgil observe that the pilgrim need never have broken one of Pier della Vigna's branches had he believed that the Polydorus episode was truth rather than fiction, a comparison that explicitly measures Dante's own poetic skill against that of his classical guide and mentor. Where Virgil failed to persuade, Dante, absorbing that failure, stages his own success.

In the midst of this complex and disturbing scene, Dante offers an intriguing observation. Above the bloody forest whirl harpies – half-human, half-bird – feeding on the leaves of these unfortunate trees. In describing the wounds these creatures make, Pier della Vigna, speaking all the while through just such a wound, observes of these attacks that: 'fanno dolore e al dolor fenestra' [they make pain, and for that pain a window] (*Inferno*, 13.102, my translation). So on the one hand, Dante deploys a metaphor of the wound as a window, on the other as a stump of wood where the pain at one end generates a reaction at the other. Both express the potentially mediatory role that wounding can play for the communication of pain, though the window configures the wound as an almost frictionless opening into depth, whereas communication through the wounded stump is far more difficult.

In the case of Pier della Vigna the wounds are torn through the bark of the tree, revealing the inner wood that bleeds its sap. Bark is an opaque surface that conceals this inner life until it is ruptured.[3] Within the poem, it is worth comparing this image with one that Dante invokes for himself at the very beginning of *Paradiso*. As the poet seeks to raise his game in order to speak clearly of the mysteries of Paradise, he calls on Apollo for inspiration: 'entra nel petto mio, e spira tue / sì come quando Marsïa traesti / de la vagina de le membre sue' [come into my breast and breathe there, as when you drew Marsyas forth from the sheath of his members] (*Paradiso*, 1.19–21).[4] This reference to the unfortunate satyr of Ovid's *Metamorphoses* is significant on two levels. First, Dante reworks the punishment in Ovid through which Marsyas is destroyed so that the flaying becomes a liberation of the soul from the body.[5] Skin is read as a synecdoche for flesh,

---

[3] Cf. Larissa Tracy, 'Face Off: Flaying and Identity in Medieval Romance', pp. 322–48, in this volume, where the Norse hero Oddr encases himself in bark for over 100 years as a form of disguise and rejuvenation.

[4] Translation: *The Divine Comedy of Dante Alighieri*, vol. 3: *Paradiso*, ed. and trans. Robert M. Durling (Oxford: Oxford University Press, 2011).

[5] Jessica Levenstein, 'The Re-Formation of Marsyas in *Paradiso* 1', in *Dante for the New Millennium*, ed. T. Barolini and H. W. Storey (New York: Fordham University Press, 2003), pp. 408–21.

a move fundamental to the Christian way of reading the body surface as the body *tout court* when, for example, the flesh is likened to a veil that conceals the soul.[6] Second, where Ovid's Marsyas is punished for his temerity after he fails to best Apollo in musical ability, Dante-Marsyas requests transcendent inspiration from his god. Like all of Dante's identifications with figures from myth and scripture, his similarity to Marsyas is fraught with ambivalence.[7] However, the implied flaying positions Dante as a martyr-witness to God's truth and as a prophet literally inspired by a divine eloquence that lifts him beyond the limited reed pipe of his vernacular poetry towards the power of scripture, that is, Apollo's lyre.[8] In the process, he seeks an unmediated identification with his creator: 'come into my breast and breathe there'. Unlike the metaphor of the broken branch from which words can only sputter indistinctly once the bark is ruptured, the image of a flayed body here is used in order to imagine an interior eloquence that can flow unimpeded by any exterior constraint. The surface is drawn clean away, the body is all wound and the soul is unsheathed, viscerally bringing what is hidden into the open.[9]

A basic distinction articulated in Elaine Scarry's work offers a modern interpretative frame for these attempts to imagine acts of wounding in relation to the release of interior states. In Scarry's words, 'Physical pain – unlike any other state of consciousness – has no referential content. It is not *of* or *for* anything. It is precisely because it takes no object that it, more than any other phenomenon, resists objectification in language.'[10] In other words, the nature of pain resists communication. As a result, the description of pain characteristically takes two forms. In Scarry's words

---

[6] Dante, of course, is not alone in deploying the skin as synecdoche for the flesh. Aquinas does the same in his commentary on Job 2.4: 'pellem pro pelle, idest carnem alienam pro carne sua' [skin for skin, that is the flesh of another for his own flesh]. Thomas Aquinas, *Expositio super Iob ad litteram*, ed. Antoine Dondaine (Rome: Ad Sanctae Sabinae, 1965), cap. II, p. 17. My translation.

[7] Robert Hollander, 'Marsyas as *figura Dantis*: Paradiso 1.20', *Electronic Bulletin of the Dante Society of America*, 27 Apr. 2010: http://www.princeton.edu/~dante/ebdsa/hollander042710.html (accessed 1 Oct. 2015).

[8] Levenstein, 'Re-formation of Marsyas', pp. 413–14.

[9] On the wider issue of the expressive body in the *Commedia*, see: David Ruzicka, '"Uno lume apparente di fuori secondo sta dentro": The Expressive Body in Dante's *Commedia*', *The Italianist* 34.1 (2014): 1–22.

[10] Elaine Scarry, *The Body in Pain: The Making and Unmaking of the World* (Oxford: Oxford University Press, 1985), p. 5. For the medievalist, Scarry's work has in some respects been superseded by Esther Cohen's more historically grounded discussions of the topic, in particular, *The Modulated Scream: Pain in Late Medieval Culture* (Chicago: University of Chicago Press, 2009). However, the distinction offered by Scarry possesses a useful analytical clarity in the present context.

once again, '[t]he first specifies an external agent of the pain, a weapon that is pictured as accompanying the pain; and the second specifies bodily damage that is pictured as accompanying the pain.'[11] These two strategies help 'to externalize, objectify, and make sharable what is originally an interior and unsharable experience', in other words they 'lift pain and its attributes out of the body and make them visible'.[12]

The Christian desire to share Christ's pain, to be crucified with Christ, became so strong in late medieval culture that it can be taken as one of that culture's defining characteristics. Interest in Christ's pain ran broad and deep. Popular enthusiasm for emulating his suffering lay at the heart of the success experienced by the Franciscan order, whose founder, Francis, shared Christ's pain so deeply that he also came to share his wounds in the stigmata. All this is well known. Theologians saw pain as the key to understanding how God became Man in the Incarnation. There was considerable disagreement about what pain Christ felt in the Passion and to what degree. One move was to divide his suffering into *dolor* (the word used by Dante of the wounded trees) and *tristitia*.[13] The first was external suffering of the physical body, the second the internal suffering of the soul. These debates were then fed back into popular discourse through the medium of sermons. Given this scrutiny of Christ's pain, it is no surprise that late medieval art practises both of Scarry's metaphors for communicating pain: the agent of pain and the mark it makes.

For example, during the thirteenth century the image of the Man of Sorrows, a Byzantine import, begins to appear in Italy.[14] This relatively impassive representation of Christ suspended in a state between life and death is then rapidly supplemented with increasingly elaborate sets of

---

[11] Scarry, *The Body in Pain*, p. 15.

[12] Ibid., p. 16.

[13] Cohen, *Modulated Scream*, pp. 198–226, for Christ's pain; and more specifically Paul Gondereau, *The Passions of Christ's Soul in the Theology of St Thomas Aquinas* (Scranton, NY: University of Scranton Press, 2009), pp. 380–403, and Donald Mowbray, *Pain and Suffering in Medieval Theology: Academic Debates at the University of Paris in the Thirteenth Century* (Woodbridge: Boydell Press, 2009), chap. 1, 'Thirteenth-Century Theological Ideas about Human Pain and Suffering and the Passion of Christ'.

[14] See, for example: A. Neff, 'Byzantium Westernized, Byzantium Marginalized: Two Icons in the *Supplicationes variae*', *Gesta* 38 (1999): 81–102; Christian Hecht, 'Von der Imago Pietatis zur Gregorsmesse: Ikonographie der Eucharistie vom hohen Mittelalter bis zur Epoche des Humanismus', *Römische Jahrbuch der Bibliotheca Hertziana* 36 (2005): 9–44; Hans Belting, *Das Bild und sein Publikum im Mittelalter: Form und Funktion früher Bildtafeln der Passion* (Berlin: Mann, 1981); and, most recently, *New Perspectives on the Man of Sorrows*, ed. Catherine Puglisi and William Barcham (Kalamazoo, MI: Medieval Institute Publications, 2013).

arma Christi, the instruments of his suffering during the Passion.[15] As Scarry would put it, these images of the agents of pain effectively 'lift pain […] out of the body and make [it] visible'. Meanwhile, the same period witnesses an explosion of interest in the marks made by the instruments of his suffering, in the wounds. This interest ranges from images in all media of Christ Crucified and covered head to toe in gore, to an emerging category depicting isolated wounds, confined initially at least to manuscript illumination. It is this type – the wound not the agent of the wound – that makes the most significant contribution to the communicative potential of Christ's flagellated body. The passages from Dante mark the extreme ends of the spectrum for such a communicative wound: to one side, the wheezing stump from which words must be forced; to the other side, the perfect release of the body liberated from its skin. However, this immediately poses a problem in a culture determined to achieve absolute and unmediated communication with the divine: Christ may have been flogged, but he was not flayed.

Indeed, in a book on flaying, the inclusion of Christ's crucified body requires some justification, though on reflection it is not entirely out of place.[16] In fact, the desire to imagine Christ's body as a flayed body and not just a flogged body leads to some interesting tensions in late medieval visual culture. The gospel writers tersely describe the scourging of Christ as a flagellation, the word that they present Jesus himself employing in anticipation of the Passion:

> Behold: we go up to Jerusalem, and all things shall be accomplished which were written by the prophets concerning the Son of man. For he shall be delivered to the Gentiles and shall be mocked and scourged (*flagellabitur*) and spit upon, and after they have scourged (*flagellaverint*) him, they will put him to death, and the third day he shall rise again.   (Luke 18.31–3)[17]

---

[15] Robert Suckale, '*Arma Christi:* Überlegungen zur Zeichenhaftigkeit mittelalterlicher Andachtsbilder', *Städel-Jahrbuch* 6 (1977): 177–208.

[16] Indeed, several articles in this collection deal with flagellation as a form of flaying. See: Jack Hartnell, 'Tools of the Puncture: Skin, Knife, Bone, Hand', pp. 20–40; Susan Small, 'Flesh and Death in Early Modern Bedburg', pp. 71–90; Valerie Gramling, '"Flesche withowtyn hyde": The Removal and Transformation of Jesus' Skin in the English Cycle Passion Plays', pp. 240–60; Sherry C. M. Lindquist, 'Masculinist Devotion: Flaying and Flagellation in the *Belles Heures*', pp. 173–207; and Emily Leverett, 'Reading the Consumed: Flayed and Cannibalized Bodies in *The Siege of Jerusalem* and *Richard Coer de Lyon*', pp. 285–307.

[17] For biblical quotations the following edition is used throughout: *The Vulgate Bible: Douay-Rheims Translation*, ed. Swift Edgar and Angela M. Kinney, 6 vols. (Cambridge, MA: Harvard University Press, 2010–13).

In due course, the punishment is exacted:

> Then therefore Pilate took Jesus and scourged (*flagellavit*) him. And
> the soldiers plaiting a crown of thorns put it upon his head, and they
> put on him a purple garment. And they came to him and said, 'Hail,
> king of the Jews,' and they gave him blows. Pilate *therefore* went forth
> again and saith to them, 'Behold: I bring him forth to you, that you
> may know that I find no cause in him.' So Jesus came forth bearing
> the crown of thorns and the purple garment. And he saith to them,
> 'Behold the Man.'   (John 19.1–5)

Superficially at least, scripture offers little license for reimagining the
flagellation as a flaying, though Christ's own words quoted above – 'all
things […] written by the prophets' – already open a door to the vivid
enrichment of the Passion narrative by recourse to the prophetic books
of the Old Testament. For the flagellation, Isaiah 1.6 proves particularly
important: 'a planta pedis usque ad verticem non est in eo sanitas; vulnus
et livor et plaga tumens, non est circumligata nec curata medicamine neque
fota oleo.' [From the sole of the foot unto the top of the head, there is no
soundness therein: wounds and bruises and swelling sores, they are not
bound up, nor *dressed*, nor fomented with oil.][18] The exploitation of this
resource in late medieval devotion to Christ's humanity was such that
the number of wounds inflicted on his body grew exponentially, until
the body's surface became all wound, bloodied throughout. From the
fourteenth century there are not only images of Christ's body entirely
red with gore but also representations of the isolated synechdochal
side-wound.[19] Standing in for the wounded body as a whole, such

---

[18] Frederick Pickering, 'The Gothic Image of Christ: The Sources of Medieval
Representations of the Crucifixion', in his *Essays on Medieval German
Literature and Iconography* (Cambridge: Cambridge University Press, 1979),
pp. 5–6. Pickering also notes the importance of Psalm 128 (129): 'supra
dorsum meum fabricaverunt peccatores' [The wicked have wrought upon
my back] (p. 3).

[19] There is now quite a substantial bibliography on the isolated side-wound.
These include (with further references): David S. Areford, *The Viewer
and the Printed Image in Late Medieval Europe* (Burlington, VT: Ashgate,
2010), pp. 229–67; and Caroline Walker Bynum, 'Violence Occluded:
The Wound in Christ's Side in Late Medieval Devotion', in *Feud, Violence
and Practice: Essays in Medieval Studies in Honor of Stephen D. White*,
ed. Belle S. Tuten and Tracey L. Billado (Burlington, VT: Ashgate,
2010), pp. 95–116. See also: Silke Tammen, 'Blick und Wunde – Blick
und Form: Zur Deutungsproblematik der Seitenwunde Christi in der
spätmittelalterlichen Buchmalerei', in *Bild und Körper im Mittelalter*, ed.
Kristen Marek (Munich: Fink, 2006), pp. 86–133; Thomas Lentes, 'Der
Blick auf den Durchbohrten: Die Wunden Christi im späten Mittelalter',
in *Deine Wunden: Passionsimaginationen in christlicher Bildtradition und
Bildkonzepte in der Kunst der Moderne*, ed. Reinhard Hoeps and Richard

representations of the side-wound retain the merest strips of skin at the perimeter. This vestigial framing is important. Without it, there is no wound or, rather, the wound becomes all encompassing, not simply bleeding into the surrounding world but engulfing it.[20] Indeed, the significance of this narrow border zone, the threshold, the lips of the wound, is clear from the beginning. In two of the earliest representations, *arma Christi* compositions from the Passional of Abbess Kunigunda and a *Vitae sanctorum* (both c. 1320), the fringe of the wound becomes the location for a prayer.[21] This choice is rather striking in the context of both Pier della Vigna's sputtering branch (of roughly the same date) and Scarry's idea of the wound as a place for the articulation of pain. Other early images of the side-wound assert a close relationship between the flagellated body, the isolated wound and Christ Crucified. In one manuscript of Gautier of Metz's *Image du monde*, for example, the enlarged side-wound occupies centre stage, but the upper third of the page contains a representation of the Crucifixion, and the lower third the column to which Christ was tied during the flagellation, with disembodied arms holding flails (Fig. 8.1).[22] A similar arrangement is found in an English Book of Hours from later in the century (1361–73).[23] This time, side-wound and flagellation change

Hoppe-Sailer (Bielefeld: Kerber, 2014), pp. 43–61 (see here also pp. 232–3, cat. no. 67, for an image of the Crucified Christ entirely red with blood); and Wolf-Dietrich Löhr, 'Die Perle im Acker: Francesco di Vannuccios Berliner "Kreuzigung" und die Eröffnung der Wunden', in *Zeremoniell und Raum in der frühen italienischen Malerei*, ed. Stefan Weppelmann (Petersberg: Imhof, 2007), pp. 160–83. Also see several of the articles in *Wounds and Wound Repair in Medieval Culture*, ed. Larissa Tracy and Kelly DeVries (Leiden: Brill, 2015), especially: Virginia Langum '"The Wounded Surgeon": Devotion, Compassion and Metaphor in Medieval England', pp. 269–90; Salvador Ryan, '"Scarce Anyone Survives a Heart Wound": The Wounded Christ in Irish Bardic Religious Poetry', pp. 291–312; Vibeke Olson, 'Penetrating the Void: Picturing the Wound in Christ's Side as a Performative Space', pp. 313–39; and Elina Gertsman, 'Wandering Wounds: The Urban Body in *Imitatio Christi*', pp. 340–65.

[20] For Christ and his wound as world-encompassing, see: Areford, *Viewer*, pp. 248–58.

[21] The Passional (Prague, National Library, MS XIV. A. 17, with arma Christi at fol. 10r) can be consulted through http://www.manuscriptorium.com, by searching the digital library for shelfmark 'XIV. A. 17' (accessed 8 Jan. 2016). See: Tammen, 'Blick und Wunde', for discussion. The *Vita sanctorum* is Brussels, Bibl. Royale Albert Ier, MS 4459–70, with the *arma Christi* on fol. 150v. See: Areford, *Viewer*, pp. 234–5.

[22] Paris, Bibliothèque nationale de France, MS Fr. 574, fol. 140v. See: Areford, *Viewer*, pp. 240–2. It can be viewed online through http://gallica.bnf.fr (accessed 15 Jun. 2015).

[23] Pommersfelden, Kunstsammlungen Graf von Schönborn, Schlossbibliothek, MS 348 (2934), fol. 9v.

Fig. 8.1 'Crucifixion; side wound and instruments of the Passion; a bishop and a cleric in prayer', in Gautier of Metz, *Image du monde, c.* 1320 (Paris, Bibliothèque nationale de France, MS Fr. 574, fol. 140v)

places and Christ appears lashed to the column. The scales in these images encourage the viewer to substitute body for wound and *vice versa*. Indeed, in the Book of Hours six angels grasp the side-wound by its lips and raise it aloft from out of a tomb, like a mandorla containing the resurrected Christ. In this case the substitution is complete: Christ has been entirely eclipsed by the open flesh of his side.

In other words, late medieval devotion to Christ's suffering humanity imagines a Passion that approaches the comprehensive brutality of flaying, even if that is not entirely warranted by scripture. Of course, there is one scriptural event in Christ's life when skin is purposefully cut from his body, the Circumcision.[24] Indeed, given late medieval investment in Christ's humanity, particularly around the twin poles of his infancy and execution, we might expect the Circumcision to have led the late medieval mind back to Christ's skin in interesting ways. As the first occasion on which Christ shed his blood, the Circumcision foreshadows the later shedding of sacrificial blood at his death. In a sense, this creates a potential space for a virtual flaying of his Passion body. The blood released in the Circumcision anticipates all the blood later shed *en route* to the cross and in the Crucifixion itself. This first bleeding is achieved not simply by opening the surface, by cutting it, but by removal of a section of that surface. Following the same logic of *pars pro toto* that allows the side-wound to stand in for the wounded body as a whole, the wound of the Circumcision is the comprehensive wounding of the Passion, but that raises the question of how to think of the severed foreskin within this trope. In fact, one of the early apocryphal accounts of Christ's infancy, the so-called Arabic Infancy Gospel of fifth- or sixth-century Syrian origin, sketches a connection between the skin removed in the Circumcision and the entire bodily surface of the adult Christ:

> And when the time of his circumcision was come, viz. the eighth day, on which the law commanded the child to be circumcised, they circumcised him in the cave, and the old Hebrew woman took the fore-skin (others say the navel-string), and preserved it in an alabaster-box of old oil of spikenard. And she had a son who was a druggist, to whom she said, *Take heed thou sell not this alabaster-box of spikenard-ointment, although thou shouldest be offered three hundred pence for it.* Now this is that alabaster-box which Mary the sinner

---

[24] 'And after eight days were accomplished, that the child should be circumcised, his name was called Jesus, which was called by the angel before he was conceived in the womb' (Luke 2.21). Holly Flora, 'Women Wielding Knives: The Circumcision of Christ by His Mother in an Illustrated Manuscript of the Meditationes vitae Christi (Paris Bibliothèque Nationale de France MS. ital. 115)', in *The Christ Child in Medieval Culture: Alpha es et O!*, ed. Mary Dzon and Theresa M. Kenney (Toronto: University of Toronto Press, 2011), pp. 145–66.

procured, and poured forth the ointment out of it upon the head and the feet of our Lord Jesus Christ, and wiped them off with the hairs of her head.[25]

In other words, oil in which the foreskin has been steeped is later used to anoint Christ's adult skin, head and foot, as if to spell out the connection of part and whole in advance of the Passion narrative. In the Gospel accounts of the anointing, Jesus himself voices the connection between the anointing and his impending fate: 'For she in pouring this ointment upon my body hath done it for my burial' (Matthew 26.12).[26] There is, however, scant evidence that this particular infancy tale played any role in late medieval piety.[27] Nevertheless, it is in the fourteenth century that the foreskin becomes the focus of a very particular type of attention. In Catherine of Siena's letters to a nun in Pisa, she states the following:

> You see very well that you are a bride and that he has espoused you –
> you and everyone else – and not with a ring of silver but with a ring
> of his own flesh. Look at that tender little child who on the eighth
> day, when he was circumcised, gave up just so much flesh as to make
> a tiny circlet of a ring.[28]

Even without interrogating this surprising image in depth, it raises some interesting points in the present context of the 'flayed' body of Christ. The devotee wears the skin of the beloved. The finger is inserted through this skin, almost like a recapitulation of Doubting Thomas and the side-wound.

---

[25] Jeremiah Jones, *A New and Full Method of Settling the Canonical Authority for the New Testament*, 3 vols. (London: J. Clark, 1726), 2:171. For an edition of the best and earliest surviving manuscript of the text, see Mario E. Provera, *Il Vangelo arabo dell'Infanzia secondo il ms. Laurenziano orientale (n. 387)* (Jerusalem: Franciscan Printing Press, 1973). The relevant section appears on pp. 72–3. This Arabic translation, now in the Laurentian library in Florence, dates to 1299.

[26] See also: Mark 14.8 and John 12.7.

[27] Kathryn A. Smith, however, has argued that it inspired the depiction of the unusual miracle of the Children in the Oven in a historiated initial in the Neville of Hornby Hours (London, British Library, MS Egerton 2781, fol. 88v). This English book of hours was composed *c.* 1335–40. The earliest depiction of the miracle occurs on a detached sheet dating to *c.* 1250–75 in the Fitzwilliam Museum, Cambridge (MS 1148–1993r). Smith suggests that increasing knowledge of Arabic texts at universities such as Paris and Oxford from the late twelfth century onwards might provide a context for an early reception of the Gospel. See: Kathryn A. Smith, *Art, Identity and Devotion in Fourteenth-Century England: Three Women and their Books of Hours* (London: British Library, 2003), p. 269 and pp. 275–8.

[28] *The Letters of Catherine of Siena*, ed. and trans. Suzanne Noffke, 2 vols. (Tempe: Arizona Center for Medieval and Renaissance Studies, 2000–1), 2:184, L T221.

Indeed, a special relationship between circumcision and side-wound as the sources for the first and last effusions of Christ's blood was emerging in the later medieval period. The isolated side-wound with its residual fringe of skin, often likened to female genitalia, can perhaps in this sense be assimilated to the prepuce. The side-wound was thought to give access to the marriage chamber in which the soul could achieve full union with Christ. The source for this idea is *Song of Songs* 2.14: 'My dove in the clefts of the rock, in the hollow places of the wall, shew me thy face, let thy voice sound in my ears: for thy voice is sweet, and thy face comely.' In Catherine's letter total identification with the object of desire, union of bride and groom (with the *Song of Songs* the fundamental text for a mystical marriage), is expressed by donning the skin of the beloved.

Catherine's foreskin-ring is perhaps an extreme outcome of the way in which Christ's body is flayed under the relentless scrutiny of the devotional gaze during the late medieval period.[29] However, the metaphorical flaying of Christ's body was also built firmly into the most venerable figures under which Christ's fleshy humanity was considered: garment and book.

The metaphor of Christ's flesh as a garment woven by the Virgin is old and rich.[30] This metaphorical robe of flesh or skin introduces additional layers of meaning to several events in Christ's life, above all in the robing and disrobing of Christ during the Passion. The repeated stripping and covering of Christ's body is one of several elements singled out for obsessive attention in late medieval devotional texts.[31] The exemplary case here, for several reasons, is the *Meditations on the Life of Christ* (hereafter *Meditations*). Written at some point in the first half of the fourteenth

---

[29] Indeed, 'scrutiny' is the right word. According to her *vita*, Christ instructs Margaret of Cortona, for example, to 'scrutinize' his wounds both within and without: 'Vade ad crucem et scruptare piagas meas intus et extra' [Go to my cross, and look at my wounds, inside and out]. Iuncta Bevegnatis, *Legenda de vita et miraculis beatae Margaritae de Cortona*, ed. Fortunato Iozzelli (Grottaferrata: Ediciones Collegii S. Bonaventurae ad Claras Aquas, 1997), p. 276. Translation from Fra Giunta Bevengnati, *The Life and Miracles of Saint Margaret of Cortona (1247–1297)*, trans. Thomas Renna and ed. Shannon Larson (St Bonaventure, NY: Franciscan Institute Publications, 2012), 5:31.

[30] See, for example: Maria Evangelatou, 'The Purple Thread of the Flesh: The Theological Connotations of a Narrative Iconographic Element in Byzantine Images of the Annunciation', in *Icon and Word: The Power of Images in Byzantium*, ed. Antony Eastmond and Liz James (Burlington, VT: Ashgate, 2003), pp. 261–79; and Elizabeth Coatsworth, 'Cloth-Making and the Virgin Mary in Anglo-Saxon Literature and Art', in *Medieval Art: Recent Perspectives, A Memorial Tribute to C. R. Dodwell*, ed. Gale R. Owen-Crocker and Timothy Graham (Manchester: Manchester University Press, 1998), pp. 8–25.

[31] Mary Dzon, 'Birgitta of Sweden and Christ's Clothing', in *The Christ Child*, ed. Dzon and Kenney, pp. 117–44.

century and available in both Latin and vernacular versions, the *Meditations* rapidly circulated throughout Europe.[32] It is perhaps the richest fruit borne out of a long tradition of medieval devotional writing focused on Christ's humanity. Scholarship has frequently turned to this text for the vivid descriptions of physical suffering during the Passion, but the devotional focus on Christ's wounds is framed by passages of dressing and undressing.[33]

It is worth following the sequence in order. After Herod clothes Christ in a 'white garment' (Luke 23.11), as if to clean the slate (as well as signal his spotless innocence), the real horror commences with the flagellation:

> Then the Lord is stripped, tied to a column and most cruelly whipped. A young man, elegant and modest, *handsome in appearance beyond the sons of men* (Ps 44.3), stands naked in front of everybody; that flesh, most innocent and tender, most pure and beautiful, undergoes the harsh and painful whips of the foulest of men.[34]

---

[32] The dating remains controversial, as does the relationship of precedence between the earliest Latin and vernacular versions. It was probably composed in central Italy. See Sarah McNamer's works: 'The Origins of the *Meditationes vitae Christi*', *Speculum* 84.4 (2009): 905–55; *Affective Meditation and the Invention of Medieval Compassion* (Philadelphia: University of Pennsylvania Press, 2009), chap. 3 in particular; 'The Author of the Italian *Meditations on the Life of Christ*', in *New Directions in Medieval Manuscript Studies and Reading Practices: Essays in Honor of Derek Pearsall*, ed. Kathryn Kerby-Fulton, John J. Thompson and Sarah Baechle (Notre Dame, IN: University of Notre Dame Press, 2014), pp. 119–37; as well as Peter Tóth and Dávid Falvay, 'New Light on the Date and Authorship of the *Meditationes vitae Christi*', in *Devotional Culture in Late Medieval England and Europe: Diverse Imaginations of Christ's Life*, ed. S. Kelly and R. Perry (Turnhout: Brepols, 2014), pp. 17–105. For an overview of the position and contribution of the *Meditations* within the larger tradition of devotional literature, see: Thomas H. Bestul, *Texts of the Passion: Latin Devotional Literature and Medieval Society* (Philadelphia: University of Pennsylvania Press, 1996), chap. 2 and pp. 48–50. In Bestul's words, the work is perhaps 'the greatest, and certainly the most popular, of the works on the Passion belonging to the Bonaventuran and Franciscan tradition'.

[33] In other contemporary texts, the framing references to dressing and undressing are more abbreviated but still present. See, for example, Paolo Pellegrini, ed., *Passione veronese* (Rome and Padua: Antenore, 2012), pp. 39–49: 'el fé vestir de una vestimenta blanca'; 'e despuià Cristo e tollo un mantello de una porpora'; 'era vestí d'una vestimenta de porpora'; 'i lo despoià de quella vestimenta de porpora e vestílo dele soe vestimente'; 'e i tollo le vestimente soe'.

[34] John of Caulibus, *Meditations on the Life of Christ*, ed. and trans. Francis X. Taney, SR, Anne Miller, OSF, and C. Mary Stallings-Taney (Asheville, NC: Pegasus Press, 2000), p. 247. Hereafter, page numbers will be given in parentheses.

Having dwelt on Christ's scourged body, the reader is directed once again
to his state of undress:

> After the Lord was untied from the column, they led him through the
> house naked, just as he was when whipped, searching for his clothes,
> which had been scattered everywhere throughout the house by those
> who stripped him. Look at him closely, suffering so, and shivering
> in the cold: for in fact *it was cold* (Jn 18:18), as the Gospel tells us.
>   (p. 247)

Despite his efforts to dress himself, Christ's tormentors find him something
else to wear:

> When he was trying to get his clothes back on, some of the most
> hateful of them made a proposal to Pilate: 'Your lordship, this man
> says he is a king. Let us clothe and crown him like a king.' And then
> taking a cloak of some kind of red silk, but old and dirty, they put
> it on him, and crowned him with thorns [Cf. John 19.2; Mark 15.17;
> Matthew 27.28].   (pp. 247–8)

Before long, however, this second robe is also removed: 'Then the Lord is
brought back inside, is stripped of that purple garment, and is now naked
before them; and he is given permission to get dressed again' (p. 249). At
this point the reader is encouraged to think of him dressing once more, first
in relation to his human nature:

> You will see him picking up his clothes thrown down on the floor,
> scattered everywhere. You will see him, with unmistakable modesty,
> reverence, and blushing, getting dressed again right in front of them,
> while they keep on ridiculing him [...] Watch him closely, and be
> moved to both devotion as well as compassion: he picks up one
> piece of clothing, then another, and in that way dresses again in front
> of them.   (p. 249)

The action is then revisited with the reader's attention directed instead
towards Christ's divinity:

> Return now to his divinity and think of that immense and eternal,
> incomprehensible and imperial Majesty incarnate, bending humbly
> to the floor, stooping and collecting his clothing, and with reverence
> and blushing, dressing himself the same as if he were the lowliest of
> men.   (p. 249)

Significantly, in the midst of this section of the meditation, attention is
directed back towards the scene of Christ's first disrobing, the flagellation:
'Showing your compassion by these thoughts, you can gaze on him
the same as, when tied to the column, he was flogged beyond reason'
(p. 249).

On arrival at Golgotha, in preparation for the Crucifixion, Christ's
clothes are removed yet again, and we are explicitly reminded that this is

not an isolated act but part of a sequence: 'Now for the third time he is stripped and appears naked in front of the entire crowd, and his wounds are reopened because the clothing stuck to his flesh' (p. 252). The reopening of the wounds draws together in the most literal fashion the woven cloth of his garment with the metaphorical weave of his flesh, a point reinforced by the next stage in this drama of veiling and unveiling as the Virgin, having clothed his divinity in the flesh of her womb at the Incarnation, now clothes him once again at the end of his life:

> Now for the first time, his mother looks at her son, held captive and made ready for the onslaught of death's agony. She is saddened beyond measure, and embarrassed, because she sees him completely naked. They did not allow him even a loin cloth. She rushes up, and gets close to him; she embraces him and girds him with her head covering. (p. 252)

The shrouding of Christ's body is also an extended affair, accompanied by long sequences scrutinizing his wounded flesh, until night draws a final veil across events:

> Since darkness was approaching, after a short pause Joseph asked our Lady to allow him to shroud the body in burial clothes and then entomb it. But she objected [...] She inspected the wounds in his hands and side, first one, then the other [...] And so, his mother examined his body carefully, for in her sadness, she felt she just had to see it. (p. 261)

The initial shrouding interrupted, the process now resumes only for Mary Magdalene to interrupt it a second time:

> Then John and Nicodemus and the others began to wrap the body and fit it with the burial cloths, as was customary with the Jews. Our Lady, however, throughout, held his head on her lap, and reserved for herself its wrapping; and Magdalene held his feet. Then when they reached his legs above the feet, Magdalene pleaded, 'Please let me wrap the feet, the place where I received his mercy.' (p. 261)

After she has pored over his broken form, she covers over his feet: 'and then, as carefully as she could and knew how, tenderly wrapped them' (p. 262). The final shrouding falls to the Virgin, the woman who swaddled him at birth: 'she wrapped that holy head in a handkerchief she had, and lovingly tied it up' (p. 262).

The cumulative effect of this obsessive catalogue is to inscribe dressing and stripping, veiling and revelation, as a central concern of the Passion narrative. Indeed, the repeating pattern regulates the various acts of the drama. More to the point, however desirable the absolute revelation of the 'flayed' body may be, such a revelation can only be desirable from the distance of prior occlusion. The repetitive cycling between the two confirms as much. A crucial step is achieved before the Crucifixion when a graphic closure of the gap between metaphor and reality occurs as Christ's beaten flesh sticks to the cloth of his robe.[35] This moment supplements a tradition in which the bloodied skin itself, with its profusion of wounds, is likened through typology to a garment.[36] In his ninth meditation on the Humanity of Christ, Anselm takes Joseph as a type of Christ:

> For what is it, O Lord, that hangs on the Cross? Hangs, I say; for past things are as present with Thee. Own It, O Father. It is the coat of Thy Joseph, Thy Son; an evil wild beast hath devoured Him, and hath trampled on His Garment in its fury, spoiling all the beauty of this His remanent Corpse, and lo, five mournful gaping wounds are left in It. This is the Garment which Thy innocent holy Child Jesus, for the sins of His brethren, has left in the hands of the Egyptian harlot, thinking the loss of His robe a better thing than the loss of purity; and choosing rather to be despoiled of His coat of flesh and go down to the prison of death than to yield to the voice of the seductress for all the glory of the world.[37]

In the thirteenth century Bonaventura took up the theme in the *Lignum vitae*, quoting Anselm verbatim in the process:

> Christ the Lord was crimsoned with His own blood, flowing in abundance: first with the sweat of the agony, then with the lashes and thorns, then with the nails, and finally with the spear-thrust. That He might become a plenteous redemption before the Lord, He wore a priestly robe of scarlet: His apparel was truly red, and His garments were like theirs that tread in the wine press. Like that of a true Joseph thrown into an abandoned cistern. His tunic was steeped as in the blood of a goat – that is, bloodshed in the likeness of sinful flesh – and sent to the Father for identification and recognition. [Quotes Anselm as above] [...] And do you, most merciful Lady of mine,

[35] This is a novel contribution made by the *Meditations* to the existing tradition. See: Bestul, *Texts of the Passion*, p. 50.

[36] The tradition includes the typological reading of Isaiah 63.1–3 as referring to Christ: 'Who is this that cometh from Edom, with dyed garments from Bosra, this beautiful one in his robe [...] Why then is thy apparel red, and thy garments like theirs that tread in the winepress? [...] I have trampled on them in my indignation, and have trodden them down in my wrath, and their blood is sprinkled upon my garments, and I have stained all my apparel'. The passage was recited in Holy Week. See: Bestul, *Texts of the Passion*, pp. 28–9.

[37] From Anselm of Canterbury's 'Ninth Meditation: Of the Humanity of Christ', consulted here: http://www.ccel.org/ccel/anselm/meditations. iv.ix.html (accessed 29 May 2015).

behold this most sacred vestment of your beloved Son, artistically woven by the Holy Spirit from your most chaste body [...].[38]

Bonaventura draws out Anselm's typological reading in opposing directions: on the one hand, towards the traditional metaphorical identification of Christ's flesh as clothing woven by the Virgin; and on the other hand, more specifically, towards the 'real' robe forced on Christ for the *ecce homo*. Bonaventura here relies more on Matthew 27.28, where the robe is scarlet – 'And stripping him, they put a scarlet cloak about him' – than Mark or John, where it is purple. In developing the typology in this way from Anselm's earlier meditation, Bonaventura's text introduces an important tension. For Anselm, the Passion is an assault on the beautiful garment of Christ's flesh, an assault that threatens to destroy its integrity by ripping five great wounds through its surface. For Bonaventura, however, the wounds themselves in their abundance seem to *generate* the integrity of the garment by coating the surface of the body a uniform and bloody scarlet.[39] Some differentiation between wounds helps to relax this tension. Not all wounds cut through the cloth in the same way. Anselm points to the five canonical wounds, but it is the side-wound that should be further singled out (as usual). The role of the side-wound as an aperture into depth that offers both shelter and access to Christ's heart has been discussed at length in studies on late medieval devotion. However, in the context of Christ's flesh as a garment, the side-wound possesses a special status. In the *Speculum amoris*, for example, the opening of the side-wound and the rending of the temple veil are drawn together as parallel acts of revelation:

> In this Passion doth likewise shine the revelation of the Angels, because the obscurities of Scripture and the mysteries of Divine secrets are here manifested and made clear by the opening of the side of Christ (*per apertionem lateris Christi*); and therefore worthily was the veil of the temple rent in sunder (*velum templi scissum est*) at his death, to the end that the hidden secrets which were in the Divine Scriptures might appear.[40]

---

[38] *The Works of Bonaventure, Cardinal, Seraphic Doctor and Saint*, vol. 1: *Mystical Opuscula*, trans. José de Vinck (Paterson, NJ: St Anthony Guild Press, 1960), pp. 128–9 (2.31: Jesus covered with blood).

[39] The tradition of Christ's body becoming entirely bloody is traced in brief in Pellegrini, *Passione*, pp. xxx–xxxi and 41–2, in reference to a double statement of the phenomenon in the Verona text: 'batèllo fortissimamentro, sí che tuta la carno ge ploveva sango [...] da ogna parto ploveva sango'. Significantly, this repetition tightly frames the moment when Christ is forced to wear a purple robe: 'e tollo un mantello de una porpora' (a statement also repeated several lines later as if to reinforce the identification of robe and wounding).

[40] James of Milan, *Stimulus amoris*, translation from *Stimulus divini amoris, that is The Goad of Divine Love*, trans. B. Lewis and rev. W. A. Phillipson

Jeffrey Hamburger has addressed this parallel between wound and rent as part of the long history identifying the temple veil and the veil of flesh.[41] By the later medieval period, the parallel has entered visual exegesis of the Crucifixion.

It is clear from the early representations of the isolated side-wound that the connections between wounding, revelation, surface, depth, garment and body were close and important to late medieval viewers. In the manuscript illumination mentioned earlier from Gautier of Metz's *Image du monde*, the depiction of the column of the flagellation in the lower third of the page does not contain Christ's body (Fig. 8.1). Rather, its absent presence is signalled by the purple robe that hangs on the wall. The robe has been set aside from the body but in its absence stands in for it, for the multitudinous wounds inflicted by the scourge and for the all-encompassing flow of blood. In the central field, the life-sized side-wound is flanked on one side by the three nails of the Crucifixion (ensuring that the absent wounds of hands and feet are also recalled). On the other side, however, are two textiles. One is a white robe, standing as though self-supporting, like a ghostly effigy. In one sense, this could be the white robe mentioned in Luke, but it seems also here to stand for the seamless robe (claimed as a relic at Trier and Argenteuil) found in John:

> The soldiers therefore, when they had crucified him, took his garments, (and they made four parts, to every soldier a part) and also his coat. Now the coat was without seam, woven from the top throughout. They said then one to another: Let us not cut it but let us cast lots for it, whose it shall be; that the scripture might be fulfilled, saying: They have parted my garments among them, and upon my vesture they have cast lots. And the soldiers indeed did these things.   (John 19.23–4)

According to tradition, the robe woven by the Virgin for the Christ Child miraculously expanded as he grew older.[42] The cloth that hangs above it on

---

(London: R. & T. Washbourne, 1907), p. 84. See most recently: Michelle Karnes, *Imagination, Meditation, and Cognition in the Middle Ages* (Chicago: University of Chicago Press, 2011), pp. 146–65. This chapter appears in the expanded version of the text produced in the early fourteenth century. See the helpful concordance in Karnes (where the relevant chapter appears as I.12), pp. 147–9.

[41] Jeffrey Hamburger, 'Body vs. Book: The Trope of Visibility in Images of Christian-Jewish Polemic', in *Ästhetik des Unsichtbaren: Bildtheorie und Bildgebrauch in der Vormoderne*, ed. David Ganz, Thomas Lentes and Georg Henkel (Berlin: Reimer, 2004), pp. 113–46.

[42] See: Gail McMurray Gibson, 'The Thread of Life in the Hand of the Virgin', at http://www.umilta.net/equal1.html (accessed 17 Mar. 2015). Cf. Gramling, '"Flesche withowtyn hyde"', p. 252.

the short pole in Fig. 8.1 is also potentially ambiguous. It has a faint purple tinge and appears to be partially transparent. The presence of the rail encourages a reading of this fabric as the temple veil, but its location here above the robe and its scale also evoke another veil, the Virgin's veil offered in the *Meditations* as a cover for Christ's modesty.[43] A deliberate gesture of polyvalence here would not be out of place given the connection running between the Virgin, the temple veil, Christ's flesh and the large wound ripped through the fabric of the latter two at the Crucifixion. Indeed, the juxtaposition of the 'seamless' robe and the yawning side-wound underscores the narrative oscillation observed above between dressing and undressing, veiling and unveiling, and the integral surface or the gaping aperture.

Although the metaphor of the veil or garment strictly applies to the totality of Christ's human body, inside and out, the image itself tends towards an articulation of the surface, the skin, as the woven element that conceals and defines an interior (even if that 'interior' expanse is the uncircumscribable realm of divinity). The elision of real and metaphorical garments is pushed to a point where the distinction between the two collapses. The pulling on and off of clothing and the accompanying sacred eroticism of the veiled and unveiled body develop a fantasy of disrobing in which the skin becomes yet another layer of revelation, not just transparent but detachable. The flow of blood across this surface like a coating of chrism raises the skin to the level of objectification desired in ritual anointing. At the same time, the violence done to this surface as it is rent open crystalizes the urge to practise vandalism on perfection.

In short, Christ's skin, as garment, *is* flayed, not just flogged. Alongside the metaphor of Christ's flesh as a garment, the other venerable image for Christ's body that potentially flays it of its skin, albeit in a rather different fashion, is the book. This metaphor has been particularly well studied in the context of the charters of Christ found from the fourteenth century onwards in England. These charters depend upon an association of Christ's skin with parchment, on which the tortures of the Passion write a binding 'contract' sealed in some cases with the side-wound. In one well-known fifteenth-century example Christ effectively unscrolls his flayed skin in front of the viewer. These charters arise out of a long tradition of interpreting Christ Crucified as a manuscript book, an association that flows naturally from the identification of Christ as the Word and his Incarnation as a fulfilment of (and replacement for) the Old Testament.[44] When the metaphor is

---

[43] Based on earlier images of the temple veil, the presence of the rail encourages this interpretation. However, in this case the representation is very abbreviated, and the veil is not obviously ripped.

[44] For some Byzantine examples, see: Derek Krueger, 'Writing and Redemption in the Hymns of Romanos the Melodist', *Byzantine and Modern Greek Studies* 27 (2003): 2–44; and Glenn Peers, *Sacred Shock: Framing Visual Experience in Byzantium* (University Park: Pennsylvania

extended to include not simply the writing of the book but its manufacture as well, it inevitably leads to an interpretation of the Passion as a kind of flaying in which, once again, the veil of Christ's flesh is reduced to its surface with a depth (or interior) that is now, in a sense, the depth of scripture, achievable by practising an exegetical reading of the skin. A late medieval example taken from *Lo specchio della Croce*, by the Dominican writer Domenico Cavalca (d. 1342), sets out these various elements at length:

> *Come Cristo in Croce sta come libro, nel quale è scritta, ed abbreviata tutta la legge; e spetialmente la carità del prossimo. ...* Tutti sappiamo che un libro non è altro, se non pelli d'agnello, bene rase, legate fra due tavole, e scritte quasi per tutto di lettere nere; ma gli principali capoversi sono lettere grosse vermiglie. Per questo modo Gesù Cristo in croce sta come libro: perocchè la sua pelle e la sua carne, la quale è agnello senza macula, e senza peccato che non fu raso, nè purificato da altri; anzi nacque tutto così puro. Ovvero possiamo dire, perchè la pelle quando si concia per scrivere, si radono gli peli ed assottigliasi; così la pelle di questo agnello fu rasa, quando gli pelarono la barba, e spogliaronlo d'ogni vestimento, e lasciaronlo nudo: al modo che si dice dell'uomo che ha perduto ogni cosa, e che è tornato al sottile. Questa pelle così nuda e pelata fu non legata, ma confitta fra due legni della croce, ed era scritta tutta di lettere nere: perocchè fu tutta lividita ed annegrita per gli colpi e per le guanciate, in tanto che dice la Scrittura, che aveva perduto ogni bellezza. ... Sonoci ancora le miniature e le lettere grosse di vermiglio: cioè le piaghe, principalmente del capo che tutte colavano sangue, e delle mani e de' piedi e del costato; le quali sono vermiglie di sangue, e sono molto grandi e grosse, come di sopra è detto. Ecco dunque come Cristo è libro, nel quale è abbreviata tutta la Scrittura; e nel quale ogni persona, secolare ed idiota, può leggere apertamente ogni perfetta dottrina.

State University Press, 2004), chap. 2, 'The Bloody Page in the Chludov Psalter'. For the Western tradition, see: David S. Areford, *Viewer*, p. 79; Jeffrey Hamburger, *St John the Divine: The Deified Evangelist in Medieval Art and Theology* (Berkeley: University of California Press, 2002), p. 178; Dieter Richter, 'Die Allegorie der Pergamentbearbeitung: Beziehungen zwischen handwerklichen Vorgängen und der geistlichen Bildersprache des Mittelalters', in *Fachliteratur des Mittelalters: Festschrift für Gerhard Eis*, ed. Gundolf Keil *et al.* (Stuttgart: J. B. Metzler, 1968), pp. 83–92; Sylvia Huot, 'Polytextual Reading: The Meditative Reading of Real and Metaphorical Books', in *Orality and Literacy in the Middle Ages: Essays on a Conjunction and its Consequences in Honour of D. H. Green*, ed. Mark Chinca and Christopher Young (Turnhout: Brepols, 2005), pp. 203–22; and Manuele Gragnolati, *Experiencing the Afterlife: Soul and Body in Dante and Medieval Culture* (Notre Dame, IN: University of Notre Dame Press, 2005), pp. 89–137.

[*How Christ on the Cross is like a book in which is written and summarised the whole law, especially the love of our neighbour. ...* We all know that a book is made out of the skin of a lamb, well-trimmed, bound between two boards, and written on almost entirely with black letters; but the rubrics [*principali capoversi*] are in large vermillion letters. In the same way, Christ stands on the cross like a book: because his lamblike skin and flesh are without blemish and without sin and were neither trimmed nor cleaned by others; but rather born entirely so pure. Or we can say instead that in order to prepare the skin for writing, the bristles are removed and it is thinned; in the same way the skin of this lamb was shorn, when they shave off his beard, and remove all of his clothing, and leave him naked: in such a fashion that it is said of someone who has lost everything that he is stripped to the bone. This skin so naked and denuded was not bound, but nailed between the two beams of the cross, and it was written all over with black letters: because it was livid and blackened all over by blows and punches, such that scripture says that it had lost all beauty. But there are also the miniatures and the large vermillion letters, that is the principal wounds of the head, all of which stream with blood, and of the hands and of the feet and of the side; which are red with blood, and are very large and wide, as was said earlier. This therefore is why Christ is a book, in which is condensed the whole of scripture; and in which every person, inexperienced or ignorant, can openly read every perfect doctrine.][45]

The immediate source for Cavalca's version of Christ as book may well have been Caesarius of Heisterbach, but he places much greater emphasis on the preparation of the parchment than the earlier writer.[46] However, once the metaphor is fully extended in this way, Cavalca has a little trouble reconciling the image of the hide skinned from the lamb with the narrative of the Crucifixion, and offers two opposing interpretations. The first is positive: the skinning and cleaning represent the purity of Christ's flesh; the second is negative: the same acts correspond to those inflicted on Christ's body as he was shaved and stripped. The act of stripping, of course, turns us back towards the metaphor of the garment.

Indeed, although these two metaphors for Christ's body – book and garment – draw attention to the bodily surface, the skin, in different ways, it would be incorrect to present them as sealed off one from the other.

[45] Domenico Cavalca, *Lo specchio della Croce: testo originale e versione in italiano corrente*, ed. P. Tito Sante Centi, OP (Bologna: PDUL Edizioni Studio Domenicano, 1992), pp. 282–5. My translation. Cavalca was based at the Dominican convent of Santa Caterina in Pisa. He probably composed the *Lo specchio della Croce* at the beginning of the 1330s.

[46] See: Richter, 'Pergamentbearbeitung', for Caesarius.

Fig. 8.2 Nicola Pisano, *Annunciation and Nativity*, marble pulpit, 1260 (Pisan style) at the Baptistery, Pisa

The ancient play on the words for text and textile, for which Arachne's tapestry in Ovid's *Metamorphoses* was perhaps the most important source, already permits an intermingling of the two. In the later medieval visual tradition, the iconography of the Annunciate Virgin also expands in a way that encourages the coexistence of both metaphors. The Virgin, previously shown spinning or weaving, is increasingly represented as reading, apparently engrossed in the scriptural passages foretelling the future passion of Christ.[47] Three brief examples illustrate the progression. In Nicola Pisano's relief of the Annunciation and the Nativity from his pulpit in Pisa, completed in 1260, the Virgin appears twice (Fig. 8.2). At the upper left, she reacts to Gabriel's message, with one hand across her heart, the other on her womb. The lower hand holds a spindle. On a diagonal stretching to bottom right, the Virgin then reappears as a monumental reclining figure. The same hand – her left – still lies across the womb, but now it is without the spindle and she reaches instead into the folds of her robe, that hang open around her stomach like the mouth of an empty bag. In a countervailing diagonal on this axis, two representations of the Christ Child appear, one to either side: the first in a sarcophagal manger; the second in a chalice-shaped bath. As if to confirm that the Virgin has woven

[47] See: McMurray Gibson, 'The Thread of Life'.

Fig. 8.3 Follower of Giroldo da Como, *Annunciation*, marble relief at the Duomo, Florence, early four-teenth century

these infant bodies from her flesh, at the bottom left her own garment runs out over the woolly backs of the shepherds' flock.

Some fifty years later, in the early fourteenth century in Florence, in another relief of the Annunciation a second sculptor adopts the metaphor of the book rather than the garment in order to articulate the Incarnation (Fig. 8.3). Here, Gabriel directs his message across an open *baldacchino* that symbolizes the Virgin. The hand of God the Father rests on its dome; inside, the dove of the Holy Spirit hovers over the words 'AVE GRATIA PLENA', which do double duty as the angelic salutation and as the Divine Word himself. Meanwhile, the flesh-and-blood Virgin has been reading from a lectern on the right. Stepping back, she has taken up her book and placed it over her womb. Instead of the woven body, the body as book is now operative. Finally, a relief from the fifteenth century, also from Florence but now in the Victoria & Albert Museum, London, combines the two (Fig. 8.4). In the central field, the Virgin holds the Christ Child. Her delicate purple veil loops round her head and is carried behind and beneath her son so that it cradles him. The veil then flows on, hanging down immediately below Christ, where it serves to cushion an open book. Veil, body and book are neatly incorporated. These three examples deploy the master metaphors for the flesh of Christ in the context of the Incarnation and Infancy, but those metaphors are also operative in images of the Passion – and in particular of the Crucifixion – at a point when violence done to the adult body might prompt a desire to see that body flayed, a desire that is only obliquely triggered in the narrative of Christ's youth.

The graphic sculptural images of Christ Crucified that begin to appear around 1300 in Europe, the so-called *crocifissi dolorosi* with which this chapter opened, offer some of the most striking manifestations of these metaphors in Christ's Passion body.[48] By the end of the fourteenth

---

[48] See, in particular: Ulrike Bergmann, ed., *Neue Forschungen zur gefassten Skulptur des Mittelalters* (Munich: Siegl, 2001); and Godehard Hoffmann, *Das Gabelkreuz in St. Maria im Kapitol zu Köln und das Phänomenon der*

Fig. 8.4 After Benedetto da Maiano (?), *Virgin and Child with the Young St John the Baptist*, painted and gilt terracotta and carved wood, 1475–1500 (Victoria and Albert Museum, London, museum no. 5-1890)

century these gruesome compendia of wounding had spread throughout Europe, from Scandinavia in the north to Sicily in the south, and from England and Spain in the west to Poland and Dalmatia in the east. The group has been compiled retrospectively by art historians and it contains considerable local variety. That said, the surviving examples suggest that itinerant sculptors were responsible for repeating works across almost the full expanse of these territories, and that the diversity is generated from a common pool of ideas about Christ's body that were selectively deployed and recombined in novel ways according – at best guess – to sculptor, patron and context. An increasing number of technical analyses over recent years mean that we are now better informed about the sophisticated manufacture of the objects themselves. They are often assembled out of multiple separately carved pieces of wood, and have multi-layered surfaces in which two-dimensional and three-dimensional features are integrated with great sophistication. Nevertheless, we remain almost entirely ignorant about contextual specifics, as the surviving works lack the usual points of reference such as inscriptions or documentation.

It is easiest first of all to see how these works might be read as 'books', just as Cavalca instructs the reader of the *Specchio della Croce* to read Christ on the cross. The best analysis in these terms has been provided by Robert Sukale in relation to the cross from S. Maria im Kapitol, Cologne, often cited as the quintessential representative of the genre (Fig. 8.5).[49] After running through the little that is known about the context for the commission – as good as nothing – Sukale turns his focus to the crucifix itself. He systematically applies the approach developed by Fredrick Pickering and James Marrow to late medieval Passion imagery.[50] These scholars have demonstrated beyond reasonable doubt that when late medieval artists and patrons sought to elaborate on the gospel accounts of Christ's suffering, they turned to Old Testament scripture as a way of generating legitimate innovations. Indeed, legitimacy appears to have been an important concern given the documented opposition to such innovation recorded for a controversial cross of this type produced for a

Crucifixi dolorosi (Worms: Werner, 2006), both with references to the earlier literature. The Italian examples are the subject of a recent doctoral dissertation by Meredith Raucher at Johns Hopkins University. I would like to thank her for discussing these works with me.

[49] Robert Suckale, 'Der Kruzifix in St. Maria im Kapitol: Versuch einer Annäherung', in *Femmes, art et religion au Moyen Âge*, ed. Jean-Claude Schmitt (Strasbourg: Presses Universitaires de Strasbourg, 2004), pp. 87–101.

[50] Pickering, 'Gothic Image'; James Marrow, 'Circumdederunt me canes multi: Christ's Tormentors in Northern European Art of the Late Middle Ages and the Early Renaissance', *Art Bulletin* 59 (1977): 167–81; and James Marrow, *Passion Iconography in Northern European Art of the Late Middle Ages and the Early Renaissance: A Study of the Transformation of Sacred Metaphor into Descriptive Narrative* (Kortrijk: Van Ghemmert, 1979).

Fig. 8.5 Unknown sculptor, crucifix at S. Maria im Kapitol, Cologne, polychromed wood, first decade of the fourteenth century (?)

London church by a German sculptor. Virtually all the distinctive features of these crucifixes, such as the visible tongues, the carefully delineated kneecaps, rib cages and backbones, the proliferation of surface wounds and so on, can be 'explained' in this fashion. Once this fundamental structuring of the image is recognized, the superabundant gore resolves into meaningful passages that can be read off the image by a viewer keyed to the paradigm. The popularity of these works suggests that such viewers were numerous. As Cavalca says, the cross is a book 'in which every person, inexperienced or ignorant, can openly read every perfect doctrine'.[51] The scriptural texts were recited in Holy Week, communicated in sermons and threaded through handbooks like the *Meditations*. In this fashion, Christ's body encourages a habit of 'reading' images that is rooted in scriptural exegesis.[52]

This exegetical model implicitly constructs Christ's body as a layered object, with a visible surface and a hidden depth. The interpretation of the Old Testament passages as prophecies of the Crucifixion requires the surface meaning of the text to be read in allegorical terms as containing a second layer of meaning that applies to Christ. As a result, the accommodation of such textual sources within the visual representation automatically supplies Christ's body with scriptural depth, marking its surface as the fulfilment of a plan already shadowed forth elsewhere. Recognition of these elements, and the corresponding movement that this generates between the image of Christ and the prophetic material, activates the different layers of meaning. This leads the viewer to oscillate between

---

[51] Cavalca, *Lo specchio della Croce*, pp. 284–5. My translation.

[52] The extent to which reading a body as a book was embedded in late medieval culture is suggested by the extension of the metaphor to other figures. See: Carolyn Muessig, 'Performance of the Passion: The Enactment of Devotion in the Later Middle Ages', in *Visualizing Medieval Performance: Perspectives, Histories, Contexts*, ed. Elina Gertsman (Burlington, VT: Ashgate, 2008), pp. 129–42 at p. 131.

contemplation of the image and of the textual material. In a kind of reversal of the scriptural model, the texts become the hidden content of the body. This means that surface and interior are maintained as closely related but distinct elements.

As well as structuring Christ's body as a 'textual' artefact, these crucifixes often also present it as a fabric, in general by exploiting the only available fabric in the Crucifixion, Christ's loincloth. The *Meditations* encourage us not only to read this as the Virgin's veil but also to imagine the prior nudity that demanded veiling, in other words to think beneath the veil. This 'thinking beneath' should not be reduced to a simple redirection of attention towards Christ's naked humanity, however important that may be in other respects. The role of the loincloth is more systematic: it becomes a means to establish the body of Christ (and the surface of that body) as a removable fabric,

Fig. 8.6 Unknown sculptor, crucifix at San Domenico e Giacomo, Bevagna, polychromed wood, *c.* 1295?

in other words a veil in its own right. The clearest examples of this are where the folds of the loincloth imitate or mirror the anatomical structure of the body. For example, in the late-thirteenth-century crucifix from the Dominican church at Bevagna in Umbria, the exaggerated and semi-abstract rhythm of the ribcage is repeated in the perizonium below (Fig. 8.6).[53] Indeed, the possibility of stripping away both cloth and flesh is further sustained at Bevagna by the manner in which Christ's body is stretched on the cross, recalling classical representations of Marsyas. More or less subtle variations on this theme can be found in many other cases in Italy and beyond. This is such a common formal strategy of wooden crucifixes that it is easy to ignore its significance. A typical element centres, for example, on

---

[53] For which see: Elvio Lunghi, *La Passione degli Umbri: Crocifissi di legno in Valle Umbra tra Medioevo e Rinascimento* (Foligno: Orfini Numeister, 2000), pp. 39–50; and the entry by Lunghi in *Dal visibile all'indicibile: crocifissi ed esperienza mistica in Angela da Foligno,* ed. Massimiliano Bassetti and Bruno Toscano (Spoleto: Fondazione Centro Italiano di Studi sull'Alto Medioevo, 2012), pp. 171–8 (cat. no. 6). Lunghi dates the work to the middle of the final decade of the thirteenth century.

the knees. On the Cologne crucifix the loincloth covers one knee but leaves the other bare (see Fig. 8.8). The anatomical structure of the concealed knee is carefully expressed beneath its fabric hood, just as it shows through from beneath the skin on the exposed knee. In combination, the juxtaposition of the knees in the foreground of the sculpture (from the perspective of a viewer in front and below) offers a key to perceiving the entire body as a series of surfaces that might be lifted away in pursuit of its hidden interior. In other words, it prompts a viewer to think of a layered surface whose layers can be successively disambiguated: from cloth to skin to flesh to bone. Although this is not the place to pursue the point at length, the articulation of the surface in late medieval sculpture, the urge to differentiate skin from subdermal features such as muscles, veins and bones, functions precisely as a multi-layered and structured visual ground for movement into depth under both models – the body as textile and the body as text.

The various metaphorical elements of Christ's communicative skin coalesce around the figure of the wound. On the one hand, the wounds form part of the 'scriptural' content of the body; on the other hand, they function straightforwardly as tears that cut into the layered surface and offer a glimpse through its fabric. However, this hardly accounts for the actual interest of these features once they are in place on the sculpture in a media-specific context. The idea of 'reading', for example, fails to capture the experience of moving around these spatially articulate sculptural works. In such a dynamic encounter, the various features do not contribute in identical fashion to a cycling between exterior and interior that functions as an extension of the obsessive veiling and unveiling of the Passion narrative in the *Meditations*. In fact, there is considerable differentiation in the roles played by the different types of wound inflicted on Christ's skin.

The wounds that appear at first to support a model of 'legibility' are the wounds of the flagellation. These frequently take the form of black-centred craters with three red rivulets running off them. Wounds, in general, are indexical symbols of a violent act. Pushing Scarry's distinction between the weapon and the wound as alternative ways of articulating pain, wounds point in two opposing directions. They potentially lead to the interior state of pain, but as indexical signs they also point back to the instrument that caused them. The wounds of the flagellation certainly function in this way. Occasionally, the craters inflicted by the knotted ropes are raised in three-dimensional relief at the rim, emphasizing the extent to which they register the impact of the flail. But these wounds essentially point to their origin twice over. The rivulets of blood function as miniature *graphic* signs of the flail. In images of the *arma Christi* from the fourteenth century, the flails of the Passion are almost invariably shown as two or three tailed. In other words, the wounds of the flagellation not only indicate their origin, they speak it as well. Given the bi-directionality of the wound as a sign, this generates a greater pressure to read *off* the surface rather than into it (and back in narrative time, rather than forwards towards revelation).

There is a second common feature of the wounds of the flagellation that differentiates them from other wounds: they tend to be arranged in a pattern, like a web of regularly spaced nodes running across the entire surface of the body.[54] Undoubtedly, this patterning serves several interrelated goals. It establishes the wounded body as meaningful or significant, reinforcing the potential 'legibility' of the proliferating wounds. The regular rhythm is also keyed to a late medieval habit of numeration as part of Passion devotion. The numbering of Christ's wounds is obsessive in this period and might easily be combined with a rhythmic counting of the rosary and the repetitions of prayer.[55] However, once in place, for a viewer, this network also supports focused devotional attention to Christ's body as a whole in three-dimensional space. The pattern pulls the eye around the form and permits the mental mapping of that form across the areas that are not initially visible. In other words, this patterning has the visual quality of establishing the continuity of a surface. When separate elements are perceived as belonging to the same pattern, this usually arises out of the belief that they share a common plane, however spatially complex that plane might be. Moreover, when looking at bodies, we generally encounter patterns of this sort when they are covered by fabrics. This means that the wounds of the flagellation as visual elements of the *crocifissi dolorosi* stabilize the presence of a bodily surface and permit the interpretation of the skin as a patterned textile.

On the journey across this patterned surface, the payoff generally centres on the side-wound, as might be expected. It is at the side-wound where the interior is most accessible, where the rhythm of bloody marks pulling the viewer over the skin is suddenly interrupted by a plunge into depth. This payoff comes in a variety of forms, but one of the most surprising and powerful involves the juxtaposition of the side-wound and the mouth along a sightline running from a significant location, such as the spot to one side notionally occupied by Mary or Longinus, or the space immediately below Christ by his wounded feet, where we might find Mary Magdalene. One of the best examples of this visual conceit occurs in a crucifix from the Dominican church in Orvieto (Fig. 8.7).[56] Christ's body is shrouded in precisely the patterned skein of flagellation marks discussed above, each with a miniature set of bloody rivulets. Seen from the canonical frontal view, these marks are among the most prominent features informing the viewer of Christ's physical pain (*dolor*). In contrast, the face, the primary screen for emotional pain (*tristitia*) is less accessible because

---

[54] Hoffmann, *Gabelkreuz*, p. 161.

[55] In general, see: Rachel Fulton, 'Praying by Numbers', *Studies in Medieval and Renaissance History* 3.4 (2007): 195–250; and Adelaide Bennett, 'Christ's Five Wounds in the Aves of the *Vita Christi* in a Book of Hours about 1300', in *Tributes in Honor of James H. Marrow: Studies in Painting and Manuscript Illumination of the Late Middle Ages and Northern Renaissance*, ed. J. Hamburger and A. Korteweg (Turnhout: Brepols, 2006), pp. 75–84.

[56] See: Lunghi, *La Passione degli Umbri*, pp. 51–64.

Fig. 8.7 Unknown sculptor,
crucifix at San Domenico,
Oriveto, polychromed
wood, late thirteenth or early
fourteenth century (?)

Christ's head has begun to sink forwards as though in death. To see the face properly, the viewer must approach the foot of the cross and look upwards, a movement that could have occurred, for example, during the Adoration of the Cross at Easter. From this acute angle, it becomes clear that Christ's eyes are in fact slightly open, communicating his inner sorrow (Fig. 8.8). However, this view from below offers an even more surprising revelation. Mouth and side-wound fall into line along the vertical axis running up towards his face. They echo each other in formal terms, and the side-wound even appears to be equipped with a row of bloody teeth just like the row of white teeth revealed in Christ's mouth as his upper lip curls back in pain. This visual analogy between wound and mouth selects from the rich set of associations clustering around the side-wound at this date, and prioritizes one that encourages the viewer to think primarily of a movement out of this aperture from depth to surface, rather than into it from surface to depth. The open mouth and gaping wound bring together a flow of blood with an imagined flow of words and therefore permit a clear communication between the exterior marks of physical pain and interior states of mind.

The crucifix from Orvieto returns us finally to where we began, with Dante and Pier della Vigna's broken stump. Pier is not just an inverted image of Christ because, like all the damned, he has disfigured the image and likeness of God within him, nor, more specifically, because of the vine

Fig. 8.8 Detail of Fig. 8.7, showing Christ viewed from the foot of the cross

in his surname that recalls Christ as the True Vine. He is also a parodic figure of Christ because his disfigured body cannot speak its pain with the clarity of communication found in Christ's suffering form. Pier's eloquence does not flow unimpeded from the branch, but spurts and sputters through the bloody sap. Likewise, his tree-body does not possess an ordered surface, full of meaning, transparent to depth or easily lifted like a veil. The bark of his skin must be broken open before any interiority – or even humanity – can be perceived within. In contrast, in the *crocifissi dolorosi* all the features of the wounded skin work together to form a meaningful surface that speaks with precision and great eloquence of both *dolor* and *tristitia*. Indeed, what makes these images particularly absorbing is not the undifferentiated overload of tortured flesh, but the finely judged differentiation that balances the communicative power of the side-wound to move a viewer inside, so to speak, toward a hidden interiority, with the power of the wound as a surface feature that takes the viewer on a journey across the skin. This means that certain wounds, the canonical five with a primary stress at this date on the side-wound, are prioritized as apertures – 'windows for pain' in Dante's words – with others supplying the patterned, potentially porous and yet essential ground through which these open. Rather paradoxically, this latter task is given over to the wounds of the flagellation. A punishment designed to obliterate the surface of the body becomes, at one level, the means of its affirmation.

9

'Flesche withowtyn hyde':
The Removal and Transformation of Jesus' Skin in the English Cycle Passion Plays

Valerie Gramling

IN all four extant medieval English dramatic cycles (York, Chester, Towneley and N-Town),[1] there is a scene towards the end of the Passion plays in which the Virgin Mary stands at the base of the cross and grieves for the torture of her son while the apostle John comforts her and explains to her and to the audience the meaning of Jesus' suffering.[2] In the N-Town cycle (late 1400s?)[3] the Virgin Mary's lament includes a description of her

---

[1] The medieval English cycle plays (sometimes called Mystery or Corpus Christi plays) were a series of short plays performed over one to three days that presented the biblical history of the world from the Creation to the Last Judgement. Though many towns and communities in England may have had their own cycles, only four relatively complete cycles are preserved in manuscript form: York (*c.* 1460–1470), Chester (1591), Towneley or Wakefield (*c.* 1475–1500) and N-Town (late 1400s). These dates are based on the earliest extant manuscripts of each cycle, but the original performances were likely much earlier. The earliest recorded performance was in York in 1378, and cycles were still being performed into the latter half of the sixteenth century; the last officially recorded cycle was performed in Coventry in 1579 (though sporadic performances may have continued into the seventeenth century). With the rise of Protestantism in England, representations of God and Jesus Christ were banned from the stage, which severely curtailed the performances of the cycle plays.

[2] York Play 36: *The Bocheres (Mortificacio Christi)*, ll. 157–82, in *The York Plays: A Critical Edition of the York Corpus Christi Play as Recorded in British Library Additional MS 35290*, ed. Richard Beadle, vol. 1 (Oxford: Oxford University Press, 2009); Chester Play 16a: *The Irenmongers Playe*, ll. 330–44, in *The Chester Mystery Cycle: Text*, ed. R. M. Lumiansky and David Mills, EETS s.s. 3 (Oxford: Oxford University Press, 1974); Towneley Play 23: *The Crucifixion*, ll. 311–502, in vol. 1 of *The Towneley Plays*, ed. Martin Stevens and A. C. Cawley, EETS s.s. 13–14, 2 vols. (Oxford: Oxford University Press, 1994); N-Town Play 32: *Road to Calvary, Crucifixion*, ll. 222–93, in vol. 1 of *The N-Town Play: Cotton MS Vespasian D.8*, ed. Stephen Spector, EETS s.s. 11–12, 2 vols. (Oxford: Oxford University Press, 1991).

[3] The exact date of the N-Town manuscript is unknown, but, as Douglas Sugano notes, it was likely 'compiled and used between 1460 and 1520' (p. 7). The primary evidence for this assumption is a date (1468) written at the end of Play 19: *The Purification*. However, it is unclear whether that date refers to the creation or compilation of the manuscript, or to a specific

son's crucified body, helping the audience to visualize what the actor's body is intended to display:

> Thow he had nevyr of me be born,
> And I sey his flesch thus al totorn –
> On bak, behyndyn, on brest beforn,
> Rent with woundys wyde.
> Nedys I must wonyn in woo
> To see my frende with many a fo,
> All to rent from top to too,
> His flesche withowtyn hyde.
>
> (ll. 238–45)[4]

Mary begins her account by reminding the audience of the mystery of the Incarnation (when God became man), testifying that 'he had nevyr of me be born'. Mary refers here to her hymen, which remained intact after Jesus was born; though her body was the vessel in which God became mortal, his birth like his conception was a miracle.[5] Yet though her body remains unbroken, his has now been torn and rent by flagellation. His bodily integrity has been split; his skin ('hyde') has been severed from his flesh.

The juxtaposition created at this moment between Mary's bodily integrity and Jesus' bodily disintegration precedes the moment of transformation when Jesus will allow his mortal body to dissolve in order to reveal and reclaim his full divinity. Mary's presence creates a dichotomy between not only integrity and disintegration but also between the eternal and the mortal, the soul and the body. Though still divine, the Jesus in this scene is primarily read by Mary (and arguably the audience) as suffering, bleeding, dying flesh. Though not immortal, Mary here represents the soul that endures separate from, yet essentially tied to, the body, watching sorrowfully as the body wastes away. Mary's lament that 'Nedys I must wonyn in woo' expresses her expectation of unending woe as she lives on after her son's torturous death. Yet as Caroline Walker Bynum has argued, Jesus' flesh was often read as an extension of his mother's, in part because he 'had no human father' but also because 'his own flesh did womanly things: it bled, it bled food, and it gave birth'.[6] Flesh was often gendered

performance. See: 'Introduction', *The N-Town Plays*, ed. Douglas Sugano (Kalamazoo, MI: Medieval Institute Publications, 2007), pp. 1–22 esp. pp. 5–12.

[4] *The N-Town Play*, ed. Sugano. All quotations are from this edition. Hereafter, line numbers are given in parentheses. SD = stage direction.

[5] In the N-Town Nativity play (Play 15), the midwives Zelomy and Salomé appear and bear witness to the miraculous birth and Mary's intact body.

[6] Caroline Walker Bynum, 'The Body of Christ in the Later Middle Ages: A Reply to Leo Steinberg', in her *Fragmentation and Redemption: Essays on Gender and the Human Body in Medieval Religion* (New York: Zone, 1992), pp. 79–117 at p. 101.

female in the Middle Ages, in part because it was subject – like Eve – to sensual temptations; the soul, which should dominate the flesh, was therefore often gendered male.[7] Jesus' flesh, like Mary's, resists sensual temptations but still fulfils the feminine role of creating and nurturing life; by allowing his flesh to be destroyed, Jesus creates eternal life for all humanity.

For both Mary and Jesus, skin creates a permeable border between the human and the divine, yet while Jesus' skin helps to delineate the distinction between his humanity and his divinity, it also creates a liminal space where both can coexist. Mary's unbroken skin protects her purity and preserves her body; Jesus' broken skin allows his flesh to be 'totorn' so his sacrifice and transformation can proceed. Yet skin is both a part of the body and not a part of the body; it continues to have form and function even after being removed from the rest of the body. Mary laments seeing her son's 'fleshche withowtyn hyde' on the cross without realizing that both her son's flesh and his hide will soon be transformed and renewed.

This distinction between body and skin, 'flesche' and 'hyde', appears in surgical and other scientific texts in the Middle Ages.[8] Skin was rarely treated as a major part of the body in these texts, but was most often discussed in relation to certain diseases or ailments (such as leprosy or haemorrhoids). Bartholomaeus Anglicus, in his thirteenth-century encyclopaedia *De proprietatibus rerum*, discusses skin in the sixty-fifth chapter (out of sixty-six) of the fifth book on the body and its parts. Much of Bartholomaeus' description, largely based on Isidore of Seville's *Etymologies*, focuses on the three names used to describe skin, each of which illuminates a unique characteristic: *cutis* because it 'is oft cut and corven'; *pellis* (from *pellere*, 'to put off') because it 'putteth off the utter griefes of the bodie'; and *corium*, meaning hide (from *caro*, 'flesh'); used after the skin has been removed from the body 'for the fleshe is covered with the Skinne'.[9] Once severed from the flesh, the skin 'has no feeling';[10] as Steven Connor notes, once the skin has been flayed, it becomes a distinctly different object, no longer connected to the body and spirit it

---

[7] See: Wendy A. Matlock, 'Feminine Flesh in *Disputacione betwyx the Body and Wormes*', in *The Ends of the Body: Identity and Community in Medieval Culture*, ed. Suzanne Conklin Akbari and Jill Ross (Toronto: University of Toronto Press, 2013), pp. 260–82 esp. pp. 272–4.

[8] See: Jack Hartnell, 'Tools of the Puncture: Skin, Knife, Bone, Hand', pp. 20–50, in this volume.

[9] *On the Properties of Things: John Trevisa's Translation of Bartholomaeus Anglicus' 'De Proprietatibus Rerum': A Critical Text*, general ed. M. C. Seymour (Oxford: Clarendon Press, 1975), 1:86. Bartholomaeus here omits an important distinction made by Isidore, who explains that *corium* should only be used for the skins of brute beasts, not humans.

[10] Ibid., p. 87.

covered and protected: 'the human or animal skin becomes simply a hide, deader than a corpse, a corpse's remnant, the corpse of a corpse'.[11]

Yet while flayed skin may be 'deader than a corpse', hides (at least those from animals) were valuable materials in the Middle Ages that could be transformed into clothing or parchment, providing physical, intellectual and/or spiritual protection and enlightenment.[12] In the N-Town play Mary's discussion of Jesus' body hints at both these transformations: in describing his flesh as 'totorn' and 'rent', she compares his bodily mutilations with ripped clothing, and in her glossing of Jesus' body for the audience, she makes it a sacred text that can be read for deeper meaning.[13] Although on stage the executioners are not seen flaying Jesus during the Crucifixion, in the last line of her speech Mary suggests that this act has indeed taken place, and in all four cycles Jesus' post-crucifixion skin is transformed and repurposed like the removed hide of an animal, occasionally as clothing (the *tunica inconsutilis*) but more commonly as a parchment preserving the sacred text of his suffering and transformation.[14]

Jesus' *tunica inconsutilis* [tunic without a seam] is a garment which, through an intimate association with his body, becomes a symbolic relic of his mortal skin when the Roman soldiers cast lots for his clothing: 'milites ergo [...] acceperunt vestimenta eius [...] et tunicam erat autem tunica inconsutilis desuper contexta per totum.' [The soldiers [...] took his garments [...] and also his coat. Now the coat was without seam, woven from the top throughout.] (John 19.23).[15] All four cycles dramatize the casting of lots scene, though only Towneley and Chester emphasize the seamless coat, which is coveted by the soldiers and Pontius Pilate for its unique construction. Its origin is not biblical, but apocryphal tradition held that the coat had been made by the Virgin Mary when Jesus was an infant,

---

[11] Steven Connor, *The Book of Skin* (Ithaca, NY: Cornell University Press, 2004), p. 11.

[12] For further discussion on wearing skin, both animal and human, in this volume, see: Frederika Bain, 'Skin on Skin: Wearing Flayed Remains', pp. 116–37; and Renée Ward, '"Thou shalt have the better cloathe": Reading Second Skins in *Robin Hood and Guy of Gisborne*', pp. 349–65.

[13] Though 'totorn' and 'rent' could each describe physical injury, the primary medieval definition of both words was the ripping of clothing. *Middle English Dictionary*, The Regents of the University of Michigan (18 Dec. 2001). Online at http://quod.lib.umich.edu/m/med/ (accessed 11 Aug. 2014) [hereafter, *MED*].

[14] This is also a common occurrence in hagiography, especially the life of St Bartholomew, which was a popular subject for artistic rendering. In this volume, see: Sherry C. M. Lindquist, 'Masculinist Devotion: Flaying and Flagellation in the *Belles Heures*', pp. 173–207; and Asa Simon Mittman and Christine Sciacca, 'Robed in Martyrdom: The Flaying of St Bartholomew in the Laudario of Sant'Agnese', pp. 140–72.

[15] Unless otherwise noted, all translations are mine.

and that it grew as he grew – just like human skin.[16] Unlike his flesh, which is torn and broken through the Passion, Jesus' *tunica inconsutilis* remains as intact as his mother's body.[17] The integrity of the *tunica inconsutilis* highlights the distinction between Jesus' flesh and his skin in these plays, for while the tears to his flesh remain even after his bodily death, his skin becomes whole again once it is removed from his earthly body.[18] This restoration suggests that, like Mary's womb, his skin is connected to his divinity, providing a space in which that divinity can be concealed and from which it can be revealed.

The association of Jesus' skin and Mary's womb is made most specifically in N-Town Play 11 – *Parliament of Heaven, Salutation and Conception* – when, in a rare pre-Nativity appearance, Filius (God the Son) appears to discuss humanity's salvation with Pater (God the Father) and Spiritus Sanctus (the Holy Spirit).[19] Filius agrees to descend to earth in order to redeem mankind, but acknowledges that in order to accomplish that he will need to put on human skin like a piece of clothing: 'Fadyr, he þat xal do þis must be both God and man – / Lete me se how I may were þat wede' (ll. 179–80). 'Þat wede' is the mantle of humanity he will need to put on over his divine essence to become human, akin to the animal skins God puts on Adam and Eve to transform them from immortal to mortal when they are expelled from Eden (Genesis 3.21). Yet while Adam and Eve are completely transformed by the skins into mortal beings, Filius must become *both* God and man, and so the human skin he will wear shall cover but not diminish his divinity.[20]

---

[16] For a discussion on how this idea of Christ's seamless coat figures in medieval text and sculpture, see: Peter Dent, 'A Window for the Pain: Surface, Interiority and Christ's Flagellated Skin in Late Medieval Sculpture', pp. 208–39, in this volume.

[17] Rosemary Woolf argues that the cycle audiences would have been familiar with the association between Mary and Jesus' seamless coat. *The English Mystery Plays* (Berkeley: University of California Press, 1972), p. 267.

[18] The resurrected Christ appears in his crucified form in the later cycle plays; even the Annunciation plays refer to his blood and wounds.

[19] This splitting of the Trinity into three separate entities who can discuss and debate is not found in the other cycle plays. Though both God the Father and God the Son appear as separate characters in other cycles, God the Son always appears as Jesus Christ, and the two characters never directly interact (though both appear in the final play of the Chester cycle on the Last Judgement). The Holy Spirit never speaks in the other cycles, and it is unclear from the texts if it was manifested on those stages in some form, or merely suggested through effects and the responses of various characters.

[20] Though stage directions from the twelfth-century Anglo-Norman *Adam* describe Adam and Eve as wearing a 'red tunic' and a 'white silk robe', respectively, later cycles both in England and on the Continent favoured costumes that signified the characters' nudity. Producers could not allow

While Filius is clear about what needs to be done, his speech also highlights the significance of how it is to be accomplished: 'Lete me se *how I may were* þat wede' (emphasis mine). Though it begins with a scene in Heaven, *Parliament of Heaven, Salutation and Conception* is ultimately an Annunciation play, showing how Filius, through the Virgin Mary, eventually does put on human skin in order to bring about man's salvation. Filius' line refers to Mary's womb as a site for God to dress himself in the 'wede' of humanity. Bishop William Durand of Mende, in his thirteenth-century *Rationale Divinorum Officiorum*, explained the sacristy of the church as a symbol of Mary's womb: 'the place where the priest puts on the sacred vestments – signifies the womb of the most blessed Mary, in which Christ clothed Himself with the sacred vestment of His flesh'.[21] In these lines, Mary's womb is described as a safe and private dressing space, a cloister in which Jesus clothes himself in flesh and skin to become human. By presenting humanity as something that can be put on over Filius' divinity, like a tunic, the writer of the N-Town play also suggests its opposite as well, that the tunic of humanity can be stripped off to reveal the divine presence.

Jesus' flagellation, during which his skin is torn and rent, is foreshadowed in the cycle Passion plays by moments of forcible unclothing and reclothing.[22] Each removal of Jesus' clothing prefigures his flagellation, as his garments are torn away from his flesh like skin so his body can be beaten, yet these initial beatings are brief and end with his tormentors dressing him in a white tunic. This act of reclothing is dramatized as an act of mockery

the actors portraying Adam and Eve to be truly naked (especially the male actor playing Eve), but clothed them in body stockings or leather suits that suggested naked skin. Meg Twycross contends that the actors of the Cornish play of Adam and Eve (described as 'aparlet in whytt lether') wore untanned and undyed leather suits that 'would thus be as near to skin in colour and texture as a simulation could get, and could be tailored close to the contours of the body in a way stiffer materials of a similar weight could not'. See: '"Apparell Comlye"', in *Aspects of Early English Drama*, ed. Paula Neuss (Cambridge: D. S. Brewer, 1983), pp. 30–49 at p. 35.

[21] *The Rationale divinorum officiorum of William Durand of Mende: A New Translation of the Prologue and Book One*, ed. and trans. Timothy M. Thibodeau (New York: Columbia University Press, 2007), p. 21. Similarly, Chaucer's Second Nun praises Mary in the prologue to her tale by stating '[t]hat no desdeyn the Makere hadde of kynde / His Sone in blood and flessh to clothe and wynde. / Withinne the cloistre blisful of thy sydis' (ll. 41–3). 'The Second Nun's Tale', in *The Works of Geoffrey Chaucer*, ed. F. N. Robinson, 2nd edn (Boston: Houghton Mifflin, 1961), pp. 208–13.

[22] Dent connects both dressing and undressing with the flaying of skin, noting that '[t]he pulling on and off of clothing and the accompanying sacred eroticism of the veiled and unveiled body develop a fantasy of disrobing in which the skin becomes yet another layer of revelation, not just transparent but detachable' ('A Window for the Pain', p. 227).

in which Jesus is dressed as a fool, yet, as Thomas Bestul notes, other medieval writers on the Passion showed how this reclothing also increased Jesus' suffering. In Bonaventure's early fourteenth-century *Meditationes vitae Christi*, '[w]hen his garments are pulled off, the wounds of the flagellation are reopened because the clothing has adhered to the flesh'.[23] In N-Town Play 30, *Death of Judas; Trials before Pilate and Herod*, Herod's use of the fool's garment reflects his desire to manipulate Jesus' skin, which he sees as something removable and replaceable. Herod orders Jesus to be stripped and beaten for refusing to speak before the king, thus initiating the first mortification of his flesh in this cycle (in other cycles Jesus is not whipped until his second trial before Pilate). Herod's followers (Primus and Secundus Judeus) 'pulle of Jesus clothis and betyn hym with whyppys', with Primus vowing to 'spare not whyl thei [the whips] last' (SD before l. 237 / l. 242). Yet Herod ultimately curtails his men's violence, preventing them from overwhelming Jesus' flesh. Herod allows his followers to whip Jesus and draw blood, but he will not let them Jesus' 'body all spyl' (l. 250).

Herod's use of 'spyl' allows for two slightly different interpretations of this moment, since 'spyl' can be read as either 'spill' or 'spoil'.[24] The Middle English 'spill' was defined as destruction or killing, and this reading would suggest that Herod stops the beating before his men kill Jesus, preferring instead to force Pontius Pilate to take responsibility for Jesus' death or release.[25] While reading 'spyl' as 'spoil' does not change this interpretation of Herod's actions or motivations, it suggests Herod is preventing a specific type of bodily torture. 'Spoil' in Middle English most commonly referred to stripping a person of clothing or an animal of skin, and, as Jesus has already been stripped of his clothing, Herod's interruption instead forestalls a literal flaying. This reading further underscores the symbolic relationship between the stripping of Jesus' garments and the later rending of his skin, since both are acts of 'spyllen'/'spoilen'.[26] Herod, however, refers to 'spyl'ing Jesus' body, not his skin; he prevents his followers not from carrying out a specific type of punishment, but from ending Jesus' life. That is a responsibility Herod cedes to Pilate. This moment ends the play, and though Jesus' flesh has been beaten, the playwright ensures that

---

[23] Thomas Bestul, *Texts of the Passion: Latin Devotional Literature and Medieval Society* (Philadelphia: University of Pennsylvania Press, 1996), p. 50.

[24] Indeed, the editors of different versions of the N-Town Plays do not agree on the meaning of 'spyl' in Herod's line: Sugano glosses it as 'spoil' (p. 257), while Spector glosses it as 'spill', which he defines as 'kill' (p. 637).

[25] In N-Town Play 30, Jesus is first taken before Pilate, who refuses to pass judgement on him because Jesus was born in Galilee and Herod is the king of that country. Herod, however, sends Jesus back to Pilate (after questioning him and having him beaten) with a message that he is giving Pilate 'powere of Jhesus' (l. 256), thus requesting that Pilate pronounce the final sentence.

[26] 'spoilen', *MED* (accessed 11 Jul. 2012).

his humanity is intact before the main action of the Passion begins. The subsequent play (*Satan and Pilate's Wife; Second Trial before Pilate*) begins with a stage direction indicating that Jesus is to be clothed in the fool's garment before the next action begins, and though the characters are ignorant of the significance, they ensure that Jesus is again covered by an artificial skin that symbolizes for the audience not only his mortality but his mortification as well.

This reclothing is only temporary, of course; later in the play, that garment will be forcibly removed by a large crowd that will 'crye for joy with a gret voys and arryn hym and pullyn of his clothis' (SD before l. 211), revealing Jesus' naked body and skin in preparation for the torments and flagellations of the Passion.[27] The removal of his clothes prefigures his flagellation, and just as his punishers attempt to strip away his social connections through the stripping of his clothes, so too do they desire to tear away his human connections through the flaying of his skin (though they do not comprehend the greater implications of their actions). Biblically, Jesus is scourged and mocked before his crucifixion, yet in re-enacting these scenes, the producers of the cycle plays not only extend the duration of his suffering[28] but also the extent of it by suggesting that Jesus is not merely beaten but actually flayed. The significance of flaying is twofold: first, it suggests that Jesus' purported (but never named) crime is high treason – which in the Middle Ages could be punished by flaying (though, as W. R. J. Barron finds, documented cases of this in England are extremely rare, if extant at all) – and second, it allows Jesus' skin to be transformed into the common by-products of animal hides: clothing and parchment.[29] For the medieval audience, the use of flaying in these plays would signify the importance of Jesus' skin and its relationship to both his humanity and divinity, guiding them to meditate on their own skin and its role as a conduit between this world and the next.[30]

[27] It is unlikely in any of the English cycles that the actor playing Jesus was literally naked on stage; possibly, he was wearing a bodysuit of white or untanned leather (such as were sometimes used to simulate the nude bodies of the prelapsarian Adam and Eve), but most likely he was wearing a loincloth. As Clifford Davidson notes, the loincloth was popular in visual depictions of the Crucifixion, and few images portray Christ as completely naked on the cross. See: Clifford Davidson, 'Nudity, the Body, and Early English Drama', *The Journal of English and Germanic Philology* 98.4 (1999): 499–522. Cf. Dent, 'A Window for the Pain', p. 226.

[28] In each English cycle there are almost twice as many plays devoted to the Passion as to the Resurrection and Assumption combined.

[29] W. R. J. Barron, 'The Penalties for Treason in Medieval Life and Literature', *Journal of Medieval History* 7 (1981): 187–202. Despite the title, Barron's article is almost exclusively about flaying.

[30] For more on flaying as a representational rather than literal act, see: Robert Mills, *Suspended Animation: Pain, Pleasure and Punishment in Medieval*

Though in none of the cycles does Pilate name Jesus' crime to the crowd, the punishment that is eventually meted out (crucifixion) was a standard punishment for treason. In the gospels, the high priests initially accuse Jesus of blasphemy, which would have traditionally been punishable by stoning, but they change their accusations when they appear before Pilate to make Jesus' crime more threatening to Rome. In his commentary on the gospel of John, Thomas Aquinas notes that Pilate is unmoved by most of the Jewish high priests' statements against Jesus, but does respond to the accusation that he has made himself 'King of the Jews'.[31] As Aquinas explains, the severity of this charge is best explained in Luke's gospel, when the high priests inform Pilate that 'Hunc invenimus subvertentem gentem nostram, et prohibentem tributa dare Caesari', as well as 'Commovet populum' [We have found this man subverting our nation, and prohibiting giving tribute to Caesar [...] exciting the people] (Luke 23.2, 5). In each cycle, the high priests carefully describe Jesus' crime to Pilate as treason, not blasphemy, most significantly in Towneley Play 22, *Scourging*: 'He callys hisself a kyng, / Ther he none is; / Thus *he wold downe bryng* / *Oure lawes*, iwys' (ll. 133–6, emphasis mine).[32] According to the high priests, Jesus has not only declared himself a king, thus going against Caesar, but has also incited the people to turn to him against Caesar and bring down Rome.

These accusations of sedition would have been of particular concern to the English in the late fourteenth century and throughout the fifteenth century (when the cycle plays were being produced). The frequent passing of various Acts of Treason demonstrates an ongoing concern with preserving the person and office of the sovereign. The Treason Act of 1351, during the reign of Edward III, defined high treason for the first time in England, while the Treason Act of 1381, passed during Richard II's reign in response to the Peasants' Revolt, specifically forbade anyone from inciting a riot or revolt; though it was revoked in 1399 with the succession of Henry IV, subsequent acts passed during Henry's reign continued to broaden and codify the definition of high treason. By accusing Jesus of proclaiming himself a king, refusing to recognize the authority of the legal sovereign and inciting the people to follow him, the high priests present Jesus as a traitor under *English* as well as Roman law.

Culture (London: Reaktion, 2005), pp. 59–82; and Larissa Tracy, *Torture and Brutality in Medieval Literature: Negotiations of National Identity* (Cambridge: D. S. Brewer, 2012), pp. 16, 62–3, 74, 92–3, 147–55.

[31] Thomas Aquinas, *Commentary on the Gospel of St. John, Part 2*, trans. Fabian R. Larcher (Albany: Magi Books, Inc., 1998), accessible online though the website of the Dominican House of Studies Priory of the Immaculate Conception. http://dhspriory.org/thomas/english/John18.htm. (accessed 15 Mar. 2012), Lecture 6.2345.

[32] *The Towneley Plays*, ed. Stevens and Cawley. All quotations are from this edition. Hereafter, line numbers will be given in parentheses.

A medieval audience would have seen this accusation of treason as both false and as a reflection of the corrupt nature of the Jewish high priests and, in the Towneley Cycle, Pontius Pilate. Though the Towneley Pilate and the high priests, Anna and Cayphas,[33] pay lip service to the rule of law throughout the cycle, their speeches and actions prove their deceitful and corrupt natures.[34] Pilate, the main villain in the Towneley Passion, announces his evil character from his first appearance in Play 20, *Conspiracy and Capture*, entering with a long speech in which he proclaims that he may 'Supporte a man today, / To-morn agans hym than. / On both parties thus I play' (ll. 31–3).[35] Before even questioning Jesus in Play 22, *Scourging*, Pilate decides that Jesus 'this day at nyght on crosse shall […] be slayn', though two lines earlier he also promises to 'fownde to be his freynd vtward, in certayn, / And shew hym fare cowntenance and wordys of vanyté' (ll. 33 / 31–2). While Anna and Cayphas are less duplicitous than Pilate, in Play 21, *Buffeting* (which as Martin Stevens and A. C. Cawley note should be 'more accurately referred to as "The Trial before Caiaphas and Annas"'), they prove willing to flout the law in ordering the buffeting of Jesus.[36] As Larissa Tracy demonstrates, in many medieval English literary texts 'torture is a symptom of corrupt governance and disregard for law in opposition to the basic elements of English identity'; to a medieval English audience, the high priests would have revealed themselves as corrupt by

---

[33] Though more commonly written as Annas and Caiaphas, these spellings reflect the names as reproduced in Stevens and Cawley's edition.

[34] G. R. Owst sees all three characters as representative of figures regularly criticized in medieval sermons: Pilate is the 'unjust [Civil Court] Judge', while Anna and Cayphas both represent the 'evil Ecclesiastical Lawyer' through whom the author can 'pillory the sins of churchmen'. See: G. R. Owst, *Literature and Pulpit in Medieval England: A Neglected Chapter in the History of English Letters and of the English People* (Oxford: Basil Blackwell, 1966), pp. 495–6.

[35] He also announces that he is the 'granser of great Mahowne' (Mohammed), a clear sign in medieval English literature that he is evil (l. 19).

[36] *The Towneley Plays*, 2:554. In Play 21, the characters of Cayphas and Anna are carefully distinguished, and much of the play becomes an argument between the two; from the beginning of the play Cayphas wants the authority to torture and kill Jesus ('Yit wold I gif of my gold, / Yond tratoure to pelt / For euer' [410–12]), while Anna repeatedly cautions Cayphas that they must follow the law ('It is best that we trete hym / With farenes' [313–14]) and should deliver Jesus to Pilate for sentencing. Yet despite appearing restrained and just, it is ultimately Anna who orders the buffeting: 'And that kyng to you take, / And with knokys make hym wake' (465–7). For a more detailed reading of this play and its reflection of contemporary politics, see: Robert S. Sturges, *The Circulation of Power in Medieval Biblical Drama: Theaters of Authority* (New York: Palgrave, 2015), pp. 21–31.

torturing and later flaying Jesus.[37] Thus, though audience members would
have recognized the severity of the high priests' charge against Jesus, they
would have understood the accusation of treason as ironic, reflecting the
high priests' correct fear that Jesus' presence signals God's new law that will
supplant the priests' old law and, by extension, their authority in society.

This concern with treason and its effect on the social body further
dovetails with the plays' presentations of Jesus' transition from mortal
to divine and the need to tear away his human skin to bring about that
transformation. By causing dissension between a sovereign and his people,
a traitor threatens the integrity of the social body, rending the fragile skin
that binds a community and a king. While there is no indication within
these plays (following biblical sources) that Jesus desires or intends to
cause such a disruption, his transformation from mortal to divine is a threat
to the integrity of the social body since it signifies the ability to transcend
social borders as well as physical ones, and, ironically, as his tormentors
peel his skin away, they hasten both his transformation and their societal
disintegration.

While in England flaying appears to have been more popular in medieval
romances than in actual practice, there are a few historical examples of it
being either threatened or carried out as a punishment for treason.[38] In 1176,
Prince Henry sentenced his vice-chancellor, Adam, to be flayed alive for the
crime of treason, though Adam escaped the punishment by pleading the
benefit of the clergy. Less fortunate was Hugh de Cressingham, treasurer
to King Edward I and the chief justice of the north; in 1297, following the
Battle of Stirling Bridge, he was reportedly flayed by the Scots, who claimed
he was 'not so much a treasurer as a traitor to the king'.[39] In this volume,
Mary Rambaran-Olm investigates the persistent myth of human skin being
removed and used as a warning to criminals who desecrated churches in
Anglo-Saxon England, though there is no evidence from the period that this
was actually done.[40] John Gower perhaps alludes to this myth in his retelling
of the popular story of the sixth-century Persian king Cambyses and the

---

[37] Tracy, *Torture and Brutality*, p. 136.

[38] Barron, 'Penalties for Treason', p. 197.

[39] *Henry Knighton's Chronicle*, ed. J. R. Lumby, Rolls Series 92 (London,
1889–95), 1:382. Qtd. in M. J. Swanton, '"Dane-Skins": Excoriation in Early
England', *Folklore* 87.1 (1976): 21–8 at p. 22. Though reported as fact by
Knighton, this may have actually been anti-Scottish propaganda.

[40] Swanton claims that remains of skin were found nailed to the doors of
several churches from Anglo-Saxon England, and that in some cases the
skin was identified as human. Several of his assumptions and conclusions
have been disproven by modern DNA analysis and by more in-depth
research into Anglo-Saxon sources, which provide no contemporary
evidence for this practice. For more on this, see: Mary Rambaran-Olm,
'Medievalism and the "Flayed-Dane" Myth: English Perspectives between
the Seventeenth and Nineteenth Centuries', pp. 91–115, in this volume.

corrupt judge Sisamnes;[41] while in most versions, after Sisamnes is flayed alive, his skin is draped over the judge's chair, in Gower's *Confessio Amantis* it is actually 'nayled on the same seete'.[42] Though the objectification of Sisamnes' skin and its placement over the judge's seat were the coda to the story, they also became the tale's enduring image. Just as traitors' heads were often impaled on pikes as warnings to future transgressors, so Sisamnes' skin becomes a tangible admonition to those who, as Gower wrote, 'wolde flitte / The lawe for the coveitise' (ll. 2992–3).

As with the skins of historical traitors, Sisamnes' severed skin is most commonly presented as both a warning and a memorial of his transgression. Yet the writers of the Latin *Gesta Romanorum* suggest another possible reading, one which elevates the removed skin to the status of a sacred relic.[43] Though the *Gesta* does not alter the seriousness of Sisamnes' offences or the gruesomeness of his punishment, in moralizing on the story's meaning, the traitor's separated skin becomes the symbol of Jesus' suffering:

> Pellis que ponitur pro memoria in sede, est Christi passio, quam homo débet habere retentam in sede cordis sui, ne contra deum et salutem anime sue delinquat, sicut scriptum est: Memorare novissima tua et in eteruum non peccabis. Christus non tantum pellem in sede crucis pro nobis dedit, sed eciam vitam.

> [The skin that was placed on the seat for remembrance is the Passion of Christ, which man should hold on the seat of his heart lest he commit offences against God or his soul's salvation. For as the

---

[41] Cambyses orders Sisamnes to be flayed alive upon discovering that the judge has taken bribes and made unjust rulings. The king then appoints Sisamnes' son, Otian, to be the new judge, and orders Sisamnes' detached skin to be placed over the judge's seat. The earliest version of this story appears in Herodotus' *Histories* (V. 25), and retellings can be found in Valerius Maximus' *Memorabilia* (VI. 3. ext. 3), the Latin *Gesta Romanorum* (Tale xxix), James Yonge's translation of the *Secreta Secretorum* (*The Gouernaunce of Prynces*), Thomas Hoccleve's *Regiment for Princes* (ll. 2675–88), and Jacobus de Cessolis' *Liber de moribus hominum et officiis nobilium super ludo scacchorum*. In this volume, see: Kelly DeVries, 'A Tale of Venetian Skin: The Flaying of Marcantonio Bragadin', pp. 51–70; and Asa Simon Mittman and Christine Sciacca, 'Robed in Martyrdom: The Flaying of St Bartholomew in the Laudario of Sant'Agnese', pp. 140–72. Robert Mills discusses the visual representation of this story in Gerard David's fifteenth-century painting. See: *Suspended Animation*, chap. 2.

[42] John Gower, *Confessio Amantis*, ed. Russell A. Peck (Toronto: University of Toronto, 1980), l. 2900.

[43] This tale is not found in the Anglo-Latin or early English versions of the *Gesta Romanorum*. The other explications of this tale in the Latin *Gesta* are consistent with standard readings: Cambyses stands in for God, the wise and all-knowing judge, and Sisamnes symbolizes sinful and wicked man.

scripture says: Remember your last judgment and into eternity you will not sin. Christ, on the seat of the cross, gave not only skin but also life for us.][44]

Once separated from the corrupt body it previously covered, Sisamnes' skin is transformed into a holy object; its lingering marks of suffering are no longer remnants of a just punishment but signifiers of Christ's sacrifice for the salvation of mankind. As in other versions of the story, the skin stretched on the judge's seat serves as an enjoiner to discourage future sin, but in the Latin *Gesta Romanorum* there is no justice or triumph in the sight of this removed skin; it is not a remnant from the particular sinner who wore it, but a reminder of general human frailty and the potential for sin in all who sit on it.

As in this meditation on Sisamnes' skin, Jesus' skin and the suffering it has undergone become a space for reflection and illumination in the later scenes of the cycle Passion plays.[45] The Virgin Mary and the apostle John initially guide the audience to a contemplation of the meaning of Jesus' suffering, written on his broken body and torn skin, and this act of translation is taken up by other characters including Jesus himself, who in the Towneley cycle glosses the wounds on his skin as a text to be witnessed and read by the audience. In Towneley Play 23, *The Crucifixion*, as Mary describes her son's wounds she begins to feel each mark on her own flesh, and implicitly asks the audience to do the same. Like the N-Town Mary, the Towneley Mary compares Jesus' skin to clothing but makes a more direct reference to her role in the production of that skin for her son: 'His robe is all to-ryffen, / That of me was hym gyffen, / And shapen with my sydys' (ll. 405–7). While 'sydys' could be used to mean Mary's hands, evoking the image of her weaving the seamless coat, it could also be defined as 'womb', referring to that sacred space in which God donned human skin.[46] Like the N-Town Mary, the Towneley Mary describes her son's skin as a hide ('all rent is thi hyde' [l. 339]), making it something not only dead but also separate from the flesh, and therefore a site on which the text of the Passion can be written and preserved.

Mary's lament is overshadowed by a lengthy monologue from Jesus in Towneley Play 26, *The Resurrection*.[47] In this play, the resurrected Jesus

[44] *Gesta Romanorum*, Tale xxix (Lugdani: apud haeredes Iacobi Iuntae, 1555), pp. 126–8 (translation mine).

[45] G. R. Owst notes various late medieval sermons on this theme which include graphic descriptions of Jesus' tortured body (*Literature and Pulpit*, pp. 508–9).

[46] The *MED* quotes Chaucer's 'The Second Nun's Tale' as an example of this usage: 'His Sone in blood and flessh to clothe and wynde / Withinne the cloistre blisful of thy sydis' (ll. 42–3). Considering the similar narrative, 'womb' seems the likeliest interpretation for the Towneley Mary's line.

[47] Jesus' speech is 120 lines long (ll. 230–350). It begins after a stage direction describing angelic voices singing 'Christus resurgens' [Christ is risen], and

reveals himself first to the audience, displaying his '[f]our hundredth woundys and v thowsand' for them to witness and contemplate, and instructing them to repent for the sins which have led to his Passion (l. 292). Martin Stevens and A. C. Cawley note that this lament was a popular topic for late medieval lyrics, and on stage 'the lament is directed to the audience, which thus serves the role of uninvolved bystanders [...] [Christ] makes all mankind responsible for the wounds inflicted upon him'.[48] Though like Mary he reflects on the necessity of his sacrifice, much of his lament echoes his description of his body and call to the audience from Play 23, *Crucifixion*: 'Behold, if euer ye sagh body / Buffet & bett thus blody' (ll. 236–7) and later 'Blo and blody thus am I bett, / Swongen with swepys & all to-swett' (ll. 525–6). Yet Jesus does not merely ask the audience to witness the marks of the Passion on his body, he insists that they read his skin to understand the full meaning of his sacrifice, turning his skin into a parchment containing a sacred text.

Skin-as-textual-space was a common image in the Middle Ages; Sarah Kay notes that medieval readers were aware of the once-living nature of parchment.[49] A mortuary roll from the fourteenth century notes the previous life of the parchment on which it is written, ironically contrasting the perpetual life of animal skin with the decay of human skin: 'Vilior est humana caro quam pellis ovina: / Cum moriatur ovis, aliquid valet illa ruina, / Extrahitur pellis et scribitur intus et extra; / Cum moriatur homo, moritur simul caro et ossa.' [Man's flesh is viler than the skin of sheep. / When sheep are dead, their skin still has some use, / For it is pulled and writ upon, both sides. / But with man's death both flesh and bones are dead.][50] Yet though this mortuary-roll text dismisses the possibility of human skin serving as manuscript material, the transformation of Jesus' skin into a parchment on which his wounds, the visible marks of his

---

ends just before the arrival of the three Marys at the tomb.

[48] *The Towneley Plays*, 2:579 n. 233–96.

[49] See: Sarah Kay, 'Flayed Skin as *objet a*: Representation and Materiality in Guillaume de Deguileville's *Pèlerinage de la vie humaine*', in *Medieval Fabrications: Dress, Textiles, Clothwork, and other Cultural Imaginings*, ed. Jane Burns (New York: Palgrave, 2004), pp. 193–205 at pp. 194–5. In this and other essays, Kay further suggests that medieval readers may have made connections between the content of some medieval manuscripts (specifically those on flaying) and the material of the manuscript itself. See: Sarah Kay, 'Original Skin: Flaying, Reading, and Thinking in the Legend of Saint Bartholomew and other Works', *Journal of Medieval and Early Modern Studies* 36.1 (2006): 35–74, and 'Legible Skins: Animals and the Ethics of Medieval Reading', *postmedieval: a journal of medieval cultural studies* 2.1 (2011): 13–32.

[50] Qtd. in *Fasciculus Morum: A Fourteenth-Century Preacher's Handbook*, ed. and trans. Siegfried Wenzel (University Park: Pennsylvania State University Press, 1989), pp. 98–9.

suffering, are recast into a sacred text was a motif in various fourteenth- and fifteenth-century manuscripts co-opted by the cycle plays.

While in the cycle plays Jesus' skin is made a space on which the text of his suffering has been written, its role as parchment is suggested rather than explicitly discussed. However, the late fifteenth-century Digby play *Christ's Burial* makes a literal comparison between Jesus' skin and parchment, and between his wounds and a sacred text. Mary Magdalene, looking on the crucified Christ and his wounds, exclaims to Joseph of Arimathea 'beholde & looke / How many bludy letters beyn written in þis buke, / Small margente her is' (ll. 271–3).[51] Joseph responds 'Ye, this parchement is strichit owt of syse', before he proceeds to gloss each bruise and drop of blood to reveal the mystery of God's love for mankind (l. 274). Joseph compares the stretching of Jesus' body on the cross to the parchmenter's stretching of a wet animal hide onto a wooden frame, an act which will transform the hide into parchment and Jesus into the Christ. This association, and Joseph's subsequent reading to the audience of the 'bludy letters' on Jesus' skin, make this scene analogous to Christ's glossing of his crucified skin in a text known as the Charter of Christ, which appears in two fourteenth- and several fifteenth-century manuscripts.[52]

The Charter of Christ, a legal document purported to be dictated by Christ himself, exists in both short and long forms and maps out a new covenant between God and man that promises heavenly rewards and eternal life to those who keep God's commandments. Jesus' earthly death seals the contract, and the short form often includes a physical seal and the image of a pierced heart with five drops of blood, signifying the Passion which brought the contract into being. British Library, Add. MS 37049 (1460–1500), a Carthusian miscellany, includes a crude illustration of a crucified Jesus standing in front of the cross, blood dripping from his side and from the nails in his hands and feet; in front of him, obscuring the lower half of his body, is the charter with its seal. Yet while this image helps suggest a relationship between Christ's suffering body and the charter, only the long form explicitly makes Christ's skin the parchment on which the document is written.

---

[51] *The Digby Plays with an Incomplete 'Morality' of 'Wisdom, Who is Christ'*, ed. Frederick J. Furnivall (Oxford: Oxford University Press, 1967). The Digby Plays are five plays found in Bodleian MS Digby 133, including plays on Mary Magdalene, Paul and the Massacre of the Innocents.

[52] Mary Caroline Spalding, whose monograph *The Middle English Charters of Christ* (Bryn Mawr, PA: Bryn Mawr College, 1914) remains the most detailed analysis and compilation of the various charters, identifies thirteen manuscripts containing the Short Charter (thirty-two lines), and fourteen manuscripts containing the Long Charter, which varies from 234 lines to 618 lines. The earliest version she finds is a Long Charter in Bodleian Library, MS Rawlinson Poetry 175, dating to the middle of the fourteenth century.

In the long form of the charter Christ states that he inscribed the document on his skin because '[n]e myght I fynd na parchemyne / ffor to laste with-outen fyne', and so for love of mankind '[m]yne awen skyn I toke þar-to' (ll. 51–2 / 54).[53] Only Jesus' skin, the liminal space that connects his humanity and his divinity, can be guaranteed to last and preserve the Charter for eternity. As he describes his Passion and crucifixion, he further explains how his earthly body was gradually transformed into the charter's parchment: first, the skin was stripped of its outer covering ('þan was I nakend wele may yhe wyten'), then cleansed ('waschen in myne awen blode') and finally stretched on the cross to dry ('Streyned to dry on þe rode tre / Als parchemyne aw for to be') (ll. 70, 77, 79–80). This last line reiterates that what he describes follows the parchmenter's standard procedure for converting animal skins into parchment (removing hair and fur, washing and then stretching and drying the skins).[54] Focusing not on the torture his body has endured but on the properly resulting 'parchemyne', Christ does not minimize his suffering but instead frames it as a transformative ritual not only from human to God but also from skin to manuscript.

Having narrated his skin's conversion into parchment, Christ continues by detailing the actual writing of the charter onto his body, and, in so doing, reads and explains the deeper significance of the text for his audience. He also expands the material description of his body as charter: the ink is made from his torturers' spit onto his 'neese' or nose (textual variants include 'neb', 'face', and 'bloode'), while the scourges or whips become the pens that engrave the letters onto his flesh:

> Here now & yhe sall wyten
> How þis charter was wryten
> Opon my neese was made þe ynk
> With Iewes spyttyng on me to stynk
> þe pennes þat þe letter was with wryten
> Was of skorges þat I was with smyten
> How many letters þare-on bene
> Rede & þou may wyten & sene
> ffyue thowsand four hundredth fifty & ten
> Woundes on me bath blak & wen.
>
> (ll. 81–90)

---

[53] All quotations are from the earliest known version of the Long Charter, in Bodleian Library, MS Rawlinson Poetry 175, fols. 94–5, as reprinted in ibid., pp. 18–42. Spalding reprints the different MS versions next to one another; there are minor word changes, but otherwise the different versions are quite consistent.

[54] For a detailed description of how parchment was made, see: Raymond Clemens and Timothy Graham, 'Part I: Making the Medieval Manuscript', in *Introduction to Manuscript Studies* (Ithaca, NY: Cornell University Press, 2007), pp. 3–17 esp. pp. 9–13.

Emphasizing the gruesome nature of this act of writing, Christ makes 5,460 both the number of letters in the charter and the number of wounds displayed on his body. The reader of this text becomes a legal witness to both the document and the suffering of Christ, enjoined by Christ to read his skin in order to 'wyten & sene' – the audience must read the Charter in order to understand the full suffering of Christ, since its every letter denotes a wound on his body. The Charter is not a historical document, however; it is a sacred contract between humanity and God, and this act of tangibly connecting with Christ's blood-as-ink and skin-as-parchment binds the readers to the compact. Created from his skin, the parchment is a relic that has touched both Jesus' humanity and his divinity. Through reading and witnessing the Charter written on his skin, the readers likewise encounter not only Jesus' suffering but also his divinity.

In the cycle plays Jesus' skin is similarly transformed into a parchment that records his suffering and his sacrifice; the audience is called to witness the transformation and to remember the words/wounds written upon it. Using the laments of Jesus, the Virgin Mary and other characters within the Passion plays, the cycle playwrights, like the character of Joseph in the Digby *Christ's Burial*, gloss the text of Jesus' skin so as to ensure that the audience not only sees the events of the Passion but also understands its deeper significance as recorded on Jesus' suffering body. Two of the cycles also describe a second type of skin-as-textual-space, an image preserving the text of the skin that allows the skin's story to be passed on even after the original text is gone[55] – the Veil of Veronica.

The story of Veronica wiping the face of Jesus as he carries his cross to Calvary, and the miracle of the image of his face being preserved in her cloth, is not found in the canonical gospels, but its popularity in the Middle Ages (in part because of its inclusion in Pseudo-Bonaventure's *Meditationes vitae Christi*) led to its being incorporated into the sixth Station of the Cross. As Ewa Kuryluk suggests, the vernicle (a medieval term for a copy of Veronica's cloth) 'is ideally suited for projection – for seeing what we want to see in it', and in her study of Veronica's legend, Kuryluk demonstrates that there were a wide variety of meanings given to the vernicle in the medieval period.[56] The vernicle preserves both Christ's divinity (through its mystical properties) and Jesus' humanity (through the suffering of the image), and so much of the contemplation of the image attempts to understand its dualism. On stage, the vernicle gains another layer from the prop representing this representation of this duality. Though the Veronica scenes in both N-Town and York are brief, they are significant in that they establish the metamorphosis of Veronica's veil from cloth to sacred relic and reinforce the theatre's ability to layer multiple significations within a

---

[55] That is, after it has been assumed into Heaven.

[56] Ewa Kuryluk, *Veronica and her Cloth: History, Symbolism, and Structure of a 'True' Image* (Cambridge: Basil Blackwell, 1991), p. 208.

single prop. As Andrew Sofer writes, Jesus 'transforms the napkin from a representational prop to a supernatural relic worthy of veneration'.[57] Yet Sofer elides the multiple transformations that occur on stage: offstage cloth becomes onstage prop that, through the action of the play, becomes Veronica's veil, which finally becomes a holy relic. This layered series of transformations reflects the larger transformation of Jesus' body being enacted on stage: from actor to the character of the suffering Jesus to redemptive sacrifice to death to resurrected divinity. Veronica's veil simultaneously contains Jesus' suffering and his resurrection, just like his onstage body.

In N-Town Play 32, Veronica runs into the crowd of 'synful pepyl' to help Jesus, wiping his face with her 'kerchy' or veil (l. 41). Jesus thanks her and tells her that 'thi whipyng doth me ese. / My face is clene that was blak to se. / I shal them kepe from all mysese / That lokyn on thi kercy and remembyr me' (ll. 45–8). What was on Jesus' face that made it 'blak to se' (dirt, sweat, blood) is unclear, but by transferring it to Veronica's veil, Jesus has created another testament to his suffering. His final words to Veronica – 'remembyr me' – echo his instruction to his disciples at the Last Supper, and just as the Eucharistic host becomes Jesus through the mystery of transubstantiation, so does Veronica's veil become the living image of Jesus through his words. The veil becomes more than a mere memorial; it becomes a true relic through Jesus' promise that all who look on the veil and remember him will be cured of 'mysese'. When he imprints his image onto the cloth, Jesus creates a representation of his skin that not only reflects his human face but also contains his divine essence; a true second skin that preserves his duality just as his earthly skin has done.

Though in York it is the Third Mary, and not Veronica, who wipes the face of Jesus, the action of the scene in York Play 34, *The Road to Calvary*, is virtually identical to that in N-Town; what distinguishes the York portrayal is that the vernicle becomes a site of resistance as well as a testament to faith. The Third Mary approaches Jesus entreating 'A, lorde, beleue lete clense thy face', and having done so immediately perceives the miraculous image left behind: 'Behalde howe he hath schewed his grace, / Howe he is moste of mayne! / This signe schalle bere witnesse / Vnto all pepull playne, / Howe Goddes sone here gilteles / Is putte to pereles payne' (ll. 184–9).[58] Unlike N-Town, Jesus does not speak during this interaction and so it is Mary's words, not his, that give the cloth meaning. Yet Jesus' silence arguably enhances the cloth's significance; it becomes his mouthpiece, visually testifying to his suffering and, in Mary's words, proving his innocence as well. While Mary asserts that the image on the cloth will bear witness to Jesus' suffering, two of the participating soldiers bear witness

---

[57] Andrew Sofer, 'Absorbing Interests: Kyd's Bloody Handkerchief as Palimpsest', *Comparative Drama* 34.2 (2000): 127–53 at p. 132.

[58] *The York Plays*, ed. Beadle. Hereafter line numbers are given in parentheses.

to *her* actions and deride her for interfering with Jesus. The first soldier calls her a 'queny' (whore) while the other reproaches her with 'casbalde' (ll. 191 / 193), and their hostility highlights the importance of the cloth as a witness both to Jesus' passion and to his innocence.[59] The soldiers chase away human witnesses, and so the cloth becomes a necessary testament. Mary warns the soldiers that '[t]his signe schall vengeaunce calle / On yowe holly in feere' (ll. 196–7), and her 'holly in feere' suggests not only that all the soldiers will be punished for their participation in the Passion, but also that they shall be punished in hellfire.[60] As in the Charter of Christ, Mary's cloth is both a relic of Jesus' skin and a testament to the sacrifice that will enable humanity's salvation; Mary warns the soldiers that by refusing to believe in the cloth and in Christ, they may be denied that salvation.

While the vernicle preserves the text of Jesus' suffering and the redemption it promises, it is a reflection of, but not a product of, his skin. It reflects not only the image of his skin but also the transformations his skin undergoes in the cycle Passion plays, being both cloth and parchment. In the cycle Passion plays, Jesus' skin is generally read as either clothing or textual space, yet in the Chester Ascension play (the most elaborate Ascension play in the cycles) the angels that witness and participate refer to his mortal skin as both clothing and parchment simultaneously. This would have also been visible in the staging of the play, in which the actor playing Jesus would have likely been costumed in a body stocking covered in red paint (or some other substance resembling blood) while the actors-as-angels, speaking from the play text, simultaneously illuminated the significance of Jesus' appearance for the audience.[61] The incorporation of both a visual and textual representation of Jesus' bloody body would have been important to a medieval audience who, as Clifford Davidson notes, 'valued the blood of Christ [...] very highly

---

[59] The exact meaning of 'casbalde' is a little obscure; literally it means 'baldhead', but that does not seem to fit this play, and the *MED* suggests that it may have been a general term of derision.

[60] The *MED* has no reference for 'feere', but both 'fere' and 'feir' could mean companions (often referring to an army). Yet while the *MED* does not give 'feere' as a form for 'fire' (or 'fir'), the *OED* lists 'feer' as an alternative fifteenth-century spelling, and it seems an appropriate usage for Mary's line.

[61] Andrea Stevens notes frequent references in both English and Continental stage records of paint being used to represent blood, though asserts that this is not 'exclusive'. See: *Inventions of the Skin: The Painted Body in Early English Drama, 1400–1642* (Edinburgh: Edinburgh University Press, 2013), pp. 51–4. Clifford Davidson speculates that the York Butchers' Guild, responsible for the *Mortificacio Christi* play, 'might well have used animal blood as a theatrical substitute for the blood of Christ'. See: Clifford Davidson, 'Sacred Blood and the Late Medieval Stage', *Comparative Drama* 31.3 (1997): 436–58 at p. 443.

indeed'.[62] In the Chester *Ascension*, the blood that stains Jesus' skin is not only a reminder of his suffering but also a promise of everlasting life for all Christians.

As Jesus ascends in Chester Play 20, *Ascension*, angels appear on stage singing and quoting from Isaiah 63.1–3:[63]

Primus Angelus cantat	Quis est iste qui venit de Edom, tinctis vestibus de Bosra? [Who is this that comes from Edom, with dyed garments from Bozrah?]
Minor Angelus respondens cantat	Iste formosus in stola sua, gradiens in multitudine fortitudinis suae? [This beautiful one in his robe, walking in the greatness of his strength?]
Jesus cantat solus	Ego qui loquor justitiam et propugnator sum ad salvandum. [I that speak for justice and am a defender to save.]
Chorus cantat	Et vestimenta tua sicut calcantium in torculari. [And your garments like theirs that tread in the winepress.]

(SD after l. 104)[64]

The garments described here (as in Isaiah) refer to Jesus' skin, which has been stained red with his blood (having been 'dyed' in his earthly struggle against evil); the angels translate this for the audience when the Third Angel asks Jesus 'Whye ys thy cloathinge nowe so reedd, / thy bodye bloodye and also head, / thy clothes also, all that binne ledd, / like to pressars of wyne?' (ll. 121–4). The angel elides Jesus' skin and clothing, both of which are covered in his blood, as he asks Jesus to explain the meaning of his suffering. While Jesus' response initially echoes his pre- and post-resurrection speeches to the audience (explaining that the blood shows his great love for mankind), he concludes by making this blood his promise to mankind that they shall be restored to flesh at the Last Judgement. As in the Charter of Christ, Jesus' blood writes the promise upon his skin for everyone to see, emphasizing the dual meanings of his resurrected corporeality: first, his risen and living body presages the human bodies that will be at Judgement Day, and second, his tangible skin preserves for eternity the text his suffering has written upon it.

---

[62] Ibid., p. 450.

[63] Bestul notes that this passage from Isaiah was 'prominent in the Holy Week liturgy' (*Texts of the Passion*, p. 29).

[64] *The Chester Mystery Cycle*, ed. Lumiansky and Mills; hereafter, line numbers are given in parentheses.

In the Chester *Ascension,* Jesus' skin is described as both clothing and textual space. In the Passion plays his clothing of skin is gradually removed in order to release the soul to eternal life, yet as it is removed it undergoes a further transformation into parchment in order to preserve the enduring text that testifies to Jesus' human life and willing sacrifice. In the Passion plays the image of skin-as-textual-space is largely separate from that of skin-as-clothing; though both appear within the plays, they are used at different moments and, thus, seem to function as related but somewhat distinct ideas. Yet in the Chester *Ascension* the two images merge as the blood observed by the Third Angel records Christ's sacrifice onto his clothing, making his skin simultaneously garment and parchment. No longer needed to contain or define humanity, Jesus' human skin does not dissolve into dust like a sloughed-off snakeskin but is instead transformed into relics that endure and testify to the meaning of his life, death and resurrection.

On the stage, clothing and parchment are not merely symbols for skin but literal representations of it, and the language of the Chester *Ascension* suggests how those layered representations may have functioned. The angels' dialogue refers to both Isaiah's prophetic text and the tangible garments the actor-as-Christ is (likely) wearing; thus, the metaphoric image becomes literally enacted upon the stage. Yet this literal enactment is also a mystery in that it exists on the stage but not off it, just as the relics created through these plays represent but do not contain truth. The audience is presented with both biblical text and visual imagery that present and gloss the Christian mystery, but cannot replicate it. Like the Corpus Christi feast, for which many of these plays were originally created, the cycle plays present Christ's body as simultaneously literal and metaphorical, tangible and intangible. Though the flaying of his skin is not enacted on the stage, the language of the plays signifies the necessary transformation that has occurred. By the end of the Passion plays, Jesus' body has become 'flesche withowtyn hyde', and that hide that has been torn from his mortal body has become the testament of his suffering and sacrifice, and will soon be the proof of his triumph over death and his promise of everlasting life. Just as the Eucharistic host could be physically divided and consumed on Earth while remaining whole in Heaven, so Jesus' skin could be removed and transformed on stage without damaging his bodily and spiritual integrity. Throughout the cycles, flayed skin remains a mystery, able to transform the body and contain the soul, yet it is also tangible evidence of bodily presence that not only reflects the body and soul but also helps to define them both.

10

No Skin in the Game:
Flaying and Early Irish Law and Epic

William Sayers

THE flaying of the human body features only marginally in the traditions of early medieval Ireland. Ireland is celebrated for its precocious and rich medieval vernacular literature, prominent in which are the epic tales of cattle-raids, wooings, exiles and violent deaths.[1] Yet there was also a substantial body of literature written in Latin, saints' lives and homilies, as well as vernacular adaptations from comparable Latin sources. It is in this latter corpus that the motif of flaying finds its fullest expression, with debatable resonances in the native tradition. This spectacular process, combining cruelty and the possibility of entertainment, is one of the more garish reifications of the human body – a divestment of personal form and integrity, and a removal of that which envelops our head, limbs and trunk, like the dissolution of a human community through total cultural loss. In contrast to the disintegration implicit in flaying, early Ireland was culturally integrated and homogeneous, with a common literary language and corpus of tradition, lore and history, and displaying a distinct awareness of nationhood.

In the medieval Irish adaptation of a Latin version of the Greek martyrdom of the apostle Bartholomew that is found in a collection of New Testament apocrypha, the irate pagan king Astreges orders Bartholomew's execution after the apostle has converted his royal brother, Polymius, and brought about the destruction of the people's idols in Albanopolis, Armenia.[2]

Ro-dluig in rig a étach corcarda ann-sin, ⁊ atbert fri-a múintir, in t-apstal do thuarcain o shúnd ar tus ⁊ a fhennad iarum, ⁊ a dichendad o chloideb fa-deóid. Tancatar tra na sacairt ⁊ téglach in rig do shaigid in apstail iar sin, co r-thuaircset he di-a ndornu, ⁊ do flescaib némnechu ⁊ do sonnaib iarnaigib, co ro-erig a fheoil ⁊ a lethar de uli, ⁊ e-sium beos oc procept do'n popul ⁊ do lucht a marbtha fesin. Ro-fhendsat he iar sin, ⁊ bensat a chroicend de, amal cech n-anmunda n-indligtech, ⁊ ro-fhuaigset a chroicend imme doridisi co ndelgi spíne ⁊ sciach

---

[1] On this precocious early literature, see most recently Elva Johnston, *Literacy and Identity in Early Medieval Ireland* (Woodbridge: Boydell Press, 2013).

[2] General information on the legend of Bartholomew in John Francis Fenlon, 'St Bartholomew', *The Catholic Encyclopedia*, vol. 2 (New York: Robert Appleton Company, 1907), *s.n. Bartholomew*. The collection was earlier known as the Pseudo-Abdias.

eterru. Atberat araile co tartsat fair fén a chroicend do iumochar fiarut na cathrach, dia creicc for indmas doib-sium. Do-riacht tra aroile fer díb chuice iar-tain co cloideb lomm i n-a láim, ⁊ do-rat dar a bragait do'n apstal de, co nu-s-dichend he amal-sin.

[Thereat the king rent his purple garment and ordered his people to smite the apostle with a club first, and then to flay him, and in the end to behead him with the sword. So the priests and the king's household seized the apostle and buffeted him with their fists and with poisonous rods and with iron staves, so that all his flesh and his skin was torn from him, while he continued exhorting the people and his murderers; next they flayed him and stripped the skin from him as from a brute beast, and sewed his skin around him again with pins of spine and thorn. Some say they made him carry his skin all over the city to sell it for money for them. Finally, one of them came up to him with a naked sword in his hand, and made a stroke with it on the neck of the apostle and in that wise beheaded him.][3]

The exact source of the Irish version is not known, but it must have followed the branch of the multi-stranded Bartholomean tradition of late Antiquity in which the martyr is not only beaten and beheaded but also flayed alive. Through a rhetorical device often found in medieval Irish literature, the account is in two articulated parts: a prolepsis (the king's judgement and order) and its realization (the execution of the command).

---

[3] *The Passion of Bartholomew*, in *The Passions and the Homilies from Leabhar Breac: Text, Translation and Glossary*, ed. and trans. Robert Atkinson (Dublin: Hodges Figgis, 1887), text, pp. 95–101 at p. 101; trans. pp. 339–45 at p. 345. The composition of the *Leabhar Breac* is dated to the first decade of the fifteenth century. No exact Latin manuscript source has been preserved. From the Renaissance onwards, flaying was an attractive motif for artists, given its dramatic and unusual character. In 'The Last Judgement', Michelangelo lends his own features to the flayed skin carried by Bartholomew. The current scholarly vogue for studying the representation of the human body in literature is anticipated, for the medieval Irish material, in Doris Edel, '"Bodily Matters" in Early Irish Narrative Literature', *Zeitschrift für celtische Philologie* 55 (2006): 69–107. Sexual and execratory functions in Irish literature are the chief subjects, but Edel adduces texts dealing with the naked body, especially its lower half, that are relevant to present concerns (see further below). On human skin in the wider context of 'body literature', see the recent collection *Reading Skin in Medieval Literature and Culture*, ed. Katie L. Walter (New York: Palgrave, 2013), which does not, however, address any Celtic evidence. For analysis of artistic renderings of Bartholomew's flaying in this volume, see: Asa Simon Mittman and Christine Sciacca, 'Robed in Martyrdom: The Flaying of St Bartholomew in the Laudario of Sant'Agnese', pp. 140–72; and Sherry C. M. Lindquist, 'Masculinist Devotion: Flaying and Flagellation in the *Belles Heures*', pp. 173–207.

The three-part order was doubtless to be found in the Irish adapter's source but it accords well with the Irish literary practices of establishing triads, here 1) beating, 2) flaying and 3) beheading. The greater, second part of the account is a narrative amplification of the reported succinct royal command. The judgement will be executed with 1) a sub-triad of fists (animate), rods (organic) and iron stakes (non-organic); 2) knives or scrapers (not named); and 3) a simple sword.

Within this overall expansion, and after the multi-media beating that lacerates both skin and flesh, flaying and its consequences become objects of a sharpened focus. Two Irish verbs are employed to designate flaying – *fennaid* and *bensaid* – and both have applications beyond the removal of skin from a human body. *Fennaid*, with its narrower semantics ('to flay, strip'), figures in the king's command as a verbal noun (*fennad*, 'flaying') and is then repeated in an active form in the description of the actual punishment. *Benaid* means more generally 'to strike' and is used here in the phrase 'to strike skin off'.[4] The flaying process is not detailed and is likely incidental to its symbolic value. Nonetheless, the act of flaying Bartholomew is highlighted in several different fashions. In terms of narrative progression it is given an overriding parallel, as the text states that the apostle continued to preach during the gruesome process, the Word thereby acting against and in negation of the removal of a basic human attribute. The flaying of a human is also likened through an isolated but explicit simile to the skinning of an animal (*anmann*).[5] The adjective *indligtech*, which the editor translates as 'brute', also meant 'lawless, beyond the law'. This is a subtle suggestion that, for the Irish, flaying may be extra-legal, and, thus, an additional reason to condemn the pagans.

The grotesque reconstruction (the skin roughly reattached with thorns, which recalls Christ's crown of thorns) and the demonstrative dimension (the apostle forced to hawk his stripped skin through the city thronged with people) are among the further means of extending the central narrative moment of the martyrdom. This combination of skin, on the way to becoming an artefact and commodity, and the preached gospel anticipates the greater phenomenon of late Antiquity and the early Middle Ages: the preparation of vellum for the transcription of the divine Word. There is also a grim pun involving *croicenn* [skin] and *creicc* [selling, buying].[6] The apostle must peddle his skin as he had earlier pitched his doctrine. Robbed of his true identity, the future saint must engage in a masquerade as a public hawker. Despite Bartholomew being set up as a constructed being, in

---

[4] *Dictionary of the Irish Language* [*DIL*], ed E. G. Quin *et al.* (Dublin: Royal Irish Academy, 1913–76), *s.v. benaid.*

[5] For a further discussion on the juxtaposition of human and animal flaying in this volume, see: Renée Ward, '"Thou shalt have the better cloathe": Reading Second Skins in *Robin Hood and Guy of Gisborne*', pp. 349–65.

[6] *DIL, s.vv.*; the two ideas come together in skin used to make a money purse.

contrast to the fabricated idols that he cast down, the roughly reattached skin cannot restore to him the original functional distinction between inside and outside that is essential to selfhood. Skin mediates between the private being and the public. Yet for the apostolic Christian who has already risked all, selfhood is not important, nor does the subjective experience of physical pain count for much, save in its equation with Christ's passion. Rather, Christian faith and the Christian mission dominate all else. Likewise, the intended exemplary punishment and the following creation of a simulacrum, a reassembled human entity that is nonetheless a monstrous profanation of God's creation, ultimately provide a demonstration of a different kind, the power of faith over contingent secular event. The royally imposed flaying must then be judged a failure. Indeed, the narrative offers no rationale as to its inclusion in the public punishment, aside from potential gruesome entertainment value. The Irish reader is left to view flaying as at the boundaries of the conceivable. Yet, while the punishment of Bartholomew is seen as highly anomalous in experiential terms, the story fits well into early medieval Irish literary praxis and is consistent with both its biographical genre and its rhetoric.

A common device in early Irish letters is for the initial word of a poem to recur as the last. The practice is called *dúnad*, or 'closing', and could range in scale from a single word to an opening motif recalled at the end of a passage. Here, the scene opens with the king rending his clothing (dyed a royal purple) out of anger at the *lèse-majesté* represented by the activity of the Christian missionary. Bartholomew's more fundamental bodily covering is also rent. When he is dispatched through beheading, a punishment consonant with an offence to the head of state, it is with a single sword characterized as *lomm* [naked], a term otherwise used of closely mown or grazed fields, devastated or plundered land. The well-articulated description then ends with the cut skin of the neck and severed head recalling the torn clothing of the head of state.

The literary development accorded the flaying motif in the Irish passion of Bartholomew clearly reveals the redactor's basic familiarity with the process (one that all rural economies would have practised on livestock) but also, perhaps, a particular interest in the punitive removal of skin, unprecedented within the larger context of early medieval Irish society and letters. For, despite this full deployment of the flaying motif, the imported account of the martyrdom of the apostle Bartholomew is quite without parallel in early Irish legendary and hagiographical writing and – even more striking – in the immeasurably greater corpora of epic narrative and legal texts. The former absence is the more readily explained, since the fifth-century missions of Palladius, Patrick and their *confrères* are depicted in later medieval sources as so immediately successful by virtue of eloquence and miracles alone, among both the Irish people and their rulers, that no missionary was obliged to die for his faith. Native Irish martyrs do not appear until the sixteenth century, as a consequence of Henry VIII's persecution of Roman Catholics.

Flaying in the European tradition – other than as a medium of Christian martyrdom – is generally associated with treason, the betrayal of one's country or polity and – a subsumed crime – disloyalty towards the head of state. Public flaying was imagined as having the potential for a horrific spectacle, as a depersonalization and dehumanization of the condemned through the loss of a fundamental human body feature even before death. The horror seems to aspire to the same scale as the offence for which it is the punishment, when state has become too large for effective personal relations, positive or negative, to suffice. Early Ireland, however, was divided into as many as 150 small kingdoms, with some rulers exercising hegemony over several tribes as great kings; occasionally one of these would accumulate sufficient power and influence to lay a claim to the high kingship, but that was never a particularly effectual office. As Proinsias Mac Cana has shown, this political pluralism, with little perceived need for unification, coordination and centralized executive power, was accompanied (perhaps complemented) by a thorough-going cultural unity: 'In the primitive Irish view of things political cohesion and centralism were evidently not in themselves an unquestionable social good, and the underlying social principle was one of co-ordination rather than consolidation.'[7] The apparent paradox is illustrated by the status of poets and men of art. Normally, one was without legal protection beyond the borders of one's own kingdom, unless sureties had been negotiated and given. But poets had immunity: the common language, the pre-eminence of their art and their distinctive dress according them an undisputed right of passage. Nonetheless, local and localized patronage remained important. Petty warfare, most often in the form of cross-border raids for slaves and cattle, was endemic. Intra-dynastic politics were equally volatile and bloody. Mac Cana would claim that early Ireland qualifies as a 'nation' on the grounds of a high degree of self-awareness and self-esteem, and of this cultural homogeneity. Royal institutions were incarnated in a king's senior officers, such as the steward (Ir. *rechtaire*). The pre-Norman state was never big, nor cohesive enough to demand and enforce submission to its authority. Authority was vested primarily in common law; kinship counted for more than professed allegiance. As a consequence, political expediency was always a prime consideration. With no sense of the state, there could be no sense of treason, though this situation would change with the Normans' introduction of legal punishment for this offence. Disloyalty was punished in battle, personal grudges in feud, not in the courts, and only exceptionally by royal fiat. Yet, *de iure* if not *de facto*, early medieval Irishmen would probably have said that legitimate sovereignty, the right and the qualities to rule, counted for even more than such kin- and tribe-based allegiance.

---

[7] Proinsias Mac Cana, *The Cult of the Sacred Centre: Essays on Celtic Ideology* (Dublin: Dublin Institute for Advanced Studies, 2011), p. 2.

The fundamental question is, then, how a medieval Irish public might have understood and reacted to the vernacular account of the martyrdom of Bartholomew, from within a culture that authorized the taking and preservation of rivals' heads, and given a literary and legal tradition which itemized the phenomena of armed conflict and legal offence in the minute detail of individual blows. The rich Irish legal literature is the logical body of texts in which to begin to seek an answer.

In D. A. Binchy's celebrated phrasing, early Ireland was 'tribal, rural, hierarchical and familiar [family-oriented]'.[8] The vast body of early medieval Irish law-texts originates in the seventh and eighth centuries and survives in manuscripts from the fourteenth to sixteenth centuries in often incomplete and corrupt form.[9] As Fergus Kelly writes, 'law-texts, wisdom-texts, sagas, histories, praise-poetry, annals, genealogies, saints' lives, religious poetry, penitentials and monastic rules all add in different ways to our understanding of early Irish society'.[10] These sources are mutually illuminating and all contribute to addressing such specific and still ill-documented aspects of the Irish *mentalité* as the world-view of pagan Ireland, which was as much overlaid as replaced by the Christianization of the country, beginning in the fifth century. The law-texts devoted to the law of persons and to offences are organized along two great coordinates: 1) the social rank and honour-price of the persons implicated, for example in the sphere of personal injury and the subsequent punishment of the guilty; 2) the practical function and often symbolic importance of the body part that is subject to injury, or even insult. Two skin-related examples illustrate how the legal system worked: 'For a grain-sized wound in the face, the lowest grade of king (*rí túaithe*) is paid 6 scruples and 2½ *séts*. An *inol* (apprentice?) with no master receives only one fleece for the same wound.'[11] Even though these injuries fall far short of the wholesale removal of skin, the rupture of the integument has serious consequences.

Within the legal framework to public life, verbal assault was taken very seriously. Irish speakers believed that satire raised blisters on the face of its victims, and thus counted as a source of disfigurement. Yet this is never likened to flaying. Blisters, in turn, suggested to others that one had been satirized (perhaps justly), and thus were an additional source of shame. Honour is closely tied to skin condition. *Face* in English and its Irish counterpart, *enech*, both serve as symbolic terms relating to status, reputation and respect,[12] suggesting that personhood in Ireland, in its both

---

[8] D. A. Binchy as quoted in Fergus Kelly, *A Guide to Early Irish Law* (Dublin: Dublin Institute for Advanced Studies, 1982), p. 3.

[9] Kelly, *Guide to Early Irish Law*, p. 1.

[10] Ibid.

[11] Ibid, p. 132; for the approximate values of these units of currency, see: p. 114.

[12] For discussions of flaying the face and beard as markers of masculinity and identity, see: Michael Livingston, 'Losing Face: Flayed Beards and

personal and public recognition, was closely tied to the external appearance of the face, body and clothing.

Notwithstanding a well-developed law of persons, the family was the key social unit, not the individual, so that fines and penalties were of consequence for the kin-group, not just the offender. Penalties commonly took the form of restitution rather than punishment. Still, legally sanctioned punishments included fines, execution (through hanging, confinement in pits, killing by sword, spear and axe), outlawry, setting adrift on the sea and, in a limited number of attested instances (all of relatively late date), various forms of mutilation. Old Irish secular laws make no mention of mutilation,[13] though some Church-inspired texts have the amputation of a hand or foot among prescribed sanctions. Ironically, Christian canon law has more provisions for capital punishment than traditional secular law.[14] It would, however, be imprudent to conclude that body mutilation was alien to pre-Christian Ireland and that such punishments were introduced along with Christian culture. According to the annals, political rivals were debarred from the kingship by forced, extra-legal tonsure, blinding or castration, impairments that would disqualify a candidate both from the role of head of state, and from serving as a generational link in a political dynasty, because of the violation of bodily integrity.[15]

Of greater relevance to the question of flaying, flogging with rods, leather straps or whips is often treated in the early law codes of many cultures, particularly as a punishment for slaves.[16] Yet, again, in contrast to the *comparanda* offered by other communities, in Ireland the recorded provisions and instances of flogging as a punishment – a humiliating violation of the integrity of what enfolds a human being – are limited to early Irish penitential literature, that is, texts of an ecclesiastical cast, like

Gendered Power in Arthurian Literature', pp. 308–21, and Larissa Tracy, 'Face Off: Flaying and Identity in Medieval Romance', pp. 322–48, both in this volume.

[13] Kelly, *Guide to Early Irish Law*, p. 221.

[14] Ibid., p. 216. For a discussion of early English injury tariffs see: *Capital and Corporal Punishment in Anglo-Saxon England*, ed. Jay Paul Gates and Nicole Marafioti (Woodbridge: Boydell Press, 2014).

[15] On the most common of these, forced tonsure, see: William Sayers, 'Early Irish Attitudes towards Hair and Beards, Baldness and Tonsure', *Zeitschrift für celtische Philologie* 44 (1991): 154–89, for the Irish legendary material; and Robert Bartlett, 'Symbolic Meanings of Hair in the Middle Ages', *Transactions of the Royal Historical Society* 6.4 (1994): 43–60, for a wider view of Britain and Western Europe. On castration and blinding, see: Charlene M. Eska, '"Imbrued in their owne bloud": Castration in Early Welsh and Irish Sources', in *Castration and Culture in the Middle Ages*, ed. Larissa Tracy (Cambridge: D. S. Brewer, 2013), pp. 149–73.

[16] Kelly, *Guide to Early English Law*, p. 221.

the martyrdom of Bartholomew.[17] For example, a thieving cleric is to be beaten with rods according to the *Penitential of Finnian*.[18] Categorically, Fergus Kelly, one of the foremost experts in early Irish law, states: 'I have found no references to flogging in the Old Irish law-texts.'[19] But it should be borne in mind that a conjuncture of base person, base crime and appropriately base punishment may have resulted in the punishment of slaves being largely ignored by the clearly elitist Irish law-texts. Kelly writes: '[The slave] has no legal protection against ill-treatment or even death at the hands of his master. His master must pay for any crime which he commits, and is entitled to compensation for offences committed against him.'[20] This is grimly but economically illustrated in the use of Old Irish *cumal* [female slave] as a unit of currency. The rather striking absence of flogging in the literary record extends to flaying as a potential punishment for violations of secular or canon law. Flaying is inevitably fatal and, thus, even when imposed on a slave would represent an economic loss, whatever its demonstrative value as a deterrent against other insubordinate or faulty behaviour or as a reassertion of power and authority.

While flaying is absent from the legal literature of early Ireland, its nature suggests affinities with martial activity, which generally has the human body as a first target of violence. The epic literature of early Ireland offers a picture consonant with the legal texts, indicating the high value attached to human skin, and the problems of its removal. Skin is the first victim of warfare. Before the sword cuts flesh and breaks bone, it rends the skin.[21] Thus, in the paramount epic of old Ireland, *Táin bó Cúailgne* (*The Cattle-Raid of Cooley*), the Ulster hero Cú Chulainn dissuades Etarcomol (a callow youth) from meeting him in single combat by slicing his clothing from his body

---

[17] One of the most striking scenes in early Irish literature is found in *Serglige Con Culainn* (*The Wasting-sickness of Cú Chulainn*), in which the hero is punished and, more importantly, humiliated by 'bird women' from the Otherworld for having hunted them in their avian form. He is beaten with a horse-whip as the women laugh at his plight. This leads to a comatose state; *Serglige Con Culainn*, ed. Myles Dillon (Dublin: Dublin Institute for Advanced Studies, 1953), ll. 74–5. On the Otherworld, see the revised perspective in William Sayers, 'Netherworld and Otherworld in Early Irish Literature', *Zeitschrift für celtische Philologie* 59 (2012): 201–30.

[18] Kelly, *Guide to Early English Law*, p. 222 n. 41.

[19] Ibid., p. 222.

[20] Ibid., p. 95.

[21] A wonder-working spear is crafted by the smith Goibniu in *Cath Maige Tuired* (*The Battle of Mag Tuired*), ed. and trans. Elizabeth Gray (Dublin: Irish Texts Society, 1982). It is presented with the following phrasing: '"Nach rind degéno mo lám-so", ol sé, "ní focertar imrold de. Nach cnes i ragae noco blasfe bethaid de íer sin"' (ll. 471–2) [No spearpoint which my hand forges will make a missing cast. No skin which it pierces will taste life afterward], p. 51.

without cutting his skin (*ní forbai ima chnes*).[22] Among the innumerable personnel of the epic is a prominent warrior among the forces of Connacht, Fer Diad, who has a *congancnes* [horn-skin] that weapons cannot pierce. Within lines of this descriptive detail, he is plied with drink, promised aristocratic sex and shamed by the threat of satire into confronting his former brother-in-arms, Cú Chulainn, in single combat.[23] The horn-skin is thought to make him invulnerable to the blows of Cú Chulainn, the sole representative of the forces of Ulster in the war. But this hero has recourse to an ignoble weapon known only to him, the *gáe bolga* [bag spear], which is cast through the water, enters the anus of its target, and expands into twenty-four barbed points. Impermeable skin is then met with treachery and evisceration.[24] This association of skin and the lower body, the locus of evacuation and procreation, is not merely fortuitous, for this linking is sustained in other texts. Evisceration guts the body rather than stripping it, effecting disintegration from within. As the possible result of a well-placed blow to the body, such disembowelment is plausible, if not common, on the battlefield, while the labour-intensive process of flaying is not.

Skin is fully implicated in another narrative moment, yet goes without explicit mention. At the close of *Togail Bruidne Da Derga* (*The Destruction of Da Derga's Hostel*) the Ulster hero Conall Cernach has returned to his father's home after the attack on, and death of, King Conaire outside the hostel of Da Derga.

Tadbaid a láim scéith. Trí .l. créchta imorro is ed ad-comaicc furri. In scíath imarro imarro-dídnestair ind lám sin is ed rus-anacht. Ind lám des imorro imo-robrad for suidiu co rrice a dí chutramai. Ro cirrad imorro ⁊ ro hathchumad ⁊ ro créchdnaiged ⁊ ro chríathrad acht congaibset na féthe frisin corp cen a etarscarad innát raba in scíath oca himdedail.[25]

[He showed his father his shield arm and the three fifties of wounds that had been inflicted upon it. His shield had protected that hand, but it had not protected his right hand. That had been attacked over

[22] *Táin bó Cúailgne: Recension I*, ed. and trans. Cecile O'Rahilly (Dublin: Dublin Institute for Advanced Studies, 1976), l. 1354.

[23] Ibid., ll. 2571–6.

[24] Ibid., ll. 3095–100. The ignoble weapon is also used as an expedient in another ethical and martial dilemma, a betrayal of kinship. In *Aided Óenfir Aífe* (*The Violent Death of Aoífe's Only Son*), in defense of Ulster's honour, Cú Chulainn deploys it against his son, Connla, whom he is seeing for the first time. *Aided Óenfir Aífe*, in *Compert Con Culainn and other Stories*, ed. A. G. van Hamel (Dublin: Dublin Institute for Advanced Studies, 1933), pp. 9–15.

[25] *Togail Bruidne Da Derga*, ed. Eleanor Knott (Dublin: Stationery Office, 1936), ll. 1527–34. This edition follows the text as found in *The Yellow Book of Lecan*, from the early fifteenth century.

two thirds of its length; it had been hacked and cut and wounded and riddled, but the sinews had not permitted it to fall off.][26]

Here sinew, flesh, and bone are seen as the essentials of a sword arm; skin is the incidental wrapper and, in convalescence, the easiest element to heal.

Rupture of the skin is also a primary concern in the epic *Scéla Mucce Meic Da Thó* (*The Story of Mac Da Thó's Pig*). The hosts of Ulster and Connacht have been invited to the same feast by the hosteller Mac Da Thó in the hope that they will fight out their respective claims to Mac Da Thó's hound, which both envy. Contention finds its origin in rival claims to the *curad mír* or 'champion's portion', the choice cut of pork from the cooking vat. The Connachtman Cet mac Magach boldly asserts his right to the prime cut and verbally bests each of the other contenders who raise a rival claim by recalling the injuries he has inflicted on them or members of their family in recent skirmishes along the border. In sequence these are: a spear thrust, a severed hand, a blinded eye, decapitation of a first-born son, a severed foot and pierced testicles – but, again, no reference to skin. Skin is, however, implied and included in each greater injury in this ordered sequence, which escalates in importance from non-descript injury to the loss of procreative ability and, thus, of a family's future.[27]

In *Togail Bruidne Da Derga*, before the concluding combat, the host assembled within the hostel is observed by an enemy scout who reports back to his leader and whose descriptions of what he has seen within are the subject of lengthy commentaries by a knowledgeable third party, who predicts the warlike acts that those observed will perform in the conflict. The narrative, reminiscent of the martyrdom of Bartholomew in this respect, proceeds in three stages: 1) description (implying potentiality) of the agents; 2) prediction of events to be carried out; 3) the account of the actual battle. But even the most outlandish and monstrous of these observed warriors, whatever injury they are capable of inflicting, will stop short of stripping their opponents of their skin:

> 'At-connarc and imdae ⁊ triar indi. [...] Imda-gní gethar gelt clithargarb finna connach a chuirp im chanag rind a ruisc roamnais tria froech finnu ferb. Cen étaigi imthaigi co certsála sís. [...] Béim búirid fri teora sústa iarnae cona secht slabradaib tredúalchaib trechisi

---

[26] *The Destruction of Da Derga's Hostel*, in *Early Irish Myths and Sagas*, trans. Jeffrey Gantz (London: Penguin, 1981), pp. 60–106 at p. 106. Numerous thumbnail portraits of Conall spread throughout the epic corpus give an unusually nuanced, almost individual picture of a complex of physical attributes; see: William Sayers, 'Portraits of the Ulster Hero Conall Cernach: A Case for Waardenburg's Syndrome?' *Emania* 20 (2006): 75–80. While hair and eyes are singled out, skin is not.

[27] *Scéla Mucce Meic Da Thó*, ed. Rudolph Thurneysen (Dublin: Stationery Office, 1935), pars. 10–14. The severed foot prefigures other lower-body injuries with procreative and generational consequences.

cona secht cendphartaib iarnaib i cind cecha slabraidi [...] m-bruit damnae cach n-ae.' '[...] con-raindfet comgním fri cach triar 7 día tuidchisead foraib imach bid indtechta tria críathar n-átha bar mbrúar la indas do-fíurad cosnaib sústaib iairn.'[28]

['I saw an apartment with three men in it. [...] Rough-haired garments all about them and no other clothing on them from head to toe. [...] Each bore an iron flail with seven chains; each chain was twisted into three strands, and each had at its end a knob as heavy as a bar for lifting ten pieces of burning metal. Huge oxhides they wore.' [...] 'They will match the performance of any trio in the hostel; if they encounter you, your fragments will pass through a corn sieve after they have destroyed you with their iron flails.'][29]

As seen in the martyrdom of Bartholomew, flaying produces a gory artefact that can then be manipulated and displayed in various fashions. While early Irish warriors did take body parts as trophies from the battlefield, skin alone was not central. On his return from his initiatory foray, for which he has been armed by his uncle King Conchobar, the youthful Cú Chulainn bears the three severed heads of the son of Nechta Scéne at his belt.[30] Heads were preserved and shown off, not so much to humiliate in death their former bearers as to highlight a warrior's prowess and intimate that he had absorbed the strength and spirit of his opponent, since in the early Celtic worldview the head was seen as the seat of the human spirit.[31] Cranial matter was removed from skulls and apparently mixed with crushed lime to make brain-balls, also displayed as trophies but capable of being used as missiles as well. Indeed, King Conchobar is struck in the head by such a ball.[32] Tongues were also taken as trophies, linking the body part to speech and such communications as boast, oath, praise and blame. Yet there is no instance of a flayed skin being cured and preserved as a battle trophy. One could imagine the removal of the outward sign of personhood, flaying, as the ultimate humiliation in early Ireland, but no evidence is at hand. Humiliation was not an objective in either legal punishment, where restitution was paramount, or war, save in revenge tales.[33]

---

[28] *Togail Bruidne Da Derga*, ll. 1262–96.

[29] *The Destruction of Da Derga's Hostel*, p. 98.

[30] *Macgnímrada* (*The Boyhood Deeds*), in *Táin bó Cúailgne*, ll. 756–8.

[31] On the practice of beheading, see most recently *Heads Will Roll: Decapitation in the Medieval and Early Modern Imagination*, ed. Larissa Tracy and Jeff Massey (Leiden: Brill, 2012). Celtic material is treated there in Larissa Tracy, '"So he smote of hir hede by myssefortune": The Real Price of the Beheading Game in *SGGK* and Malory', pp. 207–34.

[32] *The Death of Conchobar*, in *Death Tales of the Ulster Heroes*, ed. and trans. Kuno Meyer (Dublin: Hodges Figgis, 1906), pp. 343–6.

[33] When Cú Chulainn's head is severed after a defeat occasioned by magic and poison, his hand drops his sword, which cuts off an enemy hand; in

What might be called the quintessential warrior conception of the human body as the agent and target of martial activity is found in *Táin bó Cúailgne*, in an oath that the Ulster hero Fergus, in exile among the Connachtmen, swears regarding what he would do if his purloined sword were returned to him so that he might enter battle:

> Is and sin dorad Fergus in lugu sa: 'Tongu et reliqua mebsaitis lim-sa glaini fer dia m-bráigde, bráigde fear la n-dóite, dóite fer la n-uille, uille fer la rigthe, rigthe fer la n-dorndaib, dornna fer la méra, méra fer la n-ingne, ingne fer la forcléthi, forcléthi fer la medón, medón fer la slíasta, slíasta fer la n-glúne, glúne fer la colp*th*a, colpthai fer la traigthe, traigthi fer la méra, méra fer la n-i*n*gne. Doruchtfaid a méderad na h-áeru feib dodrimsired beach i l-ló áinle'. Is and sin asbert Ailill re araid: 'Domiced in claideb cuilleis toind.'

> [Then Fergus swore this oath: 'I swear by my people's oath, that I would strike men's jawbones from their necks, men's necks from their shoulders, men's shoulders from elbows, men's elbows from forearms, men's forearms and their fists, men's fists and their fingers, men's fingers and their nails, men's nails and the crowns of their heads, men's crowns and their trunks, men's trunks and their thighs, men's thighs and their knees, men's knees and their calves, men's calves and their feet, men's feet and their toes, men's toes and their nails. Their headless necks would sound in the air like a bee flying to and fro on a day of fine weather.' Then Ailill said to his charioteer: 'Bring me the sword that cuts flesh.'][34]

Fergus' oath offers a comprehensive 'head to toes' list of external body parts, seen in a complex of mostly articulated joints, rather than as bone and muscle enclosed in skin. It is not the visible exterior that is emphasized but the interior, kinetic potential (e.g., arm movement) lying below the passive skin. As a taxonomy, the enumeration consists of externally visible bodily parts marked off by the articulations of the skeleton; there are, for example, no organs or references to non-material life forces such as soul, spirit or courage – and no reference to skin. These body parts are used

---

retribution his own hand is severed. *Aided Con Culainn*, in *The Death-Tales of the Ulster Heroes*, pp. 333–40.

[34] *Táin bó Cúailgne*, ll. 4009–16; fuller discussion in William Sayers, 'Fergus and the Cosmogonic Sword', *History of Religions* 25 (1985): 30–56; and 'Pre-Christian Cosmogonic Lore in Medieval Ireland: The Exile into Royal Poetics', *Archiv für Religionsgeschichte* 14 (2012): 109–26. For further recent comment on this passage and the status of the body in early Irish literature see: Tomás Ó Cathasaigh, 'The Body in *Táin bó Cúailgne*', *Gablánach in Scélaigecht: Celtic Studies in Honour of Ann Dooley*, ed. Sarah Sheehan, Joanne Findon and Westley Follett (Dublin: Four Courts Press, 2013), pp. 131–53.

metonymically in Irish as units of measure, legal terms and so on.[35] Among the most revealing of these is *glún* [knee], which also meant 'generation, degree of consanguinity'.[36] The individual words are here used in their common, everyday sense, though the oath framework and its organization raise the whole sequence to the level of stylized, ritual discourse, giving extraordinary prominence to the human body as a cosmological essential.

The emphasis in Fergus' oath is not on killing and death as a terminal act and state. The conscious, comprehensive naming and ordering, thus re-creation and reassembly, of body parts in an oath sworn by a tribal tutelary figure or culture hero is a litany suggestive of a ritual dismemberment of a sacrificial human victim with 'the sword that cuts flesh'. As such, it has specific cosmogonic overtones. Given the gigantic size of Fergus mac Roích, all the men who are his intended victims can be taken collectively, and the Ulster host likened to a single giant being.[37] The practice of human sacrifice among the Continental Celts as documented by classical authors may be linked to conceptions of a cosmos constructed of the body parts of an originary giant being.

The Irish evidence for ritual dismemberment, even if admitted only on the conceptual level and not as an actual practice, can be matched by a complementary vision of the reassignment and reassembly of human body parts. Indian tradition, as found in the *Rig-Veda*, offers a striking parallel to the Irish account. In the first sacrifice the gods create the world from a primeval male giant, Purusha. From his mind is formed the moon, from his eye the sun and from his breath the wind. His head, navel and feet correspond respectively to the heavens, the atmosphere and the earth. The social order and the four social classes are also formed from his body: The Brahmans from his mouth, the warriors from his arms, the people from his thighs and the servants from his feet. Thus constituted, mankind has a thousand heads, eyes and feet and pervades the entire earth, even extending beyond it the length of ten fingers. Also deriving from this first sacrifice, and maintained through all repetitions of it, are seasonal time, sacred verse, its metres and formulas and religious ritual – all examples

---

[35] Early *literati* were keenly interested in Irish etymology. But they favoured the Isidorean model, where a word was split into constituent elements, over other organic images such as peeling a rind from a core. The Irish term *etarscarad* [cutting apart] then brings the study of language into the same conceptual sphere as Fergus' oath of dismemberment.

[36] Cf. the lower-body and leg wounds in *Scéla Mucce Meic Da Thó*.

[37] The name *Fergus* has been etymologized as based on Old Irish *fer* [man] + *gus* [force, vigour]. It seems a near-synonym of Irish *ferdoman* ('the makings of a man; legal minor'; cf. the Old Norse counterpart and man's name *Karlsefni*), and thus offers a close correspondence to the primal giant being implicit in Fergus' oath.

of the ordering of existence.[38] The Norse gods sacrificed the giant Ymir in comparable fashion. From his flesh they fashioned the earth, from his blood the ocean, from his bones the hills, from his hair the trees, from his brains the clouds, from his skull the heavens and from his eyebrows the middle realm in which mankind lives.[39] Despite the evident parallel to flaying as the conscious manipulation of the body, none of the creation myths of these three early cultures with a common Indo-European heritage singles out skin (as distinct from flesh) as generative of an element of the cosmos or the earth known to mankind, despite the close attention paid to the violation of such detail of the human body as cranial and facial hair.[40] This is well illustrated in Irish epic literature in the treatment of human–animal homologues.

Táin bó Cúailgne has its origins in the rivalry between two swineherds, who later assume taurine form. Given the myriad applications of animal skin, the fate of the two giant bulls is relevant in the context of Fergus' oath of dismemberment and its mirroring of cosmogonic acts. The bulls meet in a cataclysmic combat at the end of the epic. The Ulster bull, Donn Cúailgne [Dark One of Cooley], defeats the bull of Connacht, Finnbennach [Whitehorn], but the outcome is not that the loser is slaughtered, flayed and its hide put to some symbolic purpose, the ideal of which, from our modern perspective, would be to generate a vellum for recording the epic in the kind of self-referential loop so favoured by the Irish.[41] Rather, the bulls simply tear one another apart in true warrior fashion, which has an effect on the surrounding topography and toponymy,

---

[38] The myth of Purusha (Vedic hymn 10.90) is most readily available to English readers in *The Rig Veda: An Anthology, 108 Hymns Translated from the Sanskrit*, trans. Wendy Doniger O'Flaherty (New York: Penguin Books, 1981), pp. 29–32.

[39] See, among other sources for the myth of Ymir: Snorri Sturluson, *Gylfaginning*, in *Edda: Skáldskaparmál*, ed. Anthony Faulkes, 2 vols. ([London]: Viking Society for Northern Research, 1998), chap. 8.

[40] See: Sayers, 'Early Irish Attitudes'.

[41] In the epic tale *The Fate of the Children of Tuirenn* one of the supposedly impossible quests that the sons of Tuirenn are assigned in a compensation case is to recover, from the King of Greece, a pigskin that is a panacea for all ills. The text is explicit that it is not the pig that is (or was) so empowered, but only the skin; *The Fate of the Children of Tuirenn*, ed. and trans. Eugene O'Curry, *The Atlantis* 4 (1863): 157–240, excerpted in *Ancient Irish Tales*, ed. Tom Peete Cross and Clark Harris Slover, 2nd edn (New York: Barnes & Noble, 1969), pp. 49–81 at p. 62. Shape-shifting is well represented in Irish literature, often non-volitional. Skin is not singled out for description, but rather the overall form of the wolf, dog, or even insect is emphasized. In *The Fate of the Children of Tuirenn*, a man strikes himself with a wand and turns into a pig to evade pursuit (p. 54). Cf. Susan Small, 'Flesh and Death in Early Modern Bedburg', pp. 71–90, and Frederika Bain, 'Skin on Skin: Wearing Flayed Remains', pp. 116–37, both in this volume.

so that sites are later called by such names as *Finnleithe* [White(-y's) shoulder-blade]; *Áth Lúain* [ford of the loin]; and *Troma* < *trom* [liver].[42] Thus, the sacrifice and deconstruction of the bulls, representative of the forces of Ulster and Connacht, have the same results as the myth to which Fergus' oath alludes: the creation and shaping of the land. Yet here, too, the bulls' hides make no explicit contribution to topography or toponymy. The removal and subsequent deployment of skin never rises in Irish tradition to the level of a mythic motif.

One explanation for the absence of flaying in the early Irish historical and literary record is prompted by the Irish, Norse and Indian creation stories. In the basic paradigm, the different parts of the primal body become various parts of the known cosmos. The stories display the same somewhat whimsical attention to minutiae and the ephemeral: fingernails (Irish), eyebrows (Norse) and breath (Indian). It may have been that skin, although an important culturally marked 'wrapper' and fundamental to perceptions of beauty and good health, was not seen as a discrete entity, was not seen as an agent in human life. From this perspective it can be appreciated that skin is difficult to handle conceptually.[43] Today scientists classify skin as a distinct organ, but for earlier cultures it may have been seen simply as the covering or envelope of other, more recognizably distinct parts of the body such as the hand, arm or torso. The lack of agency may also have strengthened the association of skin in its totality with the lower classes and their very limited autonomy. A tale of the granting of sovereignty to a king-elect illustrates the link between unwholesome skin and subaltern status.

The identification of an individual with the makings of a just king, a relatively common motif in early Irish literature, is often achieved through a test in which the suitable candidate for the kingship is recognized by a sovereignty figure representing both legitimate rule and the land over which the king will rule. In an early European instance of the *puella senex*, or loathly lady, motif the young Níall and his half-brothers each meet an ugly hag at a well, but only Níall is willing to grant her a kiss in return for water; indeed, he is willing to lie with her. This prefigures the *hieros gamos* that underlies legitimate rule. A lengthy description of the hideous hag gives way to an account of her transformation into a beautiful young woman. These two passages reveal a keen interest in bone, flesh and skin, but in subtly different ways:

---

[42] *Táin bó Cúailgne*, ll. 4140–5.

[43] Pain occupies a comparable category in current discourse. Pain is invisible, save perhaps to modern brain imaging. All experience and, thus, appreciation are subjective; there is no agreed-on terminology of description, leaving simile and metaphor as the only recourse. See: Elaine Scarry, *The Body in Pain: The Making and Unmaking of the World* (Oxford: Oxford University Press, 1985).

Is amlaid bui in chaillech, co mba duibithir gual cech n-alt ⁊ cach
n-aigi di o mullach co talmain. Ba samalta fri herboll fiadeich in
mong glas gaisidech ba tria cleithi a cheandmullaich. Consealgad
glasgeg darach fo brith dia corran glaisfiacla bai 'na cind co roichead
a hou. Suli duba dethaighe le, sron cham chuasach. Medon fethech
brecbaindech ingalair le, ⁊ luirgi fiara fochama siad, adbronnach
leathansluaistech si, glunmar glaisingnech. Ba grain tra a tuarascbail
na cailligi. […] Tairnid fuirri iarsin ⁊ dobeir poic di. Antan immorro
ro shill fuirri iarsin ni raibi forsin domun ingen bid chaime tachim
nó tuarascbail inda si. Ba samalta fri dered snechta i claidib cach
n-alt o ind co bond di. Rigthi remra rignaidhe lé. Méra seta sithlebra.
Colpta dirgi dathailli le. Da maelasa findruine iter a troigthib mine
maethgela ⁊ lar. Brat logmarda lancorcra impi. Bretnass gelairgit i
timthach in bruit. Fiacla niamda nemannda le, ⁊ rosc rignaide romor,
⁊ beoil partardeirg.[44]

[This is how the hag looked: as black as charcoal was her every part
and her every joint from the top of her head down to the ground.
Like the tail of a wild horse was the bristling grey shock of hair that
sprouted from the crown of her head. The acorn-laden live branch
of an oak would have been severed by the sickle of green teeth that
stretched around her head to her ears. She had smoke-dark eyes
and her nose was crooked, with cave-like nostrils. Her body was all
sinewy and spotted with festering sores, and her shins were bowed
and crooked. Her knees were swollen, her ankles knobby, her green-
nailed feet as wide as shovels. The appearance of the hag was truly
loathsome. […] Then he throws himself down on her and gives her
a kiss. But then, when he looked at her, there was not in the wide
world a maiden whose bearing or appearance was more attractive
than hers. Like fresh-fallen snow in the rays of the sun was every
part of her from crown to sole. Full and regal were her forearms, her
fingers long and tapering, her legs straight and fair-skinned. Two
square-toed shoes of white metal between her little soft-white feet
and the ground. She wore a rich, deep-purple mantle, with a brooch
of polished silver holding the fold. She had bright, lustrous teeth,
large and queenly eyes, and lips as red as Parthian leather.]

The encounter concludes with this exchange: '"Is ilreachtach sin, a bean,
ol in mac." "Fir on", ol si. "Cia tusu?" or in mac. "Misi in Flaithius", ol si.'
['Many a guise, woman', said the lad. 'True enough', she said. 'Just who
are you', he said. 'I am Sovereignty', she said.][45] The diseased appearance

----

[44] Whitley Stokes, ed. and trans., 'The Death of Crimthann, and the
Adventures of Eochaid', *Revue Celtique* 24 (1903): 172–207 at pp. 196, 198,
200.

[45] My translation, based on Stokes. In 'The Anatomy of Power and the
Miracle of Kingship: The Female Body of Sovereignty in a Medieval Irish

of the skin is stressed in the portrayal of ugliness, but health and firmness of flesh are the salient points of the description of beauty and, thus, of sovereignty. Proof of Níall's kingly qualities results in the sovereignty figure sloughing off her base guise and appearing as a near-goddess, as diseased skin is replaced by healthy, without, however, any explicit evocation of flaying.

A comparable description of female beauty is found in stories associated with Étaín, the mother of Conaire (in *Togail Bruidne Da Derga*), who has several hypostases in Irish narrative and is subject to multiple rebirths, each time equally beautiful.[46] Again there is a slight emphasis on complexion and skin at the expense of flesh and bone, and on the lower body and legs. As illustrated in the portrait of Étaín, Old Irish used *tonn* [wave, foam]

Kingship Tale', *Speculum* 81.4 (2006): 1014–54, Amy C. Eichhorn-Mulligan argues that the description of the hag points to leprosy. Whatever the correspondence on points of detail, this is to miss the larger symbolism of the images in the portrait. The decay of advanced age, ill-health, darkened complexion, twisted limbs, which stand for the lack of both rectitude and rectilinearity, represent a land without a just and effective king and, by extension, a rule that, from the cosmic perspective, is illegitimate and inauthentic. On the pervasive early Irish image of bias, non-alignment, slantedness or crookedness as negative qualities that could affect royal rule, the administration of justice, the prosperity of the land and even its topography, see: William Sayers, '*Cláen Temair*: Sloping Tara', *Mankind Quarterly* 32 (1992): 241–60.

[46] 'Is and buí oc taithbiuch a fuilt dia folcud 7 a dá láim tria derc a sedlaig immach. Batar gilithir sneachta n-oenaichde na dí dóit 7 batar maethchóiri 7 batar dergithir sían slébe na dá grúad n-glanáilli. Badar duibithir druimne daeil na dá malaich. Batar inand 7 frais do némannaib a déta ina cind. Batar glasithir buga na dí súil. Batar dergithir partaing na beóil. Batar forarda míne maethgela na dá gúalaind. Batar gelglana sithfhota na méra. Batar fota na láma. Ba gilithir úan tuindi in taeb seng fota tláith mín maeth amal olaind. Batar teithbláithi sleamongeala na dí slíasait. Batar cruindbega caladgela na dí glún. Batar gerrgela indildírgi na dé lurgain. Batar coirdírgi íaráildi na dá sáil. Cid ríagail fo-certa forsna traigthib is ing má 'd-chotad égoir n-indib acht ci tórmaisead feóil ná fortche foraib.' (*Togail Bruidne Da Derga*, ll. 18–34) [At the well, the woman loosened her hair in order to wash it, and her hands appeared through the opening of the neck of her dress. As white as the snow of a single night her wrists; as tender and even and red as foxglove her clear, lovely cheeks. As black as a beetle's back her brows; a shower of matched pearls her teeth. Hyacinth blue her eyes; Parthian red her lips. Straight, smooth, soft and white her shoulders; pure white and tapering her fingers; long her arms. As white as sea foam her side, slender, long, smooth, yielding, soft as wool. Warm and smooth, sleek and white her thighs; round and small, firm and white her knees. Short and white and straight her shins; fine and straight and lovely her heels. If a rule were put against her feet, scarcely a fault would be found save for a plenitude of flesh or skin.] (*The Destruction of Da Derga's Hostel*, p. 62).

figuratively to mean 'skin', as if the body's covering were the result of a kind of organic wash, leaving a living film. Another synonym of *croicenn* [skin] is *cnes*, which is used figuratively for form, shape, complexion, external beauty.[47] It is tempting to conclude that in early Ireland skin was gendered female, flesh male; woman is superficial, comprehensive, passive, while man is material, discretionary, active. From this perspective it is possible to understand how flaying would represent more than the simple removal of an external covering, something more akin to the loss of individual identity.[48] The warrior resembles the scribe in using skin for a record, but it is his own, scarred skin and not a discrete vellum that is the medium for ambiguous testimony to past martial activity.[49]

As in the Norse account of Sigurðr roasting the heart of the dragon Fáfnir, burning the skin of his thumb, sucking on it, and thereby acquiring the ability to understand the communications of birds, the young Finn mac Cumhail burns a thumb while roasting a 'salmon of knowledge' intended for the meal of a senior poet; he puts it to his mouth, and thus gains vast knowledge and insight.[50] Again, burned skin here seems linked with the concept of comprehensiveness in its double sense of inclusiveness and understanding.[51] From this perspective, flaying would be at the far end of the dehumanizing spectrum, short of death.

Distinct from the dismemberment and disarticulation of Fergus' oath, flaying in the sense of isolating all skin from the various members that it covers represents a radical reconception of the human body, its potential dividing lines being shifted a notional 90 degrees, as the forearm is not severed from the upper arm but its skin lifted and peeled off. Instead

---

[47] In a poetic prediction of the forthcoming battle between Ulster and Connacht it is stated 'silfid crú a cnessaib curad', where *cnes* [skin] is best translated as follows: 'Blood will flow from heroes' bodies'. *Táin bó Cúalgne from the Book of Leinster*, ed. and trans. Cecile O'Rahilly (Dublin: Dublin Institute for Advanced Studies, 1967), l. 272. A consonant discussion of skin in Middle English romance is found in Katie L. Walter, 'The Form of the Formless: Medieval Taxonomies of Skin, Flesh and the Human', in *Reading Skin*, ed. Walter, pp. 119–49, in particular pp. 119–26.

[48] Eorann, wife of the maddened and now bird-like Suibhne, says in a dialogue poem 'saoth lem do chnes rochlói dath / dreasa is droighin gut rébath' [I sorrow that thy skin has lost its colour, / briars and thorns rending thee]; *Buile Suibhne (The Frenzy of Suibhne), being the Adventures of Suibhne Geilt*, ed. and trans. J. G. O'Keeffe (London: Irish Texts Society, 1913), pp. 48–9.

[49] See: William Sayers, 'The Laconic Scar in Early Irish Literature', in *Wounds and Wound Repair in Medieval Culture*, ed. Larissa Tracy and Kelly De Vries (Leiden: Brill, 2015), pp. 473–95.

[50] 'The Boyhood Deeds of Finn', ed. Kuno Meyer, *Revue Celtique* 5 (1882): 195–204, trans. Kuno Meyer, *Ériu* 1 (1904): 180–90.

[51] But thumb, skin and mouth may all be simple media, to bring salmon flesh into Finn's body.

of incision, there is subcutaneous slicing and lifting. Yet the practical experience of skinning game and domestic animals – none of which, it should be noted, were ever skinned alive – the curing of leather, its use in a wide variety of applications, even in skin-covered boats, in all these cultures argues against flaying simply being an unthought or unthinkable idea. Rather, the Irish evidence suggests that in this respect the human body was conceived as inviolate.[52]

In the absence of references to actual flaying, the epic texts do offer a symbolic substitute, with humiliation and degradation as the objectives. According to Cú Chulainn's *Macgnímrada* (*Boyhood Deeds*), which figure in the early part of *Táin bó Cúailgne*, aristocratic youths had a number of martial games and activities that complemented their training in arms. One of these was to strip a fellow – always also a rival – of his clothes. Cú Chulainn succeeds in reducing members of the boytroop to stark nakedness without so much as losing a pin from his clothing.[53] Nudity could be imagined, in social terms, as the first step toward flaying. The heroic male body is seldom seen naked in Irish narrative, willingly or unwillingly, since nakedness deprives the body of the markers of social rank. One exception is an aged warrior in *Táin bó Cúailgne*, Illiach, who is near death. He appears in his rickety war-chariot alone, stark naked, his genitals exposed, a source of mockery and humour, since nudity was widely seen as a cause for shame.[54] Conventional Irish clothing and its literary

---

[52] While the early Irish community may have welcomed the variety of artifacts made of animal skin, the crafts of the skinner and tanner would probably not have been welcome near residences, because of the smell. Tanners do not, for example, figure among the crafts represented in the seating schemata, organized by rank, of the king's hall. See: William Sayers, 'A Cut Above: Ration and Station in an Irish King's Hall', *Food and Foodways* 4 (1990): 89–110.

[53] *Táin bó Cúailgne*: 'In tan dano bá n-imdírech dognítis, dosnérged-som uli co m-bítís tornochta, ⁊ nocon ructaís-seom immorro cid a delg asa brot-som namm' [When they were engaged in the game of stripping one another, he would strip them all stark-naked but they could not even take his brooch from his mantle], ll. 558–60. There is no discrete verb here for the idea of stripping, but rather a verbal phrase 'make stark-naked' [*do-gní tornocht*].

[54] *Táin bó Cúailgne*, ll. 3366–86. An equally remarkable nude scene is found early in *Togail Bruidne Da Derga*. The young Conaire is told to proceed on foot to Tara, naked and carrying a stone in a sling, as instructed by the king of his father's bird troop, who has taken on human form, for it had been prophesied that the king-elect would be found in this condition and would then promptly be clothed in regal robes. While the narrative justifies the sling and missile by having the youngster out birding, the genital symbolism is evident; the naked youth is pristine, all potential. His transformation through clothing covers the same symbolic distance as that of the hag who turns into the fair maiden conferring sovereignty; *Togail Bruidne Da Derga*, ll. 127–52; *The Destruction of Da Derga's Hostel*, pp. 65–6.

depiction did, however, permit glimpses of the bared female body and its skin: the fair-skinned legs of the sovereignty figure as she appears to Níall, Étaín's side as she loosens her clothing to wash at the spring (*Togail Bruidne Da Derga*), Emer's young breasts seen over the yoke of her gown in *Tochmarc Emere* (*The Wooing of Emer*).[55]

The episode with Illiach occurs toward the end of the *Táin*, one of a series of brief accounts on outlandish themes that create suspense before the final clash of the hosts and bulls. They may also be seen as changes rung on the warrior body and its medical care. In addition to the naked Illiach, Cethern girds his battered body with a chariot body as a kind of exoskeleton, and there is frequent mention of 'marrow mashes', made of ox and human bones, in which wounded men may lie and quickly regain their soundness and vigour – a kind of Old Irish spa treatment.[56] Revitalized skin was not part of it. In both cases, it is bone reinforcement that is the objective, further evidence for the heroic conception of the body outlined above, and for the literally and figuratively peripheral status of skin within that understanding.

Another explanation for the near total absence of the wholesale removal of skin from the human body in Irish legal, literary and historical sources lies in what might be termed the literate 'register' and the appropriate content of its various strata. Early insular Celtic thought was marked by a distinctive kind of lateral thinking – what, from the perspective of an all-inclusive cosmos, may be termed 'thinking in homologies'. The vertical axis of hierarchy evident in social rank reflects a tripartite conception of the cosmos; the heavens or sky above; the surface of the earth, home to mankind; and the underearth and undersea. In a vast paradigm that also includes a horizontal coordinate and is more tightly and meaningfully organized than analogy, metaphor or simile, this fundamental triad is reflected in whole and in part in other organizations of the known world. Examples include the human body seen as head, upper torso and arms, lower body and legs; and society organized as king (head of the tribe), warriors (bearers of arms), and tillers of the soil and herds of animals. This organizing principle could inform narrative or plot: a king who had been unjust (law and justice belong to the aerial sphere), ineffective or cowardly in battle (martial activity), and/or exploitative or unsupportive of the legitimate reproduction of humans and animals (e.g., sexual exploitation), and the life on the land and sea in general, would die a three-fold death, realized in some instances as being struck by a falling roof beam (aerial), run through by a spear or burned (terrestrial) and drowned in a butt of beer (subterranean, submarine).[57] Then, after this three-part punishment

---

[55] *Tochmarc Emere*, in *Compert Con Culainn and other Stories*, pp. 16–68 at p. 31.

[56] *Táin bó Cúailgne*, ll. 3161–327.

[57] A classic text in this regard is *Aided Muirchertaig meic Erca* (*The Violent Death of Muichertach mac Erca*), ed. Lil Níc Dhonnchada (Dublin: Dublin

for a failed polyfunctionality, the king's head might be severed from his body. In such homological thinking, which included tripartite groupings of professions and trades, colours, instruments and tools, skin seems to have been subsumed in the conception of the lower body, along with the intestines and genitalia.[58] The consequence is the near total absence of skin in the stories of kings, save in what may be called election scenes, and its only incidental mention in tales of heroes and war, in its capacity as the cover for bone and muscle. Since labourers and slaves are not fit subjects for history or storytelling, flaying as a potential injury or punishment is *de facto* excluded from the preserved record. It may seem paradoxical to invoke an association of skin in the punitive context with the lower classes of Irish society, after having seen how prominent clear, healthy skin is in portraits of feminine beauty. However, woman's generally subaltern position in early Ireland and her association with procreation in the functional slot that mirrored the tripartite cosmos attenuate this disparity, and skin had a wide spectrum of symbolic valences according to context. A putative equation on this spectrum is between human skin and the arable surface of the earth, seen as female.

In the epic tale *Cath Maige Mucrama* (*The Battle of Mag Mucrama*), a story of dynastic succession, a ruling king makes an unjust legal decision. His foster-son immediately points out a more just solution. The old king is discredited and the way paved for the accession to the kingship of the celebrated Cormac Mac Airt.

> Fecht and didiu do-feotar caírcha glassin na rígna indí Lugdach. Táncas i rréir Meic Con. 'At-berim', or Mac Con, 'na caírig ind.' Ro boí Cormac 'na mac bic for dérgud inna farrad. 'Acc, a daeteac', orse, 'ba córu lomrad na caírech i llomrad na glasne, ar ásfaid in glassen, ásfaid ind oland forsnaib caírib.'

Institute for Advanced Studies, 1964). In this tripartite paradigm, burning counts as a warrior death, with the skin, again, the first to part of the body to be violated. See: William Sayers, '*Guin agus Crochad agus Gólad*: The Earliest Irish Threefold Death', in *Celtic Languages and Celtic Peoples: Proceedings of the Second North American Congress of Celtic Studies, Halifax, 1989*, ed. Cyril Byrne, Margaret Harry and Pádraig Ó Siadhail (Halifax: D'Arcy McGee Chair of Irish Studies, St Mary's University, 1992), pp. 65–82. We find another spectacular planned death in *Mesca Ulad* (*The Intoxication of the Ulstermen*), when Cú Chulainn and his fellows are trapped in an iron guest hall sided and faced with wood, which is then set alight; *Mesca Ulad*, ed. J. Carmichael Watson (Dublin: Dublin Institute for Advanced Studies, 1967), ll. 808–16.

[58] Additional homologically based sets are presented in tabular form in William Sayers, 'Tripartition in the Early Irish Tradition: Cosmic or Social Structure?' in *Indo-European Religion after Dumézil*, ed. Edgar C. Polomé (Washington: Institute for the Study of Man, 1996), pp. 156–83.

[Now on one occasion sheep ate the *glassen* of Lugaid's queen. The matter was brought to Mac Con for decision. 'I pronounce', said Mac Con, 'that the sheep [be forfeited] for it.' Cormac, a little boy, was on the couch beside him. 'No, foster-father', said he, 'the shearing of the sheep for the cropping of the *glassen* would be more just, for the *glassen* will grow [and] the wool will grow on the sheep.']⁵⁹

The correspondence established is greater than that of simple analogy, since the plants from the queen's garden, generally thought to be woad for dyeing, occupy the same slot or cell in the tripartite cosmos and its multiple phenomena as the wool. The act of trespass and depredation realized by the sheep is called *lommrad*.⁶⁰ This is a general term for shearing and could also be used of a shorn fleece. This forms a semantic loop in that a shearable animal is also capable of 'shearing' the turf.⁶¹ Bartholomew is dispatched with a 'naked' (*lomm*) sword in the Irish version of his martyrdom. Since a flayed animal skin could be prepared as vellum, the Irish, always attracted to word-play, called an excerpt from a manuscript passage *lommrad*, a bit of fleece taken from the larger skin. This woad/wool correspondence is paralleled in the celebrated poem called *The Lament of the Old Woman of Beare*. This aged sovereignty figure deplores the weak royal leadership that has brought blight on the land of the Beare peninsula and thus on herself. Fields that were once yellow with wheat like her golden hair are now thinned and colourless.⁶²

Other figurative use of *lommrad* extends to the devastation of the land that could be carried out by a warband. In the absence of literary references to flaying as a punishment for criminal servants and disobedient slaves in early Ireland, it is tempting, in terms of 'homological logic', to see in this use of *lommrad* an equivalent flaying of the earth, through the destruction of grass, crops and trees. The motif is well developed elsewhere in *Cath Maige Mucrama* and, indeed, is implicit in the title of the tale, since Mag

---

⁵⁹ *Cath Maige Mucrama*, ed. and trans. Máirín O Daly (Dublin: Irish Texts Society, 1975), par. 63. The earthworks of Tara collapse, to assume an angle of repose, as a consequence of the king's biased, crooked judgement; see Sayers, '*Cláen Temair*'.

⁶⁰ See: Tomás Ó Cathasaigh, 'The Theme of *lommrad* in *Cath Maige Mucrama*', *Éigse* 18.2 (1981): 211–24.

⁶¹ *DIL*, s.v. *lommrad*.

⁶² Donncha Ó hAodha, 'The Lament of the Old Woman of Beare', in *Sages, Saints and Storytellers: Celtic Studies in Honour of Professor James Carney*, ed. Donnchadh Ó Corráin, Liam Breatnach and Kim McCone (Maynooth: An Sagart, 1989), pp. 308–31. *Snomad* was used in Old Irish for the act of stripping bark from trees or skin from the human body, but in no case does it suggest complete flaying. Rather, in the legal texts it seems to refer to a graze or scrape (but not a truly bloody injury). See: *Di ércib fola*, in *Corpus Iuris Hiberniae*, ed. D. A. Binchy (Dublin: Dublin Institute for Advanced Studies, 1978), pp. 2058.25ff.

Mucrama takes its name from a plague of destructive feral pigs that ravaged and defoliated the plain.[63] Although a case can be made for the concept of flaying the earth – a reverse of cosmogonic myth in which a primal being is not turned into land, but the land into a flayed body – the case is not fully convincing. Since the land is female and its sovereignty is represented by a female figure, whose descriptions stress rectitude of form and external beauty, the arable, productive stratum of the earth, say the upper 18 inches of topsoil, streams and lakes, might well be seen as its skin. A more exact topographical flaying would then be the removal of this layer of earth that provides a seat for vegetation, through, perhaps, flooding, earthquake or mudslide or slower erosion – none particularly likely in Ireland. Furthermore, this line of thought does not bring us closer to answering the basic question of why flaying was not practised on people or on their imagined tutelary beings.

Aside from the anomaly of the translated account of the martyrdom of Bartholomew, the motif of flaying is absent, even in symbolic guise, from both medieval Irish heroic literature and accounts of royal rule over the land, the land that is always central to Irish storytelling. Yet, although the vernacular Bartholomew story, a finished literary artefact, is extrinsic to the native Irish tradition, there are multiple ways in which the story may have been fairly readily understood and appreciated as representative of an eastern culture associated with early Christianity.

The larger and perhaps still unanswered question here is why and how the notion of flaying should have been introduced in western European literature and art as a punitive act by the ruler or state, when it lacked any precedent in origin myths, the charter narratives to which early states were so eager to attach their ethos and legitimacy. The Irish evidence offers a good vantage point from which to address this question. The early Christian Church created a profile for the new faith by emphasizing humility, courage and unbroken faith on the part of its exponents and proponents, and barbarism and extravagant cruelty on the part of its opponents, idolatrous rulers, and the priests of false religions. As the Church increased in strength and organizational complexity, it assumed many of the attributes of a strong polity, attributes that might be the envy of princes and kings intent on creating secular national states. Nothing would be more likely than for the proto-state to claim supremacy in the secular sphere on a scale with the Church's claims in the religious dimension, and to assume some of the ritual and pageantry deployed by the Church in order to generate the awe it hoped would accrue for its ruler.

---

[63] In *Compert Con Culainn* (*The Conception of Cú Chulainn*) a flock of birds devastates the plain before Conchobar's seat at Emain Macha, a sure sign that the Ulstermen have fallen out of favour with the cosmic powers or that some portentous event is approaching. It will be the birth of Cú Chulainn in a remote building at one moment a hut, at another a hall; *Compert Con Culainn*, in *Compert Con Culainn and other Stories*, pp. 1–8.

These institutional borrowings could have included, on the one hand, an insistence on unquestioning, non-contingent allegiance and loyalty to the state and its head, with threatened extreme sanctions for non-compliance – treason – and, on the other, a menu of spectacular public deaths, including flaying.

In conclusion, there are multiple, somewhat complementary, possible reasons why, the martyrdom of Bartholomew excepted, the flaying of human beings does not figure in the historical records of early Ireland, while being the common fate of animals on all its farms. In medieval Irish lore, skin is not a product of the sacrificed body of a primal giant from cosmogonic myth, which might be thought to offer the most comprehensive account of the origins of social order; nor does skin contribute to the formation of the elements of the known world. Flaying is nowhere accounted an appropriate punishment (as in a Dantean *contrapasso*) for wounds and injuries that rupture a victim's skin. Satire was believed capable of raising blisters on the human face, proof that 'face', skin, its health and colour, were important complements to social worth and reputation. Metonymically, Irish words for 'skin' are even used to convey senses of human shape and form. Skin – naked, diseased, or figured as the earth's vegetal covering – is prominent in tales of kings elect. Yet no battlefield wound is likened to skinning. Although heads are taken as martial trophies and cranial matter is preserved, cured human skin is not on display. The law codes are elitist and the epic tales concerned only with the martial aristocracy, so that the absence of flaying in these may be an aspect of register. Royal misrule or natural catastrophe might turn the countryside into a wasteland but the results are never characterized as a flaying, at most only as a shearing of the land.

We must conclude that, first, skin was not seen in early Ireland as a discrete entity but as a form-giving covering and, second, its total removal from a living human body was an entirely alien concept, one first brought to Ireland with Christian hagiographical literature. This situation is cast into greater relief by the fact that the literate tradition in Ireland was dependent on the flaying of animals for the production of vellum and, thus, the written record. While Ireland's contacts with Europe were closer and richer than was long thought to be case, and Irish rulers were not ignorant of evolving concepts of kingship and statecraft on the Continent, Irish political pluralism meant that the state did not emerge as a conceptual entity in the pre-Norman period, and the punishment that European states and their kings found appropriate to treason, as a crime against the state and king, was not replicated in pre-Norman Ireland, perhaps quite simply because treason itself was not yet a functional concept in this cultural and social environment, which long remained tribal, rural and familiar.

11

Reading the Consumed:
Flayed and Cannibalized Bodies in *The Siege of Jerusalem* and *Richard Coer de Lyon*

Emily Leverett

T HE idea of flaying in the Middle Ages looms much larger in the mind and the literature than it seems to have in real life and law.[1] Flaying as an answer to treason was the ultimate rejection, disassociation and erasure of identity and, as such, highlights the deeply culturally damaging acts for which it was used as a punishment. The crime of treason held particular power, being 'as much a social as legal breach and one rooted in the viciousness of character'.[2] In late medieval romance, such viciousness is often attributed to the enemies of Christianity, particularly Saracens.[3] Flaying captured the imagination, and incidents of flaying are often moments of excessive, even fantastic, violence. As such, it should not be surprising that flaying appears in two examples of flamboyantly violent late medieval romance: the alliterative *Siege of Jerusalem* (hereafter *Siege*) and *Richard Coer de Lyon* (hereafter *RCL*).[4] Both are found in the mid-fifteenth century manuscript British Library, Add. MS 31042, also known as the London Thornton Manuscript. However, in these fourteenth-century Middle English romances, flaying is performed by Christians invoking 'in

---

[1] W. R. J. Barron, 'The Penalties for Treason in Medieval Life and Literature', *Journal of Medieval History* 7 (1981): 187–202 at p. 193. 'But in both literatures [of England and France] flaying occurs in greater frequency than the historical records of either country would seem to warrant', p. 193.

[2] Ibid., p. 188.

[3] Ibid., p. 193.

[4] *Richard Coer de Lyon* appears in two versions, labeled *a* and *b* by Karl Brunner in his 1913 edition. The *a* version contains the fantastic elements, including the flaying and cannibalizing of Saracens scenes, and is the version found in Robert Thornton's manuscript and is the text discussed in this article. Karl Brunner, ed., *Der Mittelenglische Versroman über Richard Löwenherz*, Wiener Beiträge zur Englischen Philologie 42 (Wien: W. Braumüller, 1913). The only other complete edition is found in Henry Weber's *Metrical Romances of the Thirteenth, Fourteenth, and Fifteenth Centuries: Published from Ancient Manuscripts*, vol. 2. (Edinburgh: A. Constable, 1810), pp. 3–278. All citations taken from Brunner; hereafter, line numbers given in parentheses. For a discussion on the flaying of a Venetian general by Ottoman Turks, see: Kelly DeVries, 'A Tale of Venetian Skin: The Flaying of Marcantonio Bragadin', pp. 51–70, in this volume.

a single shocking image, the primitive significance of treason', rather than by the Saracens against whom they fight and with whom such actions were often associated.[5]

Flaying of animal flesh was commonplace in the Middle Ages. It has been applied not only in cooking, but also in parchment making, in the construction of the very connections we have to that moment: books.[6] Medieval manuscripts themselves carry symbolic value just as much as the words on their pages. In the hands of a reader (or perhaps in the hands of a critic hundreds of years later), the manuscript can at once represent the immortality promised through salvation – the persistence of the body after death – while at the same time creating that message through a still-used piece of skin.[7] Books offered the opportunity to connect flaying both with the animal itself and with salvation; the heart of the saved and the body of Christ are compared to a stretched animal skin turned to parchment.[8] Sarah Kay notes that 'flayed skin can be conceptually detached from the life that once was and serve, instead, as a means to immortality'.[9] The immortality comes at a price: the damages to the animal skin '– scraping, cutting, splitting, tearing, holing, stretching, drying out – are all processes that, inflicted on a living human body rather than on a dead animal, would

---

[5] Barron, 'Penalties for Treason', p. 199. Robert Mills suggests that the flaying and execution of Goddard in *Havelok the Dane* show Havelok's sovereign justice and kingly power: 'Havelok's Bare Life', in *Reading Skin in Medieval Literature and Culture*, ed. Katie L. Walter (New York: Palgrave, 2013), pp. 57–80 at p. 74.

[6] Bruce Holsinger, 'Of Pigs and Parchment: Medieval Studies and the Coming of the Animal', *PMLA* 124.2 (2009): 616–23 at p. 619. In this volume, see: Jack Hartnell, 'Tools of the Puncture: Skin, Knife, Bone, Hand', pp. 20–50; and Frederika Bain, 'Skin on Skin: Wearing Flayed Remains', pp. 116–37.

[7] Sarah Kay has noted that in manuscripts that contain the legend of St Bartholomew the flaying is converted from punishment to sacrifice and, as such, 'symbolizes immortality as much as death'. 'Original Skin: Flaying, Reading, and Thinking in the Legend of Saint Bartholomew and other Works', *Journal of Medieval and Early Modern Studies* 36.1 (2006): 35–73 at p. 36.

[8] Holsinger, 'Of Pigs and Parchment', p. 621. For Holsinger, this connection between animal skin and human form, either literally or figuratively, elides the suffering of the animal, instead focusing on the 'suffering' of the dead animal's skin. Ultimately, he links this to the ethics of reading and studying material that is based on 'centuries of slaughter', p. 622.

[9] Sarah Kay, 'Flayed Skin as *objet a*: Representation and Materiality in Guillaume de Deguileville's *Pèlerinage de vie humaine*', in *Medieval Fabrications: Dress, Textiles, Clothwork, and other Cultural Imaginings*, ed. E. Jane Burns (New York: Palgrave, 2004), pp. 193–205 at p. 195.

be forms of torture'.[10] For the readers, 'the drama of death and redemption, enunciated in the contents of pious texts, is also enfolded in the original skin of the parchment book'.[11] Finally, Karl Steel notes that skin 'should be understood as being everywhere things persist, meet, or are. Skin intervenes in any encounter. [... T]hen by that measure, there is no way to be and not be touched, and also no way to be touched *entirely*.'[12]

At the intersection of these ideas is the flayed body. The images associated with the destruction of the flesh call into question ideas of self, both as individual and as part of the collective. Flaying is a means of banishment, a way of casting out what can never be fully (re)integrated into culture.[13] The authors of both *Siege* and *RCL* use flaying for their own production of identity – Christian and English. Furthermore, both poems include cannibalism. Both poems have flayed human flesh and consumed human flesh, and in both poems these moments are critical to the texts. The flayed, skinless bodies are consumed, either literally or metaphorically, like parchment manuscripts meant to be read, digested and, in some cases, burned. The *Siege* and *RCL* offer an opportunity for English audiences to see themselves in history. Both use the common Others of Jews and Muslims as locations for their exploration of English and Christian identity; both use flaying and cannibalism as means of creating and enforcing boundaries. The poems establish the role of England in Christian history, envisioning it as not only a part of a teleological arc, but also as a reflection of the Christian past in their present.[14] The poems turn bodies to books, and also specify how the books should be read. Within the boundaries of the text, the living Jews and Saracens are the audience for

---

[10] Kay, 'Original Skin', p. 36. While flaying is often referred to as torture in a more colloquial sense, this volume stresses the use of flaying as a form of punishment – after verdict and sentence – rather than interrogatory torture, which had a very specific definition in medieval legal culture and generally only applied to atrocities that were perpetrated in the interests of gaining a confession as 'proof'. See: Larissa Tracy, *Torture and Brutality in Medieval Literature: Negotiations of National Identity* (Cambridge: D. S. Brewer, 2012).

[11] Kay, 'Original Skin', p. 64.

[12] Karl Steel, 'Touching Back: Responding to *Reading Skin*', in *Reading Skin*, ed. Walter, pp. 183–95 at p. 18 (his emphasis).

[13] Kay, 'Original Skin', p. 40.

[14] Phillipa Hardman argues that 'this collection of texts in the London Thornton MS can thus be seen to constitute a complete history of Christian salvation from the creation through the redemption to the acts of Christ's heroes in the world, defending the Faith and overcoming God's enemies'. 'The *Sege of Melayne*: A Fifteenth-Century Reading', in *Tradition and Transformation in Medieval Romance*, ed. Rosalind Field (Cambridge: D. S. Brewer, 1999), pp. 71–68 at p. 74.

the flaying and destruction while the Christians are the authors.[15] For the external readers of these romances, especially if they read them together as Robert Thornton did, the texts provide a way of inscribing fourteenth- and fifteenth-century English into these important moments of Christian history – the 70 CE destruction of Jerusalem and Richard I's Jerusalem crusade (1189–92) – creating a vision of English identity as heroic, religiously devout and powerful.

The *Siege* begins with a vivid description of Christ's crucifixion. The story then shifts to Nathan and his conversion of Titus and Vespasian. Upon hearing the story of Christ and condemning the Jews and the Romans involved, Titus and Vespasian are healed of skin ailments. With Nero's permission, they attack Jerusalem to avenge Christ. During the romance-styled battles, Caiphas is captured, along with his priests, and flayed, hanged, set upon by cats, dogs and apes, and burnt. Vespasian returns to Rome to take over as emperor after Nero's suicide and Titus finishes the siege, during which a starving Jewess cooks and eats her child. Once in the city, Titus takes the treasures, secures Jewish slaves and razes the temple and the city. After the suicide of Pilate, Titus and his Christian Romans ride off singing to Rome.

In the past twenty-five years critical response to the *Siege* has been wide ranging. Ralph Hanna argues that the 'cheerfully sanctioned violence' of the poem had an audience among the Lancastrians.[16] Christine Chism sees the destruction of Jewish bodies as a source of empire:

> By defining, confining, and liquidating the Jewish enemy, these newly converted provincial Romans are able to heal their bodily and body-political maladies and consolidate their own disparate forces into a powerful and unified Christian image.[17]

David Lawton, too, sees the poem, particularly the hunting and hawking imagery, as 'shad[ing] the Romans' recreative activities into those of the audience, the poem itself'.[18] The result is Romans who look 'strikingly like the crusading English nobles of the late fourteenth century'.[19]

---

[15] Cf. Bain, 'Skin on Skin', pp. 127–8. Bain discusses the appropriation of Jewish skin and the anti-Judaic possibilities.

[16] Ralph Hanna III, 'Contextualizing *The Siege of Jerusalem*', *Yearbook of Langland Studies* 6 (1992): 109–21 at p. 110.

[17] Christine Chism, *Alliterative Revivals* (Philadelphia: University of Pennsylvania Press, 2002), p. 156.

[18] David Lawton, 'Titus Goes Hunting and Hawking: The Poetics of Recreation and Revenge in *The Siege of Jerusalem*', in *Individuality and Achievement in Middle English Poetry*, ed. O. S. Pickering (Cambridge: D. S. Brewer, 1997), pp. 105–17 at p. 108.

[19] Patricia Price, 'Integrating Time and Space: The Literary Geography of *Patience, Cleanness, The Siege of Jerusalem,* and *St Erkenwald*', *Medieval Perspectives* 11 (1996): 283–303 at p. 243.

Arlyn Diamond goes further, suggesting that the poem not only invites identification with the Romans as romance heroes, but also renders the violence enjoyable and 'teaches us to delight in the violence our more enlightened selves would prefer to ignore'.[20] The violence against Jews is fully embraced in the London Thornton manuscript, which 'encourages a selective reading of *The Siege*, one that sells the poem as a piece of unqualified anti-Jewish propaganda'.[21] But among some critics is a sense that the poem works against the identity-forming and anti-Judaic point of view.[22] The poem can function as a 'critique [of] violence as a means divorced from its end'.[23] Elisa Narin van Court argues that the poem reflects the lack of an 'unambiguous [or] singular' anti-Judaism in the fourteenth century. Instead, she sees a 'lively, ongoing, and deeply ambivalent concern about [Jews'] role in Christendom'.[24] Finally, several critics have dealt with the *Siege* not only as a creator of empire, but also as a means for English audiences to locate their place in Christian history and to establish an identity as *English* Christians. Suzanne M. Yeager focuses on the 'shifting cultural valence' of Rome, allowing the *Siege* to be read in two ways:

> Considered together, the exegetical reading of the poem, which interprets the Jews as a typological Christian people and views the Romans as the Antichrist, seems contradictory to the literal reading of the poem where fictitious Romans are linked to the Christian crusading forces of western Europe.[25]

---

[20] Arlyn Diamond, 'The Alliterative *Siege of Jerusalem*: The Poetics of Destruction', in *Boundaries in Medieval Romance*, ed. Neil Cartlidge (Cambridge: D. S. Brewer, 2008), pp. 103–13 at p. 113.

[21] Michael Johnston, 'Robert Thornton and *The Siege of Jerusalem*', *Yearbook of Langland Studies* 23 (2009): 125–62 at p. 128.

[22] Throughout, I will be using 'anti-Judaic', because 'anti-Semitic' signifies an ethnic distinction not usually made by medieval people, and my particular concern in this article is the religious distinction.

[23] Alex Mueller, 'Corporal Terror: Critiques of Imperialism in *The Siege of Jerusalem*', *Philological Quarterly* 84.3 (Summer 2005): 287–310 at p. 287.

[24] Elisa Narin van Court, 'Socially Marginal, Culturally Central: Representing Jews in Late Medieval English Literature', *Exemplaria* 12.2 (2000): 293–326 at p. 295.

[25] Suzanne M. Yeager, *Jerusalem in Medieval Narrative* (Cambridge: Cambridge University Press, 2008), p. 107. See also her article 'The Siege of Jerusalem and Biblical Exegesis: Writing about Romans in Fourteenth-Century England', *The Chaucer Review* 39.1 (2004): 70–102. Yeager also discusses the role of homiletic texts, including sermons on Luke, in 'Jewish Identity in *the Siege of Jerusalem* and Homiletic Texts: Models of Penance and Victims of Vengeance for the Urban Apocalypse', *Medium Ævum* 80.1 (2011): 56–84.

The dual readings show 'the role of Jerusalem shifting from a material relic sought by the English, to that of a celestial city of the soul'.[26] Roger Nicholson argues that the Jews in the Middle Ages can occupy the margins and are 'always being expelled across them, remind[ing] Europe that the border is dangerously permeable and difficult to maintain'.[27] Finally, for Suzanne Conklin Akbari, the Jews must be both preserved and destroyed: 'Symbolically the place of the Jew is in the past, providing a template for the foundation of Christian identity, a mold that, after use, must be broken.'[28] Such wide-ranging criticism bears witness to the *Siege*'s ability not only to enthral audiences, but also to challenge them, to both establish and disrupt the identity of fourteenth- and fifteenth-century English Christians. Such an audience might read themselves in either the Jews, as the persecuted chosen, or in the Romans, as crusading Christian heroes. The multiple identifications possible in the *Siege* let the English, at a geographical and temporal distance, envision themselves as a part of Jerusalem's Christian history – as both conquerors and besieged.

The *Siege* locates much of its identity anxiety in the skin of its characters. Throughout the course of the poem, that anxiety is alleviated through the perfection and destruction of skin. Before they flay Caiphas, Titus and Vespasian both suffer from skin diseases:[29]

> [Titus] hadde a maldy vnmeke   inmyddis ȝe face;
> Þe lyppe lyþ on a lumpe   lyuered on þe cheke.
> So a canker vnclene   hit clothed togedres.
> Also his fadere of flesche   a ferly bytide:
> A bikere of waspen bees   bredde in his nose
> Hyued vp in his hed –   he had hem of ȝouþe –
> And Waspasian was called   þe waspene bees after.
>
> (ll. 30–6)[30]

---

[26] Yeager, *Jerusalem in Medieval Narrative*, p. 107.

[27] Roger Nicholson, 'Haunted Itineraries: Reading *The Siege of Jerusalem*', *Exemplaria* 14.2 (Oct. 2002): 447–84 at p. 450.

[28] Suzanne Conklin Akbari, 'Placing the Jews in Late Medieval Literature', in *Orientalism and the Jews*, ed. Ivan Davidson Kalmar and Derek J. Penslar (Hanover, NH: Brandeis University Press, 2005), pp. 32–50 at p. 50.

[29] In the *South English Legendary* account of Thomas á Becket, Sir William Tracy, one of the murderers, is afflicted with a skin disease as well. He scratches the surface of his arms until he flays the skin to the bone. Only when he properly repents his part in the murder is he healed. *The Life of St Thomas of Canterbury*, in *The South English Legendary, or Lives of Saints*, ed. Carl Horstmann, EETS o.s. 87 (London: Trübner and Co., 1887), pp. 106–77 at p. 175 (ll. 2382–416). My thanks to Larissa Tracy for this reference. Cf. Introduction, p. 16.

[30] *The Siege of Jerusalem*, ed. Ralph Hanna III and David Lawton, EETS o.s. 320 (Oxford: Oxford University Press, 2003). All citations are from this volume except where otherwise noted. See also: *The Siege of Jerusalem*, ed. Michael

The curious ailments of both men affect the skin and face – including a nest of wasps breeding in Vespasian's nose. When Nathan, travelling to spread the Gospel, is brought before Titus, Titus asks if Nathan might cure his cankers. Nathan's response is that he cannot, but he tells the story of Christ, who could perform curative miracles, and of Veronica's Vernicle, which can heal.[31] Upon hearing the story, Titus rejects Caesar as a 'sinful wrecche', for Rome's participation in Christ's crucifixion (ll. 173–6). Titus is rewarded for his judgement: 'And or þis wordes were wonne to þe ende, / Þe cankere þat þe kyng hadde clenly was heled' (ll. 177–8).

After the healing, Titus sees that both Veronica and the veil are fetched and presented to Pope Peter, who accepts the veil, weeps over it and then takes it, with the Romans, to Vespasian to heal him. The 'mametes' of the Roman church crumble when the veil passes through, and a sweet odour arises, signifying its holiness (ll. 217–44). This move secures the Veil as 'an authentic Roman relic', which 'adds to the religious significance of Rome'.[32] When Vespasian sees it, he announces, 'Lo lordlynges, here þe lyknesse of Crist', and the people in the crowd weep and wring their hands over Christ's suffering (ll. 250–2). The Pope touches the veil to Vespasian and blesses him three times, after which 'Þe waspys wyten away and all þe wo after: / Þat er was lasar-liche lyȝtter was neuere' (ll. 255–6). The clearing up of the wasps and leprosy-like suffering of both Titus and Vespasian reinforces the power of faith in Christ and his relics and marks a transition from unclean to clean:

> [F]orms of bodily decay, like skin diseases, [...] mark access to full social identity. [... I]t is [the Roman leaders] who suffer skin diseases, not the Jews living under the law of Leviticus, but it is also they who become 'clean and proper' on converting to Christianity.[33]

The Roman leaders shift from corrupt to clean, their bodies blessed by miracles that position them as not only physically capable of winning the battles to come (how could Vespasian lead an army with wasps buzzing in and out of his face?), but morally capable as well. The transformation

---

Livingston (Kalamazoo, MI: Medieval Institute Publications, 2004). In this volume, Michael Livingston discusses the beard-flaying in the context of Arthurian literature. See: 'Losing Face: Flayed Beards and Gendered Power in Arthurian Literature', pp. 308–21.

[31] Valerie Gramling also discusses the significance of the Vernicle in relation to the flagellation of Christ in English Mystery Plays. In this volume, see: '"Flesche withowtyn hyde": The Removal and Transformation of Jesus' Skin in the English Cycle Passion Plays', pp. 240–60.

[32] Yeager, *Jerusalem in Medieval Narraitve*, p. 82. She also notes that, 'in the *Siege*, Rome's cultural identity is reassigned and Christianized over two hundred years prior to the actual acceptance of the Christian religion in Rome' (p. 82).

[33] Nicholson, 'Haunted Itineraries', p. 480.

from sick to healthy is a bodily representation of conversion to Christianity. Accompanied by the language of faith, Titus and Vespasian's healing prepares them to become Christian warriors. With the skin they are in ready for battle, Titus and Vespasian move from a situation in which they could not touch and be touched, to one where they will do the very violent touching.

Much has been made by critics of the appearance of the Jews in the *Siege*. As they stride from the city to battle their elaborate war-trappings echo Saracen depictions, particularly in the context of crusade romances or *chasons de geste* (ll. 445–72).[34] But in one moment in particular, despite the jewels and the massive elephants, Caiphas presents himself as thoroughly embedded in the Old Testament. Surrounded by 'lered men of þe law' who recount from psalters the psalms of David as well as the heroic stories of Joseph and Judas Maccabee (ll. 476–9), Caiphas reads from a scroll:

> Cayphas of þe kyst   kyppid a rolle
> And radde how þe folke ran   þroʒ þe rede water
> Whan Pharao and his ferde   were in þe flodde drouned,
> And myche of Moyses lawe   he mynned þat tyme.
>
> (ll. 481–4)

The specific act of reading the scrolls aloud does not pose a particular problem and, in fact, might be read positively: 'As Caiphas reads to his listeners from holy scripture, medieval audiences would have perceived in the Jews a people who experienced a long history of divine favor.'[35] However, the context suggests an alternative interpretation. The Passion opens the poem and is followed by the announcement that 'divine favor' is about to shift from the Jews to the newly Christianized Romans:

> For al þe harm þat [Christ] hadde   hasted he noʒt
> On hem þe vyleny to venge   þat his veynys brosten,
> Bot ay taried on þe tyme   ʒif þey tourney wolde;
> ʒaf hem space þat hym spilide,   þey hit spedde lyte,
> Xl winter as Y fynde   and no fewere ʒyrys
> Or princes presed in hem   þat hym to pyne wroʒt.
>
> (ll. 19–24)

The forty-year waiting period establishing Christ's mercy at the beginning

---

[34] The connection between the Jew and Saracen in the *Siege* has been discussed by several critics, including Christine Chism, who notes, 'The exotic strength of the united Jewish army links them not to the stereotypical Jew of the English cycle dramas but to the stereotypical Saracen […] in *chansons de gestes*' (*Alliterative Revivals*, pp. 17–72). See also: Mary Hamel, 'The Siege of Jerusalem as a Crusading Poem', in *Journeys Toward God: Pilgrimage and Crusade* (Kalamazoo, MI: Medieval Institute Publications, 1992), pp. 177–94.

[35] Yeager, *Jerusalem in Medieval Narrative*, p. 105.

of the poem undermines the positive portrayal of the Jews as learned and blessed. No doubt the figure of Caiphas would invoke the historical struggles and triumphs of God's chosen people, but the poem replaces those positive characters with traitors deserving to be destroyed. The audience would have known the Moses story, but the typological story of Christ would have superseded the tale. Rather than acknowledging Christ and the injustice of the Crucifixion, Caiphas reads from the Old Testament, revealing himself to be spiritually backward and the enemy of the new Christian Romans coming to avenge their Redeemer. Also, the 'roll' draws us back to the idea of parchment and of the flesh. Caiphas reads the story of the escape from Egypt on the flesh of animals. First, animal flesh as sacrifice is insufficient for salvation – this is prefigured in the Abraham and Isaac story, and made explicit in the sacrifice of Christ. Second, the parchment foreshadows Caiphas' flaying – the moment that will turn him into a piece of flesh to be read by his followers. Vespasian becomes the replacement for Caiphas, mirroring the sacrificial replacement of animal flesh with Christ's flesh.

As the New Testament hero, Vespasian relies on the image of Christ's suffering in the Passion, not a scroll, to remind his troops of their cause: 'Byholdþ þe heþing and þe harde woundes, / Þe byndyng and þe betyng þat he on body hadde' (ll. 497–8).[36] This draws attention to the suffering body of Christ, and uses imagery similar to the poem's opening:

> A pyler pyȝt was doun   vpon þe playn erþe,
> His body bonded þereto   and beten with scourgis:
> Whyppes of quyrboyle   vmbywente his white sides
> Til al on rede blode ran   as rayn in þe strete.
>
> (ll. 9–12)

While Christ's body is not flayed, his skin suffers through whips and hard leather straps.[37] Both of these could easily 'flay' the skin off his back and, indeed, that is what they seem to do, since his blood runs in the street like rain. This set of images – Caiphas reading from a parchment roll and Vespasian invoking the Crucifixion, echoing the poem's opening lines – draws a connection between the flesh, the written word and the

---

[36] I have discussed Caiphas' reading of the scroll in contrast to Vespasian's speech to his troops in terms of not only Old Testament versus New Testament, but also in terms of affective piety. See: Emily Lavin Leverett, 'An Affective Romance?: Genre Blending in *The Siege of Jerusalem*', *Medieval Perspectives* 27 (2012): 111–24.

[37] On flagellation as a mode of flaying, especially in scenes of the Crucifixion, see in this volume: Susan Small, 'Flesh and Death in Early Modern Bedburg', pp. 71–90; Sherry C. M. Lindquist, 'Masculinist Devotion: Flaying and Flagellation in the *Belles Heures*', pp. 173–207; Peter Dent, 'A Window for the Pain: Surface, Interiority and Christ's Flagellated Skin in Late Medieval Sculpture', pp. 208–39; and Gramling, '"Flesche withowtyn hyde"', pp. 243–4.

suffering of Christ. Those who find inspiration in the written word (the
Old Testament) are those who committed vicious acts of cruelty against
Christ. Caiphas reads from flayed skin highlighting the physicality of the
Jewish interpretations. Reading these bodies, the English could position
themselves as the devout heroes in their own imaginations, replacing
the literalism of Old Testament sacrifice with the repeated images of the
Passion. Audiences could also read Caiphas' book in terms of Kay's idea
of flayed skin as a means to immortality. While the audiences of the *Siege*
hold a text in their hands (or listen as someone else holds the text and reads
from it), they, too, touch dead flesh used to convey the story of mutilation
and resurrection. However, Caiphas' touch conveys no such immortality –
the story of Moses prefigures Christ's salvation, but it is not a resurrection
story. As the audience knows, there is no escape for Caiphas. His is a body
to be cast out, flayed and obliterated by fire. Christ's suffering marks his
body as a book to be read, while Caiphas' suffering marks his body as a
book to be burned.

The defeat of Caiphas in a glorious battle includes the death of the Jews,
who fell 'so þick / As hail from heuen', and the deaths of the elephants
and dromedaries (ll. 598–9, 566–72). As happens in many crusade
romances, the ground is sodden with blood. After blocking the stream to
the city 'With stokes and stones and stynkande bestes', Vespasian joins his
counsellors, including Titus, to decide on the fate of Caiphas and his twelve
priests:

> Domesemen vpon deyes   demeden swyþe
> Þat ech freke were quyk fleyn   þe felles of clene,
> Firste to be on a bent   with blonkes todrawe
> And suþ honget on an hep   vpon heye galwes,
> Þe feet to þe firmament,   alle folke to byholden,
> With hony vpon ech half   þe hydeles anointed;
> Corres and cattes   with claures ful scharpe
> Foure kagged and knyt   to Cayphases þeyes;
> Twey apys at his armes   to angren hym more
> Þat renten þe rawe flesche   vpon rede peces.
> So he was pyned fram prime   with persched sides
> Tille þe sonne doun syed   in þe somere tyme.
> Þe lerer ledes of þe lawe   a little byndþe
> Weren tourmented on a tre,   topsailes walten
> Knyt to euerech clerke   kene corres twey –
> Þat alle þe cite myȝt se þe sorrow þat þey dryuen.

>   (ll. 697–712)

The flaying is the first in a series of punishments designed both to exact
typological vengeance on Caiphas – he is essentially crucified at the end –
and to obliterate utterly the bodies of the Jewish priests. This destruction
of the Jewish bodies is about the building of Christian community: 'The
integrity of the Christian community is affirmed, its wholeness the mirror

image of the fragmented Jewish bodies in which the poem so memorably revels.'[38] The fragmentation is also about the destruction of the ideology. Since Caiphas can be associated with the books he reads, the flaying here undoubtedly brings that connection of flesh-as-writing-surface to the forefront. Caiphas' body has become a book. The body, stripped of its skin (or cover), is further associated with animals by being torn to pieces by animals. The punishment looks back to Caiphas' reading of the scrolls. Flayed, he is laid bare for all to see, including the Jews trapped in Jerusalem. In the blood and gore that must have resulted from the punishment, the man's flesh would have become unidentifiable as human. The violence dehumanizes Caiphas, and the others who have already been rendered less-than-human because of their literalist reading of the Old Testament, to mere flesh – an echo of their own parchment. The Jews see the loss of their leader. The English audience sees the graphic end of the literalists. Caiphas cannot and will not experience resurrection, but the English can. The Jews become a part of a vision of the Christian past and the English can see themselves as symbolic readers of Jewish destruction.

Finally, like many people unhappy with particular books, Vespasian demands that the remains of the Jewish priests be burnt:

> Þe kyng lete drawen hem adoun   whan þey dede were,
> Bade, 'a bole-fure betyn   to brennen þe corses,
> Kesten Cayphas þeryn   and his clerkes all,
> And brennen euereche bon   into browne askes.'
>
> (ll. 717–20)

All of the Jewish bodies are punished this way: eradicated. Burned to ashes, there is nothing left to use, nothing left to be read. This also foreshadows the coming razing of Jerusalem: 'The body of Caiphas serves as a microcosm of Jerusalem. His body is torn apart and burned to ashes, scattered to the winds; the city walls soon suffer the same fate, beaten down into "poudere".'[39]

In between the Crucifixion and the burning, many of the Jewish witnesses to the punishment and execution commit suicide:

> Þe Iewes walten ouer þe walles   for wo at þat tyme;
> Seuen hundred slow hemself   for sorrow of here clerkes.
> Somme hent hem by þe heere   and fram þe hed pulled
> And Somme doun for deil   daschen to grounde.
>
> (ll. 713–16)

This mass suicide is the earlier of two, both on the heels of horrifying

---

[38] Akbari, 'Placing the Jews', p. 37.

[39] Suzanne Conklin Akbari, 'Erasing the Body: History and Memory in Medieval Siege Poetry', in *Remembering the Crusades: Myth, Image, and Identity*, ed. Nicholas Paul and Suzanne Yeager (Baltimore: The Johns Hopkins University Press, 2012), pp. 146–73 at p. 159.

violence done to Jewish bodies. Tearing their hair for grief and flinging themselves over the walls both mark a moment of sympathy for the citizens of Jerusalem. A condemnation of violence against Jews can be read in these lines, but they also can be read as simply anti-Jew. In both possible readings, the poet emphasizes the result as connected to the actions and choices of the Jews themselves. The poem chronicles their refusals to save themselves, but the opportunity to do so positions the Jews to be read by the fourteenth- and fifteenth-century audiences as a warning – a 'strategic relatability […] that would have allowed for some degree of identification with the Jews as a people undergoing judgement'.[40] Though Titus and Vespasian are cruel and their violence condemned, the Jews of the poem still seem to have a choice in their destruction, and they choose poorly. English audiences can read their lives in both, recognizing their own tumultuous time as a reiteration of history. Like the Jews and Romans, the English Christians have their own choices to make.

Following the suicide, Vespasian commands the burning of the bodies and the scattering of the ashes to the wind, blowing them directly into the city. Those that do this call out to the Jews: '"Þer is doust for ȝour drynke," adoun to hem crieþ / And bidde hem bible of þat broþ for þe bischop soul' (ll. 717–23). It is not enough to have viciously punished and burned Caiphas and the priests in front of their own people. Vespasian reiterates their literalism one last time: the Jews are forced to consume the bodies visually, reading their destruction, and then are forced to literally consume the bodies by drinking the contaminated water. As above, this further emphasizes the Jew's exclusion from resurrection and reinforces the difference between the Christian English and Jews whose story they read. Finally, the narrator summarizes:

> Þus ended coursed Cayphas   and his clerkes twelf
> Al tobrused myd bestes,   brent at þe laste,
> In tokne of tresoun   and trey þat þey wroȝt
> Whan Crist þrow here conseil   was cached to deþ.
>
> (ll. 725–8)

Here, the punishments are directly connected to treason – defined as the crucifixion of Christ[41] – though the flaying itself is omitted in favour of the more dramatic 'mangled by beasts'. Flaying, however graphically present in the poem, was not present in England's later legal codes: '[flaying] was presumably always an exceptional punishment, justified by ancient custom rather than by written law'.[42] So the punishment in the poem occurs outside of England, performed by first-century Romans, against Jews, and in Jerusalem. In this moment the brutality is safely in the past, allowing

---

[40] Yeager, 'Jewish Identity', p. 59.

[41] Barron, 'Penalties for Treason', p. 194.

[42] Ibid., p. 191.

the audience to participate vicariously while not over-identifying. The poem, and the identification of the English with the Roman heroes, is revenge fantasy: characters with whom the audience partially identifies perform gruesome acts that serve to solidify the identity of the community, but without the risk of such violence becoming real. Though flaying is not sanctioned in English law, it can be enacted without fear in English poetry.[43] The poem creates the fantasy that the Crucifixion is treason against the English and responds with the literary fantasy of flaying as punishment.[44]

After flaying Caiphas, Vespasian is called away. Rome is without a leader, thanks to the overthrow and suicide of Nero, who chews a stick into a stake and stabs himself through the heart so that no one can have the pleasure of killing him (ll. 913–20). Nero's death is followed by a parade of horrible, corrupt and worthless emperors. The nobles of Rome send knights in armour with letters requesting that Vespasian return and become emperor. Vespasian gathers his best men, including Titus, Titus' brother and Sir Sabyn, to give him advice. Afraid of breaking his promise to raze the city to the ground, he asks what he should do. Sir Sabyn advises that Vespasian can return home and still keep his promise, and he does so through a metaphor of flaying:

> Þe dom demed was ʒer who doþ by anoþer
> Schal be soferayn hymself sein in þe werke.
> For as fers is þe freke ate ferre end
> Þat of-fleis þe fel as he þat foot holdeþ.

(ll. 989–92)

Here this deer/hunting metaphor is 'part of a widely dispersed alliterative synecdoche for concerted government'.[45] Hanna goes on to read the flayer in these lines as the 'employee', while the one holding the foot is the member of the higher class, whom he 'assume[s] to be removed from such gory manual operations'.[46] In other words, Vespasian can go home and leave the final gory siege (complete with cannibalism) to his son Titus and the others.

Given the positioning of the animal, figuratively Jerusalem, and the men surrounding it, the passage echoes the flaying of Caiphas, and Vespasian (metaphorically at least) holds the knife. The image of a deer being held

---

[43] See: Tracy, *Torture and Brutality*, and, in this volume, Larissa Tracy, 'Face Off: Flaying and Identity in Medieval Romance', pp. 322–48.

[44] Both Vespasian and Nero are figures of brutality in medieval hagiography. That one, Vespasian, here becomes a figure of Christian heroism and piety reveals the power of the narrative of Jerusalem's destruction. Since the destruction was prophetically necessary, those involved become the hands of God, rewritten as heroes even when they are traditionally not.

[45] Hanna, 'Contextualizing', p. 110.

[46] Ibid.

up by the feet so that the man at the other end can successfully and easily remove the skin echoes Caiphas' flaying followed by his being hung upside down. Once the Romans accept Titus in the position of proxy leadership, they swear on a book:

> A boke on a brode scheld   was broȝt on to swere:
> Burnes boden to þe honde   and barouns hit kyssen
> To be leel to þat lord   þat hem lede scholde,
> Sire Titus þe trewe kyng,   tille þey þe toun hadde.
>
> (ll. 1009–12)

The book on the shield brings us back again to the flesh. Caiphas and his priests have been flayed, crucified and burned, but books still remain. While the emphasis of Christian belief in this poem is directed away from reading, the touch of human flesh on inscribed animal flesh is still the way to make real and permanent the vows men take. So important to the knights is the significance of touching the book that men stretch to reach it and, those who can, kiss it – a prominent image and an intimate act.

The image of flesh torn from bone, whether by whips or flaying knives, persists across the poem. But the ultimate act of violent desperation in the poem is certainly the Jewish mother's cannibalization of her own child, and critics have made much of this scene.[47] Timothy L. Stinson has worked extensively with the *Siege* manuscripts and notes how examining variations (as opposed to looking at a single, edited text) can lead to alternative interpretations.[48] He includes the full passage detailing the mother-cannibal episode:

> O saynt Marie a Mild wyf for meschefe of fude
> hir awen barne that scho bare Made brede one the gledis

---

[47] Narin van Court reads the scene as a means of creating pity for the Jews in 'Socially Marginal, Culturally Central', p. 317, and 'The Siege of Jerusalem and Recuperative Readings', in *Pulp Fictions of Medieval England: Essays in Medieval Culture*, ed. Nicola McDonald (Manchester: Manchester University Press, 2004), p. 162; alternatively, Nicholson acknowledges the potential for sympathy, but rejects it and describes the Jews as 'trapped in the pattern of abhorrence that the poem traces' ('Haunted Itineraries', p. 481); Merrall Llewelyn Price locates the cannibal mother moment in *Siege* within the history of such cannibal stories from other Jerusalem siege narratives, with particular attention to castration anxiety. See: Merrall Llewelyn Price, *Consuming Passions: The Uses of Cannibalism in Late Medieval and Early Modern Europe*. New York: Routledge, 2003, p. 71; for further discussions of this moment, see: Akbari, 'Placing the Jews', pp. 41–2, and 'Erasing the Body', pp. 158–9; and Yeager, *Jerusalem in Medieval Narrative*, p. 105.

[48] Timothy L. Stinson, 'Makers of the Mind: Authorial Intention, Editorial Practice, and *The Siege of Jerusalem*', *Yearbook of Langland Studies* 24 (2010): 39–62.

Scho ruschede owte ribbe and rygere with rewefull wordis
Sayse Enter thare þou owte come and Etis the rybbis
and sone appon Ilke a syde oure sorowe es newe
alle withowttyn þe burghe oure bodyes to quelle
and within es hunger so hate that nere our hetris brystis
and therefore ȝelde þat þou ȝafe and aȝayne torne
Enter þare þou owte come and Etis the childe
the smelle rase of the roste righte in the strete
that fele Fastande folke felide the sauoure
and downe thay daschen the dore and hastely thay askede
why that þat mete in þat Meschefe was from men laynede
than sayde that worthiliche wife in ane wode hunger
Myn awen barne es my brede and I the bones gnawe
ȝitte hafe I sauede ȝow some and a syde fechide
Of the barne þat sho bare bot than thaire ble chaunged
and further went þay with woo wepand full sore
and sayde allas in this lyfe how lange schall we lenge
ȝitt were it better at a brayde in batelle to dye
than thus in langoure to ly and lenghthyn oure pyn.[49]

As Stinson points out, the use of 'Mary' in the first line is an invocation of the Virgin and is not given as the name of the 'Milde wyfe'.[50] Therefore, the association of the cannibal mother here with Mary mother of God and the Eucharistic connection is less immediately clear.[51] However, even with the Jewish mother not being called Mary, the Eucharistic reading is present. Opening with a cry to Mary draws attention to a parallel between St Mary and this mother.[52] The repeated emphasis on eating the child reinforces the Eucharist link – it is human flesh, a child's flesh, being devoured.[53]

Akbari writes:

> The purpose of such parodic identification is not so much to identify the Jews with Christians (and thus to humanize them), but rather to identify the Christians with the Jews, in order to articulate a notion of Christian identity that both takes Judaism as its model and eradicates it utterly.[54]

---

[49] Ibid., p. 58. For this particular passage, all quotations will be from this article. Other passages from the poem are from Hanna and Lawton. This particular passage is found in lines 1081–100 in Hanna and Lawton.

[50] Ibid., p. 59.

[51] Ibid.

[52] Mueller sees this moment as 'invit[ing] us to read this [mother] as a monstrous version of Christ's Mary' ('Corporal Terror', p. 300).

[53] This also is an invocation of Blood Libel myths about Jews consuming the flesh of Christian children as an inversion of the Eucharist.

[54] Akbari, 'Placing the Jews', p. 42.

Seeing this moment in light of the flaying of Caiphas puts it in a slightly different context. It not only parodies the Eucharist, but also echoes the earlier cannibalism and mass suicide.[55] The Jews trapped in the city have already been forced to consume the ashes of their priests. Now, one eats the flesh of a Jewish child. Upon seeing the cannibalism and the madness of the mother, many of the Jews leave, sure that suicide is better than what they are experiencing. The repetition of cannibalism and suicide highlights the roles of both the Jews and the Christians in the poem. The Christians orchestrate and create the destruction, and the Jews read that destruction. The English audience reads and understands the texts – they participate in the Eucharist – while the Jews cannot. Jewish cannibalism is literal, horrifying and without curative effect: it cannot prevent the destruction of Jerusalem or save the Jews spiritually. Whether read as sympathetic or not, these events reiterate the role of the Jews as the past, as literal and self-consuming. The Christians are the inheritors of the past and the foundation of the future. Slotted in to the Christian narrative, they see themselves as both historical (Roman) and contemporary (English) heroes, the new chosen people, whose story is not literal but symbolic, not self-consuming but spiritually revitalizing.

Titus takes the city in a final barrage of destruction and consumption. No fool, he makes sure the temple is emptied before it is completely destroyed:

> Out þe tresour to take   Tytus commaundyþ,
> Doun bete þe bilde,   brenne hit into grounde.
> [...]
> Now masouns and mynours   han þe molde souȝte
> With pykeyse and ponsone   persched þe walles;
> Hewen þrow hard ston,   hurled hem to grounde
> Þat alle derkned þe diche   for doust of þe poudere.
>
> (ll. 1263–4; 1281–4)

The temple is brought down to the earth, just like Caiphas was reduced to ashes:

> The annihilation of the walls of the city, repeated in microcosm in the annihilation of the bodies of the Jewish men, is a visible manifestation of the erasure of the community of the Jewish nation. Superseded by the Church, the community of the Jews could be seen only as the detritus of the past.[56]

The Romans, having plundered the temple and the city, reiterate

---

[55] After the codification of transubstantiation by Lateran IV, this connection between cannibalism and the Eucharist served as the basis of protest for many sects.

[56] Akbari, 'Erasing the Body', p. 159.

vengeance once more by selling the Jews: 'Ay for a peny of pris, whoso pay wolde, / Þrytty Iewes in a þrom þrongen in ropis' (ll. 1319–20). Thus, the self-consumption forced on the Jews by the Romans earlier in the poem is reiterated by the Romans' consumption of the Jews at the end.[57] The Jewish body – represented in the temple, the city and its goods, and the flesh of the people themselves – has been stripped and/ or destroyed. Veronica and her veil are in Rome, Caiphas is burnt and Jerusalem's treasure is headed to Rome. Leaving behind nothing but salted earth (ll. 1293–6), Titus and his Romans 'Wenten syngyng away and han here wille forþred / And hom riden to Rome' (ll. 1339–40). In these last lines, Rome is not merely the physical home of Titus; rather, it is the spiritual capital of Christianity. The Roman heroes have taken what they wanted, what they needed, from Jerusalem, and left the rest empty and uninhabitable. For an English audience, Rome's traitors against Christ are poetically flayed, and Rome is home to both English romance heroes defending their faith and historical heroes laying the foundation for England as a Christian nation to come. Thus, flaying plays the role it has earlier in English fiction: poetic justice. The Jewish bodies have been rendered objects – read and burned like books. As readers of the flayed-flesh book, the English can identify with the Jew's suffering, but reject the Jewish literalist mistakes and misreading, choosing instead to follow the Roman heroes.

Another tale of energetically fictionalized English history, *RCL* has been read as a romance participating in the idealizing of England as a nation. Instead of proto-Christians perpetrating a siege on Jerusalem, *RCL* deals with Richard I's life and his confrontation with a particular, monolithic image of the Saracens as 'a racialized figure of ultimate difference who condensed everything inimical to the fragile Christian selfsame'.[58] Romance as a genre, with *RCL* and *Siege* as examples, creates Saracens as enemies to be overcome; they are the source of moral and physical conflict against which the Christians in the narrative can be measured. Geraldine Heng notes that in English romance the perception of the Saracen as a monolithic Other contributed to the presentation of Christian identity that way, too:

> [Race] makes an appearance in the late Middle Ages not only through fantasmatic black, historical Jews and the collections of

---

[57] Chism notes that 'The siege culminates in the destruction of the temple, the subjection of the Jews, and the liquidation of their assets. Subjecting Jerusalem to the fierce pressures of siege, the poem reforges the city, the Jews, and the Orient [...] into pure, movable wealth' (*Alliterative Revivals*, p. 155).

[58] Jeffrey Jerome Cohen, 'On Saracen Enjoyment: Some Fantasies of Race in Late Medieval France and England', *Journal of Medieval and Early Modern Studies* 31.1 (Winter 2001): 113–46 at p. 115.

hybrid humans pressing upon the edges of civilization, but can also be found at the center of things, in the creation of that strange creature who is nowhere, yet everywhere, in cultural discourse: the white Christian European in medieval time.[59]

Through flaying, cannibalism and mangled Saracen bodies, *RCL* establishes Richard as an English and Christian hero. Much like Titus and Vespasian flaying in *Siege*, Richard goes beyond the real into fantasy. Richard is stronger, more powerful and more moral than the Saracen enemy and the 'frenemy' France. He unknowingly consumes Saracen flesh and is not corrupted by it; instead, he creates a fantasy of total power.[60] He turns the human flesh not only into food, but into a text to be read by the visiting Saracen ambassadors. While flaying might not be legal, and cannibalism is certainly disturbing, Richard succeeds by doing both. His tactics, which break boundaries of humanity, show the power of the English hero; the most violent of acts and the most polluted of meals cannot destroy him. Not only do the Saracens define the English through the differences between them, but Richard also appropriates those differences. Saracens flay and eat people as a sign of their depravity; Richard flays and eats people as a sign of dominance. He, and by extension the English, are incorruptible.

Recent critical study of *RCL* has dealt at length with discussions of the poem as a part of English national identity. For Alan S. Ambrisco, the poem's distancing of Richard and England from both the French and the Saracens 'retroactively constructs not only an identity of Richard, but a coherent identity for England as well'.[61] Nicola McDonald argues for a reading of Richard that sees him as both a conquering hero and a pious one, whose feast of Saracens is 'annihilation' for the sake of Western culture.[62] Alternatively, Suzanne Conklin Akbari reads *RCL*'s 'Eucharistic symbolism' as not only a part of building national identity, but also a reflection of the 'intertwining of religious and royal authority' during the reign of Henry IV

---

[59] Geraldine Heng, 'Jews, Saracens, "Black Men", Tartars: England in a World of Racial Difference', in *A Companion to Medieval English Literature and Culture, c. 1350–1500*, ed. Peter Brown (New York: Wiley-Blackwell, 2009), pp. 247–69 at p. 265.

[60] Nicola McDonald, 'Eating People and the Alimentary Logic of *Richard Cœur de Lion*', in *Pulp Fictions of Medieval England*, ed. McDonald (Manchester: Manchester University Press, 2004), pp. 124–50 at p. 126. A persistent contemporary legend insisted that the man who accidentally killed Richard was flayed alive, even after the king had pardoned him with his dying breath.

[61] Alan S. Ambrisco, 'Cannibalism and Cultural Encounters in *Richard Cœur de Lion*', *Journal of Medieval and Early Modern Studies* 29.3 (Fall 1999): 499–528 at p. 499.

[62] McDonald, 'Eating People', p. 143.

and Archbishop Arundel.[63] Sarah Beth Torpey finds Richard's character more ambiguous and suggests that the poem would generate discussion in a medieval audience, leaving them to discern the meaning instead of requiring a single response.[64] Suzanne M. Yeager focuses on Jerusalem and Richard's desire for it, suggesting that those traits are developed as 'expressive of English national identity'.[65] Richard's cannibalism and flaying, particularly the message he sends to the ambassadors, brings *RCL* back to reading. Richard, like Titus and Vespasian in the *Siege*, turns bodies into books. These bodies tell the tale of (English) Christian dominance in both religion and arms.

About halfway through the poem, while Richard is camped outside of Acre, he becomes ill and loses his appetite. In his sickness, he craves pork, which is hard to come by in the Saracen lands. Finally, an 'old kny3t' gives the steward a recipe to cure Richard:

> Takes a Sarezyn 3onge and ffat;
> Jn haste þat þe þeff be slayn,
> Openyd, and hys hyde off fflayn,
> And soden fful hastyly.
>
> (ll. 3088–91)

The way to cure the king and satisfy his craving for pork is to feed him a young Saracen. After preparing the 'animal', the meat is cooked in various spices, and after the king has eaten and slept, he recovers. In this case, the flaying and other preparatory actions treat the Saracen as an animal. Once the dish is served, that connection becomes clear:

> Beffore Kyng Rychard karf a kny3te,
> He eete ffastere þan he karue my3te.
> Þe kyng eet þe fflesch, and gnew þe bones,
> And drank wel afftyr, for the nones.
>
> (ll. 3109–12)

The Saracen is indistinguishable from any other meat Richard might eat. The meal goes just as the old knight said it should, and Richard eats, drinks and goes to sleep. The response of his men is laughter: 'And whenne he hadde eeten jnow3, / Hys ffolk hem tournyd away and low3' (ll. 3113–14). The boundary violation of cannibalism is rendered harmless by its results and the laughter it inspires.

---

[63] Suzanne Conklin Akbari, 'The Hunger for National Identity in *Richard Coer de Lion*', in *Reading Medieval Culture: Essays in Honor of Robert W. Hanning*, ed. Robert M. Stein and Sandra Pierson Prior (Notre Dame, IN: University of Notre Dame Press, 2005), pp. 198–227 at pp. 199–200.

[64] Sarah Beth Torpey, 'Of Cannibals and Kings: The (Monstrous) Nature of Crusading in *Richard Coer de Lyon*', *Medieval Perspectives* 23 (2008 [2011]): 105–18 at pp. 116–17.

[65] Yeager, *Jerusalem in Medieval Narrative*, p. 48.

Richard does not discover his cannibalism until after he has led a massive, successful battle against the Saracens. After a long day of killing, Richard demands the head of the pig that he had eaten. The cook tries to refuse, but is persuaded when Richard threatens to have his head cut off if he does not produce the pig's head. When the cook presents the head, he does so falling to his knees and begging for mercy (ll. 3198–210). But Richard's response to what he sees is not hostile at all:

> 'What deuyl is þis?' þe kyng cryde,
> And gan to lauȝe as he were wood.
> 'What, is Sarezynys flesch þus good?
> And neuere ers I nonȝt wyste?
> By Goddys deþ and hys vpryste,
> Schole we neuere dye for defawte,
> Whyle we may in any assawte
> Slee Sarezynys, þe flesch mowe take,
> Seþen, and roste hem, and doo hem bake,
> Gnawen here fflesch to þe bones.
> Now j haue it prouyd ones,
> Ffor hungyr ar j be woo,
> J and my ffolk schole eete moo!'

(ll. 3214–26)

Richard's delight in this moment is horrifying. It is also somewhat Eucharistic. The vow he makes 'by God's death and resurrection' never to go hungry resonates as the answer to spiritual hunger cured through the rite of communion. But cannibalism – literally eating another person, even if he is a Saracen – is problematic, too, especially when committed by a member of one's own community.[66] So it is possible that this drifts from the invocative to the parodic: 'Through the consumption of Saracen flesh, Richard takes strength from the bodies of his adversary. This eating, with its parallels to the consumption of Christ's body in the Eucharist, is a parody of the ritual enactment of that meal.'[67] He parodies the Saracens by substituting their flesh for their idea of unclean flesh: pork. The instability produced by the act is, in part, because Richard has eaten something unclean – both by eating human flesh and by consuming a Saracen. 'By eating unclean things, Richard assimilates that which is outside the boundaries of ordinary life, becoming a liminal figure.'[68] Such boundary crossing is Richard's source of power. By consuming here without negative consequence, and by recognizing the consumption as something that his own people can do, he transcends the boundary. He is capable of ingesting

---

[66] Ambrisco 'Cannibalism and Cultural Encounters', p. 509.

[67] Yeager, *Jerusalem in Medieval Narrative*, pp. 55–6.

[68] Akbari, 'The Hunger for National Identity', p. 212.

the unclean and also declaring it clean for his people. He suggests that all his people – all the English – are capable of the same.

But Richard does not stop at the possibility of eating more Saracens. Instead, he plans a meal of them, presenting Saracen ambassadors, who have come to discuss a truce, with Saracen heads for dinner. Richard himself gives instructions for the dish:

> I schal þe telle what þou schalt don.
> Priuely goo to þe prisoun,
> þe Sarezynys off most renoun,
> þat be comen off þe rycheste kynne,
> Priuyly slee hem therin;
> And ar þe hedes be of smyten,
> Looke euery name be wryten
> Vpon a scrowe off parchemyn;
> And bere þe hedes to þe kechyn,
> And in a cawdroun þou hem caste,
> And bydde þe cook seþe hem ffaste;
> And loke þat he þe her off stryppe,
> Off hed, off berde, and eke off lyppe.
> Whenne we shole sytte and eete,
> Loke þat ȝe nouȝt fforgete
> To serue hem herewiþ in þis manere:
> Lay euery hed on a platere,
> Bryng it hoot forþ al in þyn hand,
> Vpward hys vys, þe teeþ grennand;
> And loke þey be nothynge rowe!
> Hys name faste aboue hys browe,
> What he hyȝte, and off what kyn borne.

(ll. 3412–33)

The event goes as planned, terrifying the Saracen ambassadors, whom Richard mockingly reassures, insisting that he would never eat guests. He also adds that they should return and tell their 'Sawdan' that the English will never die of hunger because with one Saracen they can feed nine or ten Englishmen (ll. 3544–6). He ends by declaring that he and his men 'Into Yngelond wol we nouȝt gon, / Tyl þay be eeten euerylkon' (ll. 3561–2). Heng argues that this is a nationalistic joke laced with international aggression.[69] For Ambrisco, far from being negative, it is a sign of just how far the English will go to win.[70] For McDonald and Akbari, the significance of the act is linked to the public feasting. McDonald sees it as the Christian

---

[69] Geraldine Heng, *Empire of Magic: Medieval Romance and the Politics of Cultural Fantasy* (New York: Columbia University Press, 2003), p. 75.

[70] Ambrisco, 'Cannibalism and Cultural Encounters', p. 516.

taboo and fantasy,[71] and Akbari suggests that Richard's cannibalism is a version of sacrifice: 'just as the priest consumes the Host on behalf of the spiritual community, so Richard as king consumes the flesh on behalf of that national community'.[72] For Yeager, Richard's ability to cannibalize comes from God's favour – because Richard is blessed, he is a supernatural hero.[73] The threat of English consumption moves beyond territory and resources to the literal Saracen flesh. Those in the English audience, by extension, are also capable of this heroic feat (and feast) and can view themselves as able to conquer and consume, whether it is Saracens or the French enemy *du jour*.

All of these critical works focus on Richard's role in the cannibalizing. However, the Saracens' heads are also important. They exist not to be eaten, but to be read. Given the connection between flesh – particularly flayed flesh – and reading, the preparation of the heads is crucial to the text. Though the heads are not flayed skin, they are boiled and scraped clean of all hair, echoing the process that animal skin goes through as it is converted into parchment. Parchment is mentioned when Richard notes that the names of the Saracens should be recorded so that the heads can be correctly identified. Finally, after the cooking process, the heads are labelled and read by the Saracen visitors both literally and symbolically.

Taken together in the London Thornton manuscript, the cannibalized and flayed bodies as books in *Siege* and *RCL* become part of a larger narrative of Christian domination and destruction. These two romances appear with the crusade romances *Siege of Milan* and *Duke Roland and Sir Otuel of Spain*, a portion of the *Cursor Mundi* and a particularly graphic version of *The Northern Passion*.[74] They form a narrative of Christian history emphasizing violence and suffering, as Michael Johnston has argued:

> [T]he textual collocation Thornton has created, accompanied by the
> incipits he has composed and the textual variants he has preserved,
> encourages a selective reading of *The Siege*, one that sells the poem as

---

[71] McDonald, 'Eating People', p. 143.

[72] Akbari, 'The Hunger for National Identity', p. 214.

[73] Yeager, *Jerusalem in Medieval Narrative*, p. 76.

[74] The manuscript also contains Marian lyrics by Lydgate and other texts. For a full discussion of the manuscript, see: George R. Keiser, 'A Note on the Descent of the Thornton Manuscript', *Cambridge Bibliographic Society* 7 (1976): 346–8; Keiser, 'More Light on the Life and Milieu of Robert Thornton', *Studies in Bibliography* 36 (1983): 112–19; John J. Thompson, *Robert Thornton and the London Thornton Manuscript: BL Additional 31042* (Cambridge: Cambridge University Press, 1987); Ralph Hanna, 'The Growth of Robert Thornton's Books', *Studies in Bibliography* 40 (1987): 51–61; Ralph Hanna, *Pursuing History: Middle English Manuscripts and their Texts* (Stanford, CA: Stanford University Press, 1996).

a piece of unqualified anti-Jewish propaganda. [...] In the series of texts that Robert Thornton has gathered together in the opening of his manuscript, we meet an aggressive religiosity that finds its raison d'être in suffering: initially the suffering of Christ's body, which is subsequently transmogrified into the suffering of Jewish and Saracen bodies.[75]

After the section discussed by Johnston, the manuscript becomes slightly less coherent, and it is in this section that *RCL* appears. However, thematically it is clear that *Siege* and *RCL* have much in common. These texts speak to each other through the broken bodies of the Jews and Saracens, consumed and destroyed by the English (or English-looking) heroes. They delight in the fantasy of violent, retributive justice to reclaim, either literally or spiritually, Jerusalem. The heroes of both texts transgress both body and law, and the moments of boundary crossing allow the English audience to identify with the Christian heroes of the past.

The Jews and Saracens are not merely consumed; they are internalized. For the English, this skin-on-skin touch of the manuscript invokes their flesh, the flesh of the flayed and cannibalized, and the flesh of Christ – tortured but resurrected and present in the Eucharist. English audiences fantasize about being heroic, devout and powerful, identifying with the victorious Romans, the persecuted Jews and the incorruptible Richard I. To find their history and religious identity, the English return time and again to bloody romance.

---

[75] Johnston, 'Robert Thornton and *The Siege of Jerusalem*', p. 128.

12

Losing Face: Flayed Beards and Gendered Power in Arthurian Literature

Michael Livingston

FLAYING, as the *OED* observes, is often associated with an action 'to strip or pull off the skin or hide' from a victim's entire body (*flay* v.1a): a most horrific kind of killing or post-killing desecration of the corpse, as many articles in this volume attest. But while the meaning is now obsolete, the verb *flay* had in the late Middle Ages another, presumably less deadly, meaning: 'to tear off (a man's beard) together with the skin' (*flay* v.4b). Such an act, though certainly noteworthy for its viciousness, was more than mere punishment: since the beard can serve as a marker of masculinity, its removal shames him whose beard is torn off – shaved – against his will. Building on these same foundations, the further act of beard-*flaying* – most evident in its use as a recurring motif in Arthurian literature – both shames the flayed victim, and glorifies the victorious flayer: in sum, the flaying of beards grew within Arthurian mythology into a gendered sign of political authority.

Laura Clark, one of the few scholars to investigate this practice, has recently examined what had been a largely ignored component of Thomas Malory's *Morte Darthur*: the references to characters wearing coats made of beards.[1] Clark demonstrates the importance of the general symbolism of the beard, the history of its wear during the Middle Ages in the East and West, and the specific uses to which Malory puts these beard-coats. She concludes that in Malory's sources such beard-coats hold a 'monstrous significance' that often points towards the 'implications of unbridled imperialism', and that Malory endeavours to incorporate these meanings into his text in a way that subsumes their negative contexts and leaves King Arthur an unblemished 'worthy ruler'.[2] What follows here builds upon Clark's findings, expanding the context for her conclusions by filling in a larger history of beard-removals within medieval English Arthurian literature, including the revelation of the practice's apparent origin in Wales,

An early version of this paper was delivered at the Fortieth Meeting of the Southeastern Medieval Association, at Clayton State University in Morrow, GA, on 17 October 2014. I am grateful to the members of the audience who provided excellent feedback and suggestions on my argument.

[1] Laura Clark, 'Fashionable Beards and Beards as Fashion: Beard Coats in Thomas Malory's *Morte d'Arthur*', *Parergon* 31 (2014): 95–109.

[2] Clark, 'Fashionable Beards', p. 109.

and ultimately delving more deeply into the provocative ways in which the author of one of Malory's key sources – the Alliterative *Morte Arthure* – has utilized the received symbolism of the removal of beards. When it comes to beards, Arthur may not always be so worthy.

Scenes of beard-removal are rather common in medieval literature, and a brief look at this tradition makes clear the symbolic uses of the practice. The late alliterative poem *Siege of Jerusalem* (hereafter *Siege*), though narrating the destruction of Jerusalem in 70 CE, is an unflinchingly brutal look at the medieval world at war, from siege engines to starving citizens, from battles to executions. Amid its many graphic scenes – so many that the poet has been said to have a 'ghoulish relish for the horrible'[3] – is one that might seem strange at first glance. The Roman Emperor Vespasian, newly (and quite ahistorically) converted to Christianity after the power of Christ heals him of a wasp infestation in his nose, has sworn that he will have vengeance upon the Jews for the killing of Christ. He sends messengers to the Jews, ordering them to submit to his judgement and to hand over Caiaphas, who, as head priest of the Jews, is ultimately responsible for the death. The Jews seize these hapless messengers, bind their hands, and then 'of flocken here fax and here faire berdis' [tear off their hair and their fair beards].[4] This hair-removal accomplished, the messengers are sent back to Rome bearing blocks of cheese.

Regrettably, no critic has managed an adequate explanation for this use of cheese as an apparent mark of humiliation. The latest edition of *Siege* does, however, observe that the *Siege*-poet has an immediate precedent for the preceding beard-removal: 2 Kings (2 Samuel) 10.4–5 describes how King Hanun of the Ammonites, suspecting treachery, angrily seized the envoys of King David and shaved half of their beards before sending them away.[5] These men were so socially shamed by this degradation that David ordered them not to return to Jerusalem but to remain in Jericho until their beards had grown back. The parallel treatment of Vespasian's messengers, in the *Siege*-poet's vision, has the Roman Emperor, thus, becoming a new kind of David, this time fulfilling God's will – in a horrifically ironic reversal – through his subsequent destruction of the Jews, just as David had gone on to defeat the Ammonites. Underlying both beard-removals is the concept of shaming, and it is customary in many commentaries to view the reason for this shame to be, at least in terms of the biblical passage, the fact that 'mutilation of the beard, the symbol of a man's honor',

---

[3] Dorothy Everett, 'The Alliterative Revival', in *Essays on Middle English Literature*, ed. Patricia Kean (Oxford: Clarendon Press, 1955), p. 59. In this volume, see: Emily Leverett, 'Reading the Consumed: Flayed and Cannibalized Bodies in *The Siege of Jerusalem* and *Richard Coer de Lyon*', pp. 285–307.

[4] *The Siege of Jerusalem*, ed. Michael Livingston (Kalamazoo, MI: Medieval Institute Publications, 2004), l. 364.

[5] Ibid., pp. 94–5.

was one of 'the worst insults imaginable in those days'.[6] Unsaid in such explanations, but doubtlessly true, is the underlying fact that the wearing of the beard – outside of sideshow attractions – is a genetically masculine marker.[7] Since men grow beards and women do not, an attack on the beard of a grown man is by extension an attack on his identity as a man – on his natural virility and self-identity, and perhaps ultimately his honour.[8] This is certainly the reason that the Green Knight insults the men of King Arthur's court as 'berdlez chylder' [beardless children] in *Sir Gawain and the Green Knight*.[9] Clark, through a survey of literary examples, including such famous tales as *La Chanson de Roland* and *El cantar del mio Cid*, likewise concludes 'that beards represent the qualities of a man's character – wisdom, experience, maturity, military prowess, nobility, and honour (or the lack thereof)' – in addition to 'the more obvious and natural purpose of distinguishing men from women', as Geoffrey Chaucer's unfortunate Absolon rather famously discovers in the Miller's Tale: thinking he is kissing fair Alisoun's lips in the darkness, he begins to recognize that he has in fact kissed her exposed posterior when he observes that he feels her 'beard' upon his chin.[10]

This symbolism has considerable antiquity. While the pharaohs of ancient Egypt were meticulous shavers of body hair in life, they consistently wore – and consistently had themselves portrayed wearing – false beards, associating themselves with the bearded god of the afterlife, Osiris, who in turn represented the regular virility of the life-giving Nile. So important was this association between the god, the pharaoh and the continuance of Egyptian civilization that Hapshepsut, the famous

---

[6] *The New Oxford Annotated Bible*, ed. Bruce M. Metzger and Roland E. Murphy (Oxford: Oxford University Press, 1991), p. 397. In a brief aside on this same biblical passage, Clark claims that 'Hanun's punishment of David's men equates a clean-shaven face with bared private parts' ('Fashionable Beards', p. 97), but this seems, at best, to be a secondary or tertiary symbolism to the basic principle of shaming.

[7] Among the most famous instances of a 'Bearded Lady' is P. T. Barnum's Josephine Clofullia; for a look at public reactions to Madame Clofullia and a discussion of the plasticity of modern gender norms, see: Sean Trainor, 'Fair Bosom/Black Beard: Facial Hair, Gender Determination, and the Strange Career of Madame Clofullia, "Bearded Lady"', *Early American Studies* 12 (2014): 548–75.

[8] For an argument placing this same concept within the Renaissance, see: Will Fisher, 'The Renaissance Beard: Masculinity in Early Modern England', *Renaissance Quarterly* 54 (2001): 155–87.

[9] *Sir Gawain and the Green Knight*, ed. J. R. R. Tolkien and E. V. Gordon (Oxford: Oxford University Press, 1967), l. 280.

[10] Clark, 'Fashionable Beards', p. 101. For Absolon, see: *Canterbury Tales* I[A]3737, in *The Riverside Chaucer*, gen. ed. Larry D. Benson, 3rd edn (Boston: Houghton Mifflin, 1987), p. 75.

queen-pharaoh, appears to have worn a false beard despite her sex.[11] The people of neighbouring Assyria similarly associated the beard with the mane of a male lion and, thereby, with masculine strength and authority: a glorious beard is, thus, the most prominent feature marking many representations of the Assyrian kings. So important was facial hair to the Stoic philosopher Epictetus that he once vowed that he would accept beheading before shaving.[12] These same symbolisms surely lie behind folk narratives such as that found in the German story of 'the ungrateful dwarf', first recorded by Caroline Stahl in 1818 and popularized by the Brothers Grimm in the fairy tale of Snow-White and Rose-Red: the two girls come upon a dwarf in the forest whose beard is caught within a tree; when Snow-White uses her scissors to cut him free, he curses her for cutting his beard.[13]

Beards as a marker of manhood – and thus by extension a marker of social status – clearly remained effective through the millennia into the literature of medieval England.[14] Personal shame certainly seems to be the reason for the beard-shaving in *Siege*, building upon biblical precedent. In other cases, however, medieval English traditions ultimately stepped beyond the mere shaving of enemy beards to the far more dramatic act of *flaying* them. Though not addressed by Clark's study, whose primary focus is Malory's use of these later traditions, the extant origin of this thread of beard-flaying appears in Wales, where it is not surprisingly rooted in the very same symbolism of beard-as-masculine-marker seen in other cultures. In a recent and very perceptive study of shame and honour in the Welsh *Mabinogi*, for instance, John K. Bollard calls attention to the recurrent use in these texts of 'the traditional relationship between shame and beards', as characters repeatedly call down shame upon facial hair: 'Meuyl

---

[11] See, for instance, the colossal granite sphinx representation of the pharaoh now housed in New York's Metropolitan Museum of Art.

[12] Epictetus, *Discourses* 1.2.29.

[13] Jack Zipes, *The Great Fairy Tale Tradition: From Straparola and Basile to the Brothers Grimm* (New York: Norton, 2001), p. 772.

[14] While the literary symbolism of the beard has seemingly remained steady, it is interesting to note that the actual cultural fashion of wearing beards has not been constant. For a brief populist overview of the history of hair growth in the West, see: Charles Mackay's *Memoirs of Extraordinary Popular Delusions and the Madness of Crowds*, which devotes an entire chapter to 'The Influence of Politics and Religion on the Hair and Beard' (London: Robson, Levey and Franklyn, 1852), 1.296–303. However, changing views of personal aesthetic do not seem to have had an effect on the traditional symbolism; as Clark observes, Malory seems to have had no hesitation about utilizing the literary motif, even though the wearing of beards was not fashionable in his own day ('Fashionable Beards', p. 95). In this volume, William Sayers makes a similar connection between flaying, shame and kingship in medieval Irish sources. See: 'No Skin in the Game: Flaying and Early Irish Law and Epic', pp. 261–84, at pp. 266, 269.

ar uy maryf i', Heilyn ap Gwyn says in one notable example, 'onyt agoraf
y drws, e wybot ay gwir a dywedir am hynny.' [Shame on my beard [...]
if I do not open the door to find out whether it is true what is said about
that.][15] Bollard finds similar connections in many other works of medieval
Welsh poetry – threatening shame on beards was apparently quite popular
among the bards and their audiences – in addition to the example of 'a
legal triad stipulating the situations in which a husband may beat his
wife with impunity', which he quotes: '[S]ef yu e try e dele y maedu, am
rody peth ny delyho e rody, ac am e chaffael gan ur adan tuell, ac am unau
meuel ar e uaryf.' [These are the three [reasons] he is entitled to beat her,
for giving away something she is not entitled to give, and for catching her
with a man under a blanket, and for wishing shame on his beard.] 'Thus',
Bollard concludes, 'to say *meuyl ar dy farf* "shame on your beard" is to cast
aspersions on someone's public status, perhaps [...] on his virility.'[16]

It is this very symbolism that appears to be at work in the Welsh
Arthurian tale *Culhwch ac Olwen*. In this strange story, likely composed
in the eleventh century though now only extant in manuscripts of the
fourteenth century, a young man named Culhwch seeks as his wife
the beautiful Olwen, who unfortunately happens to be the daughter of
Ysbaddaden, the Chief Giant. Culhwch seeks out the help of his relative,
King Arthur, who agrees with his men to help fulfil the impossible tasks
that Ysbaddaden lays before Culhwch as a price for his daughter. Two of
these tasks focus specifically on beards: a leash must be made of the beard
of the great warrior Dillus the Bearded, and Ysbaddaden's own beard must
be washed and then shaved with the tusk of Ysgithrwyn, the Chief Boar. To
retrieve the beard of Dillus, Cai and Bedwyr allow the great warrior to fall
asleep, whereupon they dig a great pit under his feet and push him in. They
pluck his beard with wooden tweezers, and 'A gwedy hynny y lad yn gwbyl'
[after that they killed him outright].[17] Dillus, though killed by Arthur's men,
is noticeably not flayed; his beard-removal, like that of David's messengers

---

[15] See: John K. Bollard, '*Meuyl ar uy Maryf*: Shame and Honour in *The
Mabinogi*', *Studia Celtica* 47 (2013): 123–47 at p. 128.

[16] Ibid., p. 129. This is not to say that beards were always used in positive
connotation by the Welsh poets. To the contrary, and perhaps ironically
undercutting the general importance given to the beard within the culture,
beards can also be noted as a negative influence on the poet's physical
appearance. Thus, in 'The Poet's Beard', Iolo Goch complains of how
his 'every bristle is sharp and tough, / hard heather stabbing a girl'. *Iolo
Goch: Poems*, ed. and trans. Dafydd Johnston (Llandysul: Gomer Press,
1993), p. 104. In a personal communication, Bollard notes that similar
observations about facial hair being 'a hindrance to amorous desires' occur
in the works of Llywelyn Goch, Llywelyn ab y Moel and Rhys Goch Eryri.

[17] *Culhwch and Olwen, an Edition and Study of the Oldest Arthurian Tale*, ed.
Rachel Bromwich and D. Simon Evans (Cardiff: University of Wales Press,
1992), l. 974; the translation used here is from 'How Culhwch Got Olwen',

or those of Vespasian in *Siege*, appears to be reflective of shame alone. The fact that the hairs of his beard were painstakingly plucked while he was alive – rather than shaved *en masse* with a blade – further underscores his shameful lack of virility in the hands of his enemies; he could do nothing but suffer the prolonged pricks as, strand by strand, his proud mass of facial hair was removed. When it comes to the climactic act of shaving Ysbaddaden's beard, however, there is no plucking, and the objective does not seem to be the causing of shame.

> Ac yna y kychwynnwys Kulhwch, a Goreu uab Custennin gyt ac ef, a'r sawl a buchei drwc y Yspadaden Pennkawr, a'r anoetheu gantunt hyt y lys. A dyuot Kaw o Brydein y eillaw y uaryf, kic a chroen hyt asgwrn, a'r deu glust yn llwyr. Ac y dywawt Kulhwch, 'A eillwyt itti, wr?' 'Eillwyt', heb ynteu. 'Ae meu y minheu dy uerch di weithoh?' 'Meu', heb ynteu. 'Ac nyt reit itt diolwch y mi hynny, namyn diolwch y Arthur y gwr a'e peris itt. O'm bod i nys kaffut ti hi vyth. A'm heneit inheu ymadws yw y diot.' Ac yna yd ymauaelawd Goreu mab Custennin yndaw herwyd gwallt y penn, a'e lusgaw yn y ol y'r dom, a llad y penn a'e dodi ar bawl y gatlys. A goresgyn y gaer a oruc a'e gyuoeth.
>
> A'r nos honno y kyscwys Kulhwch gan Olwen.[18]

> [And then Culhwch, and Gorau son of Custennin with him, and those who wished ill to Ysbaddaden Chief Giant, with the things hard to find, set out for his court. And Caw of Prydyn came to shave his beard, flesh and skin to the bone, and the two ears completely.
>
> And Culhwch said, 'Are you shaved, man?'
>
> 'Yes', he said.
>
> 'Is your daughter mine now?'
>
> 'Yes', he said, 'and there is no need for you to thank me for that, but thank Arthur, the man who brought it about for you. Of my own free will, you would never have got her. And my life – it is high time to take it away.'
>
> And then Gorau son of Custennin grabbed him by the hair of his head and dragged him behind him to the mound and struck off his head and placed it on the post of the bailey. And he subdued the fort and his realm.
>
> And that night Culhwch slept with Olwen.][19]

Though the act appears off-stage, it is abundantly clear that Ysbaddaden is flayed: his beard is removed along with the flesh and the skin down to the very bone. The symbolism, like the act, is more complex than it was

in *Companion Tales to the Mabinogi: Legend and Landscape of Wales*, trans. John K. Bollard (Llandysul: Gomer Press, 2007), p. 51.

[18] *Culhwch and Olwen*, ed. Bromwich and Evans, ll. 1230–42.

[19] 'How Culhwch Got Olwen', trans. Bollard, p. 70.

with beard-shaving. Like Dillus, the chief giant loses his manhood in being overtaken by his enemies; he also loses his familial virility in having his control over Olwen removed. More than all this, however, he loses his social authority in having his realm summarily taken over. Within the context of *Culhwch ac Olwen*, therefore, beard-flaying combines the shaming of beard-shaving with a larger concept of authority within a community: flaying the beard makes literal a metaphoric removal of an individual from a position of power within the body politic.

However, the de-bearding of Ysbaddaden in *Culhwch ac Olwen* did not solidify this multivalent symbolism of beard-flaying in Arthurian tradition. That happens with the de-bearding of Rhitta Gawr, yet another Welsh giant who comes to be connected with King Arthur. The age of the Rhitta Gawr story is not known, but it is clearly part of a larger folkloric narrative in Wales. In the notes to his poem *The Doom of Colyn Dolphyn*, Taliesin Williams preserves the story of Rhitta Gawr, the 'Red Giant' who defeated two 'maniac' Welsh kings and took their beards; when he is subsequently attacked by twenty-eight more 'Kings of the Island of Britain', Rhitta the Giant defeats them all, making him a king in his own right. He de-beards his fallen foes and makes a mantle of the flayed beards that 'extended from head to heel; and Rhitta was twice as large as any other person ever seen'.[20] As evidence for the folk-tale's assumed antiquity, Williams subsequently relates it to the song 'King Ryence's Challenge', which 'was sung before Queen Elizabeth, at the grand entertainment at Kenilworth Castle, in 1575': here, King Ryence of North Wales has defeated eleven kings and made a mantle with their beards; when he demands King Arthur's beard, Arthur challenges him to a duel and defeats him.[21]

While there is no doubt that the Elizabethan 'King Ryence' belongs to the same narrative family as King Rhitta, Williams should have looked at much older sources. The beard-flaying connection between Rhitta Gawr and Arthur occurs again and again in Arthurian sources. The earliest of these extant appearances is the influential work of the Welsh cleric Geoffrey of Monmouth, *Historia regum Britanniae*, written in 1136. In this text King Arthur, after having defeated the giant of Mont Saint-Michel, compares the difficult combat with a previous one he fought:

> Praecepit intuentibus fieri silentium: dicebat autem se non invenisse alium tantae virtutis, postquam Rithonem gigantem in Aravio monte interfecit, qui eum ad praelium invitaverat. Hic namque ex barbis regum quos peremerat, fecerat sibi pelles, et mandaverat Arturo ut barbam suam diligenter excoriaret, atque excoriatam sibi dirigeret: ut quemadmodum ipse caeteris praeerat regibus, ita

---

[20] Taliesin Williams, *The Doom of Colyn Dolphyn: A Poem, with Notes Illustrative of Various Traditions of Glamorganshire* (London: Longman, Rees, Orme and Co., 1837), pp. 119–20.

[21] Williams, *Doom of Colyn Dolphyn*, p. 121.

quoque in honorem ejus caeteris barbis ipsam superponeret. Sin autem, provocabat eum ad praelium: et qui fortior supervenisset, pelles et barbam devicti tulisset. Inito itaque certamine, triumphavit Arturus, et barbam alterius cepit et spolium, et postea nulli fortiori isto obviaverat, ut superius asserebat.[22]

[Arthur said that he had not come into contact with anyone so strong since the time he killed the giant Retho on Mount Arvaius, after the latter had challenged him to single combat. Retho had made himself a fur cloak from the beards of the kings whom he had slain. He sent a message to Arthur, telling him to rip his own beard off his face and when it was torn off send it to him. Since Arthur was more distinguished than any of the other kings, Retho promised in his honour to sew his beard higher up the cloak than the others. If Arthur would not do this, then Retho challenged him to a duel, saying that whoever proved the stronger should have the fur cloak as trophy and also the beard of the man he had beaten. Soon after the battle began, Arthur was victorious. He took the giant's beard and the trophy too. From that day on, as he had just said, he had met nobody stronger than Retho.][23]

Though no direct connection can be drawn between Geoffrey and the anonymous writer of *Culhwch ac Olwen*,[24] it is fascinating to observe that the beard-flaying in the *Historia* is similarly associated with a Welsh giant. Geoffrey's tale – building upon the folklore account of the de-bearding of kings – appears to make an even more direct connection between beards and political authority. The taking of beards indicates the achievement of victories, a most gruesome and symbolic kind of trophy.

The unification of kingship, giants and testosterone-fuelled Arthurian battles cemented the symbolism of the flaying of beards as a literary sign of political power in the late Middle Ages. Following in the footsteps of Geoffrey of Monmouth, future writers of Arthuriana often made use of some variant of the Rhitta Gawr tale. In 1338, for example, the chronicler Robert Mannyng of Brunne includes a similar account of how Arthur, after killing the giant of Mont Saint-Michel (here named Dynabroke), tells the story of his defeat of the giant Ryton, who had flayed the beards from many

---

[22] Geoffrey of Monmouth, *Historia regum Britanniae*, ed. Albert Schulz (Halle: Eduard Anton, 1854), p. 142.

[23] Geoffrey of Monmouth, *History of the Kings of Britain*, trans. Lewis Thorpe (London: Penguin, 1966), p. 240.

[24] Geoffrey's status as a Welshman, based on assumptions that he was born and worked in Monmouth, has come under significant scrutiny. It may be that he was born of French-speaking parents in Monmouth, but that he spent little of his subsequent life in Wales and spoke no Welsh. See: J. C. Crick, 'Monmouth, Geoffrey of (d. 1154/5)', in the *Oxford Dictionary of National Biography* (Oxford: Oxford University Press, 2004).

kings (ll. 12,451–2); having made a cloak of the beards, Ryton demands that Arthur flay his own beard so that it can be added to it (l. 12,458). When Arthur refuses, the two fight and Arthur wins the cloak as a trophy (l. 12,475).[25] The king's victory seals his political authority over his realm.

By the fifteenth century, Rhitta-Retho-Ryton appears to have lost his supernatural status as a giant and become instead a merely barbaric man. He appears as King Rion in the *Prose Merlin*, a late Middle English translation of part of the widely read Old French Vulgate Cycle. Here the story has also been divorced from its context alongside the giant of Mont Saint-Michel: Rion is instead a formidable fellow king who must be overcome in Arthur's attempts to stabilize his realm. Rion, who threatens Arthur's lands, is described as having 'made a mantell of reade samyte furred with the beardes' of nine conquered kings. He demands Arthur's beard be sent so it can be added to this mantle, threatening otherwise to come and get it himself: 'I shall come upon thee with all myn hoste and make thy beerde be flayn and drawe from thy chyn boustously.'[26]

Unifying these appearances of beard-flaying is the barbaric monstrosity of the Rhitta figure. Even when he is, as in the *Prose Merlin*, a technically human individual, his penchant for flaying beards still represents a wildness that threatens Arthur's ostensibly more civilized court. Unlike the luxurious beard of the Assyrian king, which was meant to indicate the man's naturally superior status, the beard-coat of the monstrous figure of the giant is clearly meant to indicate his unnatural usurpation of status. Arthur's defeat of the giant thus underscores his position as the natural heir to the throne, and his ability to civilize the most barbaric corners of his realm. In defeating the one who has flayed the beards of so many kings – subsuming their virility and power in the process – Arthur demonstrably stabilizes his throne.

However, not all uses of beard-flaying in Arthuriana are quite so positive in their connotations. A notable dissenter in this tradition is the Alliterative *Morte Arthure*, which draws upon both Geoffrey of Monmouth and *Siege*, and which 'seems to be', as Marco Nievergelt has written, 'one of the most consistently elusive works of fourteenth-century English literature'.[27] Among the critical queries about the poem that have evaded resolution is the basic question of its judgement upon King Arthur: Does the poet

---

[25] Robert Mannyng of Brunne, *Chronicle, Part I*, ed. Frederick J. Furnivall, Rolls Series 87 (London: Longman, 1887), pp. 435–6. For Old Norse accounts of beard-flaying and beard cloaks, see in this volume: Larissa Tracy, 'Face Off: Flaying and Identity in Medieval Romance', pp. 322–48.

[26] *Prose Merlin*, ed. John Conlee (Kalamazoo, MI: Medieval Institute Publications, 1998), p. 293.

[27] Marco Nievergelt, 'Introduction: The Alliterative *Morte Arthure* in Context', *Arthuriana* 20.2 (2010): 3–4 at p. 3. Nievergelt's article introduces a special issue of *Arthuriana* devoted exclusively to the poem, highlighting an increasing (and welcome) critical interest in it.

ultimately aim to praise him?[28] Or does he mean to condemn him?[29] Or, intriguingly, does the poet somehow manage to do both, simultaneously holding 'contradictory viewpoints, sincerely admiring and just as sincerely rejecting worldly ideals', as Larry Benson has argued?[30] This essay is not the place to resolve these questions in any irrefutable way, but it may be that the shaming of beards within the poem provides another avenue by which we may approaching an understanding. Composed around the year 1400, this fascinating poem twice references the removal of beards, both

[28] Critical work generally on the positive side of the ledger regarding Arthur in the poem includes: John Eadie, 'The Alliterative *Morte Arthure*: Structure and Meaning', *English Studies: A Journal of English Language and Literature* 63.1 (1982): 1–12; John Finlayson, 'Arthur and the Giant of St Michael's Mount', *Medium Ævum* 32 (1964): 112–20, and 'The Concept of the Hero in "Morte Arthure"', in *Chaucer und sein Zeit: Symposium für Walter F. Schirmer*, ed. Arno Esch (Tübingen: Max Niemeyer, 1967), pp. 249–74; Henry Ansgar Kelly, 'The Non-Tragedy of Arthur', *English Studies* 63 (1982): 1–12; R. M. Lumiansky, 'The Alliterative *Morte Arthure*, the Concept of Medieval Tragedy, and the Cardinal Virtue Fortitude', *Medieval and Renaissance Studies* 3 (1967): 95–118; Richard J. Moll, *Before Malory: Reading Arthur in Later Medieval England* (Toronto: University of Toronto Press, 2003), pp. 97–122; and Elizabeth Porter, 'Chaucer's Knight, the *Alliterative Morte Arthure*, and Medieval Laws of War: A Reconsideration', *Nottingham Medieval Studies* 27 (1983): 56–78.

[29] William Matthews, in *The Tragedy of Arthur: A Study of the Alliterative 'Morte Arthure'* (Berkeley and Los Angeles: University of California Press, 1960), was one of the first critics to see an Arthur worthy only of condemnation. While Matthews argues that the king's blameworthiness is established from essentially the beginning of the poem, most subsequent scholars have been more forgiving and view Arthur in a tragic mode whereby he 'falls' into blame in the second half of the poem. See, e.g.: Mary Hamel, 'The Dream of a King: The Alliterative *Morte Arthure* and Dante', *Chaucer Review* 14.4 (1980): 298–312; Wolfgang Obst, 'The Gawain–Priamus Episode in the Alliterative *Morte Arthure*', *Studia Neophilologica* 57 (1985): 9–18; Roy J. Pearcy, 'The Alliterative *Morte Arthure*, vv. 2420–2447 and the Death of Richard I', *English Language Notes* 22 (1985): 16–27; Russell A. Peck, 'Willfulness and Wonders: Boethian Tragedy in the *Alliterative Morte Arthure*', in *The Alliterative Tradition in the Fourteenth Century*, ed. Bernard S. Levy and Paul E. Szarmach (Kent, OH: Kent State University Press, 1981), pp. 153–82; R. A. Shoaf, 'The Alliterative *Morte Arthure* and the Story of Britain's David', *Journal of English and German Philology* 81 (1982): 204–26; and Jeff Westover, 'Arthur's End: The King's Emasculation in the Alliterative *Morte Arthure*', *Chaucer Review* 32.3 (1998): 310–24.

[30] Larry Benson, 'The Alliterative *Morte Arthure* and Medieval Tragedy', *Tennessee Studies in Literature* 11 (1966): 76–7. Another proponent of just this kind of complexity is Dorsey Armstrong, 'Rewriting the Chronicle Tradition: The Alliterative *Morte Arthure* and Arthur's Sword of Peace', *Parergon* 25.1 (2008): 81–101.

to startling effect.[31] The first reference, cribbing obviously from Geoffrey's Arthurian model, once again focuses on the giant of Mont Saint-Michel. But the poet does not simply rehash the brief account of Retho the giant that Geoffrey used as a backstory to the much longer account of the giant of Mont Saint-Michel; instead, he collapses the two giants into one. In the Alliterative *Morte*, it is the giant of Mont Saint-Michel himself who wears the hideous cloak of beards, as an old woman says to King Arthur in explaining the depths of the giant's depravity:

> For both landes and lythes   full little by he settes;
> Of rentes ne of red gold   reckes he never,
> For he will lenge out of law,   as himself thinkes,
> Withouten license of lede,   as lord in his owen.
> But he has a kirtle on,   keeped for himselven,
> That was spunnen in Spain   with special birdes
> And sithen garnisht in Greece   full graithely togeders;
> It is hided all with here,   holly all over
> And borderd with the berdes   of burlich kinges,
> Crisped and combed   that kempes may know
> Ich king by his colour,   in kith there he lenges.
> Here the fermes he fanges   of fifteen rewmes,
> For ilke Estern even,   however that it fall,
> They send it him soothly   for saught of the pople,
> Sekerly at that sesoun   with certain knightes.
> And he has asked Arthure   all this seven winter;
> Forthy hurdes he here   to outraye his pople
> Til the Britones king   have burnisht his lippes
> And sent his berde to that bold   with his best bernes.
>
> (ll. 998–1012)

[He cares precious little for land or people,
and reckons nothing to riches and red gold,
but will live as he likes, a law unto himself,
without license or election, his very own lord.
He is mantled in a gown which was made to measure,
spun by specialist Spanish maids,
then gathered together most gracefully in Greece.
It is covered all over in hair, every inch of it,
and bordered with the beards of brilliant kings,
unknotted and combed, so any knight would know
each king by his color and which country he came from.
Here he rakes in revenues from fifteen realms,
for on the eve of Easter, whenever it falls,

---

[31] On the Arthurian poem's use of *Siege*, see: *Siege of Jerusalem*, ed. Livingston, p. 10 n. 30.

they pay it promptly, for the peace of their people,
have their least-afraid knights deliver it without delay.
For seven winters he awaits answer from Arthur
and will stalk this place, plaguing his people
till the King of the British crops off his beard
and it is borne by the bravest of his men to that beast.][32]

The initial connotations of this beard-flaying are typical: it indicates the giant's unnatural usurpation of political authority. But changing the owner of the cloak-of-many-beards has done more than simply streamline the story for the Alliterative *Morte*; it has fundamentally refocused the symbolism of the beard-flaying itself by harking back to the original connections between manhood and beards. The giant's wearing of so many beards marks his power and his greed, of course, but it also reflects his distinctly gendered violence. The giant's predatory sexual assaults – so brutal that he kills his victims in the course of raping them – serve as a haunting example of the powers of unchecked hyper-masculinity.

By altering the Rhitta Gawr tradition, the Alliterative-*Morte* poet not only produces a more deeply gendered interpretation of the beard-flaying than his predecessors in the Arthurian tradition, but also places in sharper focus the inherent barbarism of the flaying itself. There is, one suspects, no 'clean' way of removing a man's flesh in this manner, and there are no historical examples of real men having their beards thus flayed; it seems to have been a largely literary conceit. As a literary device, though, it is a naturally disturbing one. In the earlier, briefer versions of the Rhitta Gawr tale such sickening detail could be missed, but by shifting Rhitta into the giant of Mont Saint-Michel and giving the account of the cloak more prominence in the text, the Alliterative *Morte* gives the reader no choice but to see the beard-flaying in its essentially violent terms, against a backdrop of the giant's rape and blood-thirst and outright cannibalism. This being so, it is all the more disturbing that Arthur chooses to take possession of the giant's beard-coat, even if the destruction of the giant is, in and of itself, the proper act of a good king. For Jeffrey Jerome Cohen, one of the few critics to address the symbolism pervading this passage, this decision has far-reaching implications for Arthur's kingship within the Alliterative *Morte*:

The 'kyrtill' that the giant fashions from the kings' collected hair undermines the ideological purity of Arthur's vision of forcibly uniting disparate realms under British sovereignty, materialising Arthur's own ambition of empire into a costume with which to clothe a monstrous body.[33]

---

[32] *The Death of Arthur*, trans. Simon Armitage (New York: Norton, 2012), pp. 83, 85. Line numbers are given in parentheses in the text.

[33] Jeffrey Jerome Cohen, *Of Giants: Sex, Monsters, and the Middle Ages* (Minneapolis: University of Minnesota Press, 1999), p. 153.

Cohen's suggestion is furthered by the fact that, unlike so many of his sources, the poet's attention to the loss of beards does not end at Mont Saint-Michel. Later in the poem, beards are once again brought to the forefront of the narrative – and this time it is Arthur who commits the shaming.

Having defeated the Roman Emperor Lucius, King Arthur seizes two Roman senators found near his camp. He decides to send them to Rome to deliver his terms for the surrender of the city, but before doing so, he has them shaved:

> Then the bannerettes of Bretain   brought them to tents
> There barbours were boun   with basins on loft;
> With warm water, iwis,   they wet them full soon;
> They shoven these shalkes   shapely thereafter
> To reckon these Romanes   recreant and yelden
> Forthy shove they them to shew   for skomfit of Rome.
>
> > (ll. 2330–5)

> [Then the bannerets of Britain brought them to tents
> where barbers awaited with basins prepared;
> with warm water at once they were wetted,
> and then they shapely shaved these men,
> to show the Romans as surrendered recreants.
> So they shaved them to show the defeat of Rome.]

It is possible that this scene – which appears to be original to the Alliterative *Morte* – merely describes a shave and a haircut, but two elements suggest it represents more than that. After all, the scene is an almost perfect parallel with the actions taken by the Jews in one of the Alliterative *Morte*'s known sources, the *Siege* – actions that themselves mimic the shaming of King David's messengers, casting them in a clearly deplorable light. Arthur's decision to shave the senators thus aligns perfectly with his earlier decision to take possession of the giant's monstrous beard-coat; indeed, it is difficult not to see the shaving of the senators as Arthur's continuance of the unnatural and barbaric tradition that gave rise to the coat in the first place. Arthur, it seems, has become the very thing he sought to destroy, and in the subsequent unfolding of the poem – the dissolution of his world as Mordred usurps his kingdom and his bed and ultimately takes his life – it may be that he is condemned for it.

Beards, it seems, can carry a weight of symbolisms far more complex than we might expect. According to Aulus Gellius, the sophist Herodes Atticus was once approached by 'a man in a cloak, with long hair and a beard that reached almost to his waist', who asked for money. When Herodes asked the man what he did for a living, the man replied that he was a philosopher, and that this ought to have been obvious. Herodes replied that he saw 'a beard and a cloak; the philosopher I do not yet see'[34] – an exchange that has since been turned to a simple Latin aphorism: *Barba non facit philosophum,* 'a beard does not a philosopher make'. For Herodes' unnamed beggar, the beard was not just a marker of his masculine status, it was a symbol of both occupation and relative intellectual position, associations that tap into larger connections between facial hair and social status, not unlike those observed from the Assyrian and Egyptian kings to King Arthur and his monstrous beard-flaying enemies. It may be that Herodes was right that a beard does not make a philosopher, but, particularly within the traditions of Arthurian literature, it seems that – whether viewed in terms of gender or politics – the beard very much makes the man.

---

[34] Aulus Cornelius Gellius, *Noctes Atticae,* trans. J. C. Rolfe, Loeb Classical Library 195 (Cambridge, MA: Harvard University Press, 1927), 9.2.1–4.

Face Off:
Flaying and Identity in Medieval Romance

Larissa Tracy

F EW forms of punishment are as brutal as flaying – literally removing the skin as a way of figuratively excising the crimes and the identity of the accused. Robert Mills explains medieval notions of skin as memory: 'to flay someone alive would be to tear away the bodily surface onto which transitory memories and identities could be inscribed – only to fashion an etched parchment in its place (the dead skin), from which "timeless" moral lessons could be read'.[1] Flaying is a prominent medieval literary and artistic motif, as this volume attests; it occurs frequently in a variety of texts across the geographical and linguistic span of medieval Europe. In medieval romances like *Cligés*, *Havelok the Dane* and *Arthur and Gorlagon*, flaying features as a form of punishment, threatened or inflicted in the course of legal procedure, legitimate or illegitimate. It marks not only the bodies of those whose skin is removed, but also the reputations and identities of those who remove it. As a method of judicial interrogation or punishment, flaying leaves lasting scars even if it is not fatal – it generally precedes further abuse and execution. In *Havelok* the skin of the criminal, Godard, is removed to erase the royal identity that he sought to bestow upon himself by taking it from Havelok. In *Cligés* Fenice's skin will bear the marks of her identity as an adulteress even as she heals and is reunited with her heroic lover. In *Arthur and Gorlagon* flaying is the fatal sentence for adultery and treason. Removing skin by flaying reveals a multitude of identities for the flayer and the flayed – tyrant or adulteress.

But skin removal is not always a form of judicial punishment. The Scandinavian, or 'Viking', *fornaldarsögur* – tales of mythical heroes equivalent to romances – *Örvar-Odds saga* (*Arrow-Odd's Saga*) [hereafter *ÖO*] and *Egils saga einhenda og Asmundar saga berserkjabana* (*The Saga of Egil and Asmund*) [hereafter *EA*] include flaying episodes where the skin is removed in the heat of battle or in the fulfilment of a quest; the resulting scars are identifying markers of supernatural difference, not criminality

My thanks go out to Jeff Massey, Tina Boyer and the anonymous reader for their careful review of this piece and their helpful comments and suggestions.

[1] Robert Mills, *Suspended Animation: Pain, Pleasure, and Punishment in Medieval Culture* (London: Reaktion, 2005), p. 68.

or sanctity.[2] The mid-thirteenth-century *ÖO*[3] draws upon flaying motifs from the Arthurian tradition, such as a cloak made from kings' beards,[4] but adds another dimension to skin removal within the narrative when Oddr rips off the face of his demonic opponent. In the fourteenth-century

[2] There is another distinct genre of chivalric romances in the Norse tradition – *riddarasögur* – works 'peopled by knights' that are either adaptations of Arthurian romances or Icelandic imitations of them (Marianne E. Kalinke, *Bridal-Quest Romance in Medieval Iceland* [Ithaca, NY: Cornell University Press, 1990], pp. 6–7). But it is the specific flaying episodes of the *fornaldarsögur* that concern us here. While many of the magical aspects of the *fornaldarsögur* are stock motifs, flaying is relatively unusual. There is an analogue to the episode in *ÖO* in *Orms þáttr Stórólfssonar*, a family/legendary short story, where Ormr tears the skin off the ogre Brúsi's face, but it is one of a series of injuries Ormr inflicts on Brúsi before finally killing him by carving the 'blood-eagle' on his back – which is itself a contested literary motif. See: John McKinnell, *Meeting the Other in Norse Myth and Legend* (Cambridge: D. S. Brewer, 2005), p. 128. Anthony Faulkes suggests that the flaying motif in *Orms þáttr* comes from *ÖO* (32–4), see: Faulkes, ed., *Two Icelandic Stories* (London: Viking Society for Northern Research, 1967, repr. 2011), online at http://www.vsnrweb-publications.org.uk/Text%20Series/2IcelSt.pdf (accessed 25 Mar. 2015). But McKinnell contends that it is part of a pattern of Þórr stories, a pattern better preserved in *Orms þáttr* than in *ÖO*. He concludes that '*Orms þáttr* may have been influenced by a lost version of *ÖO*, but it is perhaps more likely that echoes of Þórr-derived motifs were commonplace in this kind of story'. However, the flaying motif does not occur as often as the other aspects of the Þórr-derived stories, like ogre or giant(ess) killing, and while Þórr does feature in both *ÖO* and *EA*, neither of these tales is simply an echo of 'myths about Þórr' (*Meeting the Other*, p. 129).

[3] There are two editions in Old Norse: *Fornaldar sögur Norðrlanda*, ed. C. C. Rafn, vols. 1–3 (Copenhagen, 1829–30), and *Fornaldarsögur Norðurlanda*, ed. Guðni Jónsson and Bjarni Vilhjálmsson, vols. 1–4 (Reykjavík: Bókútgáfan forni, 1943). All Norse quotations are taken from http://www.snerpa.is/net/forn/orvar.htm (accessed 20 Jan. 2015). There is an electronic version of the 1829 edition accessible through https://archive.org (accessed 20 Jan. 2015). All translations are from *Seven Vikings Romances*, trans. Hermann Pálsson and Paul Edwards (London: Penguin, 1985), pp. 25–137. Hereafter, page numbers are given in parentheses. *ÖO* survives in two versions, the earliest of which was composed about the middle of the thirteenth century (Pálsson and Edwards, p. 20). The older one survives in a manuscript from the early fourteenth century, and the more complete, younger version survives in a late fourteenth-century manuscript. One codex dates from c. 1300–25, part of which is found in the Royal Library in Stockholm (MS Sth. perg. 7 4to), part in Arnamagnæn Institute in Copenhagen (AM 580 4to). An eighteenth-century paper manuscript survives in the Museum of Iceland (MS AM 344 b 4to). See: Kalinke, *Bridal-Quest Romance*, pp. 4–5.

[4] See in this volume: Michael Livingston, 'Losing Face: Flayed Beards and Gendered Power in Arthurian Literature', pp. 308–21.

EA[5] the heroes encounter a skinless hag, whose face is pulled off in pursuit of a magical chessboard. But each flayed figure contradicts the assumption that its scars are monstrous, and either aids, or makes peace with, the central heroes. In most literary texts, flaying is a barbaric practice that darkens kingship, as in the twelfth-century *Cligés* and the thirteenth-century *Havelok the Dane*. But in contemporary Viking romances, flaying is most often a motif that signifies the noble transformation of the character from monster to ally; excoriation creates new identities of reconciliation rather than punishment.

Identity is a central feature of medieval romance – heroes are often disguised (either voluntarily or by circumstance), their true identities hidden behind armour, poverty or skins.[6] Contemporary with the development of medieval romance, a new generation of narratives containing scenes of flaying gained currency in the thirteenth century, due, in part, to the rapid proliferation of vernacular devotional works.[7] Sarah Kay refers specifically to translations of Jacobus de Voragine's *Legenda aurea* (*c.* 1260), which includes a series of hagiographical accounts wherein saints are subjected to a litany of tortures and punishments. The saint most commonly associated with flaying, as several contributions to this

---

[5] *EA* survives in fifteenth-century manuscripts and some later paper manuscripts in the Museum of Iceland. All Norse quotations are from: http://www.snerpa.is/net/forn/asberser.htm (accessed 20 Jan. 2015). All translations are from *Seven Viking Romances*, trans. Pálsson and Edwards, pp. 228–57. Hereafter, page numbers are given in parentheses.

[6] Renée Ward and Frederika Bain each discuss the implications of wearing skin as a means of masking identity in this volume. See: Ward, '"Thou shalt have the better cloathe": Reading Second Skins in *Robin Hood and Guy of Gisborne*', pp. 349–65; and Bain, 'Skin on Skin: Wearing Flayed Remains', pp. 116–37.

[7] Sarah Kay, 'Original Skin: Flaying, Reading, and Thinking in the Legend of Saint Bartholomew and Other Works', *Journal of Medieval and Early Modern Studies* 36.1 (2006): 35–73 at p. 41. Kay has written several influential articles on flaying, particularly in terms of animal skins and material culture. See: 'Flayed Skins as *objet a*: Representation and Materiality in Guillaume de Deguileville's *Pèlerinage de vie humaine*', in *Medieval Fabrications: Dress, Textiles, Clothwork, and other Cultural Imaginings*, ed. E. Jane Burns (New York: Palgrave, 2004), pp. 193–205; and 'Legible Skins: Animals and the Ethics of Medieval Reading', *postmedieval: a journal of medieval cultural studies* 2.1 (2011): 13–32. In this volume, William Sayers connects a graphic version of Bartholomew's execution with scant flaying references in medieval Irish secular and legal sources. See: 'No Skin in the Game: Flaying and Early Irish Law and Epic', pp. 261–84. See also: Sarah Sheehan, 'Losing Face: Heroic Discourse and Inscription in Flesh in *Scéla Mucce Meic Dathó*', in *The Ends of the Body: Identity and Community in Medieval Culture*, ed. Suzanne Conklin Akbari and Jill Ross (Toronto: University of Toronto Press, 2013), pp. 132–52.

volume note, is Bartholomew, who was executed in India for his missionary exploits.[8] The authorities in India attempt to erase the alien threat to their society by flaying the outsider. Kay writes: 'That flaying is resorted to in order to obliterate what is foreign suggests that identity can be located in one's skin.'[9] In the context of martyrdom, flaying becomes an act of sacrifice – the penultimate moment when the martyr relinquishes not only life but also the living flesh by which he or she is known. As Kay says, '[i]f one's skin is not taken but given up, and given up moreover in a sacred cause, this strengthens the capacity for flaying to symbolize immortality as much as death.'[10] The skin becomes a living artefact that survives the martyr's death as a relic. In Kay's terms, 'flaying seems to be deployed in order to reinforce belief that the outer body is merely a container of some inner reality'.[11]

The *fornaldarsögur* employ flaying differently from hagiography and romance; here, it straddles the boundary between skin taken as punishment and that given freely. Neither the Otherwordly Ögmundr in *ÖO*, nor the giantess Arinnefja in *EA*, is punished by flaying, nor do they offer their skins as trophies of martyrdom. But both sacrifice their skins – specifically, though not exclusively, the skin of the face – in the pursuit of their larger goals. If, as Jeffrey Jerome Cohen posits, the monster is a pure cultural construct – if the monster's body literally 'incorporates fear, desire, anxiety, and fantasy [...] giving them life and an uncanny independence'[12] – then the flayed monster becomes a reflection of society, its fears, its triumphs and its identity, mirrored in the replacement of monstrous skin with non-monstrous signification. In the *fornaldarsögur* – literally 'stories of ancient times', which were very popular in late-medieval Iceland[13] – the monstrous identity of the flayed figures encoded in their skinlessness is troubled by their non-monstrous actions, and they take on a potentially human identity.

These figures are monstrous already and so the loss of their flesh cannot make them more monstrous, even if it renders them more hideous. But by enduring this act, they both gain a new identity that ultimately enables

---

[8] See: Larissa Tracy, *Torture and Brutality in Medieval Literature: Negotiations of National Identity* (Cambridge: D. S. Brewer, 2012), pp. 62–3 at p. 147. In this volume, see: Asa Simon Mittman and Christine Sciacca, 'Robed in Martyrdom: The Flaying of St Bartholomew in the Laudario of Sant'Agnese', pp. 140–72; and Sherry C. M. Lindquist, 'Masculinist Devotion: Flaying and Flagellation in the *Belles Heures*', pp. 173–207.

[9] Kay, 'Original Skin', p. 41.

[10] Ibid.

[11] Ibid., p. 42.

[12] Jeffrey Jerome Cohen, *Monster Theory: Reading Culture* (Minneapolis: University of Minnesota Press, 1996), p. 4.

[13] McKinnell, *Meeting the Other*, p. 40.

them to act in support of, rather than in opposition to, the heroes in each saga. Jóhanna Friðriksdóttir writes that in these sagas, 'the boundaries between what critics have categorized as realistic and fantastic genres were blurred, or may never have existed in the first place for contemporary saga authors and audiences'.[14] As such, identity, which seems fixed in many medieval romances for the human actors, becomes a fluid plane in the *fornaldarsögur*: the hero is not always heroic, nor the monster always monstrous. Following the loss of skin, identities are lost and reformed, gender boundaries are blurred and traditional categories challenged.

In medieval Iceland, skin – specifically hides – served a variety of functions beyond the day-to-day role of household goods. As Frederika Bain explains in this collection, skin was valued as a particular component of magic, as with the infamous *nábuxur*, or 'necropants'. Her essay suggests that Icelandic skin-wearing tradition finds the act inherently sinful – though at the same time immensely powerful – even if that skin is rendered up voluntarily.[15] Flayed skin appears in a number of folktales and accounts of magic[16] and it is a feature of several Old Norse texts, even though depictions of its removal are less common. In *ÖO* skin serves a variety of identifying functions both as it is removed and as it is restored.[17] Oddr, the son of Grímr Hairy-Cheek, is an arrogant man doomed to wander the world for 300 years, unknown and obscure, occasionally coming into conflict with his nemesis, Ögmundr, a human–ogre hybrid skilled in magic.[18] During one of their physical bouts, Oddr rips the Otherworldly Ögmundr's face off as the sorcerer attempts to escape through a hole in the earth.

Both before and after his flaying, Ögmundr is marked as monstrous. His mother is an ogress who goes by the name Grimhildr (when she is around humans); his father is a human king and a great sorcerer. In addition to his demi-monstrous parentage – such hybrids are not uncommon in the medieval Icelandic tradition – Ögmundr's monstrosity is visualized in his

---

[14] Jóhanna Friðriksdóttir, *Women in Old Norse Literature: Bodies, Words, and Power* (New York: Palgrave, 2013), p. 47.

[15] Bain, 'Skin on Skin', pp. 133–6.

[16] See: Jacqueline Simpson, trans., *Icelandic Folktales and Legends* (Stroud: Tempus, 1972, repr. 2004, 2009).

[17] This story is one of the sagas concerning the multigenerational men of Hrafnista, which include *Gríms saga loðinkinna* (contemporary with *ÖO*) and *Ketils saga*, which succeeds the other two. McKinnell, *Meeting the Other*, pp. 103 and 175.

[18] The terminology varies. McKinnell refers to him as a 'giant' and an 'ogre' (p. 129), Pálsson and Edwards use 'demon' as well. He is called *fjándi*, which means 'enemy' or 'fiend'. Richard Cleasby and Gudbrand Vigfusson, *An Icelandic-English Dictionary* (1874), p. 157. The dictionary is searchable online: http://lexicon.ff.cuni.cz/html/oi_cleasbyvigfusson (accessed 2 Jan. 2016).

skin, which is 'boeð svartr ok blár' [dappled black and blue]. He has long, black hair and 'hekk flóki ofan fyrir augun, þat er topprinn skyldi heita' [a rough tussock hanging down over the eyes where his forelock should be] (p. 81). The term *flóki* refers to a section of matted hair, like wool or felt,[19] which resembles a grass lump rather than the standard *topprinn*, or lock of hair. His tussock and mottled skin identify him to Oddr and to everyone who sees him. When that skin and the trademark tussock are removed, he becomes an anonymous figure; his new identity will evolve, but it will still bring him into conflict with Oddr.

Much of Ögmundr's story is told by Rauðgrani (Red-Beard), who is Óðinn in disguise, and, as such, is an Odinic intervention – another common motif of the *fornaldarsögur*. Óðinn's interest in Oddr identifies the latter as one of the Odinic heroes, which is reinforced by several of his exploits, mirroring those of the All-Father. As an Odinic hero, Oddr takes on facets of Óðinn's divine identity: he has sex with a giantess, Hildigunnr, who bears him a son,[20] he disguises himself as a wise wanderer, and he faces impossible foes. But Ögmundr is the one described as an Otherwordly foe. Rauðgrani warns Oddr '"því at þar er ekki við mann um at eiga, sem Ögmundr er"' ['You won't be fighting a human being if you fight him'] (p. 80). However, like many Odinic heroes, Oddr ignores this advice. Ögmundr seems invincible the first time Oddr encounters him. When Ögmundr offers a flag of truce, Oddr refuses: '"Því, at ek hefi á vallt áðr við men barizt, en nú þykkjumst ek eiga við fjándr", sagði Oddr. "Ek hjó á háls þér áðan, sem mér var hægast, með sverði því, sem ek helt á, ok tók ekki á."' ['I'll tell you why', said Oddr. 'Up till now I've always believed I've been fighting men, but this time I seem to be fighting demons. I struck at your neck just now with the sword I'm holding, and it seemed an easy chance, but it didn't bite at all.'] (pp. 58–9). Ögmundr turns the tables on Oddr and accuses him of being just as monstrous (and just as difficult to kill), because he could not cut off his head either: '"Þat mun mæla mega hvárr okkar við annan, at hér sé eigi síðr átt við troll en men."' ['Each of us can say the same about the other [...] that he seems more like a troll than a man.'] (p. 59). Ögmundr recognizes the dual identity of his foe, suggesting that men and monsters are often indistinguishable from one another.

Monster–human hybridity is woven into the very fabric of Ögmundr's identity in the form of his distinctive cloak, made from the flayed beards of kings that he takes as tribute (p. 89). When Ögmundr and Oddr meet in battle (Oddr accompanied by his blood-brother Sírnir), Ögmundr throws away 'kápu minni, / þeiri er ger var / af grön jöfra' [My cloak, made / with the beards of kings] (p. 90).[21] In the ensuing fight, Oddr defeats Ögmundr

---

[19] Cleasby and Vigfusson, *An Icelandic-English Dictionary*, p. 162.

[20] McKinnell, *Meeting the Other*, p. 172.

[21] While Pálsson and Edwards translate *kápu* as 'cloak' made of beards, the similar phrase 'kápu þeirri er gör var af grön jöfra' translates as 'the cap

with brutal efficiency thanks to the help of Sírnir, who slices off a 'cartload' of Ögmundr's buttocks. This injury so shakes Ögmundr that he plunges straight into the earth. But as he does,

> Oddr greip þá báðum höndum í skegg honum með svá miklu afli, at hann reif þat allt af honum ok skeggstaðinn niðr at beini ok þar með alla ásjónuna með báðum vangafillunum, ok svá gekk upp um ennit ok aptr á miðjan haus, ok þar skildi með því, at svörðrinn slitnaði, en Oddr hafði þat, er hann helt. Jörðin luktist saman fyrir ofan höfuðit á Ögmundi, ok skildi svá með þeim.

> [Oddr got hold of his beard with both hands and jerked it so hard that he ripped off the whole beard with the skin underneath right down the bone, including the entire face and both cheeks, up the forehead and back to the middle of the crown. So they went their separate ways as the ground opened up, and Oddr kept what he was holding. The ground closed over Ögmundr's head, and that was how they parted.]   (p. 91)

Just as Ögmundr had been identifiable by his dappled skin and tussock, he is now easily recognizable by their absence. In Geoffrey of Monmouth's *Historia regum Britanniae*, King Arthur participates in a similar duel with an Otherwordly entity – the giant of Mont Saint-Michel, who also flayed his opponents' faces – and turns the tables by taking on the monstrous aspect of a beard-flayer himself.[22] Similarly, Oddr strips not only the beard and the skin from his opponent, but his entire face – the very stuff of Ögmundr's identity.

The face-flaying signifies an exchange of power – for a moment Oddr seems to have the upper hand, but Ögmundr will get away. However, Oddr's relentless pursuit of Ögmundr becomes a defining feature of his 300-year existence. Only when that feud is settled will Oddr be able to embrace his fate. In flaying the flesh from Ögmundr's face, Oddr also reclaims the beard cloak, and, thus, the masculine identities of all

---

which was made of king's beards'. Cleasby and Vigfusson, *An Icelandic-English Dictionary*, p. 218.

[22] Beard-flaying is a relatively common motif in Welsh variations of Arthurian tradition. For a fuller discussion of those examples in this volume, see: Livingston, 'Losing Face', p. 311. See also: Michael Cichon, 'Insult and Redress in "Cyfraith Hywel Dda" and Welsh Arthurian Romance', *Arthuriana* 10.3 (Fall 2000): 27–43. Beard-flaying as a means of stripping masculine identity from criminals is also a prominent literary motif. In *Chanson de Roland* the scullions who beat Ganelon before he is torn apart by horses, also 'peilent la barbe e les gernuns' [pluck out his beard and his moustache] (1823). *La Chanson de Roland*, edited with a facing page modern French translation by Léon Gautier (Tours: Mame et fils, 1872); English translation: *The Song of Roland*, trans. Glyn Burgess (London: Penguin, 1990).

the kings defeated by Ögmundr over the years. It is this exchange of masculine identities performed through the stripping of the male skin that problematizes both Arthur and Oddr as they appropriate the cloak and the monstrous identity that goes with it.[23] As a stage in his revelatory journey, Oddr absorbs the symbolic power Ögmundr gained by stripping beards. Faceless and beardless, Ögmundr is forced into hiding, until, disguised, he re-emerges as a new ruler and new adversary for Oddr, or rather, an old adversary in a different skin.

Years later, Ögmundr resurfaces as the masked Kvillánus (Quillanus), king of Novgorod, who has been a persistent and mysterious adversary: 'Hann var nokkut með undarligum hætti, því at hann hafði grímu fyrir andliti, svá at aldri sá hans ásjónu bera.' [He was a sinister-looking man, for he wore a mask covering his face so that it was never exposed.] (p. 116). The mask becomes an identifying feature – a visual trademark; it conceals the wearer's true identity while creating another. In their final confrontation, Kvillánus asks for a hiatus in the mutual battlefield slaughter in order to ask Oddr to a feast. Oddr refuses on the grounds that his opponent remains masked. Oddr first demands to know the identity of his foe:

Þá tók Kvillánus grímuna frá andliti sér ok mælti: 'Þekkir þú nokkut þetta it nauðljóta höfuð?'

Oddr kenndi þá gerla Ögmund bónda Eyþjólfsbana, því at öll merki sá þau á honum, sem Oddr haði af honum rifit skegg ok ásjónu ok aptr á mijan haus. Var þetta allt beingróit ok ekki hár á vaxit.

[Then Quillanus took the mask from his face, and said, 'Can you guess who this ugly head belongs to?'
Then Oddr realized that this gentleman was Ögmundr Eythjolf's-Killer all right, for he could still see the marks he'd given Ögmundr when he tore off his beard and face back to the middle of the crown. The flesh had healed over the bones but not a single hair grew there].

(p. 118)

The loss of his beard and the inability to grow hair on his face are permanent emasculating marks that should signify Ögmundr's inferiority to Oddr. In the Norse tradition, the inability to grow a beard, or the loss of one, was often taken as a sign of effeminacy. In *Brennu-Njals saga*, Njáll and his sons are consistently mocked for their inability to grow beards, despite Njáll's skill as a lawspeaker; beardlessness is also a standard insult in several Norse *flyting* exchanges – nasty verbal contests of wit and cunning.[24] But

---

[23] Livingston, 'Losing Face', p. 316.

[24] In chapter 38 of *Brennu-Njals saga*, Hallgerðr taunts her husband, Gunnar, for being a pacifist by comparing him to the beardless Christian Njáll: '"Jafnkomit mun á með ykkr, er hvárrtveggi er blauðr"' ['The two of you are just alike; both of you are cowards']. See: *Brennu-Njáls saga*, ed. Einar Ól.

the loss of his beard and the skin of his face also humanize Ögmundr to some degree. Even though flaying does not kill him as it might a man, he is vulnerable and can be identified by that vulnerability. Ögmundr loses his physical identity – one that marks him as monstrous – but gains an alternative identity as a king and conqueror by the mask he now wears.

Ultimately, the two opponents recognize the futility of their continued animosity, but not before each side suffers heavy losses. Ögmundr's son Svartr kills Sírnir, and Oddr beats Svartr to death with a club. Each army is obliterated so that only the two original opponents remain – Oddr and Ögmundr. Oddr is protected by his destiny and a magical shirt woven for him by the Irish princess Ölvör (who also bears him a child); Ögmundr is protected by his supernatural powers and strength. They withdraw in a stalemate, but eventually they come to an accord that Ögmundr (as Kvillánus) will rule Novgorod and Oddr will go to Gaul, and that is the end of the feud: Kvillánus sends expensive gifts to Oddr as a form of compensation with 'vináttumál ok sættarboð' [words of friendship and offers of reconciliation] (p. 120). Oddr accepts the gifts, recognizing that Kvillánus could never be beaten, being 'síðr kallast andi en maðr' [as much a phantom as a man] (p. 120). As Oddr's acceptance of Ögmundr's new identity sinks in, so does his realization that their feud is pointless. These monstrous men are evenly matched. This exchange motivates Oddr to finally settle down, marry, produce heirs and seek the fulfilment of the prophecy that will lead to his death on his home soil in Hrafnista (even though he puts on a brave face and pretends that the prophecy will not be realized).

However, Oddr does suffer from his encounter with Ögmundr, despite his victory. Ögmundr robs Oddr of his male friends and blood-brothers, thus depriving him of the homosocial bonds of masculine community.

Sveinsson, *Íslenzk Fornrit* 12 (Reykjavik: Hið Íslenzka fornritafélag, 1954), chap. 38; *Njal's Saga*, trans. Magnus Magnusson and Hermann Palsson (Harmondsworth: Penguin, 1960); and Carol J. Clover, 'Regardless of Sex: Men, Women, and Power in Early Northern Europe', *Representations* 44 (Autumn, 1993): 1–28 at p. 2. As Clover points out, *blauðr* can mean either 'soft, weak' or 'feminine' (Cleasby and Vigfusson, *An Icelandic-English Dictionary*, p. 67). Beardlessness was often associated with eunuchs. See: Shaun Tougher, 'The Aesthetics of Castration: The Beauty of Roman Eunuchs', in *Castration and Culture in the Middle Ages*, ed. Larissa Tracy (Cambridge: D. S. Brewer, 2013), pp. 48–72 at p. 60. For a discussion of masculinity and castration in the Norse sagas, see: Anthony Adams, '"He took a stone away": Castration and Cruelty in the Old Norse *Sturlunga saga*', in *Castration and Culture*, ed. Tracy, pp. 188–209. Tina Boyer analyses the implications of beard removal in the German texts *Salman und Morolf* and *Karl und Galie*. See: 'Murder and Morality in *Salman und Morolf*', *Journal of English and Germanic Philology* 115.1 (Jan. 2016): 39–60. Beardlessness is also a trait of Chaucer's Pardoner, whose gender and sexual identities have been the subject of much critical debate.

Compelled by this loss, Oddr goes into the woods and becomes a wild man – a transformation marked by his appropriation of a bark-suit that becomes a second skin. He becomes Næframaðr (Barkman; pp. 92–109), a wild man inhabiting the borders, avoiding the community of men until he reappears at a hall. After a series of *flytings* where he insults the masculinity of all the men present, a group of young men tears off the bark, revealing a new and rejuvenated Oddr:

> Ok síðan rífa þeir af honum allar næfrarnar. Hann brauzt ekki við þessu, en hann er svá búinnundir, at hann er í skarlatskyrtli rauðum, hlaðbúnum, en hár lá á herðum niðr. Hann hafði knýtt gullhlaði um höfuð sér ok var allra manna vænstr.

> [Then they tore all the bark off him, and he made no attempt to stop them. Under the bark he was wearing a red tunic of costly material, lace-trimmed; his hair fell down over his shoulder, there was a gold band round his forehead, and he looked very handsome indeed.]

> (p. 108)

The bark-suit functions as a chrysalis, a cocoon inside which the tired, sorrowful Oddr can regain his prowess and his strength to fulfil the final parts of the prophecy; the red tunic is like fresh, new skin.[25] His beauty is in marked contrast to Ögmundr's ugliness. This flaying – both of bark and skin – reveals Oddr's nobility as he assumes an air of divinity, like that of the shape-shifting gods Óðinn and Loki, or hybrid men like Bjarni (bear/man) in *Hrólfs saga kraka*, facilitating a transformation common in the *fornaldarsögur*.[26] By assuming the aspect of a tree as Næframaðr, Oddr gains wisdom and composure to face his ultimate foe, just as Ögmundr's literal and figurative loss of face allows him to remake himself into a noble and worthy king. Cohen writes that romance 'ordinarily represents the progress toward stable embodiment, toward perfect masculine-chivalric

---

[25] There is a similar episode in the English tale 'Here Begynneth a Merry Ieste of a Shrewde and Curst Wyfe Lapped in Morrelles Skin for Her Good Behauyour' (*c.* 1580), where the shrewish wife undergoes a significant transformation after being 'swaddled' in the skin of a black horse, Morel. See: Bain, 'Skin on Skin', p. 123.

[26] Transformation is a staple of medieval literature and it can be affected by the exchange of skins, as in the wolf episodes in the *Völsunga saga*, or through time spent in the forest – often because the individual's mind is clouded in madness and grief – as in Hartmann von Aue's *Iwein*. The hero lives in the forest naked, like a wild man, before he meets the lion. When he puts on clothes, he again becomes a part of the court. In the twelfth-century *Bisclavret*, Marie de France combines both tropes in her hero, who spends three days a week in the woods as a wolf and can only transform back by putting on his clothes. My thanks to Tina Boyer for her helpful suggestions regarding giants and transformation in the medieval literary tradition.

identity, with equal measures of reverence and anxiety'.[27] Oddr establishes
a masculine community to replace that taken by Ögmundr. He will lose
it all again in his final confrontation, but, for the moment, his gestation
in the bark-suit and his emergence from it are restorative. Converting (at
least nominally) to Christianity, Oddr finally meets his fate – stung by
an adder hiding in the skull of the horse he killed to avoid fulfilling the
prophecy.

In this romance, the absence or presence of skin – or a second skin
(in terms of the bark-suit that Oddr wears for over a century) – defines
both hero and villain. In shifting and exchanging skin, especially when
it is forcibly removed, Oddr and Ögmundr establish their commonalities
rather than their differences. Ögmundr, like the giant of Cohen's thesis,
'reveals the limits of selfhood, reveals that identity is intersubjective,
ex-centric, suspended across temporalities, as historically contingent as it is
monstrously incomplete. If the giant is the Other, then he is the Other as
something "strange to me although [...] at the heart of me".'[28] Constantly
at odds, Ögmundr and Oddr spur each other on. Ögmundr is a reflection
of Oddr, a necessary adversary for Oddr's self-revelation. The monster that
passes for human, cloaking itself in human skin, before that flesh mask is
ripped off to be replaced by another, more artificial mask, is particularly
threatening because 'a monster that mirrors repressed but recognizably
human aspects provokes feelings of *vulnerability*'.[29] But without Ögmundr,
Oddr cannot truly be heroic. Similarly, in *EA*, the giantess Arinnefja is a
mirror for the masculine hero, Egill; the superhuman qualities of giantesses
can physically threaten humans, but in some sagas giantesses are positive
figures whose powers and help benefit the hero.[30] Arinnefja is rendered
non-threatening, and goes through an identity quest of her own that allows
her to facilitate the successful completion of the hero's quest.

In *EA*, the former enemies Egill and Ásmundr become sworn blood-
brothers and join together to rescue the daughters of King Hertryggur
(abducted by the giant Gautr) and defend his kingdom. During their quest
the heroes find themselves in the company of Arinnefja (Eagle-Beak) and
her daughter, Skinnnefja (Skin-Beak). Arinnefja is marked not only by her
size and sexual appetite as a giantess, but also by injuries resulting from
flaying. However, rather than being menacing monsters who threaten harm
to the wandering heroes, Arinnefja and Skinnnefja take them in, nourish
them and promise to aid them in reclaiming the lost princesses. The heroes
and the giantesses exchange tales so that each knows the journeys and trials
of the others.

---

[27] Jeffrey Jerome Cohen, *Of Giants: Sex, Monsters, and the Middle Ages*
(Minneapolis: University of Minnesota Press, 1999), p. 170.

[28] Ibid., p. xv.

[29] Friðriksdóttir, *Women in Old Norse Literature*, p. 61.

[30] Ibid., p. 60.

Flaying plays an even more significant role in this narrative than in ÖO. Arinnefja's story centres on the loss of her beauty through familial and divine violence, culminating in the loss of all the skin from her body. Bullied by her seventeen sisters – among whom she was the youngest and most fair – Arinnefja calls on Þórr (Thor) for help. The thunder god has sex with each sister in turn so that the others will kill that sister in their jealousy. Finally, they are all dead, so Þórr has sex with Arinnefja, impregnating her with Skinnnefja, who is cursed by the last sister's dying breath not to thrive (p. 246). While Þórr looks out for Arinnefja, he instils in her an insatiable desire for sex.

This unquenchable need leads her to try to kidnap a man, Hringr, but his wife outsmarts her. Arinnefja is captured and, in order to save her life, must 'fara í undirheima ok sækja þrjá kostgripi: skikkju þá, sem eigi mætti í eldi brenna, ok horn þat, er aldrigi yrði allt af drukkit, ok tafl þat, sem sjálft léki sér, þegar nokkurr léki annars vegar' [go to the Underworld and fetch three treasures: a cloak that fire couldn't burn, a drinking horn that could never be emptied, and a chess set that would play by itself whenever anyone challenged it] (p. 247). Arinnefja takes half the chess set from three Otherworldly women on Mount Lucanus; when they demand it back, she refuses and challenges them to take it away, staking the half chess set against all the gold she could carry: '"Þótti þeim þat ekki ofrefli. Hljóp þá ein á mik ok greip í mitt hár ok reif af mér öðrum megin reikar ok þar með alla vangafilluna ok eyrat it vinstra."' ['They thought this wouldn't be too hard for them, and so one of them made for me, grabbed hold of my hair and tore half of it off along with my left ear and the whole of my cheek.'] (p. 247). But Arinnefja does not give up her face without a fight: she gouges out the eyes of her assailant and dislocates her hip. As with Ögmundr, flaying is a consequence of combat rather than a deliberate punishment. Both Ögmundr and Arinnefja shed their skin in a fight, marking them and shaping their identities. But in Arinnefja's fight with the women, though she loses the skin of her face, she also retaliates – she took hold of the breasts of one of the sisters and 'reif ek þau bæði af henna niðr at bringuteinum. Þar fylgdi ok með magállinn ok iðrin' [tore them both off down to the ribs and then the flesh of her belly and the entrails too] (pp. 247–8). The women flay her face, but Arinnefja eviscerates one of them, taking the act of flaying to its fatal conclusion.

Arinnefja's final and complete loss of flesh occurs in the Underworld when she goes to fetch the cloak. She meets the Prince of Darkness (Óðinn in disguise), who tells her that she can have the cloak if she can get it: '"Var þangat at hlaupa yfir eitt mikit bál. Lá ek first hjá Óðni, ok hljóp ek síðan yfir bálit, ok fekk ek skikkjuna, ok ere ek síðan skinnlaus um allan kroppinn."' ['I had to jump across a huge fire to get it. First I slept with Odin, then I jumped over the fire and got the cloak, but ever since I've had no skin to my body.'] (p. 248). The fire is a *funeral* fire, so the flaying

signifies death and rebirth.[31] Arinnefja gives the treasures to Hringr and his
wife, Ingibjörg, and swears an oath not to revenge herself on them.

While the giantess is refigured by the skin removed from her body, and
tamed out of her monstrous appetites, hides are also used in this romance
as a form of disguise. As Arinnefja's story culminates in the loss of her skin,
Egill's tale, like Oddr's, hinges on the appropriation of another, secondary
skin. Egill recounts his escape from the clutches of a giant by slaughtering a
goat, flaying off its skin, creeping inside the skin and sewing it up as tightly
as possible (p. 243). Reminiscent of Odysseus' ruse against Polyphemus,
Egill attempts to escape in the goatskin, but the giant grabs him and shakes
him loose.[32] Egill finally escapes (minus his right ear) after cutting off
the blind giant's right hand and stealing a ring with which the giant tried
to bribe him. Later, Egill comes upon a giant and a giantess fighting over
a ring; he intervenes and loses his right hand. Egill then gives the stolen
ring to a dwarf, who heals the stump and fits a socket on his sword so he
can wear it as an extension of his arm. After this disquisition, Arinnefja
presents Egill with a box that contains his severed hand. She has kept it for
him because she is the giantess whom he aided. Arinnefja rewards Egill's
courtesy and solidifies her role as ally by reattaching the hand and healing
it so that it functions perfectly. The skinless giantess, like Ögmundr, makes
an accord with her enemies which allows her to aid the heroes. The truth
of her tale is literally marked on her body, and she exchanges the story for
Egill's as she heals his hand, an act that leads John McKinnell to call her a
'proxy-mother to the failed Þórr-figure'.[33] She and Skinnnefja will join their
quest and help them bring it to a fruitful conclusion.

In these fantastic sagas giantesses are complex figures, and 'the sagas
they inhabit operate as a discursive site for a medieval discourse of gender,
sexuality, class, ethnicity, and mortality'.[34] Giantesses are relatively rare in
other Western medieval literature,[35] but they populate more than half of

---

[31] McKinnell, *Meeting the Other*, p. 178.

[32] McKinnell also notes the similarities between this episode and that in the
Odyssey (ibid., p. 184). It is also an inversion of rare punishments where a
criminal is sewn into an animal skin. See: Bain, 'Skin on Skin', p. 123.

[33] McKinnell, *Meeting the Other*, p. 184.

[34] Friðriksdóttir, *Women in Old Norse Literature*, p. 60.

[35] See: Cohen, *Of Giants*, p. xii. Cohen analyses examples of giantesses from
the Middle English *Sowdone of Babylone*, where the giantess's sudden
appearance 'is striking and perhaps suggests an ultimately northern
influence' (p. 157), and the twelfth-century Old French *Aliscans* that
may have provided the model for the *Sowdon* (p. 171). But Cohen further
argues that 'the giant is the male body writ large' (p. 157), which privileges
the popular figure of the male giant in the medieval literary tradition. The
'Saracen' sultan in the *Sowdone* frequently threatens the Christians with
flaying, though it is never carried out. As Kelly DeVries explains in this
volume, flaying was often (falsely) associated with Muslim practice after

the *fornaldarsögur*, where they are often depicted in 'binary terms as the monstrous Other, as foils to humans, as dehumanized figures, an unnatural inferior category that humans dominate'.[36] McKinnell sees Þórr's sexual exploits in *EA* as a 'witty new way of killing giantesses'.[37] He connects giantesses with 'wild nature', arguing that their 'lust makes them eager to be seduced, so behaving in an Odinic way [...] will exacerbate their mutual rivalry and make them kill each other'.[38] Arinnefja does suffer from Þórr-induced hyper-carnality, but she is spurned by the human for whom she lusts and must atone for her behaviour. This saga may be an inversion and a burlesque parody of the Odinic tradition to which *ÖO* belongs, as McKinnell suggests;[39] it may also simply be a Christian mockery of earlier, non-Christian motifs; but it also offers a different way of interpreting the roles of both the giantess and the protagonist, suggesting a greater symbiosis between magical Other and human (or superhuman, even posthuman) hero. Arinnefja has sex with Óðinn, but only as a prelude to completing a quest that strips her of her skin and her monstrous sexuality. Arinnefja is certainly a 'frightful sight', her body marked by her encounters and the violence that she has endured (and inflicted) in her own quests: besides lacking her scalp, cheek and ear, and having no skin on her body, her nose is broken and crooked, and she is missing teeth and fingers.[40] But as Friðriksdóttir explains, it is necessary to look not only at what marks the giantess as different, but also at the traits she shares with humans.[41] While the descriptions of Arinnefja and Skinnnefja signify their difference and exclusion from human community and norms – they are 'systematically marked by grotesqueness, excess, deformity, and ugliness'[42] – they also rehabilitate the hero, which allows Egill to fulfil his quest and heroic identity.

The episodes of flaying in the *fornaldarsögur* stand in stark contrast to episodes of flaying in contemporary European romances. English and Continental narratives share several other features with the *fornaldarsögur* – especially the revelation of identity – and flaying is a frequent motif. However, in these traditions flaying more often serves a punitive purpose that complicates notions of kingship.[43] Almost every modern study of

the crusades. See: 'A Tale of Venetian Skin: The Flaying of Marcantonio Bragadin', pp. 51–70.

[36] Friðriksdóttir, *Women in Old Norse Literature*, p. 60.

[37] McKinnell, *Meeting the Other*, p. 178.

[38] Ibid., pp. 178, 179.

[39] Ibid., pp. 177, 178–9.

[40] Friðriksdóttir, *Women in Old Norse Literature*, p. 63.

[41] Ibid.

[42] Ibid., p. 64.

[43] Cf. Livingston, 'Losing Face', p. 315, and Emily Leverett, 'Reading the Consumed: Flayed and Cannibalized Bodies in *The Siege of Jerusalem* and *Richard Coer de Lyon*', pp. 285–307, in this volume.

medieval literary flaying deals in some way with the thirteenth-century Middle English *Havelok*, because it contains one of the longer descriptions of this punitive process. This text is deeply concerned with royal justice, treason and a nostalgic assertion of English identity, potentially tarnished by the excessive judicial punishment – flaying and burning –inflicted on the guilty.[44]

In *Havelok* the central figures, Havelok and his (eventual) wife Goldeboru, are both dispossessed by usurping tyrants.[45] Havelok's identity as the heir to the Danish throne is obscured by the fisherman Grim, who

[44] Detailed studies on the text, context and content of the tale have only sparked the interest of critics more recently. See: Robert Mills, 'Havelok's Bare Life and the Significance of Skin', in *Reading Skin in Medieval Literature and Culture*, ed. Katie L. Walter (New York: Palgrave, 2013), pp. 57–80; Rodger I. Wilkie, 'Re-Capitating the Body Politic: The Overthrow of Tyrants in *Havelok the Dane*', *Neophilologus* 94 (2010): 139–50; Julie Nelson Couch, 'The Vulnerable Hero: *Havelok* and the Revision of Romance', *The Chaucer Review* 42.3 (2008): 330–52; Kimberly K. Bell, 'Resituating Romance: The Dialectics of Sanctity in MS Laud Misc. 108's *Havelok the Dane* and Royal *Vitae*', *Parergon* 25.1 (2008): 27–51; and several articles in Kimberly K. Bell and Julie Nelson Couch, eds., *The Texts and Contexts of Oxford, Bodleian Library, MS Laud Misc. 108: The Shaping of English Vernacular Narrative* (Leiden: Brill, 2011). I also discuss it at length in *Torture and Brutality*, pp. 16, 62–3, 74, 92–3, 147–55. Michael Swanton only touches on the occurrence of flaying in the poem: see his *English Poetry before Chaucer* (Exeter: Exeter University Press, 2002), pp. 209–20. In an earlier article, Swanton mentions it as possible evidence of actual practice. See: Michael Swanton, '"Dane Skins": Excoriation in Early England', *Folklore* 87.1 (1976): 21–8 at pp. 21–2. Swanton perpetuates the myth that Anglo-Saxons flayed sacrilegious Danes and nailed their hides to church doors, a myth since debunked, as outlined by Mary Rambaran-Olm in this volume. See: 'Medievalism and the "Flayed-Dane" Myth: English Perspectives between the Seventeenth and Nineteenth Centuries', pp. 91–115.

[45] *Havelok the Dane* is a Middle English adaptation of an Anglo-Norman story. There are at least two Anglo-Norman texts that record the deeds of this Dane: Geffrei Gaimar's *Estoire des Engleis* (c. 1135–40), and the Anglo-French *Lai d'Haveloc* (c. 1190–1220). The complete Middle English version survives in one manuscript – Oxford, Bodleian Library, MS Laud. 108, fols. 204r–219v. Thorlac Turville-Petre gives a thorough account of the earlier versions of the Havelok story and its transmission in *England the Nation: Language, Literature and National Identity, 1290–1340* (Oxford: Oxford University Press, 1996), pp. 143–55. For an edition of the original Anglo-Norman text, see: *Le Lai d'Haveloc*, ed. Alexander Bell (Manchester: Manchester University Press, 1925). Judith Weiss provides an accessible translation and introduction to the French text and its context in *The Birth of Romance in England: The 'Romance of Horn', The 'Folie Tristan', The 'Lai of Haveloc', and 'Amis and Amilun': Four Twelfth-Century Romances*

disobeys his orders to kill the boy when he realizes, through divine signs etched in the child's skin and emanating from his mouth as he sleeps, who he is. Grim takes the young prince to England and raises him among his own children into a productive working-class life. Seeking his fortune, Havelok looks for work in the kitchen of a castle where Goldeboru, whose late father, Athelwold, was venerated as an ideal example of Anglo-Saxon kingship, has been imprisoned by her guardian, Godrich. Godrich, thinking to further denigrate Goldeboru, arranges for her to marry the man he thinks is the lowly kitchen-boy, Havelok. Once the pair is married, Goldeboru sees the divine markings on her husband's body, realizes that they have a very different destiny and urges her husband to reclaim his patrimony in Denmark. Havelok successfully defeats the tyrannical Godard, who not only ordered his death but also brutally killed Havelok's sisters, and subjects him to a trial. In the course of justice, Godard is beaten, 'al quic flawen' (l. 2476),[46] and then hanged. The royal pair then returns to England, where Havelok and Goldeboru reclaim her throne, subjecting Godrich to an ignominious death by burning.

Havelok has been characterized as a male-Cinderella story concerned with issues of kingship and good governance, but the flaying episode potentially troubles Havelok's association with justice.[47] Godrich is Goldeboru's wicked foster-father, and Godard is a treacherous usurper who shamelessly murders Havelok's sisters by slitting their throats and chopping them into pieces, before threatening their younger brother and handing him over to be drowned. Considering the depth of their treachery and the abuse of power they represent, as well as their need to rule by force and fear, their trials should be a reinstitution of law and correct rule. Havelok does conduct the proceedings according to Danish and English legal tradition

---

in the French of England (Tempe, AZ: Arizona Center for Medieval and Renaissance Studies, 2009).

[46] All quotations from *Havelok* are from *Middle English Romances*, ed. Stephen H. A. Shepherd (New York: W. W. Norton, 1995), pp. 3–74. See also: *The Lay of Havelok the Dane*, ed. Walter W. Skeat, EETS e.s. 4 (London: Trübner, 1868; repr. 2008). Line numbers are given in parentheses.

[47] In *Torture and Brutality* I argue that Havelok's decision to resort to flaying as part of Godard's punishment potentially taints his rule and Others him in relation to Goldeboru who, as an English queen, does not exercise judicial brutality. In this context, Havelok, as a Dane, potentially represents anxieties of conflicting national identities within the Anglo-Scandinavian population of Lincoln and northern England, as well as emerging English sentiments of national identity in opposition to Anglo-Norman aristocratic rule in the thirteenth and early fourteenth century. Mills counters this argument, suggesting that the act of flaying actually reinforces Havelok's position as a just and good king ('Havelok's Bare Life').

(neither of which include flaying as sanctioned punishment, historically),[48] and his adherence to the will of the people and his nobles redresses the corruption of Godard and Godrich, but the brutality he exhibits remains questionable.

When Godard is trapped on the battlefield, the poet foreshadows his fate with an air of disdain: 'But Godard one (that he flowe / So the thef men dos henge, / Or hund men shole in dike slenge)' (ll. 2433–5). Godard will be flayed, as a thief is hanged or a dead dog is thrown into a ditch. His death will be ignominious, a fitting end for an evil tyrant. He will be judged first; nevertheless, his final punishment is brutal in its dispassionate delivery, and this brutality violates the integrity of Anglo-Saxon law and justice established at the beginning of the poem in praise of Athelwold's rule.[49]

To judge Godard, Havelok asks the faithful Ubbe to call together all his earls and barons, burghers and knights for a public trial that includes a jury of people drawn from across the social spectrum: 'He setten hem dun bi the wawe, / Riche and povere, heye and lowe, / The helde men and ek the grom, / And made ther the rithe dom' (ll. 2470–3). Robert Rouse writes: 'the concern for law in the romances, manifested through the romance hero's judicial crises, represents the legal anxieties of the community',[50] which may in turn represent changing interests of the romance audience. But Havelok's punishment of Godard is not presented as a judicial crisis; he calls together a parliament, which passes judgement and calls for the brutal sentence that is then carried out with almost no commentary. Rodger Wilkie argues that the legal consensus of the nobles alleviates Havelok's personal responsibility; the hero signals his legal intention, and the body

---

[48] Danish laws were very similar to the laws of the rest of medieval Europe, into which it was a fully integrated part. Per Andersen points out, however, that while interrogatory torture was introduced in other parts of Continental Europe as part of the criminal procedure to extract a confession, 'the Danish way was to turn to torture after sentencing – and then only after permission for its use had been granted by the king' (p. 1). However, flaying does not seem to have been among the catalogue of punishments used in medieval Denmark. Per Andersen, *Legal Procedure and Practice in Medieval Denmark* (Leiden: Brill, 2011). The only references in English law appear to be those to scalping in Anglo-Saxon law codes. Cf. Rambaran-Olm, 'Medievalism and the "Flayed-Dane" Myth', pp. 94–5, 100–1.

[49] Many histories and chronicles written post-Conquest engage in a competitive dialogue about the legacy of the Anglo-Saxons. See: Jay Paul Gates, 'Imagining Justice in the Anglo-Saxon Past: Eadric Streona, Kingship, and the Search for Community', *Haskins Society Journal* 25 (2013): 125–46.

[50] Robert Allen Rouse, 'English Identity and the Law in *Havelok the Dane, Horn Childe and Maiden Rimnild* and *Beues of Hamtoun*', in *Cultural Encounters in the Romance of Medieval England*, ed. Corinne Saunders (Cambridge: D. S. Brewer, 2005), pp. 69–83 at p. 72.

politic responds appropriately.[51] However, Godard's final punishment is excessive, and an air of revenge (inappropriate to state-sanctioned justice) clings to it:

> We deme that he be al quic flawen,
> And sithen to the galwes drawen
> At this foule mere tayl,
> Thoru is fet a ful strong nayl,
> And thore ben henged wit two feteres;
> And thare be writen thise leteres:
> 'This is the swike that wende wel
> The King have reft the lond, il del,
> And hise sistres, with a knif,
> Bothe refte here lif.'
> This writ shal henge bi him thare.
> The dom is demd; seye we na more.
>
> (ll. 2476–87)

Once the judgement is pronounced, Havelok, 'that stille sat so the ston' (l. 2475), remains silent and the sentence is carried out without any further discussion; however, Godard is at least allowed to confess and be shriven. In this instance, gruesome punishment is meted out with full approval of legal proceeding. The identity of the traitor has been encoded in the removal of his skin – Godard is no longer recognizable as himself, only as a traitor. As W. R. J. Barron explains, 'flaying was evidently not merely a means of inflicting a cruel death on a criminal, but of marking abhorrence of breaches of the fundamental bond of human society'.[52] So the *Havelok*-poet's choice is a striking one: either he uses it as a just recognition of the gravity of Godard's crime, or he intentionally taints Havelok as the Danish outsider prone to excessive displays of brutality that will be tempered by the balanced justice of his English queen.

Even though Havelok does not appear to revel in Godard's punishment, he ignores Godard's cries for mercy; Havelok's demeanour suggests satisfaction at the fulfilment of personal and state revenge:

> Sket cam a ladde with a knif
> And bigan rith at the to
> For-to ritte and for-to flo;
> And he bigan for-to rore
> So it were grim or gore,
> That men mithe thethen a mile
> Here him rore – that fule file!
> The ladde ne let nowith forthi,

---

[51] Wilkie, 'Re-Capitating the Body Politic'.

[52] W. R. J. Barron, 'The Penalties for Treason in Medieval Life and Literature', *Journal of Medieval History* 7 (1981): 187–202 at p. 193.

> They he criede, 'Merci! Merci!'
> That he ne flow everil del,
> With knif mad of grunden stel.
>
>   (ll. 2493–503)

Godard's unheeded pleas for mercy evoke sympathy; even though he is a tyrant and deserves harsh punishment, this goes too far. After his skin is removed, Godard (presumably still alive) is bound once again upon the pathetic mare, facing her tail, to be taken to the gallows, 'Nouth bi the gate, but over the falwes' (l. 2509) – a rough and uncomfortable ride. At the gallows he is hanged, and the poet unceremoniously proclaims his death, 'Thanne he was ded, that Sathanas' (l. 2512), but not before he chastises any who would feel sympathy for Godard or protest against the means of his execution: 'Datheit hwo recke; he was fals!' (l. 2511).

The poet's interjection seems unnecessary at this point. The public execution of traitors sent a strong signal of justice in action.[53] But the capacity to exercise mercy was also an important quality of good kingship: rulers had to be willing to leave the taste for vengeance behind and enact justice rather than pursue personal vendettas. In *Policraticus* (*c.* 1150), John of Salisbury offers advice to English kings on the correct exercise of justice, as 'for executions to be politically meaningful, they would have to be couched in terms understood by those for whom the executions were staged'.[54] According to John, 'following common physiological ideas, any excess, deprivation, or injury disrupts the internal harmony of the body social, and it is therefore the moral duty of the ruler (*medicus rei publicae*) to restore society's health by administering the law like medicine'.[55] For Godard, this is harsh medicine, indeed. The poet does not condemn this brutal form of execution outright, but he does acknowledge that there are others who might, and who might see Havelok's justice tainted by his denial of mercy to Godard. While the poem may end with 'a vision of harmony throughout society, as people not only of different ranks but also of different ethnic origins witness the coronation in London' where 'Danish and English, rich and poor, are finally integrated into one nation of England',[56] there is still a residual indictment against the application of judicial brutality that tarnishes this portrait of unity.

---

[53] Anthony Musson, *Medieval Law in Context: The Growth of Legal Consciousness from Magna Carta to the Peasant's Revolt* (Manchester: Manchester University Press, 2001), p. 19.

[54] Danielle M. Westerhof, 'Amputating the Traitor: Healing the Social Body in Public Executions for Treason in Late Medieval England', in *The Ends of the Body*, ed. Akbari and Ross, pp. 177–92 at p. 178.

[55] John of Salisbury, *Policraticus* (Lib. IV, Cap. 8), qtd. in ibid., p. 180.

[56] Thorlac Turville-Petre, '*Havelok* and the History of the Nation', in *Readings in Medieval English Romance*, ed. Carol M. Meale (Cambridge: D. S. Brewer, 1994), pp. 121–34 at p. 134.

The poet makes a distinction between Godard and Godrich, allowing 'direct comparisons between the treatment of the two traitors [...] and of the processes by which they are judged and punished', thereby engaging in a deliberate discourse of law and national identity.[57] While the English Godrich disinherits Goldeboru and violates his oath to her father (overturning the justice and peace of Athelwold's reign as a consequence), he does not resort to infanticide, so he is not subjected to the same brutal punishment of being flayed alive. He is burned at the stake instead (a punishment most often reserved for heretics). Mills sees these executions as parallel; the removal of skin by knife and fire are factors that connect English and Danish justice rather than creating a profound distinction. Mills argues that the scene of Godard's flaying 'constitutes a stripping away of inassimilable difference: skin, in *Havelok*, is the principal site for the mediation of human identity, whereas flaying – and its corollary, burning – deprive the body of the capacity to be meaningful'.[58] He further writes that the punishment of the two tyrants 'effectively deprives them of their humanity, but not in a way that supports any kind of ongoing message. Transformed into dust, or an unreadable corpse, all that Godard and Godrich can henceforth signify is death.'[59] But for medieval audiences, the spectacle of death – actual or fictional – was a signifier of power, of authority, if not always of justice.[60] It is plausible that, considering their crimes, medieval audiences would have celebrated the annihilation of Godard and Godrich's identities with the destruction of their bodies. But it is equally plausible that these deaths reflect a subtle criticism of brutality carried out in the name of justice. It is hard to imagine that former subjects and supporters, however cowed and oppressed, would condemn a traitor, even one as villainous as Godard, to the torturous penalty of being publicly flayed alive.

Godard's flaying is Havelok's first official act as king, followed by his redistribution of the lands and goods that Godard stole from him as a child; he begins his reign with a sense of judicial restoration tainted by the excessive and bloodthirsty nature of the justice, even if Godard's crimes warrant it. This taint will cling to Havelok as he and the Danes embark

---

[57] Rouse, 'English Identity and the Law', p. 75.

[58] Mills, 'Havelok's Bare Life', p. 75.

[59] Ibid.

[60] For a detailed analysis of the spectacle of pain, the significance of public execution and the meaning embedded within these acts, see: Elaine Scarry, *The Body in Pain: the Making and Unmaking of the World* (Oxford: Oxford University Press, 1985) and Jody Enders, *The Medieval Theater of Cruelty: Rhetoric, Memory, Violence* (Ithaca, NY: Cornell University Press, 1999). Scarry discusses the role of torture in destabilizing authoritarian regimes, and the illusion of power that the application of torture gives those regimes, in the first chapter of her ground-breaking study on physical violence (pp. 27–59).

to England and restore Goldeboru to her stolen throne. In dealing with Godrich, whose crimes are many but not as violent as Godard's, Havelok leaves the judgement to Goldeboru, the rightful queen of England, who enacts swift and just punishment without resorting to bloodshed or the public spectacle of flaying. While the execution of the two tyrants does present a compelling parallel, as Mills suggests (their similarities are striking),[61] the poem also heightens the sense of difference between Havelok and Goldeboru in how they reclaim their rights, how they enact justice and, potentially, how they will rule. Goldeboru tempers Havelok's vengeance; once he returns her throne to her, Havelok will be governed by her good legal sense, which includes mercy.

Other instances of excoriation in medieval romance involve issues of judicial process and interrogatory torture, and the process of flaying – either by completely removing the skin (as with Godard), or by ripping off pieces of skin with scourges and pinchers[62] – reveals an instability within the governing judicial structure, undermining the perception of these authorities as just and correct rulers. In *Erec and Enide* (*c.* 1170) Chrétien de Troyes openly condemns a set of giants for stripping the knight Cadoc of Cabruel, forcing him to ride a common nag like a thief and flogging him to the bone (ll. 4368–82).[63] Chrétien provides a similar indictment of flaying as part of interrogatory torture in *Cligés* (*c.* 1160–76).[64] In this French tale, to get the drugged Fenice to confess that she has faked her death the Salernian physicians try to trick her, threatening her if she will not speak: 'Qu'il feront de lié tel merveille / Qu'einc ne fu faite sa pareille / De nul cors de femme chaitive' [They would resort to extraordinary measures never before inflicted on the body of any unfortunate woman] (ll. 5889–91).[65]

When interrogation fails – not that Fenice could speak in her catatonic state if she had wanted to – the physicians resort to torture:

---

[61] Mills, 'Havelok's Bare Life', p. 80 n. 33.

[62] See in this volume: Susan Small, 'Flesh and Death in Early Modern Bedburg', pp. 71–90.

[63] Chrétien de Troyes, *Erec and Enide*, trans. Dorothy Gilbert (Berkeley: University of California Press, 1992).

[64] I analyse the problematic episodes of interrogatory torture in Arthurian romance in more detail, including this scene in *Cligés*, in 'Wounded Bodies: Kingship, National Identity, and Illegitimate Torture in the English Arthurian Tradition', *Arthurian Literature* 32 (2015): 1–29.

[65] All Old French citations of *Cligés* are from Bibliothèque nationale de France, MS Fr. 12560. Chrétien de Troyes, *Cligés*, in *Romans suivis des chansons, avec, en appendice, Philomena*, ed. and trans. C. Méla and O. Collet (Paris: La Pochothèque, 1994), pp. 286–494. Line numbers are given in parentheses. The English translation is from *The Complete Romances of Chrétien de Troyes*, trans. D. Staines (Indianapolis: Indiana University Press, 1990), pp. 87–169.

> Lors li redonnent un assaut
> Parmi le does de lor corroies,
> S'en perent contreval les roies,
> Et taut li batent sa char tender
> Que il en funt le sance espendre.

(ll. 5904–8)

[They then lashed her back, leaving visible marks all the way down, and gave her tender skin such a thrashing that they made the blood spurt out.]

When they realize that flaying her skin with whips does not work, they call for fire and lead, which they will pour into her palms. And if she does not confess: 'Ja endroit la metront en rost / Tant qu'ele iert tote greille' [they would place her at that very moment on the grill until she was entirely burned] (ll. 5932–3). But before they can grill her – both literally and figuratively – more than a thousand ladies burst in and defenestrate the physicians. The women act after witnessing, through a small crack in the door, 'l'angoisse et la malaventure' [the cruel torture] (l. 5942) being inflicted on Fenice, 'faisoient sofrir martyre' [forcing her to suffer martyrdom] (l. 5945). Chrétien lauds the women for jettisoning the doctors, whose bodies are crushed in the fall – necks, ribs, arms and legs broken: 'Einc mielz nel firent nules dames' [No ladies ever behaved better] (l. 5970).[66] While Chrétien may recognize the truth the physicians sought, he condemns the methods by which they attempted to discover it. Chrétien applauds the actions of the women and condemns the doctors as 'cuivert avoltre' [cowardly bastards] (l. 5930). Flaying only occupies a moment in this text, and it is recorded among the litany of torments to which Fenice is subjected in an effort to get her to reveal her deception. The focus in this scene is the damage being done to Fenice's tender skin; she will be permanently scarred by the cruelty of the Salernian doctors acting on behalf of her tyrannical foreign husband.

In the fourteenth-century Anglo-Latin (or Cymro-Latin)[67] romance

[66] L. T. Topsfield argues that Chrétien's praise is double-edged: 'Society believes the false, ignorant doctors in order to preserve its illusion about the noble and tragic death of the Empress; it destroys wise men who seek the truth'. *Chrétien de Troyes: A Study of the Arthurian Romances* (Cambridge: Cambridge University Press, 1981), p. 86.

[67] Both Siân Echard and Jeff Massey suggest that *Arthur and Gorlagon* was composed on the Welsh border, which opens other possibilities for anxieties of national identity. Siân Echard, *Arthurian Narrative in the Latin Tradition* (Cambridge: Cambridge University Press, 2005); Jeff Massey, 'The Werewolf at the Head Table: Metatheatric 'subtlety' in *Arthur and Gorlagon*', in *Heads Will Roll: Decapitation in the Medieval and Early Modern Imagination*, ed. Larissa Tracy and Jeff Massey (Leiden: Brill, 2012), pp. 183–206.

Arthur and Gorlagon, in which a king (who was formerly a werewolf) seeks to instruct King Arthur on the true nature of women, a duplicitous adulterer is flayed as a form of interrogatory torture. This story has two parts with two sets of punishment and retribution: a king is manipulated into revealing a secret to his unfaithful wife that enables her to transform him into a wolf with the mind of a man; the wolf, acting as a faithful pet, then witnesses the adultery of another king's wife with his seneschal and mauls the man. The wife has to explain her lover's wounds so she accuses the wolf of killing her child, whom she has hidden. The king is sceptical of her story and the wolf reveals the child's hiding place. With full knowledge of his duplicity, the king questions the injured seneschal, who admits nothing and tells the same lie. The king does not attempt to extract a confession, but instead confronts him with what he knows to be the truth, urging him to confess upon pain of torture. The seneschal pleads for mercy, and the king could be criticized for not granting it; however, like Havelok, he transfers the responsibility to the lords of his land, a jury of peers, who will bear the weight of the judgement. As with Godard in *Havelok*, the faithless seneschal is 'excoriatur, et laueo suspenditur' [flayed alive and then hanged] (226:29), while the queen suffers being 'equis distracta ignium globis traditur' [torn limb from limb by wild horses and given over to be burned] (226:30).[68] The guilty are savagely executed, blurring the boundaries between wolves and humans, and the story moves on without acclaim or approbation. Gorlagon relates these events dispassionately during a feast, without further commentary, suggesting that he has no concerns about the nature of the justice meted out; he shows no mercy, no compassion – he makes his former wife repeatedly and publicly kiss the embalmed head of her lover at dinner – raising questions about his fitness as king and the legitimacy of the model he presents to Arthur.[69]

[68] *Arthur and Gorlagon*, in *Latin Arthurian Literature*, ed. and trans. Mildred Leake Day (Cambridge: D. S. Brewer, 2005). *Arthur and Gorlagon* survives in one manuscript, Bodleian Library, Rawlinson MS B 149, which dates from the end of the fourteenth century to the beginning of the fifteenth century. For a fuller discussion of torture in *Arthur and Gorlagon*, see: Tracy, *Torture and Brutality*, esp. pp. 155–68. Like flaying, little early evidence survives suggesting that equine dismemberment was an actual form of execution for treason, but by the fourteenth century it had become somewhat more common in actual practice, perhaps because of the high instances of it in literary texts: a case of life imitating art.

[69] In her discussion of *Richard Coer de Lyon*, a romance begun in the thirteenth century and extant in seven manuscripts, the earliest of which is the fourteenth-century Auchinleck Manuscript, Geraldine Heng examines how popular romance 'organizes the emergence of the medieval nation, by manipulating racializing discourses through the circuit of an aggressive, cannibalistic joke'. There are several similarities between the 'cannibalistic joke' of *Richard*, which involves an ill Richard I unwittingly dining on a fat young Saracen who has been killed, opened up, flayed, boiled with

In these texts, unlike in the *fornaldarsögur*, flaying is employed by foreign kings who exert their royal will ruthlessly and who rule through fear rather than justice. Rouse sums up the interpretative debate that has been waged over episodes of literary flaying, particularly in *Havelok*: 'Some scholars have seen the pragmatic violence of the execution as an indicator of the intended audience of the poem, positioning it squarely within the realm of the tavern and the inn. Others have viewed the violence differently, seeing it as an indication of an unrealistic narrative mode – the "naive fantasy world" of the poem.'[70] Flaying does seem to play its largest role in fantasy; it looms large in the popular imagination, to borrow Kay's phrase,[71] but it did not loom large in legal fact.[72] Flaying is associated with treason in both French and English *literature*, but it was not a common punishment in *reality*. Barron says, 'It was apparently always an exceptional penalty, prescribed by ancient usage rather than written code, and reserved for punishment of crimes for which society felt a particular abhorrence.'[73] Emanuel J. Mickel rejects its use altogether, arguing 'that there is no substantiation for considering flaying to have been an "ancient usage"'.[74] As in *Havelok*, depictions of flaying draw attention only to the 'representational status of flaying in medieval culture', not to its actual practice.[75] There are occasional references to flaying (or, more correctly, scalping) in Anglo-Saxon law, and rare historical instances of the practice are recorded, mainly in English and French contexts, such as the skinning of Hughes Gérard, Bishop of Cahors, who was indicted for an attempt to poison Pope John XXII of Avignon in 1317.[76] Hanging was the most

---

saffron and served up in lieu of pork, and the somewhat cannibalistic (at least bloodthirsty) werewolf narrative in *Arthur and Gorlagon* and its final reveal of a preserved severed head on a platter at a feast. See: Geraldine Heng, 'The Romance of England: *Richard Coer de Lyon*, Saracens, Jews, and the Politics of Race and Nation', in *The Postcolonial Middle Ages*, ed. Jeffrey Jerome Cohen (New York: Palgrave, 2000), pp. 135–71 at pp. 135–6. In this volume, see: Leverett, 'Reading the Consumed', pp. 285–307.

[70] Rouse, 'English Identity and the Law', p. 75.

[71] Kay, 'Original Skin', p. 39.

[72] J. G. Bellamy, *The Law of Treason in England in the Later Middle Ages* (Cambridge: Cambridge University Press, 1970), p. 13. See also: Barron, 'Penalties for Treason'; Rambaran-Olm, 'Medievalism and the "Flayed-Dane" Myth', p. 100; and Sayers, 'No Skin in the Game', p. 265.

[73] Barron, 'Penalties for Treason', p. 197.

[74] Emanuel J. Mickel, *Ganelon, Treason, and the 'Chanson de Roland'* (University Park: Pennsylvania State University Press, 1989), p. 147 n. 303.

[75] Mills, *Suspended Animation*, p. 66; Barron, 'Penalties for Treason', p. 193.

[76] Mills, *Suspended Animation*, p. 65. Cf. Bellamy, *The Law of Treason*, p. 13. See also: Lisi Oliver, *The Body Legal in Barbarian Law* (Toronto: University of Toronto Press, 2011), and *The Beginnings of English Law*, repr. edn (Toronto: University of Toronto Press, 2012).

common form of capital punishment, though capital punishment was relatively rare throughout the Middle Ages.[77] It may be these exceptional cases to which the poet is alluding, because of the impact of flaying on the imagination. Mills writes that the significance of flaying for 'visual and literary expression' is all too apparent: 'like bodily executions more generally, skin removal had an imaginary and symbolic potency out of all proportion to its frequency in lived experience'.[78] Within medieval penal imagery, 'the network of visual and textual significations [...] transform the violated bodies of executed criminals into discourse and fantasy'.[79] The discourse inscribed on the flesh of the flayed usurper is that of authority, abuse and justice.

But flaying can also have a restorative effect, fashioning a new, positive identity for those perceived as monstrous. Just as Havelok's skin reveals his true origins and destiny, so Oddr's true identity is revealed when the bark is stripped off his body. Though both Havelok and Oddr resort to flaying their opponents, Oddr does so in the heat of battle as an attempt to stop Ögmundr's flight; the resulting injury is a just reciprocation for the beard-flaying that Ögmundr inflicts on other kings. Havelok orders punitive flaying as execution, and while it can certainly be interpreted as a just retribution for the crimes Godard perpetuated against Havelok and, thus, the person of the king, it prompts far greater horror.[80] In the Icelandic

---

[77] Trevor Dean, *Crime in Medieval Europe* (London: Pearson Education, 2001), pp. 124, 130; and Mills, *Suspended Animation*, pp. 14–15. Mills argues that chroniclers often omit records of common hangings, preferring to dwell on the rarer but more spectacular forms of execution associated with traitors; this creates a disproportionate image of violence in medieval society, contributing to a 'distorted picture of medieval penal practice' and suggesting that 'pre-modern people were accustomed to witnessing extravagant, showy execution rituals with unremitting frequency' (p. 26). And even then, many authorities (English and French included) thought capital punishment too severe to fit the popular attitudes to crime (pp. 14–15). Cf. *Heads Will Roll*, p. 8 n. 25. See also: Jay Paul Gates and Nicole Marafioti, eds., *Capital and Corporal Punishment in Anglo-Saxon England* (Woodbridge: Boydell Press, 2014).

[78] Mills, *Suspended Animation*, pp. 65–6.

[79] Ibid., p. 65.

[80] John Hines makes an interesting linguistic case for tracing the name 'Havelok' and the hero's exploits back to the Norse 'Óláfr'; he further suggests that there are connections between the occurrence of *Óláfr/*AnleifR* and the Irish *Amlaíb*, and tracks a line of descent from an Old Norse original to Old Irish, Old Welsh into Old French and then Middle English. This line of inquiry may account for the popularity of this hero in the later Middle Ages. See: Hines, 'From *AnleifR* to *Havelok*: The English and the Irish Sea', in *Celtic–Norse Relationships in the Irish Sea in the Middle Ages, 800–1200*, ed. Jón Viðar Sigurðsson and Timothy Bolton (Leiden: Brill, 2014), pp. 187–214.

fornaldarsögur monstrous beings take on sympathetic identities through the loss of their skin. Ögmundr and Arinnefja give up a precious part of what makes them recognizable, even if it is recognizable monstrosity. In Ögmundr's case, he had been hiding as human, cloaked in human skin (dappled as it was) to shroud his inhuman identity. The loss of his human skin as he escapes into the earth reveals his supernatural identity, and when he re-emerges he takes on a literal mask to hide his disfigurement. It is the scars that identify Ögmundr to Oddr and remind him of their long-standing feud. However, once the battle is done and the only two still standing among the carnage are Oddr and Ögmundr, they come to terms and achieve an accord in the face of terrible and futile destruction. For Arinnefja, the loss of skin is a trial, part of a quest that aligns her with the human knights who often quest for an enchanted chessboard.[81] She sheds the skin of an oversexualized giantess and gains the identity of a healer who aids other heroes in their quests. Friðriksdóttir writes that monstrous bodies often indicate any kind of alterity, 'sexual, racial, or cultural, often more than one at a time, justifying their exclusion and the violence with which they are treated in more than one way'.[82] Flaying may be inflicted on monsters – flaying is monstrous – but it can also transform the flayed monster into a more sympathetic actor.

Flaying in the romances leaves a mark. It changes and shapes identity: monstrous and male, just and unjust. It serves justice, but also brands those who use it as potentially unjust. Flayers and flayed often exchange identities via the removal of skin, but in the Norse romances there is no sense of condemnation, or of debilitation. In Oddr's case, his action is not calculated. It is a wound of opportunity. Likewise, Arinnefja strips the skin of her opponents as surely as they strip hers; the final loss of skin on her body is the ultimate fulfilment of her quest at the behest of a god. As Cohen writes, 'the limits of the body do not stop at the skin; the heroic individual, despite every protestation to the contrary, relies for his meaning-in-being on a network of relations that includes both the human and the inhuman'.[83] In the *fornaldarsögur* flaying reveals what is underneath the monstrous identity: Ögmundr (no worse than Oddr in his exploits) is revealed to be a just ruler as well as a fair adversary; Arinnefja is revealed to be a valiant ally who will follow the hero she heals into battle

---

[81] The idea of a giant who takes on certain chivalric attributes is not unheard of in medieval tradition. Reneé Ward and Tina Boyer both examine the intricacies of heroic identity in relation to giants in their contributions to *Heads Will Roll*, ed. Tracy and Massey. See in that volume: Boyer, 'The Headless Giant: The Function of Severed Heads in the Ahistorical (Aventiurehafte) *Dietrich Epics*', pp. 137–55; and Ward, 'To be a "Fleschhewere": Beheading, Butcher-Knights, and Blood-Taboos in *Octavian Imperator*', pp. 159–81.

[82] Friðriksdóttir, *Women in Old Norse Literature*, p. 61.

[83] Cohen, *Of Giants*, p. 176.

and help him realize his quest. Their monstrous identity has been shed along with their skin. The supernatural figures are metaphors or mirrors for society. These skinless faces attest to the vulnerability of the chivalric hero who must learn humility (and his own limits) from 'monsters'. Just as the English and Continental examples of literary flaying highlight the potential for tyranny and excess in their lessons regarding kingship, justice and identity, in both *Örvar-Odds saga* and *Egils saga einhenda* the hero sees a reflection of himself in the flayed faces of the Other.

'Thou shalt have the better cloathe': Reading Second Skins in *Robin Hood and Guy of Gisborne*

Renée Ward

R OBIN *Hood and Guy of Gisborne* is one of the earliest extant Robin Hood ballads. It survives in one mid-seventeenth-century manuscript,[1] though critics typically date the tale itself to either the late fourteenth or the early fifteenth centuries.[2] The ballad is known for what Stephen Knight and Thomas Ohlgren call 'its speed', or 'its capacity to exploit the elisions and emphases of the ballad form', and, despite its brevity, in only 234 lines (58 stanzas), the ballad contains considerable detail and action.[3] The story includes elements common to the Robin Hood myth: an antagonistic relationship between the outlaw and the Sheriff of Nottingham; a

---

I am grateful to my colleagues Elyssa Warkentin, Sheila Christie and Larissa Tracy for their feedback on this paper at various stages. This paper evolved out of a presentation for the Annual Meeting of the Canadian Society of Medievalists, St Catherine's, Ontario, 24–6 May 2014.

---

[1] It appears in the folio manuscript acquired by Thomas Percy, British Library Add. MS 27879. Percy edited and published the poem as part of his collection *Reliques of Ancient English Poetry*, 3 vols. (London: J. Dodsley, 1765). Joseph Ritson re-edited the poem shortly after Percy, including it in *Robin Hood, A Collection of All the Auncient Poems, Songs and Ballads Now Extant Relative to the Celebrated English Outlaw*, 2 vols. (London: Egerton and Johnson, 1795). The poem has since appeared in numerous collections: F. J. Child, ed., *The English and Scottish Popular Ballads*, 5 vols. (New York: Houghton Mifflin, 1882–98); J. M. Gutch, ed., *A Litell Gest of Robin Hood with other Auncient and Modern Ballads and Songs Related to the Celebrated Yeoman*, 2 vols. (London: Longman, 1847); R. B. Dobson and J. Taylor, comp., *Rymes of Robyn Hood* (London: Heinemann, 1976); and Stephen Knight and Thomas Ohlgren, eds., *Robin Hood and other Outlaw Tales* (Kalamazoo, MI: Medieval Institute Publications, 2000). All references to the ballad in this essay are from Knight and Ohlgren's edition. Hereafter, line numbers are given in parentheses.

[2] Knight and Ohlgren, *Robin Hood and other Outlaw Tales*, p. 169; Richard Firth Green, 'Violence in the Early Robin Hood Poems', in *'A Great Effusion of Blood'?: Interpreting Medieval Violence*, ed. Oren Falk, Daniel Thiery and Mark Douglas Meyerson (Toronto: University of Toronto Press, 2004), pp. 268–86 at p. 268.

[3] Knight and Ohlgren, *Robin Hood and other Outlaw Tales*, p. 170.

greenwood setting and an emphasis on the natural world; localization of the narrative, in this instance, through references to Yorkshire, Barnsdale and the town of Gisborne; an emphasis on piety, especially Robin's devotion to the Virgin; and a focus on archery, competition and the delivery of justice by Robin and his men. It also includes the common motif of strife and reconciliation in the greenwood, as Robin and Little John quarrel, go their separate ways and then, after a series of individual calamities, reunite in a scene that confirms both their solidarity and Robin's leadership.

Critics repeatedly identify the ballad as one of the most grisly of the outlaw tales. J. C. Holt describes it as a 'grim yarn', while R. B. Dobson and John Taylor note that it has an 'exceptionally violent tone'.[4] Knight similarly comments that the ballad includes 'stern stuff', remnants now inaccessible of 'some sort of ancient ferocity'.[5] Such remarks arise from the number of deaths in the ballad – five in all – as well as from the intense moments of violence connected directly to Robin, especially his decapitation, disfigurement and flaying of the bounty-hunter Guy of Gisborne's body. Indeed, Robin's murder and mutilation of Guy is the apex of the narrative's violence. More importantly, this scene has clear connections to contemporary contexts and to the social and political upheavals of the late medieval period that upset the hierarchy of the feudal system.

The cultural meaning of Robin's violence and his treatment of Guy's body reside in the animal skin the bounty-hunter wears. The hide carries a series of identities, some of which transgress species boundaries and, through their connections to social mobility and monetary economies, also transgress class boundaries. Guy's appropriation of the hide, and, thus, of these transgressive identities, threatens traditional social structures that rely upon clear divisions between both. Thus, Robin's treatment of Guy, specifically his violence towards the bounty-hunter's body, is a rejection of all that he and his second skin represent; it is an attempt to eradicate the new social order. Additionally, Robin's transferral of the hide to himself renders him an alternative source of justice, one which reinforces class boundaries and reinscribes the social hegemony of the very system that excludes him through the practice of outlawry.

The ballad opens with a dream sequence in which two strong, or 'wight' (l. 7), yeomen 'beate and bind' (l. 10) Robin and rob him of his bow. Upon rising, the outlaw declares his intent to seek out the men from his vision, and, despite John's advice that 'Sweavens are swift' (l. 13), that dreams are fleeting and therefore not necessarily important, he remains

---

[4] J. C. Holt, *Robin Hood*, 2nd edn (London: Thames & Hudson, 1989), pp. 36–7; Dobson and Taylor, *Rymes of Robyn Hood*, p. 141.

[5] Stephen Knight, *Robin Hood: A Complete Study of the English Outlaw* (Oxford: Blackwell, 1994), p. 57.

resolute.[6] The two garb themselves in their 'gowne[s] of greene' (l. 21), the markers of their unity and identity as fellow outlaws of the greenwood, and set off into the forest. Shortly thereafter, they encounter a stranger clothed in a horsehide leaning against a tree. When John offers to approach the stranger, Robin insists that he must undertake the task. In doing so, he insults his companion, who departs angrily. Robin and the stranger, who reveals he is in fact looking for the outlaw, then enter a series of exchanges.[7] They begin with an archery competition, but Robin quickly outshoots his opponent in two rounds. As the narrator makes clear, Guy, although skilled, 'cold neere shoote soe' (l. 122). After the archery contest, the bounty-hunter declares that his opponent is 'better' (l. 130) than Robin Hood, and the two finally exchange names. When Robin reveals his identity, the competition devolves into hand-to-hand combat with blades, and they fight for nearly two hours. Although Robin comes close to losing when he trips on a tree root, the outlaw finds strength through his devotion to the Virgin.[8] He surges forward from his fall, crying 'Ah, deere Lady!' (l. 155), and slays his opponent.

The slaying scene is one of the most explicitly violent moments in Robin Hood lore. After Robin kills Guy, he treats his corpse with considerable malice. First, he decapitates him. Then he impales his severed head upon the end of a bow as if it were a hunting trophy. Divorced from its body and former identity, Guy's head now signifies Robin's victory.[9] Next, Robin increases the distance between the head and its original signification:

---

[6] In this instance, John's advice is incorrect, as Robin's dream does indeed have prophetic value. His comment, though, draws upon popular medieval beliefs based upon classical dream theory, that different categories of dreams exist and that they have different levels of importance, including prophecy. Macrobius outlines the five major categories of dreams – two of which (nightmares and apparitions) he argues are not worth interpreting. The other three categories (enigmatic, prophetic and oracular) should all be examined for meaning. See: Macrobius, *Commentary on the Dream of Scipio*, trans. William Harris Stahl (New York: Columbia University Press, 1952), pp. 87–90.

[7] The series of exchanges recalls the triadic structure of the temptations/ challenges Sir Gawain faces, along with their related hunt scenes, in *Sir Gawain and the Green Knight*. I am grateful to Larissa Tracy for pointing out this connection.

[8] For more on the importance of Robin's devotion to the Virgin, especially to his position within social structures of the late Middle Ages, see: Larissa Tracy, '"For Our dere Ladyes sake": Bringing the Outlaw in from the Forest – Robin Hood, Marian, and Normative National Identity', *EIRC* 38 (Summer & Winter 2012): 35–65, esp. pp. 38–43.

[9] The severed head is a prominent and multivalent motif in pre-modern literature and culture. See, for instance, any of the essays in *Heads Will Roll: Decapitation in the Medieval and Early Modern Imagination*, ed. Larissa Tracy and Jeff Massey (Leiden: Brill, 2012).

[He] pulled forth an Irish kniffe,
And nicked Sir Guy in the face,
That hee was never on a woman borne
Cold tell who Sir Guye was.

(ll. 167–70)

Robin disfigures Guy's face so severely that it is completely unrecognizable. All trace of the head's previous identity is lost.

The outlaw's treatment of Guy's corpse connects to the narrative's construction of identities that blur the boundaries between animals and humans, and between the social categories of the three estates. These ambiguities culminate in the moment Robin slays Guy and adopts for himself the bounty-hunter's cloak – a 'capull-hyde, / Topp, and tayle, and mayne' (ll. 29–30) – a disguise that, as Stuart Kane remarks, 'allows him to cross the borders between man and animal, and outlaw and agent of authority'.[10] Robin slays Guy in an act of self-defence and his adoption of the bounty-hunter's cloak allows him later to free John, who has been captured by the Sheriff. The reunited outlaws ultimately restore order to the greenwood through their defeat of the Sheriff and his men.

Kane describes the ballad's violence, particularly those moments of violence enacted by Robin upon Guy, as 'bestialized', arguing that the horsehide signifies the latter's performance of a 'bestial' rather than human identity.[11] Yet he also admits that the second skin worn by the bounty-hunter and then by the outlaw is the skin of a 'domesticated animal'.[12] Indeed, it is not the skin of a predatory animal or of a fierce forest beast. One might expect Guy to wear a wolf or bear skin, as both 'were seen as natural competitors of the huntsmen', and their pelts were consequently prized as trophies that signified human domination over their enemies.[13] Or, one might expect him to wear a boar skin, as the boar is one of the fiercest residents of the forest and its image was often employed to attribute ferocity to humans.[14] Guy, however, wears the skin of a horse.

---

[10] Stuart Kane, 'Horseplay: Robin Hood, Guy of Gisborne, and the Neg(oti)ation of the Bestial', in *Robin Hood in Popular Culture: Violence, Transgression, and Justice*, ed. Thomas Hahn (Cambridge: D. S. Brewer, 2000), pp. 101–10 at p. 186.

[11] Ibid., pp. 105, 106.

[12] Ibid., p. 106. For the use of horsehide to 'tame' a shrewish wife, and all its 'domesticating' properties, see in this volume: Frederika Bain, 'Skin on Skin: Wearing Flayed Remains', pp. 116–37.

[13] Brigitte Resl, 'Introduction: Animals in Culture, ca. 1000–ca. 1400', in *A Cultural History of Animals in the Medieval Age*, ed. Brigitte Resl (Oxford: Berg, 2007), pp. 1–26 at p. 6. See also: Susan Small, 'Flesh and Death in Early Modern Bedburg', pp. 71–90, in this volume.

[14] Joyce Salisbury, *The Beast Within: Animals in the Middle Ages* (New York: Routledge, 1994), pp. 51 and 80.

As a ubiquitous animal within the human realm, and as 'one of the earliest domesticated animals in humanity's history',[15] the horse has a heavily humanized meaning. The poet, in fact, emphasizes the ubiquitous and humanized nature of the horse's status through semantics, and, in doing so, complicates any singular or simple understanding of what Guy's horsehide signifies. The Middle English 'capull' has no definitive meaning within the common medieval classification system for horses, and many of its associated interpretations derive from the animal's domestication. Moreover, the word's various meanings cut across the class divisions of the feudal system, which were, in the late Middle Ages, under great strain. The poet's use of 'capull', then, creates a number of possible meanings that inform whether or not the horsehide evokes a bestial or human identity, what identity Guy and Robin embody when they wear the hide, and what Robin's flaying of Guy signifies. The poet's use of the word also evokes a variety of class associations that likewise transfer to the bounty-hunter and the outlaw when they adopt the hide, rendering their social identities within the estates system potentially fluid and problematic.

Representations of the horse abound in mythology and literature, in both Eastern and Western traditions, and as an animal of extreme versatility the horse enjoys a unique status for its contributions to the development of human civilization.[16] This is an animal that humans, through force, containment and control, put to work for their own benefit. It thus constitutes a large portion of what Rosi Braidotti identifies as the 'zooproletariat', an exploited, labouring class of non-human beings put to work by humans who believed animals 'lacked a rational soul and consequently a will and sovereign subjectivity of their own'.[17] Indeed, the medieval Christian view held and perpetuated the understanding that all living beings fell under the dominion of humankind.[18] Humans use horses to move their bodies, to plough the fields and to fight their wars; exploitation of the animal was so entrenched in human culture that, by the early Middle Ages, 'firmly institutionalized distinctions between horses

---

[15] Paul H. Rogers, 'Rediscovering the Horse in Medieval French Literature', *Neophilologus* 97 (2013): 627–39 at p. 628.

[16] Rogers, 'Rediscovering the Horse', pp. 627–8; Héctor A. Segarro Soto, 'After God, we Owed the Victory to the Horses: The Evolution of the Equine Companion from Veillantif to Arondel', in *Of Mice and Men: Animals in Human Culture*, ed. Nadita Batra and Vartan Messier (Newcastle upon Tyne: Cambridge Scholars, 2009), pp. 59–66 at p. 59.

[17] Rosi Braidotti, 'Animals, Anomolies, and Inorganic Others', *PMLA* 124.2 (2000): 526–32 at p. 528.

[18] This belief arises from the text of Genesis 1.28: 'And God blessed them, saying: Increase and multiply, and fill the earth, and subdue it, and rule over the fishes of the sea, and the fowls of the air, and all living creatures that move upon the earth'. See: the *Douay-Rheims Bible Online*, www.drbo.org (accessed 15 Jun. 2015).

with varying functions were widely established'.[19] A distinct hierarchy evolved in which horses were valued – and still are – according to their breed and function.

This hierarchy closely follows that of human society, and connects to the various potential meanings of the horsehide Guy and Robin wear. Horses generally fell into three major categories during the Middle Ages: 'the destrier, or knight's war horse, the palfrey, or common traveling horse, and the sommier, or pack horse'.[20] As Bernard S. Bachrach notes, early Germanic law solidified the 'general principle [...] that a war horse had three times the value of a pack horse, and a riding horse was worth twice as much as a pack horse'.[21] A number of other sub-categories that could be loosely grouped according to the three major groups were also recognized, including, but not limited to, the *coursier* or charger, a smaller version of the war horse; the *rouncey*, a small, pony-like riding horse; the *stot* and the *sumpter*, work horses heavy enough to pull the plough or a wagon but worth more than the standard cart horse; the *mulet*, a hybrid species resulting from a donkey–horse pairing (with the donkey being the male and the horse being the female) that was used primarily as a beast of burden; and the cheapest horse of them all, the *affer*.[22] Like clothing, horses were considered indicators of an individual's actual social position, or signified social aspirations when someone rode a breed typically not associated with his or her social rank.[23] For instance, the destrier was connected explicitly to the aristocratic class, specifically to those with martial responsibilities. In England this breed was increasingly difficult to procure in the high and late Middle Ages: imported primarily by the knightly class, war horses were expensive and had shorter lifespans than other breeds because of their crucial advance positions in combat.[24] Only those with access to considerable resources could afford to buy and equip this breed.

Yet individuals did not always own or ride the animals associated with their position, particularly if they were affluent, upwardly mobile members of the third estate. One need only think of Chaucer's pilgrims in the General Prologue of *The Canterbury Tales* to find examples. The

---

[19] Bernard S. Bachrach, 'Animals and Warfare in Early Medieval Europe', *Settimane di Studio del Centro Italiano di Studi sull'Alto Medioevo* 31 (1985): 707–64 at p. 177.

[20] Rogers, 'Rediscovering the Horse', p. 630.

[21] Bachrach, 'Animals and Warfare', p. 177.

[22] See: Charles Gladitz, *Horse Breeding in the Medieval World* (Dublin: Four Courts Press, 1997), pp. 152–7.

[23] Rogers, 'Rediscovering the Horse', p. 631; and Esther Pascua, 'From Forest to Farm and Town: Domestic Animals from ca. 1000 to ca. 1450', in *A Cultural History of Animals*, ed. Resl, pp. 81–102 at p. 91.

[24] Gladitz, *Horse Breeding in the Medieval World*, pp. 158–60.

financially successful Wife of Bath can afford to ride an 'amblere' (I.469), a riding horse of high quality, and the Monk, despite belonging to an order that follows the strict rule of St Benedict, maintains an entire stable of expensive mounts (I.168).[25] Not only does the Monk own and ride horses of excellent breeding, but he also equips them with heavily decorated tack, specifically with bridles covered in loud-ringing bells (I.169–70). The mounts of the Knight and the Plowman, however, are considerably more conservative. Chaucer's narrator describes the Knight's horse, which is presumably a war horse, as of good quality and as simply equipped or attired (I.74), while identifying the Plowman's horse merely as a mare (I.541). These mounts starkly contrast with the flashy horses kept and ridden by the Monk.

Chaucer's use of the horse demonstrates how heavily humanized this animal was in medieval culture, as he uses it primarily to extend his characterizations of the pilgrims.[26] The Wife of Bath's ambler contributes to the many sexual puns associated with her character's propensity for husbands, while the costly tack of the Monk's palfrey, even the quality of the horse itself, reinforces the churchman's love of worldly and material items.[27] Both also demonstrate the material wealth and social aspirations of their owners. In contrast, the horses of the Knight and the Plowman are functional rather than ostentatious, and align with the social position of their riders within the three estates system. Yet regardless of category or description of horse, what persists across all of these examples is that meaning is imbued precisely through connection to the human world. None of these horses are wild or feral, such as the Welsh Mountain or Dartmoor ponies still present in Britain today. These are animals clearly defined through their domestication, through their function or relationship to their riders or owners.

The poet of *Robin Hood and Guy of Gisborne*, like Chaucer, highlights the horse's connections to human culture and class distinctions, but is far more ambiguous in his associations. Specifically, his use of the word 'capull' renders the horsehide's meaning polysemic. A return to *The Canterbury Tales* demonstrates a number of what John A. Fisher refers to as 'pejorative' instances of the term.[28] Chaucer uses it in connection with less savoury pilgrims, such as the Cook (IX.64–5), to identify cart horses, the lower-end working breed, and to describe the horse in the Reeve's Tale that runs away

[25] See: Geoffrey Chaucer, *The Canterbury Tales*, in *The Wadsworth Chaucer*, ed. Larry D. Benson (Boston: Wadsworth Cengage Learning, 1987).

[26] John H. Fisher, 'Chaucer's Horses', *South Atlantic Quarterly* 60 (1961): 71–9 at p. 76.

[27] On the Wife of Bath, see: Fisher, 'Chaucer's Horses', p. 76; on the Monk, see: Jill Mann, *Chaucer and Medieval Estates Satire: The Literature of Social Classes and the General Prologue to the Canterbury Tales* (Cambridge: Cambridge University Press, 1973), pp. 23 and 34.

[28] Fisher, 'Chaucer's Horses', p. 74.

(I.4088, 4105). This suggests that for Chaucer, at least, the word implied a lesser breed of horse. However, the *Middle English Dictionary* defines 'capull' more widely as 'a horse or gelding; a warhorse, cart horse, riding horse, etc.'[29] It also cites examples of these various meanings from texts contemporary to *Robin Hood and Guy of Gisborne*: *Piers Plowman* (the A and B texts) includes uses that imply both riding and pack horses; *Sir Gawain and the Green Knight* includes an example of the word in reference to a war horse; and the *Laud Troy Book* likewise employs the term in place of *destrier*.[30] In the late fourteenth and early fifteenth centuries, then, 'capull' was a highly mutable term. The poet thus identifies the second skin worn by the bounty-hunter and the outlaw with a word that, in and of itself, has no singular or definitive meaning within the common medieval classification system for horses. What the bounty-hunter's second skin signifies is as multivalent as the word with which the poet identifies it.

Despite the range of meanings 'capull' offers, only one explains the degree of violence Robin enacts upon Guy. If Guy's capull-hide is the hide of a destrier, then the hide significantly threatens established species boundaries and social hierarchies. The war horse is the pinnacle equine breed, synonymous in the Middle Ages with the figure of the knight. It is also the most impressive or domineering breed physically – a necessary feature of its physiology given the strength required to carry a knight in full armour, its own armament, and any other weapons or accoutrements. On an allegorical level the destrier is imbued with meaning connected to the knight's masculinity and martial prowess and functions, overall, as 'a symbol of his virility'.[31] Specific parts of the horse had explicit meanings within this interpretive system: 'The head with its glorious mane and upstanding ears was the quintessence of the phallic animal.'[32] The war horse is also a breed especially associated with social status. By the thirteenth century knights were firmly entrenched within the feudal system as an aristocratic class precisely because of the high cost of the martial accoutrements they required, including horses and

---

[29] *Middle English Dictionary* (MED), s.v. 'capel', www.quod.lib.umich.edu/m/med (accessed 12 May 2014). The potential for 'capel' to denote a gelding recalls Chaucer's Pardoner, whom the Host describes as so hairless, 'I trowe he were a geldyng or a mare' (I.691).

[30] *Piers Plowman* A: 'Þenne caredon heo for Caples [...] to carien hem þider' (2.132); *Piers Plowman* B: 'Grace deuised A carte [...] And gaf hym caples [...] contricioun [and] confessioun' (19.328); *Sir Gawain and the Green Knight*: 'Þe knyȝt kacheȝ his caple' (l. 2175); *Laud Troy Book*: 'The lordes hem busked [and] toke here caples' (l. 9637). For these examples, see: MED, s.v. 'capel'.

[31] Rogers, 'Rediscovering the Horse', p. 636.

[32] Beryl Rowland, *Animals with Human Faces: A Guide to Animal Symbolism* (Knoxville: University of Tennessee Press, 1975), pp. 103–4.

armour.[33] As Paul H. Rogers notes, a member of the third estate such as a villein 'would never be permitted to mount a *destrier* or a *coursier*'.[34] This breed of horse was exclusive to the aristocratic or noble class.

Thus, Guy's second skin identifies him with a social group that sits very near to the top of the social ladder. Moreover, the bounty-hunter's second skin – which includes the head, mane and tail of the horse – embodies the idealized masculine identity of the paramount martial figure, the knight. Consequently, it symbolizes the social hegemony that this member of society, through his martial duties and tenurial responsibilities, upheld. When Guy wears the capull-hide, however, his actions do not align with those of the social group whose identity he usurps. Instead, they empty the hide of its former military and class associations, linking it instead to the non-traditional monetary economy and social mobility that expanded the third estate in the late Middle Ages.

Although the narrative identifies Guy as a 'wight yeoman' (l. 25), a title that should place him in the same social group as Robin, the bounty-hunter's behaviour demonstrates that the two are most definitely not of the same sort. In fact, it suggests that even within the yeoman class a hierarchy exists and the social status of its members vary. While Robin's status is, as Richard Almond and A. J. Pollard argue, 'unambiguously' that of 'the yeoman of the forest',[35] Guy's status is less clear. As Almond and Pollard note, in the late Middle Ages the term 'yeoman' was a slippery one used to represent a range of social and class positions, including those they describe as 'proto-capitalist'.[36] This expression – proto-capitalist – is an apt one for Guy, who clearly has an interest in advancing his social position. His work as a bounty-hunter suggests as much. Guy accepts remuneration beyond his station in exchange for the capture and killing of Robin. The Sheriff of Nottingham promises Guy 'a knight's fee' (l. 204) – traditionally, a substantial grant of land[37] – in exchange for his services. Guy even suggests that this payment is more attractive to him than a monetary one, when he tells Robin that he would rather meet the outlaw than receive 'forty pound of golde' (l. 102), a considerable sum in late Middle Ages. The knight's fee, however, offers not only a fief or landholding but also the desirable social status attached to that fiefdom. The capture of Robin thus provides Guy with the greatest opportunity for social advancement within, and potentially beyond, the highest ranks of the third estate, an

[33] Sally Harvey, 'The Knight and the Knight's Fee in England', *Past & Present* 49 (Nov. 1970): 3–43 at p. 43.

[34] Rogers, 'Rediscovering the Horse', p. 631.

[35] Richard Almond and A. J. Pollard, 'The Yeomanry of Robin Hood and Social Terminology in Fifteenth-Century England', *Past & Present* 170 (Feb. 2001): 52–77 at p. 56.

[36] Ibid., p. 53.

[37] Harvey, 'The Knight and the Knight's Fee in England', p. 3.

advancement that eclipses mere financial gain by offering elevated social status and civic duties as well.

The term 'proto-capitalist' also suits Guy's choice to advance his position through the sale of his labour – specifically his fighting and killing skills. While the established landed aristocracy also, traditionally, constituted the 'warrior class', as the fourteenth century progressed this group was increasingly displaced by fighting men from the lower classes who were 'drawn to war by the prospect of profit'.[38] Yeomen, both mounted archers and foot archers, fell into this group, demonstrating that the distance between previously distinct social groups was narrowing and that 'social mobility was possible'.[39] Such social mobility upsets the established hierarchy of a system that supports itself primarily by maintaining firm boundaries between those who rule (or fight) and those who work. As a yeoman, Guy represents a range of social or class positions, including those that potentially fall into the lower aristocracy as well as those within the third estate. His actions and his identity as a bounty-hunter, though, place him firmly within the group of yeomen that belonged to the lower social group, and confirm his desire to move beyond this social position.

Guy's threat to established boundaries and hierarchies extends to those between humans and animals. More specifically, his adoption of the capull-hide, as the skin of a destrier, upsets the interspecies identity associated with martial figures. As Jeffrey Jerome Cohen and Susan Crane both point out, the permeability of species boundaries is crucial to the identity formation of the knight.[40] Simply put, the horse, rider and all of the necessary accoutrements work together in a perpetual process of becoming. Cohen calls this the chivalric circuit, a becoming that is in constant flux in which animal and human ebb and flow as they work in concert in their martial endeavour.[41] Indeed, anyone who has ever ridden a horse can appreciate this concept. Although the knight may, at times, take control while mounted, much of his work requires that the horse and rider work cooperatively, especially if they wish to survive combat. The two develop a bond that renders them more of a single identity or being, and this bond is a type of brotherhood, a relationship with the capacity for great affection.

---

[38] Andrew Ayton, 'English Armies in the Fourteenth Century', in _The Wars of Edward III: Sources and Interpretations_, ed. Clifford J. Rogers (Woodbridge: Boydell Press, 2010), pp. 303–19 at pp. 305 and 312.

[39] Ibid., pp. 315–16.

[40] Jeffrey Jerome Cohen, 'Chevalerie', in his _Medieval Identity Machines_ (Minneapolis: University of Minnesota Press, 2003), pp. 35–77; Susan Crane, 'Chivalry and the Pre/Postmodern', _postmedieval: a journal of medieval cultural studies_ 2.1 (2011): 69–87, and 'Knight and Horse', in her _Animal Encounters: Contacts and Concepts in Medieval Britain_ (Philadelphia: University of Pennsylvania Press, 2013), pp. 137–68.

[41] Cohen, 'Chevalerie', p. 76.

In *Bevis of Hampton*, for instance, Bevis initially seeks to restore his heritage but ultimately surrenders it to save the life of his beloved horse, Arondel; or, in *The Awntyrs off Arthur*, Gawain becomes mad with grief at the loss of his horse, Gresell.[42] As these examples suggest, symbiosis is the pinnacle expression of knighthood.

Guy's appropriation of the capull-hide suggests that he seeks to recreate the interspecies identity of the horse and rider within the chivalric circuit. Certainly, the hide envelops him, blurring the boundary of his human body by rendering it part of the internal materials of an animal. His use of the capull-hide, however, empties it of any associations it has with a fluid human–animal identity or with a chivalric identity. The bounty-hunter's second skin can never constitute an actual human–animal becoming, for it lacks half of the necessary sentient force. The horse itself as a living, thinking being has long since been removed. What remains is purely a material object. Guy's second skin houses an entity that is only ever human, and, therefore, fails to embody any of the species cooperation required to render effective the martial identity it evokes.

The bounty-hunter's use of the hide thus results in a perversion of its original martial, class and species signification, one that resonates with the ballad's indication of his unnatural status when he appears in the greenwood. When Robin and John first encounter the bounty-hunter, he stands with 'His body leaned to a tree' (l. 26), as if melded with the forest. Yet this connection to the natural world is not positive. Guy's figure is a dark one, and the narrator describes how a 'sword and a dagger he wore by his side, / Had beene many a mans bane' (ll. 27–8). That is, his sword and dagger (in his hands) have murdered many men. The blade with which he fights Robin evidences his former killings, as it is 'browne', or blood-stained, rather than clean, or 'bright' (l. 146), like the outlaw's blade. The contrast of blades – one soiled (dark), one clean (light) – signals that Guy is the antithesis of Robin, the true forester yeoman. Even the narrative's structure evokes the unnatural status of the bounty-hunter, for his introduction occurs within the only six-line stanza in the ballad, marking him, and it, as different, as out of step with the rest of the story. Simply put, he does not belong.

Robin's violence towards Guy's body ultimately seeks to undo the category violations the bounty-hunter and his capull-hide present, and to restore the species and class boundaries his actions transgress, by removing – figuratively flaying – the horsehide from Guy's corpse, a removal echoed in the flaying of the skin from his face. As Kane argues, Robin's violence has purpose. Guy's body defies categorization, 'and so

---

[42] Karl Steel highlights the bond, in *Bevis*, between Bevis and Arondel, and also remarks that, in *Awyntyrs*, Gawain 'mourns [Grissell] to the point of madness'. See: *How to Make a Human: Animals and Violence in the Middle Ages* (Columbus: Ohio State University Press, 2011), pp. 96, 223.

must be violently undone'.[43] More importantly, Robin's treatment of Guy's body, especially his decapitation, disfigurement and flaying of the corpse – which have strong echoes of medieval hunt rituals – marks the bounty-hunter specifically as a member of Braidotti's zooproletariat. This emphasis on his status as a labouring human-animal also reinforces his position as one within the third estate.

As numerous critics note, hunt practices culminated in the breaking or unmaking of the game, and the entire process had very specific terminology.[44] The breaking of the game – 'the process of taking apart the animal' – had three distinct stages: 'the animal was undone (split open), fleaned (flayed or skinned) and then brittled or cut into pieces'.[45] Robin enacts all three stages upon Guy's body. His initial killing blow to Guy splits the bounty-hunter's body open. More precisely, it constitutes the spaying of the game, what Ryan R. Judkins defines as killing the prey 'with a single blade thrust'.[46] Robin's removal of the corpse's capull-hide constitutes a type of flaying or skinning: the outlaw removes Guy's second skin, the outer form that carried his identity, and leaves him bare. His decapitation of the corpse and mutilation of the severed head's face contribute to the brittling process. In short, Robin does to Guy what any master of the hunt does to fallen game: he renders him 'completely unrecognizable' either as an animal or as a living being.[47] In doing so, Robin readies the body, or at least parts of the body, for a new use as his disguise, much like master hunters unmake game in order to prepare the carcass for being consumed as food or transformed into material objects. Robin's knowledge also confirms his specific status as a forester yeoman. As Almond and Pollard note, the 'foresters who worked alongside the huntsmen needed themselves to know how to conduct a hunt and how

---

[43] Kane, 'Horseplay', p. 110.

[44] For details concerning medieval hunt practices, see, for instance, Richard Almond, *Medieval Hunting*, 3rd edn (Stroud: The History Press, 2011); Susan Crane, 'Ritual Aspects of the Hunt à Force', in *Engaging with Nature: Essays on the Natural World in Medieval and Early Modern Europe*, ed. Barbara A. Hanawalt and Lisa J. Kiser (Notre Dame, IN: University of Notre Dame Press, 2008), pp. 63–84; or Ryan R. Judkins, 'The Game of the Courtly Hunt: Chasing and Breaking Deer in Medieval English Literature', *Journal of English and Germanic Philology* 112.1 (Jan. 2013): 70–92. See, in this volume: Jack Hartnell, 'Tools of the Puncture: Skin, Knife, Bone, Hand', pp. 20–50.

[45] Rebekah L. Pratt, 'From Animal to Meat: Illuminating the Medieval Ritual of Unmaking', *EHumanista* 25 (Sept. 2013): 17–26 at pp. 19–20. Pratt draws directly on Almond's explanation of the unmaking process: 'the deer was *undone* (cut open), *fleaned* (skinned), and then *brittled* (cut up)'. See: Almond, *Medieval Hunting*, p. 77.

[46] Judkins, 'The Game of the Courtly Hunt', p. 72 n. 8.

[47] Pratt, 'From Animal to Meat', p. 21.

to deal with the quarry when it was killed. They were required, as part of their craft, to know the specialized terminology of hunting and to be able to participate in the formalized rituals involved in virtually every aspect of this aristocratic pastime.'[48]

The outlaw's adoption of the capull-hide, along with his appropriation of Guy's bow, arrows and horn, symbolize his role as the master huntsman, as does his impalement of the severed head on the end of the bow. The head of fallen prey, the 'main visual trophy of the adventure [...] belonged to the master huntsman or the lord of the hunt'.[49] Similarly, the skin of the fallen prey 'would be given to the hunter which killed the animal with a bow'.[50] Although Robin does not kill Guy with his bow, he beats him outright in their archery contest and his success foreshadows the eventual defeat – or death – the bounty-hunter experiences during hand-to-hand combat. The outlaw continues to perform the hunt ritual and his role as the master huntsman when he 'sett[s] Guyes horne to his mouth, / [and] A lowd blast in it he did blow' (ll. 183–4). In other words, he blows the mort, or 'sound[s] the horn call reserved for the death' of the game.[51] This performance extends to Robin's infiltration – via his capull-hide disguise – of the Sheriff's camp. Here, he self-identifies as the master huntsman when he declares to the Sheriff (as if he is Guy, referring to Robin), 'now I have slaine the master' (l. 199). He then enacts the ceremonial distribution of the broken game among other hunters through his rescue of Little John and his gift to him of Guy's bow, which he tells his fellow outlaw is 'his boote' (l. 222). John then completes the performance when he earns his portion or share by putting the bow to good use: as the Sheriff flees, the outlaw cleaves his heart (kills him) with a well-shot arrow. Robin and John have become the hunters, Guy and the Sheriff, the hunted.

Robin's abandonment of Guy's flayed corpse in the forest confirms the low status of the bounty-hunter's body and its synonymy with labouring horses or other members of the zooproletariat. It is not uncommon, Karl Steel explains, for animal carcasses to be similarly abandoned. Non-human corpses are typically treated 'as no human body should be: the boar is eaten, the dog's corpse left in a ditch, the bird's on a dung heap, and the horse's, too, left to rot'.[52] Extant evidence suggests that, in some instances, the flesh of deceased horses would be fed to dogs, in a type of reuse, recycle or 'waste-not, want-not' mentality. According to Steel, such methods of disposal reassert 'that the horse was only an animal, that its remains, being a carcass rather than a corpse, merit only instrumental, not reverential

---

[48] Almond and Pollard, 'The Yeomanry of Robin Hood', p. 64.

[49] Almond, *Medieval Hunting*, pp. 75–6.

[50] Ibid., p. 77.

[51] Judkins, 'The Game of the Courtly Hunt', p. 72 n. 8.

[52] Steel, *How to Make a Human*, p. 59.

treatment'.[53] Robin's treatment of the recently slain Guy confirms that the outlaw views his opponent as more akin to animal than human. His treatment of the corpse is not so much irreverent as it is established practice for a butchered animal.

The outlaw's recognition of Guy's body as part of the zooproletariat does not, however, controvert its human identity. Rather, it confirms the bounty-hunter's humanity and marks him specifically as belonging to the group most often understood as chattel, the indentured, lowest ranks of the third estate that provide manual labour. As a bounty-hunter – as a killing machine who employs bladed weapons – Guy works with his hands. More importantly, Guy labours specifically for the Sheriff as a hired gun; like the *sommiers* or cart horses for hire in urban centres, he does the grunt work that the Sheriff is unwilling or unable to do himself. Indeed, *sommiers* typically have associations with the third estate, especially with agriculture and labour. In the late Middle Ages they were also increasingly associated with urban spaces, where they were often traded in horse markets or could be hired to transport 'foodstuffs and goods to, from, and around the city'.[54] The Sheriff employs Guy in a similar manner: to rid himself of his own burden, Robin Hood. Like the *sommier*, Guy's value connects directly to how well he functions for those who employ him to complete tasks that benefit their own well-being. He is a commodity, property – disposable and replaceable.

Such elisions between humans, especially members of the third estate, and animals were not uncommon in the Middle Ages. Marie de France, in her *Fables*, divides animals into three distinct categories that represent particular social groups – 'predators (the ruling classes), prey (commoners as victims), and domestic animals (also commoners)'.[55] She then uses these categories to articulate normative and non-normative class behaviours, criticizing those who express discontent with their economic and social realities. Desires for upward social mobility and the actions inspired by such desires, Marie remarks, display only 'foolishness'.[56] Chaucer, too, draws upon this literary convention in the Nun's Priest's Tale, when the fox abducts Chauntecleer. The Nun's Priest, as he describes the cacophonic barnyard chaos, likens it to – even suggests it is more unruly

---

[53] Ibid., p. 237.

[54] See: Pascua, 'From Forest to Farm and Town', p. 99.

[55] Salisbury, *The Beast Within*, p. 129.

[56] Marie de France, 'The Hare and the Deer', in *Fables*, ed. and trans. Harriet Spiegel (Toronto: University of Toronto Press, 1987), p. 25. 'The Hare and the Deer' recounts how a hare who covets the antlers of a deer beseeches the Creator to endow him with a pair. The Creator explains that the hare is not designed for such adornment, but when the hare insists that he is, she grants his request. The weight of the antlers is, of course, unbearable for the hare and he becomes immobile. Marie's lesson is that individuals should be satisfied with their lot in life rather than seeking to alter their social status.

than – the uproar caused by those who participated in the 1381 uprising. 'Certes', he declares, 'he Jakke Strawe and his meynee / Ne made nevere shoutes half so shrille' (VII.3394–5). The narrator, in one breath, elides the difference between humans, animals and barnyard foul, reinforcing the notion that members of the third estate belonged 'to another order of being […] a different race, a nonhuman'.[57]

While Robin's abandonment of Guy's body confirms the latter's position within the lowest ranks of the third estate, his exchange of the capull-hide for his own green cloak signals the reversal of their roles within the narrative and re-establishes the class boundary that separates the two yeomen.[58] Before he abandons the corpse of his enemy, the outlaw covers it with his own green cloak and says,

> Lye there, lye there, good Sir Guye,
> And with me be not wrothe;
> If thou have had the worse strokes at my hand,
> Thou shalt have the better cloathe.
>
> (ll. 171–4)

As Robin appropriates the capull-hide as a disguise, he endows his now-defeated foe with a symbol that corrects his problematic identity. Robin's green cloak, which symbolizes the greenwood, along with the brotherhood of Robin and his men, also represents his social position as forester yeoman and outlaw, a status that elevates him over Guy through its participation in the traditional social system.[59] Further, the outlaw's words to the bounty-hunter – 'Thou shalt have the better cloathe' (l. 174) – identify all that the cloak signifies as superior to the capull-hide and all that it embodies. In Robin's opinion, it is the proper marker for Guy because it undoes all of the problematic identity associations created by the capull-hide and his proto-capitalist behaviours, and places him firmly within an identity position that reinforces the feudal structure, either that of the forester yeoman or that of the outlaw.

Although Robin appropriates his now-deceased foe's horsehide in a type of social self-demotion, this action is not a move on his part to adopt permanently a new social position. The animal skin serves only as

---

[57] Lee Patterson, '"No man his reson herde": Peasant Consciousness, Chaucer's Miller, and the Structure of the *Canterbury Tales*', in *Literary Practice and Social Change in Britain, 1380–1530*, ed. Patterson (Berkeley: University of California Press, 1990), pp. 113–55 at p. 135.

[58] Similarly, King Arthur and Oddr's appropriation of their enemies' beard-cloaks reverse their roles and heroic identity. See in this volume: Livingston, 'Losing Face: Flayed Beards and Gendered Power in Arthurian Literature', pp. 308–21, and Larissa Tracy, 'Face Off: Flaying and Identity in Medieval Romance', pp. 322–48.

[59] For a discussion of outlawry as part of the traditional social structure, see: Green, 'Violence in the Early Robin Hood Poems', pp. 268–86.

a temporary tool that grants Robin access to the Sheriff of Nottingham's ranks in order to free John. Additionally, Robin's behaviour while wearing the hide emphatically rejects all of its former meaning. When Robin presents the disfigured head to the Sheriff and the Sheriff offers him a reward, the outlaw doubly declares 'Ile none of they gold, [...] / Nor Ile none of itt have' (ll. 197–8). In other words, he refuses to accept the fee intended as payment for his own death. Thus, the outlaw rejects Guy's sale of his labour. As Kimberly A. Macuare Thompson argues, '[t]hrough refusing the bounty' Robin 'is not only negating his current identity as a bounty-hunter, but he is also rejecting the "knight's fee" which would transform his status to that of a knight through yet another economic maneuver'.[60] The outlaw undoes the problematic meanings the bounty-hunter and his horsehide create, delivers appropriate justice and reinscribes the hegemony that actually excludes him. He exists temporarily within the monetary economy – just long enough to critique and reject it. In doing so, he reinforces feudal structures and, through his restoration of order, demonstrates the importance of outlawry to the maintenance of those structures.

Robin Hood and Guy of Gisborne, then, resists as it explores the social change of the late medieval period, articulating the inherently contradictory nature of the social system through the 'capull-hyde' and its multiple significations, as well as through the violence that Robin enacts upon Guy. These various meanings of 'capull' – those connected to bestial and human identities, or to class and social identities within the estates system – ultimately inform the violence within the ballad. Specifically, they shape Robin's treatment of Guy's body, which parallels the unmaking or breaking of the game within the highly ritualized medieval hunt, as well as his subsequent adoption of the hide as his own disguise. The outlaw's decapitation, disfigurement and flaying of the bounty-hunter's corpse suggest that he reads Guy's body as belonging to the lowest order of the third estate, and his act of covering the decapitated corpse with his own green mantle indicates that he seeks to return the upwardly mobile bounty-hunter to a more appropriate social position and counter the social disruption of his proto-capitalist endeavours. The violence Robin enacts upon his opponent's body also suggests that he reads the horsehide as that of a destrier, or war horse, the animal most associated with the knightly class. Guy's adoption of the horsehide empties it of its chivalric and class connections, linking it, instead, to non-traditional monetary economies and the resultant social mobility that transformed late medieval society. This provides the greatest possibility for transgressions of the species

---

[60] Kimberly A. Macuare Thompson, 'The Late Medieval Robin Hood Ballads: Economics Revisited', in *British Outlaws of Literature and History: Essays on Medieval and Early Modern Figures from Robin Hood to Twm Shon Catty*, ed. Alexander L. Kaufman (Jefferson, NC: McFarland, 2011), pp. 179–203 at p. 187.

boundaries, for it usurps the identity circuit created between a knight and all of his martial accoutrements, particularly his horse. The outlaw's actions can thus be understood as an attempt to eradicate the new social order associated with the bounty-hunter, his second skin and his employer, the Sheriff. Indeed, Robin's appropriation of the horsehide briefly renders him an alternative source of justice, one that reinscribes the social hegemony of the very system that excludes him through the institution of outlawry. However, the flaying and hide-transferral validate the skin's previous associations by temporarily incorporating them into Robin's identity. His brief adoption of the horsehide is also a confirmation of the potential fluidity of identity construction, while his ultimate rejection of the hide and that with which it is associated operates as a reinforcement of the boundaries believed to exist between human and non-human beings, and between the three estates.

EPILOGUE

Anthropodermic Bibliopegy
in the Early Modern Period

Perry Neil Harrison

FLESH, as a signifier, is fluid. As the chapters in this volume demonstrate, both the act of flaying and the removed skin itself represent a vast range of signifiers, sometimes seemingly contradictory. When practised as a punishment, Larissa Tracy correctly asserts that flaying serves to 'figuratively [excise] the crimes and the identity of the accused'.[1] However, the significance of the flayed skin does not end at the removal of identity; the dehumanizing act also provides the opportunity for transformation. For the monsters depicted in medieval Icelandic sagas, the removal of skin 'enables them to act in support of, rather than in opposition to, the heroes in each saga', allowing them fluidly to shift their roles in the romances away from the monstrous.[2] Yet, the victim of the flaying was not always the only one to undergo change. As Frederika Bain observes, for both the real-life Aztecs and the characters in literary works such as *Salman und Morolf*, the wearing of flayed skin is a way to undergo a personal metamorphosis, and 'skin-wearing is assumed to facilitate passage to an alternative state of being'.[3] Flaying has grave consequences for flayed and flayer alike, as Michael Livingston and Emily Leverett explain.[4] Finally, as several contributions to this volume suggest, the representation of Christ and St Bartholomew's flayed skins in art and literature provide audiences with means to witness and better understand both the human and the divine.[5]

I would like to extend a special thanks to Ed Frank, curator of the Special Collections of the University of Memphis Library, for his cooperation and generosity during the conducting of this study. I would also like to thank Megan May of the Abilene Christian University Brown Library for her assistance while researching this project.

[1] Larissa Tracy, 'Face Off: Flaying and Identity in Medieval Romance', pp. 322–48 at p. 326, in this volume.

[2] Ibid.

[3] Frederika Bain, 'Skin on Skin: Wearing Flayed Remains', in this volume, pp. 116–37 at p. 116.

[4] Michael Livingston, 'Losing Face: Flayed Beards and Gendered Power in Arthurian Literature', pp. 308–21; and Emily Leverett, 'Reading the Consumed: Flayed and Cannibalized Bodies in *The Siege of Jerusalem* and *Richard Coer de Lyon*', pp. 285–307, in this volume.

[5] In this collection, see: Peter Dent, 'A Window for the Pain: Surface, Interiority and Christ's Flagellated Skin in Late Medieval Sculpture',

Skin is also the substance of texts themselves – cured, scraped, stretched – it is the surface upon which these narratives, and all their incumbent meanings, are inscribed.

The variety of meanings this sign takes on is exemplified in the process of anthropodermic bibliopegy – the act of binding books in human skin. Like the flayed skin that makes up their binding, the owners of the books used them in a plethora of ways – to construct their own social and religious identity, to strike out against and dehumanize those with competing ideologies and to situate themselves within a larger social tradition. Yet, despite its variety of uses and prevalence as a plot device in modern works of horror fiction, anthropodermic bibliopegy was a historically rare occurrence. The rarity of the act notwithstanding, consistently recorded instances of its practice range from the Middle Ages until the present day, with purported examples residing in public and private libraries in both Europe and the United States.[6] Historically, the most prominent documented periods of the practice are during the late sixteenth and early seventeenth centuries, as well as a revival of popularity during the nineteenth and early twentieth centuries. While researchers have conducted tests on individual documents in order to determine their validity as artefacts, scholars have previously paid little critical attention to the reasons *why* this act would have been appealing.

As a stark reminder of the mutable nature of the human form, anthropodermic bibliopegy has served as an effective way for the owners and creators of these artefacts to both reinforce their own identity and assault the identities of ideological Others. While creators of the earliest purported anthropodermic books used the binding largely to establish their own religious identity, the surge of prominence in the late sixteenth and early seventeenth centuries used the practice as a weapon against opposing beliefs. A skin-bound edition of Louis Richeome's *L'Idolatrie Huguenote*, an early-seventeenth-century anti-Protestant polemic, demonstrates how this technique was used to both lionize the owner's own identity and demonize threats to these beliefs. Conversely, doctors in

---

pp. 208–39; Valerie Gramling, '"Flesche withowtyn hyde": The Removal and Transformation of Jesus' Skin in the English Cycle Passion Plays', pp. 240–60; Sherry C. M. Lindquist, 'Masculinist Devotion: Flaying and Flagellation in the *Belles Heures*', pp. 173–207; and Asa Simon Mittman and Christine Sciacca, 'Robed in Martyrdom: The Flaying of St Bartholomew in the Laudario of Sant'Agnese', pp. 140–72.

[6] Lawrence S. Thompson, 'Promptuary of Anthropodermic Bibliopegy', *The Book Collector's Packet* 4.2 (Oct. 1946): 15–17 at p. 17. In this article, Lawrence cites examples from 'The Newberry Library, the White Collection of the Cleveland Public, the University of California at Los Angeles Library, the Watkinson Library of Hartford, Connecticut, and the Library of Congress' (p. 17). However, he makes no claims regarding the validity of any of these documents.

the nineteenth and early twentieth centuries crafted anthropodermic books predominantly as a way to indicate their own social status and skill. Finally, the present-day creation of 'Cryobooks' subverts the historical applications of the practice by reaffirming the values of the bindings' contributors and fostering new forms of communication. These varied uses of anthropodermic bibliopegy over the course of six centuries represent the potential for human skin to serve as a mutable, but always powerful, indicator of personal identity.

Undoubtedly, the greatest source of difficulty for researchers of anthropodermic texts is the question of validity. The claim that a certain book is made of human skin is frequently unverified, and declarations regarding such bindings often do not hold up under scientific analysis. Medieval book historian Erik Kwakkel has remarked that, due to the unconfirmed nature of many of the bindings of this type, he 'thought this practice [...] was a myth'.[7] Regarding the difficulty of establishing the true, skin-bound nature of the books, Carolyn Marvin notes, 'Because there is nothing perceptibly obvious about a book bound in human skin to suggest its composition [...] it [is] especially difficult to distinguish fantasy from fact.'[8] In particular, human skin is, in many ways, similar to bovine skin, so validating claims without modern laboratory testing is nearly impossible, leading to false claims of anthropodermic bibliopegy. For example, the *Scrutinium Scriptuarum* currently held in the United States Library of Congress was renowned for having been bound in human skin, but, like a great number of these misleading artefacts, the book is actually bound in bull's hide.[9]

Scientifically verified examples of the practice during the Middle Ages are exceedingly rare, and perhaps even non-existent. Among the earliest known books believed to be bound in human skin is a French Bible dating from the late thirteenth century, though there is no available information that confirms the binding material.[10] While authentic examples of anthropodermic medieval texts are elusive, the presence

---

[7] Erik Kwakkel, 'Halloween (2): Bound in Human Skin', *Erik Kwakkel* (blog) (28 Oct. 2013), accessible through http://erikkwakkel.tumblr.com (accessed 30 Mar. 2015). In addition to the anthropodermic *L'Idolatrie Huguenote*, several additional books have undergone similar testing to verify the nature of their binding. Harvard, in particular, discovered three skin-bound documents as recently as 2014. For more information about these recent findings, see: Heather Cole, 'The Science of Anthropodermic Binding', *Houghton Library Blog*, 4 Jun. 2014, http://blogs.law.harvard.edu/houghton/2014/06/04/caveat-lecter/ (accessed 30 Mar. 2015).

[8] Carolyn Marvin, 'The Body of the Text: Literacy's Corporeal Constant', *The Quarterly Journal of Speech* 80.2 (May 1994): 129–49 at p. 133.

[9] Ibid., pp. 133–4.

[10] Samuel P. Jacobs, 'The Skinny on Harvard's Rare Book Collection', *The Harvard Crimson* (2 Feb. 2006), http://www.thecrimson.com/

of fabricated and unverified documents does prove that the idea held a place in the medieval imagination. The available accounts of this binding practice indicate a correlation between the act and religious texts, a link that would become increasingly important as anthropodermic bibliopegy became more common in subsequent centuries. In particular, a number of scientifically confirmed anthropodermic books originate from sixteenth- and seventeenth-century Europe. While the relatively small number of existing examples indicates that this manner of binding was still unusual, it became frequent enough that commonalities began to emerge. Like their medieval ancestors, many early modern documents that have been verified are religious texts of some description. One of these religious texts truly bound in human skin, currently held in the Bancroft Library at the University of California, Berkeley, is a seventeenth-century prayer book bound during the course of the French Revolution.[11] In fact, several of these anthropodermic books are of French origin, which is not entirely surprising given their religious bent and the religious, political and social turmoil facing that country during the sixteenth, seventeenth and eighteenth centuries.[12]

The French Religious Wars of the sixteenth century provided a ripe staging ground for a great many public acts of mutilation and brutality. As early as 1546 the French Parlement exercised jurisdiction over the punishments of those it deemed heretics. These punishments were highly visible and violent. In response to the discovery of a private gathering of Protestants in 1546, 'fourteen men were tortured and burned alive. A fifteenth was sentenced to witness the executions, hung by his armpits, then flogged and imprisoned.'[13] This violence was not limited to state actions. In a particularly brutal instance of mob violence, 'Two [Huguenot] lawyers [...] were hanged in the marketplace in September 1562. The crowd cut them down and mutilated them before throwing them into the river.'[14] Mutilation was a common theme in mob-related violence, particularly during the St Bartholomew's Day Massacre of 1572. As Geoffrey Treasure notes, during the massacre, 'bodies were stripped, sometimes mutilated,

---

article/2006/2/2/the-skinny-on-harvards-rare-book/ (accessed 30 Mar. 2015).

[11] Richard A. Lovett, 'Photo in the News: Book Bound in Human Skin', *National Geographic News* (11 Apr. 2006), accessible through http://news.nationalgeographic.com (accessed 30 Mar. 2015).

[12] While the majority of examples of anthropodermic bibliopegy are of French or British origin, these are by no means the only countries to have produced such artifacts. For example, Spain and Germany are each the source of verified anthropodermic books.

[13] G. R. R. Treasure, *The Huguenots* (New Haven: Yale University Press, 2013), p. 73.

[14] Ibid., p. 154.

dragged along the street and thrown into the Seine'.[15] Though this manner of public violence tapered off greatly following the 1598 Edict of Nantes, which gave Huguenots significant freedoms and made them 'in some respects a separate political entity',[16] these highly visible acts of violence were still alive in the public imagination of the early seventeenth century.

In spite of the violence during the period, there are no examples of flaying being used as a punishment during the Religious Wars. Instead, medieval ideas about the removal of skin and the crimes associated with the act led to the rise in production of anthropodermic books in France during this time. Nonetheless, the chapters of this volume prove that assigning a single, static meaning to either the act of removing flesh or the removed organ itself is far from a simple endeavour. Despite these differing shades of significance, each contributor points to the practice's larger, unifying meaning – the presence of skin, on some level, defines human identity, and the removal of this skin alters, transfers or removes this source of identity. In the words of Katie L. Walter, '[skin] also provides ways for thinking about the self, supporting but also belying the fantasy of the self's wholeness or unity'.[17] Robert Mills further explores the consequences inherent in the removal of this medium of self-perception and unity, stating, 'removing the outer surface of a human being deprives that being of its humanity, exposing the potential for an animalized, identity-less existence beneath the surface'.[18] Thus, while the act of flaying is multivalent, it can be seen as a deliberate act of dehumanization, one that removes identifying social and physical traits and transfers the victim into a subhuman stratum characterized by anonymity.

In contrast to the modern-day image of medieval brutality, Mills is quick to point out that, 'as a legal penalty, flaying seems to have played a much greater role in the imaginations of medieval people than it did in actual judicial practice'.[19] Tracy reaffirms its extraordinary use, remarking that 'flaying [...] was rarely practiced as a method of capital punishment in the medieval period'.[20] Mary Rambaran-Olm dispels the mythology of flaying

---

[15] Ibid., p. 172.

[16] Ibid., p. 228.

[17] Katie L. Walter, Introduction to *Reading Skin in Medieval Literature and Culture*, ed. Walter (New York: Palgrave, 2013), pp. 1–10 at p. 2.

[18] Robert Mills, 'Havelok's Bare Life and the Significance of Skin', in *Reading Skin*, ed. Walter, pp. 57–80 at p. 62.

[19] Ibid.

[20] Larissa Tracy, *Torture and Brutality in Medieval Literature* (Cambridge: D. S. Brewer, 2012), pp. 62–3. While punitive instances of flaying are rare, they are not completely unknown. For an account of the flaying of Peter Stubbe in sixteenth-century Germany, see in this collection: Susan Small, 'Flesh and Death in Early Modern Bedburg', pp. 71–90; for that of Marcantonio Bragadin, see: Kelly DeVries, 'A Tale of Venetian Skin: The Flaying of Marcantonio Bragadin', pp. 51–70; William Sayers, also in this volume,

in Anglo-Saxon England, while Kelly DeVries and Susan Small offer unique examples from sixteenth-century Cyprus and Germany.[21] Yet, while flaying criminals as a form of punishment was historically rare, there is an influx of anthropodermic books in sixteenth- and seventeenth-century France, and literary works of the medieval period give these early modern artefacts their most prominent source of rhetorical meaning. The dehumanizing aspects of flaying are highlighted by the crimes with which the act was associated in the literature and imagination in the Middle Ages. Several of the contributors here have reinforced W. R. J. Barron's contention that, in literature, the crime that most commonly results in the punishment of flaying was treason.[22] Literary skin removal accentuates the severity of the crime that warranted such an extreme act. Consequently, flaying as a form of capital punishment can, in part, reassert the authoritative identity of the state as well as strip the identity of the traitor. Interestingly (and perhaps fittingly) enough, just as the majority of anthropodermic bindings show signs of French origins, 'it is the French authors [...] who appear to have made most creative use of flaying as a thematic motif': Chrétien de Troyes' telling of the story of Lancelot, and Jehan Maillart's *Le Roman du comte d'Anjou*, among others, refer to flaying as a legal punishment.[23]

The association of flaying with traitorous action provides a lens through which to examine the human-skin-bound books of sixteenth- and seventeenth-century France. The extant corpus of confirmed anthropodermic volumes is too small and varied (and the history of the confirmed volumes often too uncertain) to make comprehensive statements about the actual binding practice. However, the study of the anthropodermic *L'Idolatrie Huguenote* establishes a number of the techniques' key rhetorical qualities. This document is a tremendously useful tool for discussing the context and details of anthropodermic bibliopegy, as laboratory tests have verified the book's binding.[24] The University of Memphis' Ned McWherter Library purchased the book from Burke's Bookstore of Memphis in 1985, after it had been displayed in the

analyses the absence of examples in Irish sources. See: 'No Skin in the Game: Flaying and Early Irish Law and Epic', pp. 261–84.

[21] Mary Rambaran-Olm, 'Medievalism and the "Flayed Dane" Myth: English Perspectives between the Seventeenth and Nineteenth Centuries', pp. 91–115; DeVries, 'A Tale of Venetian Skin'; and Small, 'Flesh and Death'.

[22] Though his study is often hampered by a lack of available historical information, W. R. J. Barron provides a useful perspective regarding flaying as a punishment for treason in medieval culture, see: 'The Penalties for Treason in Medieval Life and Literature', *Journal of Medieval History* 7 (1981): 187–202.

[23] Ibid., pp. 194–7.

[24] A permanent link to the catalogue entry of University of Memphis' anthropodermic copy of this book is found at: http://catalogquicksearch. memphis.edu/iii/encore/record/C__Rb1446125 (accessed 30 Mar. 2015).

Fig. 15.1 Front cover
of the anthropodermic
L'Idolotrie Huguenote

personal museum of the noted Memphis world traveller Barry Brooks for
many years.[25] In order to validate the book's binding for the sale, Burke's
sent a sample of the cover to Jerold M. Lowenstein of the San Francisco
School of Medicine, University of California. Following tests on three
separate proteins found on the sample, Lowenstein concluded that he
'[had] no doubt that the binding in question was made from human skin'
(Fig. 15.1).[26]

Unfortunately, there is no information pre-dating Brooks' purchase of
the volume; the name of the book's original owner and the identity of the
binding's unfortunate 'donor' are lost to us.[27] Nonetheless, Lowenstein's
verification of the binding as human skin is particularly important, allowing

[25] All information pertaining to the history of the anthropodermic *L'Idolatrie
Huguenote* is drawn from personal communication with Ed Frank (Curator
of University of Memphis Special Collections), 18 Dec. 2013.

[26] Jerold M. Lowenstein, 'Letter to Burke's Bookstore', University of Memphis
McWherter Library, Memphis, 3 May 1985. While early twentieth-century
tests used hair remnants to verify artifacts made from human skin, leading
to false confirmations of artifacts, Lowenstein's protein analysis specifically
identifies proteins unique to human skin. Because of this, this test allows
for a much greater degree of confidence about claims of validity. For
information about falsely identified human skins, see: Rambaran-Olm,
'Medievalism and the "Flayed Dane" Myth'.

[27] For a more complete description of the anthropodermic *L'Idolatrie
Huguenote*'s physical features, storage, and provenance, see: Perry Neil
Harrison, 'On the Binding of the University of Memphis' *L'Idolatrie
Huguenote*', *Notes & Queries* 62.4 (Winter 2015): 589–91.

researchers to confidently place the anthropodermic *L'Idolatrie Huguenote*'s binding and physical evidence within the larger context of the political and religious landscape of early seventeenth-century France. This, in turn, sheds significant light on the circumstances under which the book was produced, on the flayed skin used as its binding, and on the overall emergence of the practice.

The history surrounding the book's author, Louis Richeome, is undoubtedly the most accessible aspect of the document's past. Richeome, a Provincial Jesuit and a vehement opponent of Protestantism, wrote a number of works defending the theological beliefs and legitimacy of Catholicism and attacking those he saw to be enemies of the faith. Richeome was noted for his highly incendiary writings that actively sought to demonize the Huguenots, and he was a major contributor to a much larger ideological war between Catholicism and Protestantism that utilized polemics as its most prominent battlefield.[28] Jonathan L. Pearl reports that, in the 1603 *Plainte apologétique*, 'Richeome accused the [Jesuit] order's enemies of being "the most notable calumniators that France has seen since Luther gave birth to monsters extreme in impudence, in ignorance [and] in malice".'[29] The vilification of religious opponents persists in *L'Idolatrie Huguenote*, in which Richeome '[draws] correspondences between the pagan oracles and the Protestants', particularly the Oracle at Delphi.[30] For Richeome, this correlation was particularly damning, as he and other Catholic polemical treatise-writers of the period were of the mind that 'the Devil, in rivalry with God's prophets, established his false oracle at Delphi'.[31] Richeome's association of his political opponents with pagans and demons exemplifies, but by no means encompasses, the vitriolic nature of his writings. In short, Richeome's works were drafted for an audience who shared his hatred of the Protestants – an audience of which the owner of the anthropodermic *L'Idolatrie Huguenote* would have been a part – as a direct assault on the Huguenots. Richeome's reputation clarifies why the owner chose to bind the book in human skin, as the presence of flayed flesh would make tangible the threat of physical violence contained within the polemic's pages.

---

[28] In the years leading up to Richeome's writing of the *L'Idolatrie Huguenote*, the Huguenots often used polemics to portray themselves in beneficent opposition to the vilified Catholic Church through the commonly used construction of the Papal Antichrist. For more complete view of this debate, see: Lawrence P. Buck, *The Roman Monster: An Icon of the Papal Antichrist in Reformation Polemics* (Kirksville, MO: Truman State University Press, 2014).

[29] Jonathan L. Pearl, 'Demons and Politics in France, 1560–1630', *Historical Reflections / Réflexions historiques* 12.2 (Summer 1985): 241–51 at p. 248.

[30] Anthony Ossa-Richardson, *The Devil's Tabernacle: The Pagan Oracles in Early Modern Thought* (Princeton: Princeton University Press, 2013), p. 71.

[31] Ibid., p. 67.

Fig. 15.2 Spine and tail edge of the anthropodermic *L'Idolotrie Huguenote*

The book's spine shows that the anthropodermic cover was not the
codex's original binding (Fig. 15.2).[32] This is not surprising, because many
books in this period were purchased without a cover and later bound to the
purchaser's liking;[33] however, this reveals a great deal about the artefact's
original owner. A particular reader made a deliberate decision to bind this
book in human skin to suit his or her own preferences. The 'customized'
aspect of the book is further highlighted by the text printed on the book's
spine. Rather than reproducing the title and author of the book, the spine
bears the words '*Paolemic Huguenote par [d'Louis] Richoeme*'.[34] The inside
of the book, however, shows no signs that it was ever read: there are no
marginalia, no passages underlined, and the pages show no signs of wear or
discoloration. This suggests that the piece was specially commissioned for
display.

[32] It is important to note that, while the volume is in an overall excellent
state of preservation, the spine of the book has begun to pull away from
its binding. In large part this is due to the stiffness of the cover and the
handling of the book by modern researchers. This, however, corroborates
the theory that the book was bound in skin shortly after its publication –
the weakest part of the otherwise well-preserved book is in its binding,
indicating previous work in that region.

[33] Philip Gaskell, *A New Introduction to Bibliography* (Oxford: Oxford
University Press, 1972), pp. 146–7.

[34] Due to age and handling, the text indicating author's first name has been
rendered illegible. However, the remaining legible words leave little doubt
that the obscured word is either 'Louis' or some variant of the name.

This idea is reinforced by the words printed on the book's spine – substituted for the document's actual title. For this owner, the author and genre (a polemic by Louis Richeome) was more important than the fact that the book was a particular document, *L'Idolatrie Huguenote*. By the time of this book's binding, Richeome was an infamous polemical writer, and the claim on the spine that this is a 'polemic authored by Louis Richeome' would have called to mind his zealous political and theological stances. The ownership and display of Richeome's polemic, wrapped in human skin, aligned the book's owner with Richeome's extreme, often violent, views in a highly sensational manner – visual propaganda that reinforced the perceived animalistic qualities of the dissenting Protestants.

This artefact was also certainly crafted as a response to the Huguenots themselves, who cherished polemics as a means of defining their beliefs within the wider religious discourse of persecution. Luc Recaunt notes, 'Huguenot self-perception and identity relied heavily on the production of alternative histories', and a particularly important and effective method of generating these alternate histories was through the writing and distributing of polemical documents.[35] Huguenots situated themselves within the larger narrative of Christian history by setting their own suffering into the lineage of the Christian martyrs.[36] Huguenots sought to present themselves as innocent victims of religious oppression and, later, as being justified in their armed opposition to the Catholic Crown. Thus, the Catholic writers who rebutted the Protestant propaganda with their own polemics did not simply challenge their opponents on theological grounds, but did so on the very stage on which Huguenot identity was created and directed. In this instance, the owner of the book literally wraps his polemical response in a direct threat to the Huguenots' physical safety.

The information available about the anthropodermic *L'Idolatrie Huguenote* suggests a complex relationship between the owner's social identity and the document itself. Obviously, the owner wanted to display openly his or her anti-Huguenot sentiments through the possession and display of the book. More specifically, the most obvious reason for commissioning the binding is to instil fear because of its creation and existence. However, this trepidation extends beyond a simple fear of the grotesque nature of the artefact. While it is impossible to determine the origin of the book's anthropodermic cover, the knowledge that the owner primarily valued the book for its unique aesthetic rather than its words reveals much about how that owner wished others to view the binding. By binding an anti-Protestant text in human skin – and openly

---

[35] Luc Recaunt, 'Religious Polemic and Huguenot Identity: 1554–1619', in *Society and Culture in the Huguenot World, 1559–1685*, ed. Raymond A. Mentzer and Andrew Spicer (Cambridge: Cambridge University Press, 2002), pp. 29–43 at p. 41.

[36] Ibid., p. 30.

labelling it as a polemic against the Huguenots' beliefs – the owner clearly wished to suggest that the skin itself came from a Huguenot. Bound to the book's violent content, the flayed skin, lacking any other identifying feature, becomes associated with the subject of the book's violence, a fact that would not have been lost on its owner. Like other contemporary anthropodermic texts, there is nothing that outwardly suggests that the book is bound in human skin; however, an owner willing to invest the money to bind a book in this rare material would presumably have had little apprehension about identifying the binding's material to curious visitors.

Regardless of the source of the book's cover, the implication that the anthropodermic *L'Idolatrie Huguenote* is bound in the skin of a Huguenot places it into the lineage of the flayed 'Dane-skins' displayed on English church doors, detailed in Mary Rambaran-Olm's contribution to this collection. Much like English nationalists during the seventeenth through nineteenth centuries, who used these 'Dane skins' to 'continue a historical narrative about national character and race as unifying elements in English history',[37] the owner of the anthropodermic *L'Idolatrie Huguenote* desired to provide a public and visceral way to define his beliefs against an outside force. In each case, it is not the presence of identifying features that grant the removed skin its rhetorical significance. Rather, the new location of the skin, coupled with a cultural desire to utilize the flesh as a source of personal and group identity, work to transform the skin into a source of propaganda.

Beyond its use in defining its owner against an ideological 'Other', creating the anthropodermic *L'Idolatrie Huguenote* from the skin of a Huguenot closely links the artefact to literary flaying, the stripping of identity and the crime of treason. Since the removal of human skin carried cultural connotations of religious or social deviance, the book's cover may have been commissioned in part to associate the Huguenot 'idolaters' with the deviancies that were punished by the removal or mutilation of the flesh. Given the tumultuous political and religious climate at the time of the anthropodermic *L'Idolatrie Huguenote*'s production, a large number of the Huguenots' opponents would have certainly welcomed this association. During the early 1600s tensions were again stirring in France. While the Edict of Nantes' concessions went far in placating a great number of Protestants, many of the Edict's articles, such as the requirement of tithes to the Catholic Church and the reestablishment of Mass throughout the whole of France, ensured that a substantial degree of potentially volatile resentment remained. These tensions reached their tipping point with the Huguenot Rebellion of the 1620s.[38] This rebellion led to a renewed

---

[37] Rambaran-Olm, 'Medievalism and the "Flayed Dane" Myth', p. 108.

[38] For information regarding the Huguenot rebellions, see: Treasure, *The Huguenots*, pp. 244–68.

armed conflict between the Catholic Crown and the Protestants. With the Religious Wars, the grant to the Huguenots of social and political freedoms, and the Protestant's continued resistance all very much alive in the public mind, supporters of the zealously Catholic Richeome would have found binding the textual proof of the Huguenot's treachery in a literary symbol of treason a fitting way to assert their own anti-Protestant beliefs.

The allegation of treason extends beyond the implication of crimes committed by an individual Protestant. By surrounding the text with skin that has been stripped of its identity, the creator of the text has ensured that the exterior works in unison with the interior content to attack the Huguenots on a larger scale. Binding a book containing assaults on the Protestant's religious beliefs with a skin allegedly drawn from a symbolic traitor threatens the owner's enemies on a spiritual, political and physical level. The flayed skin surrounding the book's exterior suggests the possibility for other 'traitors' to suffer the same fate, while the interior text confronts and destabilizes the Protestants' spiritual beliefs. Furthermore, the anthropodermic binding draws upon the dual purposes behind flaying treasonous criminals; by creating this tome, the owner dehumanizes the individual 'Huguenot' making up the book's cover and the 'Huguenots' as a religious entity while, at the same time, reinforcing the owner's own anti-Protestant beliefs.

Additionally, wrapping Richeome's writing in the skin of a Huguenot is tantamount to appropriating Huguenot identity for the uses of the artefact's creator. Having been stripped of the identity contained within his/her own flesh by the act of flaying, this 'Huguenot's' skin instead becomes a weapon against his or her former political and religious faction. Therefore, the most chilling message conveyed by the anthropodermic *L'Idolatrie Huguenote* is not the physical violence of flaying, the stripping of all forms of identifying associations, or the allegations of political, religious or social deviancy, but rather the understanding that all these threats are conveyed through a medium that once shared the identity and beliefs it now oppresses. This weapon was designed to strike Huguenots on a deeply personal level as it took the form of a particularly volatile polemic – the way Huguenots traditionally established their own identity in opposition to Catholicism. As a result, by binding this document in human skin, the owner effectively attacks the Huguenots on multiple levels, stripping them of their identity and simultaneously reappropriating their bodily form, unsettling the grounds on which they primarily establish their beliefs.

While the emphasis on religious ideology would fall by the wayside, the early modern tendency for anthropodermic bibliopegy to serve as a vivid assertion of personal identity would persist during its revival in the nineteenth and early twentieth centuries. As early as 1944 Lawrence S. Thompson noted that 'the integument of homo sapiens was used time and again during the eighteenth and nineteenth centuries for covering books, often titles with macabre contents to match the covers'.[39] A great number of books from this time are commonly thought to be bound in human skin; however, like their early modern counterparts, many have not been scientifically verified. A number of these documents were tested and their binding material supposedly confirmed, but the methods available during the first half of the twentieth century are dubious at best. Thompson specifically cites 'the familiar technique of microscopic examination of vestigial remnants of hairs still clinging to the skin', used to initially confirm the validity of supposed 'Dane' skins nailed to English church doors.[40] As Rambaran-Olm has shown here, these findings have not withstood the test of time.[41]

Nonetheless, the uncertain nature of the books' binding does not diminish their rhetorical significance. By claiming that these books are bound in human skin in notes on the books' flyleaves, the artefacts' creators encourage the perception that their items are authentic. For example, one early twentieth-century flyleaf reads: 'This book was bound by me in human skin. Berlin. 1 June 1920. Paul Kersten.'[42] These notes shape the reader's perception of the text and place the artefacts into the lineage of the anthropodermic documents of early modern France, regardless of the items' validity. Like their predecessors, the nineteenth- and early twentieth-century books also reinforce the owners' personal beliefs through the removal of the flayed victims' individuality.

In one of the only dedicated studies on anthropodermic bibliopegy, Carolyn Marvin examines these nineteenth-century books, observing that the collectors of skin-bound texts during the nineteenth and twentieth centuries 'were often medical practitioners, a number of whom tanned the skin for the bindings themselves'.[43] Thompson also remarks on this affinity for tanning human skin: 'Toward the latter part of the nineteenth century several prominent American physicians began to show a pronounced interest in anthropodermic bibliopegy. At least three such volumes are in the library of the Philadelphia College of Physicians.'[44] As opposed to the anonymous owner of the anthropodermic *L'Idolatrie Huguenote*, these

[39] Lawrence S. Thompson, *Bibliologia comica; or, Humorous Aspects of the Caparisoning and Conversation of Books* (Hamden, CT: Archon, 1968), p. 35. For this article's initial publication, see: Lawrence S. Thompson, 'Notes on Bibliokleptomania', *Bulletin of the New York Public Library* 48.9 (Sept. 1944): 723–60.

[40] Lawrence S. Thompson, 'Tanned Human Skin', *Bulletin of the Medical Library Association* 34 (1946): 93–102 at p. 96.

[41] Rambaran-Olm, 'Medievalism and the "Flayed Dane" Myth', pp. 112–14.

[42] Qtd. in Marvin, 'Body of the Text', p. 134. The text of this inscription was translated from German by Betty Vadeboncœur during personal communications with Carolyn Marvin.

[43] Ibid., p. 134.

[44] Thompson, 'Tanned Human Skin', p. 97.

physicians openly associated themselves with the creation of skin-bound codices, potentially because of the scientific value of such texts. While the older book identifies the text's author and genre as a means of defining the owner in opposition to an 'Other', the physicians often use their books' flyleaves to draw attention to both themselves and their own actions, and to identify the source of their binding.

While it seems bizarre that these physicians would deliberately associate themselves with skin-bound books, they created and commissioned these anthropodermic artefacts to reinforce their professional image. Marvin suggests that physicians possessed 'a desire for personal recognition within a textual tradition of medical expertise'.[45] As medical professionals, the ability to demonstrate their access to a number of cadavers, and by extension a way to regularly hone their surgical skills, would have been an obvious benefit of associating themselves with these books.[46] Beyond this, creating and tanning their own texts showcased the physicians' skill at dissection, which potential clients would have admired. Overall, the textual notes demonstrate a great deal of pride in the act of creating anthropodermic books. Kersten proudly informs the reader that he performed the task of binding himself. Additionally, he claimed to have created six books in such a manner.[47] In response, flyleaves written by owners who did not create, but rather purchased, anthropodermic books also place a tremendous emphasis on the physicians' craft. A book signed 'mon cher docteur Bouland' expounds the merits and features of an anthropodermic book in his collection; the creator made his book by crafting the skin into vellum rather than tanning it.[48] He then directly compares this work to another tanned anthropodermic text located within his personal library.[49] Bouland's praise of the excellence of the artefact's

---

[45] Marvin, 'The Body of the Text', p. 136.

[46] The association with flayed flesh with medical expertise is not limited to nineteenth-century anthropodermic texts. For a discussion of the flayed bodies with surgery and surgeons in medieval France, see in this collection: Jack Hartnell, 'Tools of the Puncture: Skin, Knife, Bone, Hand', pp. 20–50.

[47] Lawrence notes more than ten additional physician-produced anthropodermic books. However, these were identified using the unreliable tests prevalent during the early twentieth century. See: Thompson, 'Tanned Human Skin', pp. 96–100. Cf. Rambaran-Olm's discussion of the methods used to test such artifacts in 'Medievalism and the "Flayed Dane" Myth', p. 112.

[48] The document's provenance identifies 'docteur Bouland' as Ludovic Bouland, a doctor and book collector who purchased many anthropodermic books. See: Michael Winter, 'Confirmed: Harvard Book Bound in Human Skin', *USA Today*, 4 Jun. 2014 http://www.usatoday.com/story/news/nation/2014/06/04/harvard-book-bound-human-flesh/9981335/ (accessed 31 Mar. 2015).

[49] Marvin, 'The Body of the Text', pp. 134–5.

creation confirms these books were admired in a variety of circles; in some way, these items garnered some of the admiration that the doctors sought to gain through their creation. For the nineteenth- and twentieth-century physicians associated with anthropodermic bibliopegy, the possessing and creating of these artefacts represented a strong, perhaps ostentatious, assertion of their own professional skill and value.

Additionally, Marvin suggests that the books' subject matter further assisted the physicians in shaping their social identities. She argues that the owners wished to place themselves within the 'upper-class avocation of rare-book collecting'.[50] To do this, the physicians chose to affix their anthropodermic bindings to 'rare or high culture texts'.[51] Marvin cites a human-skin-bound edition of *Des destineés de l'âme* by Arsène Houssaye, an author whose writings were popular with upper-class French society during the nineteenth century.[52] Customizing this book in such a highly individualized way indicates the owner's familiarity with the text itself, and by wrapping a book associated with high social status in a binding exemplifying the owner's expertise in his craft, the owner directly links himself and his profession with an elite social stratum.

Thus, much like the anthropodermic *L'Idolatrie Huguenote*, one of the primary reasons physicians created their own skin-bound tomes was to construct and to define their own identity. Furthermore, just as for their French predecessor, the physicians' books bolster the owners' identity while dehumanizing the flayed victims and stripping them of their identity. Occasionally, the creator's notes identify the source of the binding – at least that it is human, in some sense creating an alternative identity for the flayed flesh. Joseph Leidy's anthropodermic *Elementary Treatise on Human Anatomy* claims that its binding is fashioned from human skin and Marvin notes that, if this is true, Leidy likely gained the integument from a 'solider who died in the great Southern rebellion' during the doctor's time as a physician at the Union Army's Satterlee Army General Hospital.[53] Similarly,

---

[50] Ibid., p. 136.

[51] Ibid., p. 134.

[52] In 2014, Bill Lane, of Harvard Mass Spectrometry and Protoemics Resource Laboratory, and Daniel Kirby, of the Straus Center for Conservation and Technical Studies, confirmed the book's binding as human skin. Regarding the binding, Lane remarks, 'The analytical data, taken together with the provenance of *Des destineés de l'âme*, make it very unlikely that the source could be other than human'. Qtd. in Cole, 'The Science of Anthropodermic Binding'.

[53] Marvin, 'The Body of the Text', p. 135. Joseph Leidy's anthropodermic *Elementary Treatise on Human Anatomy* was published by Lippincott, in Philadelphia in 1861. Cf. Thompson, 'Tanned Human Skin', p. 97. Thompson notes that the book is inscribed: 'The leather with which this book is bound is human skin, from a soldier who died during the great Southern rebellion'.

physicians engaging in anthropodermic book-binding frequently drew their material from corpses that they had personally autopsied, and identified the donor as a means of commemorating their medical knowledge and practice. For instance, John Stockton Hough obtained the skin for a late 1880s anthropodermic edition of *Speculations on the Mode and Appearances of Impregnation in the Human Female* from 'Mary Lynn [...] a twenty-eight-year-old Irish widow dead of consumption at Philadelphia Hospital, the Almshouse facility where resident physicians learned their medical skills on paupers' bodies.'[54] Being reduced to the binding of a medical text, the only testament to her existence, also emphasizes Mary Lynn's poverty. Their existence on the bottom end of the social scale made the corpses of the poor prime targets for physicians looking to try their hands at anthropodermic bibliopegy, depriving the paupers of their humanizing integument and the last remnants of their living identity.

The primary similarity shared by these cadavers used for the binding of books is their difference – socially and religiously – from the books' creators. Marvin notes, 'the medical violation of the pauper's body marked it as an Other by depriving it of the dignity of its own physical boundaries'.[55] Even before they were 'Othered' on the autopsy tables, Mary Lynn and the southern soldier represented a world distinct from that of the doctors. For Hough, the corpse of an Irish pauper would have symbolized the lower class from which he was separated as an educated physician, his status and practice reified by creating anthropodermic books. Similarly, the deceased Confederate soldier would have represented an ideological opponent for Leidy, a physician at a prominent Union military hospital. Much like the owner of the anthropodermic *L'Idolatrie Huguenote*, who attacked the Huguenots by surrounding his book with their supposed skin, the physicians who crafted the nineteenth- and early twentieth-century skin-bound documents clearly sought to separate themselves on a social or ideological level from the binding's source material through their creation of the artefact, tearing the flesh from those they deemed unworthy (or inferior) and putting it to 'better' use. While this transformation is less actively combative than the threat of violence implied in the anthropodermic *L'Idolatrie Huguenote*, it still shares a fundamental intent. In each case, the creator is shaping and furthering his or her own desired identity through the stripping of the identity of an ideological 'Other'. It is in this way that the physicians who crafted skin-bound texts during the nineteenth century most actively participated in the anthropodermic tradition previously exhibited in early modern France.

While a large number of the creators of anthropodermic books practised their craft as a way to oppress an ideological 'Other' while strengthening their own individual identity and worth, the 'Cryobooks'

---

[54] Marvin, 'The Body of the Text', p. 136.

[55] Ibid., p. 141.

of the twenty-first century invert these purposes through the voluntary involvement of the bindings' contributors and the deliberate perpetuation of their identity and ideals. Through the wilful donation of skin, these documents use flesh as a medium for communication and scientific research. Cryobooks are 'small, handmade books created from human skin, pigskin, and paper'.[56] The human skin is obtained through voluntary donations from cosmetic-surgery patients, and the pages contain information on a non-pathogenic strain of HIV.[57] In these books, the details of both the donated skin and the virus are preserved for research purposes, ideally so that the artefacts will help further ongoing research on virality. At their core, these Cryobooks '[aim] to explore first hand how current use and application of retroviruses might bring another perspective to, and reconsideration of, virality as an alternative mode of inscription'.[58]

Unlike the anthropodermic *L'Idolatrie Huguenote*, whose owner's oppressive intent seeks to destroy a competing identity for the sake of reinforcing his or her beliefs, Cryobooks broaden the scope of communication through the efforts of multiple willing donors. In addition to this overall subversion, Cryobooks represent the reversal of past instances of anthropodermic bibliopegy due to both the intent of the study and the voluntary nature of the contributions of fleshly material. Also, in a turn vastly different from any previous instance of anthropodermic bibliopegy, Cryobooks do not seem to have a single 'owner', but rather are communally owned for the purpose of research; as such, the books extend their role as a signifier beyond the limits of an owner. Also, through the active donation of skin, Cryobooks seek to preserve an element of their contributors' identities as a monument to the donor, not the physician. While each artefact is made up the skin of several anonymous individuals, the books themselves nonetheless provide a lasting testament to the donors' cause. As the contributors to the books' material remain alive beyond the creation of the artefact, they can also take part in the communal ownership of the document. In this legacy, these documents demonstrate the ability for flayed skin to contribute to, rather than deny, the identity of those whose skin has been removed, and, therefore, provide a fitting mirror image to the anthropodermic texts of the previous centuries.

Through the various ways it has repurposed flayed flesh throughout its documented uses, anthropodermic bibliopegy demonstrates both the consistency and the mutability of flesh as a sign. Specifically, the anthropodermic instance of the 1608 *L'Idolatrie Huguenote* demonstrates the potential for stripped skin to both dehumanize ideological opponents and repurpose the 'anonymous' flayed skin of their adversaries as a weapon

---

[56] Tagny Duff, 'Cryobook Archives', *Canadian Journal of Communication* 37 (2012): 147–54 at p. 147.

[57] Ibid.

[58] Ibid., p. 149.

against the identity they claimed in life. Examples of the practice during the nineteenth and early twentieth centuries were less overtly violent in their purpose, but still sought to strengthen the creators' own identity at the expense of dehumanizing and removing the identity of an ideological opposite. Fittingly, the 'Cryobooks' of the twenty-first century fully invert the intent of their ancestors. These Cryobooks foster communication and reinforce and preserve the values of the 'contributor'. The sheer number of roles this practice has fulfilled over the course of six centuries speaks to both the potential for skin to speak about identity and the, oftentimes unsettling, possibility for this sign to undergo drastic change.

As this collection demonstrates, flayed skin is a mutable and versatile, but still powerful, signifier. As a legal punishment, flaying can serve as a harsh dehumanization of the victim and a stark assertion of authority (Small). Yet, not all societies assigned skin an equal level of significance, instead placing emphasis on the head and the arms, thus rendering flaying impractical as a punitive measure (Sayers). As an artefact flayed skin can function as a uniquely adaptable piece of propaganda, as well as an enduring piece of folklore and public curiosity (Harrison, Rambaran-Olm, DeVries). However, far from the purpose of intimidation and dehumanization, medieval surgeons saw skin removal as a means of healing (Hartnell). For others, the removed flesh was a means of metamorphosis and transformation (Tracy, Bain). Medieval literature provides a medium for exploring the concept of flaying, broadening the idea beyond the skin to explore the stripping of identity inherent in both the transfer of clothing and the tearing off of facial hair (Ward, Livingston, Tracy). Finally, Christ's flayed skin, both on the medieval stage and in the visual arts, granted the devout a vivid window through which to experience his suffering (Dent, Gramling), while artistic depictions of the flaying of St Bartholomew provide scholars with a template for regarding the ways values and beliefs were transferred to, and understood by, their audiences (Mittman and Sciacca, Lindquist). Like the views put forth in this book, flaying in the premodern world, despite its rarity, was too multivalent to be assigned a single, monolithic meaning. Instead, skin, even when – especially when – separated from the body, represents the fragility of the human frame. But perhaps even more, the range of meanings attributed to flayed skin demonstrates the capability of the human form to both adapt and endure.

Select Bibliography

Primary Sources

A true discourse. Declaring the damnable life and death of one Stubbe Peeter, a most wicked sorcerer who in the likenes of a woolfe, committed many murders, continuing this diuelish practise 25. yeeres, killing and deuouring men, woomen, and children. Who for the same fact was taken and executed the 31. of October last past in the towne of Bedbur neer the cittie of Collin in Germany. Trulye translated out of the high Duch, according to the copie printed in Collin, brought ouer into England by George Bores ordinary poste, the xi. daye of this present moneth of Iune 1590. who did both see and heare the same. London: E. Venge, 1590. Accessible online at http://quod.lib.umich.edu/e/eebo/A13085.0001.001/1:3?rgn=div1;view=fulltext

Abardo, Rudy. *Chiose Palatine: Ms. Pal. 313 della Biblioteca Nazionale Centrale di Firenze.* Rome: Salerno, 2005

Ælfric's Lives of Saints: Being a Set of Sermons on Saints' Days Formerly Observed by the English Church, ed. Walter W. Skeat. 4 vols. EETS o.s. 76, 82, 94 and 114. London: N. Trübner & Co., 1881–1900

Aldhelmi Opera, ed. R. Ehwald. Berlin: Apud Weidmannos, 1919

Alighieri, Dante. *The Divine Comedy,* trans. C. H. Sisson. Oxford: Oxford University Press, 1998

——— *The Divine Comedy of Dante Alighieri.* Vol. 1, *Inferno,* and vol. 3, *Paradiso,* ed. and trans. Robert M. Durling. Oxford: Oxford University Press, 1996 and 2011

Aquinas, Thomas. *Commentary on the Gospel of St John, Part 2,* trans. Fabian R. Larcher. Albany: Magi Books, 1998. Accessible online though the website of the Dominican House of Studies Priory of the Immaculate Conception. http://dhspriory.org/thomas/english/John18.htm

Árnason, Jón. *Íslenzkar þjóðsögur og æfintýri.* Leipzig: J. C. Hinrichs's Bókaverzlunar, 1862

Arrow-Odds Saga, in *Seven Vikings Romances,* trans. Hermann Pálsson and Paul Edwards. 25–137. London: Penguin, 1985

Arthur and Gorlagon, in *Latin Arthurian Literature,* ed. and trans. Mildred Leake Day. Cambridge: D. S. Brewer, 2005

Bartholomaeus Anglicus. *On the Properties of Things: John Trevisa's Translation of Bartholomaeus Anglicus' De Proprietatibus Rerum: A Critical Text,* ed. M. C. Seymour, trans. John Trevisa. Oxford: Clarendon Press, 1975

Beadle, Richard, ed. *The York Plays: A Critical Edition of the York Corpus Christi Play as Recorded in British Library Additional MS 35290.* Oxford: Oxford University Press, 2009

Bernardino de Sahagún. *Florentine Codex: A General History of the Things of New Spain.* Book 2, trans. Arthur J. O. Anderson and Charles E. Dibble. Santa Fe, NM: School of American Research, 1970

Bevegnatis, Iuncta. *Legenda de vita et miraculis beatae Margaritae de Cortona*, ed. Fortunato Iozzelli. Grottaferrata: Ediciones Collegii S. Bonaventurae ad Claras Aquas, 1997

Bevengnati, Fra Giunta. *The Life and Miracles of Saint Margaret of Cortona (1247–1297)*, trans. Thomas Renna, ed. Shannon Larson. St Bonaventure, NY: Franciscan Institute Publications, 2012

Brennu-Njáls saga, ed. Einar Ól. Sveinsson. Íslenzk Fornrit 12. Reykjavik: Hið Íslenzka fornritafélag, 1954

Brunner, Karl, ed. *Der Mittelenglische Versroman über Richard Löwenherz*. Wiener Beiträge zur Englischen Philologie 42. Vienna: W. Braumüller, 1913

Catalogue of the Hunterian Collection in the Museum of the Royal College of Surgeons in London. London: Livingstone, 1923

Catherine of Siena. *The Letters of Catherine of Siena*, ed. and trans. Suzanne Noffke. 2 vols. Tempe: Arizona Center for Medieval and Renaissance Studies, 2000–1

Cavalca, Domenico. *Lo specchio della Croce: testo originale e versione in italiano corrente*, ed. P. Tito Sante Centi, OP. Bologna: PDUL Edizioni Studio Domenicano, 1992

La Chanson de Roland, ed. and trans. Léon Gautier. Tours: Mame et fils, 1872

Child, F. J., ed. *The English and Scottish Popular Ballads*. 5 vols. New York: Houghton Mifflin, 1882–98

Chrétien de Troyes. *Cligés*, in *Romans suivis des chansons, avec, en appendice, Philomena*, ed. and trans. C. Méla and O. Collet. 286–494. Paris: La Pochothèque, 1994

—— *The Complete Romances of Chrétien de Troyes*, trans. D. Staines. Indianapolis: Indiana University Press, 1990

Dart, John. *Westmonasterium Or The History and Antiquities of the Abbey Church of St. Peters Westminster*. London: Carington Bowles, 1723

Delrío, Martín Antonio. *Disquisitionum magicarum libri sex: quibus continetur accurata curiosarum artium, et vanarum superstitionum confutatio: utilis theologis, jurisconsultis, medicis, philologis*. Repr. edn. Moguntiae: Petri Henningii, 1617

Dobson, R. B., and J. Taylor, comp. *Rymes of Robyn Hood*. London: Heinemann, 1976

Downer, L. J., ed. and trans. *Leges Henrici Primi, with Translation and Commentary*. Oxford: Clarendon Press, 1972

Egils saga einhenda og Asmundar saga berserkjabana, in vol. 3 of *Fornaldarsögur Norðurlanda*, ed. Guðni Jónsson and Bjarni Vilhjálmsson. 153–89. Reykjavík: Bókútgáfan forni, 1943

En forskreckelig oc sand bescriffuelse om mange troldfolck som ere forbrends for deris misgierninger skyld fra det aar 1589. Verlag Laurentz Benedicht: Copenhagen, 1591

Fasciculus Morum: A Fourteenth-Century Preacher's Handbook, ed. and trans. Siegfried Wenzel. University Park: Pennsylvania State University Press, 1989

Faulkes, A., ed. *Two Icelandic Stories*. London: Viking Society for Northern Research, 1967, repr. 2011

Fincel, Job. 'De mirabilibus', lib. xi, in Simon Goulart, *Admirable and memorable histories containing the wonders of our time. Collected into French out of the best authors. By I. [sic] Goulart. And out of French into English, By Ed. Grimeston.* London: George Eld, 1607. Accessible online at http://quod.lib.umich.edu/cgi/t/text/text-idx?c=eebo;idno=A01991

Fornaldar sögur Norðrlanda eptir gömlum handritum, ed. C. C. Rafn. Vols. 1–3. Copenhagen, 1829–30. Accessible online though https://archive.org

Fornaldarsögur Norðrlanda, ed. Guðni Jónsson and Bjarni Vilhjálmsson. Vols. 1–4. Reykjavik: Bókaútgáfan, 1943–4

Furnivall, Frederick J., ed. *The Digby Plays, with an Incomplete 'Morality' of 'Wisdom, Who is Christ'.* Oxford: Oxford University Press, 1967

Geoffrey of Vinsauf. *Poetria nova*, trans. Margaret F. Nims. Toronto: Pontifical Institute of Medieval Studies, 2010

Gesta Romanorum. Lugdani: apud haeredes Iacobi Iuntae, 1555

Gregory the Great. *Dialogorum Libri IV*, in *Patrologia Latina 77, S. Gregorii Papaei III* (Paris: Migne, 1862)

Grimm, Jacob. *Teutonic Mythology*, trans. James Steven Stallybrass. London: George Bell and Sons, 1883

Guiffrey, Jules. *Inventaires de Jean duc de Berry (1401–1416).* 2 vols. Paris: E. Leroux, 1894

Guigonis de Caulhiacho (Guy de Chauliac), *Inventarium sive Chirurgia magna*, ed. Michael McVaugh. 2 vols. Leiden: Brill, 1997

Gutch, J. M., ed. *A Litell Gest of Robin Hood, with other Auncient and Modern Ballads and Songs Related to the Celebrated Yeoman.* 2 vols. London: Longman, 1847

Havelok the Dane, in *Middle English Romances*, ed. Stephen H. A. Shepherd. 3–74. New York: W. W. Norton, 1995

Hedley, Thomas. *Parliament of 1610, Proceedings in Parliament 1610*, ed. Elizabeth Reed Foster. New Haven: Yale University Press, 1966

Heldris de Cornualle. *Roman de Silence*, ed. Regina Psaki. New York: Garland, 1991

'Here Begynneth a Merry Ieste of a Shrewde and Curst Wyfe Lapped in Morrelles Skin for Her Good Behauyour', in *Remains of the Early Popular Poetry of England*, ed. W. Carew Hazlitt. Vol. 4. London: John Russell Smith, 1866

Hic Mulier, in *'Custome is an Idiot': Jacobean Pamphlet Literature on Women*, ed. Susan Gushee O'Malley. Champaign: University of Illinois Press, 2004

Jacobus de Voragine. *The Golden Legend: Readings on the Saints*, ed. and trans. William Granger Ryan. Princeton: Princeton University Press, 1993

—— *Legenda aurea, vulgo Historia Lombardica dicta*, ed. Th. Graesse. 2nd edn. Leipzig: Impensis Librariae Arnoldianae, 1850

James of Milan. *Stimulus divini amoris, that is The Goad of Divine Love*, trans. B. Lewis and rev. W. A. Phillipson. London: R. & T. Washbourne, 1907

Jean Beauvoys de Chauvincourt. *Discours de la lycantropie, ou De la transmutation des hommes en loups.* Paris: J. Rezé, 1599

John of Caulibus. *Meditations on the Life of Christ*, ed. and trans. Francis X. Taney, SR, Anne Miller, OSF, and C. Mary Stallings-Taney. Asheville, NC: Pegasus Press, 2000

John of Salisbury. *Frivolities of Courtiers and Footprints of Philosophers: Being a Translation of the First, Second, and Third Books and Selections from the Seventh and Eighth Books of the 'Policraticus' of John of Salisbury*, trans. Joseph B. Pike. New York: Octagon, 1938, repr. 1972

Knight, Stephen, and Thomas Ohlgren, eds. *Robin Hood and other Outlaw Tales*. TEAMS Middle English Texts Series, 2nd edn. Kalamazoo, MI: Medieval Institute Publications, 2000

Le Lai d'Haveloc, ed. Alexander Bell. Manchester: Manchester University Press, 1925

The Lay of Havelok the Dane, ed. Walter W. Skeat. EETS e.s. 4. London: Trübner, 1868; repr. 2008

Leechdoms, Wortcunning, and Starcraft of Early England: Being a Collection of Documents Illustrating the History of Science in this Country Before the Norman Conquest, ed. and trans. T. O. Cockayne. 3 vols. London: Longman, Green, Longman, Roberts & Green, 1864–6; repr. Cambridge: Cambridge University Press, 2012

Lowenstein, Jerold M. 'Letter to Burke's Bookstore'. University of Memphis McWherter Library, Memphis, 3 May 1985

Lumiansky, R. M., and David Mills, eds. *The Chester Mystery Cycle: Text*. EETS s.s. 3. Oxford: Oxford University Press, 1974

Lydgate, John. *Fall of Princes*, ed. Henry Bergen. EETS e.s. 121–4. Oxford: Oxford University Press, 1918–19

Macrobius. *Commentary on the Dream of Scipio*, trans. William Harris Stahl. New York: Columbia University Press, 1952

Magedanz, Joseph. '*Salman und Morolf*: An English Translation with Introduction'. PhD dissertation, University of Nebraska-Lincoln, 1994

Massinger, Philip. *The Renegado*, ed. Michael Neill. London: Methuen, 2010

The Memorials of St Edmund's Abbey I, ed. T. Arnold. Rolls Series 96. London, 1890–6. Accessible online at https://archive.org/details/memorialsofstedmo1arno

Morris, Richard, ed. *The Blickling Homilies of the Tenth Century*. Part 1. EETS o.s. 58, 63 and 73. London: N. Trübner & Co., 1880

Neville, R. C. *Antiqua Explorata: Being the Result of Excavations made in and about the Roman Station at Chesterford, and other spots in the Vicinity of Audley End*. London, 1847

Newcourt, R. *Repertorium Ecclesiasticum Parochiale Londinense*, London: Benj. Motte, 1708

Nicaise, Edouard, ed. *Chirurgie de maître Henri de Mondeville*. Paris: Félix Alcan, 1893

—— *La Grande Chirurgie de Guy de Chauliac*. Paris: Félix Alcan, 1890

Njal's Saga, trans. Magnus Magnusson and Hermann Palsson. Harmondsworth: Penguin, 1960

On the Inconstancy of Witches: Pierre de Lancre's Tableau de l'inconstance des mauvais anges et demons (1612), ed. and trans. G. S. Williams. Turnhout: Brepols, 2006

Örvar-Odds saga, in vol. 1 of *Fornaldarsögur Norðurlanda*, ed. Guðni Jónsson and Bjarni Vilhjálmsson. 283–399. Reykjavík: Bókútgáfan forni, 1943. Accessible online at http://www.snerpa.is/net/forn/orvar.htm

Ovid's Metamorphoses, trans. Arthur Golding, ed. John Frederick Nims. Philadelphia: Paul Dry Books, 2000

Pagel, Julius, ed. *Die Chirurgie des Heinrich von Mondeville*. Berlin: Hirschwald, 1892

Papon, Jean. *Trias judiciel du second Notaire*. Lyons: Jean de Tournes, 1580

Pepys, Samuel. *The Diary of Samuel Pepys*, ed. Robert Latham *et al.* London: G. Bell & Sons, 1970

Percy, Thomas, ed. *Reliques of Ancient English Poetry*. 3 vols. London: J. Dodsley, 1765

Petrarch, Francesco. '*Apologia cuiusdam anonymi Galli calumnias*', in *Opera Omnia*. Basileæ: Execudebat Henrichus Petri, 1554

Petrus de Natalibus, *Catalogus sanctorum et gestorum eorum*. Lugdunum: Thomas, 1514

Pifteau, Paul, ed. and trans. *Chirurgie de Guillaume de Salicet*. Toulouse: Saint-Cyperien, 1898

Porcher, Jean. *Les Belles Heures de Jean de France, duc de Berry*. Paris: Bibliothèque nationale de France, 1953

Prieur, Claude. *Dialogue de la lycanthropie ou Transformation d'hommes en loups vulgairement dits loups-garous, et si telle se peut faire …* . Louvain: Iehan Maes & Philippe Zangre, 1596; repr. Paris: Hachette / Bibliothèque nationale, 1975

Quekett, John. 'On the Value of the Microscope in the Determination of Minute Structures of a Doubtful Nature', *Trans. of the Microscopical Society of London* 2 (1849): 152–3

Quekett, William. *My Sayings and Doings, with Reminiscences of my Life*. London: K. Paul, Trench, 1888

Richeome, Louis. *L'Idolatrie Huguenote*. Paris, 1608

Ritson, Joseph, ed. *Robin Hood, A Collection of All the Auncient Poems, Songs and Ballads Now Extant Relative to the Celebrated English Outlaw*. 2 vols. London: Egerton and Johnson, 1795

Rosenman, Leonard D., ed. *The Major Surgery of Guy de Chauliac*. Bloomington, IN: Xlibris, 2007

—— *The Surgery of Henri de Mondeville*. 2 vols. Bloomington, IN: Xlibris, 2003

—— *The Surgery of Jehan Yperman*. Bloomington, IN: Xlibris, 2002

—— *The Surgery of William of Saliceto*. Bloomington, IN: Xlibris, 2002

Rossi, Giuseppe. *Pitture a fresco del Camposanto di Pisa*. Florence: Tipografia all'Insegna di Dante, 1832; repr. Florence: Cassa di Risparmio di Firenze, 1976

The Saga of Egil and Asmund, in *Seven Vikings Romances*, trans. Hermann Pálsson and Paul Edwards. 228–57. London: Penguin, 1985

The Siege of Jerusalem, ed. Ralph Hanna III and David Lawton. EETS o.s. 320. Oxford: Oxford University Press, 2003

The Siege of Jerusalem, ed. Michael Livingston. Kalamazoo, MI: Medieval Institute Publications, 2004

Simpson, Jacqueline, trans. *Icelandic Folktales and Legends*. Stroud: Tempus, 1972, repr. 2004, 2009

Sir Gawain and the Green Knight, ed. J. R. R. Tolkien and E. V. Gordon (Oxford: Oxford University Press, 1967)

The Song of Roland, trans. Glyn Burgess. London: Penguin, 1990

Spalding, Mary Caroline, ed. *The Middle English Charters of Christ*. Bryn Mawr, PA: Bryn Mawr College, 1914

Spector, Stephen, ed. *The N-Town Play: Cotton MS Vespasian D.8*. EETS s.s. 11–12. 2 vols. Oxford: Oxford University Press, 1991

Spink, M. S., and Geoffrey Lewis, eds. *Albucasis on Surgery and Instruments: A Definitive Edition of the Arabic Text*. London: Wellcome Institute of the History of Medicine, 1973

Stevens, Martin, and A. C. Cawley, eds. *The Towneley Plays*. EETS s.s. 13–14. 2 vols. Oxford: Oxford University Press, 1994

Stiltingh, Jean (Joanne Stiltingo). 'Bartholomæus apostolus, Albanopoli in Armenia vel Albania (S.)', August V, De S. Bartholomæo Apostolo, Albanopoli in Armenia vel Albania, Seculo I, Commentarius Prævius, in *Acta Sanctorum Augusti, ex Latinis & Graecis ...* . Col. 0007A. Antwerp: Bernardus Albertus vander Plassche, 1741. Digitized edn, Cambridge: Chadwyck-Healey, 2001

Stukeley, William. *Itinerarium Curiosum*. London: Messrs. Baker and Leigh, 1724

Sugano, Douglas, ed. *The N-Town Plays*. Kalamazoo, MI: Medieval Institute Publications, 2007

Swift, Jonathan. *Prose Works*, ed. Herbert Davis. Oxford: Blackwell, 1955

Theodore Studita, *Bartholomæus apostolus, Albanopoli in Armenia vel Albania*, in *Acta sanctorum*. Bibliotheca Hagiographica Latina 1005, col. 0039A

Theophilus. *De Diversis artibus*, ed. C. R. Dodwell. Oxford: Clarendon Press, 1961

Thibodeau, Timothy M., ed. and trans. *The Rationale divinorum officiorum of William Durand of Mende: A New Translation of the Prologue and Book One*. New York: Columbia University Press, 2007

Thompson, John J. *Robert Thornton and the London Thornton Manuscript: BL Additional 31042*. Cambridge: Cambridge University Press, 1987

Valerius Maximus, *Factorum et dictorum memorabilium libri novem*. Accessible online at *The Latin Library*, http://www.thelatinlibrary.com/valmax.html

van Ghelen, Jan, *Warachtighe ende verschrickelijcke beschrijvinge van vele toovenaers ende toovenerssen: een uniek Antwerps vlugschrift uit 1589 over Duitse heksenprocessen en weerwolf Stump*, ed. Dries Vanysacker. Wildert: Carbolineum, 2003

Vasari, Giorgio. *Le vite de' più eccellenti pittori, scultori, ed architettori*, ed. Gaetano Milanesi. Vol. 4. Florence, 1879

Verstegan, Richard. *Restitution of decayed intelligence in antiquities, concerning the most noble and renowned English nation. By the study and travel of R. V.* London: Samuel Mearne, John Martyn and Henry Herringman, 1628

Warhafftige und erschreckliche Beschreibung, von einem Zauberer (Stupe Peter genandt) der sich zu einem Wehrwolff hat können machen, welcher zu Bedbur (vier meilen von Cölln gelegen) ist gerichtet worden., den 31. October, dieses 1589. Jahrs, was böser Thaten er begangen hat ... . Cologne: Nikolaus Schreiber, 1589

Winterbottom, Michael, ed. *Three Lives of English Saints*. Toronto: Pontifical Institute of Medieval Studies, 1972

Wright, C. E., and R. Quirk, eds. *Bald's Leechbook*. Baltimore: The John Hopkins Press, 1955

Wulfstan (Archbishop). *Institutes of Polity, Civil and Ecclesiastical*, ed. B. Thorpe, in *Ancient Laws and Institutes of England, Comprising Laws Enacted under the Anglo-Saxon Kings from Aethelbirht to Cnut. V. II. Containing the Ecclesiastical Laws*. Cambridge: Cambridge University Press, 2012

Secondary Sources

Agamben, Giorgio. *The Open: Man and Animal*, trans. Kevin Attell. Stanford, CA: Stanford University Press, 2004

Akbari, Suzanne Conklin. 'Erasing the Body: History and Memory in Medieval Siege Poetry', in *Remembering the Crusades: Myth, Image, and Identity*, ed. Nicholas Paul and Suzanne Yeager. 146–73. Baltimore: The Johns Hopkins University Press, 2012

—— 'The Hunger for National Identity in *Richard Coer de Lion*', in *Reading Medieval Culture: Essays in Honor of Robert W. Hanning*, ed. Robert M. Stein and Sandra Pierson Prior. 198–227. Notre Dame, IN: University of Notre Dame Press, 2005

—— 'Placing the Jews in Late Medieval English Literature', in *Orientalism and the Jews*, ed. Ivan Davidson Kalmar and Derek J. Penslar. 32–50. Hanover, NH: Brandeis University Press, 2005

——, and Jill Ross, eds. *The Ends of the Body: Identity and Community in Medieval Culture*. Toronto: University of Toronto Press, 2013

Alcoy i Pedrós, Rosa. 'La pintura gòtica', in *Art de Catalunya: Ars Cataloniae*. Vol. 8, *Pintura antiga i medieval*. 234–6. Barcelona: Edicions L'isard, 1998

Alexander, Michael. *Medievalism: The Middle Ages in Modern England*. New Haven: Yale University Press, 2007

Almond, Richard. *Medieval Hunting*. 3rd edn. Stroud: The History Press, 2011

Andersen, Per. *Legal Procedure and Practice in Medieval Denmark*. Leiden: Brill, 2011

Ankarloo, Bengt, and Stuart Clark, eds. *Witchcraft and Magic in Europe: The Middle Ages*. Phildelphia: University of Pennsylvania Press, 2002

Areford, David S. *The Viewer and the Printed Image in Late Medieval Europe*. Burlington, VT: Ashgate, 2010

Bachoffner, Pierre. 'Jérôme Brunschwig, chirurgien et apothicaire strasbourgeois, portraituré en 1512'. *Revue d'histoire de la pharmacy* 81, no. 298 (1993): 269–78

Bachrach, Bernard S. 'Animals and Warfare in Early Medieval Europe'. *Settimane di Studio del Centro Italiano di Studi sull'Alto Medioevo* 31 (1985): 707–64

Barron, W. R. J. 'The Penalties for Treason in Medieval Life and Literature'. *Journal of Medieval Literature* 7 (1981): 187–202

Baschet, Jérôme. *Les Justices de l'au-delà: les représentations de l'enfer en France et en Italie, XIIe–XVe siècle*. Rome: École française de Rome; Paris: Diffusion De Boccard, 1993

Bassetti, Massimiliano, and Bruno Toscano, eds. *Dal visibile all'indicibile: crocifissi ed esperienza mistica in Angela da Foligno*. Spoleto: Fondazione Centro Italiano di Studi sull'Alto Medioevo, 2012

Bataille, Georges. *Eroticism: Death and Sensuality*, trans. Mary Dalwood. London: Penguin, 2001

Beck, R. T. *The Cutting Edge: Early History of the Surgeons of London*. London: Lund Humphries, 1974

Bellamy, J. G. *The Law of Treason in England in the Later Middle Ages*. Cambridge: Cambridge University Press, 1970

Belting, Hans. *Das Bild und sein Publikum im Mittelalter: Form und Funktion früher Bildtafeln der Passion*. Berlin: Mann, 1981

Benati, Chiara. *'Dat Boek der Wundenartzstedye' und der niederdeutsche chirurgische Fachwortschatz*. Göppingen: Kümmerle, 2012

Benthien, Claudia. *Skin: On the Cultural Barrier between Self and the World*, trans. Thomas Dunlap. New York: Columbia University Press, 1999

Bergmann, Ulrike, ed. *Neue Forschungen zur gefassten Skulptur des Mittelalters*. Munich: Siegl, 2001

Berriot-Salvadore, Évelyne, and Paul Mironneau, eds. *Ambroise Paré (1510–1590): pratique et écriture de la science à la Renaissance. Actes du Colloque de Pau (6–7 mai 1999)*. Paris: Honoré Champion Éditeur, 2003

Bestul, Thomas. *Texts of the Passion: Latin Devotional Literature and Medieval Society*. Philadelphia: University of Pennsylvania Press, 1996

Boehm, Barbara Drake. 'The Laudario of the Compagnia di Sant'Agnese', in *Painting and Illumination in Early Renaissance Florence, 1300–1450*, ed. Laurence B. Kanter *et al*. New York: Metropolitan Museum of Art, 1994. [Exhibition catalogue.]

——, Abigail Quandt, and William Wixom, eds. *The Hours of Jeanne d'Evreux, Acc. No. 54.1.2, the Metropolitan Museum of Art, the Cloisters Collection, New York*. New York: Verlag Luzern, 2000. [Facsimile.]

Boes, Maria R. *Crime and Punishment in Early Modern Germany: Courts and Adjudicatory Practices in Frankfurt am Main, 1562–1696*. Burlington, VT: Ashgate, 2013

Boskovits, Miklós. *A Critical and Historical Corpus of Florentine Painting*. Sect. 3, vol. 9, *The Fourteenth Century: The Painters of the Miniaturist Tendency*. Florence: Giunti, 1984

Brackmann, Rebecca. *The Elizabethan Invention of Anglo-Saxon England: Laurence Nowell, William Lambarde, and the Study of Old English*. Cambridge: D. S. Brewer, 2012

Braswell, Laurel N. *Western Manuscripts from Classical Antiquity to the Renaissance: A Handbook*. New York: Garland, 1981

Briggs, Robin. *Witches and Neighbors: The Social and Cultural Context of European Witchcraft*. New York: Penguin, 1996

Brothwell, Don, and V. Møller-Christensen. 'Medico-historical Aspects of a Very Early Case of Mutilation'. *Danish Medical Bulletin* 10 (1963): 21–7

Brothwell, Don, and E. Higgs, eds. *Science in Archaeology*, 2nd edn. New York: Thames & Hudson, 1969

Brown, Elizabeth A. R. 'Death and the Human Body in the Later Middle Ages: The Legislation of Boniface VIII on the Division of the Corpse'. *Viator* 12 (1981): 221–70

Bu, Eltjo. *Medieval Manuscript Production in the Latin West: Explorations with a Global Database*. Leiden: Brill, 2011

Buck, Lawrence P. *The Roman Monster: An Icon of the Papal Antichrist in Reformation Polemics*. Kirksville, MO: Truman State University Press, 2014

Bynum, Caroline Walker. 'The Blood of Christ in the Later Middle Ages'. *Church History* 71.4 (2002): 685–714

—— *Fragmentation and Redemption: Essays on Gender and the Human Body in Medieval Religion*. New York: Zone, 1991

—— *The Resurrection of the Body in Western Christianity, 200–1336*. New York: Columbia University Press, 1995

—— 'Violence Occluded: The Wound in Christ's Side in Late Medieval Devotion', in *Feud, Violence and Practice: Essays in Medieval Studies in Honor of Stephen D. White*, ed. Belle S. Tuten and Tracey L. Billado. 95–116. Burlington, VT: Ashgate, 2010

—— *Wonderful Blood: Theology and Practice in Late Medieval Northern Germany and Beyond*. Philadelphia: University of Pennsylvania Press, 2007

Cameron, M. L. *Anglo-Saxon Medicine*. Cambridge: Cambridge University Press, 1993

Carlson, Marla. *Performing Bodies in Pain: Medieval and Post-Modern Martyrs, Mystics, and Artists*. Palgrave Studies in Theatre and Performance History. New York: Palgrave, 2010

Casey, Kathleen. 'Crime and Punishment: Anglo-Saxon Law Codes', in *The Middle Ages in Texts and Texture: Reflections on Medieval Sources*, ed. Jason Glenn. 85–92. Toronto: University of Toronto Press, 2011

Cohen, Esther. *The Modulated Scream: Pain in Late Medieval Culture*. Chicago: University of Chicago Press, 2010

Cohen, Jeffrey Jerome. *Medieval Identity Machines*. Minneapolis: University of Minnesota Press, 2003

—— *Monster Theory: Reading Culture*. Minneapolis: University of Minnesota Press, 1996

—— *Of Giants: Sex, Monsters, and the Middle Ages*. Minneapolis: University of Minnesota Press, 1999

—— 'On Saracen Enjoyment: Some Fantasies of Race in Late Medieval France and England'. *Journal of Medieval and Early Modern Studies* 31.1 (Winter 2001): 113–46

Connor, Steven. *The Book of Skin*. Ithaca, NY: Cornell University Press, 2004

Crane, Susan. *Animal Encounters: Contacts and Concepts in Medieval Britain*. Philadelphia: University of Pennsylvania Press, 2013

—— 'Chivalry and the Pre/Postmodern'. *postmedieval: a journal of medieval cultural studies* 2.1 (2011): 69–87

—— 'Ritual Aspects of the Hunt à Force', in *Engaging with Nature: Essays on the Natural World in Medieval and Early Modern Europe*, ed. Barbara A. Hanawalt and Lisa J. Kiser. 63–84. Notre Dame, IN: University of Notre Dame Press, 2008

Dale, Thomas. 'Monsters, Corporeal Deformities and Phantasms in the Cloister of Saint-Michel De Cuxa'. *Art Bulletin* 83.3 (2001): 402–36

—— 'The Nude at Moissac: Vision, Phantasia, and the Experience of Romanesque Sculpture', in *Current Perspectives in Romanesque Sculpture Studies*, ed. Kirk Ambrose and Robert Maxwell. 61–76. Turnhout: Brepols, 2011

Davidson, Clifford. 'Nudity, the Body, and Early English Drama'. *The Journal of English and Germanic Philology* 98.4 (1999): 499–522

—— 'Sacred Blood and the Late Medieval Stage'. *Comparative Drama* 31.3 (1997): 436–58

Dean, Trevor. *Crime in Medieval Europe*. London: Pearson Education, 2001

Deleuze, Gilles. *The Fold*. trans. Tom Conley. New York: Bloomsbury Academic, 1993

——, and Felix Guattari. *A Thousand Plateaus: Capitalism and Schizophrenia*, trans. Brian Massumi. Minneapolis: University of Minnesota Press, 1987

Dorveaux, Paul. *Livre des simples médecines*. Paris: Société française d'histoire de la médecine, 1913

Dückers, Rob, and Pieter Roelofs, eds. *The Limbourg Brothers: Nijmegen Masters at the French Court, 1400–1416*. Nijmegen: Ludion, 2005

—— *The Limbourg Brothers: Reflections on the Origins and the Legacy of Three Illuminators from Nijmegen*. Leiden: Brill, 2009

Dumas, Stéphane. 'The Return of Marsyas: Creative Skin', trans. John Lee, in *SK-Interfaces*, ed. Jens Hauser. 18–31. Liverpool: Liverpool University Press, 2008

Dzon, Mary, and Theresa M. Kenney, eds. *The Christ Child in Medieval Culture: Alpha es et O!* Toronto: University of Toronto Press, 2011

Echard, Siân. *Arthurian Narrative in the Latin Tradition*. Cambridge: Cambridge University Press, 2005

Egmond, Florike, and Robert Zwijnenberg, eds. *Bodily Extremities: Preoccupations with the Human Body in Early Modern European Culture*. Burlington, VT: Ashgate, 2003

Elkins, James. *The Object Stares Back: On the Nature of Seeing*. New York: Harvest, 1996

Enders, Jody. *The Medieval Theater of Cruelty: Rhetoric, Memory, Violence*. Ithaca, NY: Cornell University Press, 1999

Fay, Elizabeth. *Romantic Medievalism*. New York: Palgrave, 2002

Ferenc, Levárdy. *Magyar Anjou Legendárium*. Budapest: Magyar Helikon, 1973

Fiscalini, John, and Alan L. Grey, eds. *Narcissism and the Interpersonal Self*. New York: Columbia University Press, 1993

Foucault, Michel. *Discipline and Punish: The Birth of the Prison*, trans. Alan Sheridan. Harmondsworth: Penguin, 1979

—— *The Order of Things: An Archeology of the Human Sciences*, trans. Alan Sheridan. New York: Routledge, 2002

—— *The Spectacle of the Scaffold*, trans. Alan Sheridan. London, Penguin, 2008

Frick Art Reference Library, *Spanish Artists from the Fourth to the Twentieth Century: A Critical Dictionary*. New York: G. K. Hall, 1993–6

Friedman, John Block. 'Werewolf Transformation in the Manuscript Era'. *The Journal of the Early Book Society* 17 (2014): 35–93

Friðriksdóttir, Jóhanna. *Women in Old Norse Literature: Bodies, Words, and Power*. New York: Palgrave, 2013

Fugelso, Karl. *Studies in Medievalism XXVII: Defining Medievalism(s)*. Cambridge: D. S. Brewer, 2009

Furst, Jill Leslie. 'Flaying, Curing, and Shedding: Some Thoughts on the Aztec God Xipe Totec', in *Painted Books and Indigenous Knowledge in Mesoamerica: Manuscript Studies in Honor of Mary Elizabeth Smith*, ed. Elizabeth Hill Boone. 63–74. New Orleans: Tulane University Press, 2005

García-Ballester, Luis, *et al.*, eds. *Practical Medicine from Salerno to the Black Death.* Cambridge: Cambridge University Press, 1994

Gates, Jay Paul. 'Imagining Justice in the Anglo-Saxon Past: Eadric Streona, Kingship, and the Search for Community'. *The Haskins Society Journal* 25 (2013): 125–46

——, and Nicole Marafioti, eds. *Capital and Corporal Punishment in Anglo-Saxon England.* Woodbridge: Boydell Press, 2014

Getz, Faye. *Medicine in the English Middle Ages.* Princeton: Princeton University Press, 1998

Gilman, Sander L. *Making the Body Beautiful: A Cultural History of Aesthetic Surgery.* Princeton: Princeton University Press, 2000

Glascock, Michael, Robert J. Speakman, and Rachel S. Popelka-Filcoff. *Archaeological Chemistry: Analytical Techniques and Archaeological Interpretation.* Washington, DC: American Chemical Society, 2007

Glaze, Florence Eliza, and Brian K. Nance, eds. *Between Text and Patient: The Medical Enterprise in Medieval and Early Modern Europe.* Florence: Sismel – Edizioni del Galluzzo, 2011

Goth, Maik. 'Killing, Hewing, Stabbing, Dagger-Drawing, Fighting, Butchery: Skin Penetration in Renaissance Tragedy and its Bearing on Dramatic Theory'. *Comparative Drama* 46.2 (Summer, 2012): 139–62

Gragnolati, Manuele. *Experiencing the Afterlife: Soul and Body in Dante and Medieval Culture.* Notre Dame, IN: University of Notre Dame Press, 2005

Hamburger, Jeffrey. 'Body vs. Book: The Trope of Visibility in Images of Christian-Jewish Polemic', in *Ästhetik des Unsichtbaren: Bildtheorie und Bildgebrauch in der Vormoderne*, ed. David Ganz, Thomas Lentes and Georg Henkel. 113–46. Berlin: Reimer, 2004

—— *St John the Divine: The Deified Evangelist in Medieval Art and Theology.* Berkeley: University of California Press, 2002

Hanna, Ralph, III. 'Contextualizing *The Siege of Jerusalem*'. *Yearbook of Langland Studies* 6 (1992): 109–21

—— 'The Growth of Robert Thornton's Books'. *Studies in Bibliography* 40 (1987): 51–61

—— *Pursuing History: Middle English Manuscripts and their Texts.* Stanford, CA: Stanford University Press, 1996

Hansen, Rikke. 'Travelling Skins: Hides, Furs and Other Animal Surfaces in Art'. Presentation given at the Meet Animal Meat Conference, Uppsala University, Sweden, 2009

Heng, Geraldine. *Empire of Magic: Medieval Romance and the Politics of Cultural Fantasy.* New York: Columbia University Press, 2003

—— 'Jews, Saracens, "Black Men", Tartars: England in a World of Racial Difference', in *A Companion to Medieval English Literature and Culture, c. 1350–c. 1500*, ed. Peter Brown. 247–69. New York: Wiley-Blackwell, 2009

—— 'The Romance of England: *Richard Coer de Lyon*, Saracens, Jews, and the Politics of Race and Nation', in *The Postcolonial Middle Ages*, ed. Jeffrey Jerome Cohen. 135–71. New York: Palgrave, 2000

Henisch, Bridget Ann. *Fast and Feast: Food in Medieval Society.* University Park: Pennsylvania State University Press, 1976

Herrlingler, Rudolph. *A History of Medical Illustration.* London: Pitman, 1970

Hoffmann, Godehard. *Das Gabelkreuz in St. Maria im Kapitol zu Köln und das Phänomenon der Crucifixi dolorosi in Europa.* Worms: Werner, 2006

Holsinger, Bruce. 'Of Pigs and Parchment: Medieval Studies and the Coming of the Animal'. *PMLA* 124.2 (2009): 616–23

Holt, James Clarke. 'The Origins of the Constitutional Tradition in England', in *Magna Carta and Medieval Government.* 1–22. London: Hambledon Press, 1985

—— *Robin Hood.* 2nd edn. London: Thames & Hudson, 1989

Hoyoux, Jean. 'Reges criniti: chevelures, tonsures et scalps chez les Merovingiens'. *Revue belge de philologie et d'histoire* 26 (1948): 479–508

Huot, Sylvia. 'Polytextual Reading: The Meditative Reading of Real and Metaphorical Books', in *Orality and Literacy in the Middle Ages: Essays on a Conjunction and its Consequences in Honour of D. H. Green*, ed. Mark Chinca and Christopher Young. 203–22. Turnhout: Brepols, 2005

Husband, Timothy. *The Art of Illumination: The Limbourg Brothers and the Belles Heures of Jean de France, Duc de Berry.* New York: Metropolitan Museum of Art / New Haven: Yale University Press, 2008

Jacobs, Samuel P. 'The Skinny on Harvard's Rare Book Collection'. *The Harvard Crimson* (2 February 2006). http://www.thecrimson.com/article/2006/2/2/the-skinny-on-harvards-rare-book/

Jacquart, Danielle. *La Médecine médiévale dans le cadre parisien, XIVe–XVe siècle.* Paris: Fayard, 1998

——, and Claude Alexandre Thomasset. *Sexuality and Medicine in the Middle Ages.* Princeton: Princeton University Press, 1988

Jehaes, Els. *Optimisation of Methods and Procedures for the Analysis of mtDNA Sequences and their Applications in Molecular Archaeological and Historical Finds.* Leuven: Leuven University Press, 1998

Jones, Martin. *The Molecule Hunt: Archaeology and the Hunt for Ancient DNA.* London: Allen Lane, 2001

Jones, Peter Murray. *Medieval Medicine in Illuminated Manuscripts*, rev. edn. London: British Library, 1998

—— 'Sicut hic depingitur …: John of Arderne and English Medical Illustration in the 14th and 15th Centuries', in *Die Kunst und das Studium der Nature vom 14. zum 16. Jahrhundert*, ed. Wolfram Prinz and Andreas Beyer. 103–26. Weinheim: VCH, 1987

—— 'Staying with the Programme: Illustrated Manuscripts of John of Arderne, c. 1380–c. 1550', in *Decoration and Illustration in Medieval English Manuscripts*, ed. A. S. G. Edwards. 204–27. London: British Library, 2002

Karnes, Michelle. *Imagination, Meditation, and Cognition in the Middle Ages.* Chicago: University of Chicago Press, 2011

Kay, Sarah. 'Flayed Skin as *objet a*: Representation and Materiality in Guillaume de Deguileville's *Pèlerinage de vie humaine*', in *Medieval Fabrications: Dress, Textiles, Clothwork, and other Cultural Imaginings*, ed. E. Jane Burns. 193–205. New York: Palgrave, 2004

—— 'Legible Skins: Animals and the Ethics of Medieval Reading'. *postmedieval: a journal of medieval cultural studies* 2.1 (2011): 13–32

—— 'Original Skin: Flaying, Reading, and Thinking in the Legend of Saint Bartholomew and other Works'. *Journal of Medieval and Early Modern Studies*. 36.1 (2006): 35–73

Keiser, George R. 'A Note on the Descent of the Thornton Manuscript'. *Cambridge Bibliographical Society* 7 (1976): 346–8

—— 'More Light on the Life and Milieu of Robert Thornton'. *Studies in Bibliography* 36 (1983): 112–19

Kieckhefer, Richard. 'Radical Tendencies in the Flagellant Movement of the Mid-Fourteenth Century'. *Journal of Medieval and Renaissance Studies* 4 (1974): 157–76

Kirkup, John. *The Evolution of Surgical Instruments: An Illustrated History from Ancient Times to the Twentieth Century*. Novato, CA: Norman, 2006

Knight, Stephen. *Robin Hood: A Complete Study of the English Outlaw*. Oxford: Blackwell, 1994

Kors, Alan Charles, and Edward Peters, eds. *Witchcraft in Europe, 400–1700: A Documentary History*. Philadelphia: University of Pennsylvania Press, 2001

Kristeva, Julia. *The Powers of Horror: An Essay on Abjection*, trans. Leon S. Roudiez. New York: Columbia University Press, 1982

Lambert, Joseph. *Traces of the Past: Unraveling the Secrets of Archaeology through Chemistry*. Reading: Perseus Books, 1997

Lambert, T. B. 'Theft, Homicide and Crime in Late Anglo-Saxon Law'. *Past & Present* 214 (2012): 3–43

Largier, Niklaus. *In Praise of the Whip: A Cultural History of Arousal*, trans. Graham Harman. New York: Zone, 2007

Lawrence, Ghislaine. 'The Ambiguous Artifact: Surgical Instruments and the Surgical Past', in *Medical Theory, Surgical Practice: Studies in the History of Surgery*, ed. Christopher Lawrence. New York: Routlege, 1992

Lear, Floyd, S. *Treason in Roman and Germanic Law*. Houston: University of Texas Press, 1965

Leff, Gordon. *Heresy in the Later Middle Ages: The Relation of Heterodoxy to Dissent, c. 1250–c. 1450*. 2 vols. Manchester: Manchester University Press, 1967

Liebermann, Felix. *Die Gesetze der Angelsachsen*. 3 vols. Halle, 1898–1916

Lindquist, Sherry C. M. *Agency, Visuality and Society at the Chartreuse de Champmol*. Burlington, VT: Ashgate, 2008

—— 'The Will of a Princely Patron and Artists at the Burgundian Court', in *The Artist at Court*, ed. Stephen Campbell. 46–56. Chicago: University of Chicago Press for the Isabella Stewart Gardner Museum, 2004

——, ed. *The Meanings of Nudity in Medieval Art*. Burlington, VT: Ashgate, 2012

MacDougall, Hugh A. *Racial Myth in English History: Trojans, Teutons and Anglo-Saxons*. Montreal: Harvest House, 1982

MacKinney, Loren C. *Medical Illustrations in Medieval Manuscripts.* London: Wellcome Library, 1965

Marrow, James H. 'Circumdederunt me canes multi: Christ's Tormentors in Northern European Art of the Late Middle Ages and the Early Renaissance'. *Art Bulletin* 59 (1977): 167–81

—— 'History, Historiography, and Pictorial Invention in the *Turin-Milan Hours*', in *In Detail: New Studies of Northern Renaissance Art in Honor of Walter S. Gibson*, ed. Laurinda S. Dixon. 1–14. Turnhout: Brepols, 1998

—— *Passion Iconography in Northern European Art of the Late Middle Ages and the Early Renaissance: A Study of the Transformation of Sacred Metaphor into Descriptive Narrative.* Kortrijk: Van Ghemmert, 1979

Marzo, Antonio. 'I violenti contro sé e le proprie cose: lettura del canto XIII dell'*Inferno*', in vol. 1 of *Lectura Dantis Lupiensis*, ed. Valerio Marucci and Valter Leonardo Puccetti. 39–72. Ravenna: Longo, 2012

Matthews, David. *Medievalism: A Critical Study.* Cambridge: D. S. Brewer, 2015

Matthiae, Guglielmo. *Le porte bronzee bizantine in Italia.* Rome: Officina, 1971

McCloud, Scott. *Understanding Comics: The Invisible Art.* New York: Harper Perennial, 1994

McDonald, Nicola, ed. *Pulp Fictions of Medieval England: Essays in Popular Culture.* Manchester: Manchester University Press, 2004

McKinnell, John. *Meeting the Other in Norse Myth and Legend.* Cambridge: D. S. Brewer, 2005

McVaugh, Michael. *The Rational Surgery of the Middle Ages.* Florence: Sismel – Edizioni del Galluzzo, 2006

Meiss, Millard, and Elizabeth H. Beatson, eds. *The Belles Heures of Jean, Duke of Berry.* New York: G. Braziller, 1974. [Facsimile.]

Merback, Mitchell B. 'Living Image of Pity: Mimetic Violence, Peacemaking and Salvific Spectacle in the Flagellant Processions of the Later Middle Ages', in *Images of Medieval Sanctity: Essays in Honour of Gary Dickson*, ed. Debra Higgs Strickland. 135–80. Leiden: Brill, 2007

—— *The Thief, the Cross, and the Wheel: Pain and the Spectacle of Punishment in Medieval and Renaissance Europe.* Chicago: University of Chicago Press, 1999

Mickel, Emanuel J. *Ganelon, Treason, and the 'Chanson de Roland'.* University Park: Pennsylvania State University Press, 1989

Mills, Robert. *Suspended Animation: Pain, Pleasure and Punishment in Medieval Culture.* London: Reaktion, 2005

Mittman, Asa Simon, and Susan M. Kim. 'Locating the Devil "Her" in MS Junius 11'. *Gesta* 54.1 (Apr. 2015): 3–25

Mittman, Asa Simon, with Peter Dendle. *Research Companion to Monsters and the Monstrous.* Burlington, VT: Ashgate, 2012

Mowbray, Donald. *Pain and Suffering in Medieval Theology: Academic Debates at the University of Paris in the Thirteenth Century.* Woodbridge: Boydell Press, 2009

Musson, Anthony. *Medieval Law in Context: The Growth of Legal Consciousness from Magna Carta to the Peasant's Revolt.* Manchester: Manchester University Press, 2001

Oates, Caroline. 'Metamorphosis and Lycanthropy in Franche-Comte [*sic*] 1521–1643', in *Fragments for a History of the Human Body: Part I*, ed. Michael Feher, Ramona Naddaff and Nadia Tazi. 305–61. New York: Zone, 1989

O'Boyle, Cornelius. *The Art of Medicine: Medical Teaching at the University of Paris, 1250–1400.* Leiden: Brill, 1998

Oliver, Lisi. *The Beginnings of English Law.* Toronto: Toronto University Press, 2002, repr. 2012

—— *The Body Legal in Barbarian Law.* Toronto: University of Toronto Press, 2011

Ossa-Richardson, Anthony. *The Devil's Tabernacle: The Pagan Oracles in Early Modern Thought.* Princeton: Princeton University Press, 2013

Otten, Charlotte, ed. *A Lycanthropy Reader: Werewolves in Western Culture.* Syracuse, NY: Syracuse University Press, 1986

Owst, G. R. *Literature and Pulpit in Medieval England: A Neglected Chapter in the History of English Letters and of the English People.* Oxford: Basil Blackwell, 1966

Paatz, Walter, and Elisabeth Paatz. *Die Kirchen von Florenz: Ein kunstgeschichtliches Handbuch.* Frankfurt: Vittorio Klostermann, 1955

Park, Katharine. 'The Criminal and the Saintly Body: Autopsy and Dissection in Renaissance Italy'. *Renaissance Quarterly* 47.1 (Spring 1994): 1–33

—— *The Secrets of Women: Gender, Generation, and the Origins of Human Dissection.* New York: Zone, 2006

Parkes, Malcolm Beckwith, and Andrew G. Watson, eds. *Medieval Scribes, Manuscripts, and Libraries: Essays Presented to N. R. Ker.* London: Scholar Press, 1978

Peers, Glenn. *Sacred Shock: Framing Visual Experience in Byzantium.* University Park: Pennsylvania State University Press, 2004

Pelliccia, Alexius Aurelius. *The Polity of the Christian Church of Early, Medieval, and Modern Times,* trans. J. C. Bellett. London: J. Masters, 1883

Perkinson, Stephen. 'Likeness, Loyalty, and the Life of the Court Artist: Portraiture in the Calendar Scenes of the *Très Riches Heures*'. *Quaerendo* 38 (2008): 142–74

—— *The Likeness of the King: A Prehistory of Portraiture in Late Medieval France.* Chicago: University of Chicago Press, 2009

Pickering, Frederick. *Essays on Medieval German Literature and Iconography.* Cambridge: Cambridge University Press, 1979

Poeschke, Joachim. *Italian Frescoes: The Age of Giotto, 1280–1400.* New York: Abbeville Press, 2005

Pollington, Stephen. *Leechcraft: Early English Charms, Plantlore and Healing.* Norfolk: Anglo-Saxon Books, 2003

Pollock, Frederick. 'Anglo-Saxon Law'. *English Historical Review* 8 (1893): 239–71

——, and Frederic W. Maitland. *History of English Law.* 2 vols. Cambridge: Cambridge University Press, 1968

Poor, Sara S. 'Why Surface Reading is not Enough: Morolf, the Skin of the Jew, and German Medieval Studies'. *Exemplaria* 26.2–3 (Summer/Fall 2014): 148–62

Pouchelle, Marie-Christine. *Corps et chirurgie à l'apogée du Moyen Age.* Paris: Flammarion, 1983

Pratt, Rebekah L. 'From Animal to Meat: Illuminating the Medieval Ritual of Unmaking'. *EHumanista* 25 (Sept. 2013): 17–26

Price, Merrall Llewelyn. *Consuming Passions: The Uses of Cannibalism in Late Medieval and Early Modern Europe*. New York: Routledge, 2003

Puglisi, Catherine, and William Barcham, eds. *New Perspectives on the Man of Sorrows*. Kalamazoo, MI: Medieval Institute Publications, 2013

Réau, Louis. *Iconographie de l'art chrétien*. Vol. 1. Paris: Presses Universitaires de France, 1958

Reed, Ronald. *Ancient Skins, Parchments and Leathers*. London: Seminar Press, 1972

Resl, Brigitte, ed. *A Cultural History of Animals in the Medieval Age*. Oxford: Berg, 2007

Rouse, Richard H., and Mary A. Rouse. *Manuscripts and their Makers: Commercial Book Producers in Medieval Paris, 1200–1500*. 2 vols. Turnhout: Harvey Miller, 2000

Rouse, Robert Allen. 'English Identity and the Law in *Havelok the Dane, Horn Childe and Maiden Rimnild* and *Beues of Hamtoun*', in *Cultural Encounters in the Romance of Medieval England*, ed. Corinne Saunders. 69–83. Cambridge: D. S. Brewer, 2005

―― *The Idea of Anglo-Saxon England in Middle English Romance*. Cambridge: D. S. Brewer, 2005

Rowland, Beryl. *Animals with Human Faces: A Guide to Animal Symbolism*. Knoxville: University of Tennessee Press, 1975

Ruff, Julius R. *Violence in Early Modern Europe, 1500–1800*. Cambridge: Cambridge University Press, 2001

Russell, Jeffrey Burton. *Witchcraft in the Middle Ages*. Ithaca, NY: Cornell University Press, 1972

Salih, Sarah. 'The Medieval Looks Back', in *Troubled Vision: Gender, Sexuality, and Sight in Medieval Text and Image*, ed. Emma Campbell and Robert Mills. 223–31. New York: Palgrave, 2004

Salisbury, Joyce. *The Beast Within: Animals in the Middle Ages*. New York: Routledge, 1994

Scarry, Elaine. *The Body in Pain: The Making and Unmaking of the World*. Oxford: Oxford University Press, 1985

Schildkrout, Enid. 'Inscribing the Body'. *Annual Review of Anthropology* 33 (2004): 319–44

Sciacca, Christine, ed. *Florence at the Dawn of the Renaissance: Painting and Illumination, 1300–1350*. Los Angeles: J. Paul Getty Museum, 2012

Segarro Soto, Héctor A. 'After God, we Owed the Victory to the Horses: The Evolution of the Equine Companion from Veillantif to Arondel', in *Of Mice and Men: Animals in Human Culture*, ed. Nadita Batra and Vartan Messier. 59–66. Newcastle upon Tyne: Cambridge Scholars, 2009

Silverman, Lisa. *Tortured Subjects: Pain, Truth, and the Body in Early Modern France*. Chicago: University of Chicago Press, 2001

Simmons, Clare A. *Popular Medievalism in Romantic-Era Britain*. New York: Palgrave, 2011

Simonsohn, Shlomo. *The Apostolic See and the Jews: Documents 492–1404*. Studies and Texts 94. Toronto: Pontifical Institute of Mediaeval Studies, 1988

Smith, Pamela H. *The Body of the Artisan: Art and Experience in the Scientific Revolution*. Chicago: University of Chicago Press, 2004

——, Amy R. W. Meyers, and Harold J. Cook, eds. *Ways of Making and Knowing: The Material Culture of Empirical Knowledge*. Ann Arbor: University of Michigan Press, 2014

Smith, Susan L. 'Bride Stripped Bare: A Rare Type of the Disrobing of Christ'. *Gesta* 34.2 (1995): 126–46

—— 'The Gothic Mirror and the Female Gaze', in *Saints, Sinners, and Sisters: Gender and Northern Art in Medieval and Early Modern Europe*, ed. Jane L. Carroll and Alison G. Stewart. 73–93. Aldershot: Ashgate, 2003

Steel, Karl. *How to Make a Human: Animals and Violence in the Middle Ages*. Columbus: Ohio State University Press, 2011

Stevens, Andrea. *Inventions of the Skin: The Painted Body in Early English Drama, 1400–1642*. Edinburgh: Edinburgh University Press, 2013

Stodnick, Jacqueline, and Renée Trilling. 'Before and After Theory: Seeing through the Body in Early Medieval England'. *postmedieval: a journal of medieval cultural studies* 1 (2013): 347–53

Strauss, Walter L. *The German Single-Leaf Woodcut, 1550–1600: A Pictorial Catalogue*. 3 vols. New York: Abaris, 1975

Strehlke, Carl B. *Italian Paintings 1250–1450 in the John G. Johnson Collection and the Philadelphia Museum of Art*. Philadelphia: Philadelphia Museum of Art, 2004

Suckale, Robert. '*Arma Christi*: Überlegungen zur Zeichenhaftigkeit mittelalterlicher Andachtsbilder'. *Städel-Jahrbuch* 6 (1977): 177–208

—— 'Der Kruzifix in St. Maria im Kapitol: Versuch einer Annäherung', in *Femmes, art et religion au Moyen Âge*, ed. Jean-Claude Schmitt. 87–101. Strasbourg: Presses Universitaires de Strasbourg, 2004

Swanton, Michael. '"Dane-Skins": Excoriation in Early England'. *Folklore* 87 (1976): 21–8

—— *English Poetry before Chaucer*. Exeter: Exeter University Press, 2002

Sylwanowicz, Marta. '"And this is a wonderful instrument …": Names of Surgical Instruments in Late Middle English Medical Texts', in *Foreign Influences on Medieval English*, ed. Jacek Fisiak and Magdalena Bator. Frankfurt: Peter Lang, 2011

Terry, Allie. 'Criminal Vision in Early Modern Florence: Fra Angelico's Altarpiece for Il Tempio and the Magdalenian Gaze', in *Renaissance Theories of Vision*, ed. John Hendrix and Charles Carmen. 45–62. Aldershot: Ashgate, 2010

Terry-Fritsch, Allie, and Erin Felicia Labbie, eds. *Beholding Violence in Medieval and Early Modern Europe*. Burlington, VT: Ashgate, 2012

Thompson, C. J. S. *The History and Evolution of Surgical Instruments*. New York: Schuman's, 1942

Thompson, Lawrence S. *Bibliologia comica; or, Humorous Aspects of the Caparisoning and Conversation of Books*. Hamden, CT: Archon, 1968

—— 'Promptuary of Anthropodermic Bibliopegy'. *The Book Collector's Packet* 4.2 (Oct. 1946): 15–17

—— 'Tanned Human Skin'. *Bulletin of the Medical Library Association* 34 (1946): 93–102

Toureille, Valérie. *Crime et châtiment au Moyen Âge (Vᵉ–XVᵉ siècle)*. Paris: Seuil, 2013

Tracy, Larissa. *Torture and Brutality in Medieval Literature: Negotiations of National Identity*. Cambridge: D. S. Brewer, 2012

——, ed. *Castration and Culture in the Middle Ages*. Cambridge: D. S. Brewer, 2013

——, and Kelly DeVries, eds. *Wounds and Wound Repair in Medieval Culture*. Leiden: Brill, 2015

——, and Jeff Massey, eds. *Heads Will Roll: Decapitation in the Medieval and Early Modern Imagination*. Leiden: Brill, 2012

Treharne, Elaine. *Living through Conquest: The Politics of Early English, 1020–1220*. Oxford: Oxford University Press, 2012

Turville-Petre, Thorlac. *England the Nation: Language, Literature and National Identity, 1290–1340*. Oxford: Oxford University Press, 1996

van Dülmen, Richard. *Theatre of Horror: Crime and Punishment in Early Modern Germany*, trans. Elisabeth Neu. Cambridge: Polity Press, 1990

Vincent, Catherine. 'Discipline du corps et de l'esprit chez les flagellants au Moyen Âge'. *Revue historique* 302.3 (2000): 593–614

Wallis, Faith, ed. *Medieval Medicine: A Reader*. Toronto: University of Toronto Press, 2010

Walter, Katie L., ed. *Reading Skin in Medieval Literature and Culture*. New York: Palgrave, 2013

Way, Albert. 'Some Notes on the Tradition of Flaying, Inflicted in Punishment of Sacrilege: The Skin of the Offender being Affixed to the Church-Doors'. *Archaeological Journal* 5 (1848): 185–92

Weissman, Ronald E. *Ritual Brotherhood in Renaissance Florence*. New York: Academic Press, 1982

Wickersheimer, Ernest. *Anatomies de Mondino dei Luzzi et de Guido de Vigevano*. Paris: Droz, 1926

—— *Maître Jean Gispaden, chirurgien annécien et grenoblois de la fin du XVᵉ siècle*. Geneva: Imprimerie A. Kundig, 1926

Wilkie, Rodger I. 'Re-Capitating the Body Politic: The Overthrow of Tyrants in *Havelok the Dane*'. *Neophilologus* 94 (2010): 139–50

Wilson, Blake. *The Florence Laudario: An Edition of Florence, Biblioteca Nazionale Centrale, Banco Rari 18*. Madison, WI: A-R Editions, 1995

—— *Music and Merchants: The Laudesi Companies of Republican Florence*. Oxford: Oxford University Press, 1992

Wiseman, Susan J. 'Hairy on the Inside: Metamorphosis and Civility in English Werewolf Texts', in *Renaissance Beasts: Of Animals, Humans, and other Wonderful Creatures*, ed. Erica Fudge. 50–70. Urbana: University of Illinois Press, 2004

—— *Writing Metamorphosis in the English Renaissance, 1550–1700*. Cambridge: Cambridge University Press, 2014

Woolf, Rosemary. *The English Mystery Plays*. Berkeley: University of California Press, 1972

Wormald, Patrick. *The Making of English Law: King Alfred to the Twelfth Century.* Vol. 1, *Legislation and its Limits.* Oxford: Blackwell Publishers, repr. 2000

Yeager, Suzanne M. *Jerusalem in Medieval Narrative.* Cambridge: Cambridge University Press, 2008

—— 'Jewish Identity in *The Siege of Jerusalem* and Homiletic Texts: Models of Penance and Victims of Vengeance for the Urban Apocalypse'. *Medium Ævum* 80.1 (2001): 56–84

—— '*The Siege of Jerusalem* and Biblical Exegesis: Writing about Romans in Fourteenth-Century England'. *The Chaucer Review* 39.1 (2004): 70–102

Index